INTRODUCTIO
COMMUNICATION
STUDIES

Translating Scholarship Into
Meaningful Practice

SECOND EDITION

Edited By:

ALAN K. GOODBOY
West Virginia University

KARA SHULTZ
Commonwealth
University of Pennsylvania

Kendall Hunt
publishing company

Cover image © Shutterstock.com

www.kendallhunt.com
Send all inquiries to:
4050 Westmark Drive
Dubuque, IA 52004-1840

Copyright © 2023 by Kendall Hunt Publishing Company

ISBN: 978-1-7924-9414-7

All rights reserved. No part of this publication may be reproduced,
stored in a retrieval system, or transmitted, in any form or by any means,
electronic, mechanical, photocopying, recording, or otherwise,
without the prior written permission of the copyright owner.

Published in the United States of America

CONTENTS

OUR VISION

The field of communication studies is one of the most exciting disciplines to study. Many students agree with this assertion as communication is one of the most popular majors in college (Kramer, 2010). And many employers agree that this major equips students with a variety of competencies that are valued in the workplace including interpersonal skills, organizational skills, presentational skills, leadership, teamwork, critical thinking, reasoning, and cultural awareness (Myers et al., 2021). With research topics ranging from navigating online dating, to recognizing deception and lying, to playing videogames, communication research has produced findings that are relevant to, and may significantly enhance, our daily lives if we understand them. This textbook is designed to help you review some important communication research findings published in our peer-reviewed journals across major communication contexts (and intersections among these contexts). As Kramer (2010) noted, "unless we believe that students do not learn anything from our classes, then our research makes a difference in their personal and professional lives" (p. 435). We want to make a difference in your life with information you are likely to care about, because we, like many other scholars, believe communication scholarship does make a difference in helping people become more effective communicators (Hummert, 2009).

This edited volume is unique as our brief chapters translate research programs into simple real-life practices, suggestions, reflections, and applications across major communication contexts (computer-mediated, family, gender, health, intercultural, interpersonal, instructional, media, nonverbal, organizational, persuasion, political, science, and sport). As Frey (2009) noted, "because of its perceived lack of relevance and accessibility, to make a difference, scholarship typically has to be *translated* for use by other audiences" (p. 267). Petronio (1999) explained that "translating means that we take the knowledge discovered through research or theory and interpret it for everyday use. Translators develop pathways for converting research knowledge into practice" (p. 88). This book does precisely that it translates some of the best research findings into practice so you can be an effective communicator in a variety of real-life situations and contexts.

We believe that students who are introduced to our discipline should leave their introductory course with practical knowledge they can use in their daily lives. This perspective is rooted in the tradition of applied communication research. According to Wood (2000), applied communication scholarship adopts a pragmatic focus by "putting theory and research into the service of practice and, equally, of studying practices to refine theory in order to gain new understandings of how communication functions and how it might function differently, or better" (p. 189). Therefore, this book provides research findings from programs of published studies that have practical implications, if not direct advice, on how to communicate more appropriately and effectively. Since we know how fun and exciting the field is, we believe that students should learn about research findings that are directly relevant to them.

We are very fortunate to publish 42 brief mini-chapters that highlight major programs of communication research across critical, rhetorical, and social science perspectives. And we are even more fortunate to feature chapters from the most published and prolific communication researchers in the field. Every chapter in this book is written by experts who are exceptional scholars with impressive research agendas. We are proud to say that we have the "all-star team" of communication researchers (and their awesome graduate students) writing and translating their own research in a conversational tone. Our approach is designed to provide undergraduate students with better "take-aways" from an introductory course, show them a diverse cross-section of the state-of-the-art communication research, help them recognize major programs of research and the prolific scholars who do this research, and ultimately give them practical real-life advice grounded in scholarship. We know that translational communication scholarship can make a difference in your lives if you apply the principles and findings featured in this book. It is also our hope that you enjoy what you learn and find this translational research to be helpful advice that can aid you in the meaningful practice of communication in life.

Cheers!

Alan K. Goodboy
Professor
Peggy Rardin McConnell Research Chair
West Virginia University

Kara Shultz
Vice Provost of Undergraduate Education
Dean of Honors College
Commonwealth University of Pennsylvania

REFERENCES

Frey, L. R. (2009). What a difference more difference-making communication scholarship might make: Making a difference from and through communication research. *Journal of Applied Communication Research, 37*(2), 205–214. https://doi.org/10.1080/00909880902792321

Hummert, M. L. (2009). Not just preaching to the choir: Communication scholarship does make a difference. *Journal of Applied Communication Research, 37*(2), 215–224. https://doi.org/10.1080/00909880902792313

Kramer, M. W. (2010). It depends on your criteria. *Communication Monographs, 77*(4), 435–437. https://doi.org/10.1080/03637751.2010.523594

Myers, S. A., Goodboy, A. K., Kromka, S. M., Shin, M., Pitts, S., & Bertelsen, D. A. (2021). A curricular view of communication course offerings of National Communication Association department members. *Communication Education, 70*(4), 421–434. https://doi.org/10.1080/03634523.2021.1951313

Petronio, S. (1999). "Translating scholarship into practice": An alternative metaphor. *Journal of Applied Communication Research, 27*(2), 87–91. https://doi.org/10.1080/00909889909365527

Wood, J. T. (2000). Applied communication research: Unbounded and for good reason. *Journal of Applied Communication Research, 28*(2), 188–191. https://doi.org/10.1080/00909880009365567

AUTHOR BIOGRAPHIES

Tamara Afifi is a Professor in the Department of Communication at the University of California-Santa Barbara. Her research focuses on family and interpersonal communication in two domains: (1) how family members and relational partners communicate when they are stressed and its impact on personal and relational health, and (2) information regulation (e.g., avoidance, privacy, secrets, stress contagion effects). She is a Fellow of the International Communication Association, a Distinguished Scholar of the National Communication Association, and a former editor of Communication Monographs.

Cimmiaron F. Alvarez (M.A. University of Washington) is a Ph.D. student in the School of Communication and Information at Rutgers University. Her research interest lies at the intersection of interpersonal, family, and health communication. She primarily focuses on how people manage impressions and cope during difficult transitions. Her work has been featured in outlets such as the *Journal of Family Communication* and *Health Communication* as well as a myriad of book chapters and encyclopedia entries. She currently is the Vice Chair-Elect of the Interpersonal and Family Communication Interest Group at the Central States Communication Association.

Analisa Arroyo (Ph.D., University of Arizona) is an Associate Professor in the Department of Communication Studies at the University of Georgia. Her research interests are in health and interpersonal communication, specifically exploring how communication in close relationships is associated with individuals' well-being and relational quality. Her research can be found in some of the top peer-reviewed Communication journals, including *Communication Monographs, Communication Research,* and *Human Communication Research*, and has yielded press coverage in media outlets such as *Fox News, MSNBC, Good Morning America,* and *Fitness Magazine.* Additionally, she teaches graduate- and undergraduate-level classes in relational communication, family communication, and communication and body image.

Lamiyah Bahrainwala (Southwestern University, Georgetown) is an Assistant Professor of Communication Studies and affiliate faculty to Race & Ethnicity Studies and Feminist Studies. She is a feminist surveillance scholar who examines bizarre iterations of whiteness, global anti-Blackness, and anti-Muslim discourse. Her work has appeared in leading journals including *Communication, Culture and Critique, Feminist Media Studies,* and *Journal of International and Intercultural Communication.* Her work has been recognized with the Rhetoric Society of America (RSA) Fellows Early Career Award, and she has received numerous top paper and top article recognitions at national conferences.

Jaime Banks (Ph.D., Colorado State University) is Associate Professor in the School of Information Studies at Syracuse University. Her research is animated by questions of human-technology relations—especially those with videogame avatars and social robots—with an emphasis on perceptions of mind and morality. Her most recent work is on perceptions of moral agency and trust in robots was funded by the U.S. Air Force Office of Scientific Research, Trust and Influence Program.

Andrew C. Billings (Ph.D., Indiana University) is the Ronald Reagan Chair of Broadcasting and Executive Director of the Alabama Program in Sports Communication in the Department of Journalism and Creative Media at the University of Alabama. He teaches courses at the intersection of sports, media, and social issues. He has authored 23 books, including recent entries, *Head Game: Mental Health in Sports Media* (with Scott Parrott), *The Rise and Fall of Mass Communication* (with William Benoit), and *Mascot Nation: The Controversy Over Native American Mascots in Sports* (with Jason Edward Black). He has also authored over 230 journal articles and book chapters in outlets such as *Journal of Communication, Mass Communication & Society,* and *Journal of Broadcasting & Electronic Media.* He is currently the co-editor for the journal *Communication & Sport.* Billings' work has won numerous awards from organizations such as the International Communication Association, National Communication Association, Broadcast Education Association, and the Association for Education in Mass Communication and Journalism. His work in the classroom has also earned him many teaching awards. He has lectured in many nations around the world and has been interviewed by media over 700 times, featured in outlets such as ESPN's "Outside the Lines" and the New York Times. He has also consulted with many sports media agencies and is a past holder of the Invited Chair of Olympism at the Autonomous University of Barcelona.

Nick Bowman (PhD, Michigan State University) is an Associate Professor in the SI Newhouse School of Public Communications at Syracuse University, USA. His primary areas of expertise include research into the uses and effects of immersive and interactive media, with a specific interest in video games and virtual reality technologies. He has published more than 125 peer-reviewed manuscripts in journals focused on communication, media studies, psychology, human-computer interaction, and other academic disciplines. He is the editor of *Journal of Media Psychology* and a past editor of *Communication Research Reports*, and he is the inaugural editor of research reports for *Technology, Mind, and Behavior*. He has co-authored textbooks on mediated communication and entertainment media, and in 2020 he was named Fulbright Wu Jing-Jyi Arts and Culture Fellow in Taiwan, with a teaching and research appointment at the National Chengchi University in Taipei. Nick maintains active research collaborations with scholars across the United States, as well as groups in Belgium, Germany, and Taiwan.

Cheryl Campanella Bracken (Ph.D., Temple University) is the Vice Provost of Faculty Affairs and Development and Professor in the School of Communication at Cleveland State University in Cleveland, OH, USA. Her primary research interest focus on individuals' psychological and physiological processing of media content and form. Much of her work has focused on the role of telepresence in popular media and more recently binge watching. She has over published in outlets such as the *Journal of Communication*, *Human Communication Research*, and *Journal of Broadcasting and Electronic Media*. Additionally, she has published three books (two co-authored and one co-edited).

Tricia J. Burke (Ph.D., University of Arizona) is an Associate Professor of Communication Studies at Texas State University. Her research interests lie at the intersection of interpersonal and health communication, with a focus on navigating health-related interactions and well-being in close relationships. She also teaches classes in these areas and applies her research knowledge in her work with the university workplace wellness group and community health organizations. Tricia has published her work in a variety of journals, including *Health Communication, Communication Research, Journal of Social and Personal Relationships,* and *Journal of Family Communication,* among others. Her work has also been featured in the *Wall Street Journal* and *Time,* as well as on the *Today Show* and the *Relationship Matters* podcast.

Patrice M. Buzzanell (Ph.D., Purdue University) is Distinguished University Professor in the Department of Communication at the University of South Florida as well as Endowed Visiting Professor for the School of Media and Design at Shanghai Jiaotong University. She recently has received the 2021 Steven H. Chaffee Career Achievement Award from the International Communication Association (ICA) and the 2021 Samuel L. Becker Distinguished Service Award from the National Communication Association (NCA). Fellow and Past President of ICA, she also has served as President of the Council of Communication Associations and the Organization for the Study of Communication, Language and Gender (OSCLG). Her research coalesces around career, work-life policy, resilience, gender, and engineering design in micro-macro contexts. Her internal and external grants total around $3.5 million with her NSF funding focusing on engineering ethics scales and everyday ethical processes as well as design thinking for the professional formation of engineers that integrates socio-technical considerations and diversity, equity, inclusion, and belongingness. She also has received ICA's 2016 B. Aubrey Fisher Mentorship Award, NCA's 2016 Distinguished Scholar honor, Purdue's 2014 Provost Outstanding Mentor Award and 2015 Distinguished University Professor, the 2014 Velux Fonden Faculty Research Fellowship from the Copenhagen Business School, and feminist teacher-mentor and research awards from OSCLG, NCA, and ICA, among others.

Guo-Ming Chen is Emeritus Professor of Communication Studies at the University of Rhode Island, U.S.A. He is the founding president of the Association for Chinese Communication Studies. He served as the Executive Director and President of the International Association for Intercultural Communication Studies (IAICS). Chen's primary research interests are in intercultural communication and Chinese communication behaviors. In addition to receiving various awards and honors, Chen has published numerous books, articles, and book chapters.

Jeffrey T. Child (Ph.D., North Dakota State University) is a Professor of Communication at Kent State University in the School of Communication Studies. His primary research explores communication technology and human interaction, focusing on how people manage privacy when interacting on social media. He is a former editor of the *Journal of Family Communication*. He has over 50 research publications in journals and edited books. His research has been featured in journals like the *Journal of Family Communication, Computers in Human Behavior, Journal of the American Society for Information Science and Technology, Communication Quarterly, Communication Studies*, among others.

W. Timothy Coombs (Ph.D., Purdue University) is an advisor to the Centre for Crisis and Risk Communication and conducts research in the area of crisis communication and CSR. His research in crisis communication has won a number of awards including the Jackson, Jackson & Wagner Behavioral Science Prize from the Public Relations Society of America, the Pathfinder Award from the Institute of Public Relations in recognition of his research contributions to the field and to the practice, and the Business Impact Award from the Association for Business Communication and USC Marshall School of Business, Center for Management Communication. Dr. Coombs has won multiple PRIDE awards from the Public Relations Division of the National Communication Association for both books and research articles and was selected for the prestigious Arthur W. Page Society. Dr. Coombs was a Fulbright Scholar in Estonia in the Spring of 2013. In the Fall of 2013, he was the named NEMO Professor at Lund University, Helsingborg Campus. In 2015 he was invited to lecture at Tsinghua University, Beijing China. From 2015 to 2020 he was designated an honorary professor in the Department of Business Communication at Aarhus University. He is the past editor for *Corporation Communication: An International Journal*.

Renee L. Cowan (PhD, Texas A&M University) is an Affiliate Assistant Professor in the Knight School of Communication at Queens University of Charlotte. She teaches undergraduate and graduate courses in organizational rhetoric, organizational communication, qualitative and quantitative research, rhetorical criticism, leadership, communication theory and others. She uses qualitative, rhetorical, and quantitative methods to investigate contemporary organizational issues including: work/life issues, workplace bullying, and issues associated with the use of communication technologies in organizations. Her research appears in such peer-reviewed journals as *Human* Resource *Management Journal, Personnel Review, Management Communication Quarterly, The International Journal of Human Resource Management, Journal of Computer-Mediated Communication, Communication Education, Communication Studies, Women & Language, Communication Quarterly, Western Journal of Communication, Qualitative Research Reports in Communication, International Journal of Business Communication, Communication Research Reports*, and others.

Gregory A. Cranmer (Ph.D., West Virginia University) is an Associate Professor of Sport Communication in the Department of Communication at Clemson University, a fellow with the Robert H. Brooks Sports Science Institute, and a research fellow with the U.S. Center for Mental Health & Sport. He teaches courses focused on communication theory, research methods, and the processes associated with enacting sport communication. He has also authored over 75 journal articles and book chapters in outlets such as *Communication & Sport, Health Communication, Leadership & Organizational Development Journal, Routledge Handbook of Sport Communication, the Handbook of Communication & Sport*, and *Routledge Handbook of Sport and New Media*. He has or is currently authoring three books; the multi-award-winning *Athletic Coaching: A communication Perspective* and two forthcoming books – a Sport Communication textbook (with Natalie Brown-Devlin and Lauren Smith) and a case study book that considers the applications of communication theory and computational methods in social media research (with Brandon Boatwright). Cranmer's research has won numerous research awards from organizations such as the International Communication Association and National Communication Association.

Marianne Dainton (Ph.D. The Ohio State University) is a Professor of Communication at La Salle University in Philadelphia. She teaches interpersonal communication, intercultural communication, and communication theory. Marianne is the author of six books: *Maintaining Relationships through Communication* (co-edited with Dan Canary, published by LEA), *Applying Communication Theory for Professional Life* (co-authored with Elaine Zelley, published by Sage), *Maintaining Black Marriages: Individual, Interactional, and Contextual Dynamics* (published by Lexington Books), *Communication and Relational Maintenance* (with Scott Myers, published by Cognella), *Strategic Communication Research Methods* (with Pamela Lannutti, published by Cognella), and *Advanced Interpersonal Communication: Managing Communication Goals* (with Katie Neary Dunleavy, forthcoming from Cognella).

Her personal life is spent eating her way through the city of Philadelphia, hanging at the Jersey Shore, and trying to pass as a local while visiting foreign countries.

Stefanie Z. Demetriades (Ph.D., University of Southern California) is Assistant Professor of Communication at DePaul University and Co-Director of the Center for Media Psychology and Social Influence at Northwestern University. She teaches courses related to media and technology, health, and intercultural communication. Her research focuses on communication interventions to bridge social and health disparities, and has been published in journals including the *Journal of Communication*, *Health Communication*, and *International Journal of Communication.*

Amanda Denes (Ph.D., University of California, Santa Barbara) is an Associate Professor in the Department of Communication at the University of Connecticut. She is a Co-Editor of *The Oxford Handbook of the Physiology of Interpersonal Communication* and Editor of *Communication Reports*. She is also the recipient of a Fulbright U.S. Scholar Award from the Australian-American Fulbright Commission and a recipient of the Early Career Award from the Interpersonal Communication Division of the National Communication Association. Her primary area of specialization is interpersonal communication, with emphases in biosocial models of communication, sexual communication, and communication processes related to maintaining successful relationships. Much of her work looks at the association between communication in interpersonal relationships and people's physiological, psychological, and relational health. In particular, she is interested in why individuals disclose information about themselves to others, how they disclose that information, and the effects of such disclosures on individuals and their relationships. She specializes in investigating such phenomena in sexual contexts, such as by exploring communication during and after sexual activity and its association with individual and relational well-being.

Mike Devlin (PhD, University of Alabama) is an Associate Professor of advertising at Texas State University. Having earned his PhD in Mass Communication from the University of Alabama, he is no stranger to sport and the influence it can have on a community. Dr. Devlin's research culminates at the intersection of marketing, communication, and psychology – primarily focusing on how sport fandom impacts commercial opportunities and cultural issues. In his pursuit of understanding the complexities of sport and its fans, he has examined everything from niche sports such as mixed martial arts, to global spectacles such as the World Cup and Olympic Games. He has authored over 30 publications in nationally recognized, peer-reviewed journals, over 40 national and international conference proceedings, and several book chapters. He is also the author of the textbook *Creative Thinking and Concepting in Advertising.* His work has been featured on CNN and he has earned top paper awards from the International Communication Association, National Communication Association, and AEJMC. In 2018 he was awarded the NCA Communication and Sport Division's *Emerging Scholar Award* and the *Early Career Teaching Award* from AEJMC's Advertising Division.

Christopher M. Dobmeier (M.A. SUNY University at Buffalo) is a Ph.D. student in the Department of Communication Studies at Northwestern University. As a graduate researcher in the Center of Media Psychology and Social Influence (COM-PSI), he studies various cognitive and affective factors in the consideration of message design, and similarly, the sociopsychological mechanisms used in the processing of such messages. His projects mainly explore contexts like political entertainment and health.

Tasha N. Dubriwny (PhD, University of Georgia) is an Associate Professor in the Department of Communication at Texas A&M University. She is a feminist rhetorical scholar whose research focuses on the politics of women's health and the reproductive justice movement. Her 2013 book *The Vulnerable Empowered Woman: Feminism, Postfeminism, and Women's Health* (Rutgers University Press) was awarded the Bonnie Ritter Book Award from the Feminist and Women's Studies Division of the National Communication Association and the Outstanding Book Award from the Organization for the Study of Communication, Language, and Gender. She has published essays analyzing representations of women's health in journals such as *The Quarterly Journal of Speech*, *Women's Studies in Communication*, and *Feminist Media Studies*. She is also an award winning teacher, and her classes, from Feminist Theory to Rhetorical Criticism, take a feminist intersectional approach to grappling with power, identity, and politics.

Carsyn J. Endres (M.A. University of Cincinnati) is a doctoral student at Arizona State University. Her research explores organizational communication including areas such as: emotional labor, burnout, and resilience. Carsyn's research is primarily focused on how people manage their emotions at work. Her work has appeared in the Journal of Management Inquiry and in the Handbook of Organizational Communication Theory and Research.

Christina R. Foust (Ph.D., University of North Carolina, Chapel Hill) is Associate Professor of Communication Studies at Metropolitan State University of Denver. Her work engages rhetoric, power, and social change, in a variety of contexts, notably, social movement, political discourse, and pop culture. She is the lead editor of the book, *What Democracy Looks Like: The Rhetoric of Social Movements and Counterpublics* (with Amy Pason and Kate Zittlow Rogness), and author of the book, *Transgression as a Mode of Resistance*. Foust has published work on the intersections of social movement and social media with *Review of Communication, Journal of Contemporary Rhetoric*, and the Routledge edited volume, *Rhetoric of Social Movements: Networks, Power, and New Media* (Nathan Crick, editor). Since 2018, Foust has oriented her professional efforts to be responsive to environmental injustice and catastrophe, developing community engaged projects with students and colleagues in and around Denver. This work centers environmental education and justice, helping (re) acquaint people with their capacity for consequential action and collaboration, while "being the change" they want to see in the world.

Elisabeth Gareis (EdD, University of Georgia) is a Professor of Communication Studies at Baruch College/City University of New York. She teaches courses related to intercultural and international aspects of communication. Her research focus is on intercultural friendship and its role in prejudice reduction. Publications include books and journal articles on friendship in the context of voluntary and forced migration, the integration of nonnative speakers in migration settings, and cross-cultural differences in the communication of emotion. As a native of Germany, she is also a producer of two films on Holocaust remembrance, reconciliation, and German/Jewish friendship. Her research on intercultural friendship has been widely covered in the media (e.g., *The Chronicle of Higher Education, Inside Higher Ed, USA Today*).

Jennifer L. Gibbs (PhD, University of Southern California) is Professor of Communication at the University of California, Santa Barbara, with an affiliated appointment in the Technology Management Program (TMP). Her research focuses on self-presentation, collaboration, and relationship formation in digital contexts such as global teams, online communities, and online dating, as well as the ways in which new technologies are transforming organizations. She recently published two books (*Distracted: Staying Connected without Losing Focus* and *Organizing Inclusion*), as well as publishing over 50 peer-reviewed journal articles and book chapters in a variety of disciplines. Professor Gibbs previously served as Editor of *Communication Research* and Associate Editor of *Management Communication Quarterly*.

Alan K. Goodboy (PhD, West Virginia University) is a Professor and Peggy Rardin McConnell Research Chair of Communication Studies at West Virginia University. Dr. Goodboy is a quantitative scholar and statistics nerd, having completed over 700 hours of postdoctoral coursework in structural equation modeling. He has over 150 publications and most of his research fits into the interpersonal communication (e.g., relational turbulence in romantic relationships) and instructional communication (e.g., teaching and learning) sections of this book. Most recently, he has been collaborating on medical communication research (e.g., medical simulations) with surgery colleagues at WVU.

Laura K. Guerrero is a Professor in the Hugh Down School of Human Communication, where she studies communication in close relationships, emphasizing emotional and nonverbal communication. Her research focuses on how certain forms of communication enhance understanding and improve relationships, whereas other forms of communication make problems worse. Professor Guerrero has published more than 100 articles and chapters on these topics along with several books, including the best-selling textbook, *Close Encounters: Communication in Relationships,* and a new introductory book, *Interpersonal Encounters: Connecting through Communication.* She is the recipient of several awards, including the 2023 Western States Communication Association Distinguished Scholar Award and the 2022 International Association for Relationship Research Teaching Award.

Salvador Guzman (M.A., California State University, Los Angeles) is a doctoral student in the School of Communication and Information at Rutgers University. His research examines the intersection between racial and ethnic identity, relational and family communication, and relational uncertainty. His work primarily explores how interracial couples (re)negotiate their relationship in times of socio-political uncertainty.

Jeffrey Hall (Ph.D. University of Southern California) is a Professor of Communication Studies at the University of Kansas. Jeff was once totally enamored with trying to unravel the mysteries of flirting, so in 2013 he wrote a book about it (*The Five Flirting Styles*, Harlequin Nonfiction). That trail eventually led to researching humor in courtship and long-term romantic relationships. Around that time, he served as Chair of the Human Communication and Technology Division of the National Communication Association, and in 2022 he'll be the Chair of the Interpersonal Communication Division at the International Communication Association. Enjoying the experience of book writing, he wrote *Relating Through Technology* (Cambridge University Press), which was released in 2020. He likes talking about friendship, laughter, and keeping in touch and why we should prioritize such things in life.

Jeff Hancock is the Harry and Norman Chandler Professor of Communication at Stanford University and Founding Director of the Stanford Social Media Lab. He is also the Co-Director of the Stanford Cyber-Policy Center and the Faculty Director of the Stanford Internet Observatory. A leading expert in social media behavior and the psychology of online interaction, Professor Hancock studies the impact of social media and AI technology on social cognition, well-being, deception and trust, and how we use and understand language. His award-winning research has been published in over 100 journal articles and conference proceedings and has been supported by funding from the U.S. National Science Foundation and the U.S. Department of Defense. Professor Hancock's TED Talk on deception has been seen over 1 million times and his research has been frequently featured in the popular press, including the New York Times, CNN, NPR, CBS and the BBC.

Michael Hecht (PhD, University of Illinois) is a Distinguished Professor Emeritus of Communication Arts and Sciences at Penn State University and Co-President of REAL Prevention, LLC. Dr. Hecht specializes in culturally grounded, narrative health message design and evaluation among diverse communities. This work is community-based and guided by his Narrative Engagement Theory, Principle of Cultural Grounding, and Communication Theory of Identity. Hecht has collaboratively created several widely distributed evidence-based interventions including *keepin' it REAL,* a narrative, multicultural school-based substance use prevention curriculum, and other programs using innovative technologies to reduce adolescent substance use, risky sex among adolescents and promote HPV vaccination. He also co-developed digital include media literacy and parenting interventions. This work has been funded by the National Institutes of Health, the Merck Foundation, Robert Wood Johnson Foundation, and others. Among other awards and recognition, Hecht was chosen as the University of Illinois College of the Liberal Arts' 2020 Humanitarian of the Year, 2021 Distinguished Lecture at the Hong Kong Polytechnic University, and the 2012 Pennsylvania Rural Health Leader of the Year.

Marian L. Houser is the Interim Chair and Professor in the Department of Communication Studies at Texas State University. She is interested in a program of research that examines the intersections of interpersonal relationships and instructional communication in various contexts that include organizations, training, health campaigns, and especially the dialogue that occurs between teachers and students in the classroom. She currently is the cofounder of *CoSearch*, a research-collaboration organization, and *Living Mental Wellness*, a prevention-based organization, and co-director of the department's *BioComm Research Lab*. Dr. Houser has authored/edited two communication textbooks: *Your Interpersonal Communication: Nature/Nurture Intersection*s (Kendall Hunt) and *The Handbook of Instructional Communication* (3rd ed., Kendall Hunt). She received the Texas State University President's Award for Scholarly and Creative Activities, the Eastern Communication Association's Past President's Award for Research and named Research Fellow by the Eastern Communication Association. Dr. Houser's love for teaching also garnered her the Mariel M. Muir Excellence in Mentoring Award at Texas State University.

Ronald L. Jackson II is Distinguished University Research Professor, Department of Communication, School of Communication, Media & Film Studies at the University of Cincinnati. Recently named as a National Communication Association Distinguished Scholar and an International Communication Association Research Fellow, Dr. Ronald L. Jackson II is one of the leading communication and identity scholars in the nation. He is Past President of both the National Communication Association and the Eastern Communication Association. He is Editor Emeritus of *Critical Studies in Media Communication.* As author or editor of 16 books, his research examines how theories of identity relate to intercultural and gender communication. Specifically, within his body of work encompassing empirical, conceptual, and critical approaches to the study of masculinity, identity negotiation, Whiteness, and Afrocentricity, he explores how and why people negotiate and define themselves as they do.

Lisa B. Keränen (PhD, University of Pittsburgh) is a University President's Teaching Scholar, Associate Professor, and Chair of the Communication Department at the University of Colorado Denver and serves as Affiliate Faculty of the Center for Bioethics and Humanities on the Anschutz Medical Campus. Her research and teaching explore the intersections of rhetoric, health care, viruses, and biological risks. Her first book, *Scientific Characters: Rhetoric, Politics, and Trust in Breast Cancer Research*, received the Marie Hochmuth Nichols Award for Outstanding Scholarship in Public Address. She has also received the Karl R. Wallace Memorial Research Award from the National Communication Association and the Xiaosui Xiao Award for Outstanding Scholarship in Rhetoric from the Association for Chinese Communication Studies. Her research has appeared in venues such as *Academic Medicine, Chinese Journal of Communication, Rhetoric & Public Affairs, Quarterly Journal of Speech, Journal of Medical Humanities, Journal of International & Intercultural Communication, and more.* She is a past president of the Association for the Rhetoric of Science, Technology, and Medicine and a past director of the National Communication Association Forum.

Katherine R. Knobloch is an Associate Professor in the Department of Communication Studies and the Associate Director of the Center for Public Deliberation at Colorado State University. Her teaching and research focus on public participation and deliberative democracy, particularly the design and impact of community engagement programs. She has received National Science Foundation funding to study the expansion of the Citizens' Initiative Review and the implementation of deliberative pedagogy in chemistry classrooms and works with state and community partners to design and implement engagement programs that create opportunities for empowered local decision making. Her work has appeared in *The Journal of Applied Communication Research, Political Studies, American Politics Research, Public Administration,* and *Journal of Deliberative Democracy.* With John Gastil, she is the author of *Hope for Democracy: How Citizens Can Bring Reason Back into Politics* (Oxford, 2020).

Kevin Koban (PhD, Chemnitz University of Technology, Germany) is a postdoctoral researcher in the Department of Communication at the University of Vienna, Austria. His current research is concerned with individuals' interactions with digital systems (e.g., social machines, video games, social media) and whether the use of such systems impacts their well-being, primarily using quantitative methods. Dr. Koban's work is published in journals focusing on social machines, such as *Frontiers in Robotics and AI, Human-Machine Communication* or *Technology, Mind, and Behavior,* as well as media psychology and communication science journals, such as *Media Psychology, Psychology of Popular Media, Journal of Media Psychology, Computers in Human Behavior, Mobile Media & Communication, Journal of Medical Internet Research.*

Gary L. Kreps (Ph.D., University of Southern California) is a University Distinguished Professor in the Department of Communication at George Mason University in Fairfax, Virginia, where he directs the Center for Health and Risk Communication. His research examines the role of communication in providing high quality care, promoting public health, reducing health disparities, and informing effective health decision making related to health issues such as cancer, HIV/AIDS, and chronic disease. He is an active scholar, who has published more than 500 books, articles, and chapters concerning the applications of communication knowledge in society. His research has been funded by a number of federal and international government agencies, foundations, and corporations, and he has received many awards for his scholarship.

Jeffrey H. Kuznekoff (Ph.D., Ohio University) is an Associate Professor in the Department of Interdisciplinary and Communication Studies at Miami University. His work focuses on instructional communication, new communication technology, computer-mediated communication, and gaming. Jeff's work has been published in *Communication Education, New Media & Society,* and *Communication Research.* He is the current editor of the *Ohio Communication Journal.* Jeff teaches interpersonal communication, communication theory, and quantitative research methods.

Betty H. La France (Ph.D. Michigan State University) is a Professor of Communication Studies at Northern Illinois University. Her research interests focus on sexual communication in close relationships. She teaches undergraduate and graduate courses in interpersonal communication, research methods, and communication theory. She has published several articles in national and international journals, presented at national and international conferences, and has served on various editorial boards. Her accomplishments include several teaching and mentorship awards. She proudly serves on the Board of Directors of Northern Illinois Hospice.

Angela Y. Lee (M.A., Stanford University) is a Ph.D. candidate in Communication at Stanford University. She studies the psychology of technology in the Social Media Lab. Broadly, her research focuses on identifying pathways to improving digital well-being by helping individuals and communities have agency over their experiences with new technologies. Her work is supported by the Stanford Interdisciplinary Graduate Fellowship and the Stanford Social Impact Labs.

Timothy R. Levine (Ph.D. Michigan State University) is Distinguished Professor and Chair of Communication Studies at the University of Alabama at Birmingham (UAB). Levine's teaching and research interests include deception, interpersonal communication, persuasion and social influence, experimental research design, measurement validation, and statistical conclusions validity. He has published more than 150 journal articles. His research has been funded by the National Science Foundation, Department of Defense, and Department of Justice and his work has received press coverage from *New York Times*, *Washington Post*, NPR, NBC, CNN, Discovery Chanel, and *National Geographic*. His most recent book, *Duped: Truth-Default Theory and the Social Science of Lying and Deception*, published in 2020 by the University of Alabama Press, details his 30-year program of research on deception leading to the development and testing of Truth-Default Theory.

Jennifer A. Malkowski (Ph.D., University of Colorado Boulder) is an Associate Professor of Communication Arts and Sciences at California State University, Chico. Her research and teaching lie at the intersections of public health communication, medical professionalism, and biotechnological controversy where she explores how persuasive communication influences perceptions of and responses to health risks at both the individual and collective levels. Her work has appeared in *Health Communication*, the *Journal of Medical Humanities*, *The Review of Communication, and Journal of International & Intercultural Communication* in addition to other edited collections. She has also co-edited a special issue of *Rhetoric of Health & Medicine* that inaugurates a research trajectory for scholars invested in the public nature of health specifically as well as a forthcoming book collection entitled *Covid and... How to Do Rhetoric in a Pandemic* (University of Michigan Press) that focuses on the intersections of disease outbreak, risk communication, and social justice.

Michelle Miller-Day (PhD, Arizona State University) is a Professor of Communication Studies at Chapman University and Co-President of REAL Prevention, LLC. Her research addresses human communication and health, including areas such as substance use prevention, suicide, and families and mental health. Her community-embedded research has involved numerous creative projects to translate research findings into social change. She has collaboratively created several widely distributed evidence-based interventions including *keepin' it REAL,* a narrative, multicultural school-based substance use prevention curriculum, and other programs using innovative technologies to reduce adolescent substance use, risky sex among adolescents and promote HPV vaccination. This work has been funded by the National Institutes of Health, the Merck Foundation, Robert Wood Johnson Foundation, and others.

Brooke Molokach is a doctoral student of Communication at the University of Delaware and an affiliate of the Center for Information, Technology, and Public Life. Her research centers on the narrative-based persuasive mechanisms of disinformation and the psychological sources of resilience (such as intellectual humility) against disinformation, extremism, and affective polarization.

Stevie M. Munz (Ph.D., Ohio University) is an Associate Professor in the Department of Communication at Utah Valley University. Her research program focuses on exploring the cultural experiences of identity, power, politics, and gender. In particular, she is concerned with how human beings understand and communicate these relational, political, and social experiences. She pursues her scholarly interests along two different, but related, lines of research that examine identity in the contexts of classrooms and small-town communities. Stevie's work is published in *Communication Education, Departures, Women & Language, and The Basic Course Annual.* Stevie teaches intercultural communication, research methods, and ethnography.

Scott A. Myers (Ph.D., Kent State University) is a Professor and Peggy Rardin McConnell Endowed Teaching Chair in the Department of Communication Studies at West Virginia University, where he teaches courses in instructional, organizational, and positive communication. His research interests center primarily on the student-instructor relationship in the college classroom and the adult sibling relationship, with his research appearing in journals such as *Communication Education, Journal of Family Communication, Communication Research Reports*, and *Communication Quarterly*, among others. He is a past editor of Communication Teacher, the founding editor of the *Journal of Communication Pedagogy*, and the current editor of Journal of Family Communication. His most recent textbook—*Communication and Relationship Maintenance*—was published in 2020.

Robin L. Nabi (PhD, Annenberg School for Communication, University of Pennsylvania) is a professor of Communication at the University of California, Santa Barbara. Her research focuses on the role of emotion in media processes and effects, with particular emphasis on the persuasive effect of emotion-based messages and media use and well-being. She has served as a managing editor of Media Psychology and is a co-editor of the SAGE Handbook of Media Processes and Effects and the upcoming Oxford volume Our online emotional selves. She is a past chair of the Mass Communication Division of the International Communication Association as well as the Communication and Social Cognition Division of the National Communication Association, and she is the current Chair of the ICA Publications Committee. She is the inaugural recipient of the Innovation in Theory Award from ICA's Mass Communication Division for her work on emotional framing, and is a 2017 inductee as an ICA Fellow.

Haley Nolan-Cody (MA, The University of Texas at Austin) is a PhD student in the School of Communication and Information at Rutgers University. Her research addresses questions at the intersection of interpersonal, family, and health communication. Primarily, she studies communicative coping, resilience, and dark side processes within the family context. For example, she recently examined how people affected by substance use disorder manage this stressor in their families and communities.

Erin Oittinen (MA, University of Delaware) is a doctoral student of Communication at the University of Delaware. Erin's areas of interest include science and political communication, with current research centering on political polarization, mis- and disinformation, and the tensions between free speech and diversity, equity, and inclusion issues on college campuses.

Eli Quay received his Bachelor of Science in Communication, Technology & Culture from Bridgewater College (2020) and is currently pursuing a Master of Arts in Communication from the University of Connecticut (expected 2023). He is interested in studying both interpersonal communication and health communication, with sexual communication and sexual health being two areas which he aims to focus on. In addition to his studies, he is a graduate teaching assistant for the University of Connecticut's Department of Communication. He has taught an introductory communication course, which helps students become acquainted with the field of communication and the various specialty areas found within.

Bridget Rubenking (Ph.D, Indiana University) is an Associate Professor in the Nicholson School of Communication and Media at the University of Central Florida. She is co-author of two books, including 2020's *Binge Watching: Motivations and Implications of our Changing Viewing Behaviors* (Peter Lang). Her work has been published in journals such as *Computers in Human Behavior, Journal of Communication,* and *Journal of Broadcasting & Electronic Media.* Her line of research focuses on emotional and cognitive processing of mediated messages. Specifically, she explores how aspects of mediated content such as the presence of emotion, narrative structure, and form components of the modality media is used in influences overtime processing related to emotional and attitudinal responses, memory and learning of content, and behavioral choices. This has led her to research media multitasking, binge watching, and responses to disgust-eliciting content in entertainment messages. Her work has been cited in multiple popular press outlets, including *Forbes, ABC News, Huffington Post,* and *New York Magazine.*

Chris Sawyer is currently ranked among the top 100 most published scholars in the field of Communication Studies and maintains an active research program into the causes, symptoms, and treatments of speech anxiety. A former Chair of NCA's Communication Apprehension and Avoidance Commission, Dr. Sawyer has received recognition as a teacher-scholar including a nomination for the prestigious Minnie Stephens Piper Foundation award for college teaching excellence and was a recent recipient is a past recipient of the College of Communication Distinguished Research and Creative Activity Award. In 1983, Dr. Sawyer began his college teaching career as an instructor at Tarrant County Junior College, Northwest Campus in Fort Worth, TX and later joined the Communication Studies Department at Texas Christian University in 1999. He served as director of the Basic Speech Communication course from his appointment until 2005. A former department Chair, Dr. Sawyer currently holds the rank of Professor at TCU. He resides in Fort Worth with his wife, daughter, and two grandchildren.

Joshua M. Scacco (PhD, University of Texas at Austin) is an Associate Professor in and Associate Chair of the Department of Communication at the University of South Florida. Dr. Scacco also serves as a Faculty Researcher with the USF-Nielsen Sunshine State Survey and is a Faculty Research Associate with the award-winning Center for Media Engagement at the University of Texas at Austin. He specializes in political communication, media content and effects, and quantitative research methods. Dr. Scacco's research is focused on how emerging communication technologies influence established agents in American political life, including news organizations and the presidency. He is the coauthor, with Kevin Coe, of the book *The Ubiquitous Presidency: Presidential Communication and Digital Democracy in Tumultuous Times* (Oxford University Press, 2021). Before coming to USF, Dr. Scacco served on the faculty at Purdue University, worked in public relations at the state and federal level, and worked for a member of legislative leadership in the Pennsylvania House of Representatives as well as a U.S. senator.

Kristina M. Scharp (Ph.D, University of Iowa) is an Associate Professor in the School of Communication and Information at Rutgers University and a Director of the Family Communication and Relationships Lab. She researches the process of marginalization and the ways people cope with the major disruptions to their lives. She has over 75 publications in outlets such as the *Journal of Communication, Human Communication Research, Communication Monographs*, and *Communication Research* as well as three co-authored textbooks. Recently, she was awarded the International Communication Association's Early Career Award, NCA Family Communication Division's Distinguished Article Award, and the Leslie A. Baxter Early Career Award in Family Communication. Her work on family estrangement, in particular, has garnered attention from numerous media outlets such as *The New York Times, The Washington Post, The Conversation, The Huffington Post*, and *NPR*.

Scott M. Schönfeldt-Aultman (PhD, University of California, Davis) is a Professor in the Communication Department at St. Mary's College of California. He teaches courses addressing intercultural communication, masculinities, communication & social justice, whiteness, and drag. He has published in *Pedagogy, Culture and Society, Critical Race and Whiteness Studies, Critical Arts: A Journal of South-North Cultural and Media Studies, SAFUNDI: The Journal of South African and American Studies, Communicatio: South African Journal for Communication Theory and Research,* and the *Journal of African Cultural Studies.*

Lijiang Shen (Ph.D., University of Wisconsin-Madison) is a Professor of Communication Arts & Sciences at the Pennsylvania State University. His primary area of research considers the impact of message features and audience characteristics in persuasive health communication, message processing, and the process of persuasion/resistance to persuasion as well as quantitative research methods in communication. His research has been published in major communication and related journals. He is currently the editor of *Communication Methods and Measures.*

Natasha Shrikant is an Assistant Professor in the Department of Communication at the University of Colorado, Boulder. She uses ethnography and discourse analysis to analyze relational, institutional, and/or political ramifications of identity-negotiation in interaction. Her work focuses on negotiation of racial, ethnic, cultural, gender, and political identities in institutional contexts. Natasha has published in Communication and Discourse Studies journals such as *Communication Monographs, The Journal of International and Intercultural Communication, Language in Society, Discourse and Communication,* and *Discourse & Society.*

Kara Shultz (Ph.D., University of Denver) is the Vice Provost and Dean of the Honors College at Commonwealth University of Pennsylvania. She has worked in higher education for over 30 years as faculty member and chairperson in the Communication Studies Department at Bloomsburg University of Pennsylvania before moving into an administrative role. As an applied communication scholar, Dr. Shultz has focused on building communicative processes that support broad engagement to help organizations and communities develop shared understandings across competing perspectives to strengthen collaborative action. She has published in the *Quarterly Journal of Speech, The Howard Journal of Communications, Conflict and Diversity, The Rhetoric of Food,* and *Handbook of Communication and People with Disabilities.*

Brian H. Spitzberg is Senate Distinguished Professor Emeritus in the School of Communication at San Diego State University. He received his BA at University of Texas—Arlington (1978), his MA (1980) and PhD (1981) at University of Southern California, and his Certified Threat Management (CTM™) status in 2017. He is a Core Researcher in the Center for Communication, Health, & the Public Good, and a Co-founder & Advisory Board member in the Center for Human Dynamics in the Mobile Age, SDSU. He received the 2009 Western States Communication Association career Scholar Award, the 2011 National

Communication Association Larry Kibler Memorial Award, the 2017 Mark Knapp NCA Award for career contribution to the study of Interpersonal Communication, and the 2020 National Communication Association career Distinguished Scholar Award. His coauthored book *The Dark Side of Relationship Pursuit* won both the biennial International Association for Relationship Research Book Award (1ˢᵗ ed.: 2008) and the NCA Gerald Miller book award (2ⁿᵈ ed., 2015). He is author or coauthor of over 175 scholarly articles and book chapters, cited over 19,000 times. He has coauthored and co-edited several scholarly books on communication competence and the dark side of communication. His primary areas of research involve social media and meme diffusion, assessment, interpersonal communication skills, jealousy, conflict, threats, coercion, violence, and stalking.

Keri K. Stephens, PhD, is a Professor in Organizational Communication Technology, a Distinguished Teaching Professor, Co-Director of Technology, Information, & Policy Institute, and she directs the OPTICLab in the Moody College of Communication at The University of Texas at Austin. Her research program examines the role of technology in organizational practices and organizing processes, especially in contexts of crisis, disaster, and health. She has authored over 100 articles appearing in research journals (e.g., *Communication Theory, Health Communication, Human Communication Research, Journal of Computer-Mediated Communication, Journal of Contingencies and Crisis Management, Journal of Public Relations Research, & Management Communication Quarterly*), proceedings, and books. Her two most recent books are the national-level, award-winning book *New Media in Times of Crisis* (2019, Routledge), and the two-time, national-level, award-winning book *Negotiating Control: Organizations and Mobile Communication* (2018, Oxford University Press). Stephens has received external funding (as a PI or CoPI) from organizations like the National Science Foundation, Merck, Facebook, Tx Department of Transportation, Institute for a Disaster Resilient Texas, and Texas Water Development Board. She gave a TEDx Talk about her NSF-funded work on social media and how people were rescued from flooding during Hurricane Harvey.

Robert Stise is a PhD student at the University of Delaware. His work centers on the mechanism, impacts and usage of moral and normative views across a variety of political and social spaces.

Sarah J. Tracy (Ph.D., University of Colorado) is School Director and Professor of organizational communication and qualitative methodology in The Hugh Downs School of Human Communication at Arizona State University. Professor Tracy's scholarly work examines emotion, communication, and identity in the workplace with a focus on emotional labor, compassion, bullying, and organizational flourishing. She is a National Communication Association Distinguished Scholar, Western States Communication Association Distinguished Teacher, and Co-Founder of The Transformation Project--a consortium of faculty, students, and community members who seek to discover and promote creative change processes that encourage healthy communication patterns, collaborative group behavior, and equitable forms of social organization. Her award-winning research has resulted in two books, more than 100 scholarly essays, and she has delivered over 75 keynotes and workshops worldwide for a variety of organizations and universities. Furthermore, she regularly serves as a media resource—on topics such as workplace bullying, toxic positivity, resilience, and work-life balance—contributing to outlets such as *National Public Radio*, *The Today Show*, *The Phoenix Business Journal*, and *The Arizona Republic*.

Rachel V. Tucker is a doctoral student at the University of Connecticut in Storrs, CT. She received her M.A. at the University of Cincinnati in 2021. Her research program examines stigmatized sexual health conditions, identities, experiences and how they are managed communicatively. Her work also considers how sociocultural norms, values, and expectations related to gender and sexuality shape perceptions of and experiences with stigma, as well as how stigma is managed.

Nathan Walter (Ph.D. University of Southern California) is an Assistant Professor in the Department of Communication Studies at Northwestern University. He is Founder and Co-Director of the Center of Media Psychology and Social Influence (COM-PSI) and a faculty member at the Center for Communication and Health (CCH), both at Northwestern. Walter's research concerns the power of strategic storytelling, correction of misinformation, and the role of emotion and affect in social influence. His studies have been published in a number of leading outlets, including the *Journal of Communication*, *Communication Research*, *Human Communication Research*, and *Communication Monographs*. His most recent work, which is supported by the NIH/FDA, the Peterson Foundation, the Chicago Center for Diabetes Translation Research, and the Delaney Foundation, focuses on novel methods to debunk misinformation and change behavior.

Gust A. Yep (PhD, University of Southern California) is Professor of Communication Studies, Core Faculty of Sexuality Studies, and Faculty in the Ed. D. Program in Educational Leadership at San Francisco State University. His research examines communication at the intersections of culture, race, class, gender, sexuality, and the body with a focus on queer and trans people of color. In addition to authoring more than one hundred articles and book chapters in (inter)disciplinary journals and anthologies, he co-edited four special issues for the *Journal of Homosexuality*: Queer theory and Communication (2003), Tensions between Lesbian, Gay, Bisexual, and Transgender (LGBT) Studies and Queer Theory (2006), Sexualities and Gender in an Age of Neoliberalism (2012), and Queer Relationalities in Communication and Beyond (2022). He has been widely recognized for his teaching, mentoring, scholarship, and community work, nationally and internationally. In 2021, he was recipient of the International and Intercultural Communication Division (IICD) "Distinguished Scholar Award" and the Gay, Lesbian, Bisexual, Transgender, and Queer (GLBTQ) Communication Studies Division "Monograph of the Year" Award (coauthored with Fatima Alaoui and Ryan Lescure), sponsored by the National Communication Association (NCA). He currently serves as associate editor for *Communication and Critical/Cultural Studies, Journal of*

Applied Communication Research, Journal of Homosexuality, Journal of International and Intercultural Communication, Oxford Encyclopedia of Queer Studies and Communication, and *QED: A Journal of GLBTQ Worldmaking.*

Dannagal G. Young (Ph.D. Annenberg School for Communication at the University of Pennsylvania) is Professor of Communication and Political Science at the University of Delaware where she researches the content, psychology, effects, and appeal of political entertainment and misinformation.

Priscilla L. Young holds a master's degree in Communication Studies with emphasis on intercultural communication. She taught business communication, public speaking, and academic writing during her eight years as senior lecturer at the internationalized Peking University HSBC Business School (Shenzhen, China). While in China, she was invited to develop a one-week lecture series on intercultural communication presented at Harbin Institute of Technology's Summer International Program in 2017 and 2018. Priscilla has been an invited speaker for English, communication or media students at Agriculture University of Hebei, Baoding; Beijing International Studies University; and Shenzhen University. In the United States, Priscilla has taught at the University of Rhode Island, Johnson & Wales University, and Keiser University. Prior to university teaching Priscilla's professional career included executive director of a state chapter of a national nonprofit, assistant press secretary and special publications manager for a city mayor, public relations director for a children's museum, fund development officer for a major hospital system, and entrepreneur.

Valerie J. Young (Ph.D., University of Arizona) is an Associate Professor in the Communication Department at Hanover College in Hanover, Indiana. Her scholarship focuses on interpersonal health communication and the maintenance of romantic relationships through everyday communication processes. She teaches a variety of courses and workshops surrounding difficult conversations and effective communication skill building. She volunteers her time on wellness and community health initiatives. Her research has appeared in interdisciplinary journals such as *Journal of Social and Personal Relationships* and *Family Relations,* and others.

Shupei Yuan (Ph.D., Michigan State University) is an associate professor in the Department of Communication and an affiliate faculty in the Institute for the Study of Environment, Sustainability & Energy at Northern Illinois University. She teaches courses in the area of public relations, science communication, and environmental communication. Her research focuses on the support and factors that influence science communicators' engagement with the public, and the effects of strategic communication styles in the context of risk, science, and health communication. Shupei has published nearly forty peer-reviewed research articles, including in journals like *New Media and Society, Science Communication, Health Communication,* and *Journalism & Mass Communication Quarterly.*

COMPUTER-MEDIATED COMMUNICATION

The computer-mediated communication (CMC) context focuses on digital messages that people exchange using computer technologies. Accordingly, CMC scholars examine mediated communication across cell phones, laptop and desktop computers, social media applications, the Internet, and so on. Some major areas of research in CMC include texting, online support groups, blogging, cyberbullying, email, apps, and artificial intelligence. This section includes chapters focusing on three important areas of CMC research: (1) online dating, (2) social media and well-being, and (3) online privacy management. First, Jennifer Gibbs (University of California, Santa Barbara) examines the online dating scene to review how online daters can be more successful. Second, Jeffrey Hancock and Angela Lee (Stanford University) examine how social media use impacts our mental health and well-being. Third, Jeffrey Child (Kent State University) reviews communication privacy management (CPM) research to discuss online privacy, sharing, and disclosure in social media. Nowadays because of the sheer amount of time we spend online and on our cell phones and computers, it is important to focus our attention toward CMC research. These CMC research programs will help you navigate online dating, social media, and online disclosures. As technology continues to advance at a rapid pace, only time will tell how computer-mediated technologies and research findings will continue to change after the publication of these chapters.

HOW TO BE SUCCESSFUL
IN ONLINE DATING

Jennifer L. Gibbs
University of California, Santa Barbara

When I began studying online dating in 2003, I had no idea it would turn into an on-going research program with such importance for the field of communication. It all started when two of my friends and fellow graduate students at USC, Nicole Ellison and Rebecca Heino, invited me to collaborate with them on a project on online dating. It made sense as we all had interests in new technologies and how they were changing the way we communicate. Way back then, the World Wide Web was still relatively new and there was little scholarship on online communication, and even less published research on Internet dating (which was a brand-new phenomenon). I also had a personal interest in the topic, as I had met my husband on Match.com back in 1998, when very few people had ever tried online matchmaking. I have heard it said (and I fully agree) that research is "me-search," and the best research topics tend to be ones that are rooted in your own personal experience and passions. This is so because studying something about which you have particular knowledge and insight generally leads to more informed research, and choosing a topic that excites you provides motivation to drive and sustain your interest in the research.

A lot has changed in the online dating world in the last two decades. Overall, online dating has gone from a once stigmatized to a mainstream practice; indeed, it has become one of the most common ways for romantic partners to meet. And it does seem to work: a study found that out of Americans who married between 2005 and 2012, more than one third had met online (Cacioppo et al., 2013). Further, those who met their partners online reported lower rates of divorce and higher marital satisfaction. Early research was conducted on traditional online dating websites (e.g., Match.com, eHarmony, Yahoo Personals, and OkCupid), which required users to reveal a great deal of personal information up front in their profile (multiple photos, a narrative essay, and data fields ranging from demographic characteristics to one's political and religious views, smoking and drinking habits, and preference for children). While traditional dating sites still exist, the rise of mobile communication has made mobile

3

dating applications (e.g., Tinder, Bumble, and Grindr) more popular, which typically only ask for a few pieces of information, such as location, photo, age, and sex, and encourage quicker face-to-face meetings. Nevertheless, these location-aware apps may reveal new types of information about one's physical location (Blackwell et al., 2015); in fact, some apps even match users up based on those who have crossed paths in person.

Early online dating catered to those who face more difficulty meeting potential romantic partners in their everyday lives, including adult professionals in the workforce, older (divorced or widowed) adults, and those from marginalized groups such as LGBTQ+ or rural populations. While early research tended to focus mainly on adult, heterosexual users, scholars have shifted their attention to include underrepresented populations such as gay men (Blackwell et al., 2015; Correiro & Tong, 2016) or Muslim American women (Rochadiat et al., 2018), as well as exploring the role of intersectional identities (Marciano & Nimrod, 2021; Miao & Chan, 2021). The rise of dating apps has also made online dating more attractive to younger users, including teens and college students. In turn, the range of motivations for doing online dating has expanded beyond social or relational goals (e.g., looking for a long-term romantic relationship or a short-term sexual hookup) to include personal goals such as entertainment, self-esteem and validation, and combatting loneliness (Youngvorst & Pham, 2022). Finally, online dating has become further normalized in the COVID-19 era, with new criteria influencing decision-making about potential partners such as living situation and vaccination status, and leading to new technological enhancements including in-app voice and video features (Youngvorst & Pham, 2022).

More than just a fad or popular trend, online dating is an interesting topic for communication scholars to study, since it requires individuals to form (or at least initiate) relationships with virtual strangers in a mediated environment in which they have less visual and contextual information and fewer social cues about one another. A number of communication scholars (including myself and my colleagues) have studied questions related to how online daters present themselves, form impressions of others, and establish relationships with potential partners. This chapter reviews our knowledge on this topic, focusing on the following question: how can online daters be more successful in meeting a potential romantic partner?

PRESENTING ONESELF ONLINE

Presenting oneself and assessing others in online dating can be challenging. When you meet someone face-to-face, you have many visual and social cues to provide clues about the person and their relationship to you. The way they are dressed, physical objects they are carrying (such as a book), and the physical location in which you meet may tell you about their background and interests. You can read their body language and facial expressions to gauge their mood and how they feel about you. The other person can also use these cues to learn about you. But what about when you are just looking at a profile online? How should you present yourself in a way that is accurate yet garners attention? How do you know if someone is lying about their age, appearance, or marital status?

My colleagues and I have addressed such questions in our research. We have found that online daters navigate a tension between presenting an ideal self and an actual self (Ellison et al., 2006). On one hand, they face pressure to portray themselves in the most positive, attractive light possible in their profile, in order to stand out and be noticed amidst hundreds of other profiles. On the other hand, there are competing pressures to create honest and accurate self-portrayals if one desires a romantic relationship, since the truth will eventually come out on an in-person date. The desire to view oneself as honest may also limit the amount of deception that takes place (Mazar & Ariely, 2006). In research with a national sample of Match.com users, we found that a full 94% of our respondents strongly disagreed they had intentionally misrepresented themselves in their profile or online communication, and 87% felt such misrepresentation was unacceptable. Despite these strong claims of their own honesty, they felt that other online daters routinely misrepresented aspects such as their physical appearance, relationship goals, age, income, and marital status (Gibbs et al., 2006).

Since people are unlikely to admit to something as socially undesirable as lying in an interview or even an anonymous survey, several of my colleagues decided to measure how much online daters lie in their profiles in a more objective way, by bringing them into a lab and comparing their actual age, height, and weight with what they had claimed in their profiles. They found that a majority had indeed misrepresented one or more of these features, but that most lies were minor—such as shaving off five pounds or adding an inch to their height (Toma et al., 2008). Although blatant deception is rare, online daters do tend to exaggerate and embellish the truth (Whitty, 2008). While this certainly happens offline as well, the online dating context offers certain features that allow for increased exaggeration and embellishment. First, users are largely anonymous and the information they have about one another is initially limited to the profile. Without a shared social network (in the form of shared friends and acquaintances) to temper misinformation, online daters are free to exaggerate their virtues in order to maximize their attractiveness (Fiore & Donath, 2004). They are also communicating asynchronously (at least initially), which allows them to engage in "selective self-presentation" (Walther & Burgoon, 1992) by consciously controlling and editing their profiles to emphasize the positive and mask their negative attributes. This is not unique to online dating; we do this in other contexts such as job interviews and writing a resume. Research has found that an online dating profile is similar to a "resume" in which one tries to sell oneself to potential romantic partners rather than employers (Heino et al., 2010).

Through qualitative interviews with online dating participants, we were able to explore this issue in more depth. We found that honesty online is complicated and that misrepresentation occurs in both intentional and unintentional ways (Ellison et al., 2006). First, online daters often portray an idealized or potential future version of the self, through strategies such as identifying themselves as active in a laundry list of activities (such as hiking, surfing, and roller blading) in which they rarely participate but which are in line with how they would like to see themselves. They may also describe themselves in euphemistic terms such as "curvy" or "average" rather than admitting they are overweight. Ellison and her colleagues conceive of the profile as a "promise made to an imagined audience that future face-to-face interaction will take place with someone who does not differ fundamentally from the person represented by the profile" (Ellison et al., 2011, p. 56). In this sense, the profile is like a "psychological contract" that one could be held to by potential future dates, and it is not considered deceptive as long as it *could* be true in the future.

Misrepresentation also occurs as an attempt to circumvent technological constraints of the site. For example, online daters often "fudge" demographic information such as their age by subtracting a few years in order to avoid being "filtered out" of searches. Many online dating sites allow users to perform searches on basic demographic criteria such as age, height, weight, and geographic location. Since many users tend to perform searches using natural breakpoints (e.g., 35), it is common practice for those a few years older (36, 37, or 38) to list their age as 35 on their profile in order to appeal to a wider audience. They justify this by saying they tend to look younger or date younger people, and they often regard this as socially acceptable as long as they disclose their real age early on in their correspondence (Ellison et al., 2006). This is confirmed by an analysis of Match.com profiles that found that spikes occurred at certain (more desirable) age points that were much higher than would be expected by chance. For example, there was a disproportionate number of 29-year-old female users, eight times higher than the number of females aged 30–34 (Epstein, 2007).

Finally, online daters may unintentionally misrepresent themselves due to the limits of their own self-knowledge. We call this the "foggy mirror" effect, in which individuals represent themselves on the basis of an inaccurate self-concept that may not correspond with how others see them (Ellison et al., 2006). That is, they may not be able to accurately describe themselves because there are blind spots in their self-concept, or things about themselves that they do not know. As one of our interviewees put it, "sometimes you will see a person who weighs 900 pounds and—this is just an exaggeration—and they will have on spandex, you will think, 'God, I wish I had their mirror, because obviously their mirror tells them they look great.' It's the same thing with online" (Ellison et al., 2006, p. 13). Thus, users often unintentionally misrepresent themselves out of lack of awareness of themselves and how others may perceive them.

ASSESSING OTHERS AND FORMING RELATIONSHIPS ONLINE

Meeting people through online dating is fraught with uncertainty. There is usually no shared social network, and rather than meeting through a friend or acquaintance, users are interacting with virtual strangers. They thus face privacy risks in disclosing intimate information. Given the relative anonymity and ease of deception online, it is important for online daters to assess and vet the credibility of potential partners in order to verify their identity claims. This is more difficult since there are fewer traditional identity cues and less immediate feedback (Gibbs et al., 2011), but online environments do allow for a variety of information-seeking strategies, which refer to ways in which we seek information about others (Ramirez et al., 2002). Further, recent research suggests that pictures and textual cues may be processed independently and impact perceived attraction and impression formation in different ways (van der Zanden et al., 2022).

Although less information is available from nonverbal and social context cues, online dating participants do scrutinize the cues that are present and use them to form impressions of others, and as a result, small cues may become exaggerated or take on greater importance. For example, a profile with a typo or misspelling may be rejected based on the assumption that the profile creator is lazy or uneducated (Ellison et al., 2006). As Walther's (1996) hyperpersonal effect predicts, online daters have the tendency to idealize potential partners on the basis of limited cues, and they fill in the gaps by building up a fantasy persona that may be inaccurate and unrealistic. This may explain why the longer communicators wait to meet in person and the more they communicate online, the more likely their first meeting is to end up in rejection (Ramirez & Zhang, 2007). While a brief period of online interaction is beneficial, daters may reach a tipping point after which further interaction leads to negative outcomes when they eventually meet in person (Ramirez et al., 2015). This is especially likely to be the case if online daters perceive that potential partners are engaging in deception based on their evaluation of linguistic clues in online messages (Sharabi & Caughlin, 2019).

The process of verifying identity claims online is known as "warranting" (Walther & Parks, 2002). Warranting involves establishing a reliable link between an online persona and a "corporeally-anchored person in the physical world" (Walther et al., 2009, p. 232). Generally, messages generated by others carry more weight than information we report about ourselves (which is easier to manipulate). Support for the warranting principle has been found in several experiments finding that other-generated claims about qualities such as one's attractiveness and extraversion are more compelling than self-generated claims in social network sites (Utz, 2010; Walther et al., 2008, 2009).

For the most part, online dating participants cannot rely on other-generated accounts to warrant their identity claims. A few dating review sites have arisen where daters can rate their dates, but these have not really taken off. To compensate, online daters often engage in tactics such as "showing" rather than "telling" (Ellison et al., 2006); for example, it is more credible to demonstrate one's sense of humor by writing a clever, witty profile than by simply stating "I am hilarious" in an otherwise dull profile (Gibbs et al., 2011). Our research found evidence that online dating participants used a variety of tactics to reduce uncertainty and verify credibility of potential partners, by gathering information from both online and offline sources. The rise of social media platforms has led to new strategies of connecting with potential partners via Instagram, Facebook, or Snapchat in order to glean more naturalistic impressions of them and observe their interactions with others on these sites; this can substitute for the lack of a shared social network.

These tactics—classified as passive, active, interactive, and extractive (Ramirez et al., 2002)—include comparing profiles on multiple websites or saving emails to check for consistency, checking public records such as white pages, and "Googling" people to warrant their online claims. Some of our participants even went as far as to perform home property value searches, drawing on the rich stores of personal information accessible online. The most common strategies, however, were interactive and involved asking direct questions of the other person. Those who used more strategies to reduce uncertainty about others tended to disclose more personal information about themselves, perhaps because such "detective work" reduced their privacy concerns and made them more comfortable revealing intimate information to strangers they met online (Gibbs et al., 2011). Such individuals were also likely to have a higher sense of self-efficacy (or confidence in their own abilities) and more Internet experience.

Assessing others online is also complicated by the level of choice available, or what is known as the "paradox of choice." Having access to a large pool of eligible dating partners is convenient and affords users a great deal of choice, but this choice can also be paralyzing and lead to poor decisions. Online dating models range from "see-and-screen" sites like Match.com that allow users to browse through all user profiles and choose whom to contact to algorithmic sites like eHarmony that match users up based on compatibility algorithms, with others such as OkCupid.com blending the two by using algorithms to cull choices and letting users select from a small number of options (Tong et al., 2016). While algorithms now wield more influence over online decision-making (Courtois & Timmermans, 2021; Tong et al., 2016), and may even shape relationship success (Sharabi, 2021), all three types of models provide a great deal more choice of potential dating partners than most individuals encounter in their offline lives.

Related to the notion of expanded choice, my colleagues and I (Heino et al., 2010) observed a prevalent "market" metaphor in how online dating participants talked about their experience. Our interviewees talked about online dating as "people shopping" and used terms like "sales pipeline," "catalog," and "supermarket" to describe the process. They described viewing profiles as resumes and mentally accounting for embellishments of others, as well as trying to sell themselves. Our interviews revealed that the market metaphor encouraged a mentality in which people became more pickier and rejected profiles on the basis of trivial criteria, privileged demographic fields (age, height, and weight) rather than getting a holistic sense of the person, and regarded others as well as themselves as commodities or products to buy and sell, with an emphasis on "relationshopping" (shopping for a mate) rather than "relationshipping" (getting to know someone and developing a relationship). As one male put it, "the downside of it is, I think, that the expectations are very much of a consumer—that sort of instant karma expectation, expecting a connection with less effort" (Heino et al., 2010, p. 440).

ADVICE FOR ONLINE DATERS

Based on what we know about online dating, how can online daters be more successful? The research on misrepresentation in online dating suggests that in order to be successful, online daters should strive to present themselves in a positive and attractive yet still honest and accurate light. As in offline situations such as job interviews and first dates, it is helpful to think carefully about how you present yourself in your profile; first impressions count for a lot and are hard to change. Since people are not always aware of how others perceive them, a good strategy is to ask a friend or family member to read over one's profile and give input. Many online dating sites provide tips and advice, but we found that online daters often engage in their own recursive process of assessing others and then applying the rules to their own self-presentation (Ellison et al., 2006). For example, one may become disillusioned with profiles that only include one or two (unrealistic) photos, and then make an effort to post multiple photos of oneself in a variety of situations to portray oneself more accurately.

Despite the prevalence of at least minor misrepresentation (e.g., fudging one's age or accentuating one's appearance) in online dating, honesty is still the best policy. Gibbs et al. (2006) found that online daters who were more honest and disclosed more personal feelings and information were more likely to consider themselves successful in achieving their goals, and Baker (2005) also found that being open and honest in one's self-disclosures was one of the factors in developing successful long-term relationships. Given that others are often not completely honest in their profiles, however, it is important to find ways to "warrant" others' identity claims by looking for multiple photos, asking questions and checking for consistency, Googling them, or connecting on other social media platforms. Do not wait too long to meet in person, since it is easy to build up a fantasy persona based on limited cues that may not be completely accurate. Explicitly seeking information about potential partners can also help to avoid disappointment on a first date (Sharabi & Caughlin, 2017), and openly discussing one's mate preferences on the first date can also lead to further dates (Sharabi & Dykstra-DeVette, 2019).

Finally, emphasizing "relationshopping" may provide more choice and convenience in selecting potential partners, but online daters should not neglect the "relationshipping" aspect and expect to have an instant connection with little effort. Online dating has real advantages in providing a portal or initial introduction to individuals who may never meet otherwise, but it is just the first step. Finding the right person requires making good choices (and being able to identify which criteria will make one a good partner) initially, but the bulk of relationship development occurs offline, beyond the online dating site itself.

REFERENCES

Baker, A. J. (2005). *Double click: Romance and commitment among online couples.* Hampton Press.

Blackwell, C., Birnholtz, J., & Abbott, C. (2015). Seeing and being seen: Co-situation and impression formation using Grindr, a location-aware gay dating app. *New Media & Society, 17*(7), 1117–1136. https://doi.org/10.1177/1461444814521595

Cacioppo, J. T., Cacioppo, S., Gonzaga, G. C., Ogburn, E. L., & VanderWeele, T. J. (2013). Marital satisfaction and break-ups differ across on-line and off-line meeting venues. *Proceedings of the National Academy of Sciences, 110*(25), 10135–10140. https://doi.org/10.1073/pnas.1222447110

Corriero, E. F., & Tong, S. T. (2016). Managing uncertainty in mobile dating applications: Goals, concerns of use, and information seeking in Grindr. *Mobile Media & Communication, 4*(1), 121–141. https://doi.org/10.1177/2050157915614872

Courtois, C., & Timmermans, E. (2021). Cracking the Tinder code: An experience sampling approach to the dynamics and impact of platform governing algorithms. *Journal of Computer-Mediated Communication, 23*(1), 1–16. https://doi.org/10.1093/jcmc/zmx001

Ellison, N. B., Hancock, J. T., & Toma, C. L. (2011). Profile as promise: A framework for conceptualizing veracity in online dating self-presentations. *New Media & Society, 14*(1), 45–62. https://doi.org/10.1177/146144481141039

Ellison, N. B., Heino, R. D., & Gibbs, J. L. (2006). Managing impressions online: Self-Presentation processes in the online dating environment. *Journal of Computer-Mediated Communication 11*(2), 415–441. https://doi.org/10.1111/j.1083-6101.2006.00020.x

Epstein, R. (2007). The truth about online dating. *Scientific American Mind, 18*(1), 28–35. https://www.jstor.org/stable/24939564

Fiore, A. T., & Donath, J. S. (2004). Online personals: An overview. In *Proceedings of the Conference on Human Factors in Computing Systems.* New York: ACM, 1395–1398.

Heino, R. D., Ellison, N. B., & Gibbs, J. L. (2010). Relationshopping: Investigating the market metaphor in online dating. *Journal of Social and Personal Relationships, 27*(4), 427–447. https://doi.org/10.1177/0265407510361614

Gibbs, J. L., Ellison, N. B., & Heino, R. D. (2006). Self-Presentation in online personals: The role of anticipated future interaction, self-disclosure, and perceived success in Internet dating. *Communication Research, 33*(2), 152–177. https://doi.org/10.1177/0093650205285368

Gibbs, J. L., Ellison, N. B., & Lai, C. H. (2011). First comes love, then comes Google: An investigation of uncertainty reduction strategies and self-disclosure in online dating. *Communication Research, 38*(1), 70–100. https://doi.org/10.1177/0093650205285368

Marciano, A., & Nimrod, G. (2021). Identity collision: Older gay men using technology. *Journal of Computer-Mediated Communication, 26*(1), 22–37. https://doi.org/10.1093/jcmc/zmaa016.

Mazar, N., & Ariely, D. (2006). Dishonesty in everyday life and its policy implications. *Journal of Public Policy & Marketing, 25*(1), 1–21. https://doi.org/10.1509/jppm.25.1.117

Miao, W., & Chan, L. S. (2021). Domesticating gay apps: An intersectional analysis of the use of Blued among Chinese gay men. *Journal of Computer-Mediated Communication, 26*(1), 38–53. https://doi.org/10.1093/jcmc/zmaa015

Ramirez, A., Sumner, E. M., Fleuriet, C., & Cole, M. (2015). When online dating partners meet offline: The effect of modality switching on relational communication between online daters. *Journal of Computer-Mediated Communication, 20*(1), 99–114. https://doi.org/10.1111/jcc4.12101

Ramirez, A., Walther, J. B., Burgoon, J. K., & Sunnafrank, M. (2002). Information-seeking strategies, uncertainty, and computer-mediated communication: Toward a conceptual model. *Human Communication Research, 28*(2), 213–228. https://doi.org/10.1111/j.1468-2958.2002.tb00804.x

Ramirez, A., & Zhang, S. (2007). When online meets offline: The effect of modality switching on relational communication. *Communication Monographs, 74*(3), 287–310. https://doi.org/10.1080/03637750701543493

Rochadiat, A. M. P., Tong, S. T., & Novak, J. M. (2018). Online dating and courtship among Muslim American women: Negotiating technology, religious identity, and culture. *New Media & Society, 20*(4), 1618–1639. https://doi.org/10.1177/1461444817702396

Sharabi, L. L. (2021). Exploring how beliefs about algorithms shape (offline) success in online dating: A two-wave longitudinal investigation. *Communication Research, 48*(7), 931–952. https://doi.org/10.1177/0093650219896936

Sharabi, L. L., & Caughlin, J. (2017). What predicts first date success? A longitudinal study of modality switching in online dating. *Personal Relationships, 24*(2), 370–391. https://doi.org/10.1111/pere.12188

Sharabi, L. L., & Caughlin, J. (2019). Deception in online dating: Significance and implications for the first offline date. *New Media & Society, 21*(1), 229–247. https://doi.org/10.1177/1461444818792425

Sharabi, L. L., & Dykstra-DeVette, T. A. (2019). From first email to first date: Strategies for initiating relationships in online dating. *Journal of Social & Personal Relationships, 36*(11), 3389–3407. https://doi.org/10.1177/0265407518822780

Toma, C. L., Hancock, J. T., & Ellison, N. B. (2008). Separating fact from fiction: An examination of deceptive self-presentation in online dating profiles. *Personality and Social Psychology Bulletin, 34*(8), 1023–1036. https://doi.org/10.1177/0146167208318067

Tong, S. T., Hancock, J. T., & Slatcher, R. B. (2016). Online dating system design and relational decision making: Choice, algorithms, and control. *Personal Relationships, 23*(4), 645–662. https://doi.org/10.1111/pere.12158

Utz, S. (2010). Show me your friends and I will tell you what type of person you are: How one's profile, number of friends, and type of friends influence impression formation on social network sites. *Journal of Computer-Mediated Communication, 15*(2), 314–335. https://doi.org/10.1111/j.1083-6101.2010.01522.x

Walther, J. B. (1996). Computer-mediated communication: Impersonal, interpersonal, and hyperpersonal interaction. *Communication Research, 23*(1), 3–43. https://doi.org/10.1177/009365096023001001

Walther, J. B., & Burgoon, J. K. (1992). Relational communication in computer-mediated interaction. *Human Communication Research, 19*(1), 50–88. https://doi.org/10.1111/j.1468-2958.1992.tb00295.x

Walther, J. B., Van Der Heide, B., Hamel, L. & Shulman, H. (2009). Self-generated versus other-generated statements and impressions in computer-mediated communication: A test of warranting theory using Facebook. *Communication Research, 36*(2), 229–253. https://doi.org/10.1177/0093650208330251

Walther, J. B., Van Der Heide, B., Kim, S., Westerman, D., & Tong, S. T. (2008). The role of friends' appearance and behavior on evaluations of individuals on Facebook: Are we known by the company we keep? *Human Communication Research, 34*(1), 28–49. https://doi.org/10.1111/j.1468-2958.2007.00312.x

Walther, J. B., & Parks, M. R. (2002). Cues filtered out, cues filtered in: Computer-mediated communication and relationships. In M. L. Knapp & J. A. Daly (Eds.), *Handbook of interpersonal communication* (3rd ed., pp. 529–563). Sage.

Whitty, M. (2008). Revealing the 'Real' me, searching for the 'Actual' you: Presentations of self on an internet dating site. *Computers in Human Behavior, 24*(4), 1707–1723. https://doi.org/10.1016/j.chb.2007.07.002

Youngvorst, L. J., & Pham, T. (2022, online). Virtual dating and the COVID-19 pandemic: Investigating motives, predictors, and outcomes. *Human Communication & Technology*.

van der Zanden, T., Mos, M. B. J., Schouten, A. P., & Krahmer, E. J. (2022). What people look at in multimodal online dating profiles: How pictorial and textual cues affect impression formation. *Communication Research, 49*(6), 863–890. https://doi.org/10.1177/0093650221995316

UNDERSTANDING THE RELATIONSHIP BETWEEN SOCIAL MEDIA AND WELL-BEING

Jeffrey Hancock & Angela Y. Lee
Stanford University

INTRODUCTION

Social media has dramatically transformed how we connect with one another and the world. Platforms like Facebook, Instagram, Twitter, and TikTok have rewired our social lives, providing unprecedented opportunities for people to chat with friends, join new communities, create their own content, and connect with the world at large. At the same time, however, they also introduce the potential for individuals to encounter harmful or offensive content (Kim et al., 2021; Kumar et al., 2023) to compare their lives to the curated feeds of their friends and role models (Cingel et al., 2022; Meier & Johnson, 2022) and to avoid other obligations by offering nearly limitless possibilities for distraction (Hall & Liu, 2022; Reinecke et al., 2022).

How might the integration of social media use into our daily lives come to bear on our well-being? Recent years have seen an outpouring of concerns about the potential for social media use to exacerbate mental health problems like depression, anxiety, loneliness, and body insecurity (Meier & Reinecke, 2021; Orben, 2020). At the individual level, many everyday social media users fear they spend too much time online and express reservations about their ability to navigate the culture of constant connectivity that social media affords (Cheng et al., 2019; Lanette et al., 2018; Lee et al., 2021). These concerns are often shared by parents, teachers, and public health practitioners working with children and adolescents (Rideout et al., 2022). As social media proliferates across the world—and young people join at earlier ages—institutions like UNICEF and the Substance Abuse and Mental Health Services Administration have emphasized the need to understand how engagement with these platforms might influence our mental health and well-being (Fore, 2021; SAMHSA, 2023).

13

In this chapter, we summarize the state of the field on the relationship between social use and psychological well-being—with an emphasis on explaining how and why social media can affect different people in different ways. We also identify ongoing challenges and open questions facing the field and discuss several promising new future directions that may advance our understanding. Finally, we conclude by offering several empirically-based recommendations for how to optimize the use of social media.

WHAT WE KNOW: THE STATE OF THE LITERATURE ON SOCIAL MEDIA USE AND WELL-BEING

Few questions in the field of communication have received the degree of empirical and public attention as the relationship between social media use and psychological well-being. Much of this work has been motivated by the urgent need to understand the causes of the youth mental health crisis: a concerning uptick in adolescent depression, hopelessness, and loneliness that began in the early 2010s and has persisted through recent years (American Academy of Pediatrics, 2021). According to the Center for Disease Control and Prevention, young people today experience 40% more feelings of persistent sadness and suicidal ideation than youth from a decade ago (Youth Risk Behavior Surveillance System, 2022). These reports have been matched by a distressing increase in youth hospitalizations related to self-harm (Youth Risk Behavior Surveillance System, 2022).

Many have questioned whether the rise of social media platforms may be to blame. In particular, some scholars have noted that the onset of the mental health crisis coincides with the entrée of smartphones into the mainstream, theorizing that the introduction of social media into society may have catalyzed new mental health problems among vulnerable adolescents (Twenge & Farley, 2021; Twenge and Martin, 2020). Indeed, numerous observational studies demonstrate a substantial negative correlation between heavy social media use and well-being (Meier & Reinecke, 2021). In an analysis of a nationally representative sample of American and British teens, Twenge and Martin (2020) found that people who regularly spent many hours online each day (e.g., 5+ hours) were at higher risk of experiencing depressive symptoms and having thoughts of suicide. Furthermore, released files from the social media corporation Meta revealed that internal research had raised concerns that Instagram and Facebook use could harm adolescents' mental health, particularly for young girls (Wells et al., 2021). As a result, some scholars and journalists have called for greater regulation of social media as an effort to protect younger generations from its adverse effects (Haidt, 2021).

The extant literature on social media and well-being, however, does not provide clear-cut evidence that social media is primarily harmful, or that it is responsible for the increase in anxiety observed in teens over the last decade. To date, hundreds of studies have examined the impact of social media on diverse indicators of well-being; using myriad empirical methods; across different communities, populations, and nations. Some substantiate concerns about the detrimental effects of social media on mental health, finding that increased use corresponds to heightened levels of loneliness, worse self-esteem, and decreased life satisfaction (Andreassen et al., 2016; Appel et al., 2016; Verduyn et al., 2017). However, many other studies find that using social media can *improve* mental health, such as by increasing their social connection, reducing symptoms of depression, and increasing their day-to-day enjoyment of life (Burke et al., 2010; Ellison et al., 2011, 2014). To further complicate matters, still other studies find minimal associations between social media and well-being. For instance, one particularly notable project followed a cohort of participants over eight years and asked them to track their social media use and experience of depression (Coyne et al., 2020). To their surprise, they found no relationship—there were no differences in depression between those who spent more or less time on social media.

How can we make sense of these conflicting findings? When confronted with divergent results across many studies, scientists often conduct a *meta-analysis:* an analytical review of previous work that produces an estimate of "overall effects" by aggregating the findings of individual studies. To better understand how social media affects well-being, we conducted our own meta-analysis by identifying 226 studies that examined this relationship (spanning a total of over 275,000 participants) (Hancock et al., 2022). By looking at the results of all of these studies together, we found that social media use was *not* associated with a combined overall measure of well-being ($r = .01$, *n.s.*). This is not because social media has *no* effect on well-being, but rather that there are likely both positive and negative effects for well-being associated with social media use, and those effects are likely different for different people. For instance, we found that for the average person, spending more time on social media was associated with an increase in social connection (also known as *relational well-being*) but also with an increase in feelings of depression and anxiety. Other meta-analyses and reviews conducted by other researchers find a similar pattern of small, mixed effects (Meier & Reinecke, 2022; Odgers & Jensen, 2020; Orben, 2020)—indicating that while there appear to be real harms that can result from social media use, there are also real benefits as well.

These findings suggest it is important for us to account for both the positive and negative effects of social media. While we should by no means turn a blind eye toward its potential harms, we also should not overlook the tangible benefits that social media can bring. For some people, social media is a lifeline to crucial sources of emotional support and communities where they feel like they belong.

MAKING SENSE OF HETEROGENEITY: IMPORTANT DIFFERENCES IN SOCIAL MEDIA EFFECTS ON WELL-BEING

The results of our meta-analysis also highlight the importance of considering *heterogeneous social media effects.* As we discussed above, some studies found negative associations between social media use and well-being and others found more positive relationships. Though this may appear to be conflicting, it makes sense if we remember that social media can affect different people in different ways. Indeed, it should not be surprising that social media effects are not "one-size-fits-all." Consider your own social media use. We all use unique combinations of social media in different ways, for different amounts of time, and in different social contexts—not to mention the myriad types of content and contacts with which we interact.

A new line of research on *person-specific effects* embraces this individuality by examining how social media affects different people in different ways (Valkenburg et al., 2021, 2022). Instead of trying to understand how social media affects most people *most* of the time—such as when examining between-group differences—this framework focuses instead on tracking how social media affects specific individuals. For example, a longitudinal study tracking the effect of social media use on positive and negative emotions over three weeks found that spending time on social media harmed well-being for 28% of adolescents, improved it for 26%, and had no effect for the remaining teens (Beyens et al., 2021). Similar patterns of heterogeneous social media effects have also been observed for other forms of well-being, including individuals' satisfaction with their relationships (Pouwels et al., 2021). As a result, instead of asking "Is social media good or bad for people?," this framework instead asks us to consider the question, "For *whom* is social media enhancing or harmful? And under what circumstances?" Below, we unpack some of the main factors that may explain why social media can affect different people in different ways.

Platforms and Affordance Differences. It may be an oversimplification to ask how social media affects well-being as there really is no single form of social media given the wide range of platforms and apps and the diverse activities that users can engage in within a platform. Instead, each individual's social media use can be understood as their unique *social media ecology,* consisting of the specific combination of applications they use—some of which may be better for their well-being than others (Rhee et al., 2021; Zhao et al., 2016). Indeed, these effects can vary from person to person. For example, using Instagram may be particularly beneficial for some users and harmful for others.

One way of understanding these differences is by considering *affordances,* or the specific ways of interacting with others that platforms facilitate (Treem & Leonardi, 2013). For example, text-based platforms like Twitter and Reddit afford users the ability to read through threaded discussions and commentaries, whereas video-based platforms like TikTok afford people the ability to watch and rewatch multimodal content. Certain affordances, like the ability to communicate anonymously, can be enhancing or harmful under different circumstances. Anonymous or pseudonymous messaging (i.e., under a username or social media handle) can make it easier for people to share their true thoughts and seek emotional support without worrying about how their vulnerability may be perceived by their friends or family (Luo & Hancock, 2020). In particular, there can be significant psychological benefits to feeling that one's innermost thoughts and feelings are being seen, heard, and recognized, even in an anonymous format (Ma et al., 2016)—as is often seen in many anonymous support groups, such as those for survivors of abuse and harassment (Andalibi et al., 2016). On the other hand, the same affordance of anonymous messaging can also embolden people to say hurtful things to others by reducing the threat of consequences from their actions. Indeed, cyberbullying is often enacted by anonymous perpetrators who post messages online that they would not normally say to another person face-to-face (Giumetti & Kowalski, 2022; You & Lee, 2019).

Content Differences. Exposure and engagement to certain forms of social media content may be enhancing, whereas others may be harmful. For instance, there is a clear relationship between seeing harmful, offensive, or toxic messages (i.e., cyberbullying) and worsened mental health (Giumetti & Kowalski, 2022; Viner et al., 2019). Even if hateful content is not targeted toward the individual, merely seeing others be harassed or attacked online can be detrimental to well-being—particularly if the target belongs to a shared identity group. For example, a review of studies on Black social media users' well-being found that exposure to images and videos of racial discrimination or targeted violence was a significant source of psychological distress (Park et al., under review).

While it should be no surprise that seeing such negative forms of content may harm well-being, exposure to positive representations of others' lives can also exacerbate mental health problems—particularly if they portray idealized or curated content that makes people feel worse about themselves in comparison. In both online and offline settings, individuals seek to put their "best foot forward" and present themselves in a positive light to others. On social media, this often manifests in the form of perfected and edited photos depicting the highlights from people's parties, vacations, achievements, and celebrations (Schreurs & Vandenbosch, 2022). Seeing these idealized versions of others' lives can harm people's self-esteem and body image if they begin to compare the unpolished realities of their everyday lives to the carefully constructed self-presentations of others (Kleemans et al., 2018; Schreurs & Vandenbosch, 2022).

Behavioral Differences. The ways that people engage with social media can also affect their well-being. While actions like liking, commenting, reacting, or scrolling may seem second-nature to many social media users, research indicates that some of these behaviors tend to be more associated with positive outcomes than others. In a series of studies, Verduyn et al. (2017) found that using social media *passively* to browse through content is often associated with poorer well-being. In particular, people tended to feel worse when they perceived their scrolling to be mindless, unintentional, or a waste of time (Cheng et al., 2019; Lee et al., 2021). On the other hand, using social media *actively* to engage with friends, comment and react to posts, and connect with other people is associated with greater life satisfaction and reduced psychological distress because these behaviors tend to strengthen individuals' relationships.

Crucially, it is important to remember that active use is not always enhancing and passive use is not always harmful (Meier et al., 2022; Valkenburg et al., 2022). Indeed, there are many instances of active social media use that can undermine well-being for the self or for others. Consider a social media user who spends an hour arguing with people on Reddit threads (Kumar et al., 2023), or another individual who likes and shares content that glorifies problematic alcohol consumption (Westgate & Holliday, 2016). Though active, these ways of using social media can be harmful. Conversely, it is easy to think of examples where passive social media use may be beneficial to well-being. It may be particularly restorative for someone to spend an hour on social media watching videos of animals, crafts, or stand-up comedy if they have had a long day and need to take some time to use media to reduce their stress (Knobloch-Westerwick et al., 2020).

Motivational Differences. The reasons why people choose to use social media can also have important implications for their well-being. Theory and research on uses and gratifications reveal that people use social media to pursue numerous activities that are intended to fulfill some kind of need or move them closer to some kind of goal (Whiting & Williams, 2013). These uses can include those which are conventionally perceived as more "productive"—such as using social media to build professional connections, to learn new skills, or to build a brand online—as well as those which focus on providing comfort or distraction, such as simply using social media to avoid other tasks. Using social media can improve or harm well-being, depending on whether people are pursuing enhancing or harmful goals.

For example, social media use that is motivated by a desire to connect and maintain relationships is known to be particularly beneficial. Indeed, some of the strongest and most consistent benefits of social media use can be found in individuals' relational well-being— the strength of their friendships and relationships—because they help people maintain lines of communication despite distance. Using social media to stay in touch can be particularly meaningful if they are in a community where they have few opportunities for in-person interaction. In few cases has this *social compensation* been more impactful than during the COVID-19 pandemic? In a notable series of studies, Metherell et al. (2022) and Vuorre et al. (2021) found that adolescents with social media were substantially less lonely than their offline peers during the pandemic-induced lockdowns because they were able to access their social networks.

On the other hand, however, using social media to obtain social validation can be problematic. It is easy for social media users to depend on likes, comments, and follows to gauge their sense of social standing. Unlike face-to-face interactions, the networked nature of social media profiles provides quantifiable, easily accessible metrics about what others think. While turning to numbers like "how many people like your photo" can provide quick boosts to one's self-esteem, it can be problematic to depend on social media for self-worth, especially over the longer term (de Vries et al., 2016; Sabik et al., 2020).

Mindset Differences. Even when people use social media for the same amount of time, or in the same ways, people can also *interpret* their social media use in ways that are consequential to their well-being. Think about the last time that you spent 20 minutes on your social media platform of choice. Did you think that it was a waste of time, or did you think that it was meaningful? Did you feel that you were using it intentionally, or did you feel like it was hard to resist its pull?

A growing body of research reveals that the answers people bring to questions like these can change how people respond to using social media—for better or for worse. Just as people can have mindsets about whether their intelligence is *growable* or *fixed* (Dweck, 2008; Rege et al., 2021), we also hold *mindsets* about the role of social media in our own lives that shape how understand the time we spend online (Lee et al., 2021). Whether actively aware of it or not, people have mindsets about how much *agency* they have over social media (i.e., "Am I in control of my social media use, or is it exerting control over me?") and the *valence* of its anticipated effects in their lives (i.e., "Is social media generally good or bad for me?"). Crucially, these mindsets can be as consequential to well-being as the time spent on it. In a series of studies, Lee and Hancock (2023) found that people who viewed themselves as in control of their social media use (i.e., a high agency mindset) not only reported greater life satisfaction and perceived social support, but also less depression, anxiety, and stress. In contrast, people who held the mindset that they had little control over their social media use (i.e., a low agency mindset) experienced significantly more mental health issues.

Population Differences. It is also important to consider how social media may influence well-being of different demographics and identity groups. For instance, there is growing recognition that social media can have more pronounced effects on people of different genders. Specifically, prolonged social media use appears to be more harmful for women's mental health (Orben et al., 2022; Twenge, 2022), with studies finding that it can increase depression and anxiety, in addition to undermining self-esteem and body image. This is often theorized to be because of the pervasive emphasis on physical appearance and the idealization of thinness that is often promoted on these platforms. Furthermore, women may be subject to greater harassment and cyberbullying on social media, which can exacerbate these negative effects.

In addition to differences based on gender, social media may also have varying effects on well-being across different developmental periods. Adolescents and young adults, for example, may be particularly sensitive to the impact of social media, as they are in a phase of life when identity formation, peer relationships, and body image concerns are especially salient (Orben et al., 2021). During this time, social media can amplify social comparison and competition, leading to feelings of inadequacy and anxiety. In contrast, because older adults have social networks that tend to be shrinking, they may find tremendous value in social media's affordances for connecting with old and new friends. The relationship between social media and well-being is likely to change across the lifespan, though more work is needed in this area.

ADVICE FOR SOCIAL MEDIA USERS: HOW CAN YOU OPTIMIZE YOUR USE OF SOCIAL MEDIA?

Just as social media can encompass a variety of different platforms, features, and types of content, its effects on our mental health are also multifaceted. Although we know that social media is related to well-being in different ways for different people, people can *optimize* their experiences with social media by adopting the belief systems and practices that help them maximize the benefits from social media while minimizing its harms (Lee & Hancock, 2023).

First, it is important to reflect on the role that social media plays in your life. Consider trying a *personal social media audit*, paying attention to the ways in which you are using social media and thinking critically about the reasons underlying your use. In addition to tracking how much time you spend online, it can also be valuable to attend to the content you are engaging with and how it makes you feel. For example, are you watching videos on TikTok because you want to learn more about your favorite artist, or because you want to take a quick break from chores? Or are you spending your time online because you are procrastinating on an important task or trying to ignore an impending deadline? Which kinds of content make you feel more positive about yourself, and which tend to have a negative effect on your mood? Actively reflecting on the nuances of your individual social media use and interacting with your well-being can help you come up with a plan for optimizing your engagement.

In doing so, it is important to remember that you have *agency* over how you use social media and how it makes you feel. As research on social media mindsets indicates, it can be valuable to focus on the ways in which you have control over what you see, what you do, and what goals you use social media to achieve. Specifically, you can use social media in *agentic ways* by choosing to use it to pursue activities that you find personally meaningful, whether this involves exploring new interests, connecting with friends, or just watching videos or listening to music. Being intentional and deliberate about how and why you use social media can help you obtain more benefits from the time you spend on it.

Crucially, if you are starting to feel that your social media use is out of your control, you can try some of the following techniques to regain a sense of agency. For example, you can assert control over the content in your social media feed by actively curating which accounts you follow. If you notice that seeing content from certain influencers or friends from college makes you feel worse about yourself, you can "spring clean" your social media by unfollowing them or blocking them. If these feel too harsh, you can also consider "restricting" certain accounts or making use of features like the "not interested" button on TikTok or the "show me less" tool on Facebook. On the other hand, you can also cultivate a more optimal feed by engaging more with content that brings you happiness.

If you feel that you are spending more time than you would like to on social media, consider reflecting on the specific ways in which you may be able to manage your use—like reducing social media use before bed to ensure that you can get a good night's sleep. Many people find that taking a break from social media helps them reassess the role it plays in their lives and be more critical about the ways in which they would *ideally* like to use social media.

Finally, it is important to know that you do not need to do this alone. The culture of "constant connectivity" afforded by social media can make it difficult for us to learn how to optimize our use. However, this can be a community effort. Having open conversations about social media with our friends, family members, and partners can help us gain clarity on how to make the most out of these technological tools. While everyone can benefit from such dialogue, these conversations may be particularly beneficial for children and adolescents who are still learning to manage their social and interpersonal relationships in an increasingly digital world. Indeed, parents, teachers, and caregivers can support young people in thinking critically about the ways in which they engage with social media and scaffold the skills they need to use it intentionally. Honesty, empathy, and curiosity—rather than judgment—are essential to healthy conversations. We can help one another make the most out of our experiences with social media by paying attention to how it makes us feel, taking action to optimize our use, and listening to one another as we all learn to live and learn in our digitally connected world.

REFERENCES

American Academy of Pediatrics (October 19, 2021). AAP-AACAP-CHA Declaration of a National Emergency in Child and Adolescent Mental Health. https://www.aap.org/en/advocacy/child-and-adolescent-healthy-mental-development/aap-aacap-cha-declaration-of-a-national-emergency-in-child-and-adolescent-mental-health/

Andalibi, N., Haimson, O. L., De Choudhury, M., & Forte, A. (2016, May). Understanding social media disclosures of sexual abuse through the lenses of support seeking and anonymity. In *Proceedings of the 2016 CHI Conference on Human Factors in Computing Systems* (pp. 3906–3918).

Beyens, I., Pouwels, J. L., van Driel, I. I., Keijsers, L., & Valkenburg, P. M. (2021). Social media use and adolescents' well-being: Developing a typology of person-specific effect patterns. *Communication Research*. Advance online publication. https://doi.org/10.1177/00936502211038196

Centers for Disease Control & Prevention (2021). Youth risk behavior survey: Data summary and trends report (2011-2021). https://www.cdc.gov/healthyyouth/data/yrbs/pdf/YRBS_Data-Summary-Trends_Report2023_508.pdf

Cheng, J., Burke, M., & Davis, E. G. (2019, May). Understanding perceptions of problematic Facebook use: When people experience negative life impact and a lack of control. In *Proceedings of the 2019 CHI Conference on Human Factors in Computing Systems* (pp. 1–13).

Cingel, D. P., Carter, M. C., & Krause, H. V. (2022). Social media and self-esteem. *Current Opinion in Psychology*, 101304. https://doi.org/10.1016/j.copsyc.2022.101304

De Vries, D. A., Peter, J., De Graaf, H., & Nikken, P. (2016). Adolescents' social network site use, peer appearance-related feedback, and body dissatisfaction: Testing a mediation model. *Journal of Youth and Adolescence, 45*, 211–224. https://doi.org/10.1007/s10964-015-0266-4

Dweck, C. S. (2008). Can personality be changed? The role of beliefs in personality and change. *Current Directions in Psychological Science, 17*(6), 391–394. https://doi.org/10.1111/j.1467-8721.2008.00612.x

Fore, H. (Feb. 8, 2021). Growing concern for well-being of children and young people amid soaring screen time. https://www.unicef.org/press-releases/growing-concern-well-being-children-and-young-people-amid-soaring-screen-time

Giumetti, G. W., & Kowalski, R. M. (2022). Cyberbullying via social media and well-being. *Current Opinion in Psychology,* 101314. https://doi.org/10.1016/j.copsyc.2022.101314

Haidt, J. (2021). The dangerous experiment on teen girls. *The Atlantic.* https://www.theatlantic.com/ideas/archive/2021/11/facebooks-dangerous-experiment-teen-girls/620767/

Hall, J. A., & Liu, D. (2022). Social media use, social displacement, and well-being. *Current Opinion in Psychology,* 101339. https://doi.org/10.1016/j.copsyc.2022.101339

Kim, J. W., Guess, A., Nyhan, B., & Reifler, J. (2021). The distorting prism of social media: How self-selection and exposure to incivility fuel online comment toxicity. *Journal of Communication, 71*(6), 922–946. https://doi.org/10.1093/joc/jqab034

Kleemans, M., Daalmans, S., Carbaat, I., & Anschütz, D. (2018). Picture perfect: The direct effect of manipulated Instagram photos on body image in adolescent girls. *Media Psychology, 21*(1), 93–110. https://doi.org/10.1080/15213269.2016.1257392

Knobloch-Westerwick, S., Mothes, C., & Polavin, N. (2020). Confirmation bias, ingroup bias, and negativity bias in selective exposure to political information. *Communication Research, 47*(1), 104–124. https://doi.org/10.1177/0093650217719596

Kumar, D., Hancock, J., Thomas, K., & Durumeric, Z. (2023, April). Understanding the behaviors of toxic accounts on reddit. In *Proceedings of the ACM Web Conference 2023* (pp. 2797–2807).

Lanette, S., Chua, P. K., Hayes, G., & Mazmanian, M. (2018). How much is' too much'? The role of a smartphone addiction narrative in individuals' experience of use. *Proceedings of the ACM on Human-Computer Interaction, 2*(CSCW), 1–22.

Lee, A. Y., & Hancock, J. (2023). Social media mindsets: A new approach to understanding social media use & psychological well-being. *PsyArXiv.*

Lee, A. Y., Hancock, J. T., & Ellison, N. B. (2021). To use or be used? The role of agency in social media use & well-being. *Frontiers in Computer Science, 5*, 24.

Lee, A. Y., Katz, R., & Hancock, J. (2021). The role of subjective construals on reporting and reasoning about social media use. *Social Media + Society, 7*(3). https://doi.org/10.1177/20563051211035350

Luo, M., & Hancock, J. T. (2020). Self-disclosure and social media: motivations, mechanisms and psychological well-being. *Current Opinion in Psychology, 31*, 110–115. https://doi.org/10.1016/j.copsyc.2019.08.019

Ma, X., Hancock, J., & Naaman, M. (2016, May). Anonymity, intimacy and self-disclosure in social media. In *Proceedings of the 2016 CHI Conference on Human Factors in Computing Systems* (pp. 3857–3869).

Meier, A., & Johnson, B. K. (2022). Social comparison and envy on social media: A critical review. *Current Opinion in Psychology*, 101302. https://doi.org/10.1016/j.copsyc.2022.101302

Meier, A., & Reinecke, L. (2021). Computer-mediated communication, social media, and mental health: A conceptual and empirical meta-review. *Communication Research, 48*(8), 1182–1209. https://doi.org/10.1177/00936502209582

Metherell, T. E., Ghai, S., McCormick, E. M., Ford, T. J., & Orben, A. (2022). Digital access constraints predict worse mental health among adolescents during COVID-19. *Scientific Reports, 12*(1), 19088. https://doi.org/10.1038/s41598-022-23899-y

Orben, A. (2020). Teenagers, screens and social media: A narrative review of reviews and key studies. *Social Psychiatry and Psychiatric Epidemiology, 55*(4), 407–414. https://doi.org/10.1007/s00127-019-01825-4

Orben, A., Przybylski, A. K., Blakemore, S. J., & Kievit, R. A. (2022). Windows of developmental sensitivity to social media. *Nature Communications, 13*(1), 1649. https://doi.org/10.1038/s41467-022-29296-3

Pouwels, J. L., Valkenburg, P. M., Beyens, I., van Driel, I. I., & Keijsers, L. (2021). Some socially poor but also some socially rich adolescents feel closer to their friends after using social media. *Scientific Reports, 11*(1), 21176. https://doi.org/10.1038/s41598-021-99034-0

Rege, M., Hanselman, P., Solli, I. F., Dweck, C. S., Ludvigsen, S., Bettinger, E., ... & Yeager, D. S. (2021). How can we inspire nations of learners? An investigation of growth mindset and challenge-seeking in two countries. *American Psychologist, 76*(5), 755–767. https://doi.org/10.1037/amp0000647

Reinecke, L., Gilbert, A., & Eden, A. (2022). Self-regulation as a key boundary condition in the relationship between social media use and well-being. *Current Opinion in Psychology, 45*, 101296. https://doi.org/10.1016/j.copsyc.2021.12.008

Rhee, L., Bayer, J. B., Lee, D. S., & Kuru, O. (2021). Social by definition: How users define social platforms and why it matters. *Telematics and Informatics, 59*, 101538. https://doi.org/10.1016/j.tele.2020.101538

Rideout, V., Peebles, A., Mann, S., & Robb, M. B. (2022). *Common Sense census: Media use by tweens and teens*. Common Sense.

Sabik, N. J., Falat, J., & Magagnos, J. (2020). When self-worth depends on social media feedback: Associations with psychological well-being. *Sex Roles, 82*, 411–421. https://doi.org/10.1007/s11199-019-01062-8

Schreurs, L., & Vandenbosch, L. (2022). Should I post my very best self? The within-person reciprocal associations between social media literacy, positivity-biased behaviors and adolescents' self-esteem. *Telematics and Informatics*, 101865. https://doi.org/10.1016/j.tele.2022.101865

Substance Abuse and Mental Health Services Administration (2023). https://www.samhsa.gov/coe-social-media-mental-wellbeing

Treem, J. W., & Leonardi, P. M. (2013). Social media use in organizations: Exploring the affordances of visibility, editability, persistence, and association. *Annals of the International Communication Association, 36*(1), 143–189. https://doi.org/10.1080/23808985.2013.11679130

Twenge, J. M. (2020). Why increases in adolescent depression may be linked to the technological environment. *Current Opinion in Psychology, 32*, 89–94. https://doi.org/10.1016/j.copsyc.2019.06.036

Twenge, J. M., & Farley, E. (2021). Not all screen time is created equal: associations with mental health vary by activity and gender. *Social Psychiatry and Psychiatric Epidemiology, 56*, 207-217. https://doi.org/10.1007/s00127-020-01906-9

Twenge, J. M., Haidt, J., Lozano, J., & Cummins, K. M. (2022). Specification curve analysis shows that social media use is linked to poor mental health, especially among girls. *Acta Psychologica, 224*, 103512. https://doi.org/10.1016/j.actpsy.2022.103512

Twenge, J. M., & Martin, G. N. (2020). Gender differences in associations between digital media use and psychological well-being: Evidence from three large datasets. *Journal of Adolescence, 79*, 91–102. https://doi.org/10.1016/j.adolescence.2019.12.018

Valkenburg, P., Beyens, I., Pouwels, J. L., van Driel, I. I., & Keijsers, L. (2021). Social media use and adolescents' self-esteem: Heading for a person-specific media effects paradigm. *Journal of Communication, 71*(1), 56–78. https://doi.org/10.1093/joc/jqaa039

Valkenburg, P. M., Meier, A., & Beyens, I. (2022). Social media use and its impact on adolescent mental health: An umbrella review of the evidence. *Current Opinion in Psychology, 44*, 58–68. https://doi.org/10.1016/j.copsyc.2021.08.017

Verduyn, P., Ybarra, O., Résibois, M., Jonides, J., & Kross, E. (2017). Do social network sites enhance or undermine subjective well-being? A critical review. *Social Issues and Policy Review, 11*(1), 274–302. https://doi.org/10.1111/sipr.12033

Viner, R. M., Gireesh, A., Stiglic, N., Hudson, L. D., Goddings, A. L., Ward, J. L., & Nicholls, D. E. (2019). Roles of cyberbullying, sleep, and physical activity in mediating the effects of social media use on mental health and wellbeing among young people in England: A secondary analysis of longitudinal data. *The Lancet Child & Adolescent Health, 3*(10), 685–696. https://doi.org/10.1016/S2352-4642(19)30186-5

Vuorre, M., Orben, A., & Przybylski, A. K. (2021). There is no evidence that associations between adolescents' digital technology engagement and mental health problems have increased. *Clinical Psychological Science, 9*(5), 823–835. https://doi.org/10.1177/2167702621994549

Wells, G., Horwitz, J., and Seetharaman, D. (2021). Facebook knows Instagram is toxic for teen girls, company documents show. *The Wall Street Journal.* https://www.wsj.com/articles/facebook-knows-instagram-is-toxic-for-teen-girls-company-documents-show-11631620739?mod=hp_lead_pos7andmod=article_inline

Westgate, E. C., & Holliday, J. (2016). Identity, influence, and intervention: The roles of social media in alcohol use. *Current Opinion in Psychology, 9*, 27–32. https://doi.org/10.1016/j.copsyc.2015.10.014

Whiting, A., & Williams, D. (2013). Why people use social media: a uses and gratifications approach. *Qualitative Market Research, 16*(4), 362–369. https://doi.org/10.1108/QMR-06-2013-0041

You, L., & Lee, Y. H. (2019). The bystander effect in cyberbullying on social network sites: Anonymity, group size, and intervention intentions. *Telematics and Informatics, 45*, 101284. https://doi.org/10.1016/j.tele.2019.101284

Zhao, X., Lampe, C., & Ellison, N. B. (2016, May). The social media ecology: User perceptions, strategies and challenges. In *Proceedings of the 2016 CHI Conference on Human Factors in Computing Systems* (pp. 89–100).

EFFECTIVE PRIVACY MANAGEMENT AND DISCLOSURE PRACTICES ON SOCIAL MEDIA: SHARING AND PROTECTING OURSELVES

Jeffrey T. Child
Kent State University

Without question, social media use fulfills an important role today for many individuals to engage and connect with close and distant friends, romantic interests, family members, acquaintances, businesses, and colleagues (Child & Westermann, 2013; Frampton & Child, 2013; Petronio et al., 2021). Greater use of social media across time has increased for all demographic groups, but so have concerns about privacy and security given the information that we freely share about ourselves online in order to be social and connect with others (Auxier & Anderson, 2021; Rainie, 2018). The focus of my scholarly research agenda for the last fifteen-plus years has been to understand how young adults manage their privacy on social media and respond to evolving privacy concerns when interacting on various social media platforms. The goal of this chapter is to help you understand ways to engage in mindful privacy management practices when interacting online with various audiences through social media.

SITUATING ONLINE PRIVACY REGULATION WITHIN COMMUNICATION PRIVACY MANAGEMENT THEORY

When I began studying privacy and disclosure practices online close to 20 years ago, the landscape of online places where young adults would interact was dramatically different than today (Child & Starcher, 2020; Child et al., 2008). The most popular place at that time to interact online socially with others on the Internet was the diary-based website MySpace.com, which quickly became eclipsed by Facebook which is now being challenged by growth in a range of smaller platforms like Instagram, Snapchat, and TikTok (Auxier & Anderson, 2021; Child & Petronio, 2011; Child et al., 2008; Petronio et al., 2021). Various social media platforms will continue to come and go but engaging in effective privacy regulation and disclosure practices on whatever platform is selected for online interaction with others will persist as an important goal.

During the early 2000s, parental voices to influence with adult children about effective privacy regulation and disclosure practices in digital online spaces were mostly nonexistent (Child et al., 2008). Today, parents and children talk quite a bit about how to effectively regulate and manage privacy online and extend these conversations across generations of family members by even helping socialize grandparents with knowledge about how to effectively engage in online digital spaces (Child & Petronio, 2011; Child & Westermann, 2013; Child et al., 2015). The way that I have made connections across time, platforms, and variations in social media use patterns is by trying to tie together findings from multiple studies with CPM theory as the guiding framework for exploration of understanding user behaviors related to online privacy regulation and disclosure practices. Next, I briefly review some of the major concepts about this theory and how the theory impacts our general understanding of privacy regulation and disclosure on social media.

Sharing and Protecting Access to the Self Are Both Important Goals. One difference between CPM theory and prior theorizing (i.e., social penetration theory) is that according to CPM theory, greater sharing of private information with others does not necessarily lead to deeper intimacy between the individuals (Petronio, 2002; Petronio et al., 2021). As such, CPM theory contends that both learning how to effectively connect and be social with others by opening up our privacy boundaries is just as important as learning how not to share too much private information about ourselves online and stipulating privacy rules with others to help protect private information from not being compromised (Petronio & Child, 2020).

One nuance of achieving these mutual goals in a social media space is to keep in mind the properties of the medium of interaction (Child & Petronio, 2015). In social media spaces, sometimes people encounter privacy breakdowns and breeches because they interact in a public space in too private of a way (Child et al., 2011, 2012; Petronio et al., 2021). By this, they sometimes put too much personal information out for others to consume and can forget that others can and do pay attention to what we disclose online through mediated lurking practices (Child & Starcher, 2016). The semi-permanent nature of content that we disclose online can also relate to privacy breakdowns (Child & Petronio, 2015). Meaning, when we post thoughts, videos, or images through social media, it can be hard to take that content back or fully control it. People try to accomplish these goals through different kinds of privacy rules.

Regulating Privacy Effectively Through Coordinating Privacy Rules with Others. An important premise of CPM theory is that a rules-based process guides how we share and protect private information about ourselves with others as well as the expectations that we have for how information we share might subsequently be shared with third parties (Petronio, 2002; Petronio et al., 2021). At the individual level, *core considerations* (like culture, personality, and contextual factors) influence our privacy management and disclosure practices in a range of consistent ways across time (Petronio, 2013). In social media, this can be something like the influence of sharing practices on different platforms or how family members socialize us to manage private information in desired ways online (Child & Petronio, 2011; Child et al., 2015). *Catalyst considerations* for privacy rules include the situational and variable ways that we may come to adapt practices to different circumstances to share or protect private information where either goal feels more appropriate to achieve in the moment (Petronio & Child, 2020). For example, if someone shared they were struggling with the loss of a parent on social media on a parent's birthday and you decide to share part of your own parental loss story online to connect with them, you have more than likely regulated your private information due to a catalyst privacy rule influence. Catalyst influences on privacy rules are the flexible ways that our privacy rules remain adaptive to different situations that may arise.

When we share private information with others, CPM theory suggests that we must coordinate our expectations for how others should act as proprietors of that information or they will come to rely on whether or not to further share information based on their own individual expectations and preferences (Child et al., 2008; Petronio, 2002; Petronio et al., 2022). To effectively coordinate these kinds of privacy rules in digital spaces individuals need to specify who else can and can not know specific information shared (i.e., linkage rules), how much actual information people can and can not know (i.e., permeability rules), and when people can and can not make their own decisions about sharing private information shared with them with others (i.e., ownership rules; Child et al., 2008). Coordinating privacy rules for groups on social media to follow can be harder to accomplish given the sizes of most people's social media networks and the combination of both strong and weak ties facilitated by people on different social media sites (De Wolf et al., 2014).

Effective privacy management on social media can happen through a range of strategies. This includes socializing with others about the rules they should use to manage information we share with them, monitoring our actual disclosure choices, and using the technology features associated with different social media platforms effectively (Child & Petronio, 2011; De Wolf et al., 2014; Petronio & Child, 2020). One way to prevent fewer breakdowns is to exercise caution as an individual in how much private information is shared online by making effective use of vague-booking or strategic ambiguity when information is shared within a social network (Child & Starcher, 2016; Child et al., 2008). This can effectively get people information who can interpret your coded language online while also blurring the specificity of it for others who are not the intended targets for the private information. Another strategy is to make use of privacy settings, groups, and technology in order to be able to say what you want to a specific, rather than a general, social media audience (Child, 2023). When privacy rules do not function effectively, content deletion practices are one-way individuals can respond to privacy breakdowns and can help to correct privacy missteps (Child et al., 2011, 2012).

Responding Effectively to the Inevitability of Privacy Breakdowns. CPM theory contends that despite our best efforts to regulate private information effectively, we will ultimately encounter situations where our privacy expectations are misaligned with actual practices. Privacy turbulence is the theoretical mechanism for readjusting privacy and disclosure norms so they function as intended as an ongoing process (Petronio, 2002). In some instances, we learn the most from when our privacy does not function as intended (Petronio 2013; Petronio et al., 2022). People can experience minor distributions in privacy management to complete breakdowns.

In the context of social media, privacy breakdowns can occur given the difficulty to coordinate privacy expectations with diverse kinds of individuals who have access to parts of what we share with them. A type of unexpected privacy breakdown can occur when someone screen grabs content with another device and shares it how they desire despite our expectations (Child et al., 2011, 2012; Petronio et al., 2022). An intentional privacy breech is different from an unintentional one, where the individual simply does not know what is expected of them as a co-owner of content shared with them (Petronio et al., 2022). Content initially circulated on social media can continue to live a life of its own, even despite our best efforts to try to control that content in desired ways (Child, 2023). Because privacy breakdowns are inevitable, CPM theory functions as a type of system-based theoretical framework because it specifies mechanisms for getting back to balance in terms of privacy intentions and expectations aligning with actual practices. Now, I turn to discuss more evidence-based insights about how you might understand and regulate your own privacy on social media in interacting online.

EVIDENCE-BASED INSIGHTS FOR EFFECTIVE PRIVACY MANAGEMENT ON SOCIAL MEDIA

Social media allows us to interact with people across contexts of life (Child & Petronio, 2011, 2015). One implication of this is that people can develop complex disclosure and privacy management practices to accommodate the diversity of a social media network. In this section, I explore how our personality dispositions impact the choices we make to either protect or provide greater access to our thoughts. Next, I examine how family members come to interact and use social media to enhance the overall quality of their relationships. Then, I turn to discuss the world of work and how having colleagues a part of a social media space can necessitate engaging in content deletion practices to prevent privacy breakdowns from occurring. Finally, I end the chapter by discussing the individual goals that we pursue when interacting on social media impact how we can manage our privacy effectively.

PERSONALITY-BASED DISPOSITIONS IMPACT SOCIAL MEDIA PRIVACY MANAGEMENT PRACTICES

One of the first things that I discovered through a range of research studies about privacy management and regulation online is that our personality attributes for how we function in our face-to-face lives matter in terms of privacy regulation expectations and practices employed on social media (Child & Agyeman-Budu, 2010; Child et al., 2008, 2012). Self-monitoring skills, concern for appropriateness, and disinhibition predict when we open up and close down our privacy boundary on social media in interesting ways. People who highly monitor themselves and what they may say to someone face-to-face exercise the same cautiousness on social media, ultimately disclosing less private information than low self-monitors, who tend to share more of their private information when interacting with others on social media (Child et al., 2008). In terms of disinhibition, people who have higher disinhibition levels engage in lower levels of privacy management on social media (Child et al., 2012). As such, aspects of who we are as people can transcend the medium of interaction we choose for engaging people in getting to be a part of our private and public words (Child & Petronio, 2015).

One interesting personality trait that had an unexpected relationship to privacy management practices was vague-booking (Child & Starcher, 2016). Our study found that individuals who frequently engage in posting strategically ambiguous messages, or what we call vague-booking, often share more of their private information online than those who do not use the strategy. We suspect that people who are often drawn to post messages like "my life is awful" or "well this day sucks" are sometimes people who need validation and want to see that people want to hear more about their private information before sharing more content. However, when people were more aware and concerned about any mediated lurking that was occurring on their social media sites, vague-booking provided a mechanism to protect their privacy and engage in more privacy management. As such, personality dispositions can sometimes cluster in ways that help prevent privacy breakdowns from occurring.

Families Connect and Share Private Information Freely Through Social Media. Families use social media as another way to engage in the sharing of private information and connect with one another (Child & Petronio, 2015; Child & Westermann, 2013; Child et al., 2015). Furthermore, the ways that families socialize with members of the unit to manage private information (i.e., family privacy orientations) carry influence in terms of how people come to manage privacy on social media (Child et al., 2015). For example, in one study we examined the way that young adults were socialized to share private information more openly or in a more protected manner with family members in face-to-face interactions. Individuals who were more open overall with their family members in face-to-face settings would also communicate with family members more openly through Facebook as well as engage in more follow-up conversations offline with family members about content disclosed initially on Facebook (Child et al., 2015).

Furthermore, the study also found that young adults do the most socializing of general privacy management on social media with their grandparents and parents whereas they talk with siblings more about ways to prevent privacy breakdowns and mishaps from occurring (Child et al., 2015). An important contribution of this research demonstrates a reverse privacy socialization pattern than what usually occurs within the home. Namely, when children are young, parents help socialize us in knowing what to say and not disclose to people inside and outside of the family unit. In the social media space, younger generations are often the privacy socialization voices for older generations in helping them to understand appropriate ways to manage privacy online because younger generations tend to be on top of new technology innovations more so than older generations (Child & Petronio, 2015; Child et al., 2015; Petronio, 2002).

Scholarship supports that adult children do not see their parents wanting to engage with them through social media as a type of invasion of their privacy (Ball et al., 2013; Child & Westermann, 2013). However, when parents are a part of a young adult's social media space they can use the technology to try to monitor and invade the privacy of their college-aged children (Ledbetter, 2019). Most parents and young adults use social media technology to enhance relational connections and closeness rather than engage in invasive behaviors (Ball et al., 2013; Ledbetter, 2019). Research also supports that most young adults accept parents into their social media spaces without scrubbing content prior to adding them into the space (Child & Westermann, 2013). However, research by Ledbetter (2019) confirms that when parents use technology and other means to invade the privacy of their college-aged children, these practices are related to increased levels of psychological distress in the college-aged children.

The World of Work and the Interface of Social Media and Privacy Management. Individuals must think about including colleagues in a social media space and how having increased access to personal information may result in privacy breakdowns. How organizations socialize members to treat privacy within the workplace impacts the way that individuals respond to social media friend requests. For example, Frampton and Child (2013) found similar trends to parental social media request processing in so much that most working professionals accept their colleagues as a part of their social media spaces freely without scrubbing content first. However, when an organization stressed that people should mostly keep one's personal life away from the work context, working professionals were more likely to deny a coworker's request to be a part of their social media space. Finally, the individual coworker also matters. The study found that people who experience higher levels of coworker communication satisfaction are more likely to accept a colleague into a social media space than when the levels are lower.

However, having coworkers as a part of social media space has implications for experiencing privacy breakdowns. In a different study, one of the main reasons that individuals would remove content from their social media spaces was due to a fear of repercussions and/or employment security issues (Child et al., 2011, 2012). The study found that most social media users would experience the need to remove content from their social media accounts because of evolving privacy concerns related to impression management triggers, safety and personal identity triggers, relational triggers, and fear of legal and/or disciplinary triggers. Interestingly, a minority of participants indicated that they would never engage in content deletion practices and these people would come to this decision for one of two reasons. They either were very cautious and would anticipate every potential privacy breakdown beforehand when crafting messages or they were high risk takers and did not care what people thought about what they posted (Child et al., 2011, 2012). However, most of us do not anticipate every possible privacy breakdown that can occur and care deeply about how people see us, necessitating revisiting what we post and removing content periodically.

One practical implication of this research is to remember that most people who do not know us well will come to form impressions about us based upon the limited information that we post. In many cases, the impressions being formed by others can be inconsistent with the desired expectations and result in the need to engage in content deletion or clarification practices. Interestingly, most people anticipated the need to scrub content from their social media sites rather than responding to reactive privacy breakdowns brought to their attention by others (Child et al., 2011, 2012). One implication of this research is that social media users care deeply about privacy and actively return to what they post to mitigate privacy breakdowns.

The Goals We Pursue Impact Social Media Disclosure and Privacy Breakdown Patterns. When people interact through social media, they can facilitate different social interaction goals (Child et al., 2012). Research supports that these various interaction goals impact how much privacy management people engage in on social media and consequently, the need to engage in content deletion practices to curb privacy breakdowns (Petronio et al., 2021). We created 19 items from open-ended research about the various types of social interaction goals that social media users might pursue. The items resulted in six different interaction goals (or privacy rule orientations). When posting content on social media, individuals can (1) privilege their own perspectives predominately; (2) use social media in a consequence-driven manner; (3) have a strategic or purposive approach to what gets posted; (4) focus on a sharing orientation; (5) a protective orientation; or (6) be unbothered and unworried about what kind of content gets posted.

Interestingly, these six orientations resulted in different social media privacy management patterns and practices. For example, the sharing orientation results in less privacy management whereas the consequence-driven goal or orientation results in more privacy management. We then used the open-ended data about the types of content deletion practices (Child et al., 2011) to create seven distinct deletion motivations. People engaged in deleting content to (1) management conflict, (2) protect their personal identity and safety, (3) lessen the fear of retribution, (4) increase employment security, (5) control impression management, (6) regulate emotions, and (7) engage in relational cleansing after a breakup. One main conclusion of the study was that whenever someone was more open they were also more likely to need to make deletions related to multiple of these motivations. The study illustrates that ultimately how people use social media matters in understanding disclosure and privacy management practices and ultimately when content needs to be removed as a response to privacy turbulence (Child et al., 2012). The study helps illustrate that privacy management practices are tied to a range of goals and outcomes that may be relevant to different kinds of people.

Some important practical recommendations flow from this work related to effectively managing privacy on social media. First, there is benefit in not posting content to an entire network but rather to think about the content, the audience, the level of vulnerability, and how the information may take on a life of its own after posting (Child, 2023; Petronio et al., 2021). This requires that when sharing thoughts on social media engaging in a purposive practice where mindfulness about potential privacy breaches and breakdowns are considered. Finally, remember that each social media platform and site has unique nuances in relation to privacy management (Auxier & Anderson, 2021). For example, do not assume that because snaps disappear from Snapchat that it is a safe place to post whatever you want. People can easily screengrab or capture the content posted with a second digital device.

CONCLUSION

This chapter situates the study of privacy regulation and disclosure within CPM theory (Petronio, 2002). The chapter illustrates the ways that context, personality, and individual interaction goals factor into how people regulate privacy on social media and come to experience privacy breakdowns. As more diverse platforms and users continue to gravitate toward social interaction online, considering effective privacy management practices can help in crafting healthy and fulfilling relationships that easily move between online and offline spaces and places with fewer privacy breakdowns.

REFERENCES

Auxier, B., & Anderson, M. (2021, April 7). *Social media use in 2021*. Pew Research Center. https://www.pewresearch.org/internet/2021/04/07/social-media-use-in-2021/

Ball, H., Wazner, M. B., & Servoss, T. J. (2013). Parent-child communication on Facebook: Family communication patterns and young adults' decisions to "friend" parents. *Communication Quarterly, 61*(5), 615–629. https://doi.org/10.1080/01463373.2013.822406

Child, J. T. (2023). Opening closed doors: Managing identity and privacy with social media. In D. O. Braithwaite, K. R. Rossetto, J. T. Child, & J. T. Wood (Eds.), *Casing interpersonal communication: Case studies in personal and social relations* (3rd ed., pp. 109–114). Kendall Hunt.

Child, J. T., & Agyeman-Budu, E. A. (2010). Blogging privacy management rule development: The impact of self-monitoring skills, concern for appropriateness, and blogging frequency. *Computers in Human Behavior, 26*(5), 957–963. http://dx.doi.org/10.1016/j.chb.2010.02.009

Child, J. T., Duck, A. R., Andrews, L. A., Butauski, M., & Petronio, S. (2015). Young adults' management of privacy on Facebook with multiple generations of family members. *Journal of Family Communication, 15*(4), 349–369. https://doi.org/10.1080/15267431.2015.1076425

Child, J. T., Haridakis, P. M., & Petronio, S. (2012). Blogging privacy rule orientations, privacy management, and content deletion practices: The variability of online privacy management activity at different stages of social media use. *Computers in Human Behavior, 28*(5), 1859–1872. https://doi.org/10.1016/j.chb.2012.05.004

Child, J. T., Pearson, J. C., & Petronio, S. (2008). Blogging, communication, and privacy management: Development of the blogging privacy management measure. *Journal of the American Society for Information Science and Technology, 60*(10), 2079–2094. https://doi.org/10.1002/asi.21122

Child, J. T., & Petronio, S. (2011). Unpacking the paradoxes of privacy in CMC relationships: The challenges of blogging and relational communication on the internet. In K. B. Wright & L. W. Webb (Eds.), *Computer-mediated communication in personal relationships* (pp. 21–40). Peter Lang.

Child, J. T., & Petronio, S. (2015). Privacy management matters in digital family communication. In C. J. Bruess (Ed.), *Family communication in the age of digital and social media* (pp. 32–54). Peter Lang.

Child, J. T., Petronio, S., Agyeman-Budu, E. A., & Westermann, D. A. (2011). Blog scrubbing: Exploring triggers that change privacy rules. *Computers in Human Behavior, 27*(5), 2017–2027. https://doi.org/10.1016/j.chb.2011.05.009

Child, J. T., & Starcher, S. C. (2016). Fuzzy Facebook privacy boundaries: Exploring mediated lurking, vague-booking, and Facebook privacy management. *Computers in Human Behavior, 54*, 483–490. https://doi.org/10.1016/j.chb.2015.08.035

Child, J. T., & Starcher, S. C. (2020). Measurement issues and trends in family communication research. In E. Graham & J. Mazer (Ed.), *Communication research measures* (3rd ed., pp. 20–35). Routledge.

Child, J. T., & Westermann, D. A. (2013). Let's be Facebook friends: Exploring parental Facebook friend requests from a communication privacy management (CPM) perspective. *Journal of Family Communication, 13*(1), 46–59. https://doi.org/10.1080/15267431.2012.742089

De Wolf, R., Willaert, K., & Pierson, J. (2014). Managing privacy boundaries together: Exploring individual and group privacy management strategies in Facebook. *Computers in Human Behavior, 35*, 444–454. https://doi.org/10.1016/j.chb.2014.03.010

Frampton, B. D., & Child, J. T. (2013). Friend or not to friend: Coworker Facebook friend requests as an application of communication privacy management theory. *Computers in Human Behavior, 29*(6), 2257–2264. https://doi.org/10.1016/j.chb.2013.05.006

Ledbetter, A. M. (2019) Parent-child privacy boundary conflict patterns during the first year of college: Mediating family communication patterns, predicting psychosocial distress. *Human Communication Research, 45*(3), 255–285. https://doi.org/10.1093/hcr/hqy018

Petronio, S. (2002). *Boundaries of privacy: Dialectics of disclosure.* SUNY Press.

Petronio, S. (2013). Brief status report on communication privacy management theory. *Journal of Family Communication, 13*(1), 6–14. https://doi.org/10.1080/15267431.2013.743426

Petronio, S., & Child, J. T. (2020). Conceptualization and operationalization: Utility of communication privacy management theory. *Current Opinion in Psychology, 31*, 76–82. https://doi.org/10.1016/j.copsyc.2019.08.009

Petronio, S., Child, J. T., & Hall, R. D. (2021). Communication privacy management theory: Significance for interpersonal communication. In D. O. Braithwaite & P. Schrodt (Eds.), *Engaging theories in interpersonal communication* (3rd ed., pp. 314–327). Sage.

Rainie, L. (2018, March 27). *Americans' complicated feelings about social media in an era of privacy concerns.* Pew Research Center. https://www.pewresearch.org/fact-tank/2018/03/27/americans-complicated-feelings-about-social-media-in-an-era-of-privacy-concerns/

FAMILY COMMUNICATION

The family communication context focuses on how family members (spouses, children, siblings, grandparents, etc.) communicate with one another. Family communication scholars often examine how family members' communication maintains familial bonds or disrupts family functioning. Some major research areas in family communication include parenting, communication in adoptive families, family stories and storytelling, family rituals, and marriage. This section includes chapters focusing on three important areas of family communication research: (1) family distancing and parent–child estrangement, (2) communicating closeness with siblings, and (3) topic avoidance and secrets in parent–adolescent relationships. First, Kristina Scharp, Cimmiaron Alvarez, Salvador Guzman, and Haley Nolan-Cody (Rutgers University) review family estrangement research and discuss how family members voluntarily and intentionally distance themselves. Second, Scott Myers (West Virginia University) reviews sibling communication research to discuss how siblings communicate with each other to remain close. Third, Tamara Afifi (University of California, Santa Barbara) reviews family information regulation research to discuss how topic avoidance and secrets impact family relationships. Family relationships are some of the longest-lasting and most important relationships in our lives. It is important to consider how our family communication affects us, and these chapters can help you navigate family distancing, maintain closeness with a brother or sister, and understand secrets in the family.

UNDERSTANDING FAMILY DISTANCING: TAKING A CLOSER LOOK AT PARENT–CHILD ESTRANGEMENT

Kristina M. Scharp, Cimmiaron F. Alvarez, Salvador Guzman, &
Haley Nolan-Cody
Rutgers University

Back when I (KMS) was in graduate school, I became interested in the idea that some families require more communication to construct their identity inside of the family and present that identity to others (i.e., discourse dependence; Galvin, 2014). Even though all families require communication, families that lack blood and legal ties often suffer the most societal stigma and are considered second, or sometimes, even third best to those that have those blood/legal ties (see Scharp & Thomas, 2020). This misconception is problematic because there are many ways people can have (and create for themselves) a happy family independent of shared biology or through legal connections. This led me to ask the question, "If the culture thinks that families without blood/legal ties are somehow inferior, then are ALL biological families really the gold standard?" "Are ALL people bound by blood truly happy together?" The answer to both these questions is a resounding ... NO.

Thus, I began to study family estrangement. Family estrangement is a process of decreasing interdependence when at least one family member voluntarily and intentionally distances themselves from another family member because of an often, ongoing negative relationship (Scharp, 2019). A large-scale survey suggests that over 25% of Americans identify as being estranged from at least one family member (Pillemer, 2020). Because this is one of the primary processes I study and because you likely know someone who is estranged from a family member (or you might be estranged yourself), we spend the majority of this chapter using estrangement as the primary example. Yet, people might distance themselves for all different reasons, some for even prosocial reasons like emerging adults who leave home for college.

Indeed, in conducting research on estrangement, I connected with scholars publishing about other types of family distancing processes that were not the same but still related. In particular, I connected with Dr. Elizabeth Dorrance Hall (Michigan State University) who was studying family member marginalization (i.e., being the Black sheep of the family; 2018; Dorrance & Wilson, 2021). Together, we developed the Family Communication and Relationships Lab where we began researching a variety of distancing processes such as parental alienation (Scharp et al., 2020, 2021), college student adjustment (Dorrance Hall et al., 2020, 2021), and (foster) adoption (Scharp & Thomas, 2020; Thomas & Scharp, 2017). Together, we have begun to theorize about family distancing specifically, and relational distancing more broadly, acknowledging that accomplishing and maintaining distance is inherently tied to how much access people have to ideological, material, and relational resources (i.e., power).

With this in mind, we will begin by introducing different types of family distancing before turning to the ways adult children distance themselves from their parents and how they maintain that distance. Lastly, we will discuss some of the ways family distancing research has disrupted assumptions about what it means to be a family.

TYPES OF FAMILY DISTANCING

Depending on the circumstances, family distancing might be voluntary, but in other instances, completely involuntary (Scharp & Dorrance Hall, 2019). Specifically, pulling away and parting mutually are two types of voluntary family distancing whereas being pushed out and removed by a third party are two instances of nonvoluntary distance.

Pulling Away. Pulling away occurs when one member attempts to pull away from the rest of the family (Scharp & Dorrance Hall, 2019). One process of pulling away might occur when adult children want to estrange themselves from a parent. What is important to note is that estrangement is not a one-time event, but rather frequently takes the form of an on-again/off-again relationship (Scharp et al., 2015). Even though people want distance, they sometimes feel internal guilt for pulling away and/or external pressure from friends and family members to reconcile. Yet, most adult children who distance themselves from their parents do not want to reconcile and engage in a variety of strategies that we will discuss to accomplish and maintain distance (Scharp, 2019).

Parting Mutually. Rather than one family member pulling away from another, both family members might decide they want distance or that distance is appropriate (Scharp & Dorrance Hall, 2019). Reasons for parting mutually might include natural life course events, such as a child leaving home for college (Dorrance Hall et al., 2020) or a decision to migrate to a different country (see Scharp et al., 2021). For example, Basigner and Knobloch (2018) examined how parents coped with their child's U.S. military service online. Even though the desire for distance was mutual, parents still missed their child and coped by seeking support, relating to others, and recognizing positive outcomes of their child's military service (Basinger & Knobloch, 2018).

Pushed Out. Individuals might feel pushed out of their family when they are continually left out or ignored, although they desire to stay in the family's in-group (Scharp & Dorrance Hall, 2017). Dorrance Hall (2018) defines family member marginalization (i.e., being the Black sheep; FMM), as a process when a person "feels fundamentally different from other members and are often excluded or disapproved of by several members of their family" (p. 308). Dorrance Hall and Wilson (2021) identified three dimensions of FMM: (1) disapproval, (2) difference, and (3) exclusion. Disapproval occurs when family members question or express displeasure with a person's choices. Difference pertains to what extent an individual feels similar or dissimilar to their family based on attitudes, background, values, and appearance. Exclusion depicts whether the family includes or ostracizes the individual. Taken together, these components can leave a person feeling as though they have been pushed out of their family.

Removed by Third Party. Unlike the other three types of family distancing where at least one individual seeks distance, external factors (e.g., government intervention, natural disaster, and illness) might also separate families (Scharp & Dorrance Hall, 2017, 2019). Migrants who travel to the United States and must leave their families, for example, could have done so because of natural disasters or civil unrest. Parent alienation is an example of third-party interference when, after a divorce, one parent consciously or even subconsciously turns their child against the other parent (Scharp et al., 2020). Another example is when the State removes a child and places them in the foster care system (see Baxter et al., 2014; Nelson & Thomas, 2022; Thomas, 2015; Thomas et al., 2017). These studies illustrate the ways in which external factors can involuntarily separate family members despite their desire to, in many cases, remain together. In the next section, we address what it's like for people when one person wants distance (i.e., to pull away) and the other person wants to maintain the family relationship in the context of parent–child estrangement.

ACCOMPLISHING AND MAINTAINING FAMILY DISTANCE

For those seeking to distance themselves from a family member, one of the most popular questions we get asked is, "How do people accomplish and maintain distance in a culture that contends a family is forever?" To answer this question in the context of parent–child estrangement, Scharp (2019) conducted a constructivist grounded theory of family distancing. Scharp identified eight characteristics or _distance continua_ that constitute the estrangement continuum: (1) communication quality, (2) communication quantity, (3) physical distance, (4) presence/absence of emotion, (5) positive/negative affect, (6) desire to be a family, (7) role reciprocity, and (8) legal action, which ultimately translate to distancing behaviors. These continua reflect the variety of ways people might gain distance from their family.

The Eight Continua of Parent–Child Estrangement. The first distance continuum characterizes _communication quality_, which alludes to the extent to which interactions are both "satisfactory" and "intimate" (p. 437). The second continuum, _communication quantity_, details the presence and/or absence of communication. For example, some adult children might speak to their parents more frequently but not discuss anything of importance whereas others might speak less frequently but have a more meaningful discussion (i.e., communication quality). *Physical distance* is also a central role in estrangement. Although some family members live within the same household or in close vicinity to one another, other members might live thousands of miles away and actively stay away. The fourth distance continuum pertains to the *presence/absence of emotion*, which determines whether a person feels anything for the other person. If the other person elicits an emotional response, *positive/negative affect* describes whether those feelings are *good* or *bad*. Further, family members might also grapple with whether or not they want to reconcile, even though most adult children report that is not their goal (i.e., *desire to be a family*). The seventh continuum, *role reciprocity*, captures whether family members behave like a family and fulfill family roles (e.g., caretaking). Lastly, *taking legal action* is the eighth component by which family members utilize legal strategies to decrease their interdependence with other family members (e.g., emancipation, name changes, and amendments to legal documents).

Movement and Maintenance Across the Distance Continua. Indeed, as we demonstrate in this chapter, estrangement is not uniform, but rather a negotiated and dynamic process. Family members might move back and forth, recalibrating their distance and moving across the continua. Of course, not all family members seek movement and instead look toward maintaining their distance. This, however, can become complicated as maintenance behaviors for one individual might constitute distance for another. As Scharp (2019) posits, "movement toward greater distance and maintenance along/on the continuum are sometimes the same behavior in varying degrees" (p. 441). Here, we briefly map 10 communication behaviors that help people accomplish and maintain distance: (1) decreasing meaningful contact, (2) reducing amount of contact, (3) moving away and (4) staying away, (5) decreasing feeling, (6) increasing negative affect and (7) holding on to negative affect, (8) reducing relationship effort, (9) ignoring role expectations, and lastly, (10) taking legal action.

The first behavior, decreasing meaningful contact, work to limit the depth and breadth of information shared, as well as de-identifying with family members. Resisting the notion that family relationships are forever, reducing the amount and quality of contact emphasizes the importance of communication in what makes a relationship. Further, moving and staying away from family members can help people avoid unwanted contact and family rituals (e.g., see Galvin, 2014). In other words, limiting physical access can help people maintain their safety and/or avoid unwanted interactions at family events. A family member might also experience decreased feelings over time as they negotiate how to maintain familial distance. In addition, increasing negative affect and holding on those emotions work to help people maintain distance despite pressures for reconciliation. Avoiding attempts to reconnect and reducing relationship efforts also illustrates a family member's desire to withdraw or no longer be part of that family. Lastly, a family member might ignore ascribed familial roles and tasks they feel are part of their "jobs" in their families (e.g., caretaking and providing supportive communication), sometimes officially cutting ties through legal action (e.g., name change or emancipation).

The Importance of Acknowledging Power. What distancing strategies people engage in and the extent to which they do so often depends on how much access they have to power. Sometimes power rests in ideology and social norms. For example, the culture celebrates children who leave their home for college and discourages those who want to become estranged from their parents (even if the adult child has a good reason for doing so). These beliefs make distancing easier for some people and harder for others (i.e., power). Other times, access to material resources might dictate how much power a person has to gain distance from their family. For example, children often do not have the financial resources to gain distance from their parents until they can earn enough money to live independently. Power might even come in the form of relationships. In other words, some people can gain distance because they can rely on others to provide necessities whereas some people do not. For example, adult children might be able to gain distance from one parent if they have grandparents willing to support them. Thus, understanding distance often also requires understanding the power dynamics at play. Furthermore, people might need to overcome multiple barriers at the ideological, material, and relational levels. In this regard, gaining and maintaining distance can be extremely effortful and require extensive support. In this next section, we discuss ways to research on family distancing has helped tackle some of the ideological misconceptions that make gaining distance from a family member so difficult.

DISRUPTING ASSUMPTIONS ABOUT FAMILY RELATIONSHIPS

Perhaps the most useful way family distancing research has made a difference is by disrupting misconceptions about what family distancing is, what it means, and how it can be productive. Disrupting this misconception is important considering people have such a bias for closeness that they might inadvertently stifle someone's opportunity for growth (e.g., taking an opportunity far away) or even encourage them to return to an abusive family relationship because they believe people should always forgive their families (Scharp & Dorrance Hall, 2019).

Scharp and Dorrance Hall (2019) identify multiple ways that family distancing might yield benefits for those who desire it. For example, everyday examples of prosocial family distancing might include children who leave home for college, people joining military service, or moving for a better employment opportunity. More serious examples (but still prosocial) might include gaining distance from an abusive family relationship, deciding to place a child for adoption, or seeking residential treatment for substance abuse issues. Regardless, distance has the potential to help people live safer, healthier, and better lives. Nevertheless, family distancing can have negative ramifications, especially for those pushed out of the family or those who have been affected by third-party interference. In the future, researchers should consider linking family distancing to health outcomes to better understand how distance might impact a person's life, especially given how distancing is often an ambivalent experience (e.g., Scharp, 2021).

Other ways family distancing research has disrupted misconceptions is through studies that expose ideologies that stigmatize people who have gained distance from a family member. For example, in a study about the meaning of the parent–child relationship, Scharp and Thomas (2016) identified a cultural ideology that suggested that parents and children were forever connected through biology, that family webs insinuated unending obligations, and that shared history was irreplaceable. Despite being widely accepted by the culture, they also identified an alternative way of understanding the parent relationship based on relational maintenance, reciprocal care, love, and survival. By highlighting a different way to be a family, they challenged, (1) the genetic/biological definition of family, (2) the idea that family relationships are nonvoluntary and do not require maintenance, (3) that family conflict will eventually be resolved without consequence, (4) the idea of closeness as a strictly positive experience, and (5) even the way the word "estranged" suggests estrangement is an event as opposed to a process. Upending these misconceptions has been important not only for how scholars think about families but also for normalizing the experience of estrangement. Likely because of some of these misconceptions, it was not until the early 2010s before scholars began to empirically study the process of family estrangement in any discipline.

Another study about estrangement and uncertainty revealed that adult children who distanced themselves from their parents experienced something called parental love uncertainty (Scharp & McLaren, 2018). In other words, they expressed uncertainty about whether their parents loved them. Although people often seek to reduce their uncertainty, adult children actively worked to maintain their parental love uncertainty because either their parents loved them and treated them poorly or their parents did not love them. Because neither answer was satisfactory, adult children illustrated that not all parents love their children or behave that way. Even though this finding can be difficult to process, disrupting this misconception might empower people in abusive family relationships to gain the distance they need.

An important part of this ongoing work is disseminating it to a larger audience. This work has been translated into several popular press articles on the widely-read news outlets (e.g., *New York Times*, and *Washington Post*) and websites such as *Psychology Today* and *The Conversation,* which translate research findings into tangible recommendations (e.g., https://theconversation.com/what-is-family-estrangement-a-relationship-expert-describes-the-problem-and-research-agenda-164852). In addition, collaboration with counselors on this topic assist professionals in understanding the very nuanced processes of family distancing and thus determining the proper treatment plan for patients in these circumstances. Given how many people experience family distancing and how long it has been ignored, letting people know that they are not alone has been an essential part of helping people understand their own experiences.

CONCLUSION

In conclusion, family distancing can include multiple processes (e.g., alienation, marginalization, and adoption) whereby a family member might: (1) pull away from their family, (2) be pushed out of their family, (3) part mutually, or (4) be removed by a third party (Scharp & Dorrance Hall, 2019). Although people traditionally think of family relationships as nonvoluntary, distance can be a healthy solution to an unhealthy family environment (e.g., estrangement) or simply part of the life course (e.g., going away to college). If gaining distance from your family is your goal, research suggests that you could do some combination of (1) reducing the quantity and/or quality of communication with your family member, (2) move and/or stay away to avoid physical contact, (3) reduce your emotional response and/or increase your negative feelings, (4) refrain from acting like or meeting the expectations of being a family member, (5) avoid reconciliation, and/or (6) take legal action (Scharp, 2019). Regardless of what action best fits your situation, remember that setting boundaries is an individual process and dependent on power; this means that what works for one person might not work for another. Nevertheless, family distancing is very common and can be essential for people in abusive and unhealthy family relationships.

REFERENCES

Basinger, E. D., & Knobloch, L. K. (2018). A grounded theory of online coping by parents of military service members. *Journal of Social and Personal Relationships*, *35*(5), 702–721. https://doi.org/10.1177/0265407517694769

Baxter, L. A., Norwood, K. M, Asbury, B., & Scharp, K. M., & (2014). Narrating adoption: Resisting adoption as "second best" in online stories of domestic adoption told by adoptive parents. *Journal of Family Communication*, *14*(3), 253–269. https://doi.org/10.1080/15267431.2014.908199

Dorrance Hall, E. (2018). The communicative process of resilience for marginalized family members. *Journal of Social and Personal Relationships*, *35*(3), 307–328. https://doi.org/10.1177/0265407516683838

Dorrance Hall, E., Scharp, K. M., Sanders, M., & Beaty, L. (2020). Family communication patterns and the mediating effects of support and resilience on students' concerns about college. *Family Relations*, *69*(2), 276–291. https://doi.org/10.1111/fare.12386

Dorrance Hall, E., Shebib, S., & Scharp, K. M. (2021). The mediating role of helicopter parenting in the relationship between family communication patterns and resilience in emerging adults. *Journal of Family Communication*, *21*(1), 34–45. https://doi.org/10.1080/15267431.2020.1859510.

Dorrance Hall, E., & Wilson, S. R. (2021). Explicating dimensions of family marginalization and types of marginalized family members. *Journal of Social and Personal Relationships*, *38*(7), 2099–2120. https://doi.org/10.1177/02654075211003981

Galvin, K. M. (2014). Blood, law, and discourse: Constructing and managing family identity. In L. A. Baxter (Ed.), *Remaking "family" communicatively* (pp. 17–32). Peter Lang.

Nelson, L. R., & Thomas, L. J. (2022). "I am my home": Aged out foster youth's discursive constructions of home. *Western Journal of Communication, 86*(2), 174–193. https://doi.org/10.1080/10570314.2022.2048415

Pillemer, K. (2020). *Fault lines: Fractured families and how to mend them.* Random House.

Scharp, K. M. (2021). Thematic co-occurrence analysis: Advancing a theory and qualitative method to illuminate ambivalent experiences. *Journal of Communication, 71*(4), 545–571. https://doi.org/10.1093/joc/jqab015

Scharp, K. M. (2019). "You're not welcome here": A grounded theory of family distancing. *Communication Research, 46*(4), 427–455. https://doi.org/10.1177/0093650217715542

Scharp, K. M., & Dorrance Hall, E. (2017). Family marginalization, alienation, and estrangement: Questioning the nonvoluntary status of family relationships. *Annals of the International Communication Association, 41*(1), 28–45. https://doi.org/10.1080/23808985.2017.1285680

Scharp, K. M., & Dorrance Hall, E. (2019). Reconsidering family closeness: A review and call for research on family distancing. *Journal of Family Communication, 19*(1), 1–14. https://doi.org/10.1080/15267431.2018.1544563

Scharp, K. M., Geary, D. E., Wolfe, B. H., Wang, T. R., & Fesenmaier, M. A. (2021). Understanding the triggers and communicative processes that constitute resilience in the context of migration to the United States. *Communication Monographs, 88*(4), 395–417. https://doi.org/10.1080/03637751.2020.1856395

Scharp, K. M., Hansen, R., Kubler, K., & Wang, T. R. (2021). Making meaning of parental alienation using relational dialectics theory. *Personal Relationships, 28*(1), 169–189. https://doi.org/10.1111/pere.12356

Scharp, K. M., Kubler, K. F., & Wang, T. R. (2020). Individual and community practices for constructing communicative resilience: Exploring the communicative processes of coping with parental alienation. *Journal of Applied Communication Research, 48*(2), 207–226. https://doi.org/10.1080/00909882.2020.1734225

Scharp, K. M., & McLaren, R. M. (2018). Uncertainty issues and management in adult children's stories of their estrangement with their parents. *Journal of Social and Personal Relationships, 35*(6), 811–830. https://doi.org/10.1177/0265407517699097

Scharp, K. M., & Thomas, L. J. (2016). Family "bonds": Making meaning of parent-child relationships in estrangement narratives. *Journal of Family Communication, 16*(1), 32–50. http://dx.doi.org/10.1080/15267431.2015.1111215

Scharp, K. M., & Thomas, L. J. (2020). A child for every family?: Characterizations of "adoptable" foster children in online permanency advocacy publications. *Journal of Social and Personal Relationships, 37*(7), 2098–2117. https://doi.org/10.1177/0265407520918668

Scharp, K. M., Thomas, L. J., & Paxman, C. G. (2015). "It was the straw that broke the camel's back": Exploring the distancing processes communicatively constructed in parent-child estrangement backstories. *Journal of Family Communication, 15*(4), 330–348. https://doi.org/1 0.1080/15267431.2015.1076422

Thomas, L. J. (2015). *Fostering resilience: Exploring former foster children's narratives* (Doctoral dissertation). http://ir.uiowa.edu/etd/1775

Thomas, L. J., Jackl, J. A., & Crowley, J. L. (2017). "Family? … not just blood": Discursive constructions of "family" in adult, former foster children's narratives. *Journal of Family Communication, 17*(3), 238–253. https://doi.org/10.1080/15267431.2017.1310728

Thomas, L. J., & Scharp, K. M. (2017). "A family for every child": Discursive constructions of "ideal" adoptive families in online foster adoption photolistings that promote adoption of children from foster care. *Adoption Quarterly, 20*(1), 44–64. http://dx.doi.org/10.1080/10926755.2016. 1263261

COMMUNICATING CLOSENESS WITH SIBLINGS

Scott A. Myers
West Virginia University

If you are like most people, you have at least one sibling. And, according to adult sibling researchers Geoffrey Greif and Michael Wooley, if you are like most people, you generally rate your sibling relationships as important, feel supported by your siblings, and consider your relationships to be emotionally close. At the same time, you may experience feelings of ambivalence or conflict toward a sibling or feel relationally closer to one sibling than you might feel to other siblings (Greif & Wooley, 2016). These ratings, feelings, and considerations are all part of what communication sibling researcher Alan Mikkelson (2014) terms the paradoxical nature of the sibling relationship: a long-lasting, involuntary, and permanent relationship in which its participants simultaneously think, behave, and communicate toward one another in loving yet hateful, comforting yet irritating, and supportive yet discouraging ways toward one another.

As a researcher who has studied adult sibling relationships over the past 20 years, I can attest that the communication behaviors in which individuals engage with their siblings mirror this paradoxical nature. Yet, whether adult siblings elect to purposely remain actively involved in each other's lives or keep abreast of one another through a third party (e.g., parent and another sibling), communication technology (e.g., texting and email), or social media (e.g., Instagram and Twitter), the adult sibling relationship typically is characterized by some semblance of relational closeness. Two factors that are known to influence both the breadth and the depth of adult sibling relational closeness are the type of sibling relationship to which two people belong and the lifespan stage of the sibling relationship in which the individuals are located, which is the focus of this chapter.

ADULT SIBLING RELATIONSHIP TYPE

The first factor that affects how adult siblings communicate closeness with each other is the perceived relational quality of their relationship. Deborah Gold (1989) created a five-category typology of adult sibling relationships rooted in relational quality: intimate, congenial, loyal, apathetic, and hostile. In an *intimate* sibling relationship, individuals experience a strong sense of relational closeness and psychological investment, willingly provide each other with emotional and instrumental support when needed, and rarely experience envy or resentment. Despite the geographical distance that may separate them, they often consider themselves to be best friends. In a *congenial* sibling relationship, much like intimate siblings, they do not let envy or resentment govern their relationships, but instead of considering each other to be "best" friends, they consider themselves to be "good" friends. As "good" friends, they remain emotionally and psychologically involved in each other's lives—even though they are more likely to disagree and argue with one another than intimate siblings—and provide each other with support and care, although this support and care often must be solicited by the sibling in need.

In a *loyal* sibling relationship, individuals consider their relationships to be bound by their shared family background and a sense of obligation to offer support and care when needed. Although they recognize the importance of the sibling bond and respond quickly to their siblings in a time of crisis, they are not as emotionally involved with their siblings as intimate and congenial siblings and are more likely to openly express disapproval about their siblings (e.g., sibling's lifestyle, relational partner, or occupation). In an *apathetic* sibling relationship, contact is minimal and individuals lack emotional involvement in the relationship. They tend to act indifferently toward one another—making little effort to behave otherwise—and rarely think about each other. Apathetic siblings are hesitant to either take instrumental or emotional support from a sibling or offer it to a sibling. In a *hostile* sibling relationship, individuals purposely avoid contact with one another and openly express their disapproval of, disdain toward, or disgust about their sibling. They not only fail to provide emotional and instrumental support for each other, but they also outright reject any request for help from each other.

Relationship Maintenance Behaviors. Intrigued by this typology, my colleague Alan Goodboy and I were interested in examining whether the frequency of those behaviors that adult siblings use to maintain their relationships would differ among intimate, congenial, loyal, apathetic, and hostile siblings (Myers & Goodboy, 2010). These behaviors—known as relationship maintenance behaviors—are the things that people do and say in order to keep their relationships moving forward or to prevent their relationships from becoming stagnant (Canary & Stafford, 1994). Five common behaviors adult siblings use to maintain their relationships are (1) *positivity*, which refers to communicating with a sibling in a cheerful and optimistic manner; (2) *assurances*, which refers to expressing a desire to remain involved in the sibling relationship; (3) *openness*, which refers to directly discussing the nature of the sibling relationship; (4) *networks*, which refers to siblings sharing common affiliations and memberships; and (5) *tasks*, which refers to sharing and completing those activities unique to the sibling relationship (Canary & Stafford, 1992; Stafford & Canary, 1991).

In this study, we obtained two findings. First, we found that the congenial sibling relationship type was the most commonly reported type of sibling relationship, followed by the intimate, the loyal, and the apathetic/hostile relationship types. Second, we discovered that individuals who classified their sibling relationships as intimate used the positivity, assurances, openness, networks, and tasks relationship maintenance behaviors more frequently than individuals who classified their sibling relationships as congenial, loyal, or apathetic/hostile. Individuals who classified their sibling relationships as congenial used the five maintenance behaviors more frequently than individuals who classified their sibling relationships as loyal as did individuals who classified their sibling relationships as loyal rather than apathetic/hostile.

Several years later, my colleague Kelly Odenweller and I were interested in whether individuals who classified their sibling relationships as intimate, congenial, loyal, or apathetic/hostile would report differences in the frequency with which their sibling used the five relationship maintenance behaviors with them (Myers & Odenweller, 2015). Not surprisingly, we found that individuals who classified their sibling relationships as either intimate or congenial reported that their sibling used all five maintenance behaviors with them more frequently than individuals who classified their sibling relationships as either loyal or apathetic/hostile. Furthermore, we found that individuals who classified their sibling relationships as loyal reported that their sibling used the five behaviors with them more frequently than individuals who classified their sibling relationships as apathetic/hostile. And, similar to the Myers and Goodboy (2010) study, participants classified their sibling relationship type most often as congenial, followed by loyal, intimate, and apathetic/hostile.

We were further interested in discovering whether intimate, congenial, loyal, and apathetic/hostile sibling types differed in their affective feelings toward one another, namely, their commitment to the sibling relationship, the trust they placed in the sibling, their feelings of communication and relational satisfaction associated with the sibling relationship, and the extent to which they liked and loved their sibling. Individuals who classified their sibling relationships as either intimate or congenial reported the same levels of commitment, trust, communication satisfaction, relational satisfaction, and liking. Those individuals who classified their sibling relationships as congenial, however, reported greater levels of affective feelings than individuals who classified their sibling relationships as either loyal or apathetic/hostile; individuals who classified their sibling relationships as loyal reported greater levels of affective feelings than individuals who classified their sibling relationships as apathetic/hostile.

Affectionate Communication. The findings of these aforementioned studies made me wonder whether intimate, congenial, loyal, and apathetic/hostile siblings also differed in their expressions of affectionate communication (Myers, 2015), which refers to "an individual's intentional and overt enactment and expression of feelings of closeness, care, and fondness" (Floyd & Morman, 1998, p. 145). In this study, I hypothesized that individuals who classified their sibling relationships as intimate would use affectionate communication at a higher rate, consider the use of affectionate communication to be more important, and consider the use of affectionate communication to be more appropriate than individuals who classified their sibling relationships as congenial, loyal, or apathetic/hostile. This hypothesis was supported: Individuals in intimate sibling relationships used affectionate communication the most frequently and considered the use of affectionate communication as both more important and appropriate than individuals in congenial, loyal, and apathetic/hostile sibling relationships.

In a related vein, three of my graduate students and I discovered that adult siblings use affectionate communication as an additional relationship maintenance behavior (Myers et al., 2011). Interestingly, we also found that they are more likely to use affectionate communication strategically (i.e., purposely and consciously) than routinely (i.e., unintentionally and out of habit), suggesting that when it comes to maintaining their relationships, siblings may intentionally think about how to do so.

ADULT SIBLING RELATIONSHIP LIFESPAN

Another factor that affects the manner in which adult siblings communicate closeness to one another is related to their location in the adult sibling relationship lifespan, which progresses through three stages: emerging adulthood, early and middle adulthood, and late adulthood (Myers & Rittenour, 2012). *Emerging adulthood* occurs when individuals are between the ages of 18 and 25 years (Arnett, 2000) and reflects a time period when they no longer consider themselves to be adolescents yet do not necessarily consider themselves to have reached adulthood (Arnett, 2015). During this stage, individuals become more interested in their relationships with their friends and their romantic partners and less interested in their sibling relationships in that they begin to distance themselves emotionally and physically from their siblings and decrease their involvement (e.g., shared activities and time) in their day-to-day interactions with their siblings (Arnett, 2015; Scharf et al., 2005).

Early and middle adulthood reflects the time period when individuals are between 26 and 54 years of age (Myers & Goodboy, 2006). As individuals move through this second stage, they no longer reside with their families of origin and become actively involved in establishing their own family. As individuals focus on their spouses or significant others, their children, and their careers (Connidis, 1992), involvement in their sibling relationships is viewed as less obligatory (White, 2001) and more voluntary (Goetting, 1986). Once individuals reach the age of 55, the *late adulthood* stage begins (Myers & Goodboy, 2006). During this stage, the sibling relationship takes on a renewed importance as individuals face retirement, declining health and functional status, and, ultimately, the deaths of spouses, relatives, and friends (Connidis, 1992; Gold, 1987). It is not uncommon for late adulthood siblings to intensify their emotional bond and increase both the breadth and the depth of their communication with each other (Gold, 1987).

Commitment. Despite the differences in sibling communication that occur during the emerging adulthood, early and middle adulthood, and late adulthood stages, researchers have noted that siblings generally remain committed to one another across the sibling lifespan. To investigate the role that commitment plays in the adult sibling relationship, my colleagues Christine Rittenour, Maria Brann, and I explored whether sibling commitment remains stable or fluctuates across the three stages (Rittenour et al., 2007). We discovered that commitment remained stable across the lifespan; that is, regardless of the adult sibling lifespan stage, siblings reported that they were highly committed to their relationships. We further found that across these three stages, siblings who provided each other with communication-based emotional support and used social support behaviors remained committed to the sibling relationship.

With this finding in mind, my colleague Leah Bryant and I were interested in identifying the ways that emerging adult siblings express their commitment behaviorally to each other (Myers & Bryant, 2008b). In this study, we identified 11 categories of commitment behaviors and discovered that not only do emerging adult siblings use all 11 behaviors regularly, but also that their use of these behaviors is tied positively to the communication and relational satisfaction they associate with their sibling relationship.

The first five categories centered on the provision of some form of social support. *Tangible support* occurred when siblings provided each other with needed goods or services such as preparing or purchasing meals, providing transportation, loaning money, or purchasing gifts. *Emotional support* consisted of expressions of caring and concern directed toward each other (e.g., "I offer him support and positivity"). *Informational support* occurred when siblings needed advice, guidance, or feedback about the events occurring in their lives (e.g., their schoolwork, their jobs, and their relationships). *Esteem support* arose when siblings wanted to demonstrate their positive effect for each other such as attending activities in which their siblings were participating (e.g., sporting events, band concerts, and school functions) or providing an ego boost that they believed their sibling desperately needed (e.g., "To show my commitment, I often compliment him and give him confidence"). *Network support* emerged when siblings included each other in their activities and same groups of friends.

The sixth and seventh categories centered on how siblings expressed intimacy with each other through their daily routines. *Everyday talk* referenced the communication that occurred between siblings on a regular basis (whether it was face-to-face, cell phone, email, or text messaging) about their daily mundane activities (e.g., jobs, school, chores, and errands). *Shared activities* centered on activities in which siblings participated together on a regular basis that are just as mundane such as playing video games, watching television, or having the same interests (e.g., "We both like the same music so I am constantly introducing her to new bands that I think she might like"). While both of these categories involved routine behaviors through which commitment was conveyed indirectly, the eighth and ninth categories involved the communication of messages that strategically and specifically expressed commitment toward a sibling. *Verbal expressions* consisted of direct verbal statements (e.g., "I tell my brother I love him every time I see him") whereas *nonverbal expressions* consisted of direct nonverbal behaviors (e.g., "Every time I see my sister, as a sign of greeting we give a kiss on the cheek to each other and a hug").   The 10th category is *protection*, which were the purposeful efforts made to shield siblings from negative or hurtful people, situations, or influences. Protection was used generally (e.g., "I will always have his back, whether he is right or wrong. Blood is thicker than water, and I will defend him in any situation") or would arise when the sibling was in a potentially troublesome or bothersome situation (e.g., "Being the only girl, and the youngest, [my brother] is very protective of me and keeps a close eye on me, particularly with males or potential boyfriends"). The eleventh category is *intimate play*, which was the physical (and sometimes antisocial) behaviors siblings used with each other. As one participant stated, "it's just playful fighting between brothers. A punch to say hello and a punch to say goodbye. Most often I get put in a headlock just walking by."

Verbal Aggressiveness. Verbal aggressiveness is another way in which adult siblings communicate closeness across the lifespan, albeit possibly a lack of closeness. Considered to be a destructive communication trait, verbal aggressiveness is a message behavior that attacks an individual's self-concept in order to deliver psychological pain (Infante & Wigley, 1986). To probe the presence of verbally aggressive messages used by siblings across the three adult sibling lifespan stages, Alan Goodboy and I examined the rate at which siblings directed verbally aggressive messages toward each other over a four-week period (Myers & Goodboy, 2006). In this study, we obtained two findings. First, we discovered that siblings in the emerging adulthood stage reported receiving verbally aggressive messages at a higher rate than siblings in either the early and middle adulthood stage or the late adulthood stage. These verbally aggressive messages attacked the sibling's intelligence, teased their sibling about their relationships with others, called the sibling uncomplimentary nicknames, made fun of the sibling's physical appearance, threatened to get the sibling in trouble, pointed out the sibling's faults, and told their siblings that they lack common sense. Second, across the three stages of the adult sibling lifespan, when adults are the recipients of these verbally aggressive messages from a sibling, they like and trust their siblings less and are less committed to their sibling relationship.

My colleague Leah Bryant and I then conducted a study where we asked emerging adults to provide us with an example of a verbally aggressive message they received from a sibling and assess the message in terms of its perceived hurtfulness, perceived intensity, and perceived intentionality (Myers & Bryant, 2008a). Although we identified seven types of verbally aggressive messages uttered by siblings, no significant differences in perceived hurtfulness, intensity, or intent emerged among these types. That is, despite the verbally aggressive content associated with each type, no one type was considered to be more hurtful, intense, or intentional than any other message type.

The first type is *name calling*, which involved the use of a derogatory, disparaging, or malevolent term directed toward a sibling. These terms could be general (e.g., "My sister called me an idiot") or based on a behavior the sibling did not like or appreciate (e.g., "He called me 'gay' because I wouldn't go get his phone charger"). The second type is *insults*, which identified siblings' ineptitude in some aspect of their lives and often centered on attacking their abilities, intelligence, or appearance. The third type is *withdrawal*, which occurred when siblings wanted to make it clear that they did not want to be in the presence of one another. These messages were conveyed verbally (e.g., "Why don't you just stay at school because no one wants you here") and nonverbally (e.g., "My sister will go weeks without speaking to me if she is upset").

The fourth type is *physical acts or threats (real or implied)*, which involved the threat of engaging in a violent or aggressive act with a sibling. While most threats were physical (e.g., "Roger told me he would 'punch me in the face' if I interfered with his relationship again"), other threats resembled intimidation or blackmail (e.g., "One time, my brother threatened me, and told me that if I didn't drive him to his friend's house he would tell our mom something that I had done in the past that he knows that she wouldn't approve"). The fifth type is *repudiating the relationship*, which siblings used as a way to either deny or reject the sibling relationship (e.g., "Your opinion doesn't count since you don't live here anymore") or as a way to question the sibling's place in the family (e.g., "She told me ... that she wished she could have a different sister, because if I was a real sister I wouldn't have treated her the way that I did").

The sixth type is *unfair comparison*, which unjustly compared one sibling's situation to another sibling's situation. These comparisons often revolved around siblings' education and academic prowess: "While I was telling my sister about a hard test that I had just taken, she rolled her eyes and sighed repeatedly. Then she proceeded to tell me how much harder her classes were then [sic] mine and said that I have nothing to complain about." The seventh type is *negative affect*, which conveyed a dislike, hatred, or general disdain toward the sibling such as "I hate you, I can't wait until you go back to school."

CONCLUSION

The research findings are clear: when adult siblings use relationship maintenance and affectionate communication behaviors with each other, behaviorally express their commitment to each other, and refrain from using verbally aggressive messages with each other, their relationships ultimately reflect a higher level of relational closeness. Furthermore, adults who classify their sibling relationships as intimate, congenial, or loyal and maintain an active presence in each other's lives throughout the emerging adulthood, early and middle adulthood, and late adulthood stages of the sibling relationship lifespan place themselves in a position to better develop and maintain relational closeness with their siblings.

To sustain your current level of closeness—or perhaps to increase your feelings of closeness—take a moment and consider the behaviors you currently use to communicate closeness with your siblings. Based on what you have read in this chapter, answer these questions:

1. Would you classify your sibling relationship as intimate, congenial, loyal, or apathetic/hostile? To what extent does this classification affect whether you use relationship maintenance and affectionate communication behaviors as a way to maintain closeness with your sibling?

2. Which relationship maintenance behaviors do you use to maintain your relationships? Why? How does this use of relationship maintenance behaviors accurately portray the type of relationship you have?

3. How often do you use affectionate communicate behaviors with a sibling? How appropriate and important is it to you to engage in affectionate communication with your sibling?

4. In which stage of the adult sibling lifespan is your relationship located? How do the characteristics of this stage affect how you communicate closeness with your sibling?

5. What behaviors do you use to express commitment to your sibling relationship? How does your use of these behaviors mirror how satisfied you are with your relationship?

6. How often do you direct verbally aggressive messages toward a sibling? What is the content of these messages? Is your use of these messages intended to be playful or hurtful, intense, and intentional?

7. How strategically do you communicate closeness with your sibling through your use of relationship maintenance and affectionate communication behaviors, behavioral expressions of commitment, and verbally aggressive messages? Which of these behaviors do you tend to use more routinely with your sibling?

REFERENCES

Arnett, J. J. (2000). Emerging adulthood: A theory of development from the late teens through twenties. *American Psychologist, 55*(5), 469–480. https://doi.org/10.1037/0003-066X.55.5.469

Arnett, J. J. (2015). *Emerging adulthood: The winding road from the late teens through the twenties* (2nd ed.). Oxford University Press.

Canary, D. J., & Stafford, L. (1992). Relational maintenance strategies and equity in marriage. *Communication Monographs, 59*(3), 244–267. https://doi.org/10.1080/03637759209376268

Canary, D. J., & Stafford, L. (1994). Maintaining relationships through strategic and routine interactions. In D. J. Canary & L. Stafford (Eds.), *Communication and relational maintenance* (pp. 1–22). Academic Press.

Connidis, I. A. (1992). Life transitions and the adult sibling tie: A qualitative study. *Journal of Marriage and the Family, 54*(4), 972–982. https://doi.org/10.2307/353176

Floyd, K., & Morman, M. T. (1998). The measurement of affectionate communication. *Communication Quarterly, 46*(2), 144–162. https://doi.org/10.1080/01463379809370092

Goetting, A. (1986). The developmental tasks of siblingship over the life cycle. *Journal of Marriage and the Family, 48*(4), 703–714. https://doi.org/10.2307/352563

Gold, D. T. (1987). Siblings in old age: Something special. *Canadian Journal on Aging, 6*(3), 199–215. https://doi.org/10.1017/S0714980800008424

Gold, D. T. (1989). Sibling relationships in old age: A typology. *International Journal of Aging and Human Development, 28*(1), 37–51. https://doi.org/10.2190/VGYX-BRHN-J51V-0V39

Greif, G. L., & Wooley, M. E. (2016). *Adult sibling relationships.* Columbia University Press.

Infante, D. A., & Wigley, C. J., III. (1986). Verbal aggressiveness: An interpersonal model and measure. *Communication Monographs, 53*(1), 61–69. https://doi.org/10.1080/03637758609376126

Mikkelson, A. C. (2014). Adult sibling relationships. In K. Floyd & M. T. Morman (Eds.), *Widening the family circle: New research on family communication* (2nd ed., pp. 19–34). Sage.

Myers, S. A. (2015). Using Gold's typology of adult sibling relationships to explore sibling affectionate communication. *North American Journal of Psychology, 17*(2), 301–310.

Myers, S. A., & Bryant, L. E. (2008a). Emerging adult siblings' use of verbally aggressive messages as hurtful messages. *Communication Quarterly, 56*(3), 268–283. https://doi.org/10.1080/01463370802240981

Myers, S. A., & Bryant, L. E. (2008b). The use of behavioral indicators of sibling commitment among emerging adults. *Journal of Family Communication, 8*(2), 101–125. https://doi.org/10.1080/15267430701857364

Myers, S. A., Byrnes, K. A., Frisby, B. N., & Mansson, D. H. (2011). Adult siblings' use of affectionate communication as a strategic and routine relational maintenance behavior. *Communication Research Reports, 28*(2), 151–158. https://doi.org/10.1080/08824096.2011.565276

Myers, S. A., & Goodboy, A. K. (2006). Perceived sibling use of verbally aggressive messages across the lifespan. *Communication Research Reports, 23*(1), 1–11. https://doi.org/10.1080/1746490500535798

Myers, S. A., & Goodboy, A. K. (2010). Relational maintenance behaviors and communication channel use among adult siblings. *North American Journal of Psychology, 12*(1), 103–116.

Myers, S. A., & Odenweller, K. G. (2015). The use of relational maintenance behaviors and relational characteristics among sibling types. *Communication Studies, 66*(2), 238–255. https://doi.org/10.1080/10510974.2014.930918

Myers, S. A., & Rittenour, C. E. (2012). Demographic and relational predictors of adult siblings' use of relational maintenance behaviors. *Journal of the Communication, Speech & Theatre Association of North Dakota, 24*(1), 1–17.

Rittenour, C. E., Myers, S. A., & Brann, M. (2007). Commitment and emotional closeness in the sibling relationship. *Southern Communication Journal, 72*(2), 169–183. https://doi.org/10.1080/10417940701316682

Scharf, M., Shulman, S., & Avigad-Spitz, L. (2005). Sibling relationships in emerging adult-hood and in adolescence. *Journal of Adolescent Research, 20*(1), 64–90. https://doi.org/10.1177/0743558404271133

Stafford, L., & Canary, D. J. (1991). Maintenance strategies and romantic relationship type, gender and relational characteristics. *Journal of Social and Personal Relationships, 8*(2), 217–242. https://doi.org/10.1177/0265407591082004

White, L. (2001). Sibling relationships over the life course: A panel analysis. *Journal of Marriage and Family, 63*(2), 555–568. https://doi.org/10.1111/j.1741-3737.2001.00555.x

"IT'S OKAY TO KEEP SOME THINGS TO YOURSELF": THE FUNCTIONALITY OF TOPIC AVOIDANCE AND SECRETS IN PARENT–ADOLESCENT RELATIONSHIPS

Tamara D. Afifi
University of California, Santa Barbara

Parents of adolescents and young adults are sometimes conflicted about how much information to ask them about their private lives. For instance, my oldest daughter went off to college this year. I know it is normal and healthy for her to keep information from me about what she does at college. At the same time, I want to know she is safe. As college students, you face similar dilemmas regarding what information and how much information you disclose to your parents. Do you tell your parents everything about what you do with your friends? How openly do you talk to your parents about your sexual attitudes and behaviors or alcohol use? What makes some adolescents and young adults more likely than others to talk to their parents about important issues? There are likely good reasons why adolescents and young adults do not tell their parents everything. Many parents may also prefer that their children not tell them things. There are also likely circumstances where children want to tell their parents something and know that they should talk to them about it, but still choose to withhold it.

This chapter highlights some of the recent research in the field of communication on topic avoidance and secrets. In particular, this chapter will focus on topic avoidance, disclosure, and secret keeping in parent–adolescent/young adult relationships. The goal of this chapter is to answer the questions: "What role do topic avoidance and secrets play in parent–adolescent/young adult relationships? What impact do topic avoidance and secrecy they have on family relationships? In order to answer these questions, differences among related concepts will briefly be addressed, followed by a discussion of how these topics used to be studied in the field of communication and how scholars study them currently.

TOPICS THAT ARE COMMONLY AVOIDED OR KEPT SECRET AND THE IMPORTANCE OF CONTEXT

Before diving into the research in this area, it is important to distinguish among a few concepts. Topic avoidance, secret-keeping, and disclosure are ways that people regulate information and privacy boundaries. One of the primary distinctions that need to be made is between topic avoidance and secrets. Topic avoidance refers to a topic that people purposefully refrain from discussing with someone, but that the other person typically knows exists (Afifi et al., 2007). Secrets, on the other hand, involve information that is purposefully withheld or concealed from another person. For example, if Chantel's parents know she drinks in high school but Chantel refrains from bringing it up with her parents, this would be topic avoidance. However, if Chantel smoked marijuana and did not tell her parents, it would be a secret. Because secret-keeping requires that information is hidden from others, secrets tend to be more negative than topics that are avoided and often have more negative consequences if they are revealed. Keeping a secret also requires more cognitive energy than choosing not to talk about something (Bok, 1983). Nevertheless, some secrets are positive (e.g., a surprise birthday party or present and pregnancy). In addition, not all secrets are deceptive. Secrets are deceptive if the person who is keeping the secret is creating a false impression. Other times, people are keeping a secret simply because they are not close enough to someone to share the information or do not believe it is any of the other person's business (privacy concerns). Nevertheless, it is important to remember that secrets and topic avoidance are very common. In fact, approximately 95% of people have a secret of some sort (Afifi et al., 2007; Vangelisti, 1994).

Topic avoidance and secrets are also ways people keep information private. Privacy is often a larger umbrella term that encompasses topic avoidance and secrets and involves information that people think they "own" (Petronio, 2002). For example, people often think they own the information they put on their social media. They can partially control the information they share with others by enabling or denying certain people access to the information (i.e., through privacy control settings). However, in the end, personnel who work at social network organizations and other people (e.g., the police) can still access, and consequently "co-own" information people put on their social media. The only real way to protect their private information from being shared is to avoid sharing it. Avoidance, secrecy, and disclosure become ways in which people regulate their private information.

Much of the early research on information regulation focused on the topics that adolescents avoid talking about with their parents or keep secret from them. For example, Guerrero and Afifi (1995) found that adolescents commonly avoid the topics of sex, friendships, and activities they engage in with their friends, dating relationships, negative things that have happened or failure events, and the state of their relationships, with their parents. Parents also refrain from talking about certain topics with their children. In particular, they often withhold information about their health, finances, and conflict with their spouse from their children (Afifi et al., 2005). Likewise, Vangelisti (1994) notes in her research on family secrets that there are intra-family secrets or secrets that certain family members keep from other family members and whole family secrets or secrets that the entire family keeps from "outsiders" or people outside the family. In addition, there are different types of topics that are kept secret. Vanglisti (1994) identified three types of secrets: (1) taboo topics, (2) rule violations, and (3) conventional secrets. Taboo secrets are potentially the most hurtful in families because they tend to be stigmatized or condemned by society. Examples of taboo secrets include addictions, violence, and adultery. Rule violations involve breaking family rules, such as if you were cohabitating against your parents' wishes or were partying when you were living with your parents and you were not supposed to be partying. Conventional secrets are topics, such as getting bad grades or health problems, which some people might consider inappropriate to bring up for conversation.

A topic that continues to be commonly studied is adolescents' avoidance of talking about sex and other risky behaviors (e.g., alcohol, drugs, and self-harming behaviors) with their parents. One of the central findings across this body of literature is that the more open parents are with their children talking about sex (and other risky behaviors), the less likely the children are to delay their sexual debut, the less risky behaviors they are likely to engage in, and they are more likely to talk to their parents and their parents about their sexual attitudes and behaviors (Bianchi et al., 2019). For example, Hurst et al. (2022) found that when adolescents (average age = 15 years) had families who were high in conversation orientation (or greater openness to discussing a wide array of sensitive topics) and low in conformity orientation (parents having lower expectations for their children conforming to their own standards, behaviors, and beliefs), they had greater sexual self-efficacy (confidence in one's sexual decision-making) and intentions to communicate about sex with their romantic partner. Families that were the opposite had less sexual self-efficacy and intentions to communication with their partner about sex.

Even though research still tends to focus on the frequency of conversations about sex between parents and adolescents, recent research has begun to examine the content and quality of those conversations (e.g., Coffelt, 2010; Holman & Koenig-Kellas, 2018; see also Flores & Barroso, 2017 for review). For instance, Holman and Koenig-Kellas (2018) asked adolescents and young adults to reflect on the memorable conversations they had about sex with a parent. Six memorable message types emerged from these conversations: *underdeveloped, safety, comprehensive talk, warning/threat, wait,* and *no talk.* The adolescents and young adults wanted more comprehensive discussions from their parents. Out of all of the types of conversations, *Comprehensive-talk* and *safety* were reported as the most effective. Indeed, more research is necessary that focuses on the content, effectiveness, and what kind of talk adolescents desire from their parents when talking about sex and other risky behaviors.

There are also considerable myths about sex talk that tends to drive the research in this area (Afifi et al., 2020). One myth is that conversations about sex between parents and children are a one-time event. In families that have greater conversation orientation, conversations about sex are likely (and should be) a process that occurs throughout the lifespan. The conversations evolve in content and quality depending upon the age of the child. A parent might talk about body parts with a young child, progress to discussions about the act of sex as the child turns 8 or 9, and then have more specific conversations as the child starts to think about dating. These conversations with their parents then shift even more as the child enters college, if they have they have children, and as they enter perimenopause (Afifi et al., 2020). Another myth is that the conversations about sex are always top-down from the parent to the child. Because of the open communication environment that has been established, children who grow up in families with higher conversation orientation likely have children who initiate conversations about sex as well. Sex talk, therefore, becomes multi-directional. Researchers, however, continue to study sex conversations solely from a top-down, unidirectional perspective.

Additional research is also necessary that examines actual conversations between parents and children about sex. Even though there are ethical and practical challenges to conducting this research, we have done this in our research and found it to be incredibly important (Afifi et al., 2008). We had 118 parents and adolescent/young adult pairs (ages 14–21) come into the laboratory. We asked them to choose three out of four commonly avoided topics to talk about with each other: (1) the child's sexual attitudes and behaviors, (2) negative things the child has done, (3) the parents' relationship, and (4) marriage and divorce in general. To make the parents and children more comfortable (and for ethical reasons), they were allowed to omit one of the topics. Of the four topics, 60% of the sample chose not to talk about the topic of sex, which is a fairly good indication itself of how much this topic is avoided in parent–child relationships. However, we took the remaining dyads and analyzed their communication patterns when talking about the child's sexual attitudes and behaviors. The quantitative portion of the study revealed that when parents were receptive, informal, and composed during the conversation, their adolescents were less anxious and, in turn, were less avoidant. When the child also perceived that their parent was a competent communicator, the child was less anxious and less avoidant during the conversation.

In addition to sex, risky behaviors in general often tend to be avoided or kept secret from parents. As Michelle Miller-Day has long argued (see Miller-Day, 2008), research is necessary that examines different types of family environments and messages about drugs and alcohol and their effectiveness in preventing their abuse. Shin et al. (2019) found that expressiveness or an open family environment and structural traditionalism (parents who emphasize power and obedience) were inversely associated with adolescent (9th graders') substance use, whereas conflict avoidance was positively associated with it. In addition, adolescents with parents that used a more indirect communication style (e.g., hinting and nonverbal cues) rather than directed confrontation reported the lowest substance use. One could interpret from these findings that having a family that is open but that does not pressure a child with direct questioning repeatedly, as well as clear rules and standards is associated with less substance use.

In addition to risky behaviors, another topic that is commonly avoided or kept secret that has recently been the focus of a considerable amount of research is adolescents' mental health. Perhaps because of generational gaps and stigma, parents often do not understand their child's mental health challenges or make them feel bad for not being able to simply "get over it" (Haughton & Afifi, 2023). This tends to produce a considerable amount of avoidance and secrecy. The extent to which parents and adolescents talk openly about mental health is also highly dependent upon culture. For example, even though parents across all cultures have difficulties talking about mental health with their adolescents, parents in Black, Latinx, and Asian families might have even greater difficulty than White parents talking about it with their children because it is more stigmatized in these cultures and less community support (Haughton & Afifi, 2023). Adolescents have reported feeling more risks than benefits to disclosing the secret of having a mental illness to others, given the potential for bullying, misunderstanding, and discrimination in the public (Mulfinger et al., 2019). When adolescents know their peers face similar mental health challenges, it helps them to disclose (Mulfinger et al., 2019). Indeed, having parents who talk openly about mental health and who are emotionally supportive fosters an environment where adolescents and young adults feel comfortable talking about mental health challenges and it can enhance well-being.

Similarly, talking openly about mental health in families also encourages adolescents and young adults to disclose about their own challenges (Haughton & Afifi, 2023). In fact, Rafferty et al. (2022) found in their interviews with young adults that the quality of the relationship, reciprocity in sharing health information, and having an open family communication environment throughout their childhood facilitated open discussions about health (in general) with their parents. Taniguchi-Dorios et al. (2022) also found in their daily diary logs with college students that when parents were more emotionally supportive when their college-age child disclosed to them about their mental health, the child reported better well-being.

There are numerous other topics that adolescents and young adults avoid or keep secret from their parents, but those mentioned above are among the top ones being addressed currently in the literature. In addition to understanding what topics adolescents avoid discussing with their parents, it is important to understand why they withhold the information.

REASONS FOR AVOIDANCE AND SECRETS

People avoid or keep secrets for many reasons, which can serve both positive and negative functions. Individuals often withhold information because they are not close to someone, are afraid of getting hurt or being judged (self-protection), are afraid of hurting the relationship (relationship protection), want to protect another person from being hurt (other protection), or simply want to maintain their privacy (see Afifi et al., 2007). For example, adolescents and young adults might be afraid to tell their parents that they received a bad grade on an exam for fear of being judged or looked down upon by their parents (self-protection). Or, if a child is a staunch Democrat and the parent is a staunch Republican, neither one of them might talk about politics to preserve their relationship (relationship protection).

When people are deciding whether to disclose something, they weigh the risk involved with disclosing it. According to CPM theory (Petronio, 2002), revealing private information is risky and people create metaphorical boundaries around themselves that ebb and flow with the degree of risk involved with a disclosure. The less that people trust others, the more rigid their privacy boundaries become and the less likely they are to disclose private information to them. When the information being withheld is negative or potentially harmful, people often engage in avoidance or secrecy for protection reasons: protection of the self, their relationship, and/or other people (Afifi et al., 2005).

Avoidance and secrets, however, can also serve important and positive functions. According to relational dialectics theory (Baxter, 2010) and CPM theory (Petronio, 2002), people need a balance of openness and closedness to maintain healthy relationships. Within romantic relationships, partners need to disclose information to learn more about their partner and grow closer to him/her. However, they also need to keep some information to themselves to maintain a sense of privacy. There are many instances where a secret is neutral or positive (e.g., a surprise birthday party) and there is very little risk involved with revealing it. When people are privy to a secret, it can also create a cohesive bond between the people who are keeping the secret (Vangelisti & Caughlin, 1997). Secrecy in adolescence can sometimes help maintain boundaries and close connections (Finkenauer & Hazam, 2000; Finkenauer et al., 2005). Secrecy in adolescence is also expected and natural (Solis et al., 2015). Adolescents often have secrets that they keep from their parents, especially compared to their best friends and this can give them a feeling of autonomy (Solis et al., 2015). Secrets that are shared among adolescents can also create feelings of closeness among them (Finkenauer et al., 2009).

When secrets are kept from others, however, it can also create feelings of exclusion and prohibit adolescents from forming close relationships with those from whom the secrets are being kept (Elsharnouby & Dost-Gozkan, 2020). Consequently, while adolescents may become closer to each other if they are keeping secrets from other adolescents and their parents, it could create an emotional wedge between the parents and adolescents (Finkenauer et al., 2009).

CONSEQUENCES FOR PERSONAL AND RELATIONAL HEALTH

Even though avoidance and secrets do serve positive functions, they can have negative health and relational consequences. Topic avoidance and secrets are often associated with dissatisfaction and worse well-being in families and romantic relationships. For instance, secret-keeping in families on one day has been associated with greater secret keeping in future days and correspondingly poorer family relationships (Smetana et al., 2010). When newlyweds think that their partner is keeping a secret from them, it often makes them feel rejected and excluded (Finkenauer, 2009). Even though secrets are natural and expected in adolescence, but they can create a sense of distance between parents and adolescents and negatively affect the adolescents' well-being (Baudat et al., 2022). For example, Elsharnouby and Dost-Gozkan (2020) found that among 1097 middle school adolescents (ages 14–16), those who reported the best well-being (life satisfaction, problem-solving confidence, and lowest anxiety) kept fewer secrets from their mothers (and parents in general) compared to their best friends. Those with the worst well-being kept more secrets from both parents and best friends. Topic avoidance has also been found to be dissatisfying in a variety of relationships, including dating relationships and parent–child relationships (Afifi et al., 2007). People are bothered by their own avoidance but tend to be especially bothered if they believe others are avoiding them (Caughlin & Golish, 2002). If someone thinks another person is avoiding or keeping something secret from them, he/she may wonder what it means about their relationship, given that healthy relationships are often equated with openness in the United States (Afifi et al., 2017).

A significant amount of research has also shown that the disclosure, particularly secrets that are traumatic, tends to be health-promoting (e.g., Gortner et al., 2006). The act of sharing a secret, whether it is done verbally or through writing, is beneficial to one's health (Smyth & Pennebaker, 2001). Pennebaker has found that young adults who write about their traumatic events rather than keep them secret tend to have better physical health over time (Petrie et al., 1998). There is a whole sub-field of narrative medicine designed to help patients reframe their trauma through writing personal narratives.

Nevertheless, people often assume that disclosure is always better for physical and relational health when it can also have negative consequences. Whether or not disclosure has positive or negative consequences often depends upon the purpose of the disclosure (e.g., whether it is cathartic or helps someone make sense of something) and the response one receives after revealing it. For example, Cornejo et al. (2021) found that when DACA students were told for the first time by a parent that they were undocumented, some of them were quite angry at the disclosure and it provide a significant amount of uncertainty regarding their identity. In another instance, my research team and I (Afifi et al., 2017) asked 251 college students who were dating to think of a stressor that they could not stop thinking about (or cognitively ruminating about) and to keep daily diary logs for two weeks. We randomly assigned them to one of four conditions for the first week: (1) to talk about the stressor with their dating partner every day, (2) to avoid talking about the stressor with anyone, including their dating partner, (3) to write about their stressor but not talk about it with anyone, including their dating partner, or (4) a control group where they were not told anything. After one week was over, we lifted the restrictions and everyone went back to normal for the remaining week. We found that writing about one's stressor reduced anxiety the most over the course of the week. Talking continuously about one's stressor to one's dating partner harmed the dating relationship the most and encouraged the most brooding. The effect of verbal rumination on the relationship, however, depended upon the emotional support provided by the partner and the ability of the partner to help positively reframe the stressor. Research also shows that when people disclose too much negative information to each other, it can result in stress contagion effects where one person's stress spills over onto another (Afifi et al., 2020). In short, topic avoidance, secrets, and disclosures can have positive or negative effects on relationships. It is how they are used, and their functions, that are important.

REFERENCES

Afifi, T. D. (2003). "Feeling caught" in stepfamilies: Managing boundary turbulence through appropriate privacy coordination rules. *Journal of Social and Personal Relationships, 20*(6), 729–756. https://doi.org/10.1177/0265407503206002

Afifi, T. D., Afifi, W. A., Morse, C., & Hamrick, K. (2008). Adolescents' avoidance tendencies and physiological reactions to discussions about their parents' relationship: Implications for post-divorce and non-divorced families. *Communication Monographs, 75*(3), 290–317. https://doi.org/10.1080/03637750802342308

Afifi, T. D., Basinger, E. D., & Kam, J. A. (2020). The extended theoretical model of communal coping: Understanding the properties and functionality of communal coping. *Journal of Communication, 70*(3), 424–446. https://doi.org/10.1093/joc/jqaa006

Afifi, T. D., Caughlin, J., & Afifi, W. A. (2007). Exploring the dark side (and light side) of avoidance and secrets. In B. Spitzberg and B. Cupach (Eds.), *The dark side of interpersonal relationships* (2nd ed., pp. 61–92). Erlbaum.

Afifi, T. D., Olson, L., & Armstrong, C. (2005). The chilling effect and family secrets: Examining the role of self protection, other protection, and communication efficacy. *Human Communication Research, 31*(4), 564–598. https://doi.org/10.1111/j.1468-2958.2005.tb00883.x

Afifi, T. D., Parrish, C., & Haughton, C. (in press). Parent-child communication about sex. In T. A. Coffelt (Ed.), *Interpersonal sexual communication across the lifespan.* Peter Lang Publishing.

Afifi, T. D., Shahnazi, A., Coveleski, S., Davis, S., & Merrill, A. (2017). Testing the ideology of openness: The comparative effects of talking, writing, and avoiding a stressor on rumination and health. *Human Communication Research, 43*(1), 76–101. https://doi.org/10.1111/hcre.12096

Baudat, S., Mantzouranis, G., Petegem, S. V., & Zimmermann, G. (2022). How do adolescents manage information in the relationship with their parents? A latent class analysis of disclosure, keeping secrets, and lying. *Journal of Youth and Adolescence, 51*, 1134–1152. https://doi.org/10.1007/s10964-022-01599-0

Baxter, L. (2010). *Voicing relationships: A dialogic perspective.* Sage.

Bianchi, D., Morelli, M., Baiocco, R., Cattelino, E., Laghi, F., & Chirumbolo, A. (2019). Family functioning patterns predict teenage girls' sexting. *International Journal of Behavioral Development, 43*(6), 507–514. https://doi.org/10.1177/01650254198730

Bok, S. (1983). *Secrets: On the ethics of concealment and revelation.* Vintage Books.

Caughlin, J. & Golish, T. (2002). An analysis of the association between topic avoidance and dissatisfaction: Comparing perceptual and interpersonal explanations. *Communication Monographs, 69*(4), 275–296. https://doi.org/10.1080/03637750216546

Coffelt, T. (2010). Is sexual communication challenging between mothers and daughters? *Journal of Family Communication, 10*(2), 116–130. https://doi.org/10.1080/15267431003595496

Cornejo, M., Kam, J., & Afifi, T. D. (2021). Discovering one's undocumented immigration status through family disclosures: The perspectives of College Students with Deferred Action for Childhood Arrivals (DACA). *Journal of Applied Communication Research, 49*(3), 267–285. https://doi.org/10.1080/00909882.2021.1896022

Elsharnouby, E., & Dost-Gözkan, A. (2020). Adolescents' well-being with respect to the patterns of disclosure to and secrecy from parents and the best friend: A person-centered examination. *Journal of Youth and Adolescence, 49*, 1687–1701. https://doi.org/10.1007/s10964-020-01246-6

Finkenauer, C., Frijns, T., Engels, R. C. M. E., & Kerkhof, P. (2005). Perceiving concealment in relationships between parents and adolescents: links with parental behavior. *Personal Relationships, 12*(3), 387–406. https://doi.org/10.1111/j.1475-6811.2005.00122.x

Finkenauer, C., & Hazam, H. (2000). Disclosure and secrecy in marriage: Do both contribute to marital satisfaction? *Journal of Social and Personal Relationships, 17*(2), 245–263. https://doi.org/10.1177/0265407500172005

Finkenauer, C., Kubacka, K. E., Engels, R., & Kerkhof, P. (2009). Secrecy in close relationships: Investigating its intrapersonal and interpersonal effects. In T. Afifi & W. Afifi (Eds.), *Uncertainty, information management, and disclosure decisions* (pp. 300–320). Routledge.

Flores D., & Barroso J. (2017). 21st century parent-child sex communication in the United States: A process review. *Journal of Sex Research, 54*(4–5), 532–548. https://doi.org/10.1080/00224499.2016.1267693

Gortner, E. M., Rude, S. S., & Pennebaker, J. W. (2006). Benefits of expressive writing in lowering rumination and depressive symptoms. *Behavior Therapy, 37*(3), 292–303. https://doi.org/10.1016/j.beth.2006.01.004

Guerrero, L. K., & Afifi, W. A. (1995). Some things are better left unsaid: Topic avoidance in family relationships. *Communication Quarterly, 43*(3), 276–296. https://doi.org/10.1080/01463379509369977

Holman, A., & Koenig-Kellas, J. (2018). "Say something instead of nothing": Adolescents' perceptions of memorable conversations about sex-related topics with their parents. *Communication Monographs, 85*(3), 357–385. https://doi.org/10.1080/03637751.2018.1426870

Hurst, J. L., Widman, L., Maheux, J. A., Evans-Paulson, R., Brasiliero, J., & Lipsey, N. (2022). Parent–child communication and adolescent sexual decision making: An application of family communication patterns theory. *Journal of Family Psychology, 36*(3), 449–457. https://doi.org/10.1037/fam0000916

Miller-Day, M. (2008). Talking to youth about drugs: What do late adolescents say about parental strategies? *Family Relations, 57*, 1–12.

Mulfinger, N., Rusch, N., Bayha, P., Muller, S., Boge, I., Sakar, V., & Krumm, S. (2019). Secrecy versus disclosure of mental illness among adolescents: I. The perspective of adolescents with mental illness. *Journal of Mental Health, 28*(3), 296–303. https://doi.org/10.1080/09638237.2018.1487535

Petronio, S. (2002). *Boundaries of privacy: Dialectics of disclosure.* SUNY Press.

Rafferty, K. A., Coffelt, T. A., & Miller, N. (2022). Understanding criteria that predict private health information disclosures between emerging adults and their parents. *Western Journal of Communication, 86*(1), 19–38. https://doi.org/10.1080/10570314.2021.1995622

Shin, Y., Miller-Day, M., & Hecht, M. (2019). Differential effects of parental "drug talk" styles and family communication environments on adolescent substance use. *Health Communication, 34*(8), 872–880. https://doi.org/10.1080/10410236.2018.1439268

Smatana, J., Villaloubos, M., Rogge, R., & Tasopoulos-Chan, M. (2010). Keeping secrets from parents: Daily variations among poor, urban adolescents. *Journal of Adolescence, 33,* 321–331.

Taniguchi-Dorios, E., Thompson, C. M., & Reid, T. (2022): Testing a model of disclosure, perceived support quality, and well-being in the college student mental illness context: A weekly diary study. *Health Communication.* Advance online publication. https://doi.org/10.1080/10410236.2022.2086841

Vangelisti, A. L. (1994). Family secrets: Forms, functions and correlates. *Journal of Social and Personal Relationships, 11*(1), 113–135. https://doi.org/10.1177/0265407594111007

Vangelisti, A. L. & Caughlin, J. P. (1997). Revealing family secrets: The influence of topic, function, and relationship. *Journal of Social and Personal Relationships, 14*(5), 679-705. https://doi.org/10.1177/0265407597145006

GENDER COMMUNICATION

The gender communication context offers us a unique opportunity to investigate one of the most fundamental parts of ourselves—our gender identities. The study of gender and communication allows us to learn about how these gender identities influence our personal and public communication with others. Gender communication researchers explore the constructed nature of gender roles as situated within a particular culture. Although our understandings of the ideas "masculine" and "feminine" have come to seem natural and unchanging, these concepts may alternatively be understood as flexible and as created through communicative practices. In the following chapters, you will be asked to explore how our own communicative practices can condone, contribute to, or resist the cultural construction of gender stereotypes. This section includes three chapters representative of gender communication research: (1) feminist contributions to public discourse theory, (2) critical perspectives on the ways in which popular media script our gender, and (3) queer communication theory and research. First, Tasha Dubriwny (Texas A&M University) examines the politics of women's health utilizing a postfeminist as a guiding framework as she explores how feminist theories regarding empowerment, agency, and self-determination have been "taken up," used, and/or transformed in contemporary culture. In particular, Dubriwny examines how issues of reproduction, sexuality, and women's expected roles are at the heart of feminist arguments for women's empowerment. Second, Ronald Jackson II (University of Cincinnati) and Natasha Shrikant (University of Colorado, Boulder) show how negative portrayals of Black men in the media can affect individual stereotypes and everyday interracial interactions among the as popular media script our bodies, our race, and our gender. In particular, Jackson and Shrikant examine racial scripts, characterizing Black male bodies as foreign, and gender scripts, attributing a particular type of masculinity to the Black male body and how negative portrayals of Black men in the media can affect individual stereotypes and everyday interracial interactions among the public resulting in disproportionate mistreatment of marginalized groups. Third, Gust Yep (San Francisco State University) and Scott Schönfeldt-Aultman (Saint Mary's College of California) examine how queer theory and trans studies tell us more about communication at the intersections of gender and sexuality along with race, class, and nation. Through dialogue, they explore Gust's work on queer theory and trans studies to analyze power, gender, and sexuality and their shaping of social relations/hierarchies and normalization so that we might our how our own assumptions and practices reinforce or disrupt heteronormativity and heteropatriarchy. Throughout these three chapters, you are challenged to become a more critical receiver of communicative messages that reinforce gender stereotypes and to use your critical insights to examine the implications and possibilities of your own communication habits.

RHETORICS OF EMPOWERMENT AND WOMEN'S HEALTH

Tasha N. Dubriwny
Texas A&M University

A recent advertisement for Adidas features a diverse cast of women (from Sudanese basketball player and coach Asma Elbadawi to Ellie Goldstein, a British model with Down syndrome) and a powerful motivational message. As the images of women flash across the screen, soaring music plays and a narrator declares, "It's impossible. To take hold of the world's spotlight overnight. Create your own uniform. Be a cover model. A powerful athlete. Or compete as a transwoman. Impossible? No. I'm possible" (Adidas, 2022). Although somewhat unique in its deliberately international focus, the Adidas ad is not unique in its message of empowerment for women. Communication scholars use the term "femvertising" to describe advertising campaigns that seem to promote gender equality. Although femvertising campaigns that promote female empowerment clearly work to sell products (messages of empowerment produce positive brand attitudes and strong emotional connections with female consumers), some scholars, like myself, question the larger messages behind femvertising campaigns and other popular message of women's empowerment (Tsai et al., 2021, p. 20). We might ask, for example, what kind of empowerment do we secure when empowerment is equated with the purchase of commodities (athleisure wear, beauty products, vitamins, birth control, and so forth)?

In my research on the politics of women's health, I answer questions like these by turning to the concept of postfeminism. Postfeminism does not refer to a time "after feminism." Instead, feminist media and rhetorical scholars use the term to describe a sensibility that informs many media and cultural products in which feminist messages of empowerment and self-determination are co-opted and depoliticized through an emphasis on individuality, self-surveillance, consumerism (see Dubriwny, 2012, p. 23; Windels et al., 2020, p. 19). In this chapter, I use postfeminism as a guiding framework to ask, in the specific context of women's health, "*How have feminist theories regarding empowerment, agency, and self-determination been 'taken up,' used, and/or transformed in contemporary culture?*"

WHY WOMEN'S HEALTH?

Communication scholars interested in postfeminist culture have investigated the postfeminist depoliticization of empowerment and self-determination across any number of topical areas, including entertainment media and politics (e.g., Anderson, 2017). Women's health—from when, where, and how women receive health care to how medical knowledge constructs understandings of women's bodies—is an area particularly ripe for an analysis of postfeminist culture because of women's historical struggles to become empowered in relation to their bodies and the medical industry. As Barbara Ehrenreich and Deidre English explain, biomedicine has been "strategic to women's oppression" as a source of sexist ideology and discrimination (as cited in Woods, 2013, p. 269). The history of medical treatment of women is perhaps too long and complicated for this short chapter, but we can take our cue from the work done by feminist women's health movement activists who set out in the late 1960s and 1970s to challenge and reshape medical practice.

Women's health movement activists challenged the use of the male body as the norm in understandings of health and disease, drew awareness to the pathologization of women's bodies and natural processes (like menstruation), and advocated for patient empowerment through self-determination, access to medical knowledge, and appreciation of women's own knowledge—their experiential knowledge—of their bodies (Dubriwny, 2012, pp. 14–23). In the vision of feminist activists, empowerment in terms of women's health meant many things: the right to speak back to physicians, to be informed, to decide on the course of one's medical care, to embrace the female body as natural and good, to enact bodily self-determination, and to prioritize women's knowledge of their bodies, all while maintaining a critical (or questioning) stance toward the medical industry (Dubriwny, 2012; Kline, 2010; Morgen, 2002). Importantly, empowerment here is not only about individual agency and self-determination, but also about empowering a collective—in this case, women—to challenge and reshape the medical industry to suit their needs. In the remainder of this chapter, I turn to three ways in which messages of empowerment about women's health have been transformed in our postfeminist culture.

EMPOWERMENT AS SELF-WORK

A quick scan of weight loss programs, from the rebranded WW (formerly Weight Watchers) to the more recent Noom (a program "designed by psychologists"), demonstrates at least one consistent theme: an enormous amount of time spent on the self as a project. These types of programs ask participants—most often women—to engage in numerous self-monitoring activities through each day as they try to reshape their bodies. Women discipline their own bodies (counting calories, restricting food, and engaging in exercise) as encouraged by the diet and wellness industries. Such self-disciplining and the focus on the self-as-project is one way in which feminist notions of empowerment have been transformed in postfeminist culture. To be clear, it is not wrong to try to be healthy, but what's at stake when empowerment is equated with a focus on the self?

Let's consider one example, from the work of Marissa Doshi who does research on popular health-related apps that are aimed at women. Doshi and her research assistant retrieved 200 apps targeting various aspects of women's health (sexual health, mental health, fitness, and so forth). They coded the apps' conceptual categories, and then isolated three main themes or idealizations of the "healthy women": the Barbie, the goddess, and the entrepreneur (2018, p. 187). Doshi argues that the apps configure achieving traditional body ideals (thin, youthful, and appropriately muscular) as empowering, and one of the key modes of empowerment is the disciplining and surveillance of the female body. Women can, for example, use the "iPeriod" app to record detailed data about their menstrual cycles. As Doshi explains, such apps position the female body as an "entrepreneurial project requiring constant monitoring and attention to achieve success" (2018, p. 193). The problem is that although women are empowered through these apps to develop detailed knowledge of their own bodies, the apps fail to recognize systemic factors that may hinder achieving health goals (2018, p. 194). Responsibility for health is placed squarely and solely on women's shoulders. In this way, the apps participate in a particularly pernicious part of postfeminist culture: they focus empowerment on women's individual capacities to maintain health but ignore larger structural inequalities (2018, p. 196; see also Dubriwny, 2012). More recently, with dramatic changes in U.S. abortion law (discussed more in my concluding thoughts), period tracking apps' mode of empowerment has also been called into question by feminist activists and legal scholars concerned that such apps could be used to penalize those seeking or considering an abortion (Torchinsky, 2022). Using period-tracking apps may increase women's vulnerability to state control over their medical decisions.

I have also highlighted how empowerment has been transformed in postfeminist health discourses to focus primarily on women's surveillance and disciplining of their bodies and, through the lack of attention to structural and systemic issues, this empowerment places responsibility for achieving a healthy state in women's hands. My work on cultural discourses about postpartum depression is a good example. I analyzed numerous popular narratives about postpartum depression, from Brooke Shields' book *Down Came the Rain* to mainstream news coverage of postpartum depression. What I found was that new mothers are positioned as risky subjects; that is, they are constructed as women vulnerable to a potent mix of hormones and genetics that, after birth, might lead to depression. Women are urged to engage in self-surveillance of their emotional and behavioral states, to take up a "clinical gaze" and recognize when their experiences might fall outside of the "norm" and need medical treatment (Dubriwny, 2012, p. 89). Empowerment through self-surveillance using the language of diagnosis ties new mothers directly to a medical understanding of childbirth and motherhood, and the solution for new mothers is also medical: treatment through antidepressants.

In this research, I recognized the importance of treating depression, but I also offered two critiques of how empowerment has been transformed into self-surveillance leading directly to medical treatment. First, I draw attention to the construction of motherhood that women are being asked to uphold as they review their emotions and behaviors. Women face expectations to perform to a standard of good motherhood in which mothering is depicted as always joyful; women are expected to find fulfillment in mothering, be selfless in relation to their children, and have an instinctual ability to nurture their children (Dubriwny, 2012, p. 70). This construction of motherhood is raced and classed (White, upper-middle-class women are consistently represented as ideal good mothers), but it is an idealization that no woman can live up to. Postfeminist discourse about postpartum depression directly engages expectations for good motherhood by asking women to engage in surveillance and medicalization of feelings (sadness and anger) and behaviors (sleeplessness and tears) that do not meet cultural expectations for good mothering. Does medical treatment then become the short-term solution to a problematic understanding of motherhood? Second, as women are empowered to engage in self-surveillance, our attention is once again focused on the self. Postfeminist empowerment as self-work draws our attention away from structural issues. To fully empower women during the postpartum period, we need to empower them as a collective to change the context of mothering: for example, to have more social support networks, paid maternity leave, and affordable childcare.

SELF-DETERMINATION AS CHOICE

I want to now turn to a discussion of how self-determination has been transformed through postfeminist health discourse. As envisioned by women's health movement activists, self-determination meant the ability to have control over one's body in the face of a medical institution that had a long history of failing women. To fully enact self-determination, women as a collective needed to have full knowledge about their bodies, medical research, and treatment options. In my research on women's health, I argue that self-determination is now largely understood through the phrase "choice." Many feminist rhetorical scholars have recognized that "choice" has potential to both empower and discipline women, as choice aligns with the idea of women's agency, but is also typically embedded within larger discursive and material structures that constrain women (Hayden & O'Brien Hallstein, 2010). As I have previously argued, "As subjects who make choices, women are represented in [postfeminist] discourse about their health as free to construct their own lives … However, their choices are not limitless; they are choices are shaped by highly gendered expectations for womanhood, [and] prevailing market forces" (Dubriwny, 2012, p. 26). To make this argument clearer, it might help to consider a few examples.

Carly Woods's (2013) work on advertisements for oral contraceptives that are designed to suppress menstruation demonstrates how choice holds the promise of self-determination but is "co-opted to promote controversial choices that reinforce sexist stereotypes" (p. 267).

Although each of the campaigns for Yaz, Loestrin, and Seasonale/Seasonique use different strategies, together they work to suggest that women can be empowered by choosing to suppress their menstrual cycles. For example, describing Seasonique's campaign, Woods notes, "Contemporary women are urged to take Seasonique so that their lives will be minimally disrupted, without the pain or nuisance of menstruation that previous generations of women had no choice but to endure" (2013, p. 278). Women exert self-determination over their bodies, then, by choosing a contraceptive that allows them to menstruate when they want. But, who is the "they" in the advertisements? And what kind of lifestyle is supported by this discourse of choice? Woods notes that it is remarkable that the advertisements feature White, heterosexual, middle-class women and outline a life with a traditionally gendered script: dating, marriage, and childbirth (2013, p. 279). Further, the campaigns continue a long medical and cultural tradition of stigmatizing and pathologizing menstruation (menstruation is depicted as unwanted and unclean). Thus, while oral contraceptives that suppress menstruation may be useful for many women and people with female bodies, the choice offered to women relies on sexist stereotypes of menstruating women and propels a problematic ideal of the non-menstruating body as normal (2013, p. 280).

In my research in three different areas, the HPV vaccine Gardasil, the rise in prophylactic mastectomies, and VBACs, or vaginal births after cesareans, I also explore how choice is a problematic form of self-determination because of the limited choices offered to women and the ways in which certain choices emerge in public and medical discourses as the "right" choice (Dubriwny, 2012; Dubriwny & Ramadurai, 2013). For example, in the complicated case of prophylactic mastectomies, I describe how a previously unthinkable treatment (the removal of healthy breasts) has become an expected choice for women who have the BRCA gene mutations (Durbriwny, 2012). Women with the BRCA1 and BRCA2 gene mutations have a substantially increased risk (as high as 90% for some women) for breast cancer over the course of their lifetimes. For these women, many of whom identify as "previvors" (survivors of a predisposition to a disease), empowerment is based on the ability to make individual choices for the prevention of cancer. The choices are limited: increased surveillance (frequent MRI scans), chemoprevention, and prophylactic surgery. As I analyzed public discourse and women's narratives, I was disturbed by the easy acceptance of prophylactic mastectomies, especially given the relatively recent history in which women's health activists fought against the radical mastectomy as the standard treatment for breast cancer.

What is intriguing about the case of prophylactic mastectomies is that they become what I describe as a "compulsory choice" for women, a choice that is not really a choice at all. As represented in mainstream discourse, the risk of cancer for women with the BRCA mutations is unacceptable and they must act to prevent cancer. The reason why cancer is unacceptable (again, as depicted in public discourse) relies on the most traditional identity for women: motherhood. For example, one woman described her choice of a prophylactic mastectomy as a way to preserve her ability to have a family in the future. Other reports suggested that prophylactic mastectomies allowed women to continue their role as mothers to their current children without the specter of cancer looming over them (Dubriwny, 2012, p. 54–57). Simply put, cancer is unacceptable because with cancer, women cannot fulfill their familial responsibilities. The choice of a prophylactic mastectomy appeals to women's empowerment, but it also reifies the sense that women's most important role in life is motherhood. The empowered woman's choices, in this case, are occurring in a highly moralized context in which the choice of prophylactic mastectomy is "ensconced within traditional expectations about both motherhood and heterosexual partnerships" (Dubriwny, 2012, p. 63).

I suggested above that the case of prophylactic mastectomies was complicated, and it certainly is. Cancer is devastating. Mothers should be able to live and raise their children. What I do as a rhetorical scholar is draw attention to how public discourse is shaping our understanding of particular issues. In the case of prophylactic mastectomies, self-determination becomes a choice of surgery that women are expected to make in order to maintain a traditional nuclear family.

AGENCY AS PERFORMING TRADITIONAL GENDER ROLES

Given my discussion of the examples above that illustrate how empowerment and self-determination have been transformed into a focus on disciplining the body and enacting the "correct" medical choices, I'm sure it's not surprising that the third issue that I want to highlight regarding the postfeminist transformation of empowerment is the revitalization of very traditional gender roles for women. Expectations for women to be good mothers, wives, and daughters filter through postfeminist health discourse, directly implicating the construction of what choices are "good" for women to make, the normalization of particular understandings of healthy (note that the healthy body is very often one the replicates harmful beauty standards), and justifications for why women should maintain their health in the first place. To think through the implications of grounding women's agency in traditional gender roles, I want to return briefly to my research on prophylactic mastectomies. As represented in mainstream discourse, the choice of prophylactic mastectomies are thoroughly embedded within the heterosexual matrix, or naturalized understandings of gender that support masculine hegemony and heterosexist power (Dubriwny, 2012, p. 65). My concern with this postfeminist transformation of empowerment is that it ties women's personhood to children and husbands. Women are empowered in this discourse to choose prophylactic mastectomies not because they matter in and of themselves, but because they matter to their families. Taking care of families, protecting fertility—these are certainly real issues that many women encounter throughout their lives. We might ask ourselves, however, what it means to represent the empowered woman as one who is always either mothering or preparing to be a mother. Similarly, in my work on mainstream discourse about the HPV vaccine, I note that young women are represented as choosing the vaccine to maintain their fertility. HPV vaccination campaigns revolved around twin themes of empowerment and choice, but the discourse is disempowering in areas where feminists have worked for decades for women's collective empowerment: women's role in the home, familial and sexual relationships, and reproduction (Dubriwny, 2012, p. 141).

CONCLUDING THOUGHTS

In June 2022, the Supreme Court overturned *Roe v. Wade*, the 1973 ruling that gave women the (limited) right to access abortion care in the United States. Abortion is a complicated topic and one that I have not concentrated on in this chapter. However, as my concluding sentence in the previous section indicates, issues of reproduction, sexuality, and women's expected roles are at the heart of feminist arguments for women's empowerment. It is worth noting that the language of empowerment has been strategically deployed by the antiabortion lobby and in antiabortion legislation. Angela Roberti describes the "pro-woman" anti-abortion frame as a co-optation of the feminist language of empowerment: such a frame "situates the state as empowering women through regulatory abortion policy" including ultrasound mandates and educational informed consent policies (Roberti, 2022, p. 140). The circulation of rhetorics of empowerment on all sides of the abortion debate should certainly encourage us to think carefully about *how* women are "empowered" in the United States in a post-*Roe* landscape. If women and people with uteruses can no longer access abortion-related care (including potentially care during and after a miscarriage) in their home states, have they been empowered? Given the feminist emphasis, particularly visible in the activism of the women's health movement, on self-determination and the right to determine the course of one's medical care, I would suggest the answer is no.

My overview of the research on postfeminist women's health discourse has pointed to the ways in which feminist notions of empowerment, self-determination, and agency have been transformed in contemporary culture into a focus on the self as project with women empowered to engage in self-surveillance and craft lives that align with traditional understandings of womanhood. The language of empowerment, as the overturning of *Roe* suggests, can also be configured to increase regulations and restrict women's access to medical care. I hope that as you engage in health discourses, you can now take a more thoughtful approach to understanding the modes of empowerment being offered to you. How are you being empowered? What choices can you make? How do your choices align with (or resist) larger power structures and gender inequalities? Although I have focused this chapter on women's health and empowerment, all of us should consider the political implications of rhetorics of empowerment as they function in our lives.

REFERENCES

Adidas (2022, February 14). *I'mpossible* [Video]. Youtube. https://www.youtube.com/watch?v=fujboh-W7Sk

Anderson, K. V. (2017). Deflowering the voting virgin: Piety, political advertising, and the pleasure prerogative. *Quarterly Journal of Speech, 103*(1/2), 160–181. https://doi.org/10.1080/00335630.2016.1241891

Doshi, M. J. (2018). Barbies, goddesses, and entrepreneurs: Discourses of gendered digital embodiment in women's health apps. *Women's Studies in Communication, 41*(2), 183–203. 10.1080/07491409.2018.1463930

Dubriwny, T. (2012). *The vulnerable empowered woman: Feminism, postfeminism, and women's health*. Rutgers University Press.

Dubriwny, T., & Ramadurai, V. (2013). Framing birth: Postfeminism in the delivery room. *Women's Studies in Communication, 36*(3), 243–266. https://doi.org/10.1080/07491409.2013.830168

Hayden, S. & O'Brien Hallstein, L. (2010). *Contemplating maternity in an era of choice: Explorations into discourses of reproduction*. Lexington Books.

Kline, W. (2010). *Bodies of knowledge: Sexuality, reproduction, and women's health in the second wave*. University of Chicago Press.

Morgen, S. (2002). *Into our own hands: The women's health movement in the United States, 1969-1990*. Rutgers University Press.

Roberti, A. (2022). Empowering women by regulating abortion? Conservative women lawmaker's cooptation of feminist language in US abortion politics. *Politics, Groups, and Identities, 10*(1), 139–145.

Torchinsky, R. (2022, June 24). How period tracking apps and data privacy fit into a post-*Roe v. Wade* climate. *National Public Radio*. https://www.npr.org/2022/05/10/1097482967/roe-v-wade-supreme-court-abortion-period-apps

Tsai, W. H. S., Shata, A., & Tian, S. (2021). En-gendering power and empowerment in advertising: A content analysis. *Journal of Current Issues & Research in Advertising, 42*(1), 19–33. https://doi.org/10.1080/10641734.2019.1687057

Windels, K., Champlin, S., Shelton, S., Sterbenk, Y., & Poteet, M. (2020). Selling feminism: How female empowerment campaigns employ postfeminist discourses. *Journal of Advertising, 49*(1), 18–33. https://doi.org/10.1080/00913367.2019.1681035

Woods, C. S. (2013). Repunctuated feminism: Marketing menstrual suppression through the rhetoric of choice. *Women's Studies in Communication, 36*(3), 267–287. 10.1080/07491409.2013.829791

SCRIPTING THE BLACK MASCULINE BODY

Ronald Jackson II
University of Cincinnati

Natasha Shrikant
University of Colorado, Boulder

INTRODUCTION

The moment a child is plopped down in front of the television, while mommy and/or daddy go off and do things around the house, a child begins to learn things not previously introduced by the family. Of course, there are messages that are consistent with what this child has already learned at home, but there are new messages as well. According to TV-Free America, a Washington, DC-based think tank and advocacy organization, kids will have watched nearly 15,000 hours of television by the age of 10. They further explain that by the age of 65, the average American has watched a sum total of 9 years worth of television. That's 4,733,538.90 minutes of TV! That's a lot of consumption by anyone's standards; however, this chapter is not so much interested in proving how many hours one watches TV or even whether one is actually ever exposed to media. It's clear already that we are major consumers of all media, not the least of which is television. Instead, this chapter is about what messages, narratives, and stereotypes individuals are taught by the media and how these messages shape social perceptions of cultural others. Quite simply put, there are three overarching points you must remember from this chapter:

- All media teach messages—some good and some bad.
- Every prominent message is like a script that you are expected to play out.
- If you are oblivious to what you are being taught you will subconsciously consume messages that ultimately affect your behavior and/or perceptions toward others.

To address these themes, we have selected to discuss the scripting theory or paradigm. More specifically, we ask, "how do popular media script the Black masculine body, and what are the consequences of this scripting for social relations?"

WHAT IS "SCRIPTING"?

Although this concept has been discussed by a few scholars, most notably Duke University professor Robyn Wiegman in her book *American Anatomies*, Ronald Jackson's work has applied the idea of scripting to communication studies. As with any theatrical script, the script is the text, and the act of scripting is the writing of the text. Therefore, to script some-one else's body is to actively inscribe or figuratively place oneself, worldview, or perceptions onto someone else. To put it another way, the concept of scripting is whole lot like what happens with graffiti or even film production. The graffiti artist finds a canvas or wall and begins to mark all over it with creative inscriptions. Often times, the end product is a sign or symbol that reflects something about who the artist is or who the artist is representing. Likewise when a film producer develops a movie that is stereotypical he or she is scripting the lives of each character. In the act of writing the script the producer is also imposing his or her own presumptions, perhaps through research, about how people might act who look like that character. This may eerily resemble real life, and often times that is the intention. Even in a fictive story, there have to be some recognizable real-life elements with which audi-ences can resonate. So, with the theory of scripting, the body is theorized as a canvas, which is figuratively written upon by another. The term "scripting" is used to signify that human beings, through all kinds of discourse including media, assign meaning to their perceptions of others in an effort to structure their observations and reflections concerning differences. This is really fascinating when applied to race and culture and it happens every single day.

Imagine for a moment you are watching television and a commercial comes on. Keep in mind you are not in "critical" or "intellectual" mode. You are really relaxed when you are suddenly startled by what you see on television. In this commercial, a white hand reaches down to pick up a toothbrush; the other hand is used to glide on the toothpaste in a swirl-like fashion. As the toothbrush with the white swirl toothpaste is lifted to the teeth, the camera gets a tight, close-up shot of a black outlined medium-sized, bodiless, transparent figure dancing all over the teeth. The white toothpaste is applied to the agitated teeth, and as the black outlined figure is being dissolved, the voiceover script reads, in a most frantic tone, "Oh no, we have to get rid of the evil plaque man." The commercial closes. No face is ever shown. This commercial may seem rather innocent on the surface, but if you are attuned to hearing commercials and other media that disparage minority groups it is actually quite disappoint-ing. The advertisement has several implications. First, from a critical perspective, after the voiceover was heard it became clear that this figure, which appeared to be without body or gender was actually a man. And, no matter how much the viewer wanted to believe that the black outline meant nothing, the commercial implicitly suggested via both the symbolic black outline and the voiceover that the figure is Black. If you say the concluding line enough times, you will notice how your tongue is inclined to replace "plaque" with "Black." Some may dismiss this interpretation as mere paranoia, but we contend it is beyond coincidence that the other mechanics of the commercial work hand-in-hand with what is depicted in the commercial. This is one example of how scripting works. There are often implicit messages imposed on others' bodies that correlate with real-life, everyday stereotypes.

There are many ways in which racial scripts emerge in the media. One only needs to think about feel-good movies like *Crazy Rich Asians* and *Night School* or more serious dramas like *Get Out* to see how racialized bodies are often treated and understood. To put it bluntly, the notions of race and racial scripting are about bodies that have been assigned social meanings. As a result, we as media consumers unknowingly or subconsciously set up social cognitions about race that conform to mass-mediated stereotypes. Through this process of social conformity and media reinforcement, we gradually come to know dialectically what it means to be Black by negating what it means to be quintessentially White; similarly, we also come to know what it means to be female in relation to what it dialectically means to be male, or what it means to be nonbinary in contrast to what it means to be cisgender. The media rarely offer a complete composite of blackness, femaleness, and gender identity. Consequently, this act of negation is the linchpin of soured interracial and cross-gendered relations in the United States.

SCRIPTING THE BLACK MASCULINE BODY

In our research, we study how Black bodies have become surfaces of racial representation. Unfortunately, much of the mass media represents African Americans as out of control, undereducated, poor, violent, angry, incapacitated, and criminal although admittedly we have seen significant progress in the last 20 years with the advent of TV shows like *Queen Sugar, Love Is, Cherish the Day,* and movies like *If Beale Street Could Talk* and *Black Panther.* There are a few ways that stereotypes about Black bodies are countered and replaced in the media with more positive stereotypes like the talented and athletic Black person. The number of media representations we see of successful, positive, healthy, educated, normal Black citizens in the media are far outweighed by the sheer force of the negative, harmful, and stereotypical images. If it is true that media teach audiences via messages and that communication scholars George Gerbner and Larry Gross were correct when they indicated that there is a direct relationship between television viewing and cultivated effects on viewers' attitudes and behaviors, then it is no wonder that racism, sexism, and all forms of social exclusion persist in American society.

The media has taught us that if there is a violent crime it is likely being committed by someone Black. We are taught that poverty is just another word for Black, and therefore a ghetto is a place where Black people live. We are taught to be scared of Black men and to avoid being alone with them because they are innately violent. This carrousel of vicious media stereotypes cements a kind of fear that has led to some police officers feeling more quickly threatened by Black citizens than nonblack ones, and as a result, these individuals hasten to discharge their weapons more quickly when they see Black bodies. The media has taught us a script—Black skin is a signifier of danger. This script is *written upon* Black bodies without their consent. It is a heavy burden to carry for every Black citizen in the United States, especially given the often fatal consequences. We need not look any further than the cases of Trayvon Martin, Sam DuBose, Sandra Bland, George Floyd, Breonna Taylor, Michael Brown, Eric Garner, Walter Scott, Ahmaud Arbery, Tamir Rice, and others. Each one of these names evokes the public memory of their lives tragically lost to horrific violence due to racism.

As a consequence of the previously mentioned racial representations of Blacks in media, in real-life, nonblack people become attuned to negative stereotypes of Black people, while many other possible characterizations of African Americans are swept under the rug. Presently, the mass media are currently the primary channels through which race is socially constructed by society. Once the scripting of different races or racialized bodies begins, it is like a machine that is difficult to turn off. People's minds automatically or subconsciously activate the stereotypes they have learned in the media. They may not even know they are acting on those stereotypes. For example, have you ever gone to a store or mall in a predominantly Black or Hispanic poor neighborhood and found yourself suddenly afraid to leave your door unlocked or your electronics exposed on the front seat? Now take a moment to recall whether you do the same thing at a store or mall in what appears to be a predominantly White, middle-to upper-middle-class neighborhood. Your reaction in each scenario is a subconscious (and may be even a conscious) reflex that instinctively combines your personal background with what you think you know about the people who live in that vicinity. Alternatively, if you are, for example, a Black man in any of these settings, have you noticed nonblack people distancing themselves from you, acting afraid, or treating you as a potential criminal? If you are not and have not grown up around Blacks or Latinos, but you do recall hearing plenty of crime news stories about these groups or you recall images from movies or other media that reinforce negative stereotypes about these groups as being violent, then this is the information that you will use when interacting with these groups.

Interestingly, the way humans perceive the differences between racial bodies is by observing bodies' corporeal zones, or parts of the body that mark it as being of a particular type. This is what we call preverbal communication. For Black bodies, these corporeal zones sometimes include nappy hair, thick lips, and darker-than-White skin complexion. Although perceptions of these visual individual differences may not always have negative consequences, people cannot ignore corporeal zones. They perceive them and from them script the body with particular ideologies. One very ordinary set of scripts in our society is that of blackness and whiteness, which are often presented racially as though they are the complete opposite of one another. Of course, the colors themselves in a crayon box do seem quite opposite, but you must admit this is an odd way to think of human beings, particularly of entire cultures.

Yet, the Black–White dichotomy continues to live, even in what some have called our "postracial society." You should know there is no such thing. Here are a couple of illustrations of this Black–White dialectic at work. As mentioned earlier, Black bodies have been characterized as violent; by contrast, White bodies have been socially constituted as nonviolent, normal, kind, mild-mannered, humane, educated, and often middle-class or affluent. The news perpetuates these characterizations, chastising Black bodies for violent behavior, and de-vilifying White bodies when they commit acts of violence.

A primary example of this is in the coverage of admitted White supremacist Dylann Roof's shooting of a bible study group. On Wednesday, June 17, 2015, *USA Today* reported, "A man accused in a deadly shooting rampage" entered Mother Emmanuel AME Church, an historic Black church in Charleston, Carolina during a Wednesday night bible study. He was warmly welcomed, and he decided to stay for much of the bible study. After 45 minutes, the Pastor asked everyone to bow their heads for prayer and that is when Roof took the opportunity to open fire shooting these 9 individuals with approximately 74 bullets while yelling racial epithets. He spared the life of one individual so she could tell the story. This individual explained that during the massacre nine people were murdered. After an intensive manhunt, he was arrested the following day in North Carolina. The *Charlotte Observer* reported that the Shelby Police Chief Jeff Ledford indicated that when he was arrested Dylann Roof was "polite" and "quiet." To add insult to this devastating tragedy, after being apprehended by the police, several newspapers reported that Roof complained he was hungry; so a couple of officers kindly decided to stop and get him a meal from Burger King while he was in custody. It is almost unbelievable that after admitting to this pernicious act of executing nine innocent strangers that the officers would be so concerned about Roof's hunger pangs. Evidence shows that Dylann admitted he committed the crime, and officers found a manifesto he had written, which stated, "I have no choice. I am not in the position to, alone, go into the ghetto and fight … I chose Charleston because it is the most historic city in my state, and at one time had the highest ratio of blacks to Whites in the country. We have no skinheads, no real KKK, no one doing anything but talking on the internet. Well someone has to have the bravery to take it to the real world, and I guess that has to be me."

The Roof case illustrates the double standards applied to White and non-white citizens. Throughout the trial, we heard Dylann Roof referred to as "Mr. Roof." References to him were dignified and respectful. No national news outlets were known to refer to him as a monster or savage. He was not even identified as being threatening. He was deemed compliant, kind, and polite. Interestingly, other studies have examined how Blacks, Whites, and Latinos are portrayed in the news. In 2020, Travis Dixon and colleagues analyzed how Blacks, Latinos, and Whites are portrayed as lawbreakers. Blacks were found to be almost two and a half times more likely to be portrayed as lawbreakers than Whites. However, in reality, Blacks were arrested less frequently than Whites and Latinos. Dixon and associates (2020) argue that these news representations serve to further ingrain the stereotype of the Black male as a violent criminal … News reports play a large role in scripting the Black male body as violent and criminal. This inscription has large implications for the African American community because it encourages racial profiling and police brutality toward African American males.

Racial profiling is a very pervasive part of society (Dixon et al., 2018). Although racial profiling is only acknowledged after a heinous occurrence of police brutality, it actually exists in many different contexts such as shopping, banking, housing, and academics (Davis, 2001; Kincheloe et al., 1997; MacDonald, 2003; Meeks, 2000). Davis (2001) provides numerous statistics about the occurrence of racial profiling that occurs with Black drivers and Meeks (2000) presents narratives and testimony about Black male experience with racial profiling, thus validating that racial profiling is indeed extremely prevalent. Police brutality toward Black male youth is also a widespread phenomenon. In 2015, a Black male, Sam DuBose, was pulled over and killed by an off-duty, out-of-jurisdiction police officer because when he was asked to step out of the car after being stopped for expired license plates, he explained he had a disability that would not let him do that easily (Hunt, 2015).

The importance of news stories like these is that "these cases are not about police making arrests; they are about people's humanity being seized" (Jackson, 2006, p. 65). Racial profiling is a new form of lynching, or as Jackson terms it, symbolic lynching. Racial profiling, and the mass media's contribution to it, in essence, characterizes Black male bodies in a particular way, just as slaves were characterized as violent bucks, and then impose penalties on this particular, marginalized group. After all, after Black bodies have been established as generally violent, who will question the disproportionate amount of Black arrests made in the United States? Or the representation of criminals as being primarily Black on the news? The anxiety created by the media has led to a reciprocal relationship between the media and community relations. One feeds off the other and in the end, the inscription of the violent Black brute becomes more and more difficult to resist. The other stereotypes work in the same way. Think about euphemisms like "urban," which signify lower income, inner-city communities where minorities live. Now, consider the board game called Ghettopoloy, in which players build crack houses and projects on their stolen properties. Wealth consists of a ghetto stash and hustler cards. Examples of characters include a Pimp and a Hoe. This board game, designed by David Chang, capitalizes on what outsiders see as the "ghetto experience." Video games such as *Grand Theft Auto* perform the same function, using a "virtual ghettocentric imagination," (Watkins, 1998, p. 250) to allow players to control and exploit their own voyeurism via virtual gangstas. If one becomes proficient at the game there are levels where racial epithets are quite common. Here, the scripts about minorities are devastating, and laced with an entertainment device where it can appeal to the subconscious mind.

SUMMARY

Scripting is a complicated process that occurs over time. Although scripts can be challenged, changed, and reconstructed, they often still hold remnants of older scripts. The complete process of scripting bodies is referred to as body politics. In body politics, there is a scripter (i.e., the mass media or someone who holds authority), the scripted (e.g. the Black male body), and the inscription (i.e., violent, incapacitated, and exotic). All of these aspects come together to characterize a body in a particular way. Furthermore, scripting is a historical process. One needs to examine both the history of inscriptions and the current consequences of those inscriptions in order to properly explore Black male corporeal politics.

There are several stereotypical scripts that currently characterize black males: exotic and strange, violent, incompetent and uneducated, sexual, exploitable, and innately incapacitated. These scripts are a combination of racial scripts, characterizing Black male bodies as foreign, and gender scripts, attributing a particular type of masculinity to the Black male body. As a result of these inscriptions, some people have xenophobic attitudes toward Black males. These attitudes, however, are not a recent invention that can be accredited solely to mass media representations. The survival of these attitudes and stereotypes is also dependent on people preserving them over time through messages presented to children at the earliest ages all the way through adulthood.

The purpose of this chapter was to explore the process of scripting and inscription of meanings onto Black male bodies; however, you can substitute any marginalized group and find similar results. We can imagine scripting studies that analyze scripts about gay people, women, or any cultural group. Scripting, or how people characterize and make sense of the other, is a historical process that can be rewritten over time. In this chapter, we have seen examples of how the process of inscription occurs. Most importantly, we have explained how mass media portrayals of marginalized groups link to everyday race relations in the United States. We have shown that negative portrayals of Black men in the media can affect individual stereotypes and everyday interracial interactions among the public. Furthermore, on a larger scale, these negative representations are connected to disproportionate mistreatment of marginalized groups as evidenced by mediated racial (mis)representations, crime news reports, racial profiling, and police brutality. As communication scholars, it is important to note the impact that communicative media can have on society, and to be critical of the information presented to us, and not allow scripts to control how we treat others, but instead to always treat our fellow citizens humanely and with dignity and respect.

REFERENCES

Dixon, T. L., Bauer, E., & Josey, C. L. (2018). How news frames prime non-Whites as social problems. In P. D'Angelo (Ed.), *Doing news framing analysis 2: Empirical and theoretical perspectives* (pp. 343–361). Routledge.

Dixon, T. L., Weeks, K., Sevilla, M. & Tolbert, A. (2020). Stereotypes of Black/African American populations. In A.C. Billings & S. Parrot (Eds.), *Media stereotypes: From Ageism to xenophobia.* Peter Lang Publishing.

Hunt, A. (2015). *What Sam DuBose's rap sheet tells us about him and the police.* Cincinnati Enquirer. https://www.cincinnati.com/story/news/2015/08/10/sam-duboses-rap-sheet-tells-us/31356367/.

Jackson, R. L. (2006). *Scripting the black masculine body: Identity, discourse, and racial politics in popular media*. State University of New York Press.

Jackson, R., & McDonald, A. (2019). The violence of white entitlement and the hypocrisy of earned merit. *Departures in Critical Qualitative Research, 8*(4), 64–68. https://doi.org/10.1525/dcqr.2019.8.4.64

Jan, T. (2009, July 20). *Harvard professor Gates arrested at Cambridge home*. MetroDesk. http://www.boston.com/news/local/breaking_news/2009/07/harvard.html

Kincheloe, J. L., Steinberg, S. R., & Gresson, A. D. (1997). *Measured lies: The bell curve examined*. St. Martin's Press.

MacDonald, H. (2003). *Are cops racist?: How the war against the police harms black Americans*. Ivan R. Dee Publisher.

McCormack, S. (2015/2017). *Cops bought Dylan Roof Burger King after Charleston shooting*. Huffington Post. https://www.huffpost.com/entry/dylann-roof-burger-king_n_7645216

Meeks, K. (2000). *Driving while black: What to do if you are a victim of racial profiling*. Broadway Press.

Watkins, S. C. (1998). *Representing: Hip hop culture and the production of Black cinema*. University of Chicago Press.

Wiegman, R. (1995). *American anatomies: Theorizing race and gender*. Duke University Press.

GENDER, SEXUALITY, POWER, AND VIOLENCE: QUEER THEORY AND TRANS STUDIES IN COMMUNICATION

Gust A. Yep
San Francisco State University

Scott M. Schönfeldt-Aultman
Saint Mary's College of California

Public and academic discussion of queer and trans bodies and identities has increased dramatically in the new millennium. As areas of study, the first comprehensive collections of research using queer theory (Yep, Lovaas, & Elia, 2003a) and trans studies (Spencer & Capuzza, 2015) were published in the communication discipline in the last two decades. Since then, a number of studies have appeared in communication journals and edited volumes. This chapter focuses on one of Gust's research programs—his work on queer theory and trans studies in the field of communication (Elia, Lovaas, & Yep, 2003; Elia & Yep, 2012; Slagle & Yep, 2007; Yep, 2002a, 2003, 2005, 2007, 2009a, b, 2010a, 2013a, 2016, 2017, 2020a, b; Yep, Alaoui, & Lescure, 2019, 2020, in press; Yep & Chivers, 2016, 2017; Yep & Conkle, 2013; Yep & Elia, 2007, 2012; Yep & Lescure, 2014, 2015, 2019; Yep, Lescure, & Allen, 2015, 2022; Yep, Lescure, & Russo, 2019; Yep, Lovaas, & Elia, 2003a, b, c; Yep & Ochoa Camacho, 2004; Yep, Olzman, & Conkle, 2012; Yep, Russo, & Allen, 2015; Yep, Russo, Allen, & Chivers, 2017; Yep, Russo, & Lescure, 2015; Yep & Shimanoff, 2013). A lot of the research in queer theory, however, has been characterized, in Gamson's words, as "speaking some kind of high-falutin' pig Latin" (2003, p. 385). More recently, McCann and Monaghan (2020) note "queer theory is difficult to define" (p. 1). To provide a friendly introduction to queer theory and trans studies in communication, we decided to "queer" this chapter. To do so, we are presenting the ideas in the form of a dialogue between two colleagues rather than using the format of a more traditional expository essay. Our conversation was broadly guided by the question "How might queer theory and trans studies tell us more about communication at the intersections of gender and sexuality along with race, class, and nation?"

LOCATING OURSELVES IN THE DIALOGUE

We have always found it important to situate ourselves and to be self-reflexive in the work and writing that we do. Gust grew up in three cultures—Chinese, Peruvian, and U.S. American—and identifies as "Asianlatinoamerican" (Yep, 2002b, p. 60). He lives in the San Francisco Bay Area with Pierre, an affectionate and inquisitive Pomeranian he adopted from a local dog rescue organization. He is a Professor of Communication Studies, Core Graduate Faculty of Sexuality Studies, and Faculty in the doctoral program in Educational Leadership at San Francisco State University. Scott grew up in the southern United States most of his life and has lived in the San Francisco Bay Area since 1995. He is a Professor of Communication at Saint Mary's College of California. He identifies as a cisgender White, middle-upper class, heterosexual, neurotypical, able-bodied man. Scott and Gust met when Scott was a student of Gust's in a master's program in Communication in the late nineties. Since then, we have been coauthors and copresenters on conference panels and have had many conversations together. We share similarities in our approaches to teaching (employing critical pedagogy) and in politics, as well as a love of good food and tea. The dialogue is a distillation of the conversations we have had over the years regarding matters such as gender, sexuality, race, culture, and identity.

A DIALOGUE ABOUT QUEER THEORY AND TRANS STUDIES IN COMMUNICATION

Scott: Most of us have heard the terms "queer" and "trans" before. I wonder if you can say more about what queer theory is and does and if you can also say something about how queer theory gets employed by you and others in the field of communication.

Gust: The first thing I want to say is that queer theory is not a traditional theory per se; most people think of a theory as a kind of contained system and logic of description and explanation of a specific kind of phenomenon. Queer theory is more of an interdisciplinary, intellectual movement influenced by critical theory, cultural studies, feminism, postmodernism and poststructuralism. It offers us specific ways of looking, understanding, and explaining power relations in society, so, in that sense, it is theory. Queer theory has affected the way we think about identity, social relationships, social structures, cultural institutions, and power relations in society.

Scott: What do you mean when you say that queer theory has something to do with power relations in society? I also wonder how this may connect to how you employ "transing" in your work.

Gust: First, I want to clarify that I'm using power in a Foucauldian sense—power as relational, ubiquitous, and productive and not simply repressive (Foucault, 1990). So, based on this notion of power, we can see that power is always already embedded in all of our relationships, such as interpersonal relations (e.g., relationship with our boss), social relations (e.g., the ways we group and categorize people), social institutions (e.g., family), or cultural ideologies (e.g., heteropatriarchy). The way that we employ power is not always visible, so in that sense we are not always aware of it. As Foucault (1990) suggests, the power of power is to maintain its invisibility. We are always affected by power. The project of queer theory is to use specific analytical tools for us to become more conscious of how power is operating in our social relationships, with particular attention to how gender and sexuality structure social life.

Queer theorists recognize and acknowledge the history of the term "queer" that is deployed to degrade, to dehumanize, and to pathologize sexual minoritarian subjects. But they are reclaiming the term to resignify it and give it new meaning and to gesture toward a political project of social justice. The term "queer" can be used as a noun and as a verb. Most people think of "queer" as a noun—as someone who is odd (strangeness) or someone who is lesbian or gay (identity). As a verb, queer theory uses the term to describe a process of making something familiar and taken-for-granted into something unfamiliar and strange so that it can be analyzed and examined.

Similarly, transing is a term and a deconstructive tool used to analyze gender in relation to other forms of difference, such as race and nation (Yep, Russo, & Allen, 2015). It maintains that gender is (a) intersectional (e.g., the meanings and experiences of gender are always already working through conceptions of race, class, sexuality, body, and nation, among others), (b) simultaneously an individual performance (e.g., how one dresses) and an administrative structure (e.g., gender in government identification cards), (c) multiple (e.g., gender galaxy) rather than dualistic (e.g., gender binary), and (d) embodied by people and as such, we should pay attention to how people experience—and live—in their gendered bodies rather than imposing gender meanings and categories on people (e.g., assuming that little girls should act in feminine ways). By using queering and transing, queer theory and trans studies provide important tools for analysis.

Scott: Can you give another example of such analysis? You mention awareness of power.

Gust: In terms of how power might be operating in a text, in a social relation, in a specific situation. For instance, most people think about marriage as something naturally occurring when two individuals are in love which each other and want to build a life together. Marriage, for these people, is simply a natural part of the life cycle. Most people probably do not think about marriage as something to be analyzed. What queer theory does is look at marriage and its power relations. It would look at the history of marriage, pointing out that marriage was really not so much about love, but about property ownership and the maintenance of wealth, and that it was not until the early 20th century that marriage was seen as the culmination and expression of love between two individuals. This whole notion of marrying for love is a relatively new concept that permeates the way that we think about dating and romantic relationships in a lot of contemporary cultures (Yep, 2013b).

Scott: So many people don't think about all of these consequences because they feel they are not—or don't think they are—affected by them.

Gust: Everyone is affected but in different ways, depending on their social location and how their identities intersect. For example, a white, middle-class, nonbinary, asexual, able-bodied, U.S. citizen is affected differently than an African, upper-class, cisgender, lesbian with a disability, and a recent immigrant to the United States.

Scott: You've just highlighted intersectionality of different identities. I sometimes like to think in metaphors, so what metaphor would you use to describe intersectionality?

Gust: Intersectionality is like a cake. It is made out of a lot of different ingredients, like flour, sugar, eggs, perhaps chocolate chips. None of those are in themselves the cake. The egg is not the cake, the sugar is not the cake. The cake is more than each of the individual ingredients. So, when we talk about race, class, gender, sexuality, ability, and nation, a person is not just their race, because they also have gender, sexuality, and so on. We can't just say this person is a ciswoman without also looking at the other elements that make her a whole person.

In mainstream U.S. culture, we tend to think of identity in additive ways. For example, we might ask a lesbian of color if her race is more important than her gender or sexuality. In the process, we are asking her to fragment herself into parts and to determine what aspects of her identity are more important, when in fact, she is a whole person, which means that all of these factors are operating simultaneously in any given social situation. In this sense, intersectional identities are multiplicative rather than additive (Yep, 2002b, 2016; Yep & Lescure, 2019).

Scott: I've also heard you talk about "thick intersectionalities," about biographies and lived experiences. I wonder if you can talk about how thick intersectionalities differ from the intersections we were just talking about.

Gust: Well, there are different ways of doing intersectionalities and of doing race, class, gender, sexuality, ability, and nation. One way is the "roster-like" approach to intersectionality when one simply lists the various different identities of a person, which is, in my view, simplistic and superficial (Yep, 2010b, 2016; Yep & Lescure, 2019).

Scott: Why simplistic and superficial? And what makes the kind of intersectionality you're advocating "thick"?

Gust: Because it is a process of listing several identity markers without paying attention to how a person lives and how the person's history and biography affect their communication and relationships. So, for instance, we might have someone whose identities might be labeled as white, middle-class, cismale, straight, able-bodied, and U.S. American.

Scott: You realize that sounds like my identities, ones that get centered a lot and that get constructed as normative—and when they're legitimately critiqued, too often it results in folks claiming victimized identity.

Gust: Yes. On the surface, one can make a number of assumptions about your life, privileges, and politics—if we simply stayed with those superficial markers. But as we have gotten to know each other, we have learned about each other's biographies, histories, and personal and social struggles and in that process, I could say that we have a lot of similarities, even though on the surface we appear very different. Thick intersectionalities pays attention to the particularities of our lives and our life journeys and how they are affected by the intersections of race, class, gender, sexuality, ability, and nation (Yep, 2010b, 2016; Yep & Lescure, 2019).

Scott: In other words, thick intersectionalities avoid essentializing, while also recognizing the reality of differences as lived by people—differences that have varied and significant material consequences within societal systems and structures.

Gust: We get to know people as unique individuals rather than as a simple combination of social categories. That's not to suggest that race, class, gender, sexuality, ability, and nation don't matter but that we need to attend to the ways that they are embodied and lived in the world.

Scott: It seems to me that making assumptions about people based on an additive approach or from a simplistic intersectional perspective is pretty commonplace. There doesn't appear to me to be lots of interrogation of discourses of race, class, gender, sexuality, ability, and nation in mainstream U.S. media or in many everyday relationships and conversations. If we think specifically about discourses of sexuality and normalization, this brings us to the notions of heteronormativity and heteropatriarchy. I know you've thought, spoken, and written a lot about these. Can you talk more about them?

Gust: One of the aims of queer theory is to examine the process of normalization, that is, the process by which we make certain practices unquestionable and taken-for-granted in a culture. Earlier I mentioned that marriage is normalized and so is heterosexuality. Queer theory examines them so that they can be understood in terms of power relations in society. One of the primary concerns of queer theory is to uncover the processes of normalization in general, and normalization in relationship to gender and sexuality in particular (Yep, 2009b). But normalization isn't just a queer theory project: it's an aim of critical theory. One way to think about it is that queer theory is using the normalization of gender and sexuality as a starting point for the analysis of social relations. For example, queer theory focuses on heteronormativity, which is the normalization of heterosexuality (Yep, 2002a, 2003, 2005, 2009b). When I say normalization of heterosexuality, I mean the seemingly natural, given, assumed, unquestionable status given to heterosexuality in social relations (Yep, 2002a, 2003). When we look at heterosexuality more closely, however, we can see that it depends on the gender binary (e.g., ciswomen and cismen attracted to and desiring each other), a major concern in trans studies (Yep, Russo, & Allen, 2015; Yep, Russo, Allen, & Chivers, 2017; Yep, Russo, & Lescure, 2015).

Let's illustrate this with an example. Kris is a nonbinary person and identifies as they/them. Kris' uncle has known Kris as "my little niece," and imagines Kris growing up, getting married to a man, and having that man's children. Implicit in this set of assumptions is that the normal and natural way to be in the world is to be heterosexual and cisgender. Such assumptions imply that heterosexuality and the gender binary are unquestionable and inevitable and can be used to call Kris' identity and personhood into question when they deviate from them (e.g., they do not want to get married, they do not want to have children, and they are attracted to all genders). So, I'm posing this question: what happens to this young person, the "niece," when they find that they are discovering their sexuality, their wishes, and their aspirations as an individual? Some would suggest that they may see heterosexuality and the gender binary as the only "right" options. This is what we might term "compulsory heterosexuality" and cisgenderism. In this sense, the normalization of heterosexuality—or heteronormativity—and the gender binary—or cisgenderism—becomes a site of violence (Yep, 2002a, 2003; Yep, Russo, & Allen, 2015; Yep, Russo, Allen, & Chivers, 2017; Yep, Russo, & Lescure, 2015).

Scott: A site of violence? You mean that violence might be inflicted upon Kris? By their uncle? By society? By family?

Gust: Well, I want to use the notion of violence more broadly. Violence is, in my view, the process of harming someone, physically, psychologically, symbolically, or all of the above (Yep, 2003; Yep, Russo, & Allen, 2015). For example, if the uncle insists on using feminine pronouns when Kris is nonbinary, he is inflicting injury on their personhood.

Scott: Yes, and he will have much support in society and from the injurious discourses circulating within society, given the refusal, resistance, and/or lack of understanding so many folks have regarding pronoun usage and sexualities that aren't gender- and heteronormative. Those discourses, and the social structures from which they emerge and within which they circulate contribute to the valuation of what is considered appropriate personal and social activity. You're suggesting that the uncle's perspective and insistence on particular pronoun usage coupled with the social structures work to impose upon people, not just upon the "niece," but upon the uncle, too, a sense of what is proper, appropriate, and normative, and that these are a violent enforcement of heteronormativity and gender normativity, not in the least because of the emotional and psychological experience and repercussions of such enforcement upon both the "niece" and uncle. One might also suggest that heteropatriarchy allows more space for the uncle to make such comments without obvious consequences, and that he might even benefit by making such comments in that it reaffirms his own heterosexuality and status as a cisgender, non-transman.

Gust: Absolutely! The uncle is operating not just within the structures of heteronormativity and the gender binary, but also within the structures of heteropatriarchy. By heteropatriarchy, I mean a systemic social arrangement that upholds the dominance of cismen over ciswomen through the institution of heterosexuality (Yep, 2003). As I mentioned earlier, heterosexuality is dependent on the coherence of gender in the form of the gender binary (Yep, Russo, Allen, & Chivers, 2017). What happens to heterosexuality if we have a relationship between a cisperson and a nonbinary one?

Scott: Well, I think heterosexuality gets disrupted and challenged, and that the social structures of heteronormativity and heteropatriarchy get called upon to try to reestablish and reinforce the gender binary and normative sexuality. I understand those structures as the traditional family (e.g., breadwinning husband and housewife , husband as head of household), the church (e.g., predominantly male-led, literal interpretations of scripture regarding gender, sexual, and marital relations), the legal system (e.g., inheritance benefits for married couples, definition of rape), the educational system (e.g., selective study of male-dominant and heterosexual histories, the predominance of male heroes and straight, cisgender characters in children's books), mass media (e.g., the focus on male sports, the news coverage on trans athletes and bans) and the like.

Gust: Here we see how gender and sexuality might work to mutually reinforce each other to create and maintain normativity. More recent work on queer theory is focusing on normativity within cultural contexts, nationally and transnationally (Yep, 2013a; Yep, Alaoui, & Lescure, 2020; Yep, Lescure, & Russo, 2019). Similarly, recent work on trans studies is attempting to center the voices of trans subjectivities and relationalities (Yep, Alaoui, & Lescure, 2019). Moving from individual normativities (e.g., sexual identity, gender identity) and cultural norms (e.g., heteronormativity, cisnormativity) to social relations, I have been interested in examining and understanding how people relate to each other in nonnormative ways—what I call "queer relationalities" (Yep, 2017, 2020; Yep, Alaoui, & Lescure, in press).

Scott: Oh, that's a fascinating concept. Say more.

Gust: In simple terms, queer relationalities might be understood as sexual minoritarians' ways of relating, engaging, and connecting with others under the regime of heteropatriarchy (Yep, 2017, 2020). These modes of relationality and sociality are largely culturally unintelligible, that is, ignored, neglected, erased, and trivialized in mainstream heteronormative culture (Yep, Alaoui, & Lescure, in press). For example, a knowing look of recognition that another person is sexually or gender nonnormative is a form of queer relationality. As you might imagine, this world of queer relationality is vast and communication scholars should, in my view, start paying more attention to it.

Scott: I know you're only touching the surface here. When we think about queer relationality and gender and sexual normativity, we also are pondering whether or not to endorse those forms of normativity or to transgress against them, right? Any suggestions or thoughts about this struggle?

Gust: I want to make a distinction between transgression and intervention. Trangression is the process through which individuals either consciously or less consciously break away from or do not conform to normativities. One example would be dressing differently, such as going to class to teach in shorts and a T-shirt when you normally wear more formal attire, to call attention to the performativity of the various dimensions of identity (of a professor, in this case). A transgression is essentially an act (or acts) that fail to conform to normativities. Intervention, on the other hand, is a deliberate act (or series of acts) that call our attention to the underlying power dynamics that govern specific forms of normativity (Yep, 2008).

Scott: So interventions are intentional efforts to disrupt normativity …

Gust: … and to call attention to its underlying aims and purposes.

Scott: I wonder if such calling attention requires specific mention of what one is challenging. For instance, if one wears particular kinds of clothing with the intent to have students question normative practices of gender and sexuality broadly, does one have to specifically say that's what one is doing in order to "call attention" or does just wearing it do that? Does this determine whether it is an intervention or transgression? I'm asking because it seems to me that an intervention, and the instance I mention here, is marked by political intention and motive for progressive change. Perhaps one's constant dressing differently with political intent and motivation for progressive change is more transgression than intervention, though if one specifically comments on why one dresses the way one does, it moves into intervention because one is deliberately attempting to undermine one's own privileges and power that one receives otherwise. I suppose I am suggesting that acts marked by political intention and motive for progressive change are not in themselves interventions unless they actually serve to call attention (be it through specific mention or not) to the underlying power dynamics that govern specific forms of normativity.

Gust: Yes, interventions are deliberate acts to produce progressive social change. These changes can be small or large (Yep, 2008). They can also occur at the individual level—like some of one's heterosexual students starting to think about their heterosexual privilege— and at the systemic level—like some of the students in your example, regardless of gender identity, getting together to organize to promote and support trans rights in their state.

CONCLUSION

In this dialogue, we discussed some of the aims of queer theory and trans studies, including the concepts of queering and transing. We highlighted their efforts to analyze power, gender, and sexuality and their shaping of social relations/hierarchies and normalization. We also explored the concepts of intersectionality and thick intersectionalities, which pay attention to histories and biographies and the particularities of race, class, gender, sexuality, ability, and nation. In our discussion, we noted queer theory's examination of heteronormativity and the violence inherent in it. We mentioned how heterosexuality is utterly dependent on the gender binary, which is a site of violence for gender nonnormative people. We concluded with an explanation of transgressions and interventions.

There are several direct communicative implications of our dialogue. These consist of (1) becoming more conscious of the significance of power in everyday interactions and in social structures and institutions; (2) striving to be more aware of one's own and each person's particular social realities that shape their lived experiences; (3) recognizing that intersections of identity complicate our understanding of people and everyday communicative encounters; (4) becoming more aware of how gender and sexuality are normalized; (5) not assuming that gender and sexuality are clear categories and not making simplistic assumptions about them; (6) observing how we reinforce normalization for ourselves and others via personal, cultural, and social practices; and (7) seeking to practice transgressions and interventions, and to acknowledge them, in efforts to disrupt normativity, even when one is benefitting or receiving privilege from heteronormativity and heteropatriarchy.

REFERENCES

Elia, J. P., Lovaas, K. E., & Yep, G. A. (2003). Reflections on queer theory: Disparate points of view. In G. A. Yep, K. E. Lovaas, & J. P. Elia (Eds.), *Queer theory and communication: From disciplining queers to queering the discipline(s)* (pp. 335–337). Harrington Park Press.

Elia, J. P., & Yep, G. A. (2012). Sexualities and genders in an age of neoterrorism. *Journal of Homosexuality, 59*(7), 879–889. https://doi.org/10.1080/00918369.2012.699826

Foucault, M. (1990). *The history of sexuality: Vol. 1. An introduction.* Vintage.

Gamson, J. (2003). Reflections on queer theory and communication. In G. A. Yep, K. E. Lovaas, & J. P. Elia (Eds.), *Queer theory and communication: From disciplining queers to queering the discipline(s)* (pp. 385–389). Harrington Park Press.

McCann, H., & Monaghan, W. (2020). *Queer theory now: From foundations to futures.* Red Globe Press.

Slagle, R. A., & Yep, G. A. (2007). Taming Brian: Sex, love, and romance in *Queer as Folk.* In M. L. Galician & D. Merskin (Eds.), *Critical thinking about sex, love, and romance in the mass media: Media literacy applications* (pp. 189–202). Erlbaum.

Spencer, L. G. & Capuzza, J. C. (Eds.). (2015). *Transgender communication studies: Histories, trends, and trajectories.* Lexington Books.

Yep, G. A. (2002a). From homophobia and heterosexism to heteronormativity: Toward the development of a model of queer interventions in the university classroom. *Journal of Lesbian Studies, 6*(3/4), 163–176. https://doi.org/10.1300/J155v06n03_14

Yep, G. A. (2002b). My three cultures: Navigating the multicultural identity landscape. In J. N. Martin, T. K. Nakayama, & L. A. Flores (Eds.), *Readings in intercultural communication: Experiences and contexts* (2nd ed., pp. 60–66). McGraw-Hill.

Yep, G. A. (2003). The violence of heteronormativity in communication studies: Notes on violence, healing, and queer world-making. In G. A. Yep, K. E. Lovaas, & J. P. Elia (Eds.), *Queer theory and communication: From disciplining queers to queering the discipline(s)* (pp. 11–59). Harrington Park Press.

Yep, G. A. (2005). Heteronormativity. In J. T. Sears (Ed.), *Youth, education, and sexualities: An international encyclopedia* (pp. 395–398). Greenwood.

Yep, G. A. (2007). The politics of loss and its remains in *Common Threads: Stories from the Quilt. Rhetoric & Public Affairs, 10*(4), 681–699. https://www.jstor.org/stable/41940330

Yep, G. A. (2008). The dialectics of intervention: Toward a reconceptualization of the theory/activism divide in communication scholarship and beyond. In O. Swartz (Ed.), *Transformative communication studies: Culture, hierarchy and the human condition* (pp. 191–207). Troubador.

Yep, G. A. (2009a). Gay, lesbian, bisexual, and transgender theories. In S. W. Littlejohn & K. A. Foss (Eds.), *Encyclopedia of communication theory* (Vol. 1, pp. 421–426). Sage.

Yep, G. A. (2009b). Queer theory. In S. W. Littlejohn & K. A. Foss (Eds.), *Encyclopedia of communication theory* (Vol. 2, pp. 817–821). Sage.

Yep, G. A. (2010a). Rolando and Tatiana: Living at the intersections of race, class, gender, sexuality, and nation. In C. M. Noland, J. Manning, & J. MacLennan (Eds.), *Case studies of communication about sex* (pp. 46–54). Cambridge.

Yep, G. A. (2010b). Toward the de-subjugation of racially marked knowledges in communication. *Southern Communication Journal, 75*(2), 171–175. https://doi.org/10.1080/10417941003613263

Yep, G. A. (2013a). Queering/quaring/kauering/crippin'/transing "other bodies" in intercultural communication. *Journal of International and Intercultural Communication, 6*(2), 118–126. https://doi.org/10.1080/17513057.2013.777087

Yep, G. A. (2013b). Privilege and culture. In A. Kurylo (Ed.), *Inter/Cultural Communication: Representation and construction of culture in everyday interaction* (pp. 163–184). Sage.

Yep, G. A. (2016). Toward thick(er) intersectionalities: Theorizing, researching, and activating the complexities of communication and identities. In K. Sorrells & S. Sekimoto (Eds.), *Globalizing intercultural communication: A reader* (pp. 86–94). Sage.

Yep, G. A. (2017). Further notes on healing from the violence of heteronormativity in Communication Studies. *QED: A Journal in GLBTQ Worldmaking, 4*(2), 115–122. https://doi.org/10.14321/qed.4.2.0115

Yep, G. A. (2020a). Queer relationalities in the era of social distancing. *QED: A Journal in GLBTQ Worldmaking, 7*(3), 167–173. https://doi.org/10.14321/qed.7.3.0167

Yep, G. A. (2020b). Towards a performative turn in intercultural communication. *Journal of Intercultural Communication Research, 49*(5), 484–493. https://doi.org/10.1080/17475759.2020.1802325

Yep, G. A., Alaoui, F. Z. C., & Lescure, R. M. (2019). Transing Sin-Dee-Rella: Representations of trans women of color in Sean Baker's *Tangerine*. In R. A. Lind (Ed.), *Race/gender/class/media 4.0: Considering diversity across audiences, content, and producers* (4th ed., pp. 154–158). Routledge.

Yep, G. A., Alaoui, F. Z. C., & Lescure, R. M. (2020). Relationalities in/through difference: Explorations in queer intercultural communication. In S. Eguchi & B. M. Calafell (Eds.), *Queer intercultural communication* (pp. 19–45). Rowman & Littlefield.

Yep, G. A., Alaoui, F. Z. C., & Lescure, R. M. (in press). Mapping queer relationalities: An exploration of communication at the edges of cultural unintelligibility. *Journal of Homosexuality*.

Yep, G. A., & Chivers, N. T. (2016). Fetuao's dilemma: Negotiating gender and sexuality in the hypermasculine world of rugby. In D. Tucker & J. Wrench (Eds.), *Casing sport communication* (pp. 292–300). Kendall Hunt.

Yep, G. A., & Chivers, N. T. (2017). Intersectionality. In Y. Y. Kim & K. L. McKay-Semmler (Eds.), *The International encyclopedia of intercultural communication* (Vol. 2, pp. 1532–1537). Wiley-Blackwell.

Yep, G. A., & Conkle, A. (2013). The new gay domesticity: Homonormativity in ABC's *Brothers and Sisters*. In R. A. Lind (Ed.), *Race/Gender/Media 3.0: Considering diversity across audiences, content, and producers* (3rd ed., pp. 218–224). Pearson.

Yep, G. A., & Elia, J. P. (2007). Queering/quaring blackness in *Noah's Arc*. In T. Peele (Ed.), *Queer popular culture: Literature, media, film, and television* (pp. 27–40). Palgrave-Macmillan.

Yep, G. A., & Elia, J. P. (2012). Racialized masculinities and the new homonormativity in LOGO's *Noah's Arc. Journal of Homosexuality, 59*(7), 890–911. https://doi.org/10.1080/00918369.2012. 699827

Yep, G. A., & Lescure, R. M. (2014). Kauering "home" in Ang Lee's *The Wedding Banquet*. In E. Patton & M. Choi (Eds.), *Home sweat home: Perspectives on housework and modern domestic relationships* (pp. 167–182). Rowman & Littlefield.

Yep, G. A., & Lescure, R. M. (2015). The practice of normativities in everyday life. In D. B. Goltz & J. Zingsheim (Eds.), *Queer praxis: Questions for LGBTQ worldmaking* (pp. 93–106). Peter Lang.

Yep, G. A., & Lescure, R. M. (2019). A thick intersectional approach to microaggressions. *Southern Communication Journal, 84*(2), 113–126. https://doi.org/10.1080/1041794X.2018.1511749

Yep, G. A., Lescure, R. M., & Allen, J. (2015). Queering aging? Representations of Liberace's intimate life in HBO's *Behind the Candelabra*. In N. Jones & B. Batchelor (Eds.), *Aging heroes: Growing old in popular culture* (pp. 65–76). Rowman & Littlefield.

Yep, G. A., Lescure, R. M., & Allen, J. (2022). Intercultural same-sex relationships: Masculinities, sexualities and communication across borders. In J. Manning & C. Noland (Eds.), *Contemporary studies of sexuality and communication: Theoretical and applied approaches* (2nd ed., pp. 197–211). Kendall Hunt.

Yep, G. A., Lescure, R. M., Russo, S. E. (2019). Queer intercultural communication. In J. Nussbaum (Ed.), *The oxford research encyclopedia of communication*. Oxford University Press. DOI: 10.1093/acrefore/9780190228613.013.170

Yep, G. A., Lovaas, K. E., & Elia, J. P. (Eds.). (2003a). *Queer theory and communication: From disciplining queers to queering the discipline(s)*. Harrington Park Press.

Yep, G. A., Lovaas, K. E., & Elia, J. P. (2003b). Queering communication: Starting the conversation. In G. A. Yep, K. E. Lovaas, & J. P. Elia (Eds.), *Queer theory and communication: From disciplining queers to queering the discipline(s)* (pp. 1–10). Harrington Park Press.

Yep, G. A., Lovaas, K. E., & Elia, J. P. (2003c). A critical reappraisal of assimilationist and radical ideologies underlying same-sex marriage in LGBT communities in the United States. *Journal of Homosexuality, 45*(1), 45–64. https://doi.org/10.1300/J082v45n01_03

Yep, G. A., & Ochoa Camacho, A. (2004). The normalization of heterogendered relations in *The Bachelor. Feminist Media Studies, 4*(3), 338–341.

Yep, G. A., Olzman, M., & Conkle, A. (2012). Seven stories from the "It Gets Better" Project: Progress narratives, politics of affect, and the question of queer world-making. In R. A. Lind (Ed.), *Produsing theory in a digital world: The intersection of audiences and production in contemporary theory* (pp. 123–141). Peter Lang.

Yep, G. A., Russo, S. E., & Allen, J. (2015). Pushing boundaries: Toward the development of a model for transing communication in (inter)cultural contexts. In L. G. Spencer & J. C. Capuzza (Eds.), *Transgender communication studies: Histories, trends, and trajectories* (pp. 69–89). Lexington Books.

Yep, G. A., Russo, S. E., Allen, J., & Chivers, N. T. (2017). Uniquely *Glee*: Transing racialized gender. In R. A. Lind (Ed.), *Race and gender in electronic media: Challenges and opportunities* (pp. 55–71). Routledge.

Yep, G. A., Russo, S. E., & Lescure, R. M. (2015). Transing normative boyhood masculinity in Alain Berliner's *Ma Vie en Rose. Boyhood Studies: An Interdisciplinary Journal, 8*(2), 43–60. https://doi.org/10.3167/bhs.2015.080204

Yep, G. A., & Shimanoff, S. B. (2013). The U.S. Day of Silence: Sexualities, silences and the will to unsay in the age of empire. In S. Malhotra & A. Carrillo-Rowe (Eds.), *Silence and power: Feminist reflections at the edges of sound* (pp. 139–158). Palgrave Macmillan.

HEALTH COMMUNICATION

The health communication context focuses on how we speak about our health and interpret health-related information. As active consumers of health care, we decide how we process health messages directed toward us and how we respond. Health communication scholars study topics such as patient-caregiver communication, health promotion campaigns, stigma, and illness identity. This section includes chapters focusing on three important areas of health communication research: (1) drug use prevention in children, (2) communicating about weight, and (3) strategic health communication during the pandemic. First, Michelle Miller-Day (Chapman University, REAL Prevention) and Michael Hecht (REAL Prevention) explore their worldwide health intervention and curriculum (keepin' it REAL) that has been very successful at keeping kids off drugs. Second, Tricia Burke (Texas State University), Analisa Arroyo (University of Georgia), and Valerie Young (Hanover College) discuss how partners talk about weight-related and body-related communication in close relationships. Third, Gary Kreps (George Mason University) discusses how strategic health communication can help with health promotion and care during the COVID-19 pandemic. Our health is so important to us. Fortunately, healthy decisions and outcomes can be enhanced in people's conversations and decision-making processes. Health communication research provides us with many answers that can literally save lives (if people listen). We hope these chapters help you consider the role that communication plays in your health and the health of others.

KEEPIN' IT REAL WHEN DEVELOPING NARRATIVE HEALTH MESSAGES

Michelle Miller-Day, Chapman University, REAL Prevention
Michael L. Hecht, REAL Prevention

INTRODUCTION

Think about the last time that you felt some pressure to drink alcohol, vape, or use a substance such as marijuana. Pressure can come from others in a social context explicitly ("we are doing tequila shots, come on and have some!") implicitly (friends are passing a joint and it is handed to you), or come from inside yourself ("everybody is de-stressing right now by drinking. I'm feeling stressed out too. Maybe I should join them?"). If you cannot think of a time you felt some pressure to indulge, then good for you! For everyone else, you have a lot of company. We are bombarded daily with advertising and marketing messages to use illicit substances for fun or relaxation and many of us are faced with both implicit and explicit pressure to partake. All of these messages are of interest to us as researchers, but the work that we will be discussing in this chapter is located at the intersection of interpersonal, intrapersonal, health, and intercultural communication. In particular, our substance use prevention research examines the personal stories of others to identify messages received from others in social contexts (interpersonal communication) along with messages that we give ourselves (intrapersonal communication) about substance use. We then translate that information into health interventions (health communication) for kids and adapt these interventions for a variety of cultural groups (intercultural communication).

NARRATIVES ABOUT DRUGS–HOW WE LEARNED TO KEEP IT REAL

The health intervention we discuss in this chapter is our kid-centric substance use prevention curriculum titled *keepin' it REAL* (*kiR*). This prevention curriculum is now believed to be the most widely used program of its kind reaching over 2 million youth per year in the United States, as well as hundreds of thousands around the world, and it all started with kids' stories. We say that *kiR* is "kid-centric" because it was built around kids and their stories. Our first step as academics was to of course become well-read on the current research about kids and their lives. But, most importantly, we talked to hundreds and hundreds of kids from all around the United States. We asked them to tell us stories about their experiences in risky situations, particularly when they were offered illicit drugs explicitly or implicitly. These stories told us a lot about what happens when drugs are offered, how the kids see drugs, and what we can do to prevent drug use.

Stories are powerful tools because they are both a way of thinking as well as a style of communicating (Hecht & Miller-Day, 2007). What do we mean by this? People are inherently storytellers. Think of the cave pictures and the stories they tell about hunts and other events. Think about how we learn about our families and the world—through the stories family members tell us about our ancestors and about their lives, through stories they read to us that teach us about values and beliefs, and through the stories we see in the media. In fact, we remember things in story form. Try remembering a historical fact—it will often be in the context of a story about an event and people. And, while not everyone is a storyteller, most of us talk in story form at least some of the time. Think about the last time you met someone—did you try to understand each other's story (i.e., where they are from and what is their major). So, understanding the stories kids tell us about drugs is likely to reveal how they see drugs and drug use, the choices they make, as well as what can be done to influence them to make healthy choices.

DRUG NARRATIVES

Looking at patterns across different stories we can identify larger narratives. For example, think about the stories you tell about your college experience so far. One student's individual story may differ somewhat from another student's story, but there is likely to be a common theme cutting across many of the stories. A theme reflecting a larger shared experience. In our work across the United States, we have learned that there are some consistent patterns that emerge across teens' drug offer and refusal stories. The larger narrative is fairly consistent within the United States urban and rural communities, as well as across other international cultures for whom we have adapted the *kiR* program including Mexico, Nicaragua, the UK, Brazil, Guatemala, and Spain. Our analyses of teens' stories tell us about the "who, what, where, and how" of drug offers.[1]

Who Offers. Contrary to the stereotype, most drug offers come from friends and family rather than strangers. While acquaintances and strangers are responsible for a certain portion of the offers, a large majority come from those who are close to the kids with whom we talked. As a result of offers occurring in the context of personal relationships, there can be a lot of implicit pressure to accept these offers.

What Gets Offered. Again, in contrast to public images of a meth or prescription drug epidemic, alcohol and tobacco (both smoked and chewed) are far and away the most frequently offered substances for most groups of youth under the age of 18. For example, in a recent rural study, over 70% of the offers involved these substances (Pettigrew et al., 2011). One exception is our work among Mexican American youth, where marijuana is offered with relatively higher frequency than tobacco (but not alcohol).

How Offered. Our research suggests that while a variety of strategies are used to offer substances, the most frequent style is what we call a simple offer or mere availability. In both, the substance is made available without pressure or influence. For example, a simple offer might be, "You want a dip?" or "Do you want a beer?"

When influence is used, the offerer will try to minimize risks, appeal to group norms, talk about benefits, or some combination strategy (e.g., minimize risks and show benefits). For example, someone might minimize risks by saying, "Just do it, just do it, you won't get caught if you're with me" or "Aw, come on. It's just, it's harmless."

Others might appeal to group norms, utilizing a bandwagon strategy of "everyone's doing it." For example, someone might say, "Come on, we're all smoking" or "Awww, you're such a wuss." Sometimes, the normative pressure is internal; that is, coming from personal pressure. Kids pressure themselves to act a certain way so they will fit in or be liked. In this situation, offerers do not put pressure on the kid to use (although that pressure can be implicit), but rather, the kid brings it on him or herself. For example, one kid told us:

> Like, the first thing that goes through your mind is that if you don't do it, will your friends still like you? And then, you have that second thought, like, "Well, maybe it's not that bad." But then, like, it's, like, your body's telling you, "No, don't do it because it'll hurt you." Like, "Don't do it, 'cause you'll hurt me." But then your mind's telling you, "Well, maybe your friends won't like you if you don't do it." So it's like a mind-over-matter type thing.

Others talk about benefits of use. For example, one kid reported being told, "Oh, did you guys try this? It's so awesome, like, it's good, it tastes like fruit and stuff." Another was offered pot and told, "It feels good to be like that."

---

1 See Alberts et al. (1991) and Pettigrew et al. (2011) for examples of more detailed information on early analyses.

How Substances Are Resisted or Refused. Drug resistance or refusal strategies have been at the heart of adolescent substance use prevention since the 1980s when Nancy Reagan coined the "Just Say No" campaign strategy. Our research suggests that there are four ways of refusing drug offers. These became known as "real," an acronym for remembering Refuse (simple no), Explain (no with an explanation), Avoid (avoid the situation or the offer), and Leave (leave the situation) (Alberts et al, 1991; Pettigrew et al., 2011). We have found these strategies are used by people from kindergarten through college and recently found they also were used to resist sexual pressure. But we are not the only ones to find these strategies—their existence was confirmed by Harrington (1995) and others.

Refuse. Refuse is the simplest strategy—at least the least complex one. All it requires is saying "no" or shaking one's head "no." However, one's style of communication is particularly important. To be effective, this must be done with confidence, assertiveness, or even with an element of aggression.

Explain. Explain is a little more complex communication strategy because it requires us to justify our reasoning. An example might be, "No thanks, I have to pick my parents up at the airport and cannot be high when I see them." However, as Langer (1989) has shown, even a "nonreason" reason can work. A simple example would be when asking for a pencil, saying, "Can I have a pencil I need one." Not really an explanation but in explanation form (I want "x" because "y"). So, some kids say, "No, I don't want a beer because I don't drink."

Avoid. Avoid is the most complex strategy. We know that means it should come last, but RELA does not make for a good acronym. In any case, there are both proactive and reactive avoidance strategies. Proactive strategies prepare for or anticipate drug offers. One proactive way to avoid this is by not putting yourself in a situation where an offer will be made. Think about a typical Friday night—do you know what party is likely to have lots of alcohol? Other substances? Avoiding would mean not going to the party. Perhaps a bit risky and more complicated are reactive strategies such as avoiding the rooms at the party where beer is served or consumed. Even more complicated, is a verbal avoidance. For example, when offered a beer at a party, one young woman said she wanted to dance instead. Others accept the offered beer but do not drink it. Still, others carry a beer (or apple juice that looks like beer) around a party so they will not be asked again.

Leave. The final strategy, leave, involves removing yourself from a situation in which drugs are offered. While this sometimes is paired with an explanation of why you are leaving, it is largely about the action of going. Some kids employ elaborate leave strategies. At a younger age, they may arrange for their parents to be the reason they have to leave. Some even think of a texting code so their friends can help them get out of the situation (e.g., inviting them to another party; making it so their ride is going).

All of these strategies can be relatively straightforward. Our research suggests that leave is used most frequently by older adolescents and young adults who have the means to leave by themselves or by more sophisticated younger communicators who can figure out how to get out of the situation.

Relationships. Regardless of the strategy, one of the key challenges for all age groups is how to refuse without insulting others or losing friends. Sometimes the issue is all in our head—internal or personal pressure because we think people will not like us unless we fit in. Other times, however, it is real. Kids really do say to each other, "you can't hang out with us unless you drink or smoke." Then people may have to choose between being part of a certain group and doing what they think is best. Tough choices, but nobody said being healthy was easy.

TRANSLATING NARRATIVES INTO DRUG PREVENTION MESSAGES

We have always been interested in describing the social process of drug offers as academic research, but we have also been motivated to translate that knowledge into health promotion. Fortunately, there were some theories to guide us and we were developing others to perfect this approach such as communication competence theory (Spitzberg & Cupach, 1984) and narrative engagement (Miller-Day & Hecht, 2013; Polkinghorne, 1988).

Our goal then, is to teach knowledge, motivation, and skills (communication competence theory) through engaging, narrative role models. We do this by using indigenous narratives to construct lessons. In other words, the information and skills we want to convey and the motivation we want to provide is to depict stories told by other youth—kids telling about real events that occurred to real kids and telling a larger narrative of communicating resistance. We describe this kid-centric approach as "from kids, through kids, to kids." These stories create narrative engagement (i.e., create interest, realism, and identification) because the youth recognize themselves and their peers in the stories and find them appealing. The narratives also provide role models (using social cognitive theory)[2] that teach youth how to resist drug offers (knowledge), enhance the perceived need to resist through social norms (motivation), and the strategies for accomplishing this (skills of competent communication). Since the stories shared in the program come from other kids, they are not "preachy" and we avoid using fear appeals because research shows they are less effective for this age group (Hasting et al., 2004). The stories ground the curriculum in a kids-eye view of the world, making the kid-centric while reflecting ethnic, gender, regional, and other identities (cultural grounding) (see Hecht & Krieger, 2006).

You are probably thinking, this is all well in theory, but how can you do all these things at once? It all starts with the effective presentation of stories. If the research is done well, we will have identified prototypical narratives reflecting cultural styles of thought and conversation that can be used to develop classroom materials. Elsewhere, the overall curriculum development has been described (Gosin et al., 2003). But, here we focus on effectively translating the adolescents' narratives into videos illustrating and teaching resistance skills.

---

2 For more about the use of role models and Social Cognitive Theory see Bandura (1986, 1989).

REAL VIDEOS

The goal of the videos in the *keepin' it REAL* curriculum is to teach communication and life skills while communicating an antidrug use norm. While the videos focus on the four refusal skills (REAL), they also teach decision-making and risk assessment. At the same time, by showing youth refusing offers they convey the impression that "cool" kids are not doing drugs and it is OK to be drug-free. Finally, we hope that after they practice these skills, they will feel like they can resist and resist effectively. This is called "refusal efficacy." All this is accomplished by creating realistic and interesting models for the four resistance skills with which youth can identify.

Since the initial development of the program, we have had a variety of cultural adaptations and updated versions of the program videos.[3] In each version, we follow a similar process when developing the videos. First, we recruited students and faculty from high schools in the local communities. We then conducted training sessions with the video production teams in which we overview the narrative philosophy of *kiR* and then present the four refusal strategies conceptually and provided exemplar narratives elicited in interviews with students from the community. The teams then create dramatic recreations of the strategies through an iterative process. Students draft script concepts and receive feedback from the project team. Then they draft scripts and again received feedback. We finalize scripts and the videos are shot. A "rough cut" or draft video is reviewed before the final edit.

Finally, in all adaptations of the *kiR* program, we produce a "making of the videos" that introduces the high school students who create the videos and highlight their reasons for being involved with the production. This video is used to start the program on the first day and not only introduces the concepts but also to increase identification with the teens in the videos. We choose high school students as the source of the message because they are "near peers"—slightly older members of their own community and age cohort. We are proud to report that some of the students who produced the videos in our original curriculum won regional Emmy awards for their work. At the same time, not only do the overall 10 lessons reduce alcohol, tobacco, and marijuana use (Hecht et al., 2006), but our analyses indicate that if students watched at least four videos with no other content, the curriculum has a similar effect (Warren et al., 2006). As a result, the *kiR* curriculum has been selected by the Surgeon General of the United States as one of the most effective culturally-grounded evidence-based prevention programs in the United States (2016) and is distributed nationally by Discovery Health and ETR Publishing, REAL Prevention, and Youthlight books. In 2009, the *kiR* curriculum was adopted for national and international distribution by D.A.R.E. America.

KEEPIN' IT D.A.R.E.

D.A.R.E. America has a long history in school-based drug prevention. Started in 1983 in Los Angeles, California, D.A.R.E. has grown into what is believed to be the largest school-based

---

3 For more information on some of these various cultural adaptations see Colby et al. (2013), Kulis et al. (2019), Cutrin et al. (2021), and Marsiglia et al. (2019).

drug prevention program in the world. While they have had great success disseminating their programs and their D.A.R.E. officers have proven to be highly effective prevention teachers (Hammond et al., 2008), the outcomes from their programs have been less than desirable. As a result, D.A.R.E. decided to adopt an existing evidence-based prevention program rather than create a new program of their own. We felt honored with the selected *kiR*. However, we did not realize what this meant for the further translation of the curriculum.

All school-based curricula involve three constituencies—the kids, the schools, and the prevention scientists. We had a long history of working with these in our community-based research practices. We view these constituencies as collaborators rather than clients or merely our target audience. As prevention scientists, we are committed to a curriculum that works for the kids that the teachers can teach. D.A.R.E., however, brings in other communities.

The first of these is D.A.R.E. America, itself a private, nonprofit organization led by former law enforcement officials. D.A.R.E. also consists of educators, mostly former and current teachers, as well as active law enforcement officers around the country. As an organization for almost 40 years at the time we write, D.A.R.E. has developed its own culture that reflects, in part, the law enforcement community. While they see themselves as involved in what is known as "community-based policing," they are still cops residing within a cop culture. As a result, the organization does not change rapidly. In addition, it has lived with constant criticism from the press and scientific community due to unfavorable research results in the past. As you can imagine, a trusting partnership was slow to build.

In addition to the D.A.R.E. itself, the program utilizes officers to deliver the curriculum in schools and they constitute a separate constituency. These officers work for local police forces that provide this service to the schools. This is sometimes part of their larger role as school resource officers. Within their own police organizations, they are sometimes derisively referred to as "kiddy cops," making their jobs a bit harder. As preventionists, they face the unique challenge of coming into someone else's classroom for a limited, usually for a 10-week period. Thus they are typically "outsiders" who represent authority and are unfamiliar with the students when the lessons start. They are still quintessential cops, yet at the same time, they have extensive training in public presentations, drug prevention, and classroom facilitation, making them more open to prevention science than many of their contemporaries. However, they are not teachers, and thus the curriculum itself—the written and visual resources that make us the lessons—needs to reflect the officers' needs as implementers;—a process we came to call "DARE-ification" or "DARIFYING" the lessons. We drafted, revised, pilot tested, redrafted, revised, and kept going until everyone was satisfied with the adapted program. Ultimately, the curriculum was implemented by D.A.R.E. in 2009 to very positive feedback within the organization and schools.

As evidenced by a three-year, multi-longitudinal study of D.A.R.E.'s programs, the keepin' it REAL curriculum has improved D.A.R.E.'s outcomes (Prevention Strategies, 2022). We also know that there has been a 25% increase in participation by middle school students since adopting *kiR*. We also know that the partnership has expanded to a new elementary curriculum that goes into the field starting January 2012. This means that in the U.S. alone, over 2 million youth are enrolled in *kiR*. This is in addition to youth in 45 countries around the world. This is an incredible opportunity to really see communication theory in practice; to teach about safe and responsible choices, improve self-control, planning, communication, and relationship skills, help them understand risks and consequences as well as the perspective of others, and learn to get and give help. Of course, in the end, we hope that students who receive the curriculum will lead healthier and safer drug-free lives. We are not naïve enough to think the *kiR* is the be all and end all in prevention or that we can save the world. But if we can "move the curve" on their skills and decrease unhealthy behaviors, it will all be worth it.

REFERENCES

Alberts, J. K., Miller-Rassulo, M., & Hecht, M. L. (1991). A typology of drug resistance strategies. *Journal of Applied Communication Research, 19*(3), 129–151. https://doi.org/10.1080/00909889109365299

Bandura, A. (1986). *Social foundations of thought and action: A social cognitive theory.* Prentice Hall.

Bandura, A. (1989). Human agency in social cognitive theory. *American Psychologist, 44*(9), 1175–1184. https://doi.org/10.1037/0003-066X.44.9.1175

Colby, M., Hecht, M. L., Miller-Day, M., Krieger, J. L., Syvertsen, A. K., Graham, J. W., & Pettigrew, J. (2013). Adapting school-based substance use prevention curriculum through cultural grounding: An exemplar of adaptation processes for rural schools. *American Journal of Community Psychology, 51,* 190–205. https://doi.org/10.1007/s10464-012-9524-8

Cutrín, O., Kulis, S., Maneiro, L., MacFadden, I., Navas, M. P., Alarcón, D., ... & Marsiglia, F. F. (2021). Effectiveness of the Mantente REAL program for preventing alcohol use in Spanish adolescents. *Psychosocial Intervention, 30*(3), 113–122. https://doi.org/10.7440/res64.2018.03

Gosin, M., Marsiglia, F. F., & Hecht, M. L. (2003). *keepin' it REAL*: A drug resistance curriculum tailored to the strengths and needs of pre-adolescents of the Southwest. *The Journal of Drug Education, 33*(2), 119–142. https://doi.org/10.2190/DXB9-1V2P-C27J-V69V

Hammond, A., Sloboda, Z., Tonkin, P., Stephens, R., Teasdale, B., Grey, S. F., & Williams, J. (2008). Do adolescents perceive police officers as credible instructors of substance abuse prevention programs? *Health Education Research, 23*(4), 682–696. https://doi.org/10.1093/her/cym036

Hastings, G., Stead, M., & Webb, J. (2004). Fear appeals in social marketing: strategic and ethical reasons for concern. *Psychology and Marketing, 21*(11), 961–986. https://doi.org/10.1002/mar.20043

Harrington. N. G. (1995). The effects of college students' alcohol resistance strategies. *Health Communication, 7*(4), 371–391. https://doi.org/10.1207/s15327027hc0704_5

Hecht, M. L., & Krieger, J. K. (2006). The principle of cultural grounding in school based substance use prevention: The Drug Resistance Strategies Project. *Journal of Language and Social Psychology, 25*(3), 301–319. https://doi.org/10.1177/0261927X06289476

Hecht, M. L., & Miller-Day, M. (2007). The Drug Resistance Strategies Project as translational research. *Journal of Applied Communication Research, 35*(4), 343–349. https://doi.org/10.1080/00909880701611086.

Kulis, S. S., Marsiglia, F. F., Medina-Mora, M. E., Nuño-Gutiérrez, B. L., Corona, M. D., & Ayers, S. L. (2021). Keepin'It REAL—Mantente REAL in Mexico: a cluster randomized controlled trial of a culturally adapted substance use prevention curriculum for early adolescents. *Prevention Science, 22*, 645–657. https://doi.org/10.1007/s11121-018-0956-8

Langer, E. J. (1989). *Mindfulness.* Addison Wesley.

Marsiglia, F. F., Medina-Mora, M. E., Gonzalvez, A., Alderson, G., Harthun, M., Ayers, S., ... & Kulis, S. (2019). Binational cultural adaptation of the keepin'it REAL substance use prevention program for adolescents in Mexico. *Prevention Science, 20*, 1125–1135. https://doi.org/10.1007/s11121-019-01034-0

Miller-Day, M., & Hecht, M.L. (2013). Narrative means to preventative ends: A Narrative engagement framework for designing prevention interventions. *Health Communication, 28*(7), 657–670. https://doi.org/10.1080/10410236.2012.762861

Pettigrew, J., Miller-Day, M., Krieger, J., & Hecht, M. L. (2011). Alcohol and other drug resistance strategies employed by rural adolescents. *Journal of Applied Communication Research, 39*(2), 103–122. https://doi.org/10.1080/00909882.2011.556139

Polkinghorne, D. E. (1988). *Narrative knowing and the human sciences.* State University of New York Press.

Prevention Strategies (January, 2022). An Evaluation of the "D.A.R.E.: keepin' it REAL" Elementary School Program Executive Summary. University of North Carolina, Greensboro.

Spitzberg, B. H., & Cupach, W. R. (1984). *Interpersonal communication competence.* Sage. U.S. Department of Health and Human Services (HHS), Office of the Surgeon General (2016). *Facing addiction in America: The Surgeon General's report on alcohol, drugs, and health.* HHS.

Warren, J. R., Hecht, M. L., Wagstaff, D. A., Elek, E., Ndiaye, K., Dustman, P., & Marsiglia, F. F. (2006). Communicating prevention: The effects of the keepin'it REAL classroom videotapes and televised PSAs on middle-school students' substance use. *Journal of Applied Communication Research, 34*(2), 209–227. https://doi.org/10.1080/00909880600574153

WEIGHT-RELATED COMMUNICATION: HELPFUL, HURTFUL, AND UNAVOIDABLE

Tricia J. Burke Analisa Arroyo Valerie J. Young
Texas State University University of Georgia Hanover College

The three of us started researching weight communication as graduate students at the University of Arizona. Tucson is pretty warm year-round and has a "West Coast" vibe. As a result, we noticed a lot of emphasis on body type and appearance as a proxy for "health," often upheld by this notion that we all have a moral obligation—a preoccupation—to be and look fit. These expectations for maintaining a toned and tanned physique may conflict with a typical college student lifestyle, however, with late nights and less-than-healthy eating and drinking patterns. In studying communication in close relationships, we naturally developed research interests around how people talk about their health behaviors and goals with other important people in their lives (e.g., romantic partners, friends, and family).

As communication scholars, we take seriously our role in highlighting the ways in which health communication transactions impact people's well-being. Together, we have examined communication in terms of interpersonal health promotion (i.e., social support and social influence messages) and body image conversations (i.e., "fat talk"). Given that messages of health and wellness are connected to body size and weight (Mackert & Schorb, 2022), weight-related topics of conversation—like diet and exercise—are common in interpersonal relationships. These are tough conversations to have, however, because of social pressures and stigma surrounding body size and weight, as well as the relational and personal context involved.

In general, the heightened focus on weight as an indicator of health propagates unrealistic body standards that undermine individuals' body image specifically, and their mental and physical health more broadly. While our intention in talking with others about weight and health behaviors may be honorable (after all, we are *supposed* to want them to live well and be healthy!), they can also be hurtful conversations (after all, *none of your business*!). These conversations are challenging because they unearth societal expectations about how we look and act and do not always reflect the positive acceptance of who we are—regardless of body size and health status. In this chapter, we review research about communication patterns concerning health behaviors in close relationships and describe some of the relational and social pressures concerning weight-related behaviors in relation to health.

HEALTH PROMOTION IN CLOSE RELATIONSHIPS

Close relationships are an important context in which to understand health promotion (Umberson, 1992), particularly when it comes to certain lifestyle behaviors, as our friends, family members, and romantic partners participate in these behaviors with us—we eat together, walk together, sit on the couch together, etc. Research in this area generally focuses on romantic partners and suggests that partners try to motivate (Dailey et al., 2010), influence, and support (Burke & Segrin, 2014) each other to be healthier. Because these conversations also occur outside of romantic relationships, we designed a study to understand health promotion messages across three different close relationship types: romantic partners, family members (especially mothers), and friends.

We collected data from women at three different universities; 198 answered questions about their communication with their mothers, 269 answered questions about their romantic partner, and 170 answered questions about a close friend. Mothers' weight-related communication was the most consistently associated with the daughters' outcomes (physical activity, healthy eating, body appreciation, body dissatisfaction), followed by romantic partners, with limited results for friends (Arroyo et al., 2020). Similarly, in comparing the different forms of communication, *social influence* was the most consistently associated with these outcomes.

Social influence is often understood in terms of positive and negative messages. Positive influence messages evoke positive emotion, whereas negative influence messages evoke negative emotion (Butterfield & Lewis, 2002). If I say to my friend "Let's train for a 10k together. It will be fun!" it reflects positive influence, but if I say "I am going to be disappointed in you if you don't do this 10k with me," it reflects negative influence. When positive types of messages are part of a relationship, we see a cycle of positivity (more positive communication, positive feelings about one's partner, and more health-promoting behavior choices). But negatively framed messages, such as making a partner feel guilty when they make unhealthy choices or pressuring them to change, can be counterproductive. This pattern was evident in the mother-daughter results from our study. Specifically, positive social influence from mothers was related to more healthy eating, body appreciation, and physical activity, whereas the opposite was true for negative social influence from mothers (Arroyo et al., 2020).

Although romantic partners were not the most prominent source of health promotion in that study, research has consistently shown that romantic relationships are consequential when it comes to health promotion (Burke & Segrin, 2014; Markey et al., 2015; Young & Burke, 2017). Getting takeout and playing video games sounds like a fun night in, but we need to be careful about doing these kinds of activities often because perceiving one's relationship to be a source of "unhealthy" behaviors is associated with lower well-being and relationship satisfaction (Young & Burke, 2017). It is not surprising, then, that key areas of health promotion in romantic relationships include getting one's partner to change what they eat, how much they eat, and the type and amount of exercise their partner gets (Young et al., 2019). These kinds of health promotion and regulation happen in same-sex and opposite-sex relational partners.

Whereas gay men are especially likely to try to regulate their partners' eating behaviors, lesbian women are more likely to engage in regulation when coupled with a heavy partner (Markey et al., 2015). This kind of regulation may not be recommended, however. When people encourage and compliment their partner using positivity, their partners report that it works—they do more healthy things and fewer unhealthy things (Young et al., 2019). On the other hand, when people use more negative messages to get their partner to be healthy (like trying to guilt a partner into exercise), their partners actually report *more unhealthy* behaviors.

These findings show that communication about diet and exercise can be tricky, particularly because weight and health are personal topics. They are intricately connected to individuals' presumed responsibility and worth. No one wants to feel like they are nagging their partner to exercise or like they are being judged by their partner for not exercising enough. As a result, when designing health promotion messages, we understand that they might not always be well-received, and we may consider *perceived constraints* against communicating these messages (Burke & Segrin, 2017) or avoiding these topics altogether (Ray et al., 2019). In other words, people might hesitate to engage in weight-related health promotion with a partner if they feel that it might harm their relationship.

Our research demonstrates that there are several constraints that might limit our expression of influence. These can include relational resources constraints like, "It is better for our relationship to avoid talking about my partner's exercise," arousal management constraints like, "Discussing my partner's exercise makes me uncomfortable," and interaction goal constraints like, "I don't want to discuss my partner's exercise because I want to respect their privacy" (Burke & Segrin, 2017; Ray et al., 2019). When we are less worried about these constraints, we are more likely to use influence messages to encourage our partners to engage in healthier behaviors (Burke & Segrin, 2017) and less likely to engage in topic avoidance (Ray et al., 2019). Although it is advisable to use care in communicating weight-related messages in close relationships, avoiding these topics may be problematic, as people engage in fewer healthy diet and exercise behaviors when their partners avoid these discussions (Ray et al., 2019).

In addition to influence, partners motivate each other to be healthier by communicating health-specific social support messages (Burke & Segrin, 2014). Supportive messages reflect reminders and compliments about engaging in diet and exercise (Burke & Segrin, 2014)—which might sound like: "it's been a while since you played basketball; why don't you set up a game this week?"—or seeking support for goals (Crowley et al., 2020)—which may sound like: "I need to do a yoga class. Will you watch the kids so I can go?" In our research on opposite-sex partners' communication and health behaviors, we found that men who perceive positive influence messages from their partners also perceive more support from their partners, which is then related to them engaging in healthier diet and exercise behaviors (Burke & Segrin, 2014). In contrast, men who perceive negative influence messages from their partners perceive lower support from their partners, which is then related to them engaging in fewer healthy diet and exercise behaviors.

Clearly, supportive messages are valuable when it comes to promoting healthy behaviors and relational and mental well-being, and may even help during conversations about body image. For instance, in another study, we found that perceiving partner health support (e.g., "my partner is supportive of my attempts to exercise") was related to lower conflict in relationships (Burke et al., 2012). Additionally, research on body-related communication between same-sex partners suggests that communicating with partners while completing a body image assessment together helped individuals reexamine their body ideals, which benefited their body satisfaction (Markey et al., 2017). These findings highlight the importance of understanding weight communication related to body image.

SOCIAL COMPONENTS OF WEIGHT COMMUNICATION AND BODY IMAGE

In addition to conversations about our partners' bodies and behaviors, another way that weight-related communication occurs in our close relationships involves discussing our own bodies with others. One way we do this is through "fat talk," or the everyday comments we make about our body shape, size, and weight. Examples include: "I need to go on a diet," "I know I shouldn't eat this," or "Does this make me look fat?" These comments are self-evaluative and often negative. Because we are taught that bodies are connected to self-worth, these sorts of comments are interpersonal reinforcements of sociocultural norms around our bodies, teaching us and others that our bodies object to be evaluated.

Many scholars who originally investigated fat talk were interested in the social norms of it: who did it and why? However, given the prevalence of individuals who are dissatisfied with their bodies in one way or another, we thought these comments might be driven by actual beliefs about one's body, which might be consequential to well-being. In one study, we investigated undergraduate men's and women's body weight, mental health, and engagement in fat talk across a two-week span. At the end of these two weeks, we found that people who reported being more dissatisfied with their bodies also reported engaging in more fat talk and that engaging in more fat talk was related to higher levels of depression and perceived pressure to be thin (Arroyo & Harwood, 2012). It seems, then, that fat talk is more than a normative behavior, and more than something we do because other people—friends, family, partners, strangers—do it. Instead, it seems to be rooted in individuals' negative beliefs about their bodies.

We wondered what impact society's objectification of our bodies plays in this process. That is, society treats our—especially women's—bodies as objects for the use, pleasure, and evaluation of others. Fat talk, then, is an extension of *objectification* into the realm of inter-personal relationships; individuals engage in fat talk as a way to self-objectify, treating their own bodies as objects as a site of evaluation. Our research investigated this prediction in a sample of women and found that self-objectification was related to engaging in more fat talk, and fat talk, in turn, was related to lower well-being, in the form of higher body dissatisfaction, drive for thinness, bulimic tendencies, and depression (Arroyo et al., 2014).

Because fat talk is a normative and expected behavior among women, wherein women conform to the norms of their peers and make self-disparaging comments to "fit in," we extended our previous research to study young women and a close friend. To some degree, this sort of talk fosters relational connection, intimacy, and closeness, but we found that female friends who engage in more fat talk with one another also report higher body dissatisfaction, drive for thinness, bulimia, depression, and dieting behaviors (Arroyo et al., 2014). This finding highlights another problem with fat talk, which is that fat talk invites more fat talk (Arroyo et al., 2014). So, in order to understand ways to counteract this problematic behavior, we examined responses to fat talk in a sample of female friends. We found that women who thought that their friends were more accepting of them during fat talk interactions (showed positive regard, warmth, and attentiveness during interactions) reported less binging and purging behaviors, and healthier eating and exercise behaviors (Arroyo et al., 2017).

These kinds of body-related communication also occur on social media. It is likely that you have seen friends post their daily workouts or stats on social media. We were curious about how these online, mediated posts may be related to interpersonal communication about our bodies. On one hand, our research indicates that individuals may be maintaining sociocultural pressures about the body online, with interpersonal and mass communication working together to cultivate an ideal body image that could be damaging to one's self-concept. Indeed, we found that seeing friends' fitness posts more frequently was related to engaging in more self-disparaging comments about their own bodies and weight-related behaviors (Arroyo & Brunner, 2016); this relationship was especially strong for individuals who had the tendency to engage in social comparisons with others. On the other hand, though, we found that when people saw more exercise-related posts from their social media connections, they reported being more concerned about their weight (Burke & Rains, 2018), as well as higher levels of healthy eating behaviors and exercising (Arroyo & Brunner, 2016). Again, for people who tended to make upward social comparisons—or comparing oneself to someone of superior fitness—seeing more exercise-related posts from social media connections was related to more positive exercise attitudes (Burke & Rains, 2018).

Together, these results suggest that viewing body-related posts on social media may encourage individuals to engage in healthy behaviors. Yet, doing so does not come without consequence, as it is also related to people's self-disparaging comments, body dissatisfaction, and being more concerned about their weight. This research represents a cyclical pattern for how people use social media and interpersonal communication to identify a need to change or improve their own bodies. These sociocultural norms and expectations are significant because they may precipitate health promotion conversations in close relationships.

CONCLUSION

This chapter summarizes some of our research on weight-related communication. These conversations are so common that we may not notice them, question their potential consequences, or realize how they perpetuate social ideals. Although we may have good intentions in trying to improve our own and our close others' well-being, we want to acknowledge the complex findings presented here. There are certainly instances in which communication may promote healthy behaviors, but there are plenty of instances in which it can undermine our health, well-being, and relationships.

Our research demonstrates that it is important to consider the context when creating these messages and to try to take a supportive, rather than a regulatory, approach. In other words, think carefully about how the message might be received by another person and come up with a message that sounds affirming ("Hey, I've been wanting to try this new salad recipe; do you want to try it with me?" or "What do you think about inviting some friends to go for a hike this weekend?") rather than derogatory ("If you keep neglecting your health, you are not going to be around for our son's high school graduation" or "I am getting rid of all of the junk food in our house because you can't control yourself.").

Keep in mind that your friends or romantic partners may have different ideas about what it means to be healthy or unhealthy—and that these meanings are typically rooted in dominant sociocultural discourses, as well as personal experiences and history. Try talking about these meanings and behaviors without judgment. It is important to remember that the concepts of "health" and "wellness" are socially constructed and may fail to foster acceptance for ourselves and our close others—and that we are all more than *just* bodies.

REFERENCES

Arroyo, A., & Brunner, S. (2016). Negative body talk as an outcome of friends' fitness posts on social networking sites: Body surveillance and social comparison as potential moderators. *Journal of Applied Communication Research, 44*(3), 216–235. https://doi.org/10.1080/00909882.2016.1192293

Arroyo, A., Burke, T. J., & Young, V. J. (2020). The role of close others in promoting weight management and body image outcomes: An application of confirmation, self-determination, social control, and social support. *Journal of Social and Personal Relationships, 37*(3), 1030–1050. https://doi.org/https://doi.org/10.1177/0265407519886066

Arroyo, A., & Harwood, J. (2012). Exploring the causes and consequences of engaging in fat talk. *Journal of Applied Communication Research, 40*(2), 167–187. https://doi.org/10.1080/0090988 2.2012.654500

Arroyo, A., Segrin, C., & Harwood, J. (2014). Appearance-related communication mediates the link between self-objectification and health and well-being outcomes. *Human Communication Research, 40*(4), 463–482. https://doi.org/10.1111/hcre.12036

Arroyo, A., Segrin, C., Harwood, J., & Bonito, J. A. (2017). Co-rumination of fat talk and weight control practices: An application of confirmation theory. *Health Communication, 32*(4), 438–450. https://doi.org/10.1080.10410236.2016.1140263

Burke, T. J., & Rains, S. A. (2018). The paradoxical outcomes of observing others' exercise behavior on social network sites: Friends' exercise posts, exercise attitudes, and weight concern. *Health Communication, 34*(4), 475–483. https://doi.org/10.1080/10410236.2018.1428404

Burke, T. J., Randall, A. K., Corkery, S. A., Young, V. J., & Butler, E. A. (2012). "You're going to eat *that*?" Relationship processes and conflict among mixed weight couples. *Journal of Social and Personal Relationships, 29*(8), 1109–1130. https://doi.org/10.1177/0265407512451199

Burke, T. J., & Segrin, C. (2014). Examining diet- and exercise-related communication in romantic relationships: Associations with health behaviors. *Health Communication, 29*(9), 877–887. https://doi.org/10.1080/10410236.2013.811625

Burke, T. J., & Segrin, C. (2017). Weight-related social control in couples: Associations with motives, constraints, and health behaviors. *Communication Research, 44*(3), 348–366. https://doi.org/10.1177/0093650215590606

Butterfield, R. M., & Lewis, M. A. (2002). Health-related social influence: A social-ecological perspective on tactic use. *Journal of Social and Personal Relationships, 19*(4), 505–526. https://doi.org/10.1177/0265407502019004050

Crowley, J., Burke, T. J., Denes, A., Allred, R., & Carberry, E. (2020). Relational turbulence in the wake of weight transitions: A Support marshaling analysis. *Personal Relationships, 27*(3), 630–651. https://doi.org/10.1111/pere.12335

Dailey, R. M., Richards, A. A., & Romo, L. K. (2010). Communication with significant others about weight management: The role of confirmation in weight management attitudes and behaviors. *Communication Research, 37*(5), 644–673. https://doi.org/10.1177/0093650210362688

Mackert, N., & Schorb, F. (2022). Introduction to the special issue: Public health, healthism, and fatness. *Fat Studies, 11*(1), 1–7. https://doi.org/10.1080/21604851.2021.1911486

Markey, C. H., Gillen, M. N., August, K. J., Markey, P. M., & Nave, C. S. (2017). Does "body talk" improve body satisfaction among same-sex couples? *Body Image, 23*, 103–108. https://doi.org/10.1016/j.bodyim.2017.08.004

Markey, C. N., Markey, P. M., August, K. J., & Nave, C. S. (2015). Gender, BMI, and eating regulation in the context of same-sex and heterosexual couples. *Journal of Behavioral Medicine, 39*(3), 398–407. https://doi.org/10.1007/s10865-015-9700-z

Ray, C., Burke, T. J., Young, V. J., & Curran, M. A. (2019). Enacting social control to encourage healthier partner diet and exercise behavior: Considering the roles of constraints and topic avoidance. *Southern Communication Journal, 84*(5), 301–313. https://doi.org/10.1080/1041794X.2019.1644665

Umberson, D. (1992). Gender, marital status and the social control of health behavior. *Social Science & Medicine, 34*(8), 907–917. https://doi.org/10.1016/0277-9536(92)90259-S

Young, V. J., & Burke, T. J. (2017) Self, partner, and relationship motivations for healthy and unhealthy behaviors, *Health Psychology Report, 5*(3), 219–226. https://doi.org/10.5114/hpr.2017.65221

Young, V. J., Burke, T. J., & Curran, M. A. (2019). Interpersonal effects of health-related social control: Positive and negative influence, partner health transformations, and relationship quality. *Journal of Social and Personal Relationships, 36*(11–12), 3986–4004. https://doi.org/10.1177/0265407519846565

STRATEGIC USE OF HEALTH COMMUNICATION: IMPLICATIONS FOR RESPONDING TO THE COVID-19 PANDEMIC

Gary L. Kreps
George Mason University

INTRODUCTION

This chapter examines the applications of strategic health communication to enhance the delivery of care and the promotion of health during critical public health emergencies, such as the COVID-19 pandemic. Pandemics are complex health problems that are difficult to respond to, especially when they first arise because there is so much that we do not know about them. To respond effectively to the COVID-19 pandemic, we needed to find out what the causes of the pandemic were, how the virus spread, what the best available strategies were for preventing contagion, how we could diagnose when people become infected, and what the best strategies are for treating infection. Over the course of the pandemic, we have learned a lot about these important issues, but there is still much more we need to learn to cope with this and future pandemic health risks effectively. As we learned more about the COVID-19 virus, we found that even partial answers to important questions helped health officials to communicate relevant pandemic information to key public audiences to help these people determine how to best protect themselves, their family members, friends, and others from becoming infected with the virus and helped them to decide what they should do if they did contract the virus. Sadly however, there have been serious problems with public health communication about the COVID-19 pandemic, especially in the United States, where many people have been (and many still are) confused and misinformed about COVID health risks and about the best strategies for preventing and responding to these risks.

This chapter begins with a description of the study of health communication to identify key topics, issues, and strategies that are most relevant to effective communication during a pandemic. Then, the chapter presents key principles about how strategic, evidence-based health communication can be applied to responding to serious pandemic health threats. We have learned that the kinds of communication problems that have occurred during the COVID pandemic are not unique. There are often serious communication problems related to the delivery of care and promotion of health, especially when confronting complex, new, and evolving health problems. Unfortunately, we often underestimate the complexities of communicating meaningfully about these kinds of challenging health problems. Too often, health care and health promotion efforts are guided by good intentions, precedent, and expedience that have led to mistakes, while these efforts should have been guided by strategic health communication knowledge. We have learned that the complexity of achieving health goals, such as informing health-related decision-making and encouraging the adoption of recommended health promotion behaviors, demands strategic evidence-based guidance from relevant health communication research and theory.

DEVELOPMENT OF HEALTH COMMUNICATION INQUIRY

Health communication has developed as a rapidly growing and exciting applied area of inquiry that examines the powerful influences of human and mediated communication on health care and health promotion (Kreps & Bonaguro, 2009). Health communication inquiry is typically problem-based, focused on explicating, examining, and addressing important and troubling health care and health promotion issues. These issues often include difficulties in promoting active coordination and collaboration in the delivery of health care, challenges to promoting adoption of recommended health behaviors, demands to reduce and ultimately eliminate inadvertent errors that jeopardize the quality of health care, attempts to meet unmet health information needs for supporting informed health decision-making, and the quest to overcome serious inequities in care that lead to health disparities and poor health outcomes (Kreps, 2011a; Neuhauser & Kreps, 2010). These are serious issues that demand attention from health communication scholars to help refine health promotion activities and improve health outcomes, especially during public health emergencies, such as the COVID-19 pandemic. How can we use health communication inquiry to enhance health outcomes during health crises?

COMMUNICATION AND HEALTH OUTCOMES

The applied nature of health communication inquiry is firmly grounded in the broadly accepted conclusion, based on a wide body of research, that developing effective health communication programs can facilitate improvements in the delivery of care and the promotion of health. In this way, health communication scholars can ultimately help enhance health outcomes (Kreps & Maibach, 2008; Parrott, 2008). Unfortunately, it appears that health care and health promotion practitioners have often been slow to recognize and implement the best health communication knowledge to help them accomplish their complex health promotion goals. (We have learned this the hard way during the COVID pandemic).

Ask yourself, how often health communication research has been used to guide the development, implementation, and evaluation of public health education and promotion programs? (Not often enough)! How often does health communication research guide health care delivery strategies for eliciting full diagnostic information, accomplishing informed consent, or promoting adherence to health care recommendations? (Very rarely)! Too often, health care and promotion programs and practices are not guided by relevant health communication research. The complexity of achieving desired health communication goals, such as influencing entrenched health behaviors (such as smoking, nutrition, exercise, and safer sexual practices) and promoting informed health-related decision-making (such as engaging in disease screening, adopting prevention behaviors, or getting vaccinated) demand strategic guidance from relevant and rigorous research and theory. This chapter will describe how this can be done.

A large and developing body of health communication research powerfully illustrates the centrality of communication processes in achieving important health care and health promotion goals (Kreps, 2011a; Kreps & Bonaguro, 2009). Previous work has reported a series of seminal studies that illustrate the powerful influences of communication strategies and programs on health knowledge, behaviors, and outcomes (Kreps, 2017a; 2017b; 2012; Kreps & O'Hair, 1995). For example, research by Greenfield et al. (1985) clearly demonstrates the positive influences of increased patient/provider participation in directing health care treatment on achieving desired health outcomes. Kreps and Chapelsky Massimilla (2002) also report many studies that illustrate the positive effects of communication interventions on cancer-related health outcomes.

Communication research increasingly informs the development of public health policies and legislation, including policies to prevent and respond to serious health risks, promote equity in health care, and improve media coverage of important health issues (Atkin & Smith, 2010; Guttman, 2010; Kunkel, 2010; National Cancer Institute, 2008, Noar et al, 2009; Siu, 2010). Yet, there is so much more that can be done by health communication scholars to improve public health and wellness. While health communication scholarship has already made important contributions to improving health promotion, health communication inquiry has the potential to make even more important and wide-ranging contributions to improving public health. This is evident now due to the unprecedented problems with contagion, hospitalizations, and deaths experienced during the COVID-19 pandemic.

ADDRESSING IMPORTANT HEALTH COMMUNICATION ISSUES

To really make a positive difference in health outcomes, health communication scholars must carefully identify and examine the critical issues confronting at-risk populations, health care providers, family caregivers, and others participating in the modern health care system and then design studies to address these important health problems. The COVID-19 pandemic is a vivid example of one of these critical health issues that demand effective communication, but many other serious health problems demand good communication of relevant health information. These difficult health challenges may involve confronting deadly diseases (such as cancer, heart disease, and HIV/AIDS, coping with environmental calamities (such as floods, hurricanes, tsunamis, and forest fires), as well responding to acts of violence, warfare, and terrorism that too often threaten lives and well-being. We need studies that will examine the key communication factors that influence these critical health issues. Major health issues in modern society are covered regularly by the popular media (radio, television, magazines, and newspapers), reported by independent agencies in major reports and news conferences (such as reports prepared by the Institute of Medicine), and studied by important federal health agencies like the National Institutes of Health and the Centers for Disease Control and Prevention. A sampling of the repercussions of these serious problems include limited access to care when needed, low quality of health care services provided for many consumers (especially during emergencies when health care delivery systems are overloaded and many consumers need intensive care), medical errors that often occur in the delivery of care during complex and novel health crises, inequities in health outcomes between privileged and less privileged populations, limited availability and access to relevant health information, lack of sensitivity in the delivery of care, ineffective health education and health promotion programs, poor consumer adherence with health recommendations, and failure to engage in recommended behaviors to help detect and avoid health risks. Health communication scholars need to design studies to examine the communication factors that are related to these important public health issues (Kreps, 2022).

Current evidence suggests that most, if not all, of these important health issues are directly related to the effectiveness of health communication. For example, some of the serious issues that threaten the delivery of high-quality care, including the insidious recurrence of medical errors, lack of consumer adherence with treatment recommendations, and poor levels of active consumer participation in health care decision-making have all been linked to the effectiveness of health communication (Greenfield et al., 1985, Kreps & Bonaguro, 2009). Evidence suggests that these health care delivery issues are closely related to miscommunication and misinformation, lack of provider-consumer cooperation, and poor health information sharing (DiMatteo, & Lepper, 1998; Kreps et al., 2011). Similarly, serious disparities in health outcomes for poor, at-risk, vulnerable, and minority populations have also been related to the effectiveness of health communication

(Dutta & Kreps, 2013; Kim & Kreps, 2022). Evidence suggests that disparities in health outcomes are closely related to poor consumer access to relevant health information, lack of consumer understanding about prevention and treatment opportunities, ineffective communication relationships between health care providers and consumers, as well as mistrust and intercultural communication barriers within the modern health care system (Eysenbach & Kohnler, 2002; Kreps, 2006). Challenges with achieving health promotion goals have also been connected to the effectiveness of public health communication education, campaign, and intervention programs designed to influence health behaviors (Dutta-Bergman, 2005; Hornik, 2002; Kreps, 2007, 2011a). These are all critical communication issues that deserve close attention from health communication researchers. Ambitious health communication studies need to be designed to directly address the serious communication problems that limit the effectiveness of health care and health promotion. Such studies should focus in on examining the critical communication processes at play in the delivery of care and promotion of health, while also examining the larger societal, institutional, and cultural communication influences on health and health care.

THE NEED TO CAREFULLY STUDY HEALTH COMMUNICATION ISSUES

To improve health care and health promotion, health communication scholars must take their work seriously, conduct large-scale studies evaluating health communication programs, practices, and policies, going the extra mile to translate health communication research into practice (Kreps et al., 2002). Taking health communication scholarship seriously means not only asking important health communication research questions, but also conducting rigorous and far-reaching studies that generate valid, reliable, and generalizable data that can effectively inform health care and health promotion practices (Kreps, 2001; Kreps, 2011b). Serious health communication researchers take great care to meticulously design studies to accurately measure key health communication concepts, processes, and outcomes with both precision and depth. This must involve efforts to widely disseminate and implement findings by actively translating and transforming raw health communication research findings into practical and usable health care/promotion programs and policies. This demands that researchers carefully test the efficacy of interventions by monitoring outcomes (both positive and negative outcomes) of carefully implemented health communication programs within representative health care systems serving at-risk populations.

To really make a difference, health communication scholarship must provide important insights into best practices for delivering health care and promoting health. Research must chronicle what works well and what is causing problems in the delivery of care and promotion of health. The quality of research that health communication scholars conduct is directly related to the potential for this research to inform health policies and practices. Care must be taken to rigorously design and conduct health communication studies to generate the most accurate, valid, and revealing data to demystify the many complexities of health care and health promotion. New models and theories should be developed, tested, and refined to help describe and predict the intricate influences of communication within health systems. Innovative methods should be employed to study the complex communication processes that enable the effective delivery of care and the promotion of health.

The demand for engaged health communication research that examines communication practices and recommends refined policies is most apparent when considering the glaring need to evaluate the failed communication responses in the United States to the COVID-19 pandemic (Kim & Kreps, 2020; Kreps, 2021). What have we learned from the problems experienced in the U.S. during the pandemic concerning the rampant spread of dangerous health misinformation and disinformation, politically motivated conspiracy theory campaigns that confused the public about causes, effects, and responses to the pandemic, concerted efforts by public figures (including former President Trump) to discourage the public from following prevention guidelines (such as social distancing and mask-wearing), hostile public attacks on the credibility and motivations of noted health experts who recommended adoption of evidence-based public health prevention mandates, and growing public hesitance toward accepting life-saving vaccinations that all combined to allow the COVID virus to spread wildly and kill more than one million Americans, more deaths per capita than any other nation? We need engaged health communication research to guide public communication responses that can help avoid similar health tragedies when confronting future serious societal health threats (Kreps, 2022).

Establishing Relevant Partnerships

A major strategy for translating health communication inquiry into practice depends on developing meaningful interdisciplinary, interprofessional, and community-based partnerships with scholars, health care providers, consumers, administrators, government agency representatives, support organization members, and public policymakers. These collaborative partnerships are instrumental in helping health communication scholars effectively design, implement, and institutionalize the best evidence-based health communication strategies and interventions within society. It is clear that although health communication scholars have important expertise concerning the process of communication, they certainly do not have many of the answers needed about how health care systems work, how consumers behave, and how to influence institutional and public health policies. Establishing collaborations with key health care system partners can help provide needed expertise and answers for addressing these important application issues effectively.

A good first step for developing meaningful health communication research partnerships is to establish research collaborations with scholars from other related disciplines, such as public health, health education, epidemiology, the social sciences, and health professional fields. For example, Kreps and Maibach (2008) make a strong case for the synergistic opportunities that can derive from collaborations between health communication and public health scholars, citing complementary, yet distinct, areas of expertise, theoretical grounding, methodological orientation, and intervention strategies. Major federal funding agencies have begun requesting grant applications from research that represent different, yet complementary, disciplines and research areas (Kreps, in-press-A). These funding agencies recognize the unique contributions, benefits, and insights that multidisciplinary research cooperation can provide.

Community-based collaborations are also critically important for supporting the applications of health communication research into practice. Good partners for increasing the applications of health communication knowledge include representatives from government agencies, health care delivery systems, nonprofit associations, social service agencies, advocacy organizations, consumer groups, at-risk populations, and even corporations. It is only through these community-based collaborations that we can effectively translate compelling research findings into products, programs, policies, and practices that will be adopted within the modern health care system. Community partners have the embedded health system expertise that communication scholars desperately need to collaboratively introduce new health communication programs into health systems and help to refine these programs so they will work effectively over time.

Community participative research and intervention programs have shown great potential to facilitate applications of research results into health care practices (Minkler, 2000; Minkler & Wallerstein, 2002). Community partners can help health communication scholars learn the best inside strategies for gathering meaningful data from respondents, for interpreting research results within the framework of cultural contexts, for designing usable and effective communication interventions, for testing these interventions in action within real health settings, and for implementing and sustaining these interventions within social systems (Neuhauser, 2001; Neuhauser & Kreps, in-press). Actively engaging community partners in the applied research process can impart a strong sense of ownership in the research and intervention processes among these community partners, that can have major influences on minimizing potential community resistance to accepting the interventions and encouraging cooperation in the implementation and institutionalization of health communication programs, tools, and policies (Kreps, 2007).

Developing, Sustaining, and Disseminating Effective Health Communication Programs

It is imperative that health communication scholars not only conduct relevant health communication research, but also take concerted efforts to use their research findings to guide the development of evidence-based health communication programs to enhance the delivery of care and promotion of health. Exemplar health communication programs can include evidence-based policies and practices for the delivery of care (such as protocols for conducting patient interviews, guidelines for making decisions about triaging patients for treatment priority in emergency rooms, and forms for guiding and recording informed consent for treatment), health education tools and media (such as interactive tailored websites for helping smokers learn about strategies for smoking cessation, video games for sensitiz-ing adolescents about the importance of good nutrition, and online training programs for helping health care providers develop skills for communicating with patients from diverse backgrounds), strategic health communication campaigns (such as media campaigns that encourage parents to get their children vaccinated, school-based programs to educate chil-dren about the dangers of drug abuse, and comprehensive multimedia education programs to help new parents care for their children). Not only can health communication scholars provide relevant data for guiding the development of these health care and health promotion programs, but they can also gather formative evaluation data for refining these programs and summative evaluation data for assessing program impact and value (Abbatangelo-Gray et al., 2007; Kreps, 2002).

It is also important to develop new and effective strategies for disseminating relevant health communication knowledge to health care system participants who can use this information for accessing needed care, guiding health-related decision-making, and pro-moting health and well-being. A first step for broad dissemination of health communica-tion research findings is to expand publication and presentation of health communication research in scholarly outlets outside of the communication discipline, including at relevant conferences and in important journals from related disciplines (such as public health, health education, health psychology, health sociology, medicine, nursing, and other health profes-sional fields), and well as at interdisciplinary conferences and health journals. These presen-tations and publications can help spur interdisciplinary collaborations, and many of these scholarly outlets have greater exposure to the popular media and health professionals than most communication conferences and journals. However, scholarly conferences and jour-nals may be unfamiliar venues for those without advanced scientific training and are not likely to reach many health care consumers, caregivers, health care administrators, public health officials, or policymakers.

Efforts need to be taken to identify appropriate communication channels for eas-ily reaching and influencing broader audiences of consumers, caregivers, administrators, government officials, and other policymakers. For example, popular magazines, websites, blogs, radio and television programs, newspapers, and special audience presentations can have greater public reach than typical scholarly outlets. Moreover, health communication research must be translated out of academic jargon and into language and images that are familiar and meaningful to targeted audiences (see for example, Kreps & Goldin, 2009). Health communication scholars must learn how to become public scholars and develop needed communication skills to reach and influence diverse audiences, including commu-nicating effectively with vulnerable and at-risk populations. Participation in health fairs, media interviews, briefings for administrators and government representatives, public pre-sentations, public forums, training programs for health care providers and consumers, and publication of popular articles in different online and print outlets can go a long way in broadening dissemination of health communication knowledge. Interactive dissemination programs can encourage the exchange of questions and answers about health communication issues that can clarify the meanings and implications of health communication research. Some fruitful interactive channels for health communication dissemination include participation in support groups (both online and in-person groups), training programs, and websites that allow information exchange.

CONCLUSION

By conducting relevant engaged and translational research and disseminating this work widely, health communication scholars can develop, implement, and sustain important health communication programs, tools, policies, practices, and intervention to enhance health outcomes. This is especially important when we consider how such research could help to avoid the kinds of serious communication problems experienced in the United States when responding to the COVID-19 pandemic.

U.S. government agencies could have improved the ways they responded to the COVID-19 pandemic by engaging in strategic, evidence-based health and risk communication activities. For example, formative health communication evaluation research concerning the pandemic could have been used to help identify the key audiences who were at greatest risk from the pandemic, what their primary information needs were related to the pandemic, the best information sources and communication channels to use with different audiences, and the most influential, understandable, and usable relevant messages to provide to specific audiences to help guide good decision-making about preventing spread of the virus and responding effectively when people became infected. Important information sources, including representatives from the Office of the President, Congress, the CDC, the FDA, local public health departments, health care providers, media sources (reporters, writers, and celebrities), first responders, and other influential sources should have worked collaboratively to establish the most accurate and up-to-date pandemic information messages and guidelines to uniformly share with the public for minimizing confusion and encouraging public adherence with health promotion recommendations. In addition, far-reaching and regularly updated communication campaigns should have been developed that utilized a variety of media channels, including television, radio, newspapers, and social media to provide clear, coordinated, relevant, and updated information about the pandemic to counter potential misinformation and promote public understanding about the seriousness of the pandemic health risks. In addition, local in-person and multi-level mediated public information exchange programs (forums, call centers, talk shows, chat rooms, etc.) should have been established to enable people to seek information, recommendations, and referrals and to access needed social support during the pandemic. If these kinds of strategic communication programs had been implemented effectively, contagion could have been significantly reduced and many lives could have been saved. However, these kinds of health communication guidelines should be implemented for guiding responses to future public health crises.

As a student of health communication, you can learn how to access relevant and accurate information to promote your own health, navigate the health care system, and serve as an effective advocate for your friends and family who may be confronting health issues. Your communication skills and insights can enable you to help reduce health risks and support health promotion efforts. Health communication inquiry is a most relevant and exciting area of study that has direct implications for improving health outcomes.

REFERENCES

Abbatangelo-Gray, J., Kennedy, M.G., Cole, G.E., Baur, C., Bernhardt, J., Cho, H., Denniston, R., Farrelly, M., Figueroa, M.E., Hornik, R., Kreps, G.L., Middlestadt, S., Parrott, R., Slater, M., Snyder, L., & Storey, D. (2007). Guidance for evaluating mass communication health initiatives: Summary of an expert panel discussion sponsored by the Centers for Disease Control and Prevention. *Evaluation and the Health Professions, 30*(3), 229–253. https://doi.org/10.1177/0163278707304041

Atkin, C.K., & Smith, S.W. (2010). Improving communication practices to reduce breast cancer environmental risks. *Health Communication, 25*(6–7), 587–588. https://doi.org/10.1080/10410236.2010.496836

DiMatteo, M.R., & Lepper, H.S. (1998). Promoting adherence to courses of treatment: Mutual collaboration in the physician-patient relationship. In L.D. Jackson & B.K. Duffy (Eds.). *Health communication research: A guide to developments and directions.* (pp. 75–86). Greenwood Press.

Dutta, M.J., & Kreps, G.L. (Eds). (2013). *Reducing health disparities: Communication Interventions.* Peter Lang Publishers.

Dutta-Bergman, M. J. (2005). Theory and practice in health communication campaigns: A critical interrogation. *Health Communication, 18*(2), 103–122. https://doi.org/10.1207/s15327027hc1802_1

Eysenbach, G., & Kohnler, C. (2002). How do consumers search for and appraise health information on the world wide web? Qualitative study using focus groups, usability tests, and in-depth interviews. *British Medical Journal, 324m*, 573–577. https://doi.org/10.1136/bmj.324.7337.573

Guttman, N. (2010). Using communication research to advance the goals of the National Health Insurance law in Israel: Deliberative methods to elicit public value priorities. *Health Communication, 5*(6–7), 613–614. https://doi.org/10.1080/10410236.2010.496837

Greenfield, S., Kaplan, S., & Ware, J. Jr. (1985). Expanding patient involvement in care: Effects on patient outcomes. *Annals of Internal Medicine, 102*, 520–528. https://doi.org/10.7326/0003-4819-102-4-520

Hornik, R. C. (2002). *Public health communication: Evidence for behavior change.* Lawrence Erlbaum.

Kreps, G. L. (2022). Addressing challenges to effectively disseminate relevant health information. *World Medical & Health Policy*, *14*(2), 220–224. https://doi.org/10.1002/wmh3.528

Kim, D.K., & Kreps, G.L. (2022). (Eds.). *Global health communication for immigrants and refugees: Cases and strategies*. Routledge.

Kim, D. K. D., & Kreps, G. L. (2020). An analysis of government communication in the United States during the COVID-19 pandemic: Recommendations for effective government health risk communication. *World Medical & Health Policy*, *12*(4), 398–412. https://doi.org/10.1002/wmh3.363

Kreps, G. L. (2021). The role of strategic communication to respond effectively to pandemics. *Journal of Multicultural Discourses*, *16*(1), 12–19. https://doi.org/10.1080/17447143.2021.1885417

Kreps, G.L. (2012). Translating health communication research into practice: The importance of implementing and sustaining evidence-based health communication interventions. *Atlantic Communication Journal*, *20*(1), 5–15. https://doi.org/10.1080/15456870.2012.637024

Kreps, G.L. (2017a). Online information and systems to enhance health outcomes through communication convergence. *Human Communication Research*, *43*(4), 518–530, https://doi.org/10.1111/hcre.12117

Kreps, G.L. (2017b). Transdisciplinary health communication research across the continuum of care. In C. Lambert & M. Grimm (Eds.), *Health communication as a transdisciplinary field* (pp. 13–22). Nomos Verlag.

Kreps, G.L. (2011a). Translating health communication research into practice: The influence of health communication scholarship on health policy, practice, and outcomes. In T. Thompson, R. Parrott, & J. Nussbaum, (Eds.), *The Handbook of Health Communication* (2nd ed., pp. 595–608). Routledge.

Kreps, G.L. (2011b). Methodological diversity and integration in health communication inquiry. *Patient Education and Counseling*, *82*(3), 285–291. https://doi.org/10.1016/j.pec.2011.01.020

Kreps, G.L. (2007). Health communication at the population level—Principles, methods and results. In L. Epstein (Ed.) *Culturally appropriate health care by culturally competent health professionals: International workshop report* (pp. 112–120).

The Israel National Institute for Health Policy and Health Services Research, Kreps, G.L. (2006). Communication and racial inequities in health care. *American Behavioral Scientist*, *49*(6), 760–774. https://doi.org/10.1177/0002764205283800

Kreps, G.L. (2001). Consumer/provider communication research: A personal plea to address issues of ecological validity, relational development, message diversity, and situational constraints. *Journal of Health Psychology*, *6*(5), 597–601. https://doi.org/10.1177/13591053010060051

Kreps, G. L. (2002). Evaluating new health information technologies: Expanding the frontiers of health care delivery and health promotion. In R. G. Bushko (Ed.), *Future of health technology* (pp. 205–212). IOS Press.

Kreps, G.L., & Bonaguro, E. (2009). Health communication as applied communication inquiry. In L. Frey & K. Cissna (Eds.) *The Handbook of Applied Communication Research* (pp. 970–993). Lawrence Erlbaum.

Kreps, G.L., & Chapelsky Massimilla, D. (2002). Cancer communications research and health outcomes: Review and challenge. *Communication Studies, 53*(4), 318–336. https://doi.org/10.1080/10510970209388596

Kreps, G.L., & Goldin, R. (2009). Why you should vaccinate your child against H1N1. STATS. http://stats.org/stories/2009/vaccinate_child_h1n1_nov17_09.html

Kreps, G.L., Gustafson, D., Salovey, P., Perocchia, R.S., Wilbright, W., Bright, M.A., & Muha, C. (2007). The NCI Digital Divide Pilot Projects: Implications for cancer education. *Journal of Cancer Education, 22 (Supplement 1),* S56–S60. https://doi.org/10.1007/BF03174347

Kreps, G.L. & Maibach, E.W. (2008). Transdisciplinary science: The nexus between communication and public health. *Journal of Communication, 58*(4), 732–748. https://doi.org/10.1111/j.1460-2466.2008.00411.x

Kreps, G.L., & O'Hair, D. (Eds.). (1995). *Communication and health outcomes.* Hampton Press.

Kreps, G.L., Villagran, M.M., Zhao, X., McHorney, C., Ledford, C., Weathers, M., & Keefe, B.P. (2011). Development and validation of motivational messages to improve prescription medication adherence for patients with chronic health problems. *Patient Education and Counseling, 83*(3), 365–371. https://doi.org/10.1016/j.pec.2011.04.029

Kreps, G.L., Viswanath, K., & Harris, L.M. (2002). Advancing communication as a science: Opportunities from the federal sector. *Journal of Applied Communication Research, 30*(4), 369–381. https://doi.org/10.1080/00909880216589

Kunkel, D. (2010). Media research contributes to the battle against childhood obesity. *Health Communication, 25*(6–7), 595–596. https://doi.org/10.1080/10410236.2010.497019

Minkler, M. (2000). Using participatory action research to build healthy communities. *Public Health Reports, 115*(2–3), 191–197. https://doi.org/10.1093/phr/115.2.191

Minkler, M., & Wallerstein, N. (2002). *Community based participatory research for health.* Jossey-Bass. National Cancer Institute. (2008). *The role of the media in promoting and reducing tobacco use.* Tobacco Control Monograph No. 19. Bethesda, MD: U.S. Department of Health and Human Services, National Institutes of Health, National Cancer Institute. NIH Pub. No. 07-6242.

Neuhauser, L. (2001). Participatory design for better interactive health communication: A statewide model in the USA. *The Electronic Journal of Communication, 11* (3 & 4).

Neuhauser, L., & Kreps, G.L. (in press). Participatory design and artificial intelligence: Strategies to improve health communication for diverse audiences. In N. Green, S. Rubinelli, & D. Scott. (Eds.). *Artificial Intelligence and Health Communication.* American Association of Artificial Intelligence Press.

Neuhauser, L., & Kreps, G.L. (2010). Ehealth communication and behavior change: Promise and performance. *Social Semiotics, 20*(1), 7–24. https://doi.org/10.1080/10350330903438386

Noar, S.M., Palmgreen, P., Chabot, M., Dobransky, N., & Zimmerman, R.S. (2009). A 10-year systematic review of HIV/AIDS mass communication campaigns: Have we made progress? *Journal of Health Communication, 14*(1), 15–42. https://doi.org/10.1080/10810730802592239

Parrott, R. (2008). A multiple discourse approach to health communication: Translational research and ethical practice. *Journal of Applied Communication Research, 36*(1), 1–7. https://doi.org/10.1080/00909880701799345

Siu, W. (2010). Fear appeals and public service advertising: Applications to influenza in Hong Kong. *Health Communication, 25*(6–7), 580. https://doi.org/10.1080/10410236.2010.496829

INTERCULTURAL COMMUNICATION

The intercultural communication context affords us the opportunity to explore the ways in which culture is a pervasive, yet for the most part, unconscious and taken for granted part of our everyday lives. It is clear that culture, in all its variations, is the manifestation of what it means to belong with a group of people. We express our culture through communication and it is in communication that the differences between our cultural values are exposed. In the following chapters, you will be asked to explore the ways in which our own culture influences our interactions with others and methods for increasing our intercultural communication competence. The following chapters explore intercultural interactions across both the local and everyday cross-cultural types of encounters and the international cross-cultural exchanges. First, Elisabeth Gareis (Baruch College) explores the challenges to communication in forming and maintaining successful intercultural friendships, explains the potential for intercultural friendship to increase cross-cultural knowledge, raise global awareness, and reduce prejudice, and provides advice on how you can form intercultural friendships in college. Second, Guo-Ming Chen and Priscilla Young (University of Rhode Island) discuss how we can best increase our intercultural communication competence when we encounter people from different international cultures during travel, study, or business interactions. Chen and Young provide a model of Intercultural Communication to help you become a successful global citizen. In the third chapter of this section, Lamiyah Bahrainwala (Southwestern University) reviews how can we read data with a more critical surveillance lens and how surveillance shapes our ideas of race, disability, and terrorism. Bahrainwala compels us to attend to Critical Surveillance Studies and how this can help us see *how* technologies are not neutral, and *why* sorting is a political act.

HOW CAN INTERCULTURAL FRIENDSHIP HELP REDUCE PREJUDICE?

Elisabeth Gareis
Baruch College

It has been said that college is the best time in life—a time for experiencing the freedom of adulthood without adult responsibilities, such as family and career obligations. Even if some of these responsibilities are already part of your life, college allows you to explore interesting subjects, discover new paths, and meet people that you would otherwise not have met, such as international students from other countries. The United States attracts the largest number of students from around the world (Institute for International Education, 2020). Chances are that your college, too, has a sizeable number of international students. The combination of freedom to explore and a diverse student population at most colleges, make campuses the ideal place for forming intercultural friendships.

I was 22 years old when I came to the United States as an international student from Germany. My goal was to improve my English proficiency, learn about American culture, and make friends. Soon after I arrived, however, I noticed that friendship networks tended to be segregated: Americans largely socialized with other Americans, and international students with students from their own countries or other international students. I took a different approach and made it a point to seek out interactions with Americans; soon, most of my friends were Americans. However, my observations about the networks of my fellow students had made me curious, and I decided to conduct research on the topic of intercultural friendship for my doctoral dissertation and later, after I graduated, as part of my scholarly work as a professor.

Intercultural friendship is a most intriguing topic. Scholars have found that intercultural friendship can help achieve veritable miracles. It can increase the life satisfaction of international students (Rohrlich & Martin, 1991), help improve their language skills (Ward & Masgoret, 2004), promote cross-cultural adjustment (Zhang & Goodson, 2011), and make them feel less homesick (Hendrickson et al., 2011). In students from the host country (e.g., American students at home in the United States), friendships with international students serve to increase cross-cultural knowledge, raise global awareness, and foster international goodwill (Todd & Nesdale, 1997). But perhaps the greatest value of intercultural friendships is that, in both sojourners and hosts, intercultural friendship can help reduce prejudice.

This chapter will focus on the following questions: How can intercultural friendship help reduce prejudice? What are the challenges of forming intercultural friendships? And what is the advice for finding intercultural friends at college?

INTERCULTURAL FRIENDSHIP AND PREJUDICE REDUCTION

Intercultural communication is a relatively new area of academic study. Interest in the topic first blossomed in the 1950s after World War II and during the Civil Rights era in the United States. Scholars searched for ways to achieve positive intercultural relations. Arguably the most seminal book of that time is Allport's *The Nature of Prejudice* (1954). In it, Allport introduces the contact hypothesis, which states that social contact between different groups can reduce prejudice—especially if four conditions are met: equal status between the members of the groups, common goals, cooperation, and institutional support. Imagine, for example, that a group of U.S. American students and a group of Nigerian students want to form an amateur soccer team. Initially, there may be two ingroups (one American and one Nigerian), with each one seeing the other group as the outgroup. However, if all students in this mixed team are fairly good players (equal status), want to win the upcoming tournament (common goal), work together to achieve the goal (cooperation), and are supported by the college administration (institutional support), Allport's four conditions are fulfilled and chances are that any prejudice the students had will decrease or even vanish.

Allport's book is one of the most cited books in the field of intergroup relations. In fact, his contact hypothesis proved to be so fertile that in the decades since, countless studies have been conducted to investigate the concept further. Some of these studies have discovered that friendship plays a significant role in prejudice reduction. Pettigrew (1997) even determined that "the potential for friendship is an essential, not just facilitating, condition of optimal intergroup contact" (p. 183). What's more, Pettigrew found that intergroup friendship not only affects a person's perception of their friend's culture (e.g., an American student's perception of Nigerian culture, in our soccer team example) but that the positive effect generalizes to other outgroups as well. The American soccer player, for example, will have more positive feelings not just about Nigerian culture but about other cultures as well—simply by having made an intercultural friend. May be even more surprising, Wright et al. (1997) discovered that the reduction of prejudice through intercultural friendship also transfers indirectly to ingroup members who do not have an outgroup friend themselves but only know of another ingroup member's friendship. In other words, once the sister of our American soccer player knows about her brother's friendship with the Nigerian student, she too will likely experience a reduction in prejudice as a result. This effect is called the extended contact effect.

To summarize, intercultural friendship helps reduce prejudice in the friends about each other's cultures, in the friends concerning other outgroups, and even in people who are in the friends' networks but who do not have intercultural friendships themselves. How can intercultural friendship have such a far-reaching effect? Pettigrew (1997) theorized that intergroup friendship helps reduce prejudice because (1) individuals learn about the outgroup that they are in contact with, (2) develop empathy for the outgroup, (3) start to like and identify with the outgroup, and finally (4) reappraise their own ingroup; i.e., "gain distance from their own group and form a less provincial perspective on other groups in general" (p. 173). By realizing that one's own cultural norms, customs, and lifestyles are not the only way to organize the world, other cultures become humanized and are seen in a more positive light.

Later, Pettigrew and Tropp (2008) conducted a meta-analysis (i.e., examined the data from a large number of studies concerning the contact hypothesis) and found that the most influential factors for prejudice reduction are the decrease in anxiety and the increase in empathy that come with intercultural friendship formation. In other words, people become less fearful about interacting with culturally others and are able to take the perspective of the outgroup and empathize with their concerns.

CHALLENGES OF INTERCULTURAL FRIENDSHIP FORMATION

The powerful effect of intercultural friendship on attitudes toward other cultures holds immense promise for positive intercultural relations and peace. Unfortunately, intercultural friendships are not as common as one would wish. One of the most frequent complaints of international students, for example, is the lack of meaningful contact with host nationals (e.g., Kudo & Simkin, 2003). Indeed, studies in the United States, the United Kingdom, Australia, and New Zealand have found that more than 30 (in some places 80) percent of international students have no host-national friends (e.g., Bochner et al., 1985; Gareis, 2012; Nesdale et al., 1995; Ward & Masgoret, 2004).

This lack of friendships becomes understandable when we look at the factors that help or hinder intercultural friendship formation. The first factor is cultural similarity or dissimilarity. Humans tend to socialize with others who are similar to them—in culture, age, educational level, and other aspects. The saying "birds of a feather flock together" expresses this notion well. The respective academic theory is called the similarity-attraction effect (Byrne, 1969). Similarity is attractive because it affirms one's identity and makes communication easy. When you meet someone from your own culture, you can readily predict their behavior (e.g., what they are going to say or do when they greet you, etc.). This gives you so-called attributional confidence. By contrast, when you meet someone from another culture with different communication patterns, values, and customs, predicting behavior is more difficult, and your expectations (e.g., of eye contact and gestures) are often not met. This process is called expectancy violation (Burgoon & Ebesu, 2005). Cultural differences can be relatively minor (e.g., as is the case between the United States and Canada), making violations minimally disruptive. However, when cultures differ greatly (e.g., as is the case between the United States and China), expectancy violations can occur so frequently and may cause so much uncertainty and anxiety that individuals may choose not to pursue relationships. Overcoming cultural distance takes effort; for some, the cost of forming a friendship across cultures outweighs the benefits (Robinson et al., 2020).

The good news is that the uncertainty and anxiety that comes with meeting culturally different others can be managed and reduced. According to the anxiety/uncertainty management theory by Gao and Gudykunst (1990), you can do so, for example, by eliciting and providing self-disclosure; that is, asking questions, showing interest, and sharing information about yourself.

You should also know that it is mostly the beginning stages of friendship formation—the orientation and exploratory stages—that are affected by intercultural complexities and can throw a budding relationship off balance. At the later stages—the affective and stable stages—interaction will become more personal and cultural dissimilarities retreat into the background (Gudykunst, 1985; Gudykunst et al., 1987). A key to reaching the latter stages is communication.

This brings us to the next factors influencing intercultural friendship formation: communication and intercultural competence. If you are an international student, communication competence is first of all, proficiency in the host language (Gareis et al., 2011). But it is also the realization that you need interest and regular exposure to acquire unfamiliar communication practices. If you are a domestic student, it helps to be mindful that visitors may not be familiar yet with colloquial English and the cultural references that are often the basis of humor and that you may need to paraphrase and explain. Beyond communication competence, both sojourners and hosts benefit from intercultural competencies, including attitudes (e.g., recognizing the life-enhancing role of intercultural interactions), knowledge (e.g., about one's own culture and about other cultures), and skills (e.g., the ability to view issues from multiple perspectives) (Spitzberg & Changnon, 2009).

Another factor helping or hindering intercultural friendship formation is motivation. In the ideal case scenario, both sojourners and hosts are keen on making contact with each other—the sojourners to immerse themselves in the new culture, and the hosts to welcome them and share in the mutual exchange. But sometimes sojourners, as well as hosts, lack motivation; for example, if students are focused only on the task of getting a degree and therefore make little time for exploring the other opportunities that college life offers. But even well-meaning students can get demotivated. When you first arrive at college, you frequently make friends early on: during orientation, in your dorm, and in your first classes.

Because entering a new environment can be stressful, these initial friends are often friends from your own culture, resulting in a monocultural American network if you are American or a monocultural Chinese network if you are Chinese, for example. Same-culture friends fulfill an important role because they can provide security and comfort in a new environment, but once a monocultural network exists, there is little need to venture out and establish intercultural relationships (Brown, 2009). When social-media contacts with long-established friendships back home further satisfy your social needs (Hotta & Ting-Toomey, 2013), there may be no motivation left for reaching across cultural lines.

For international students, there is the additional challenge of the host environment and host receptivity. Intercultural contact does not happen automatically; it needs institutional support. Sometimes the college environment lacks in leisure activities that are conducive to intercultural contact, for example, causing sojourners to feel constrained in their recreation (Glass et al., 2014). Other times, the host community is not receptive to international visitors; that is, the host community does not exhibit the attitudes, openness, generosity, goodwill, and support that would make for optimal contact (Kim, 2001; Williams & Johnson, 2011). When sojourners are not embraced by the host community, stereotypes are often at play. Stereotypes can appear positive (e.g., the stereotype of Asians as high achieving) or negative (e.g., the stereotype of Asians as unwilling to adapt); in both cases, the stereotypes can create a sense of threat for the hosts; for example, if they fear that Asians create competition (Maddux et al., 2008) or that they may displace the local culture (Collins, 2006). The situation is exacerbated when sojourners are seen banding together in groups. In a study in the United Kingdom, Peacock and Harrison (2009) found that the attitude among domestic U.K. students was one of passive xenophobia; they viewed international students as distant and excluding, with no opening for interaction. By the same token, international students often deplore a perceived lack of interest or even discrimination on part of the hosts (Lee and Rice, 2007). Again, stereotypes are often the basis of such lack of interest or discrimination. A stereotype about East Asian males, for example, is that they lack masculinity. The distress that a lack of receptivity based on stereotypes can cause is heartbreakingly illustrated by a male East Asian interviewee in one of my studies. He evaluated his difficulty in making American friends by saying: "I think Americans don't need to make Asian male friends" (Gareis, 2012, p. 319).

A final factor is friendship patterns. If individuals do become friends, they may find that there is yet one more challenge to overcome. Although friendship is a relationship type that is present in most cultures, and definitions of friendship around the world often include similar characteristics, there are few universals. In fact, Hruschka (2010), found only three characteristics common to all the cultures that he studied: mutual aid based on need, positive affect, and gift-giving. One characteristic in which friendship patterns differ is the level of engagement and closeness, and the United States represents a special case in this respect. Hofstede (2001) asserts that in individualistic cultures, such as the United States, "ties between individuals are loose" (p. 225). Hofstede also found that U.S. culture ranks high in short-term orientation. May be as a result of this combination, American friendships are often described as easy to establish and fun, but also as superficial, noncommittal, and short-lived (e.g., Bellah, et al., 1985). Other cultures' friendship patterns tend to be more intense and higher in commitment and duration. This difference can cause frustration among sojourners and hosts alike. An East Asian student in the United States, for example, commented that she and her American friend "don't really talk something deeply in the heart" [sic], expressing disappointment about the level of closeness in her friendship (Gareis, 2012, p. 319). In defense of U.S. friendship patterns, Baumgarte (2016) highlights the positive aspects of American friendships. He describes them as independent, including, and idealist (i.e., with a focus on enjoying each other's company, being friendly, and upbeat), as opposed to those of contrast cultures, which from the American perspective appear intervening, excluding, and realist (i.e., with a tendency for giving advice, having close friendships at the exclusion of others, and seeing good as well as not-so-good characteristics in friends). The frustrations caused by these different definitions of friendship have been so confounding that as early as the 1950s, when study abroad first become popular, Du Bois (1956) cautioned American students about establishing friendships with international students for fear of disappointment. Likewise, current orientation handbooks for international students often warn sojourners that U.S. friendships are less intense and enduring than those elsewhere (e.g., Althen & Bennett, 2011).

ADVICE FOR FINDING INTERCULTURAL FRIENDS

All of the abovementioned challenges can be overcome—with awareness, communication, interest ... and some flexibility. The reward can be life-changing. Intercultural friendships have tremendous benefits: civically by reducing prejudice and improving cross-cultural attitudes, academically by expanding your horizon and increasing your communication repertoire, and professionally by internationalizing your network for future collaborations. On a personal level, they are among the most enriching experiences that you as a college student can have. If you do not have intercultural friends and want to embark on this adventure or if you have some experience but want to broaden your range, the following recommendations can help.

My advice is to start by investigating whether there are existing programs at the college that foster intercultural contact (e.g., by contacting the international student office or student affairs). You can also check whether assignments in your classes can foster intercultural contact. Many classes, for example, feature group or pair assignments; you could ask your professor to be placed with an international student or in a group that is created on the basis of diversity (for an example, see Gareis & Jalayer, 2018 and Gareis et al., 2019). Once you are in contact with someone from a different culture, try to get to know them. Initiate conversation and activities together. Alternatively, you could brainstorm pursuits that fulfill the four conditions of the contact hypothesis (equal status, common goals, cooperation, and institutional support) and that have friendship potential (i.e., by including repeated interaction and being meaningful). As an international student, I met my best American friends in the university choir, for example. The choir met four times a week, went on tours, and many students stayed for several terms—ideal conditions for making friends. We had a fantastic time. Similar activities include sports, hiking, camping, and all kinds of student clubs.

Another great way to make friends are buddy or conversation partner programs. Does your college have such a program? If not, you could create one (for instructions, see Aaron et al., 2018). At my college, a number of students and faculty advisors founded a student-coordinated conversation partners program that matches native and non-native speakers of English. The premise is for each pair to meet at least six times per semester for at least one hour; at the end of the semester, many of the partners have become friends. Participants comment that the program "took them out of the comfort zone" and that they met people "they would not have met otherwise." These comments show that we often need a little push to begin the journey of intercultural friendship.

Connections do not happen automatically simply because international and domestic students go to the same college. If nobody gives you a push, do it yourself. Garner the courage and seek out relevant leisure activities, establish contact with culturally different classmates, or start an initiative at your college to bring together students from varying backgrounds. By forging connections, you will definitely learn and grow . . . and may end up having the kind of experience that makes college so exciting and memorable.

REFERENCES

Aaron, R., Cedeño, C., Gareis, E., Kumar, L., & Swaminathan, A. (2018). Peers to peers: Developing a student-coordinated conversation partners program. *Journal of International Students, 8*(3), 1319–1330. http://doi.org/10.5281/zenodo.1254586

Allport, G. (1954). *The nature of prejudice.* Addison-Wesley.

Althen, G., & Bennett, J. (2011). *American ways: A guide for foreigners in the United States* (3rd ed). Intercultural Press.

Baumgarte, R. (2016). Conceptualizing cultural variations in close friendships. *Online Readings in Psychology and Culture, 5*(4), https://doi.org/10.9707/2307-0919.1137

Bellah, R. N., Madson, R., Sullivan, W. M., Swidler, A., & Tipton, S. M. (1985). *Habits of the heart.* University of California Press.

Bochner, S., Hutnik, N., & Furnham, A. (1985). The friendship patterns of overseas students and host students in an Oxford University residence. *Journal of Social Psychology, 125*(6), 689–694. https://doi.org/10.1080/00224545.1985.9713540

Brown, L. (2009). Worlds apart: The barrier between East and West. *Journal of International and Intercultural Communication, 2*(3), 240–259. https://doi.org/10.1080/17513050902985323

Burgoon, J. K., & Ebesu, H. A. S. (2005). Cross-cultural and intercultural applications of expectancy violations theory and interaction adaptation theory. In W. B. Gudykunst (Ed.), *Theorizing about intercultural communication* (pp. 149–172). Sage.

Byrne, D. (1969). Attitudes and attraction. In L. Berkowitz (Ed.), *Advances in experimental social psychology* (Vol. 4) (pp. 36–89). Academic Press.

Collins, F. L. (2006). Making Asian students, making students Asian: The racialisation of export education in Auckland, New Zealand. *Asia Pacific Viewpoint, 47*(2), 217–234. https://doi.org/10.1111/j.1467-8373.2006.00308.x

Du Bois, C. (1956). *Foreign students and higher education in the United States.* American Council on Education.

Gao, G., & Gudykunst, W. B. (1990.) Uncertainty, anxiety, and adaptation. *International Journal of Intercultural Relations, 14*(3), 301–317. https://doi.org/10.1016/0147-1767(90)90017-Q

Gareis, E. (2012). Intercultural friendship: Effects of home region and sojourn location. *Journal of International and Intercultural Communication, 5*(4), 309–328. https://doi.org/10.1080/17513057.2012.691525

Gareis, E., Goldman, J., & Merkin, R. (2019). Promoting intercultural friendship among college students. *Journal of International and Intercultural Communication, 12*(1), 1–22. http://doi.org/10.1080/17513057.2018.1502339

Gareis, E., Merkin, R., & Goldman, J. (2011). Intercultural friendship: Linking communication variables and friendship success. *Journal of Intercultural Communication Research, 40*(2), 155–173. https://doi.org/10.1080/17475759.2011.581034

Gareis, E., & Jalayer, A. (2018). Contact effects on intercultural friendship between East Asian students and American domestic students. In Y. Ma & M. A. Garcia-Murrilo (Eds.), *Understanding international students from Asia in American Universities: Learning and living globalization* (pp. 83–106). Springer.

Glass, C. R., Gómez, E., & Urzua, A. (2014). Recreation, intercultural friendship, and international students' adaptation to college by region of origin. *International Journal of Intercultural Relations, 42,* 104–117. https://doi.org/10.1016/j.ijintrel.2014.05.007

Gudykunst, W. B. (1985). A model of uncertainty reduction in intercultural encounters. *Journal of Language and Social Psychology, 4*(2), 79–98. https://doi.org/10.1177/0261927X8500400201

Gudykunst, W. B., Nishida, T., & Chua, E. (1987). Perceptions of social penetration in Japanese–North American dyads. *International Journal of Intercultural Relations, 11*(2), 171–189. https://doi.org/10.1016/0147-1767(87)90017-4

Hendrickson, B., Rosen, D., & Aune, R. K. (2011). An analysis of friendship networks, social connectedness, homesickness, and satisfaction levels of international students. *International Journal of Intercultural Relations, 35*(3), 281–295. https://doi.org/10.1016/j.ijintrel.2010.08.001

Hofstede, G. (2001). *Culture's consequences* (2nd ed.). Sage.

Hotta, J. & Ting-Toomey, (2013). Intercultural adjustment and friendship dialectics in international students: A qualitative study. *International Journal of Intercultural Relations, 37*(5), 550–566. http://dx.doi.org/10.1016/j.ijintrel.2013.06.007

Hruschka, D. J. (2010). *Friendship: Development, ecology, and evolution of a relationship.* University of California Press.

Institute for International Education. (2020). *Project atlas: 2020 release.* https://iie.widen.net/s/g2bqxwkwqv/project-atlas-infographics-2020

Kim, Y. Y. (2001). *Becoming intercultural: An integrative theory of communication and cross-cultural adaptation.* Sage.

Kudo, K., & Simkin, K. A. (2003). Intercultural friendship formation: The case of Japanese students at an Australian university. *Journal of Intercultural Studies, 24*(2), 91–114. https://doi.org/10.1080/0725686032000165351

Lee, J. J., & Rice, C. (2007). Welcome to America? International student perceptions of discrimination. *Higher Education, 53*(3), 381–409. https://doi.org/10.1007/s10734-005-4508-3

Maddux, W. W., Galinsky, A. D., Cuddy, A. J. C., & Polifroni, M. (2008). When being a model minority is good . . . and bad: Realistic threat explains negativity toward Asian Americans. *Personality and Social Psychology Bulletin, 34*(1), 74–89. https://doi.org/10.1177/0146167207309195

Nesdale, D., Simkin, K., Sang, D., Burke, B., & Fraser, S. (1995). *International students and immigration.* Australian Government Publishing Service.

Peacock, N., & Harrison, N. (2009). "It's so much easier to go with what's easy" "mindfulness" and the discourse between home and international Students in the United Kingdom. *Journal of Studies in International Education, 13*(4), 487–508. https://doi.org/10.1177/1028315308319508

Pettigrew, T. F. (1997). Generalized intergroup contact effects on prejudice. *Personality and Social Psychology Bulletin, 23*(2), 173–185. https://doi.org/10.1177/0146167297232006

Pettigrew, T. F., & Tropp, L. R. (2008). How does intergroup contact reduce prejudice? Meta-analytic tests of three mediators. *European Journal of Social Psychology, 38*(6), 922–934. https://doi.org/10.1002/ejsp.504

Robinson, O., Somerville, K., & Walsworth, S. (2020). Understanding friendship formation between international and host-national students in a Canadian university. *Journal of International and Intercultural Communication, 13*(1), 49–70. https://doi.org/10.1080/17513057.2019.1609067

Rohrlich, B. F., & Martin, J. N. (1991). Host country and reentry adjustment of student sojourners. *International Journal of Intercultural Relations, 15*(2), 163–182. https://doi.org/10.1016/0147-1767(91)90027-E

Spitzberg, B. H., & Changnon, G. (2009). Conceptualizing intercultural competence. In D. Deardorf (Ed.), *The Sage handbook of intercultural competence* (pp. 1–52). Sage.

Todd, P., & Nesdale, D. (1997). Promoting intercultural contact between Australian and international university students. *Journal of Higher Education Policy and Management, 19*(1), 61–76. https://doi.org/10.1080/1360080970190108

Ward, C., & Masgoret, A. M. (2004). *The experiences of international students in New Zealand: Report on the results of the national survey.* Wellington, New Zealand: International Policy and Development Unit, Ministry of Education. http://www.educationcounts.govt.nz/publications/international/14700

Williams, C. T., & Johnson, L. R. (2011). Why can't we be friends? Multicultural attitudes and friendships with international students. *International Journal of Intercultural Relations, 35*(1), 41–48. https://doi.org/10.1016/j.ijintrel.2010.11.001

Wright, S. C., Aron, A., McLaughlin-Volpe, T., & Ropp, S. A. (1997). The extended contact effect: Knowledge of cross-group friendships and prejudice. *Journal of Personality and Social Psychology, 73*(1), 73–90. https://doi.org/10.1037/0022-3514.73.1.73

Zhang, J., & Goodson, P. (2011). Predictors of international students' psychosocial adjustment to life in the United States: A systematic review. *International Journal of Intercultural Relations, 35*(5), 139–162. https://doi.org/10.1016/j.ijintrel.2010.11.004

INTERCULTURAL COMMUNICATION COMPETENCE

Guo-Ming Chen & Priscilla Young
University of Rhode Island

Most people probably do not think a lot about how culture affects communication, and vice versa. Generally, we communicate with others the way that our families communicated with us. We listened to and watched the way our parents spoke to and behaved around others, and we followed suit. So, why the interest now in what is called intercultural communication? Is not everybody basically the same? After all, we are all human beings.

Well, think about these questions: Do you expect to live in the same place where you grew up for the rest of your life? Will the population where you live remain as it is, with no new people moving there? Will the people you work with be of the same background as you, having the same cultural heritage and speaking the same native language? What if you travel to a different country? Will customs be the same? How would you react when speaking to a person who does not make eye contact or who politely agrees with all you say? What if you waved at someone whose reaction made you wonder what you did wrong?

These are only a smattering of examples of how culture affects who we are and how we communicate both verbally and nonverbally. The trick, however, is to learn that these behaviors are not necessarily the same for people with backgrounds different from ours. Even more important is to learn that just because we do something in a particular way does not mean that others are wrong when they do things in their own way. No one culture is better than another. It just is different. So, in the spirit of questioning consider the following: How can we best increase our intercultural communication competence when we encounter people from different international cultures during travel, study, or business interactions? This chapter attempts to answer this question by exploring the concept of "intercultural communication competence."

INTERCULTURAL COMMUNICATION COMPETENCE

So what is "intercultural communication competence" (ICC)? ICC can be simply defined as an individual's ability to execute effective and appropriate communication behaviors in order to achieve one's communication goals in an intercultural context. Over the years, intercultural communication scholars have attempted to figure out what are the elements of ICC (e.g., Abe & Wiseman, 1983; Chen, 2009, 2010a; Dai & Chen, 2020; Dai & Martin, 2022; Gjoci & Gjoci, 2020; Hammer et al., 1978; Haslett, 2020; Lustig & Koester, 2009; Ruben & Kealey, 1979; Spitzberg & Changnon, 2009; Wiseman & Abe, 1986). After a thorough review of the literature of ICC study, Chen (2014) found that the elements specified by scholars can be categorized into four dimensions, and each dimension is comprised of four components (see Figure 1).

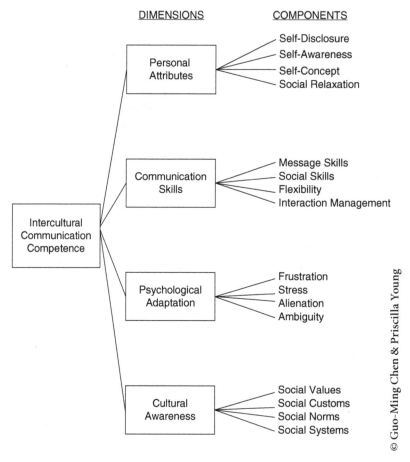

Figure 1. The dimensions and components of intercultural communication competence.

Figure 1 shows that an interculturally competent person possesses four sets of abilities when interacting with people from different cultural backgrounds:

1. Personal attributes—referring to having a positive personality, which includes knowing how to disclose oneself appropriately (self-disclosure), knowing oneself (self-awareness), seeing oneself positively (self-concept), and showing little anxiety in interaction (social relaxation).

2. Communication skills—referring to knowing how to interact well, which includes being skillful in the verbal and nonverbal language of one's cultural counterpart (message skills), being empathic (social skills), knowing how to behave in different contexts (flexibility), and knowing when to initiate, take turns, and terminate a conversation (interaction management).

3. Psychological adaptation—referring to the ability to cope with culture shock, which includes coping with the feelings of frustration, stress, alienation, and uncertainty caused by the ambiguous situation due to cultural differences.

4. Cultural awareness—referring to the understanding of the cultural conventions of one's counterpart, including social values, social customs, social norms, and social systems.

Figure 1 is a nice illustration of the content of ICC. In order to make the model of ICC even more precise, Chen and Starosta (1996) and Chen (2010b) went one step further to transform Figure 1 into a more aesthetic and theoretical model (see Figure 2), which indicates that ICC can be examined from three perspectives: (1) cognitive—intercultural awareness, (2) affective—intercultural sensitivity, and (3) behavioral—intercultural adroitness. The three perspectives represent the three sides of the equilateral triangle of ICC. Let's use this model to learn more about ICC.

Figure 2. A model of intercultural communication competence.

INTERCULTURAL AWARENESS

The cognitive perspective of ICC, indicating the ability of intercultural awareness, refers to the understanding of distinct cultural features of one's counterpart. It is a process of learning about the beliefs and values or the way of thinking of persons from another culture (Chen & Starosta, 1998–9). To know cultural differences is the first step to reduce ambiguity or uncertainty of intercultural interaction. This will in turn lead to less discomfort, confusion, and anxiety in the process of adapting to a new cultural environment.

According to Kluckhohn (1948), culture is a map. If the cultural map in one's mind is accurate, one will not get lost when interacting with people from that specific culture. It is similar to a geographical map. If the information on the map correctly reflects the streets of the area, one will get to the destination easily. A culture is also like an essay which always has a "theme" running through it (Turner, 1968). In order to know a culture, one needs to know how to properly draw the cultural map or pull out the cultural theme. The cultural map or cultural theme can be demonstrated by studies on cultural values from scholars like Kluckhohn and Strodbeck (1961), Hall (1976), and Hofstede (1984).

Kluckhohn and Strodbeck (1961) pointed out that cultural values can be understood from five universal problems faced by all human societies: (1) human nature, (2) the relationship between human and nature, (3) time orientation, (4) activity orientation, and (5) relational orientation. Hall (1976) classified human culture into high-context culture and low-context culture. In high-context cultures, such as China and Japan, people tend to be more indirect in expressing themselves and more able to read nonverbal cues; while in low-context cultures, like Switzerland and the United States, people tend to be more verbally expressive and direct in interaction. Hofstede (1984) examined cultural values from the business perspective and found five dimensions, including individualism versus collectivism, power distance, uncertainty reduction, masculinity versus femininity, and Confucian dynamism.

Not being aware of the cultural conventions of one's counterpart often leads to misunderstanding in the process of intercultural interaction, which may result in interpersonal conflict, failure in business transactions, or war between nations. The following are a few daily-life examples of cultural differences for you to see how many you are aware of:

1. In Malaysia, people do not use their left hand to eat, hold things, or shake hands, because they think the left hand is not clean.

2. In Korea, gifts should not be wrapped in white paper.

3. In business negotiations, North Americans typically use a factual approach based on logic, Saudi Arabians use an affective approach based on emotions, and Russians use an axiomatic approach based on ideals (Glenn et al., 1977).

4. Mexicans emphasize interpersonal relationships more than being "on time," thus the way they perceive time tends to be polychromic, which means that they may schedule several events at the same point of time.

There are many ways to assess the degree of one's intercultural awareness (e.g., Kitao, 1981; Kohl, 1988; Moran et al., 2010; Saville-Troike, 1978; Yu & Van Maele, 2018). Appendix A is an instrument for testing intercultural awareness developed by Chen (1995). The underlined nation can be replaced by any nation you like, but remember to reverse the scores of different items based on the cultural values of the nation you select for the test.

INTERCULTURAL SENSITIVITY

The affective perspective of ICC is represented by intercultural sensitivity. This refers to, based on the awareness of cultural characteristics of one's counterpart, the ability to further develop a positive feeling or emotion toward cultural differences in the process of intercultural communication. This positive emotion includes one's willingness or motivation to understand, acknowledge, respect, and even accept differences between the two cultural beings or groups (Chen & Starosta, 1997). It is important to know that intercultural awareness as the foundation of ICC must be accompanied with intercultural sensitivity in order to reach the authentic state of intercultural understanding. Chen's (1995) study showed that in certain situations (e.g., in a competitive business negotiation), without being interculturally sensitive or using one's heart to understand and empathize with the cultural differences, interactants may take advantage of their counterparts because of the understanding of their counterparts' culture.

Interculturally sensitive persons usually possess six distinct personal characteristics (Bennett, 1986; Triandis, 1977; Yum, 1989): (1) self-esteem—a strong sense of self-value or self-worth, (2) self-monitoring—the ability to detect the situational constraints in order to behave appropriately, (3) open-mindedness—the willingness to accept differences, (4) empathy—to see the other's point of view from that person's perspective, (5) interaction involvement—responsiveness, perceptiveness, and attentiveness in interaction, and (6) suspending judgment—not jumping to conclusions without having sufficient information. Appendix B is a more recent and valid instrument developed by Chen and Starosta (2000), which readjusts the factors of intercultural sensitivity. You can answer the questions to gauge your level of intercultural sensitivity.

INTERCULTURAL ADROITNESS

The ultimate goal of knowing and being sensitive to cultural differences is to perform effectively at the behavioral level of intercultural interaction (Cheung et al., 2022). Intercultural adroitness (or intercultural effectiveness) speaks for the behavioral perspective of ICC. It refers to the ability to achieve one's communication goals in intercultural interaction through behavioral performance (Chen, 2007). In other words, intercultural adroitness is demonstrated by one's verbal and nonverbal communication skills that enable the person to be successful and productive in the process of intercultural communication. It is important to remember, however, that the definition of ICC includes appropriateness, so effective

communication behaviors must be regulated by this principle because in intercultural interaction one may use unethical means (e.g., violating the cultural rules of one's counterpart)
to effectively but inappropriately attain the communication goal.

Studies show that those effective intercultural communication skills include five elements (e.g., Cupach & Imahori, 1993; Martin & Hammer, 1989; Wiseman, 2003): (1) message skills—the ability to employ one's counterpart's verbal and nonverbal behaviors, (2)
interaction management—the ability to initiate, take turns, and terminate a conversation,
(3) behavioral flexibility—the ability to attend to various information and to use appropriate
communication strategies, (4) identity management—the ability to maintain one's counterpart's personal and cultural identities, and (5) relationship cultivation—the ability to establish the interdependent and reciprocal relationship with one's counterpart. Appendix C is
a valid instrument developed recently by Portalla and Chen (2010), which you can use to
measure your ability of intercultural adroitness.

Finally, you may wonder how can people acquire the ability of ICC. Intercultural training
is the answer for this. Scholars and practitioners from different disciplines have developed a
variety of intercultural training programs to help people become competent in intercultural
interaction. Chen and Starosta (2005) organized those common intercultural training programs into five models: (1) the classroom model—usually applying the curricular offerings
of an education system, (2) the simulation model—involving participants in an environment that closely resembles a specific culture, (3) the self-awareness model—training people
how psychological forces operate in groups and how their own behaviors influence others,
(4) the cultural awareness model—focusing on the understanding of cultural knowledge of
one's counterpart, (5) the behavioral model—teaching trainees specific behavioral skills of a
specific culture, and (6) the interaction model—directly asking participants to interact with
people from a specific culture. Intercultural training is the practical part of intercultural
communication study. If you are interested in it, you can use the references at the end of this
chapter to gain more information about the topic (e.g., Landis et al., 2003) or take a course
dedicated to the topic of Intercultural Communication.

CONCLUSION

The globalization trend continues to dominate the 21st century. As a college student, you will
face international students and scholars from different cultures on campus on a daily basis;
you may study abroad to fulfill your college course or travel around the world just because
the transportation and communication technology makes transnational movement so easy,
convenient and less expensive; you will compete in the global job market after graduation. All
these point to the importance of becoming a global citizen in order to succeed in contemporary
human society. Being a successful global citizen means to be able to communicate effectively
and appropriately in different cultural contexts. This chapter aims to examine the knowledge
and skills for being competent in intercultural communication by specifying the dimensions

and components of a model of ICC. Instruments used to measure the ability of each dimension of ICC were also included so that you can assess your own degree of ICC and further improve it if necessary through participating in different kinds of intercultural training.

From the research perspective, it is clear that the approach taken in this chapter to explore the concept of intercultural communication competence is based on the tradition of functionalism or discovery paradigm. In other words, the approach assumes that the elements of ICC can be systematically identified and empirically tested, so that people can acquire ICC through a more scientific method, such as a well-designed intercultural training program. One needs to be aware that in addition to functionalism, there are alternative approaches to the study of ICC. For instance, as Young (1996) pointed out, the study of intercultural communication can be addressed from the critical perspective, through which power or ideology embedded in the historical context is involved in understanding the intercultural communication process. In this sense, ICC is conceived as "speaking authentically, accurately, and appropriately with regard to the social relationship, as well as a willingness on the part of those in positions of power to cooperate with those who resist domination" (Kelly 2008, p. 267). To better understand ICC, it will be wise to integrate not only the views from different perspectives (e.g., Liu et al., 2022) but also from different methodological approaches.

REFERENCES

Abe, H., & Wiseman, R. L. (1983). A cross-cultural confirmation of the dimensions of intercultural effectiveness. *International Journal of Intercultural Relations, 7*(1), 53–67. https://doi.org/10.1016/0147-1767(83)90005-6

Bennett, M. J. (1986). A developmental approach to training for intercultural sensitivity. *International Journal of Intercultural Relations, 10*(2), 179–196. https://doi.org/10.1016/0147-1767(86)90005-2

Chen, G. M. (1995). *International e-mail debate and intercultural awareness.* Manuscript prepared for a grant project sponsored by the Fund for the Improvement of Postsecondary Education (PIPSE).

Chen, G. M. (2007). A review of the concept of intercultural effectiveness. In M. Hinner (Ed.), *The influence of culture in the world of business* (pp. 95–116). Peter Lang.

Chen, G. M. (2009). Intercultural communication competence. In S. Littlejohn & K. Foss (Eds.), *Encyclopedia of communication theory* (pp. 529–532). Sage.

Chen, G. M. (2010a). *A study of intercultural communication competence.* China Review Academic Publishers.

Chen, G. M. (2010b). *Foundations of intercultural communication competence.* China Review Academic Publishers.

Chen, G. M. (2014). Intercultural communication competence: Summary of 30-year research and directions for future study. In X-d. Dai & G. M. Chen (Eds.), *Intercultural communication competence: conceptualization and its development in cultural contexts and interactions* (pp. 14–40). Cambridge Scholars.

Chen, G. M., & Starosta, W. J. (1996). Intercultural communication competence: A synthesis. *Annals of the International Communication Association, 19*(1), 353-383. https://doi.org/10.1080/23808 985.1996.11678935

Chen, G. M., & Starosta, W. J. (1997). A review of the concept of intercultural sensitivity. *Human Communication, 1,* 1–16.

Chen, G. M., & Starosta, W. J. (1998-9). A review of the concept of intercultural awareness. *Human Communication, 2,* 27–54.

Chen, G. M., & Starosta, W. J. (2000). The development and validation of the intercultural sensitivity scale. *Human Communication, 3,* 1–15.

Chen, G. M., & Starosta, W. J. (2005). *Foundations of intercultural communication.* University Press of America.

Cheung, R. Y., Jiang, D., Yum, Y. N., & Bhowmik, M. K. (2022). Intercultural sensitivity and prosocial behavior towards South Asians in Hong Kong: Mediating mechanisms of warmth and stigma. *International Journal of Intercultural Relations, 86,* 56–63. https://doi.org/10.1016/j.ijintrel.2021.11.002

Cupach, W. R., & Imahori, T. T. (1993). Identity management theory: Communication competence in intercultural episodes and relationships. In R. L. Wiseman & J. Koester (Eds.), *Intercultural communication competence* (pp. 112–131). Sage.

Dai, X-d., & Chen, G. M. (2020). Conceptualizing cultural integration competence. *China Media Research, 16*(2), 13–23.

Dai, X-d., & Martin, J. (2022). Perspectives and approaches to intercultural communication competence: Toward a theoretical synthesis. In Y. Miike & J. Yin (Eds.), *The handbook of global interventions in communication theory* (pp. 456–473). Routledge.

Gjoci, N., & Gjoci, E. (2020). Exploring intercultural competence at the macro and micro scale: A case study from Albanian University students. *Journal of Intercultural Communication, 52,* 32–51.

Glenn, E. S., Witmeyer, D., & Stevenson, K. A. (1977). Cultural styles of persuasion. *International Journal of Intercultural Relations, 1*(3), 52–66. https://doi.org/10.1016/0147-1767(77)90019-0

Gudykunst, W. B., & Kim, Y. Y. (1992). *Communicating with strangers.* McGraw-Hill.

Hall, E. T. (1976). *Beyond culture.* Anchor.

Hammer, M., Gudykunst, W., & Wiseman, R. (1978). Dimensions of intercultural effectiveness. *International Journal of Intercultural Relations, 2*(4), 382–393. https://doi.org/10.1016/0147-1767(78)90036-6

Haslett, B. (2020). A face model of intercultural communicative competence: Integrating non-Western and Western communication. *China Media Research, 16*(2), 24–39.

Hofstede, G. (1984). *Culture's consequences.* Sage.

Kelly, W. (2008). Applying a critical metatheoretical approach to intercultural relations: The case of U.S.-Japanese communication. In M. K. Asante, Y. Miike, & J. Yin (Eds.), *The global intercultural communication reader* (pp. 263–279). Routledge.

Kitao, K. (1981). The test of American culture. *Technology & Mediated Instruction, 15,* 25–45.

Kluckhohn, F. K., (1948). *Mirror of man.* Harper Collins.

Kluckhohn, F. K., & Strodbeck, F. L. (1961). *Variations in value orientations.* Row, Peterson.

Kohls, L. R. (1988). Models for comparing and contrasting cultures. In J. M. Reid (Ed.), *Building the professional dimension of educational exchange* (pp. 137–153). Intercultural Press.

Landis, D., Bennett, J. M., & Bennett, M. (Eds.) (2003). *Handbook of intercultural training.* Sage.

Liu, Y., Liu, J., & King, B. (2022). Intercultural communicative competence: Hospitality industry and education perspectives. *Journal of Hospitality, Leisure, Sport & Tourism Education, 30*, 100371. https://doi.org/10.1016/j.jhlste.2022.100371

Lustig, M. W., & Koester, J. (2009). *Intercultural competence: Interpersonal communication across cultures.* Allyn and Bacon.

Martin, J. N., & Hammer, M. R. (1989). Behavioral categories of intercultural communication competence: Everyday communicators' perceptions. *International Journal of Intercultural Relations, 13*(3), 303–332. https://doi.org/10.1016/0147-1767(89)90015-1

Moran, R. T., Harris, P. R., & Moran, S. V. (2010). *Managing cultural differences: Global leadership strategies for the 21ˢᵗ century.* Elsevier.

Portalla, T., & Chen, G. M. (2010). The development and validation of the intercultural effectiveness scale. *Intercultural Communication Studies, 19*(3), 21–37.

Ruben, B. D., & Kealey, D.J. (1979). Behavioral assessment of communication competency and the prediction of cross-cultural adaptation. *International Journal of Intercultural Relations, 3*, 15–47.

Saville-Troike, M. (1978). *A guide to culture in the classroom.* InterAmerica Research Associates.

Spitzberg, B. H., & Changnon, G. (2009). Conceptualizing intercultural competence. In D. K. Deardorff (Ed.), *The Sage handbook of intercultural competence* (pp. 2–52). Sage.

Triandis, H. C. (1977). Cross-cultural social and personality psychology. *Personality and Social Psychology Bulletin, 3*(2), 143–158. https://doi.org/10.1177/014616727700300202

Turner, C. V. (1968). The Sinasina "big man" complex: A central cultural theme. *Practical Anthropology, 15*(1), 16–22. https://doi.org/10.1177/009182966801500103

Wiseman, R. L. (2003). Intercultural communication competence. In W. B. Gudykunst (Ed.), *Cross-cultural and intercultural communication* (pp. 191–208). Sage.

Wiseman, R. L., & Abe H. (1986). Explication and test of a model of communicative competence. *Human Communication Research, 13*(3), 3–33. https://doi.org/10.1111/j.1468-2958.1977.tb00518.x

Young, R. E. (1996). *Intercultural communication: Pragmatics, genealogy, deconstruction.* Multilingual Matters.

Yu, Q., & Van Maele, J. (2018). Fostering intercultural awareness in a Chinese English reading class. *Chinese Journal of Applied Linguistics, 41*(3), 357–375. https://doi.org/10.1515/cjal-2018-0027

Yum, J. O. (1989). *Communication sensitivity and empathy in culturally diverse organizations.* Paper presented at the 75th Annual Conference of the Speech Communication Association, San Francisco.

APPENDIX A. INTERCULTURAL AWARENESS INSTRUMENT

Directions: Here are several statements about <u>American</u> cultural values. Please indicate the extent to which you feel that each statement describes what you think. There are no right or wrong answers. Just answer honestly how you feel by indicating:

> 5 = Strongly Agree
> 4 = Agree
> 3 = Not Decided
> 2 = Disagree
> 1 = Strongly Disagree

_____ 1. <u>Americans</u> are individualists.
_____ 2. <u>Americans</u> are doing-oriented.
_____ 3. <u>Americans</u> believe that life is basically sad.
_____ 4. <u>Americans</u> are high in family mobility.
_____ 5. <u>Americans</u> emphasize spiritual life.
_____ 6. <u>Americans</u> are open in the family role behavior.
_____ 7. <u>Americans</u> are less formal in social interaction.
_____ 8. <u>Americans</u> seldom express their opinions openly.
_____ 9. <u>Americans</u> emphasize social rank.
_____10. <u>Americans</u> often refer to each other by first name.
_____11. <u>Americans</u> are not action-oriented.
_____12. <u>Americans</u> believe that they are in control over their environment.
_____13. <u>Americans</u> rely on intermediaries in social interaction.
_____14. <u>Americans</u> express their opinions directly.
_____15. <u>Americans</u> are less democratic in the family role behavior.

_____16. <u>Americans</u> emphasize change more than tradition.
_____17. <u>Americans</u> do not emphasize status.
_____18. <u>Americans</u> emphasize the future more than the past.
_____19. <u>Americans</u> believe that human nature is unchangeable.
_____20. <u>Americans</u> believe that people are controlled by the supernatural.

Note: The underlined nation's name can be replaced by another nation.
Items to be reversed (i.e., 5=1, 4=2, 2=4, 1=5): 3, 5, 8, 9, 11, 13, 15, 17, 19, 20

APPENDIX B. INTERCULTURAL SENSITIVITY SCALE

Direction: Below is a series of statements concerning intercultural communication. There are no right or wrong answers. Please work quickly and record your first impression by indicating the degree to which you agree or disagree with the statement. Thank you for your cooperation.

5 = strongly agree	
4 = agree	
3 = uncertain	Please put the number corresponding to your answer in the
2 = disagree	blank before the statement
1 = strongly disagree	

_____ 1. I enjoy interacting with people from different cultures.

_____ 2. I think people from other cultures are narrow-minded.

_____ 3. I am pretty sure of myself in interacting with people from different cultures.

_____ 4. I find it very hard to talk in front of people from different cultures.

_____ 5. I always know what to say when interacting with people from different cultures.

_____ 6. I can be as sociable as I want to be when interacting with people from different cultures.

_____ 7. I do not like to be with people from different cultures.

_____ 8. I respect the values of people from different cultures.

_____ 9. I get upset easily when interacting with people from different cultures.

_____10. I feel confident when interacting with people from different cultures.

_____11. I tend to wait before forming an impression of culturally-distinct counterparts.

_____12. I often get discouraged when I am with people from different cultures.

_____13. I am open-minded to people from different cultures.

_____14. I am very observant when interacting with people from different cultures.

_____15. I often feel useless when interacting with people from different cultures.

_____16. I respect the ways people from different cultures behave.

_____17. I try to obtain as much information as I can when interacting with people from different cultures.

_____18. I would not accept the opinions of people from different cultures.

_____19. I am sensitive to my culturally-distinct counterpart's subtle meanings during our interaction.

_____20. I think my culture is better than other cultures.

_____21. I often give positive responses to my culturally different counterparts during our interaction.

_____22. I avoid those situations where I will have to deal with culturally-distinct persons.

_____23. I often show my culturally-distinct counterpart my understanding through verbal or nonverbal cues.

_____24. I have a feeling of enjoyment toward differences between my culturally-distinct counterpart and me.

Note. Items 2, 4, 7, 9, 12, 15, 18, 20, and 22 are reverse-coded before summing the 24 items (i.e., 5=1, 4=2, 2=4, 1=5). Interaction Engagement items are 1, 11, 13, 21, 22, 23, and 24, Respect for Cultural Differences items are 2, 7, 8, 16, 18, and 20, Interaction Confidence items are 3, 4, 5, 6, and 10, Interaction Enjoyment items are 9, 12, and 15, and Interaction Attentiveness items are 14, 17, and 19.

APPENDIX C. INTERCULTURAL ADROITNESS SCALE

Direction: Below is a series of statements concerning intercultural communication. There are no right or wrong answers. Please work quickly and record your first impression by indicating the degree to which you agree or disagree with the statement. Thank you for your cooperation.

5 = strongly agree	
4 = agree	
3 = uncertain	Please put the number corresponding to your answer in the
2 = disagree	blank before the statement
1 = strongly disagree	

_____ 1. I find it is easy to talk with people from different cultures.

_____ 2. I am afraid to express myself when interacting with people from different cultures.

_____ 3. I find it is easy to get along with people from different cultures.

_____ 4. I am not always the person I appear to be when interacting with people from different cultures.

_____ 5. I am able to express my ideas clearly when interacting with people from different cultures.

_____ 6. I have problems with grammar when interacting with people from different cultures.

_____ 7. I am able to answer questions effectively when interacting with people from different cultures.

_____ 8. I find it is difficult to feel my culturally different counterparts are similar to me.

_____ 9. I use appropriate eye contact when interacting with people from different cultures.

_____ 10. I have problems distinguishing between informative and persuasive messages when interacting with people from different cultures.

_____11. I always know how to initiate a conversation when interacting with people from different cultures.

_____ 12. I often miss parts of what is going on when interacting with people from different cultures.

_____ 13. I feel relaxed when interacting with people from different cultures.

_____ 14. I often act like a very different person when interacting with people from different cultures.

_____ 15. I always show respect for my culturally different counterparts during our interaction.

_____ 16. I always feel a sense of distance from my culturally different counterparts during our interaction.

_____ 17. I find I have a lot in common with my culturally different counterparts during our interaction.

_____ 18. I find the best way to act is to be myself when interacting with people from different cultures.

_____ 19. I find it is easy to identify with my culturally different counterparts during our interaction.

_____ 20. I always show respect for the opinions of my culturally different counterparts during our interaction.

Note. Items 2, 4, 6, 8, 10, 12, 14, 16, and 18 are reverse-coded before summing the 20 items (i.e., 5=1, 4=2, 2=4, 1=5). Behavioral Flexibility items are 2, 4, 14, and 18, Interaction Relaxation items are 1, 3, 11, 13, and 19, Interactant Respect items are 9, 15, and 20, Message Skills items are 6, 10, and 12, Identity Maintenance items are 8, 16, and 19, Interaction Management items are 5 and 7.

CRITICAL SURVEILLANCE STUDIES: LIVING ETHICALLY IN A SURVEILLANT WORLD

Lamiyah Bahrainwala
Southwestern University

What exactly is surveillance, and why would Communication Studies scholars study it? Surveillance is an organized method of watching people and gathering data in order to influence them (Lyon, 2007, among others). Watching, gathering, influencing: all three are necessary for an act to rise to the definition of "surveillance"—so casual people-watching at a coffee shop or following someone on social media would not count. So why would Communication Studies scholars study it? Well, we have at least two reasons: first, we *communicate* the need to surveil (and are persuaded into becoming surveillance agents ourselves) and second, we communicate the *results* of surveillance. Both these communicative functions help structure our societies and can reveal what and who we place at the center of our social values.

As I mentioned a moment ago, Communication Studies scholars study how surveillance data *is communicated,* which is shaped by how this data is *sorted. How* we organize data about people, and then use that data to *influence* people, reveals our values and structures of our societies. Here is an example: in 2019, I attended a celebration recognizing innovative government employees (Guhin, 2019), and one clever team won the "epidemic research" category by studying scooter-related injuries. You know the scooters I'm talking about—the motored kind that is a cheap alternative to Uber. How on earth were they able to tap into funds set aside for epidemiologists? Well, they argued, the use of these scooters seemed to "spread" during music festivals and major events and produced a specific recurring injury: concussions. This creative reasoning won that team funding and recognition: by sorting their data into an "epidemic of concussions" rather than "scooter accidents," they were able to make an entirely different argument and influence their audience to give them money from a different pot. Undoubtedly, there is a politics to sorting data, and it determines how we interpret it.

So let's consider how data sorting can go badly and produce deeply troubling, racist consequences. Let's look at health data once again: the United States Centers for Disease Control and Prevention (CDC) decided to look at Yelp reviews to help track underreported outbreaks of food poisoning (Newman, 2014). Since Yelp offers a convenient "star" sorting mechanism, why not use that public data to trace cases of food harm? After all, getting food poisoning at a restaurant would lead to one or two-star reviews, which would be easy to gather and sort. The CDC used computer sorting to gather data about reviews that mentioned the words "vomit" and "diarrhea." However, one journalist noted that this system overlooked the likelihood that Yelpers were much more likely to bring up food poisoning if they had eaten at an "ethnic" restaurant; that is, a restaurant serving non-European food (Simmons, 2014). Thus, taking the sorted Yelp data at face value would have told a skewed and profoundly racist story. *How* we surveil and sort data matters, and reveals our politics.

This brings us to the question: how can we read data with a more critical surveillance lens? And how would that help us understand how surveillance shapes our ideas of race, disability, and terrorism?

CRITICAL SURVEILLANCE STUDIES: SURVEILLANCE IS NOT NEUTRAL BECAUSE TECHNOLOGY IS NOT NEUTRAL

So far, the examples I have provided begin to explain both the nature and the need for *Critical Surveillance Studies,* which is the focus of this chapter as well as Communication Studies scholars studying surveillance. Critical Surveillance Studies look at how data is sorted in biased ways that exclude and minoritize various groups. What this means is that Critical Surveillance Studies is *feminist in nature*: it relies on the seminal work of Black feminist surveillance scholars who have shown the relevance of race, gender, ability, national origin, class, and other demographic markers in how we sort data. This can help us identify, and thus resist, using a "universal human template" when building the spaces where we live, work, and learn. Let me offer some examples of what insights we glean through a Critical Surveillance approach: Safia Noble notes that a Google search of "girls" produces images of children playing, but a search of "Black girls" produces highly sexualized results and links to pornography websites (Noble, 2018). Thus, the Google search filters are clearly not a neutral technology. We may also consider biometric surveillance, like fingerprinting, to be the ultimate neutral technology. However, fingerprints of certain groups can wear away, particularly manual laborers, the elderly, and those who have received treatment for cancer (Harmon, 2009), which can force additional surveillance on them. So we see how supposedly neutral technology is, well, not neutral at all. Critical Surveillance Studies and the work of

Black feminist surveillance scholars take a second look at this data and argue how it structures our society—from who we police to who we consider to be a child.

But what does it mean to "take a second look" at such data? Critical Surveillance Studies applies *intersectionality* to studying discourse about surveillance, which means looking at how race, ability, social class, age, gender, national origin, and migration history all mediate how we gather and sort data. In the paragraph above, I mentioned how fingerprinting particularly affects the elderly, cancer patients, and folks who work with their hands, thus making age, disability, and social class relevant. However, because Latinx individuals are overrepresented in manual work from forestry to construction and warehousing (Dubina, 2021), race, ethnicity, and migration become salient when critiquing fingerprinting as well. What compounds this problem is that many such manual jobs are also considered essential, and during COVID-19 this disproportionately exposed Latinx workers to the disease as they could not stop coming to work (University of Illinois Chicago School of Public Health, 2021). Yet another example of surveilled data that demands an intersectional approach is data about intimate partner violence. Women of color, particularly Black and indigenous women, are disproportionately likely to experience such violence (Stockman et al., 2015). When women report such violence, police departments typically take photographs of injuries—but bruising, swelling, and discoloration appear very differently on darker skin (Moore, 2015, p. 107–124), making those injuries seem less serious and easier to dismiss. We see, then, that race and gender *both* impact this form of photographic data, but the technology that collects this data—the camera—purports to be neutral. More to the point, such surveillance technology implicitly values light-skinned victims and disadvantages, dark-skinned women, which is why an intersectional, critical, Black feminist surveillance approach would expose this.

OUR METHODS OF SURVEILLANCE REVEAL WHAT WE VALUE

As we are beginning to see, there are significant consequences to interpreting data *without* an intersectional eye. Consider the statistics on accidental child drownings in the United States. The CDC estimates that roughly 4,000 children die from drowning annually and sorts this data by age, disability, gender, race, and ethnicity. The CDC also reports that Black children drown at *nearly eight times the rate of White children* in swimming pools (Drowning Facts, 2022). Alongside this horrific statistic, the CDC lists some common reasons for drowning—"not being able to swim" and "location"—without accounting for race. However, an intersectional Critical Surveillance reading of that data would reveal some important context: that sand is particularly hard on natural Black hair, creating a barrier of access to swimming on beaches (something Black communities have long discussed, of course); that pools have historically been restricted from Black individuals by White agents (NPR, 2008); and that pools and water parks often restrict modest swimwear, which can exclude Muslim girls and Black Muslim girls. When pools and beaches carry such barriers to access, it is no surprise that Black children are half as likely as White children to know how to swim (NPR, 2008). Therefore, "not knowing how to swim" or listing "minorities" as more likely to drown does not adequately account for the specific circumstances Black children and Black Muslim children face. Any support programs developed accordingly would continue to overlook Black swimmers' needs—from lifeguard training to public pool policies. Critical Surveillance Studies offer an intersecting approach to gathering, sorting, and interpreting such data to fundamentally alter our approaches to public welfare. The more intersectionally we examine surveillance data, the better we will be able to develop support systems that show Black children that they matter.

You will recall that we identified two areas of focus in Critical Surveillance Studies: how we *sort* data (which we have covered) and how we communicate the *need* for surveillance. Let's turn our attention to the latter. Citizens have to be made compliant to increasingly invasive surveillance—after all, no one was taking off their shoes or pulling out liquids and laptops at airports 20 years ago—and these escalating surveillance measures have to be justified. Additionally, private citizens are increasingly being told to conduct "lateral surveillance," or watch over and report each other. To go back to the airport example for a moment, consider all the "if you see something, say something" signs that *you,* the average traveler, are meant to act upon. Consider the "neighborhood watch" signs you encounter: it is meant to be neighbors keeping an eye out for people who are "suspicious" or "don't belong" in the neighborhood, and report them. Given this increasingly invasive surveillance, and the fashioning of ordinary citizens into vigilantes, it is essential to justify the need for surveillance.

A Critical Surveillance approach examines these justifications for surveillance to understand what our society values. Once again, it does so by critiquing such messaging using intersectionality: what does it mean to "see" and "say something" at an airport? What is a neighborhood watch person meant to do, beyond "watch?" An intersectional look shows that TSA scanners at airports "out" disabled and trans individuals who may have pacemakers or metal in their skeletons, or breast and penis prostheses (Dubrofsky & Magnet, 2015, p. 5). Meanwhile, consider how the "see something/say something" exhortation particularly hurts Arab-Semitic looking individuals, who have been reported as suspicious for carrying a pressure cooker to a friend's home for a potluck (Reeves, 2017, p. 137) or taking cups of water into the toilet to wash themselves per Islamic custom (Hijek, 2012). And then surveillance is often justified through race-based fear. Consider how, during a morning stroll in 2015, a 57-year-old South-Asian named Sureshbhai Patel was tackled and paralyzed by Alabama police because a neighborhood "watcher" identified him as a suspicious "skinny Black man" (Stephens, 2015). We see here how anti-Blackness and lateral surveillance work together to create an imagined threat. Simone Browne discusses how Blackness has been constituted as fundamentally *always out of place* through the early biometric technology of branding, which marked all Black individuals as out of place if they were not on their "assigned" plantation. Meanwhile, when I was a graduate student at the University of Texas at Austin in 2012, I recall campus being evacuated because of a bomb threat that the phone operator described as being made by a person with a "Middle Eastern accent" (White, 2012). Given that several languages are spoken in the Arabian Peninsula, this description is perplexing, but it works with racialized surveillance logics of threat. A Critical Surveillance approach pins down how we communicate the *need* for surveillance, and how the notion of "threat" is culturally constructed.

RACIALIZING RISK: THE PANOPTICON AND THE BAN-OPTICON

In both these examples (of Sureshbhai Patel and the bomb threat), we see the same idea: the state has racialized risk, *and it does this communicatively.* Didier Bigo terms this racialization of risk the ban-opticon (2008). Citizen vigilantes are encouraged to react based not just on what they are *seeing,* but increasingly on what they are *feeling.* Marnie Ritchie terms this "feeling for the state," (2015) and describes such experience of threat as "prerational" (2020), making it both spontaneous and difficult to interrupt. Thus, the vague messaging we see about surveillance (seeing "something," looking out for "suspicious" people) is not only intentional but designed to shift audiences away from *seeing* to *feeling.* Such cutting-edge feminist work from Critical Surveillance scholars in Communication Studies shows how surveillance—which comes from the French word meaning "watch from above"—is discreetly moving away from literal watching to *feeling.* You may recall how a Black child named Trayvon Martin was followed and murdered in 2012 by a neighborhood watch vigilante named George Zimmerman, because Zimmerman "felt" Martin was "up to no good" and "on drugs or something" (per Zimmerman's 911 call). We see Zimmerman assigning a threat in response to how he is *feeling* about Martin's mere presence. Complicating this is the fact that neighborhood watch groups are actually trained by the police (Reeves, 2017, p. 77–85), which means that everyday citizens are now tracking and profiling through racialized *feelings of threat.* Following Bigo's ban-opticon, we know that such tracking, profiling, and sorting of risk is racialized. Such sorting makes a Critical Surveillance eye crucial to *unsorting* the data and parse out race and risk.

It is worth noting that the term *ban-opticon* itself derives from *panopticon,* the first prison designed by architect Jeremy Bentham that continues to shape contemporary surveillance cultures. This structure, which Bentham designed with the aim to eliminate punishment of inmates, consists of a darkened central guard tower surrounded by a colosseum with hundreds of small, backlit cells. The idea is for a guard in the central watchtower to keep an eye on hundreds of inmates at once, who are permanently on display yet isolated from one another. Bentham reasoned that this would eventually train inmates to self-surveil while also preventing planned rebellions. Michel Foucault notes that long-term "surveillant cultures" arose from the design of this first prison structure (1995) and are visible in everyday public spaces today. Consider how retail stores have visible cameras, which may well be broken, to encourage costumes to self-surveil while feeling permanently on display. We see open office-plans that increase worker visibility while isolating them in cubicles. Foucault calls this trickling-down panoptic culture *panopticism.* But yet again, Critical Surveillance Studies deepens our understanding of panopticism by exposing how "constant visibility" is acutely experienced by Black individuals, trans individuals, women, and nonbinary individuals. Over and over again, we see the need for a Critical Surveillance approach in contemporary surveillance discourse to highlight issues of race, dis/ability, and gender inequities in surveillance.

OPACITY AND TRANSPARENCY: DISCURSIVELY CREATING THE TERRORIST

Finally, Critical Surveillance Studies have traced the rise of a persistent trope in rhetorics of safety: transparency discourse. Transparency discourse sorts objects, people, and behaviors into categories of safety and encourages looking *inside* objects and bodies to determine risk, intent, and threat. Think about how casually you might use the phrase "I wanted to be totally transparent" to imply that you are acting in good faith. This is not a coincidence: we see this value placed on transparency in myriad realms, from medical care for pregnant people via ultrasounds to carceral practices of looking into oral and anal cavities. Rachel Hall notes how the frenzied media coverage of Saddam Hussein's capture focused on his oral cavity search; a voyeuristic tour of his jail cell; and an obsession with the underground hole he was found hiding in (2015, p. 61–66). This desire to look into Muslim and Arab bodies is particularly pervasive: I examined dozens of YouTube videos of Muslim men in various Western countries standing on public streets, blindfolded with arms held open, to present themselves as "safe," demonstrating how both transparency *and* disability are meant to "neutralize" a "terrorist threat" (Bahrainwala, 2019). We also find that the Nike Pro Hijab, which purports to target Muslim women's needs, makes the hijab itself more "surveillable" (Bahrainwala & O'Connor, 2019) with a form-fitting, contoured design that achieves the same "transparency chic" (Hall, 2015, p. 25–35) achieved by individuals stripping off their outer layers, shoes, and headgear to demonstrate "safeness" during airport scans. And this transparency rhetoric is worldwide: to "destigmatize" conversations about menstruation, for instance, wealthy (largely cis-male) actors in the Indian film industry began unwrapping sanitary pads on video to "demystify" them (News18, 2018)—a bizarre performance that decidedly left out rural, non-English speaking Indian audiences who menstruate.

Make no mistake: this obsession with transparency can be deadly because it marks dark skin and disability as impediments to visibility—and therefore red flags. You will recall that certain bodies are considered persistently "opaque" because technology—like lighting and TSA scanners—are made keeping light skin, straight-textured hair, form-fitting clothing, and uncovered heads in mind. Furthermore, when airport security looks inside shoes, bags, and bodies through x-ray imaging, it puts pregnant, disabled, trans, Muslim, and Sikh individuals (who wear headcoverings) at risk. Consider, then, how much *more* invasive these transparency measures might be for a Black Muslim woman who wears a pacemaker—one whose skin, hair, headcovering, and disability all potentially trigger additional surveillance. And return to the murder of Trayvon Martin, we see how the opacity assigned to this Black child became fatal: his murderer, George Zimmerman, repeatedly mentioned that Martin's hands were concealed in his pockets; that he was wearing a hoodie, and that his (dark) skin was dimly visible. Transparency rhetorics are deadly, and we interrupt them through an intersectional Critical Surveillance approach.

LIVING ETHICALLY IN A SURVEILLANT WORLD

So if we had to summarize the nature and uses of Critical Surveillance Studies, we might say that it:

1. Uncovers templates of which bodies and which movements are "norm-al;"
2. It reveals our values through how we sort data; and
3. It recognizes how to surveil, and thus structure society, more inclusively and effectively

While it's understandable to feel discouraged by the pervasiveness of surveillance and ongoing invasions of privacy, it is worth remembering that surveillance is essential to the functioning of democracy and the protection of the most vulnerable. We *need* systems in place to track and sort data so that we may engage in civic activities, like voting, and allocate support to our most vulnerable. And so, instead of becoming pessimistic, we must turn our attention to how we *sort* the data (Lyon, 1994, p. 218–225) and how this sorting impacts our interpretation of who should receive support and who should be policed. Thus, by compelling us to take an intersectional look at gathered data, Critical Surveillance Studies help us see *how* technologies are not neutral, and *why* sorting is a political act. When we reject the idea that technology and sorting are "neutral," we equip ourselves to better understand the communications we receive as we move through our world, helping us live more freely, safely, and equitably.

REFERENCES

Bahrainwala, L. (2019). Blind Submission. *Communication, Culture & Critique, 12*(4), 519–534. https://doi.org/10.1093/ccc/tcz027

Bahrainwala, L., & O'Connor, E. (2019). Nike unveils Muslim women athletes. *Feminist Media Studies, 22*(3), 469–484. https://doi.org/10.1080/14680777.2019.1620822

Bigo, D. (2008). Globalized (in) security: the field and the ban-opticon. In *Terror, insecurity and liberty* (pp. 20–58). Routledge.

Drowning Facts (2022, March 10). *Centers for Disease Control and Prevention.* https://www.cdc.gov/drowning/facts/index.html

Dubina, K. (2021, September 15). Hispanics in the Labor Force. U.S. Department of Labor Blog. https://blog.dol.gov/2021/09/15/hispanics-in-the-labor-force-5-facts

Dubrofsky, R. E., & Magnet, S. A. (2015). *Feminist surveillance studies.* Duke University Press.

Foucault, M. (1995). *Discipline & punish: The birth of the prison.* Translated by Alan Sheridan. Vintage Books.

Guhin, B. (2019, August 27). *Celebrate the people who are supporting our community at the 2019 Civic Futures Awards.* Medium. https://medium.com/civiqueso/celebrate-the-people-who-are-supporting-our-community-at-the-2019-civic-futures-awards-c4256845cad6

Hall, R. (2015). *The transparent traveler.* Duke University Press.

Harmon, K. (2009, May 29). Can you lose your fingerprints? Scientific American. https://www.scientificamerican.com/article/lose-your-fingerprints/

Hijek, B. (2012, May 29). Muslim family detained at airport over bathroom ritual. Sun Sentinel. https://www.sun-sentinel.com/sfl-mtblog-2012-05-muslim_family_detained_at_airp-story.html

Lyon, D. (2007). *Surveillance studies: An overview.* Polity.

Lyon, D. (1994). *Electronic eye: The rise of surveillance society.* University of Minnesota Press.

Moore, K. D. (2015). Held in the light: Reading images of Rihanna's domestic abuse. In R. E. Dubrosky & S. A. Magnet (Eds.), *Feminist surveillance studies* (pp. 107 – 124). Duke University Press.

Newman, M. (2014). *Yelp Reviews Help Track Food Illnesses. The New York Times.* https://www.nytimes.com/2014/05/23/dining/reviews-on-yelp-help-track-illness.html

News18 (2018, February 6). PadMan Challenge Unites Bollywood; Celebrities Break Taboo Surrounding Menstrual Hygiene. https://www.news18.com/news/movies/padman-challenge-unites-bollywood-kjo-deepika-anushka-alia-break-taboo-surrounding-menstrual-hygiene-1651983.html

Noble, S. U. (2018). *Algorithms of oppression: How search engines reinforce racism.* NYU Press.

NPR (2008, May 6). Racial History of American Swimming Pools. https://www.npr.org/2008/05/06/90213675/racial-history-of-american-swimming-pools

Reeves, J. (2017). *Citizen spies: The long rise of America's surveillance society.* NYU Press.

Ritchie, M. (2015). Feeling for the state: Affective labor and anti-terrorism training in US hotels. *Communication and Critical/Cultural Studies, 12*(2), 179–197. https://doi.org/10.1080/14791420.2015.1023816

Ritchie, M. (2020). Fusing race: The phobogenics of racializing surveillance. *Surveillance & society, 18*(1), 12–29. https://doi.org/10.24908/ss.v18i1.13131

Simmons, A. (2014). *Gastronomic Bigotry.* Slate. https://slate.com/human-interest/2014/06/ethnic-restaurants-and-food-poisoning-the-subtle-racism-of-saying-chinese-food-caused-your-stomachache.html

Stephens, C. (2015, February 12). Alabama police fire, arrest the officer who badly injured Indian grandfather during sidewalk stop. Alabama Local News. https://www.al.com/news/2015/02/adison_police_fire_and_arrest.html

Stockman, J. K., Hayashi, H., & Campbell, J. C. (2015). Intimate partner violence and its health impact on ethnic minority women. *Journal of Women's Health, 24*(1), 62–79. https://doi.org/10.1089/jwh.2014.4879

University of Illinois Chicago School of Public Health (2021, February 2). Black, Hispanic Americans are Overrepresented in Essential Jobs. https://publichealth.uic.edu/news-stories/black-hispanic-americans-are-overrepresented-in-essential-jobs/

White, A. (2012, Sept. 14). UT Bomb Threat Declared a Hoax; Response Questioned. The Texas Tribune. https://www.texastribune.org/2012/09/14/ut-campus-cleared-after-bomb-threat-no-weapons-fou

INTERPERSONAL COMMUNICATION

The interpersonal communication context focuses on how we convey messages in our close and connected relationships. These close relationships (e.g., romantic relationships and friendships) are initiated, maintained, and terminated, by our interactions and communication decisions. Some major areas of research in interpersonal communication include relational uncertainty, social support, conflict, and affection. This section includes chapters focusing on three important areas of interpersonal communication research: (1) relationship maintenance, (2) jealousy, and (3) sexual communication. First, Marianne Dainton (La Salle University) reviews how couples stay together by keeping their romantic relationships in a desired state. Second, Laura Guerrero (Arizona State University) reviews how partners experience and respond to jealousy in their romantic relationships. Third, Amanda Denes, Rachel Tucker, and Eli Quay (University of Connecticut) review research on communication before, during, and after sexual activity. Since most of us commit (at least temporarily) to a romantic relationship at some point in life (and you might have a partner right now), these research programs will help you understand how to build, maintain, and communicate effectively in romantic relationships. After all, it is communication that can make or break your love life.

ROMANTIC RELATIONSHIP MAINTENANCE

Marianne Dainton
La Salle University

According to the U.S. Census, about 34% of marriages end in divorce, with the rates significantly higher for second marriages and among older Americans (Mayol-García et al., 2021). Yet, Americans believe in love. According to some recent statistics, 94% of Americans believe in true love, and over 70% believe in soul mates (Brooks, 2021). So, why the relatively high divorce rate? One possibility is related to your beliefs about love. Scholars have identified two different beliefs about love: a destiny belief and a growth belief (Knee, 1998). People who hold a destiny belief are those who believe in soul mates; they believe in perfect matches and that love conquers all. Unfortunately, when the inevitable problems arise, they tend to become disillusioned and leave the relationship. Conversely, individuals who have growth beliefs believe that relationships are built over time. They are more likely to engage in relationship maintenance behaviors, both in terms of preventative and corrective measures. For that reason, they are more likely to avoid the types of disillusionment that lead to divorce.

For the past 30 years, my research has focused on the communication associated with maintaining romantic relationships. First, I should explain what I mean by relationship maintenance. There are actually several different ways you can think about it (Dindia & Canary, 1993). The first way is to consider whether the couple is still together, regardless of whether they are happy or not. We all know people who stay in a relationship for a long time but seem to be miserable in the relationship. Using this first way of defining maintenance, it does not matter whether the individuals are happy, only that they are still together. The second way to define maintenance is as the efforts the couple uses to keep their relationship in a preferred state. In this scenario, it is not enough to just keep the relationship intact, the partners have to achieve a desired level of happiness, love, commitment, or intimacy, for example. Lastly, relationship maintenance might center on keeping a relationship in repair. Unlike the previous definitions, which focus more on "prevention" of problems, this definition centers on "fixing" things when they break. For example, maintenance would involve efforts to resolve an existing conflict, negotiate how to live with an ongoing disappointment, or dealing with discovered deception. My own research uses the second way of thinking about maintenance. I am interested in not only how couples manage to remain together happily, but also how other important components of the relationship are sustained. What keeps people in love? How do we remain committed to our partners?

This chapter is divided into three distinct areas of focus associated with maintaining romantic relationships. The first section focuses on the types of communication that serve to maintain relationships. The second section addresses the question of why some people engage in maintenance and others do not. The last section focuses on the how the relationship is affected by the use of maintenance behaviors.

MAINTENANCE BEHAVIORS

One of the first studies that specifically focused on relationship maintenance was conducted by two communication scholars (who happened to be in a long-distance romantic relationship at the time). Laura Stafford and Dan Canary (1991) first asked 77 people to respond to the question "What do you do to maintain your relationship?" Based on the answers they received, Stafford and Canary created a questionnaire to measure how frequently people reported that they engaged in particular behaviors, which they distributed to nearly 1000 people who were in a romantic relationship at the time they completed the survey. They used a statistical technique called factor analysis to explore the results of the survey, which uncovered five maintenance behaviors. The first was **positivity**, which refers to efforts to be cheerful and optimistic around the partner. **Openness** means having serious discussions about the relationship. **Assurances**, the third strategy they uncovered, is when people reassure their partner about their love and commitment to the relationship. The fourth strategy Stafford and Canary (1991) uncovered was **social networks**, which means relying on common family and friends. Finally, **sharing tasks** refers to completing responsibilities that the couple face.

My own research has extended the results of this original study in three important ways. First, Stafford and Canary focused on *strategies* that people used to maintain relationships, but my own experience suggested that people are not always consciously thinking about their relationship and intentionally engaging in behaviors in order to maintain their relationship. Instead, I thought that people often engage in *routine* maintenance behavior; behavior that is not consciously thought about or intentionally acted in order to maintain the relationship.

For example, I suspect that giving your partner a kiss goodbye before leaving for work is just part of a daily routine, and not something that a person thinks "oh, I have to kiss him good-bye so that our relationship succeeds." In a series of studies, my colleagues and I sought to identify the routine nature of relationship maintenance. These studies confirmed the original five behaviors I just described, as well as two additional maintenance behaviors: conflict management and advice (Dainton & Stafford, 1993; Stafford et al., 2000). **Conflict management** refers to proactive ways to deal with conflict such as apologizing when you are wrong and being patient and forgiving with the partner. **Advice** means providing a "reality check" for your partner and serving as a sounding board for his or her complaints.

Once we uncovered these additional behaviors, I was interested in further exploring the extent to which these behaviors were performed routinely or strategically. Dr. Brooks Aylor and I conducted a survey asking people how often they performed each of the seven behaviors strategically (with the explicit goal of maintaining the relationship) and how often they performed the same behavior routinely (without really thinking about why they were performing the behavior). We found that positivity and tasks were performed more routinely than strategically, but that no behaviors were performed more strategically than routinely (Dainton & Aylor, 2002). Interestingly, we also found no relationship between the routine use of a behavior and a strategic use of a behavior. What that means is that the same person who uses assurances strategically is unlikely to also use assurances routinely; it's not that some people just like to use particular behaviors. Instead, clusters of behaviors seem to be used routinely, and clusters of behaviors are likely to be performed routinely. Aylor and I hypothesized that in long-term relationships people might use routine maintenance, but if something happens to break a couple's routine, the relationship partners might switch to strategic maintenance (Dainton & Aylor, 2002). In that case, strategic maintenance might better be understood using the fourth definition of maintenance, which centers on "repair" rather than prevention of problems.

The second way I have critiqued and extended the original Stafford and Canary (1991) study has been through a focus on negative maintenance behaviors. The original five strategies, and the updated seven behaviors, all have a bias toward positive behavior. That is, most of us would agree that these are positive things to do in a relationship. But all of us know that relationships include both positive and negative behavior, good times and bad. Accordingly, my student Jaime Gross and I copied the original methods used by Stafford and Canary (1991) in order to develop a measure of negative maintenance behaviors. We first asked a sample of people about the negative things they do for relationship purposes (Dainton & Gross, 2008). We then turned this data into survey items and conducted a survey asking people to respond to the frequency with which they performed these behaviors. Using factor analysis, we identified six negative maintenance behaviors. The first negative maintenance behavior is **jealousy induction**, which is an intentional effort to make the partner jealous. Second is **avoidance**, which refers both to avoiding the partner as well as avoiding topics that might lead to arguments. **Spying** is third. Not surprisingly, this involves checking the partner's mail or phone or actively talking to the partner's friends to gather information. Next is **infidelity**. Believe it or not, some people report behaviors ranging from flirting to having sex with other people so that he or she can prevent boredom. **Destructive conflict** is the fifth type of negative maintenance; unlike the more positive conflict management identified earlier, this behavior refers to controlling behavior and seeking arguments. The final behavior is **allowing control**, which references breaking plans with family or friends to be with the partner, avoiding activities that the individual previously enjoyed because the partner does not like them, and letting the partner make decisions for him or her.

Finally, given the growth in social and new media, more recently my research has shifted to focus on how relationship maintenance is achieved through social media. I developed a scale to study social media maintenance that measures three prosocial behaviors—**positivity**, **assurances**, and **openness**—and one negative behavior, **online monitoring** (which is conceptually similar to the spying behavior identified by Dainton & Gross, 2007; Dainton, 2013). Several studies have used this measure and have concluded that in general relationship maintenance via social media can complement other forms of maintenance, but it cannot replace face-to-face maintenance in close relationships (Dainton & Stokes, 2015; Stewart et al., 2014).

WHAT PREDICTS MAINTENANCE BEHAVIOR?

The second major question my research has addressed has been to determine what predicts the use of maintenance behavior. Certainly, an understanding of what people do to maintain relationships, strategically or routinely, positively or negatively, and across a variety of different communication channels is important. But clearly not everyone engages in maintenance behaviors, otherwise, relationships would never end. My research has focused on four distinct variations: Sex and gender differences in the use of maintenance, cultural adaptations, differences in relationship type, and theoretical predictions.

SEX AND GENDER DIFFERENCES

From the very beginning of scholarly research into relationship maintenance, scholars have been interested in whether men and women perform maintenance in a similar fashion. The results from a host of studies indicate that although men and women typically use the same maintenance behaviors, women tend to use more maintenance overall (see Aylor & Dainton, 2004). However, we should be very careful about the use of the terms *sex* and *gender*. *Sex* refers to biological differences, so if we said women engage in more maintenance than men we would be suggesting that there are biological reasons for this pattern. *Gender*, on the other hand, focuses on how people are raised to behave. If you are looking at gender differences in communication, then you would be focusing on how feminine people, masculine people, and androgynous people (i.e., people high in both masculinity and femininity) behave. Because previous research found that there are very few biological differences in communication (Canary & Hause, 1993), I conducted two studies looking at how gender might be related to relationship maintenance.

First, I worked with Stafford and Haas to determine whether sex or gender is a better predictor of the use of maintenance (Stafford et al., 2000). Interestingly, we found a rather small correlation between sex and gender ($r = .13$). What this means is that knowing whether someone is a male or female does not help particularly to determine if they are masculine or feminine. Put in another way, not all men are masculine and not all women are feminine. In this study, we found that if you control for someone's gender role, there were only two significant relationships between biological sex and the use of maintenance: women were slightly more likely to use openness and shared tasks. Instead, we found that femininity was the single best predictor of all seven pro-social maintenance behaviors. The takeaway piece of advice is that if you want a maintained relationship, you should make sure your partner has either a feminine or androgynous gender role.

In the second study, Aylor and I looked at sex and gender differences in the routine and strategic use of maintenance behaviors (Aylor & Dainton, 2004). Replicating the study I did with Stafford et al., we found that gender role was a stronger predictor of maintenance than sex, with sex predicting only one maintenance behavior: the routine use of openness. More interestingly, we found that femininity was a better predictor of routine maintenance, and masculinity was a better predictor of strategic maintenance. This suggests that feminine people tend to think about relationship maintenance as simply part of a daily routine, whereas masculine people tend to operate on a "if it ain't broke, why fix it" model. That is, masculine people tend to approach maintenance as something that is done only when there is a problem that needs to be solved.

CULTURAL ADAPTATIONS

Most of the research that I have discussed so far has focused primarily on White couples. Because life experiences are often different for persons of color, I have conducted several studies focused on the experience of relationship maintenance among Black couples and among interracial couples. Taking a culturally sensitive stance, I first conducted in-depth interviews with Black married couples to identify the maintenance behaviors they used in their marriages (Dainton, 2017a). Notably, the respondents identified the same maintenance behaviors that we had used in previous research, but they identified some differences in the meanings of these behaviors. For example, many of the Black couples suggested that they were "brutally honest" with each other. Although this is analogous to the openness maintenance behavior, the intensity of the description reflects research that has found that the typical Black communication pattern is more direct and expressive than the typical White communication pattern (Hecht et al., 1989). In addition, the couples indicated that they perceived positivity to be inauthentic, and therefore violated the importance of honesty (Dainton, 2017a). Finally, the couples that I interviewed suggested that social networks could be problematic, and they tended to try to keep other people "out of our relationship."

Following the depth interviews I did a large-scale survey of 494 married individuals, among whom 260 were Black and 232 were White. The results of this study indicated variations in the use of maintenance, with the White individuals reporting that they used more assurances and social networks than the Black individuals, and the Black individuals reporting that they used more jealousy induction and infidelity than the White individuals. However, race explained very little of the variance in maintenance enactment, meaning that although these differences were statistically significant, there is little practical significance to these results.

DIFFERENCES IN RELATIONSHIP TYPE

You may have noticed that I have been using the neutral term "relationship partner" throughout this chapter. That's because not all romantic relationship types are the same, and a great deal of research has sought to compare married and dating relationships. First, there are clear differences in the maintenance efforts in dating and married relationships. Stafford and Canary (1991) found that married people were more likely than dating people to use assurances and that dating people were more likely than married people to use openness. Similarly, my work with Stafford (Dainton & Stafford, 1993) indicated that married people were more likely to engage in sharing tasks, whereas dating couples were more likely to use mediated communication to sustain their relationship.

One way to think about these differences might be to think about these groups as ultimately demonstrating different relationship lengths rather than different types of relationships. In my own work, I have found that people engage in less maintenance over time (Dainton, 2000), although the most accurate way to describe this is with a U-shaped curve (Dainton, 2008). That is, after an early high in the amount of maintenance, the use of maintenance steadily drops over time, with it increasing again later in life (usually associated with after the children have left the home). Historically, research has indicated that the birth of children is negatively associated with relationship maintenance, but (good news for prospective parents out there!), it seems that this U-shaped curve is true for both parents and nonparents (Dainton, 2008).

What is particularly interesting is that although these behaviors are used less frequently over time, people tend to keep their expectations for their partner's use of the behavior fairly high (Dainton, 2000). This sets them up for potential dissatisfaction, as their expectations are not being met. The best advice I can give for this is that we ought to change our expectations as our relationship changes; "happily ever after" is a pretty difficult standard to achieve.

THEORETICAL PREDICTIONS

It is the rare student who looks forward to a class in communication theory. However, theory often provides us with important insights in how we should behave in everyday life. In my own work, I have used three different theories to help me to understand why some people engage in maintenance and others do not.

The first theoretical approach is social exchange, which takes an economic approach to understanding relationships. Social exchange theory focuses on the rewards and costs associated with being in a relationship. In this approach, the partner's use of positive maintenance behaviors would be considered a reward, and one's own use of positive maintenance is considered a cost. Stafford and Canary's original maintenance study used social exchange theory (Canary & Stafford, 1992, 2001; Stafford & Canary, 1991), with a particular focus on one type of social exchange theory called equity theory. The simple explanation of equity theory is that people are happiest when they are receiving the same proportion of rewards to costs as their partner (Sprecher, 1986). If an individual is putting more into the relationship than what s/he is getting out of it, the relationship would be considered under-benefitted, and if the reverse is true—the person is getting more out of it than what they are putting into it—the relationship is considered over-benefitted. Typically, about 50% of people in relationships consider themselves to be in equitable relationships, with the remaining 50% divided equally between those who think they are under-benefitted and those that think they are over-benefitted. Stafford and Canary (1991) found partial support for this approach, finding that, in general, people who think they have an equitable relationship engage in more pro-social maintenance.

My own research reaches much the same conclusion; equity principles do predict the use of maintenance some of the time. However, it does not provide a particularly robust explanation for maintenance. In one study, I compared the extent to which equity theory, reciprocal exchange (i.e., if my partner uses assurance then I use assurances too), and self-interest (i.e., the only thing that matters is receiving maintenance behaviors) explained relationship maintenance (Dainton, 2017b). The study found that all three factors mattered, but that equity explained very little in the use of maintenance. Moreover, equity also does not predict the use of negative maintenance behaviors. That is, one would expect people in equitable relationships would use fewer negative behaviors, and that those in under-benefitted relationships might use more negative maintenance behaviors. However, we found only one relationship between equity and negative maintenance, with over-benefitted people using avoidance less than the other two groups (Dainton & Gross, 2008).

The second theoretical approach is uncertainty reduction theory, which argues that uncertainty is detrimental to relationship stability (Berger, 1987). Two particular forms of uncertainty appear to be most associated with romantic relationships: future uncertainty and mutuality uncertainty. According to Knobloch and Solomon (1999), future uncertainty refers to an individual's feelings of being unsure where the relationship is going, and mutuality uncertainty refers to an individual's insecurity about whether the partner feels the same way that he or she does. In several studies, I have found some evidence that the use of relationship maintenance behaviors is a means for managing uncertainty (e.g., Dainton & Aylor, 2001). In fact, in a direct test of competing theoretical predictions, certainty (the opposite of uncertainty) was a better predictor of the use of positive maintenance behaviors than was equity, although both certainty and equity together did predict an individual's use of positivity, openness, and conflict management (Dainton, 2003). Of interest, uncertainty also seems to predict the use of negative maintenance behaviors, with uncertain individuals engaging in more of all six of the negative maintenance behaviors (Dainton et al., 2017).

The final theoretical approach I have used is attachment theory. Attachment theory suggests that our early relationship with caregivers (usually parents) influences how we see all of our adult relationships (Bartholomew, 1990). Four attachment styles have been identified in research. **Secure** individuals have positive self-esteem and hold positive views of others. **Preoccupied** individuals have negative views of themselves and positive views of others. These people tend to be overly focused on the relationship and have a tendency to "smother" their partners with care. **Fearful avoidant** types have negative views of both themselves and others. These individuals are terrified of being hurt and are most likely to desire being in a relationship but be too afraid to do so. Finally, the **dismissive** attachment style has a positive view of self and a negative view of others. These individuals are most likely to be game-players who do not value, and do not pay attention to, their relationships with others.

My research has determined that attachment theory successfully predicts positive maintenance use, with secure individuals engaging in all seven pro-social behaviors more than any other group, and dismissive individuals engaging in less of all seven behaviors than any other group (Dainton, 2007). However, the use of maintenance by the other two attachment groups is less clear-cut; I found that preoccupied and fearful-avoidant individuals are less likely to use positivity or positive conflict management, but are more likely to use assurances. It seems that these individuals are quite good at expressing love but are not so good at engaging in behaviors that would make them more loveable.

I have also studied how attachment styles influence the use of negative maintenance behaviors (Goodboy et al., 2017). This research indicates that secure individuals were less likely to use negative maintenance behaviors with the exception of avoidance, and that preoccupied and dismissive individuals were more likely to use all six negative maintenance behaviors. More importantly, Goodboy and Bolkan (2011) found that dismissive and fearful avoidants were more likely to use the negative maintenance behaviors regardless of how satisfied they were.

THE EFFECTS OF MAINTENANCE BEHAVIORS

Throughout this chapter, I have talked about a number of different positive and negative maintenance behaviors, but I should caution you that not all behaviors "count" equally. That is, some of these behaviors are much more important than others. Across a number of studies, my own research and that of my colleagues have found that using assurances (both routine and strategic), routine positivity, and positive conflict management is associated with greater relationship satisfaction (e.g., Dainton, 2000; Dainton & Gross, 2008; Stafford & Canary, 1991; Stafford et al., 2000). Conversely, using the negative maintenance behaviors of allowing control, destructive conflict, infidelity, and jealousy induction is negatively associated with satisfaction (Dainton & Gross, 2008; Goodboy et al., 2010).

What is surprising to most people is that using openness—even though it is considered a positive strategy—has been negatively related to satisfaction in virtually all studies (e.g., Dainton, 2000; Dainton & Aylor, 2002; Stafford et al., 2000). Before you start keeping secrets and lying to your partner, you need to remember that correlation does not equal causation. That is, because of statistical limitations, it might simply be that unhappy people use openness, and not that openness leads to unhappiness. Picture the "big relationship talk." Most people avoid it unless and until they are so unhappy they have to express their unhappiness. Also of interest, and unlike in the White samples that make up most studies of maintenance, when I compared the impact of maintenance behaviors for married Black individuals and married White individuals, I discovered that the use of openness is not a negative predictor of satisfaction for Black couples (Dainton, 2017a). Accordingly, there are cultural differences in how openness affects a relationship.

Also of interest, you might recall that social networks were identified by the Black couples I interviewed as a tension in their relationship (Dainton, 2017a). Social networks do not typically emerge as a significant factor in predicting relationship satisfaction or commitment in the majority of studies using a White sample. However, when I studied interracial couples use of maintenance I found that social networks were associated with satisfaction and commitment (Dainton, 2015). I suspect that ongoing social challenges associated with interracial relationships make having a solid support system especially useful for these types of relationships.

In the very beginning of this chapter, I indicated that I believe that maintenance has broader implications for relationships than just the link between maintenance and satisfaction. To summarize other findings (e.g., Dainton et al., 1994; Goodboy et al., 2010; Stafford & Canary, 1991), feelings of love are associated with positivity and tasks. Liking is most associated with positivity, assurances, and relying on social networks, and the use of negative maintenance behaviors is associated with the decreases in liking. Control Mutuality (agreeing on who has the right to influence the other in the relationship) is associated with positivity, assurances, and social networks. As for commitment, the most consistent finding is that assurances and sharing tasks are the best pro-social maintenance behaviors and that all six negative behaviors are associated with lower levels of commitment. Clearly, using assurances and positivity makes the most difference in the maintenance of desired relationship states.

I mentioned an important axiom saying that "correlation doesn't equal causation" just a few paragraphs ago. I should mention that originally maintenance was viewed as both a cause and consequence of relationship characteristics like satisfaction. That is, we believed that satisfied people used maintenance, which leads to satisfaction, which leads to maintenance, and so on. Since the original study in 1991, we now know this is not the case. Dainton and Stafford (2000) got their first clue when they conducted a study to see what predicted maintenance. They were surprised to find that satisfaction did not predict the use of any maintenance behaviors, and commitment had only a slight effect on a few behaviors. Directly testing this finding, Canary, Stafford, and Semic (2002) surveyed married couples once a month for three months and found that the use of maintenance predicts feelings of satisfaction, commitment, and love, but the reverse is not true. In addition, they found that the effects of maintenance fade rather quickly, so maintenance has to be continuously enacted if you want to sustain your preferred level of satisfaction, love, and the like.

CONCLUSION

Thirty years after beginning a sustained program of research into relationship maintenance, we can conclude that using specific maintenance behaviors, especially being reassuring and being positive, leads to a more satisfying and committed relationship. We know that gender is more strongly associated with using relationship maintenance behaviors than sex is, so forget about the whole "Men are from Mars, Women are from Venus" thing. We know that relationship maintenance efforts fade over time, which is likely why people tend to become less satisfied over time. However, some types of people are more likely to use more maintenance and remain more satisfied than others.

As key take-ways about maintaining romantic relationships, consider some of the principles of relationship maintenance developed by Dainton and Myers (2020):

Principle 1: Cultural prescriptions influence the maintenance process in important ways;

Principle 2: Maintenance occurs on multiple different communication channels, but mediated maintenance complements, rather than substitutes for, face-to-face maintenance in close relationships;

Principle 3: People engage in both functional and dysfunctional maintenance activity;

Principle 4: The two maintenance behaviors that most influence relational qualities are positivity and assurance.

REFERENCES

Aylor, B., & Dainton, M. (2004). Biological sex and psychological gender as predictors of routine and strategic relational maintenance. *Sex Roles, 50*, 689–697. https://doi.org/10.1023/B:SERS.0000027570.80468.a0

Bartholomew, K. (1990). Avoidance of intimacy: An attachment perspective. *Journal of Social and Personal Relationships, 7*(2), 147–178. https://doi.org/10.1177/0265407590072001

Berger, C. R. (1987). Communicating under uncertainty. In M. E. Roloff & G. R. Miller (Eds.), *Interpersonal processes: New directions in communication research* (pp. 39–62). Sage.

Brooks, A. C. (2021, September 9). Stop waiting for your soul mate: Love isn't destiny. That's what makes it sweet. *The Atlantic.* https://www.theatlantic.com/family/archive/2021/09/soul-mates-love-destiny/620014/

Canary, D. J., & Hause, K. S. (1993). Is there any reason to research sex differences in communication? *Communication Quarterly, 41*(2), 129–144. https://doi.org/10.1080/01463379309369874

Canary, D. J., & Stafford, L. (1992). Relational maintenance strategies and equity in marriage. *Communication Monographs, 59*(3), 243–267. https://doi.org/10.1080/03637759209376268

Canary, D. J., & Stafford, L. (2001). Equity in the preservation of personal relationships. In J. H. Harvey & A. Wenzel (Eds.), *Close romantic relationships: Maintenance and enhancement* (pp. 133–151). Erlbaum.

Canary, D. J., Stafford, L., & Semic, B. A. (2002). A panel study of the associations between maintenance strategies and relational characteristics. *Journal of Marriage and Family, 64*(2), 395–406. https://doi.org/10.1111/j.1741-3737.2002.00395.x

Dainton, M. (2000). Maintenance behaviors, expectations, and satisfaction: Linking the comparison level to relational maintenance. *Journal of Social and Personal Relationships, 17*(6), 827–842. https://doi.org/10.1177/0265407500176007

Dainton, M. (2003). Equity and uncertainty in relational maintenance. *Western Journal of Communication, 67*(2), 164–186. https://doi.org/10.1080/10570310309374765

Dainton, M. (2007). Attachment and marital maintenance. *Communication Quarterly, 55*(3), 283–298. https://doi.org/10.1080/01463370701490083

Dainton, M. (2008). The use of relationship maintenance behaviors as a mechanism to explain the decline in marital satisfaction among parents. *Communication Reports, 21*(1), 33–45. https://doi.org/10.1080/08934210802019413

Dainton, M. (2013). Relationship maintenance on Facebook: Development of a measure, relationship to general maintenance, and relationship satisfaction. *College Student Journal, 47,* 113–121.

Dainton, M. (2015). An interdependence approach to relationship maintenance in interracial marriage. *Journal of Social Issues, 71*(4), 772–787. https://doi.org/10.1111/josi.12148

Dainton, M. (2017a). *Maintaining Black marriages: Individual, interpersonal, and contextual dynamics.* Lexington Books.

Dainton, M. (2017b). Equity, equality, and self-interest in marital maintenance. *Communication Quarterly, 64*(3), 247–267. https://doi.org/10.1080/01463373.2016.1227346

Dainton, M., & Aylor, B. A. (2001). A relational uncertainty analysis of jealousy, trust, and the maintenance of long-distance versus geographically-close relationships. *Communication Quarterly, 49*(2), 172–188. https://doi.org/10.1080/01463370109385624

Dainton, M., & Aylor, B. A. (2002). Routine and strategic maintenance efforts: Behavioral patterns, variations associated with relational length, and the prediction of relational characteristics. *Communication Monographs, 69*(1), 52–66. https://doi.org/10.1080/03637750216533

Dainton, M., Goodboy, A. K., Borzea, D., & Goldman, Z. W. (2017). The dyadic effects of relationship uncertainty on negative relational maintenance. *Communication Reports, 30*(3), 170–181. https://doi.org/10.1080/08934215.2017.1282529

Dainton, M., & Gross, J. (2008). The use of negative strategies for relationship maintenance. *Communication Research Reports, 25*(3), 179–191. https://doi.org/10.1080/08824090802237600

Dainton, M. & Myers, S. A. (2020). *Communication and relational maintenance.* Cognella.

Dainton, M., & Stafford, L. (1993). Routine maintenance behaviors: A comparison of relationship type, partner similarity and sex differences. *Journal of Social and Personal Relationships, 10*(2), 255–272. https://doi.org/10.1177/026540759301000206

Dainton, M., & Stafford, L. (2000). Predicting maintenance enactment from relational schemata, spousal behavior, and relational characteristics. *Communication Research Reports, 17*(2), 171–180. https://doi.org/10.1080/08824090009388763

Dainton, M., Stafford, L., & Canary, D. J. (1994). Maintenance strategies and physical affection as predictors of love, liking, and satisfaction in marriage. *Communication Reports, 7*(2), 88–98. https://doi.org/10.1080/08934219409367591

Dainton, M., & Stokes, A. (2015). College students' romantic relationships on Facebook: Linking the gratification for maintenance to Facebook maintenance activity and the experience of jealousy. *Communication Quarterly, 63*(4), 365–383. https://doi.org/10.1080/01463373.2015.1058283

Dindia, K., & Canary, D. J. (1993). Definitions and theoretical perspectives on maintaining relationships. *Journal of Social and Personal Relationships, 10*(2), 163–173. https://doi.org/10.1177/026540759301000201

Goodboy, A. K., & Bolkan, S. (2011). Attachment and the use of negative relational maintenance behaviors in romantic relationships. *Communication Research Reports, 28*(4), 327–336. https://doi.org/10.1080/08824096.2011.616244

Goodboy, A. K., Dainton, M., Borzea, D., & Goldman, Z. W. (2017). Attachment and negative relational maintenance: Dyadic comparisons using an actor-partner interdependence model. *Western Journal of Communication, 81*(5), 541–559. https://doi.org/10.1080/10570314.2017.1302601

Goodboy, A. K., Myers, S. A., & Members of Investigating Communication (2010). Relational quality indicators and love styles as predictors of negative relational maintenance behaviors in romantic relationships. *Communication Reports, 23*(2), 65–78. https://doi.org/10.1080/08934215.2010.511397

Hecht, M., Ribeau, S., & Alberts, J. K. (1989). An Afro-American perspective on interethnic communication. *Communication Monographs, 56*(4), 385–410. https://doi.org/10.1080/03637758909390271

Knee, C. R. (1998). Implicit theories of relationships: Assessment and prediction of romantic relationship initiation, coping, and longevity. *Journal of Personality and Social Psychology, 74*(2), 360–370. https://doi.org/10.1037/0022-3514.74.2.360

Knobloch, L. K., & Solomon, D. H. (1999). Measuring the sources and content of relational uncertainty. *Communication Studies, 50*(4), 161–278. https://doi.org/10.1080/10510979909388499

Mayol-García, Y., Gurrentz, B., & Kreider, R. M. (2021, April). Number, timing, and duration of marriages and divorces: 2016. *Current Population Reports, P70–167.* U.S. Census Bureau.

Sprecher, S. (1986). The relation between inequity and emotions in close relationships. *Social Psychology Quarterly, 49*(4), 309–321. https://www.jstor.org/stable/2786770

Stafford, L., & Canary, D. J. (1991). Maintenance strategies and romantic relationship type, gender and relational characteristics. *Journal of Social and Personal Relationships, 8*(2), 217–242. https://doi.org/10.1177/0265407591082004

Stafford, L., Dainton, M., & Haas, S. (2000). Measuring routine and strategic relational maintenance: Scale development, sex versus gender roles, and the prediction of relational characteristics. *Communication Monographs, 67*(3), 306–323. https://doi.org/10.1080/03637750009376512

Stewart, M. C., Dainton, M., & Goodboy, A. K. (2014). Maintaining relationships on Facebook: Associations with uncertainty, jealousy, and satisfaction. *Communication Reports, 27*(1), 13–26. https://doi.org/10.1080/08934215.2013.845675

COMMUNICATIVE RESPONSES TO JEALOUSY: HOW TO COPE WITH THE GREEN-EYED MONSTER

Laura K. Guerrero
Arizona State University

Jealousy has been the subject of plays, movies, poems, and songs for centuries. Shakespeare called jealousy the green-eyed monster in *Othello*. In contemporary times, Nick Jonas sang that jealousy gives him a "right to be hellish" in his hit song, *Jealous*. Jealousy is fascinating in part because it is connected to love and hate but also to protection and possession. How people communicate about jealousy plays a key role in determining if jealousy has negative or positive effects on relationships (Andersen et al., 1995; Guerrero, 2014; White & Mullen, 1989). Thus, this chapter centers around two questions: How do people communicate about jealousy and are some types of jealous communication more helpful or harmful than others?

Before answering those questions, it is important to define jealousy within the context of romantic relationships. *Romantic jealousy* is a cognitive, emotional, and behavioral reaction to a real or perceived threat to a romantic relationship by a rival (Guerrero & Andersen, 1998b; Pfeiffer & Wong, 1989; White & Mullen, 1989). Notice that the threat only needs to be perceived. Sometimes jealousy is based on a real threat, but other times jealousy is prompted by unwarranted worries and suspicions. For example, researchers have found that when people creep a lot on their partner's social media, they are likely to see things that worry them (Elphinston & Noller, 2011; Muise et al., 2009; Utz et al., 2015). Think about constantly checking a partner's Instagram likes or Snapchat score. Such actions can trigger all sorts of suspicions even if the partner is innocent. Jealous thoughts and feelings can also be fleeting or pervasive. Carson and Cupach (2000) noted that chronic jealousy is often marked by rumination, which "can be described as obsessive worry about the security of the relationship" (p. 309). Similarly, Bryson (1991) noted that jealous individuals sometimes experience emotional devastation, a syndrome that can include feeling helpless, insecure, confused, fearful, inadequate, depressed, exploited, and taken for granted.

Certain types of communication, however, can help individuals cope with jealousy effectively and alleviate these types of negative thoughts and emotions. Communicative responses to jealousy are behavioral reactions to jealousy that have "communicative value" and "the potential to fulfill individual and relational goals" (Guerrero et al., 1995, p. 272). Messages have communicative value when they are sent with intent and/or interpreted as meaningful by others. In the context of jealousy, messages are sometimes constructed to try to meet goals such as bolstering self-esteem, maintaining a relationship, reducing uncertainty, and retaliating against a cheating partner (Guerrero & Afifi, 1998, 1999). Communicative responses to jealousy have been grouped under four broad categories: constructive, destructive, avoidant, and rival-focused (Guerrero et al., 2011).

CONSTRUCTIVE COMMUNICATIVE RESPONSES TO JEALOUSY

Although jealousy is often regarded as a negative reaction that has aversive consequences for individuals and relationships, jealousy also has a bright side. Jealousy can reflect love, inject excitement and appreciation into a taken-for-granted relationship, reinforce commitment, and rekindle feelings of attraction and passion (Guerrero & Andersen, 1998b, Pines, 1992). Two communicative responses to jealousy have been identified as generally constructive because they promote positive feelings and relationship satisfaction (Bevan, 2013; Guerrero et al., 1995, 2011). Constructive responses to jealousy are also related to feeling hurt and threatened (Denes et al., 2015; Guerrero et al., 2005) and wanting to maintain the relationship (Guerrero & Afifi, 1998). One of the constructive responses, *integrative communication,* focuses on problem-solving, constructive criticism, and supportive communication. Integrative communication strategies include calmly questioning the partner about her or his actions and feelings, explaining one's own feelings, and discussing what can be done in the future to prevent jealousy. The other constructive response, *compensatory restoration,* entails trying to maintain the relationship by using tactics such as increasing affection, being a better partner, and spending more time together. Such tactics are often designed to highlight the benefits of the current relationship in comparison to the rival relationship.

Responding to jealousy using these types of constructive communication can be beneficial. Such responses are more likely when partners have stronger communal orientations, which means that they are highly responsive to each other's needs (Cayanus & Booth-Butterfield, 2004), and when they are highly invested in the relationship (Bevan, 2008). Integrative communication, in particular, is related to commitment (Bevan, 2008) and to feeling less uncertainty about the relationship (Bevan & Tidgewell, 2009). One study showed that when women reported responding to jealousy using constructive communication, both they and their partners reported being happier in their relationship (Guerrero, 2014).

One reason constructive responses are beneficial is that partners respond favorably to them. Participants in a study by Yoshimura (2004) read scenarios depicting different ways that their partner might express jealousy to them. Those who read the scenario that represented positive communication (e.g., a combination of integrative communication and compensatory restoration) reported that they would be especially likely to discuss their feelings with their partner, try to be a better partner in the future, and express remorse by appearing hurt or crying. Thus, constructive communicative responses may elicit a more positive response from the partner than other types of communicative responses to jealousy.

Some research, however, suggests that constructive communication alone may not be enough to combat the potentially negative effects of jealousy. Constructive communicative responses are most effective when they are combined with the genuine expression of negative emotions such as hurt (Andersen et al., 1995). In other words, it is not always enough to sit down and have a calm discussion with one's partner. Jealous individuals may also want to show their partner some of their feelings so that their partner empathizes with them. There appears to be a fine line, however, between expressing one's jealous feelings openly and communicating those emotions in a hostile manner.

Indeed, it may be difficult to express jealousy constructively when emotions are strong and jealous thoughts are pervasive. When this is the case, emotions take over and it becomes challenging to cope with jealousy effectively. Research has supported this idea. For example, Guerrero et al. (2005) found that people said they used constructive responses when they were annoyed, but not when they were angry. Anger was related to more negative responses, such as yelling or making accusations. Bryson (1991) also found that people who experience emotional devastation are unlikely to react to jealousy constructively. Similarly, when people ruminate about their jealous feelings, they are more likely to use all of the communicative responses to jealousy (including compensatory restoration) except for integrative communication (Carson & Cupach, 2000). Taken together, these studies show that when jealousy is accompanied by intense negative feelings and pervasive thoughts, it is difficult for people to engage in integrative communication.

Compensatory restoration, on the other hand, tends to be used when jealous individuals experience intense emotional and cognitive jealousy (Bevan, 2008) and see their relationship as essential to their happiness (Carson & Cupach, 2000). Too much compensatory restoration, however, can backfire if it is perceived as desperate or clingy behavior (Guerrero, 1998). For example, spending extra time together and saying "I love you" more often can help strength the bond between two people, but if one person is doing these things continually, the other person may feel smothered and want more space. The ideal mix of constructive responses to jealousy, then, may consist of high levels of integrative communication with some compensatory restoration and empathy-inducing emotional expression mixed in.

DESTRUCTIVE COMMUNICATIVE RESPONSES TO JEALOUSY

In contrast to constructive responses, Guerrero and her colleagues (2011) identified a set of destructive behaviors that tend to make jealousy worse. These destructive responses, which include negative communication, counter-jealousy inductions, and violent communication, are designed to control the partner or make the partner feel bad. They are also linked to negative emotions such as feeling fearful, upset, and angry (Denes et al., 2015; Guerrero et al., 2005). Many different behaviors fall under the category called *negative communication*, including giving cold or dirty looks, acting rude, arguing, pulling away, administering the "silent treatment," and showing anger. These behaviors are likely perceived as punishing by the partner, but they do not cross the line into physical violence.

Violent communication, in contrast, includes behaviors such as hitting or pushing one's partner, throwing dishes or other objects, and threatening physical harm. People in heterosexual relationships are more likely to respond violently to jealousy when they experience intense negative emotions, regardless of whether the threat is from a different or same-sex rival (Denes et al., 2015; Guerrero et al., 2005). Despite this, jealousy-induced violence is relatively rare, although people who do resort to violence often list jealousy as a cause (Guerrero & Andersen, 1998a). This may seem confusing at first, but think of it this way. Among all the ways people can respond to jealousy, violent communication is rare; but among the small population of people who report becoming violent in their relationships, jealousy is often cited as a reason for violence. Obviously, violent communication should be avoided at all costs. Some people may lose control when jealous or use violence (or threats of violence) as a way to try to control their partner and stop them from seeing others. No matter why it is used, however, violent communication almost always leads to relationship destruction in the long run.

Counter-jealousy inductions, which involve trying to make the partner jealous, are a third form of destructive communication about jealousy. When people feel jealous, they sometimes want to make their partner feel jealous in turn. Sometimes counter-jealousy inductions are used as a way to get back at the partner and even the score. Other times, they are used to check for a reaction with the hope that the partner will realize how attractive they are and not want to lose them. Baxter and Wilmot (1984) referred to this as a type of "secret test" that allows people to reduce uncertainty about their partner's feelings. So, if Jordan is jealous because Spencer has been spending time with an attractive coworker, Jordan might start making flirtatious comments on people's social media to see if Spencer notices or cares. If Spencer notices, this might reassure Jordan, but it could also start conflict between the two of them. Indeed, counter-jealousy inductions like this can be used to try to maintain a relationship (Cayanus & Booth-Butterfield, 2004; Fleischmann et al., 2005), but they can also backfire, with people reporting that they are less happy in their relationships if they or their partner use counter-jealousy inductions (Guerrero, 2014). People who have game-playing or obsessive styles of love are also more likely to engage in counter-jealousy inductions (Goodboy et al., 2012), so such strategies may be part of a larger pattern of drama in some relationships.

These three destructive responses to jealousy are harmful to relationships in other ways. Not surprisingly, people who use these three responses report being relatively unhappy in their relationships (Andersen et al., 1995; Dainton & Gross, 2008; Guerrero et al., 2011). In fact, using versus not using destructive responses helps explain why jealousy is related to low levels of satisfaction in some relationships but not others. When jealous people engage in destructive responses, not only do they report less relational satisfaction, but their partners do too (Guerrero, 2014). People may be especially likely to use destructive communication when they are experiencing anxious or possessive types of jealousy (Barelds & Barelds-Dijkstra, 2007). Anxious jealousy involves constantly worrying about losing one's partner to someone else. Possessive jealousy refers to feeling a need to keep tabs on a partner so that rivals cannot get close enough to threaten the relationship. When people have a history of experiencing these types of jealousy, they may find it difficult to control destructive impulses and to remain calm when the next incident of jealousy strikes.

AVOIDANT COMMUNICATIVE RESPONSES TO JEALOUSY

Both constructive and destructive forms of jealous communication involve actively sending a message to one's partner. Avoidant responses, which include silence and denial, are more passive or reactive (Guerrero et al., 2011). *Silence* involves becoming quiet and not saying very much (if anything) about one's jealous feelings. For example, if Garrett is upset that his girlfriend, Olivia, was flirting with an old friend at a party, he might be less talkative than usual when she returns to his side. If he is purposely giving her the "silent treatment," his behavior would fall under negative communication, but if he is quiet because he just does not feel like talking, then Garrett's behavior would be classified as silence. *Denial*, on the other hand, involves inhibiting emotions and pretending not to be jealous. So, if Olivia asks Garrett, "What's wrong? You're so quiet" and he responds by saying "nothing" and trying to act as if he is not upset, then Garrett would be using the denial strategy.

The jury is still out on whether avoidant responses to jealousy are related to being more or less happy in a relationship. Some studies have found that people are less satisfied in their relationships if they report using avoidant responses (e.g., Andersen et al., 1995). Other studies have found that there is no relationship between avoidant responses and satisfaction (e.g., Guerrero, 2014; Guerrero et al., 2011). One study found that silence and denial were related differently to satisfaction (Irvin, 2007). In this study, people reported being the happiest with their relationships when they used silence but not denial to cope with jealousy. This may be because there are times when it is inadvisable to talk about one's jealous feelings too much. Perhaps Garrett has nothing to worry about; Olivia just has a vivacious personality and was excited to see an old friend. Given time he might learn that Olivia's flirtation with this old friend was harmless and that there was no need to disclose jealous feelings that quickly passed. However, if Olivia asks him about his feelings and he denies them, then this could reflect a deeper communication problem between the two of them.

RIVAL-FOCUSED COMMUNICATIVE RESPONSES TO JEALOUSY

The responses discussed so far focus on communicating with one's partner. However, there are three people involved in a jealousy triangle—the jealous person, the jealous person's partner, and the rival. There are times, then, when the jealous individual communicates with the rival or uses communication to try to find out more information about the rival relationship. Indeed, when people are jealous they often feel uncertain about their partner's feelings and intentions (Afifi & Reichert, 1996; Guerrero & Afifi, 1999). Some forms of rival-focused communication can help alleviate this uncertainty.

Four specific types of rival-focused communication have been identified: surveillance, rival contacts, signs of possession, and rival derogation. *Surveillance* occurs when the jealous person tries to find out about or interfere with a rival relationship by engaging in behaviors such as creeping on the partner's social media, calling the partner to see who he or she is with, and spying on the partner. *Rival contacts* involve directly talking to the rival. Jealous individuals sometimes ask rivals questions to assess the seriousness of the threat they pose. They might also confront them and tell them to stay away from their partner. *Signs of possession*, in contrast, involve letting rivals know that one's partner is taken. For example, Garrett might introduce Olivia to a rival as "my girlfriend" and put his arm around her so everyone knows they are together. Finally, *rival derogation* occurs when the jealous individual makes negative comments about the rival. Garrett might tell Olivia that her old friend has "sure let himself go" or mention that he has been unemployed for a while. The key here is that the jealous individual is trying to make the rival look less appealing. In a way, this strategy is similar to compensatory restoration, except that instead of trying to make oneself look better, the jealous person tries to make the rival look worse.

Some rival-focused responses appear to be less helpful than others depending on the situation. Using surveillance behavior can be healthy if it helps alleviate jealousy or protect the relationship from serious threats from third parties (Buss, 1988). In addition, people who want to maintain their relationships are likely to use surveillance (Guerrero & Afifi, 1998). There is a limit, however, on how much surveillance is healthy. One study showed that people who reported using surveillance tended to be happier in their relationships, as long as surveillance was *not* accompanied by high levels of rumination about their jealous feelings (Elphinston et al., 2013). When surveillance provides reassurance and reduces worries, it may be effective, but when it instead leads to rumination (or is prompted by rumination), it can intensify jealous feelings. This may explain why some studies have found surveillance to be related to relational satisfaction (e.g., Elphinston et al., 2013), whereas others have found surveillance to be related to relational *dis*satisfaction (Guerrero, 2014; Guerrero et al., 2011).

Similarly, signs of possession can signal that a partner is overly possessive, or they can signal love and protectiveness. Some studies have shown that people who report using signs of possession when they get jealous also say they are happy in their relationships, although this finding appears stronger for men than women (Guerrero, 2014; Irvin, 2007). Derogating or contacting the rival does not appear to be smart strategy for coping with jealousy since people who use these responses, or have a partner who uses them, tend to report lower levels of relationship satisfaction (Bevan, 2008; Guerrero, 2014; Guerrero et al., 2011).

So, what do all of these different findings mean? When taken together they seem to indicate that too much rival-focused communication is unhealthy for individuals and relationships. A small dose of surveillance behavior may help reduce uncertainty and alleviate a jealous person's concerns. However, too much surveillance can be intrusive and even threatening, and it can also signal a lack of trust. Similarly, some signs of possession may ward off potential rivals and let a partner know that they are loved but too many signs of possession may suggest that the jealous person is overly clingy and paranoid. Therefore, if a jealous person feels a need to engage in rival-focused communication, it is advisable to use such behaviors in moderation. It would also be better to reduce uncertainty about jealous feelings by talking to the partner and using integrative communication, rather than by using surveillance.

CONCLUSION

Jealousy is inevitable in most relationships. But many of its negative consequences can be avoided by using the right communication. When people feel jealous, they should understand that sometimes behaviors that seem threatening are not. Perhaps jealousy is unfounded. The best way to find out is to use integrative communication. People should also avoid getting caught in the trap of emotional devastation and rumination. Dwelling on jealous feelings makes it more difficult to respond in a constructive manner, and creeping on someone's social media makes rumination more likely. Jealous individuals should avoid using destructive communicative responses, as well as certain types of avoidant and rival-focused communication, such as denial and rival derogation, which only make a bad situation worse. Other responses, such as silence, surveillance, and signs of possession, appear to be helpful in some situations but harmful in others. The best strategy of all may be to express one's emotions sincerely and calmly while using a lot of integrative communication and moderate amounts of compensatory restoration. Knowing this recipe for constructive communication may help individuals tame the green-eyed monster and stop themselves from being hellish when jealous.

REFERENCES

Afifi, W. A., & Reichert, T. (1996). Understanding the role of uncertainty in jealousy experience and expression. *Communication Reports, 9*(2), 93–103. https://doi.org/10.1080/08934219609367642

Andersen, P. A., Eloy, S. V., Guerrero, L. K., & Spitzberg, B. H. (1995). Romantic jealousy and relational satisfaction: A look at the impact of jealousy experience and expression. *Communication Reports, 8*(2), 77–85. https://doi.org/10.1080/08934219509367613

Barelds, D. P. H., & Barelds-Dijkstra, P. (2007). Relations between different types of jealousy and self and partner perceptions of relationship quality. *Clinical Psychology and Psychotherapy, 14*(3), 176–188. https://doi.org/10.1002/cpp.532

Baxter, L. A., & Wilmot, W. W. (1984). "Secret tests": Social strategies for acquiring information about the state of the relationship. *Human Communication Research, 11*(2), 171–201. https://doi.org/10.1111/j.1468-2958.1984.tb00044.x

Bevan, J. L. (2008). Experiencing and communicating romantic jealousy: Questioning the investment model. *Southern Communication Journal, 73*(1), 42–67. https://doi.org/10.1080/10417940701815626

Bevan, J. L. (2013). *The communication of jealousy.* Peter Lang.

Bevan, J, L., & Tidgewell, K. D. (2009). Relational uncertainty as a consequence of partner jealousy expressions. *Communication Studies, 60*(3), 305–323. https://doi.org/10.1080/10510970902956057

Bryson, J. B. (1991). Modes of responses to jealousy-evoking situations. In P. Salovey (Ed.). *The psychology of envy and jealousy* (pp. 45–62). Guilford.

Buss, D. M. (1988). From vigilance to violence: Tactics of mate retention in American undergraduates. *Ethology and Sociology, 9*(5), 291–317. https://doi.org/10.1016/0162-3095(88)90010-6

Carson, C. L., & Cupach, W. R. (2000). Fueling the flames of the green-eyed monster: The role of ruminative thought in reaction to romantic jealousy. *Western Journal of Communication, 64*(3), 308–329. https://doi.org/10.1080/10570310009374678

Cayanus, J. L., & Booth-Butterfield, M. (2004). Relationship orientation, jealousy, and equity: An examination of jealousy evoking and positive communicative responses. *Communication Quarterly, 52*(4), 237–250. https://doi.org/10.1080/01463370409370195

Dainton, M. & Gross, J. (2008). The use of negative behaviors to maintain rel ationships. *Communication Research Reports, 25*(3), 179–191. https://doi.org/10.1080/08824090802237600

Denes, A., Lannutti, P. J., & Bevan, J. L. (2015). Same-sex infidelity in heterosexual romantic relationships: Investigating emotional, relational, and communicative responses. *Personal Relationships, 22*(3), 414–430. https://doi.org/10.1111/pere.12087

Elphinston, R. A., Feeney, J. A., Noller, P., Connor, J. P., & Fitzgerald, J. (2013). Romantic jealousy and relationship satisfaction: The costs of rumination. *Western Journal of Communication, 77*(3), 293–304. https://doi.org/10.1080/10570314.2013.770161

Elphinston, R. A., & Noller, P. (2011). Time to face it! Facebook intrusion and the implications for romantic jealousy and relationship satisfaction. *Cyberpsychology, Behavior, and Social Networking, 14*(11), 631–635. https://doi.org/10.1089/cyber.2010.0318

Fleischmann, A. A., Spitzberg, B. H., Andersen, P. A., & Roesch, S. C. (2005). Tickling the monster: Jealousy induction in relationships. *Journal of Social and Personal Relationships, 22*(1), 49–73. https://doi.org/10.1177/0265407505049321

Goodboy, A. K., Horan, S. M., & Booth-Butterfield, M. (2012). Intentional jealousy-evoking behavior in romantic relationships as a function of received partner affection and love styles. *Communication Quarterly, 60*(3), 370–385. https://doi.org/10.1080/01463373.2012.688792

Guerrero, L. K. (1998). Attachment-style differences in the experience and expression of romantic jealousy. *Personal Relationships, 5*(3), 273–291. https://doi.org/10.1111/j.1475-6811.1998. tb00172.x

Guerrero, L. K. (2014). Jealousy and relational satisfaction: Actor effects, partner effects, and the mediating role of destructive communicative responses to jealousy. *Western Journal of Communication, 78*(5), 586–611. https://doi.org/10.1080/10570314.2014.935468

Guerrero, L. K., & Afifi, W. A. (1998). Communicative responses to jealousy as a function of self-esteem and relationship maintenance goals: A test of Bryson's dual motivation model. *Communication Reports, 11*(2), 111–122. https://doi.org/10.1080/08934219809367693

Guerrero, L. K., & Afifi, W. A. (1999). Toward a goal-oriented approach for understanding communicative response to jealousy. *Western Journal of Communication, 63*(2), 216–248. https://doi. org/10.1080/10570319909374637

Guerrero, L. K., & Andersen, P. A. (1998a). The dark side of jealousy and envy: Desire, delusion, desperation, and destructive communication. In B. H. Spitzberg & W. R. Cupach (Eds.), *The dark side of relationships* (pp. 33–70). Erlbaum.

Guerrero, L. K., & Andersen, P. A. (1998b). The experience and expression of romantic jealousy. In P. A. Andersen & L. K. Guerrero (Eds.), *The handbook of communication and emotion: Research, theory, applications, and contexts* (pp. 155–188). Academic Press.

Guerrero, L. K., Andersen, P. A., Jorgensen, P. F., Spitzberg, B. H., & Eloy, S. V. (1995). Coping with the green-eyed monster: Conceptualizing and measuring communicative responses to romantic jealousy. *Western Journal of Communication, 59*(4), 270–304. https://doi. org/10.1080/10570319509374523

Guerrero, L. K., Hannawa, A. F., & Babin, E. A. (2011). The communicative responses to jealousy scale: Revision, empirical validation, and associations with relational satisfaction. *Communication Methods and Measures, 5*(3), 223–249. https://doi.org/10.1080/19312458.2011.596993

Guerrero, L. K., Trost, M. L., & Yoshimura, S. M. (2005). Romantic jealousy: Emotions and communicative responses. *Personal Relationships, 12*(2), 233–252. https://doi.org/10.1111/ j.1350-4126.2005.00113.x

Irvin, A. (2007). *Jealousy and relational satisfaction in long-distance versus proximal dating relationships.* Unpublished honor's thesis, Arizona State University, Tempe.

Muise, A., Christofides, E., & Desmarais, S. (2009). More information than you ever wanted: Does Facebook bring out the green-eyed monster of jealousy? *CyberPsychology & Behavior, 12*(4), 441–444. https://doi.org/10.1089/cpb.2008.0263

Pfeiffer, S. M., & Wong, P. T. P. (1989). Multidimensional jealousy. *Journal of Social and Personal Relationships, 6*(2), 181–196. https://doi.org/10.1177/026540758900600203

Pines, A. M. (1992). *Romantic jealousy: Understanding and conquering the shadow of love.* St. Martin's Press.

Utz, S., Muscanell, N., & Khalid, C. (2015). Snapchat elicits more jealousy than Facebook: A comparison of Snapchat and Facebook use. *Cyberpsychology, Behavior, and Social Networking, 18*(3), 141–146. https://doi.org/10.1089/cyber.2014.0479

White, G. L., & Mullen, P. E. (1989). *Jealousy: Theory, research, and clinical applications.* Guilford Press.

Yoshimura, S. M. (2004). Emotional and behavioral responses to romantic jealousy expressions. *Communication Reports, 17*(2), 85–101. https://doi.org/10.1080/08934210409389378

HIGHLIGHTS FROM RESEARCH ON COMMUNICATION BEFORE, DURING, AND AFTER SEXUAL ACTIVITY

Amanda Denes, Rachel V. Tucker, & Eli Quay
University of Connecticut

In television, movies, and everyday life, we are consistently exposed to messages about sex. Whether thinking about sex or talking about it with others, we receive messages from an early age that sex is a common part of relationships. Although not everyone chooses or has a desire to engage in sexual activity, it is nonetheless a common behavior in intimate relationships. Sexual activity can include a wide range of behaviors, from deep kissing to fondling to penetrative sexual activity (Peck et al., 2016). Given this broad definition, it is easy to see why so many people report that sexual activity is part of their life.

Communication researchers play a vital role in understanding sexual activity by studying the ways that people send, receive, and process messages about sex. Interpersonal communication scholars, in particular, have focused on understanding how relational partners talk about sex, whether that be conversations about safer sex practices, sexual needs and desires, or sexual histories. This chapter focuses on one domain of sexual communication research—communication that occurs within the sexual encounter itself. This includes communication immediately before sexual activity occurs, during the sexual activity, and right after sexual activity, sometimes referred to as "pillow talk." Together, this chapter will explore communication processes during sexual episodes, with a focus on college students' experiences.

SEXUAL COMMUNICATION AMONG COLLEGE STUDENTS

Many people assume that college life is filled with sexual activity, but what do the numbers regarding college students' sexual behavior really look like? A national survey administered by the American College Health Association (ACHN) in the spring of 2020, before the onset of COVID-19, found that approximately 40.2% of college students reported never having sex at all (ACHN, 2020). Out of the other 59.8% of college students who did report ever having sex, 33.7% of those students reported having sex within the last two weeks (ACHN, 2020). The fall 2021 version of the survey reported that 49.2% of college students reported never having sex, while a little more than half of the other 50.8% of students had sex within the past two weeks (ACHN, 2021). The bottom line: college students are having sex and even a world-changing pandemic did not change that fact.

These statistics help us understand the frequency of sexual activity among college students, but for communication researchers and students, we are particularly interested in understanding college students' *communication* about sex. Communicating about sexual topics can be difficult, resulting in partners withholding information and a lack of understanding about their partner's sexual likes and dislikes (Byers, 2011). Exploring the causes and consequences of sharing sexual information is important, though, as couples' communication about sex is consistently linked to greater sexual and relationship satisfaction (Mallory, 2022). Technology also provides a way for college students to talk about sex. A majority of college students report that they are willing to discuss sex over technological avenues such as texting and private messaging on social media (Tannebaum, 2018). Talking about sex via various technologies may also have benefits for in-person communication. For example, Tannebaum (2018) found that students who had used technology to communicate with their partners about sex tended to feel more comfortable engaging in sexual communication in a face-to-face setting as well. With this broad base for understanding the frequency of college students' sexual activity and some recent trends in research on sexual communication, we now turn our attention to the specific context of communication before, during, and after sexual activity.

COMMUNICATING BEFORE SEXUAL ACTIVITY

There are many topics partners may discuss before engaging in sexual activity. These can range from conversations about consent to talking about their sexual needs, preferences, and desires to discussing safer sex topics, such as condom use, contraception, and sexually transmitted infections (STIs). This section reviews some key findings from recent research that explores topics of communication that occur prior to sexual activity.

INITIAL CONSENT AND SEXUAL REFUSAL

Before sexual activity, it is important for partners to communicate about whether or not (and if so, how) they want to engage in sexual activity. This involves communicating about consent. The definition of consent has evolved over time, but in recent years, many states, organizations, and institutions have begun to adopt affirmative consent policies.

These policies define *consent* as "a knowing, voluntary, and mutual decision among all participants to engage in sexual activity" that "can be given by words or actions as long as those words or actions create clear permission regarding willingness to engage in sexual activity" (The New York State Senate, 2017). Consent can be communicated verbally through spoken statements and/or nonverbally through behaviors and actions (Jozkowski et al., 2014; Marcantonio et al., 2021). For example, some people provide verbal consent by saying that they would like to engage in sexual activity or by making suggestive comments. Individuals might also provide nonverbal consent through their actions, such as by grabbing or putting on a condom, removing their clothing, or positioning their body to engage in a particular sexual activity (Marcantonio et al., 2021). Alternatively, partners may communicate that they want to delay, halt, or abstain from sexual activity through messages of *sexual refusal* (Dalton, 2022). Like consent, sexual refusal can be expressed verbally through spoken statements (e.g., saying they would like to wait or explaining they are not ready) or nonverbally through behaviors and actions (e.g., pushing someone away or distancing themselves; Coffelt, 2018; Dalton, 2022). Because consent and refusal can involve both verbal and nonverbal cues, it is important to be mindful of a sexual partner's words *and* actions when obtaining consent. Additionally, it is important to keep in mind that consent is an ongoing process and it can be given and taken away at any time. Sexual partners should get consent before *and* during sexual activity and make sure to listen to one another, clarify boundaries, and only engage in sexual activities that both partners are comfortable with (Dalton, 2022).

SEXUAL NEEDS, DESIRES, AND PREFERENCES

Other topics that partners may communicate about before sexual activity are their sexual needs, desires, and preferences. This involves discussing sexual activities that a person would or would not like to try and those that they find (un)pleasurable and (un)enjoyable. There are many reasons why partners may want to discuss or avoid talking about their sexual preferences (Hullman et al., 2022; Kuang & Gettings, 2021; Rehman et al., 2019). For example, a person may want to talk with their partner about the sexual activities they find most pleasurable, but they may also be worried about how their partner will view them after sharing this information, or they may worry about how the information will affect their relationship (Hullman et al., 2022; Rehman et al., 2019). Individual differences can also impact a person's comfort in communicating about their sexual needs, desires, and preferences. For example, research has found that the more confident partners are in their ability to communicate effectively about their sexual preferences, the more likely they are to discuss these topics (Hullman et al., 2022; Kuang & Gettings, 2021). Although discussing sexual needs, desires, and preferences can be challenging, it can also improve sexual and relationship satisfaction (Mallory, 2022), and is thus an important topic for sexual communication researchers to explore.

SAFER SEX PRACTICES

A final topic that arises between sexual partners before engaging in sexual activity is safer sex practices. Communication about these topics can be initiated by one or all partners involved in the sexual interaction. During these conversations, partners may discuss a range of topics aimed at mitigating risks associated with sexual behavior. For example, partners might talk about whether they currently have an STI, the last time they were tested for STIs, their sexual history, and preferences regarding condom use. However, these topics are often avoided because they are perceived as being risky (Brannon & Ray, 2021). For example, one partner may avoid talking about STIs because they are worried it may affect the way the other partner views them and their relationship (Rehman et al., 2019). This is especially true for people who have been previously diagnosed with an STI and might feel embarrassed and ashamed to share this information (Coffelt et al., 2021). Despite the challenges associated with communicating about these topics, they are important to discuss, as they directly affect the sexual health, safety, and well-being of partners.

COMMUNICATING DURING AND AFTER SEXUAL ACTIVITY

Whereas communication before sexual activity can help ensure a safe, consensual, and satisfying sexual experience, communication during and after sexual activity can enhance sexual partners' sexual satisfaction and connection with one another. This section first reviews research on communication between sexual partners during sexual activity. Then, we turn our attention to communication after sexual activity, sometimes referred to as "pillow talk."

COMMUNICATION DURING SEXUAL ACTIVITY

Sexual activity is often an intimate and passionate activity between people who are sexually and/or emotionally attracted to one another. But it's not just the sexual act(s) that can enhance connection between partners, it's also what they *say* during the sexual activity. A growing line of research has started to shed light on the things that people say during sex and how that is connected to larger relational well-being. For example, researchers have found that the more people report that they engage in nonverbal and/or verbal communication during sex, the more they report being sexually satisfied (Babin, 2013; Brogan et al., 2009). Jonason and colleagues (2016) also looked at the *content* of communication during sexual activity by examining types of erotic talk. They found two broad types of erotic talk during sexual activity: individualistic erotic talk, which is communication focused on expressing one's own needs or desires, and mutualistic erotic talk, which is communication focused on the relationship or coordination between partners (Jonason et al., 2016). They found that people who reported more of either type of erotic talk during sexual activity also reported more sexual satisfaction and that people who reported more mutualistic erotic talk also reported greater relationship satisfaction. This makes sense when considering that mutualistic erotic talk is focused on relational dynamics and thus may reflect positive feelings about the relationship more broadly. In our own research, we found that the more people told their partner positive things they felt about them during sex (which was broadly assessed by asking participants how much they agreed or disagree with statements like "I expressed some positive feelings for my partner to him/her"), the more likely they were to report that they had experienced an orgasm, and disclosing these feelings or engaging in mutualistic erotic talk were both connected to feeling more relationally satisfied (Denes et al., 2020a). In another study, we similarly found that talking more during sex (which, again, was broadly assessed with items such as "My partner talks during sex") was associated with greater sexual satisfaction and, in turn, greater sexual satisfaction was associated with greater relationship satisfaction (Bennett & Denes, under review).

Researchers have also considered whether certain personality traits or dispositions predict the likelihood of a person communicating during sex. For example, Babin (2013) found that people who had more apprehension or anxiety communicating about sexual issues generally, safer sex practices, or sexual dislikes reported engaging in less verbal or nonverbal communication during sex, whereas people who felt confident about themselves sexually (which is called *sexual self-esteem*) reported engaging in more verbal and nonverbal communication during sex. We similarly found that sexual self-esteem and sexual assertiveness were linked to communicating more during sexual activity (Bennett & Denes, under review). Together, these studies demonstrate that it is not only just engaging in sexual activity that helps partners feel close and connected, but also the things that they say or do during sex.

COMMUNICATION AFTER SEXUAL ACTIVITY

The image of a couple lying in bed together after sexual activity, whispering sweet nothings and basking in a euphoric glow, is one commonly seen in television and movies. But does "pillow talk" really help couples enjoy the final moments of the sexual episode? Our research over the past decade has sought to answer that question by examining factors that predict pillow talk, or communication after sexual activity, as well as by exploring the impact of pillow talk on individuals and their relationships.

In much of our research on pillow talk, we ask people to complete an online survey within two hours of engaging in sexual activity, which we define as any activity "below the belt" (in other words, any sexual activity that involves genital contact). Most of our studies have focused on college students' experiences and have helped us understand the role of pillow talk in young adult relationships. Much of this research has also considered how hormonal or physical changes that occur due to sexual arousal and climax might impact people's pillow talk. For example, one of the first studies in this line of work examined whether orgasm predicted pillow talk. The idea was that when people orgasm, they experience a surge in the hormone oxytocin and that hormone is linked to feelings of trust, bonding, and intimacy. In other words, if people orgasm, they should experience a surge in oxytocin and that might make them feel especially intimate and close with their partner and facilitate positive communication. As expected, the study found that people who reported orgasming from the sexual activity were more likely to disclose positive thoughts and feelings to their partner after sex, and such communication was associated with greater feelings of trust, satisfaction, and closeness (Denes, 2012).

We have now conducted several studies linking orgasm to people's communication after sexual activity, suggesting that the intimate afterglow of sex might create an environment that allows sexual partners to be open and vulnerable about their feelings. Our studies have also found that orgasm is linked to perceiving greater benefits and fewer risks to pillow talk, which, in turn, predict greater positive disclosures after sex and greater relationship satisfaction (Denes, 2018). More recently, we conducted a study that directly measured oxytocin, in order to see whether hormonal surges during sexual activity were connected to pillow talk like we suspected. We had college students collect saliva samples at home immediately before and after the next time they engaged in sexual activity with their romantic partner. We then tested those samples for oxytocin and looked at whether changes in hormone levels from before to immediately after sexual activity were linked to their general tendencies to communicate after sex. We found that men's oxytocin levels after sex (but not *changes* in their oxytocin levels from before to immediately after sex) were associated with perceiving greater benefits and fewer risks to sharing their thoughts and feelings during pillow talk (Denes et al., 2021). For women, oxytocin levels were not connected to general tendencies to communicate after sexual activity. However, for both women and men, the more benefits and fewer risks they saw to communicating after sex, the more they disclosed positive thoughts and feelings to their partner during pillow talk. These findings might suggest that general hormone levels, rather than changes in hormone levels during a sexual episode, are more meaningful in understanding sexual communication patterns.

Beyond the link between orgasm, oxytocin, and pillow talk, our research team wondered what other factors might impact college students' communication after sexual activity. We conducted a study where we asked college students to fill out a survey after each time they engaged in sexual activity for two weeks. Looking at averages across the two weeks, we found that people who consumed more alcohol prior to sexual activity perceived fewer benefits to pillow talk, and their communication was less positive and personal (Denes & Afifi, 2014). We also explored the hormone testosterone, which has been linked to more dominant behavior and may suppress the effects of oxytocin. We found some evidence that higher testosterone impedes sexual communication, as people with higher testosterone levels saw fewer benefits and greater risks to disclosing after sex, and their post sex communication was less intentional and less positive (Denes et al., 2017). In both studies, we also found that, for individuals who experienced orgasm from the sexual activity, some of the negative links between alcohol or testosterone and pillow talk disappeared, perhaps suggesting that the glow or euphoria of sexual climax might nullify some of the potentially negative impacts of consuming alcohol or higher testosterone.

All of this research seemed to suggest that pillow talk was a generally good thing in relationships, but we wanted to determine whether it could really *help* sexual partners. That led us to conduct a study to see if increasing pillow talk might create a sense of connection between partners that helps them manage difficult times (Denes et al., 2020b). We designed a "pillow talk experiment" where we asked some couples to double their pillow talk and we compared them to a control group of couples who were not given any instructions related to their pillow talk. After three weeks, we had all the couples come to the communication laboratory and have a conversation about a stressor or difficulty they'd been dealing with in their relationship. We took measurements of cortisol, sometimes called the "stress hormone," before and after the conversation and also had couples complete a survey assessing their relationship satisfaction. We found that for men (but not for women) who doubled their pillow talk, their relationship satisfaction increased, however, physical stress responses were largely unaffected by the intervention. Although our other studies revealed positive links between pillow talk and relational well-being for women and men, this study suggested that increasing pillow talk may have unique benefits for men.

FINAL TAKEAWAYS FOR COLLEGE STUDENTS' SEXUAL COMMUNICATION

The research reviewed throughout this chapter offers important implications for college students' sexual communication. First, it is important to recognize that while many college students are sexually active, many are not. In fact, research over the past decade reveals that young adults' sexual activity is on the decline (e.g., Ethier et al., 2018; Twenge et al., 2017). Perceptions that everyone is engaging in casual sex are likely overstated and many students want options beyond those offered by college hookup culture (Wade, 2017). The takeaway is that there are plenty of people who decide to engage in sexual activity and plenty who do not–you should do whatever you feel comfortable with and makes you happy. For those who want and choose to engage in sexual activity, clear communication about sexual boundaries (including giving and obtaining consent throughout a sexual experience and talking about safer sex practices) and sharing sexual needs, desires, and preferences are important for ensuring that both partners are respected and have a satisfying experience.

Communication during and after sexual activity also matters. Although it comes with the risk of being vulnerable, sharing positive thoughts and feelings during or after sexual activity is linked to sexual and relationship well-being, and thus may contribute to feelings of intimacy and connection during sexual activity. However, alcohol may impede those benefits, particularly if it is used as a substitute for developing closeness and intimacy. It is also important to recognize and appreciate that each person has a unique biological makeup, and hormones and genes may impact how comfortable or confident a person feels communicating. Does this mean that we are all stuck with whatever we were born with? Absolutely not—hormones are just one piece of the puzzle of understanding sexual communication, and recognizing this fact can make us more informed about our communication, our bodies, and our relationships. Hopefully, this chapter has made it clear that sexual communication is a complex process and there are many factors that impact verbal and nonverbal behavior across the sexual episode. Ultimately, research on communication before, during, and after sexual activity highlights the importance of studying communication during sexual episodes and its impact on sexual and relational well-being.

REFERENCES

American College Health Association (2020). *NCHA III: Undergraduate student reference group executive summary, spring 2020*. https://www.acha.org/documents/ncha/NCHA-III_SPRING-2021_UNDERGRADUATE_REFERENCE_GROUP_EXECUTIVE_SUMMARY_updated.pdf

American College Health Association (2021). *NCHA III: Undergraduate student reference group executive summary, fall 2021*. https://www.acha.org/documents/ncha/NCHA-III_FALL_2021_UNDERGRADUATE_REFERENCE_GROUP_EXECUTIVE_SUMMARY.pdf

Babin, E. A. (2013). An examination of predictors of nonverbal and verbal communication of pleasure during sex and sexual satisfaction. *Journal of Social and Personal Relationships, 30*(3), 270–292. https://doi.org/10.1177/0265407512454523

Bennett-Brown, M., & Denes, A. (under review). Testing the communication during sexual activity model: An examination of the associations among personality characteristics, sexual communication, and sexual and relationship satisfaction.

Brannon, G. E., & Ray, M. A. (2021). Participant-reported experiences of conversations about sexually transmitted infections with romantic partners: Perceptions of ownership and privacy. *Health Communication*. Advance online publication. https://doi.org/10.1080/10410236.2021.1981563

Brogan, S. M., Fiore, A., & Wrench, J. S. (2009). Understanding the psychometric properties of the sexual communication style scale. *Human Communication, 12*(4), 421–445.

Byers, S. E. (2011). Beyond the birds and the bees and was it good for you?: Thirty years of research on sexual communication. *Canadian Psychology, 52*(1), 20–28. https://doi.org/10.1037/a0022048

Coffelt, T. A. (2018). Sexual goals, plans, and actions: Toward a sexual script emerging adults use to delay or abstain from sexual intercourse. *Western Journal of Communication, 82*(4), 416–438. https://doi.org/10.1080/10570314.2017.1400095

Coffelt, T. A., Ritalin, R., & LeFecvre, L. (2021). Revealing and receiving sexual health information. *Health Communication, 36*(2), 136–145. https://doi.org/10.1080/10410236.2019.1669128

Dalton, E. D. (2022). Framing sexual refusal experiences among emerging adult women: Politeness theory in unscripted territory. *Communication Studies, 73*(1), 17–35. https://doi.org/10.1080/10510974.2021.2011356

Denes, A. (2012). Pillow talk: Exploring disclosures after sexual activity. *Western Journal of Communication, 76*(2), 91–108. https://doi.org/10.1080/10570314.2011.651253

Denes, A. (2018). Toward a post sex disclosures model (PSDM): Exploring the associations among orgasm, self-disclosure, and relationship satisfaction. *Communication Research, 45*(3), 297–318. https://doi.org/10.1177/0093650215619216

Denes, A., & Afifi, T. D. (2014). Pillow talk and cognitive decision making processes: Exploring the role of orgasm and alcohol on communication after sexual activity. *Communication Monographs, 81*(3), 333–358. https://doi.org/10.1080/03637751.2014.926377

Denes, A., Afifi, T. A., & Granger, D. A. (2017). Physiology and pillow talk: Relations between testosterone and communication post sex. *Journal of Social and Personal Relationships, 34*(3), 281–308. https://doi.org/10.1177/0265407516634470

Denes, A., Crowley, J. P., & Bennett, M. (2020a). Between the sheets: Investigating young adults' disclosures during sexual activity. *Personal Relationships, 27*(2), 484–501. https://doi.org/10.1111/pere.12324

Denes, A., Crowley, J. P., Dhillon, A., Bennett-Brown, M., Stebbins, J. L., & Granger, S. W. (2021). Exploring the role of oxytocin in communication processes: A test of the post sex disclosures model. *Communication Monographs.* Advance online publication. https://doi.org/10.1080/03637751.2021.1957490

Denes, A., Crowley, J. P., Winkler, K. L., Ponivas, A. L. P., Dhillon, A., & Bennett, M. (2020b). Exploring the effect of pillow talk on relationship satisfaction and physiological stress responses to couples' difficult conversations. *Communication Monographs, 87*(3), 267–290. https://doi.org/10.1080/03637751.2020.1726424

Ethier, K. A., Kann, L., & McManus, T. (2018). Sexual intercourse among high school students—29 states and United States overall, 2005–2015. *Morbidity and Mortality Weekly Report, 66*(51–52), 1393–1397. https://doi.org/10.15585/mmwr.mm665152a1

Hullman, G. A., Weigel, D. J., & Brown, R. D. (2022). How conversational goals predict sexual self-disclosure decisions. *The Journal of Sex Research.* Advance online publication. https://doi.org/10.1080/00224499.2022.2035310

Jonason, P. K., Betteridge, G. L., & Kneebone, I. I. (2016). An examination of the nature of erotic talk. *Archives of Sexual Behavior, 45*(1), 21–31. https://doi.org/10.1007/s10508-015-0585-2

Jozkowski, K. N., Sanders, S., Peterson, Z. D., Dennis, B., & Reece, M. (2014). Consenting to sexual activity: The development and psychometric assessment of dual measures of consent. *Archives of Sexual Behavior, 43*(3), 437–450. https://doi.org/10.1007/s10508-013-0225-7

Kuang, K., & Gettings, P. E. (2021). Uncertainty management in sexual communication: Testing the moderating role of marital quality, relational closeness, and communal coping. *Health Communication, 36*(11), 1368–1377. https://doi.org/10.1080/10410236.2020.1751401

Mallory, A. B. (2022). Dimensions of couples' sexual communication, relationship satisfaction, and sexual satisfaction: A meta-analysis. *Journal of Family Psychology, 36*(3), 358–371. https://doi.org/10.1037/fam0000946

Marcantonio, T. L., O'Neil, A. M., & Jozkowski, K. N. (2021). Sexual consent cues among sexual minority men in the United States. *Psychology & Sexuality.* Advance online publication. https://doi.org/10.1080/19419899.2021.1936141

The New York State Senate (2017, August 18). *Section 6441: Affirmative consent to sexual activity.* https://www.nysenate.gov/legislation/laws/EDN/6441

Peck, B., Manning, J., Tri, A., Skrzypczynski, D., Summers, M., & Grubb, K. (2016). What do people mean when they say they "had sex"? Connecting communication and behavior. In J. Manning & C. Noland (Eds.), *Contemporary studies of sexuality & communication: Theoretical and applied perspectives.* Kendall Hunt.

Rehman, U. S., Balan, D., Sutherland, S., & McNeil, J. (2019). Understanding barriers to sexual communication. *Journal of Social and Personal Relationships, 36*(9), 2605–2623. https://doi.org/10.1177/0265407518794900

Tannebaum, M. (2018). College students' use of technology to communicate with romantic partners about sexual health issues. *Journal of American College Health, 66*(5), 393–400. https://doi.org/10.1080/07448481.2018.1440585

Twenge, J. M., Sherman, R. A., & Wells, B. E. (2017). Sexual inactivity during young adulthood is more common among US Millennials and iGen: Age, period, and cohort effects on having no sexual partners after age 18. *Archives of Sexual Behavior, 46*(2), 433–440. https://doi.org/10.1007/s10508-016-0798-z

Wade, L. (2017). What's so cultural about hookup culture? *Contexts, 16*(1), 66–68. https://doi.org/10.1177/1536504217696066

INSTRUCTIONAL COMMUNICATION

The instructional communication context focuses on how instructors and students communicate inside and outside of the classroom. Some major areas of research in instructional communication include effective teaching behaviors (teacher clarity, humor, relevance, and confirmation) and student communication and learning outcomes (student participation, communication apprehension, motivation, and learning). This section includes chapters focusing on three important areas of instructional communication research: (1) writing and sending emails, (2) coping with public speaking anxiety, and (3) texting in class. First, Keri Stephens (University of Texas at Austin), Marian Houser (Texas State University), and Renee Cowan (Queens University of Charlotte) discuss how students can craft and send more productive emails to their professors. Second, Chris Sawyer (Texas Christian University) reviews how students can better cope with public speaking anxiety. Third, Jeffrey Kuznekoff (Miami University) and Stevie Munz (Utah Valley University) examine student texting in class, which is a common student habit, and how impacts learning and notetaking. As a college student, these research findings have a direct relevance to your lives because you will write many emails, give several speeches, and have the urge to text during class. We want you to have an enjoyable and successful college experience.

DID I REALLY SEND THAT? CRAFTING EFFECTIVE EMAILS TO PROFESSORS

Keri K. Stephens
University of Texas at Austin

Marian L. Houser
Texas State University

Renee L. Cowan
Queens University of Charlotte

WARNING: You are about to read actual email messages sent from students to professors. Grammar and punctuation have not been altered in any way:

Message 1 (sent unsigned): *My parents are mad that I signed up for your 350 lab class. They think it's too late. They still want me to come home every weekend. So is there any way I can be placed into one of your lab classed that are earlier or another day?*

Message 2: *Howdy Mr. Smith. I'm in your Thursday night class. I want to let you know/ask you if it's cool if I can attend your Tuesday night class on Oct. 20th. I know we have a test but on the 15th I have floor seats for the beyonce concert and I don't want to mis it =]...Gracias.*

Message 3: *hey teach, so sorry i was absent yesterday. These legal matters are killing me. but im not making excuses. i was just wondering if it would be too much trouble to let me know where i stand on absences in both my classes i am fortunate enough to have you as an instructor for. im trying to get my lawyer to help me work my court appearances around my class schedule. Thanks.*

Message 4: *Dr.Smith, I spoke with you abut this already, and the fact that I couldn't even make it to the bathroom without going on myself. Its not that I didn't want to come to class, it wa s matter of I could not physically make it to class one, and two why would you want me to spread that to the rest of the class and then put them and or you out for a week or so? This is ridicules, how are we expected to be in class when its not physically possible. Next time I'll just come to class an dpuke on the floor or shit mypants, if that will make you happy and keep mepassing the class. See you in class.*

INTRODUCTION

It is highly likely these students, if given the opportunity to review their email message, would wonder "Wow! Did I really send that?" While these are extreme examples, almost every professor who has taught for more than a year has a similar extreme email case to share. It is difficult to speculate what causes students to decide to hit the send key after composing these messages. Is it the stress that students feel about making that "A," or is the message written so quickly that the student does not think twice about how a professor might react toward their less-than-ideal message? Regardless of the reason, it is highly likely that students do not have their requests granted when their emails are misunderstood, confusing, and do not meet the expectations of the professors.

This chapter focuses on using research to better understand how students can best use email to communicate with professors. As there is considerable evidence to suggest that the student-instructor relationship is extremely valuable and creates many positive outcomes for the student, it is important to understand the impact of proper versus improper messages (Frymier & Houser, 2000; Pogue & Ahyun, 2006; Savic, 2018; Witt et al., 2004). The following example will be used throughout this chapter and is a more common type of email many students send to professors today—one resembling a text message. This message is very casual in tone and is considered quite informal; nonetheless, students who send these emails are evaluated quite harshly (Blackburne & Nardone, 2018):

> Subject: mting?
> Hey, I read chapter 9 and attended class but still don't get it. r u going 2 b in your office this afternoon can I come by if you are. tb

This chapter begins by discussing the concept of audience analysis and frames this to elaborate on the professor–student communication relationship. In addition, specific features of email messages are examined, followed by a discussion of email use beyond college and into the workplace. When you complete this chapter, you should be more aware of the benefits of thinking about your email before you hit the send key.

USING EMAIL WITH PROFESSORS

Email is a dominant form of professor–student communication and interaction (Kim et al., 2016; Pate et al., 2022), and much of this email is sent from mobile phones (Carr & Stefaniak, 2012). Research on email use in this context can really help students understand why they need to carefully consider their email use and the specific actions within them that bother professors. This form of written communication is personal and often one-on-one, so it provides an ideal opportunity to build a relationship or ruin a potential relationship.

PROFESSORS: AN IMPORTANT AUDIENCE

Communication students are typically taught to analyze their audience before they attempt to communicate. Audience analysis is often stressed in the public speaking context where students learn to craft openings that capture the attention of the audience and include details in the speech body that appeal to them (Beebe et al., 2010). This analysis is also very important in interpersonal interactions because these communication events typically occur more frequently than speeches and audience analysis increases the effectiveness of communication. This is especially the case when the audience is a professor and the message from the student is a request of some type.

Research suggests that requests are the most frequent type of email message sent from a student to a professor (Duran et al., 2005). Virtually every student will need to make a request of a professor at some time during their college career. Some requests are very simple, such as setting up a meeting during or outside of office hours. Other requests require a bit more persuasion, such as a request to miss class or have an assignment regraded. How you craft your email message has a direct impact on (1) whether the professor complies with your request, (2) their perception of your credibility, and (3) whether they like you (Bolkan & Holmgren, 2012; Stephens et al., 2009). Well-written, grammatically correct, and organized messages are received more positively (Blackburne & Nardone, 2018; Bunz & Campbell, 2004; Sims, 2015; Waldvogal, 2007). This helps overcome the issue of imposing additional costs or burdens—e.g. time to read and comprehend the message—on the message receiver. Well-crafted emails demonstrate goodwill on the part of the students because they have taken their time to write the message (Jessmer & Anderson, 2001) and thus, the professor views them as more credible (Sims, 2015; Stephens et al., 2011). Professors are also more motivated to work with students when they receive polite emails, and thus, their willingness to grant special requests increases (Bolkan & Holmgren, 2012).

Many students nod their heads at this point because this makes sense when they stop and think about their audience. This is, after all, a professor who has some amount of authority over them. But often students simply do not stop to think before typing the message, or they say, "If they know me, then it does not matter if I send a sloppy email." Students also defend their decisions for sending quick overly casual emails to professors by claiming, "My professor is young and so it is different because we are both in the same generation and quick messages are acceptable." These may seem like logical conclusions, but the research does not support these rationalizations.

MILLENNIAL PROFESSORS AND EMAIL

Few people will argue that the members of Generation Y (or Millennials) and those even younger in Generation Z and Alpha use technology differently than people in prior generations (Lancaster & Stillman, 2002). Students and young faculty born between 1982 and 2000 are considered part of the Millennial generation because of their advanced technology use and most traditional college-aged students are considered part of this generation or the more recent Generation Z or Alpha. Research suggests these more current generations are confident in how they use technology (Howe & Strauss, 2000) and they tend to violate email quality and structure expectations more often than people over 30 years of age (Extejt, 1998). Stephens et al. (2009) specifically examined whether there were differences in how younger professors viewed email violations when compared to professors from older generations. In their study of perceptions of students' overly casual emails, they found very few age effects on email perceptions. Thus, regardless of age, professors had very similar negative reactions to overly casual emails. So, younger professors did not view these professional email violations more permissively, suggesting students should proceed cautiously.

However, their study did find that younger professors are engaged in more text messaging (Stephens et al., 2011), and throughout the higher education community, there are increasing informal reports that some professors request that students text them in addition to using email. This does not, however, suggest students have free reign to send casual and sloppy messages. Research also suggests that email is used more by an older generation, while younger people rely on mobile phones, text messaging, and instant messaging (Kim et al., 2007)

FAMILIARITY AND EMAIL

It makes sense that once people become more familiar, email formality can decrease, but the research on professor–student email conversations does not suggest this. In their experimental study examining the effect of familiarity on a professor's willingness to comply with a simple request for a meeting with a student, Stephens et al. (2009) discovered the results differed depending on whether professors' or students' opinions were asked. In their study, familiarity (how well they know a student) did not affect how a professor evaluates a student's credibility, their attitude toward a message, their feeling of liking, or their willingness to grant a meeting. Students *believed* that when professors did not know the student sending the message, they were more willing to grant a meeting request if the message was more formally constructed (Stephens et al., 2011). This suggests that students might pay closer attention when they do not know a professor, but then become less worried about message quality when they become more familiar with them. Keep in mind that this is only one study and that these findings might differ depending on the context. But remember that regardless of familiarity with a student, a professor's view on the email does not change. So, students need to continue to remain professional in their email communication even as they get to know their professors.

WHAT ABOUT GRAMMAR AND PROFESSIONALISM

People often think that others will forgive them for grammar errors because they are sending email from their mobile phone. Could this possible be true? Carr and Stefaniak (2012) studied exactly this issue and discovered this was not necessarily the case. Though they did find that people who sent grammatically incorrect email messages from an iPhone were viewed as slightly more professional than people sending grammatically incorrect emails from a nonmobile device, those who sent grammatically flawed messages were always seen as less professional than those with grammatically correct messages.

MOVING BEYOND GRAMMAR ERRORS

One explanation for why students and other young people use grammatically incorrect and less professional language in email is because they spend much of their time communicating through text messaging; the evidence for cause, however, is not strong (Plester & Wood, 2009). Studies have found that adults often consider using textese—language and shortcuts typical in a text message—inappropriate (Kemp & Clayton, 2017). Textese includes slang and abbreviations like LOL (laughing out loud). But how do younger adults view this form of messaging? Recent research studied 8th graders and asked them to rate their fellow students depending on the level of textese in their messages. Even 8th graders rated their peers as less intelligent, having a lack of attention to details, and utilizing an inappropriate writing style when they used a considerable amount of text-message-like shortcuts (Kemp et al., 2021).

In another study looking specifically at student emails, Blackburne and Nardone (2018) found that an email behavior even worse than making grammatical errors is having an overly familiar tone before the recipient believes there has been appropriate rapport. Specifically, being rude or overly critical is the worst tone, followed by being sarcastic, and then being too frank. By the way, many of us are probably too frank because this category includes greetings like "Hey!" More appropriate tones are courteous and professional, such as "Dear Dr. Stephens" (Blackburne & Nardone, 2018). And if you think that student pursuing higher degrees, like a medical education are more professional with their email, you are partly correct. They are better than undergraduates, but they tend to use subject lines inappropriately and they did not include adequate closings that identify themselves clearly (Kim et al., 2016).

A DAY IN THE LIFE OF A PROFESSOR

To better understand why professionalism in communication matters in a college environment, let's examine what it is like to be in a professor's shoes. When a student's email appears in the professor's inbox, it is highly likely to be mixed with 25–50 other messages. Many of these messages come from other students and not necessarily students in the same class. In addition to students' emails, professors receive emails about departmental committees, university news, research grant information, letters of recommendation requests from former students, textbook adoption materials, volunteer requests from student organizations, and emails from coauthors and journal editors, just to mention a few. Combine the broad diversity of the messages with the reality that professors have busy days and many of the research findings regarding how professors examine and evaluate email messages make a lot of sense.

Pulling these findings together, it becomes clear there is a type of organizational and institutional norm that guides professors' interpretations of emails. Professors are in an organizational role where their job includes teaching and evaluating student work. Thus, receiving a carelessly constructed email from any student might make that role more prominent and create a situation where students are harshly evaluated for their sloppiness (Stephens et al., 2011). Professors worry when they receive emails with grammatical errors and shortcuts because they dread having to read and grade papers (which are often much longer) from a student who opts not to take the time to write a proper email.

WRITING EFFECTIVE EMAILS FOR PROFESSORS

So far, this chapter has focused primarily on the perception of students who write overly casual and grammatically incorrect email messages, but research also provides guidance on the specific components of email messages that likely matter the most. For example, do you like long emails that drone on for pages? Probably not, and the research says that most of us prefer concise emails that are well-crafted and to the point (Crowther & Goldhaber, 2001).

There are some differences in opinions concerning what is problematic, especially when comparing professors and students. Two specific email items were found especially frustrating for professors: the absence of the author's name in the message and the use of shortcuts like those found in text messages (Stephens et al., 2009). Both of these issues bothered students significantly less than professors. Again, try and put yourself in a professor's shoes; this might help to clarify the following research findings. For example, imagine reading a message, in an inbox full of unread messages that are unsigned. The professor looks everywhere in the message to figure out who sent it but only finds the email address kl523478@txstate. edu. The professor thinks, "Do I have a student with the initials KL in any of my 4 classes?" Then the professor wonders if the letters are even the student's initials. In a frustrated state, the professor does not know how to respond. Now imagine being a professor and receiving an email from a student that includes the acronym "LOL." The professor wonders, "Does that student want me to laugh out loud, or are they sending me an uncomfortable amount of love?" Of course, this assumes the professor is familiar with text message acronyms and is related to another research finding regarding professors' dislike of shortcuts.

So what about openings, closings, signature blocks, and the all-important subject line? Research provides some guidance on these issues as well. "Hey" or "Howdy" is a bit abrupt for a professional email (Blackburne & Nardone, 2018) and simply avoiding a greeting altogether is not prudent. Several research studies suggest that people need to include greetings such as Dear, or Hello as well as the person's name (Bunz & Campbell, 2004; Waldvogal, 2007). In a study of faculty perceptions of impoliteness, having an appropriate opening had the most impact on their perceptions of the students (Savic, 2018). In addition, unless advised otherwise, you should never refer to your professor as Mr. or Mrs. when Dr. is their formal title

(Yagoda, 2003). If you do not know your professors' titles you should simply ask them or look them up on the Internet to see if they have completed their Ph.D. When you are ending your message, you should include a closing as it sends an appropriate politeness cue (Bunz & Campbell, 2004; Savic, 2018), and be sure to sign your name as the author of the message (Stephens et al., 2009). It is also extremely important to use the subject line and to include specificity that will encourage others to open the message (Crowther & Goldhaber, 2001). People are increasingly overloaded, and email is to blame in many situations (Farhoomand, & Drury, 2002).

Sims (2015) offers a helpful framework, The Five P's, for thinking about writing emails to professors and in the workplace. Have a *personal*, individualize greeting and closing. Be *precise* by including an accurate subject line. Be *prepared* implies you have included the information you need before sending the message. *Politeness* means using a formal tone and being courteous. Finally, *proofread* your work for grammar, in addition to accuracy and tone.

Avoiding email pitfalls and crafting thoughtful messages will not go unnoticed which is especially important if you are making a request. A final consideration is to understand that your email address sends a message about who you are as a person. Imagine being a professor and receiving an email from *biglovemama@gmail.com*. Many students never consider that their actual email address sends an additional message above and beyond the content of the message. Not only does this send the wrong message to a professor, but it is also unprofessional as you consider graduating and entering the workplace (and perhaps even asking for that valuable letter of recommendation).

USING EMAIL BEYOND COLLEGE

While there will be varied organizational norms for how to use email in the places you work, much of what we have discussed here provides a conservative approach for you to manage your impression as you begin your career. Wilson (2005) warns college graduates to pay close attention because sending improper emails can send a negative impression to important and powerful audiences such as managers, colleagues, and customers. One of the advantages of taking a communication course is that you learn how to observe others and adapt your communication to fit their needs and create a win-win situation for both of you. Not all organizations will want extremely formal emails, so it is important for you to learn how this tool is appropriated in a given environment (Ducheneaut & Watts, 2005). Also, consider that mobile devices like iPhones are frequently used in workplace environments and sending and receiving messages from these smaller devices presents challenges to crafting well-written messages with limited character subject lines (Stephens et al., 2009). A good workplace email reference guide is *Send*, by Shipley and Schwalbe (2008), op-ed editor of the *New York Times* and Hyperion Books' editor-in-chief. This popular press book provides humorous, yet real examples of how people have ruined careers by not being cognizant of email etiquette. They also provide many tips for how to successfully communicate through email.

USING EMAIL WITH OTHER COMMUNICATION TECHNOLOGIES

Email is still a dominant form of communication between many students and professors, (Smith et al., 2017) and it is often considered a professional way to communicate (Stephens & Heller, 2010). Yet it is important to remember that email is not used in isolation because students and working professionals often use a mix of communication technologies that include text messages, social media, instructional tools like Blackboard/Canvas, phone, and even face-to-face (FtF) communication (Stephens et al., 2008). Recent research suggests that using a combination of communication technologies—e.g. email followed by FtF communication—is more persuasive than simply using email of FtF repetitively (Stephens & Rains, 2011). In their study of using multiple messages to persuade college students to visit career services, Stephens and Rains (2011) found that overload—defined as having more messages than people want—plays a pivotal role in why a mix of communication technologies matters. These findings point to another tip when interacting with professors—vary the medium you use to communicate. Instead of sending repeated emails, it is often prudent to handle some conversations in person rather than send repeated emails.

CONCLUSION

If you have not yet felt a bit uncomfortable about past email messages you have sent, you are probably in the minority. Most of us are guilty of firing off a last-minute email or using shortcuts to compose an email on a mobile device. These mistakes can be costly. This chapter should have reminded you that the messages you send to professors are worth the time to get the message correct and your message understood. Hopefully, you understand more about how your audience (a professor) views your message in the context of the other 25–50 waiting in their inbox. It does not matter how well you know your professor or if your professor is young, professionalism is expected in this environment. Even though it is tempting to use shortcuts, especially when you are using mobile phones, do not include them in emails. Remember to sign your emails with your name, use descriptive subject lines, and focus on appropriate greetings. It is important that you learn how these mistakes impact your life as a college student because if you remember the importance of professionalism now, it will serve you well in your professional career. btw…gtg!

REFERENCES

Beebe, S. A., Beebe, S. J., & Ivy, D. K. (2010). *Communication: Principles for a lifetime* (4th ed.). Allyn and Bacon.

Blackburne, B. D., & Nardone, C. F. (2018). Beyond grammar: Tracking perceptions of quality in student e-mail. *Journal of Technical Writing and Communication, 48*(4), 412–440. https://doi.org/10.1177/0047281617730532

Bolkan, S., & Holmgren, J. L. (2012). "You are such a great teacher and I hate to bother you but…": Instructors' perceptions of students and their use of email messages with varying politeness strategies. *Communication Education, 61*(3), 253–270. https://doi.org/10.1080/03634523.2012.667135

Bunz, U., & Campbell, S. W. (2004). Politeness accommodation in electronic mail. *Communication Research Reports, 21*(1), 11–25. https://doi.org/10.1080/08824090409359963

Carr, C. T., & Stefaniak, C. (2012). Sent from my iPhone: The medium and message as cues of sender professionalism in mobile telephony. *Journal of Applied Communication Research, 40*(4), 403–424. https://doi.org/10.1080/00909882.2012.712707

Crowther, G., & Goldhaber, G. (2001, August/September). Face-to-face or e-mail: The medium makes a difference, *Communication World,* 23–26.

Ducheneaut, N., & Watts, L. A. (2005). In search of coherence: A review of e-mail research. *Human-Computer Interaction, 20*(1–2), 11–48. https://doi.org/10.1080/07370024.2005.9667360

Duran, R. L., Kelly, L., & Keaton, J. A. (2005). College faculty use and perceptions of electronic mail to communication with students. *Communication Quarterly, 53*(2), 159–176. https://doi.org/10.1080/01463370500090118

Extejt, M. M. (1998). Teaching students to correspond effectively electronically. *Business Communication Quarterly, 61*(2), 57–67. https://doi.org/10.1177/108056999806100208

Farhoomand, A. F., & Drury, D. H. (2002). Managerial information overload. *Communications of the ACM, 45*(10), 127–131. https://doi.org/10.1145/570907.570909

Frymier, A. B., & Houser, M. L. (2000). The teacher-student relationship as an interpersonal relationship. *Communication Education, 49*(3), 207–219. https://doi.org/10.1080/03634520009379209

Howe, N., & Strauss, W. (2000). *Millennials rising: The next great generation.* Vintage.

Jessmer, S., & Anderson, D. (2001). The effect of politeness and grammar on user perceptions of electronic mail. *North American Journal of Psychology, 3*(2), 331–346. https://docview/89176765/fulltextPDF/6B53FA29FE81450FPQ/1?accountid=7118

Kemp, N., & Clayton, J. (2017). University students vary their use of textese in digital messages to suit the recipient. *Journal of Research in Reading, 40*(S1), S141–S157. https://doi.org/10.1111/1467-9817.12074

Kemp, N., Graham, J., Grieve, R., & Beyersmann, E. (2021). The influence of textese on adolescents' perceptions of text message writers. *Telematics and Informatics, 65,* 101720. https://doi.org/10.1016/j.tele.2021.101720

Kim, H., Kim, G. J., Park, H. W., & Rice, R. E. (2007). Configurations of relationships in different media: FtF, email, instant messenger, mobile phone, and SMS. *Journal of Computer-Mediated Communication, 12*(4), 1183–1207. https://doi.org/10.1111/j.1083-6101.2007.00369.x

Kim, D.-H., Yoon, H. B., Yoo, D.-M., Lee, S.-M., Jung, H.-Y., Kim, S. J., Shin, J.-S., Lee, S., & Yim, J.-J. (2016). Etiquette for medical students' email communication with faculty members: a single-institution study. *BMC Medical Education, 16*(1), 129. https://doi.org/10.1186/s12909-016-0628-y

Lancaster, L. C., & Stillman, D. (2002). *When generations collide: Who they are, why they clash, how to solve the generational puzzle at work.* HarperCollins.

Pate, A. N., Fleming, L., Jones-Bodie, A., Wagner, J. L., Fleming, J. W., Davis, C., & Brown, M. (2022). Impact of communication method and timeliness on student and faculty perception of professionalism and value. *American Journal of Pharmaceutical Education, 86*(2), 115–123. https://doi.org/10.5688/ajpe8391

Plester, B., & Wood, C. (2009). Exploring relationships between traditional and new media literacies: British preteen texters at school. *Journal of Computer-Mediated Communication, 14*(4), 1108–1129. https://doi.org/10.1111/j.1083-6101.2009.01483.x

Pogue, L., & Ahyun, K. (2006). The effect of teacher nonverbal immediacy and credibility on student motivation and affective learning. *Communication Education, 55*(3), 331–344. https://psycnet.apa.org/doi/10.1080/03634520600748623

Savić, M. (2018). Lecturer perceptions of im/politeness and in/appropriateness in student e-mail requests: A Norwegian perspective. *Journal of Pragmatics, 124,* 52–72. https://doi.org/10.1016/j.pragma.2017.12.005

Shipley, D., & Schwalbe, W. (2008). *Send: The essential guide to email for office and home.* Random House, Inc.

Sims, C.-D. L. (2015). Competency and connection: Undergraduate students and effective email messages. *Communication Teacher, 29*(3), 129–134. https://doi.org/10.1080/17404622.2015.1028557

Smith, M., Chen, Y., Berndtson, R., Burson, K., Griffin, W. (2017). Office hours are kind of weird: Reclaiming a resource to foster student-faculty interaction. *InSight: A Journal of Scholarly Teaching, 12,* 14–29. http://www.insightjournal.net/

Stephens, K. K., Cowan, R. L., & Houser, M. L. (2011). Organizational norm congruency and interpersonal familiarity in email: Examining messages from two different status perspectives. *Journal of Computer Mediated Communication, 16*(2), 228–249. https://doi.org/10.1111/j.1083-6101.2011.01537.x

Stephens, K. K., & Heller, A. (2010). 2010 US Census Coverage Measurement Residence Hall Report, Washington DC, US Census Bureau.

Stephens, K. K., Houser, M. L., & Cowan, R. L. (2009). R U able to meat me: The impact of students' overly casual email messages to instructors. *Communication Education, 58*(3), 303–326. https://doi.org/10.1080/03634520802582598

Stephens, K. K., & Rains, S. A. (2011). Information and communication technology sequences and message repetition in interpersonal interaction. *Communication Research, 38*(1), 101–122. https://doi.org/10.1177/0093650210362679

Stephens, K. K., Sørnes, J. O, Rice, R. E., Browning, L. D., & Sætre, A. S. (2008). Discrete, sequential, and follow-up use of information and communication technology by managerial knowledge workers. *Management Communication Quarterly, 22*(2), 197–231. https://doi.org/10.1177%2F0893318908323149

Waldvogal, J. (2007). Greetings and closings in workplace email. *Journal of Computer-Mediated Communication, 12*(2), 456–477. https://doi.org/10.1111/j.1083-6101.2007.00333.x

Wilson, E. V. (2005). Persuasive effects of system features in computer-mediated communication. *Journal of Organizational Computing and Electronic Commerce, 15*(2), 161–184. https://doi.org/10.1207/s15327744joce1502_4

Witt, P. L., Wheeless, L. R., & Allen, M. (2004). A meta-analytical review of the relationship between teacher immediacy and student learning. *Communication Monographs, 71*(2), 184–207. https://psycnet.apa.org/doi/10.1080/036452042000228054

Yagoda, B. (2003, June 13). What should we call the professor? *The Chronicle of Higher Education, 49*(40), B20. Retrieved from http://chronicle.com

HOW CAN STUDENTS BETTER COPE WITH PUBLIC SPEAKING ANXIETY IN THE COLLEGE CLASSROOM?

Chris R. Sawyer
Texas Christian University

We begin this chapter with a short vignette about a student named Miriam, a college sophomore taking her first course in communication. Confident in every other aspect of her academic life, she avoids any class requiring public speaking. However, her university requires a basic speech course for graduation, and today Miriam is giving her dreaded first speech in that class. Detailed, hard-working, and always prepared, Miriam has devoted most of her preparation time to researching and writing multiple drafts of her presentation. Miriam did not make much effort in rehearsing delivery because her main goal was to muddle through this assignment by reading from her extensive notes. Suddenly she realizes that she is the next to make a presentation. Her heart begins to pound, and her breathing becomes shallow. Worrisome thoughts race through her mind. The instructor calls her name, and soon afterward, the "moment of truth" finally arrives. Standing behind a lectern, she faces her fellow students for the first time. How will Miriam react to this new situation? Will her anxiety symptoms continue to escalate, making this the single most stressful event of her life? Perhaps she will discover that presenting speeches is not so bad or might even enjoy the experience. What about the reactions of the audience and her teacher? How will they perceive her performance? Will they see through her attempts to cover up her insecurities or not notice them?

Modern communication scholars have posed these questions, and many others like them, when trying to account for speakers' anxiety levels before, during, and after they give public speeches. Those new to this issue are often amazed to discover its complexity and the richness of theories offered to explain it. Despite the tireless efforts of many prominent scholars, a complete account of speech anxiety has yet to appear in scholarly writings.

The purpose of this chapter is to present a summary of how one simple approach to this problem, called narrow banding (Behnke & Sawyer, 1998), has helped to advance our knowledge of how students can better manage the negative effects of speech anxiety in the college classroom.

EARLY SPEECH ANXIETY RESEARCH

For more than 70 years, communication scholars have attempted to examine the relationships among the various forms of public speaking state anxiety. In his summary of early "stage fright" research, Clevenger (1959) was uncertain whether the methods used to measure anxiety at that time were valid. Moreover, it was unclear to him whether those methods represented different aspects of the same construct or if definitional problems were at fault. Shortly after Clevenger's paper was published. However, it became evident that conceptual weaknesses impeded the progress of early speech anxiety researchers.

Spielberger (1966) differentiated state and trait anxiety using factor analytic techniques pioneered by Cattell and Scheier (1958). A state is a transitory condition, which means that it varies over time. Traits, however, are stable and may reflect basic individual differences such as personality dimensions. Essentially, what distinguishes traits from states comes down to "how do you generally feel" (trait) versus "how do you feel at a given moment in time," usually "right now" (state). Before Spielberger, communication scholars often used ambiguous or excessively broad measures of anxiety in their research. The State-Trait Anxiety Inventory (STAI A-State) (Spielberger et al., 1970) overcame these limitations and became the most widely used measure of public speaking state anxiety in empirical studies (Sawyer, 2016).

Spielberger's state-trait distinction was a valuable breakthrough for communication scholars. McCroskey's (1982) Personal Report of Communication Apprehension (PRCA-24) has impelled scholars to ask deeper questions about human nature, test new generalizations, achieve scientific progress, and improve communication instruction (Sawyer, 2018a). Trait measures of anxiety, like the PRCA-24, are useful because the way speakers describe their general speech anxiety today tends to be very similar to how they will report it in the future. As a result, instruments such as the PRCA-24 can help identify students who might suffer discomfort on future speech assignments. On the other hand, public speaking state anxiety refers to how speakers feel during a particular speech, as opposed to all others they have ever presented (Behnke & Sawyer, 1998). Because each speaking situation is unique, speakers will not respond the same way whenever they make a presentation. Moreover, unlike traits, states fluctuate with time, making them useful for answering various questions where the trait approach would be impractical. The work covered in this chapter focuses on state rather than trait communication apprehension.

MEASUREMENT AND CONCEPTUAL ISSUES

Before discussing the contributions of this research, you should know several concepts and some basic vocabulary. First, the most common method of conducting speech anxiety research is asking speakers to share their experiences using interviews and surveys. Self-reported data of this type are easy to obtain and usually provide good accounts of feelings, worry, and other psychological variables. In other speech anxiety research, trained observers watch video recordings of speeches looking for telltale signs of nervousness. However, one cannot see every aspect of anxiety with the naked eye. The third and last strategy involves directly measuring physical changes in a speaker's body, such as increased heart rate and blood pressure brought on by the stress of giving a speech (Sawyer, 2017a, b). Although weak associations exist between psychological, physiological, and behavioral measures of speech anxiety, each way of knowing and observing contributes unique information to our understanding of the problem. Together these approaches to speech anxiety research are called the three modes of experience. Although speakers' self-reported anxiety is most useful to our work, we have also used physiological (Roberts et al., 2004; Sawyer & Behnke, 2014) and behavioral (Finn et al., 2003) indices of speech anxiety.

Another idea is "unrolling the ball of string." Imagine that you are holding a ball of cotton string in the palm of your hand. Unwinding it, you realize that the ball consists of different colored stands of twine and yarn connected end-to-end. As an analogy, "unrolling the ball of string" means measuring state anxiety at particular moments throughout the speech rather than for the speech as a whole. This approach reveals insights into speakers' reactions left undetected when researchers ask them to describe their overall feeling during a presentation. Some of these have surprising results, especially for students enrolled in introductory courses.

Unrolling the ball of string leads us to the concept of state anxiety milestones. Milestones are specific moments before, during, and immediately following a public speech during which specific psychological events occur (Behnke & Sawyer, 1999). In much of our research, we ask speakers to tell us how they felt at various times, such as one minute before speaking, during the first and last minutes of their presentations, and for the minute immediately following their speeches. These are the anticipation, confrontation, adaptation, and release milestones. The use of milestones to gauge the state anxiety levels of speakers is also called narrow-band measurement (Behnke & Sawyer, 1998).

SPEECH STATE ANXIETY PATTERN TYPES

Speaker anxiety during each milestone reveals at least two competing emotional processes: habituation and sensitization (Behnke & Sawyer, 2001a; Finn et al., 2003). When examined across the four milestones, most speakers report their highest level of psychological state anxiety during the anticipation milestone, approximately 1 minute before presenting the speech. Anxiety levels begin to decline during the first minute of speaking, also known as the "moment of truth" or confrontation milestone. State anxiety levels then continue to decrease through the last minute of the speech and the minute after the speech or adaptation and release milestones. Habituation is the tendency for humans to become progressively more comfortable in the presence of fear arousing stimulus (Sawyer, 2018b). Mathematically, habituation is a monotonic decreasing function of anxiety across the four milestones.

Approximately two-thirds to three-quarters of all speakers studied in pattern studies display this overall shape and are called habituators.

Generally, a secondary pattern accounts for the remaining speakers and reflects a contrary process called sensitization. For these speakers, psychological anxiety is elevated during the anticipation milestone but rises dramatically and peaks during the confrontation stage. Anxiety then declines gradually during the remainder of the speech and through the release milestone. Speakers who display this inverted V-shaped pattern are called sensitizers. We have been able to establish several concerning speakers with this pattern type. Sensitizers adapt more slowly to public speaking than habituators (Sawyer & Behnke, 2002a) and experience more body sensations of distress (Horvath et al., 2004; Witt et al., 2006). Compared to habituators, sensitizers report higher levels of anxiety sensitivity (Behnke & Sawyer, 2001b), affect intensity, and sensitivity to punishment (Clay et al., 2005). Sensitization during public speaking appears to be the function of high-trait anxiety combined with reactivity to stressful stimuli (Harris et al., 2006; Roberts et al., 2005).

MAKING SENSE OF THE FINDINGS

Each of the findings discussed above is consistent with recent advances in understanding how emotions are processed. Specifically, anxiety is part of the human stress response, a species-specific survival mechanism shaped by natural selection, regulated by neural anatomy, and observable in human physiology (Sawyer, 2020). It consists of a constellation of symptoms or reactions, including increased physiological arousal (increased heart rate), heightened vigilance, stress reactions, and rumination or worry, which reflect our evolutionary development as a species (Gray & McNaughton, 2000; LeDoux, 2015). Our vignette at the start of the chapter contained many of these characteristics. Miriam's speaking behavior, which we did not describe, would likely reflect a condition known as behavioral inhibition, including monotone vocal cues, deadpan facial expressions, and rigid or nonexistent gestures (Finn et al., 2003; Mulac & Sherman, 1974). According to this perspective, once behavior inhibition sets in, it will continue to influence speaker behaviors until the level of perceived threat diminishes.

Interestingly, state anxiety naturally declines with exposure to a feared stimulus, so long as speakers experience little or no real harm (McNally, 2007). Suppose that Miriam avoids speaking in public because she worries that audiences will behave unfavorably toward her. In this case, a supportive audience will promote the habituation response because what the speaker fears seldom materializes. One anxiety management strategy that uses this principle is exposure therapy (Foa et al., 2006). Under this strategy, a therapist or clinician presents a fear stimulus that is strong enough to evoke a mild to moderate anxiety reaction. Then, while continued exposure to the stimulus is maintained, the therapist controls or reduces any negative consequences. Thus, exposure therapy helps speakers to adjust their anxiety responses, much like resetting a thermostat when weather conditions change.

A convenient method for implementing exposure therapy in the communication class-room is the TRIPLESPEAK assignment (Dubner & Mills, 1984). In TRIPLESPEAK, the teacher divides the speech class into four groups. Students assigned to one of the groups are speakers, while the other groups serve as the audience. Every speaker makes a brief presentation to each of the audience in turn. These brief multiple exposures have the effect of reducing the threat of giving a speech. As the perceived threat diminishes, speakers become less inhibited, more comfortable, and experience less distress. Moreover, habituation during these initial presentations continues to help speakers on subsequent assignments (Finn et al., 2009b).

To summarize, this chapter covers several principles. First, anxiety affects speakers' physiological, behavioral, and psychological reactions. Consequently, it is among the greatest barriers to student success in introductory communication courses, especially those requiring public speaking assignments. Next, instruments like the PRCA-24 measure traits which resist change over time. Therefore, it is more appropriate to focus on states when assessing students' progress. Otherwise, substantial gains in speaker confidence will go undetected when using trait measures alone. Besides, only about half of the variance in speech state anxiety is a function of trait anxiety. The remaining 50% stems from speaker adaptation while speaking, along with some situational variance (Harris et al., 2006). Third, "unrolling the ball of string," called public speaking state anxiety, requires looking at specific moments in which critical events occur, called milestones. Habituators differ from sensitizers mainly at the "moment of truth" or confrontation. Therefore, preparing students for the first minute of the presentation may be critical to how much they benefit from class speaking assignments. Last, instructors can embed exposure within various classroom assignments such as TRIPLESPEAK. As a result, students can get the benefits of greater confidence during confrontation without the embarrassment of feeling singled out for special treatment.

Most stage fright researchers are motivated by the compassionate impulse to help others and relieve discomfort. Here are four suggestions based on the information presented in this chapter that could potentially enhance your life as a public speaker.

Do not forget to breathe. Many of the anxious speakers we have studied report physical sensations such as chest pressure, palpitations, and shortness of breath. Proper breathing can neutralize the symptoms of the fight-flight reflex to some degree. A few minutes before your speech, consciously take deep breaths, inhaling through your nose and filling your abdomen. Hold each breath for a few seconds, and then exhale quietly through your nose. You should start feeling more relaxed within a few cycles of deep breathing. Also, breathing from your stomach when giving speeches can help you to project your voice so that you can be heard clearly by everyone in the audience.

Remember, the worst part is over very early. The physical symptoms of state anxiety are uncomfortable for a reason. They act like an alarm system warning you of some potential threat. Over the years, we have learned that those speakers who can get through the "moment of truth" at the outset of a presentation become progressively less anxious as they continue to speak. Consequently, it would be best if you spoke continuously for at least the first minute of the presentation. We recommend rehearsing your speech's initial minute or two and taking notes or other memory aids with you to the podium. After speaking for about a minute or so, you should experience fewer stress sensations and greater comfort.

Most audiences can not tell how nervous you are. Beginning public speakers often worry that their audiences will be able to detect how anxious they are. Despite the intense physical sensations and racing thoughts associated with stage fright, most audiences do not notice speakers' anxiety. Researchers who have studied the communication of public speaking anxiety report that audiences underestimate speaker nervousness, making their detection of anxiety low (Sawyer & Behnke, 2002b). One explanation is that emotions are primarily communicated through the face and the voice. Anxious speakers often have subdued vocal and facial cues. Speakers are more inhibited at the beginning of their speeches and become increasingly expressive as they feel more comfortable. Audiences see and hear less of your anxiety when you start speaking, though some can slip through. Later, audiences will pick up more of your emotions as you become less anxious. Although these facts might not alleviate all your concerns, you should not focus on how much anxiety your audience can see or hear.

Start small and work your way up. Once you have learned the fundamentals of preparing and giving speeches during your introductory communication course, make a point to give short presentations occasionally in front of small but friendly audiences outside of class. Volunteering to make an announcement to a small social gathering of friends is an excellent place to start. Look for opportunities to speak and gradually increase the length of your speeches, presenting them to slightly larger groups each time. Most of our students who have used this strategy report greater confidence when making formal public speeches at large gatherings.

Many great orators throughout history began their careers with fear and trepidation. Despite this, they became confident and well-composed speakers with diligent practice and the support of others. The same can be true for you.

REFERENCES

Behnke, R. R., & Sawyer, C. R. (1998). Conceptualizing speech anxiety as a dynamic trait. *Southern Communication Journal, 63*(2), 160–168. https://doi.org/10.1080/10417949809373086

Behnke, R. R., & Sawyer, C. R. (1999). Milestones of anticipatory public speaking anxiety. *Communication Education, 48*(2), 165–172. https://doi.org/10.1080/03634529909379164

Behnke, R. R., & Sawyer, C. R. (2001a). Patterns of psychological state anxiety in public speaking as a function of anxiety sensitivity. *Communication Quarterly, 49*(1), 84–94. https://doi.org/10.1080/01463370109385616

Behnke, R. R., & Sawyer, C. R. (2001b). Public speaking arousal as a function of anticipatory activation and autonomic reactivity. *Communication Reports, 14*(2), 73–85. https://doi.org/10.1080/08934210109367740

Cattell, R. B., & Scheier, I. H. (1958). The nature of anxiety: A review of thirteen multivariate analyses comprising 814 variables. *Psychological Reports, 4*(3), 351–388. https://doi.org/10.2466/pr0.1958.4.3.351

Clay, E., Fisher, R. L., Xie, S., Sawyer, C. R., & Behnke, R. R. (2005). Affect intensity and sensitivity to punishment as predictors of sensitization (arousal) during public speaking. *Communication Reports, 18*(1–2), 95–103. https://doi.org/10.1080/08934210500310007

Clevenger, T. (1959). A synthesis of experimental research in stage fright. *Quarterly Journal of Speech, 45*(2), 134–145. https://doi.org/10.1080/00335635909385732

Dubner, F. S., & Mills, F. O. (1984). Triplespeak: A teaching technique to multiply successful speech performance. *Communication Education, 33*(2), 168–172. https://doi.org/10.1080/03634528409384734

Finn, A. N., Sawyer, C. R., & Behnke, R. R. (2003). Audience-perceived anxiety patterns of public speakers. *Communication Quarterly, 51*(4), 470–481. https://doi.org/10.1080/01463370309370168

Finn, A. N., Sawyer, C. R., & Schrodt, P. (2009b). Examining the effect of exposure therapy on public speaking state anxiety. *Communication Education, 58*(1), 92–109. https://doi.org/10.1080/03634520802450549

Foa, E. B., Huppert, J., & Cahill, S. P. (2006). Emotional processing theory. In B. O. Rothbaum (Ed.), *Pathological anxiety: Emotional processing in etiology and treatment* (pp. 3–24). Guilford Press.

Gray, J. A., & McNaughton, N. (2000). *The neuropsychology of anxiety: An enquiry into the functions of the septo-hippocampal system (oxford psychology series)* (2nd ed.). Oxford University Press.

Harris, K. B., Sawyer, C. R., & Behnke, R. R. (2006). Predicting speech state anxiety from trait anxiety, reactivity, and situational influences. *Communication Quarterly, 54*(2), 213–226. https://doi.org/10.1080/01463370600650936

Horvath, N. R., Hunter, M. C., Weisel, J. J., Sawyer, C. R., & Behnke, R. R. (2004). Body sensations during speech performance as a function of public speaking anxiety type. *Texas Speech Communication Journal, 29*(1), 65–72.

Ledoux, J. (2015). *The emotional brain: The mysterious underpinnings of emotional life* (15th ed.). Simon & Schuster.

McCroskey, J. C. (1982). Oral communication apprehension: A reconceptualization. *Annals of the International Communication Association, 6*(1), 136–170. https://doi.org/10.1080/23808985.1982.11678497

McNally, R. J. (2007). Mechanisms of exposure therapy: How neuroscience can improve psychological treatments for anxiety disorders. *Clinical Psychology Review, 27*(6), 750–759. https://doi.org/10.1016/j.cpr.2007.01.003

Mulac, A., & Sherman, A. (1974). Behavioral assessment of speech anxiety. *Quarterly Journal of Speech, 60*(2), 134–143. https://doi.org/10.1080/00335637409383219

Roberts, J. B., Finn, A. N., Harris, K. B., Sawyer, C. R., & Behnke, R. R. (2005). Public speaking state anxiety as a function of trait anxiety and reactivity mechanisms. *Southern Journal of Communication, 70*(2), 161–167. https://doi.org/10.1080/10417940509373321

Roberts, J. B., Finn, A. N., Harris, K. B., Sawyer, C. R., & Behnke, R. R. (2005). Public speaking state anxiety as a function of trait anxiety and reactivity mechanisms. *Southern Communication Journal, 70*(2), 161–167. https://doi.org/10.1080/10417940509373321

Sawyer, C. R. (2016). Communication apprehension and public speaking instruction. In *Communication and learning* (pp. 397–426). De Gruyter. https://doi.org/10.1515/9781501502446-017

Sawyer, C. R. (2017a). Physiological measurement: Blood pressure. In M. Allen (Ed.), *SAGE encyclopedia of communication research methods*. Sage. https://doi.org/10.4135/9781483381411.n430

Sawyer, C. R. (2017b). Physiological measurement: Blood pressure. In M. Allen (Ed.), *SAGE encyclopedia of communication research methods* (pp. 1239–1242). Sage. http://dx.doi.org/10.4135/9781483381411.n430

Sawyer, C. R. (2018a). Communication apprehension. In *Oxford research encyclopedia of communication*. Oxford: Oxford University Press. https://doi.org/10.1093/acrefore/9780190228613.013.764

Sawyer, C. R. (2018b). Habituation and communication. In *Oxford bibliographies of communication*. Oxford University Press. https://doi.org/10.1093/OBO/9780199756841-0208

Sawyer, C. R. (2020). Developmental psychophysiology and the human stress response during communication. In *The handbook of communication science and biology* (pp. 332–343). Routledge. https://doi.org/10.4324/9781351235587-28

Sawyer, C. R., & Behnke, R. R. (1999). State anxiety patterns for public speaking and the behavior inhibition system. *Communication Reports, 12*(1), 33–41. https://doi.org/10.1080/08934219909367706

Sawyer, C. R., & Behnke, R. R. (2002a). Reduction in public speaking state anxiety during performance as a function of sensitization processes. *Communication Quarterly, 50*(1), 110–121. https://doi.org/10.1080/01463370209385649

Sawyer, C. R., & Behnke, R. R. (2002b). Behavioral inhibition and the communication of public speaking state anxiety. *Western Journal of Communication, 66*, 412–422. https://doi.org/10.1080/10570310209374747

Spielberger, C. D. (1966). *Anxiety and behavior*. Academic Press.

Spielberger, C. D., Gorusch, R. L., & Lushene, R. E. (1970). Manual for state-trait anxiety inventory. Consulting Psychological Corporation.

Witt, P. L., Brown, K. C., Roberts, J. B., Weisel, J., Sawyer, C. R., & Behnke, R. R. (2006). Somatic anxiety patterns before, during, and after giving a public speech. *Southern communication journal, 71*(1), 87–100. https://doi.org/10.1080/10417940500503555

INSTRUCTIONAL COMMUNICATION: RESEARCH ON TEXTING AND NOTE-TAKING

Jeffrey H. Kuznekoff
Miami University

Stevie Munz
Utah Valley University

INTRODUCTION

In Spring 2011, I (Jeff) was enrolled in the last graduate class I would ever take and, coincidently, that class also resulted in a surprise research topic that informed most of my future work. The class focused on instructional communication and nearly all of my classmates were other doctoral students at Ohio University (OU). Most of us were attending OU through scholarships that included teaching about two undergraduate-level communication courses each semester. Nearly all of us had a couple of years of teaching experience but, as still somewhat new teachers, we had a lot to learn about teaching and a class in instructional communication was a great way to learn more about communicating effectively as a teacher. One of our class sessions was devoted to talking about new technologies and teaching.

At one point during the class, when each of us was sharing how we use technology as a teacher, one of the other graduate students asked about student technology use. They wanted to know if other instructors had also noticed their students using their mobile phones during class. The general consensus was that everyone had noticed more students texting or checking social media sites while in class and that this was a relatively new occurrence. I thought back to when I started at OU in Fall 2008 and, back then, it was relatively rare to see students texting during class. At that point in time, the iPhone was a little over a year old and most people on campus had flip phones. However, by 2011 it seemed like most of our students had some sort of smartphone that they were bringing and using during class and that use was something fairly new. The conversation quickly shifted to the question of what effect texting during class would have on student learning.

For context, I am an earlier adopter of technology. So much so that I missed my own brother's birthday to stand in line to get the original iPhone, which the AT&T store ran out of before I got one (something my brother reminded everyone of during his best man toast at my wedding). That earlier question, what effect texting during class would have on student learning, was directed to me since I study CMC and new communication technology. At that point, communication research did not have a great answer to that question or a good understanding of how technology use might also have an influence on student note-taking. Those unanswered questions ended up being the start of several research projects that would be fundamental to my, and Stevie's, careers.

TEXTING RESEARCH

To answer the unresolved questions from that class session, I worked with Dr. Scott Titsworth (Kuznekoff & Titsworth, 2013) to develop an experimental study that would help to answer those questions. At that point in time, past communication research used self-report data to look at perceptions of mobile phones in the college classroom (Campbell, 2006) and to examine how mobile phone usage might influence student learning (Wei et al., 2012). However, we thought that developing an experiment would allow us to gain additional insight into this area of research. An experiment has several advantages over self-report data, which is when participants in a study are asked to report their own attitudes, beliefs, behaviors, etc. (Lavrakas, 2008). Sometimes participants will report what they think the researcher wants to hear or perhaps report information that makes them appear more socially acceptable. An experiment can potentially avoid these issues and allows researchers to carefully control or manipulate particular aspects of a study (i.e., variables) in order to measure the effect those manipulations have.

We developed a way to simulate text messages or social media content that would automatically be pushed to a student's mobile device during a study session. Students who attended our study session were randomly assigned, by a computer, to either receive a new message every 30 seconds or every 60 seconds. During this study session, students watched a 12-minute video lecture, were asked to take notes on that lecture as they would in one of their regular classes and to respond to each message they received on their device. All of the messages we used had content that was entirely unrelated to the lecture content. We also had a group of students who were given the same instructions as the other groups but with the key exception of being told **not** to use their mobile devices at all during the session. At the end of each session, students reviewed their notes and took two tests that measured how much they learned from the video lecture.

This setup allowed us to create three groups, each of which viewed the same video lecture, took notes on that lecture, and took the same tests of student learning. After our study sessions were over, we graded the tests of student learning and recruited independent coders who graded the quality of notes each student took. We then sorted all of the students into the groups they were assigned to control group (no text messages), the group receiving text messages every 60 seconds (low-distraction group), and the group receiving text messages every 30 seconds (high-distraction group); and then we used several statistical tests to compare the average grade each group received on the tests of student learning and on their notes.

Our main finding was that students who were in the high-distraction group scored about 13% points lower on one of our tests of learning (a multiple-choice test) than the students who were not using their mobile device at all. The students in the high-distraction group also scored lower on the quality of notes they took and recalled less information from the lecture than the control group. Our findings helped to answer our initial question of what effect texting during class would have on student learning. In this case, actively using mobile devices generally hurt student learning and reduced the quality or completeness of notes that students took. However, one of the key limitations from our study was the type of messages we asked students to respond to. In our original study, we only used messages that were entirely unrelated to the lecture content. By the time our study was published, instructors were starting to use mobile devices as a way for students to send messages to their professor during class (Tyma, 2011), and more recently, scholars have examined how classroom participation can be enhanced via services like Twitter (Denker et al., 2018). To address this limitation, we decided to do another, slightly more complex study, that would expand what we found in our initial research.

That new study (Kuznekoff et al., 2015) used the same basic setup as the original study but did change a couple of key points. We kept the control group and we kept the frequency of messaging the same (i.e., 30 seconds or 60 seconds); however, we added on two other modifications that increased the complexity of the study. One of those modifications was randomly assigning students to groups that either had to respond to a message or create their own original message. The other modification was whether the message was focused on content related to the course lecture or unrelated to the course lecture. Both of those modifications also included the two levels of message frequency. So, instead of our original study that had three total groups, we ended up with a study that had a total of nine groups of students. In addition to manipulating how frequently students received messages, we also manipulated if they responded to or created a message, and also manipulated if the content of the messages was related or unrelated to the lecture content.

Similar to the first study, those students who did not text scored 10–17% points higher on our multiple-choice test, recalled more information from the lecture and had higher quality notes than those students who were engaged in texting unrelated to course content. However, what we found out was that those students who were engaged in texting related to course content did not suffer from the same negative effects as those who were texting about unrelated content. Instead, the students who scored the worst on our tests of student learning were those who were responding to or composing messages that were unrelated to the course content, and this was especially the case for those students doing that activity frequently (i.e., sending/receiving a message every 30 seconds). What this tells us is that it is certainly possible to use a mobile device in class but the key to doing that successfully is to remain engaged in the course content and to resist the urge to engage with content unrelated to the course.

While we hope our two studies help both students and professors to make informed decisions about how to use mobile devices during class, we also know that student device usage is changing. For example, one trend is students using laptops or tablets during class for note-taking. Our past studies connect to this issue; however, using technology to take notes is a very important area for students and teachers to consider. While we might initially think that laptops or tablets allow students to take higher quality notes (because students can type faster than they can write), research has tended to show the opposite, and understanding why that is the case is critical for students to make informed decisions about how they use technology in the classroom.

DING. DING. DING.

The familiar sounds of alert notifications from text messages, social media, and emails permeate the classroom. Students flow into the classroom with a variety of mobile and wearable technological devices. I (Stevie) watch as one student, glances down at her shiny Apple Watch and gently nods as she scrolls though message. She gently taps the screen with her palm, dismissing the notification, and arranges her MacBook on the desk. Her presence in the classroom is laden with mobile connectivity both to her personal and student life. As the teacher, I take a moment to reflect on my own smartwatch, laptop, and my "teacher desk" fully equipped with Internet, and projection capabilities. Today, we are watching a YouTube video about Appalachia. In a mere few seconds, the video loads and we are whisked off to the rolling hills of a region thousands of miles away from our desert oasis. "Be sure to take notes on the film," I say in a firm tone. "Encouraging them to take notes is important, Stevie" I think to myself.

As teachers, we observe our students feverishly type on their tablets and laptops and we contemplate if they are taking notes about class content. Providing deliberate cues for students to take notes is considered an important teaching strategy to encourage note-taking in the classroom. In order to help students in this process, a teacher may prompt students verbally or provide students with complete or partial notes. Titsworth and Kiewra (2004) found that lecture cues and note-taking positively raised student achievement. Students recorded more details and organizational points from the lecture than their counterparts who listened to a cue-free lecture. The importance of note-taking for student information recall and processing is well documented in the literature (see Kiewra & Benton, 1988; Titsworth 2001, 2004). While it is clear that student note-taking can have a positive influence on student learning, how students take notes, distractions, and multitasking all impact the quality of those notes. It is worth noting that the way you take notes and the conditions under which you take notes both matter, and these factors impact the quality of student notes.

As a student, you have likely taken notes on a laptop or tablet in class. You may have even become frustrated with a "no technology" policy in the classroom, which forced you to take notes the old-school way—with a paper and pencil. Have you asked yourself why the teacher had this policy? One reason may be that s/he is familiar with the less than favorable research regarding the effects of note-taking on laptop and tablets on student learning. Often when we type our notes on a keyboard, we are inclined to take verbatim notes rather than processing a teacher's lecture through our own thoughts and ideas (Stacy & Cain, 2015). Put another way, when we take verbatim notes, we tend to act as a transcription machine and focus too much on typing out exactly what the speaker is saying as quickly as we can. We avoid personalizing our notes and therefore, lessen the learning experience that occurs when we handwrite our notes. Even though it is likely faster for you to type your notes on a keyboard than handwrite them, note-takers that take handwritten notes record higher quality notes with paraphrasing and visual depictions (Luo et al., 2016). This process forces you to more meaningfully process what the speaker is saying, think about their message, and then decide how to write that material down in a meaningful way (Mueller & Oppenheimer, 2014). That is a more active process than simply typing out exactly what the speaker just said and moving on the next word (i.e., literally in one ear and out the other). It is important to remember that the goal of taking notes in a class is for you to have materials to review later on. Having a superior set of notes to review for an upcoming exam would be pretty nice, right? Or may be having high quality notes to look back on in the following semester or for a future class project might be helpful?

You might be thinking, "Okay, I'm not going to take notes on my laptop, but I do like to browse the Internet occasionally during class." Using your technology in the classroom for nonclassroom purposes is known as cyberslacking or cyberloafing. Recently, researchers reported students to spend more than half of a class period using technology for nonclass purposes (Ragan et al., 2014). If you are spending any significant amount of time on your laptop or mobile device for personal use during class, you are likely negatively impacting your learning. In some ways, technology allows us to be more easily distracted and therefore less likely to think through what a professor is saying or take meaningful notes. Technology is ubiquitous in the classroom, so as a student, you have to be more aware of how it impacts your learning and more intentional in how you use it.

As learners, we all face the nagging desire to multitask on our laptops or tablets. We click open a social media site or check the status of a delivery, while attempting to remain attuned and engaged in a conversation. Right now, you might be reading this chapter on a tablet or laptop with a variety of tabs open at the ready for browsing. Sana and colleagues (2013) determined that when learners attempt to complete multiple tasks at the same time, both tasks suffer. In short, we are not good multitaskers and our research supports this finding, too (Kuznekoff & Titsworth, 2013; Kuznekoff et al., 2015). Being distracted or off-task from the lecture in class was found to result in poorer academic performance in comparison to students who were not distracted (Wood et al., 2012). A problem with using a laptop or tablet to take notes in the classroom and also being distracted by nonclass material is cognitive strain. Our brain is already more strained by trying to take notes on a laptop or tablet in comparison to long form handwritten note-taking. When we attempt to take notes on a laptop or tablet and browse nonclass related material on the Internet or send and receive mobile messages, academic performance suffers (Sana et al., 2013). All of the tasks you are attempting to perform access similar mental resources, which diminishes your ability to fully complete any tasks.

SUGGESTIONS FOR STUDENTS

So, now what? First, we believe that it is important to recognize that the classroom, and your workplace, are filled with technology, so you need strategies for how to manage it. College is really the last place that you can develop those strategies in an environment in which help is readily available. Ultimately, it is up to you to develop technology habits that help aid your learning. Your instructors can certainly offer advice, but you will likely need to carefully reflect on what strategies work for you and which ones do not. Most colleges and universities have a learning or study center that often offers a variety of services to help aid students in their learning. We definitely recommend seeing if the center at your institution has resources or workshops available for how to use technology effectively in the classroom or workplace.

Second, we suggest thinking carefully about the negative impact of multitasking on your learning and on your work. You might recognize that you become distracted or disengaged during a class period because of environmental factors like lack of sleep, temperature in the classroom, or personal ongoings in your life. Once you understand why you are multitasking, you can begin to intentionally engage with self-control and mindfulness in how you use technology. In addition, your use of technology in a class meeting or group work session can give off messages, even if those messages are unintentional. If you are in class or in a workgroup and are unable to break away from your mobile device, it sends the message that you are not engaged in that meeting or in the class content. That likely is not a habit you want to get into and, instead, being able to exercise self-control and focus your attention on where it needs to be is likely an important habit to develop, especially for your eventual career after you graduate.

Third, take notes the old-school way—by hand with a pen and paper. If you do use a tablet or laptop to take notes, be exceedingly careful that you are not multitasking and resist the urge to become a transcription machine. The research continues to overwhelmingly support long-form note-taking because of the positive effects on student learning and information recall. You must use a laptop for note-taking, mimic the process used for long-form note-taking. That means mentally think about the content/message from the speaker, think of how to encode that information in your notes in a meaningful way, and perhaps even use the advantages of technology to help improve your notes. For example, you could color code different sections of your notes or perhaps highlight pieces of content to draw your attention to them later on.

Lastly, we know that being mentally present during class is critical for your learning. Putting devices away if they become distracting (i.e., self-regulation) and opting for long-form note-taking are just two ways that you might enhance your presence in the classroom. In addition, we would encourage you to carefully reflect on what strategies or habits help you to learn. Communication research has a lot to offer to help you in that reflection and, instructional communication research in particular, is well suited to help you address that and other important questions.

REFERENCES

Campbell, S. W. (2006). Perceptions of mobile phones in college classrooms: Ringing, cheating, and classroom policies. *Communication Education, 55*(3), 280–294. https://doi.org/10.1080/03634520600748573

Denker, K. J., Manning, J., Heuett, K. B., & Summers, M. E. (2018). Twitter in the classroom: Modeling online communication attitudes and student motivations to connect. *Computers in Human Behavior, 79*, 1–8. https://doi.org/10.1016/j.chb.2017.09.037

Kiewra, K. A., & Benton, S. L. (1988). The relationship between information-processing ability and notetaking. *Contemporary Educational Psychology, 13*(1), 33–44. https://doi.org/10.1016/0361-476X(88)90004-5

Kuznekoff, J. H., Munz, S. M., & Titsworth, B. S. (2015). Mobile phones in the classroom: Examining the effects of texting, Twitter, and message content on student learning. *Communication Education, 64*, 344–365. https://doi.org/10.1080/03634523.2015.1038727

Kuznekoff, J. H., & Titsworth, B. S. (2013). The impact of mobile phone usage on student learning. *Communication Education, 62*(3), 233–252. https://doi.org/10.1080/03634523.2013.767917

Lavrakas, P. J. (2008). *Encyclopedia of survey research methods* (P. Lavrakas, Ed.). Sage.

Luo, L., Kiewra, K. A., & Samuelson, L. (2016). Revising lecture notes: How revision, pauses, and partners affect note taking and achievement. *Instructional Science, 44*(1), 45–67. https://doi.org/10.1007/s11251-016-9370-4

Mueller, P. A., & Oppenheimer, D. M. (2014). The pen is mightier than the keyboard: Advantages of longhand over laptop note taking. *Psychological Science, 25*(6), 1159–1168. https://doi.org/10.1177/0956797614524581

Ragan, E. D., Jennings, S. R., Massey, J. D., & Doolittle, P. E. (2014). Unregulated use of laptops over time in large lecture classes. *Computers & Education, 78*, 78–86. https://doi.org/10.1016/j.compedu.2014.05.002

Sana, F., Weston, T., & Cepeda, N. J. (2013). Laptop multitasking hinders classroom learning for both users and nearby peers. *Computers & Education, 62*, 24–31. https://doi.org/10.1016/j.compedu.2012.10.003

Stacy, E. M., & Cain, J. (2015). Note-taking and handouts in the digital age. *American Journal of Pharmaceutical Education, 79*(7), 107. https://doi.org/10.5688/ajpe797107

Titsworth, B. S. (2001). The effects of teacher immediacy, use of organizational lecture cues, and students' notetaking on cognitive learning. *Communication Education, 50*(4), 283–297. https://doi.org/10.1080/03634520109379256

Titsworth, B. S. (2004). Students' notetaking: The effects of teacher immediacy and clarity. *Communication Education, 53*(4), 305–320.

Titsworth, B. S., & Kiewra, K. A. (2004). Spoken organizational lecture cues and student notetaking as facilitators of student learning. *Contemporary Educational Psychology, 29*(4), 447–461. https://doi.org/10.1016/j.cedpsych.2003.12.001

Tyma, A. (2011). Connecting with what is out there!: Using Twitter in the large lecture. *Communication Teacher, 25*(3), 175–181. https://doi.org/10.1080/17404622.2011.579911

Wei, F. F., Wang, Y. K., & Klausner, M. (2012). Rethinking college students' self-regulation and sustained attention: Does text messaging during class influence cognitive learning? *Communication Education, 61*(3), 185–204. https://doi.org/10.1080/03634523.2012.672755

Wood, E., Zivcakova, L., Gentile, P., Archer, K., De Pasquale, D., & Nosko, A. (2012). Examining the impact of off-task multi-tasking with technology on real-time classroom learning. *Computers & Education, 58*(1), 365–374. https://doi.org/10.1016/j.compedu.2011.08.029

MEDIA COMMUNICATION

Beginning with the invention of writing and paper, humans have sought to amplify and extend their communication across time and space. The context of media communication examines both the use of particular media and critiques the forms and practices of the media in contemporary society. Media has served as a large influence in shaping our sense of who we are, how we are positioned in the world, and what is important to pay attention to (and subsequently what we can ignore and thereby dismiss as unimportant). The following chapters explore the proliferation, influence, and place of contemporary forms of media in our everyday lives as we receive (mis)information, play video games, and binge-watch television. First, Stefanie Demetriades (DePaul University), Nathan Walter (Northwestern University), and Christopher Dobmeier (Northwestern University) examine the consequences, from trivial to tragic, of misinformation in the media, the underlying cognitive biases and mechanisms that allow misinformation to thrive, and strategies that we can use to combat our susceptibility to it. Next, Nicholas Bowman (Syracuse University) explores the influence and effects of video games and the functional role video games play in our daily lives helping us manage our moods and achieve (at least temporary) psychological well-being and enjoyment. Finally, Bridget Rubenking (University of Central Florida) and Cheryl Campanella Bracken (Cleveland State University) investigate the impact of our increased control over viewing content in the streaming age. Rubenking and Bracken consider the relatively recent "new normal" of the focused, attentive way of viewing serial television content, known as binge-watching, and study the motivations and effects of binge-watching on viewers.

HOW POWERFUL IS MISINFORMATION IN THE MEDIA, WHY IT HAPPENS AND HOW TO STOP IT?

Stefanie Z. Demetriades
DePaul University

Nathan Walter
Northwestern University

Christopher M. Dobmeier
Northwestern University

A mystical Medieval plant sprouting whole sheep from its branches (Crew, 2013); tiny fully-formed men, created in a 17th-century nobleman's lab and gifted with the ability to see the future (Swancer, 2018); concoctions of rattlesnake venom to cure assorted ailments, hawked in the American West of the 1890s (Shapiro, 2018). Fantastical as they seem today, each of these claims was at some point in history held up as fact by otherwise apparently reasonable people. Of course, we have countless contemporary examples of misinformation as well, from widespread political conspiracy theories to beliefs that vaccines cause autism. The specifics may change over the centuries, but the underlying mechanisms that keep these kinds of false claims afloat remain the same. In recent years, researchers in communication and social psychology have uncovered important insights about what these mechanisms might be, and why they can make it so difficult to correct misinformation.

This chapter provides an overview of misinformation and its correction, starting with an explanation of the term, and then considering evidence from research and theory about why misinformation maintains such a strong grip—and what might be done to loosen it.

MISINFORMATION IN CONTEXT

"Misinformation" refers to factually inaccurate information that is not supported by solid evidence or expert opinion (Walter & Tukachinsky, 2020). It is important to note that by this definition, misinformation is agnostic about intent. You may have heard the related term *dis*information, which refers to false information that is intentionally designed to mislead people, often for political gain. Disinformation is a special subcategory of misinformation, but the broader term includes both erroneous information as well as deliberately false or misleading claims.

As the examples at the start of this chapter demonstrate, misinformation is hardly new; false claims and stories have been with us throughout human experience. In recent years, however, misinformation has exploded in prominence. The rise of social media is a major factor, creating unprecedented opportunities for false claims to travel far wider and faster than ever before (Vosoughi et al., 2018). Meanwhile, public trust in governments and institutions is declining (Kennedy et al., 2022), political polarization is on the rise (Desilver, 2022), and misinformation has gained mainstream footholds among prominent public figures—like former U.S. President Donald Trump, who racked up an extraordinary 30,573 documented false or misleading claims during his term (Kessler et al., 2021). Taken together, these trends create especially fertile ground for misinformation to flourish.

THE CONTINUED INFLUENCE EFFECT

Given the sheer amount of misinformation circulating in this media and sociopolitical landscape, it is hardly surprising that people are so often exposed to it. More surprising is that the effects of misinformation hang on so tenaciously even in the face of direct contradiction with factual evidence, a phenomenon researchers describe as a "continued influence effect" (Walter & Tukachinsky, 2020). There has been a massive increase in worldwide efforts to try to counter misinformation in recent years (Funke & Flamini, 2022; Stencel, 2019). And yet the evidence on whether these efforts are successful is mixed at best: while some studies have found that correcting misinformation can be effective, others suggest that people generally disregard corrections, or soon revert back to their earlier inaccurate beliefs (Walter & Tukachinsky, 2020).

So, what is going on here? In the following sections, we consider insights from theory and research about the underlying mechanisms and biases that shape how people retain and process information. Each of these frameworks offers a potential explanation for why misinformation has such a tenacious grip—and what strategies might help to loosen it.

MEMORY

Human memory is limited and deeply flawed, and this essential cognitive constraint provides perhaps the most straightforward explanation for the lingering effects of misinformation: people simply are not good at remembering what is true and what is not. To begin, people tend to vastly overestimate the accuracy of their recollections, putting more trust in memories of dramatic events than those of mundane events, even though both are equally prone to error and distortion (Talarico & Rubin, 2007). Matters are further complicated because memory is so susceptible to suggestion and manipulation. Research has consistently found that personal recollection is an extremely unreliable record of the past: people tend to remember events in ways that match up with information that is been provided to them, even if that information is inaccurate or entirely fabricated (Puddifoot, 2020). In one set of studies, researchers were even able to "implant" false memories of an event from the participants' childhood by using a combination of repeated misinformation, leading questions, social pressure, and visualization exercises. The participants were eventually unable to distinguish the false memory from other memories of their own, and remembered it vividly— even though the incident in question had never actually happened (Shaw, 2020).

Given its lapses and malleability, faulty memory is certainly a compelling piece of the puzzle in terms of how misinformation might initially take hold. But memory alone does not explain why people *continue* to believe misinformation against evidence to the contrary. For that, we need to consider not just how we retain information, but also how we process it.

MENTAL MODELS

With every experience and observation, we gather up countless data points about the world. In order to make sense out of what would otherwise be a chaotic mess of data, our brains create cognitive maps that turn all of this input into useable information. These "mental models" supply a template for meaning, so that when we encounter new information it can be integrated alongside existing memories as part of a coherent, subjective reality (Johnson & Seifert, 1994). Importantly, these can vary significantly from person to person, so the same information may be interpreted in diverse ways, depending on what fits best with an individual's mental model (Jones et al., 2011). What's more, we tend to avoid uncomfortable discrepancies in our view of ourselves or the world (Festinger, 1957; Steele, 1988). Rebuilding an entire mental model is a major and disruptive task, so there is a strong incentive to instead tweak the interpretation of a bit of information to fit the existing framework, or to simply ignore it altogether.

The more someone has invested in a mental model, the more entrenched their beliefs can become. This may be a key reason that convoluted conspiracy theories are so pernicious and difficult to unwind: they are not just about a single erroneous claim, but rather woven into a highly coherent mental model and bound up with a person's beliefs, values, and sense of identity.

SOURCE CREDIBILITY AND CONFIRMATION BIAS

Decades of research have made it clear that the actual content of a message is just one relatively small piece of how people evaluate information. Source credibility—the perceived level of expertise and trustworthiness of the source of the message—also carries a great deal of weight (Petty & Cacioppo, 1986). It may be tempting to think that credibility is dependent on innate characteristics of the sources themselves. In reality, however, source credibility is largely in the eye of the beholder. If information aligns with a person's preexisting beliefs, they are more likely to perceive the source of that information as credible—and conversely, if a source presents information that contradicts a person's beliefs and worldview, the more likely they are to dismiss that source as untrustworthy. Case in point: an experimental study of exposure to misinformation during the highly polarized 2016 U.S. Presidential election (Swire et al., 2017). In this study, participants rated their belief in a mix of factual and misleading statements that President Trump made on the campaign trail. They then received information that affirmed the factual statements as true and retracted the misinformation as inaccurate. Notably, the results indicated that the actual veracity of information had relatively little impact on people's beliefs; instead, they were mainly influenced by the perceived credibility of the person verifying Trump's statements.

FLUENCY AND REPETITION

Another possible explanation of misinformation's continued influence focuses not on the content of the claim, but rather on the subjective experience of processing that message (also referred to as "metacognitions"). The ease or difficulty of processing a message can affect how people evaluate its accuracy. As succinctly summed up by Schwarz et al. "when thoughts flow smoothly, people nod along" (2016, p. 85). For instance, a thought-provoking experiment by Newman et al. (2014) found that participants were more likely to trust people with easier-to-pronounce names compared to the same information attributed to someone with a more difficult-to-pronounce name. Following a similar line of reasoning, Walter et al. (2020) showed that fact-checking messages with complex language were less likely to correct misinformation compared to easier fact-checking articles.

Mere repetition has also emerged as another subtle way to reinforce myths by making them feel more fluent and familiar. This proposition has gathered considerable empirical support showing that people interpret the familiarity of repeated claims as a marker of accuracy (Berinsky, 2017; Foster et al., 2012). At first glance, this should not present a major problem, since repeated claims would ostensibly represent the social consensus around an issue; yet, research has shown that repetition seems to increase acceptance even if every reiteration comes from the same source (Weaver et al., 2007). This troubling finding may help explain how a relatively small but coordinated group of people can effectively push rumors and lies, as in the case of the unfounded belief that the 2020 U.S. Presidential elections were rigged (Yang & Khan, 2022).

NEGATIVITY BIAS

Consider the following headlines: *Planned Parenthood is Trafficking in Fetal Tissue for Profit, The COVID-19 Pandemic was Orchestrated by Pharmaceutical Companies*; and, *Ukrainian President Volodymyr Zelensky Fled to Poland and Abandoned His People After the Russian Invasion.* Beyond being patently false, what these headlines share in common is that they are all tremendously negative, which often gives them the upper hand in the battle against the less scintillating truth. This phenomenon is known as the "negativity bias," and it suggests that humans are hardwired to pay closer attention to and more easily recall negative information (Taylor, 1991).

When it comes to misinformation, the dominance of negativity can manifest in a number of ways, including the dissemination and adoption of falsehoods. If individuals are more likely to remember and pass along information about negative events (Bebbington et al., 2017), social media with its never-subsiding tide of negative and unverified content seems to offer the perfect breeding ground for misinformation. It is no coincidence that false news, especially highly negative stories, has been found to spread "significantly farther, faster, deeper, and more broadly than the truth in all categories of information" (Vosoughi et al., 2018, p. 1).

POTENTIAL REMEDIES TO MISINFORMATION'S CONTINUED INFLUENCE

Given all this evidence about our flawed memories and biased cognitive processes, the odds may seem heavily stacked in favor of misinformation. The good news, however, is that these same theoretical insights about how people process information can also be applied to developing potential remedies. This final section of the chapter looks at some of emerging evidence about what works to counter misinformation.

You have probably come across countless examples of "myth vs. fact" lists and messages online, offering a side-by-side comparison of a false claim and the corrected information. This is a common strategy, but unfortunately, the research shows that this kind of straightforward negation—simply identifying a claim as false—is not going to be effective in most cases (Walter & Tukachinsky, 2020). In one study, for example, researchers tested a "myth-busting" message about flu vaccines. They found that people who saw the message soon jumbled the myth versus fact in their memories, and wound up remembering the false information, rather than its correction, as true (Skurnik et al., 2007). In short, simply refuting a false claim is not enough; in fact, by repeating the claim, the correction can paradoxically wind up backfiring and making the misinformation more memorable and familiar.

So, if correction alone does not work, what does? Remember that the theory of mental models suggests that people like full, coherent maps or stories to contextualize information. If belief in misinformation is a key part of that story, the result is a bit like playing Jenga—pulling that one piece out can risk destabilizing the whole structure, so people are more reluctant to let go of it (Johnson & Seifert, 1994). A more productive route is to fill the gap with an alternative explanation that keeps the model intact but updated (Lewandowsky et al., 2012). That means not only providing a correction, but also explaining the basis for that correction in a way that still coheres with a person's broader worldview. For example, van der Meer and Jin (2020) tried to correct misinformation about a highly-infectious influenza strain, comparing the efficacy of a simple rebuttal (brief bullet points) and factual elaboration (a detailed description about why the virus is a severe threat). In line with the mental model literature, the findings suggest that a more comprehensive explanation helped to correct people's misconceptions, while simply negating a specific piece of information had little effect.

Keeping in mind the importance of source credibility, the impact of a correction also depends on where and how it is presented. After all, if a person believes that the COVID-19 pandemic is part of a vast government conspiracy, assurances that the vaccine is safe from an official like Dr. Anthony Fauci are not likely to be convincing—they may even fit into that person's mental model as further evidence of a government coverup. Research suggests the most effective corrections should ideally come from the very same source as the misinformation because they are more likely to be perceived as authentic and uncompromised by ulterior motives.

These kinds of strategies can help to mitigate the ongoing influence of misinformation, but they are all essentially damage-control after the fact. A more proactive strategy is to try to prevent misinformation from taking hold to begin with. Social media companies like Twitter, YouTube, and Facebook have begun implementing more stringent content standards, including flagging or removing posts with inaccurate information or banning repeat offenders from the platform entirely (Shu & Shieber, 2020). Governments are also exploring regulations to stem the flow of misinformation (Funke & Flamini, 2022). Policies like this could have a significant impact, but they are subject to all manner of political, social, and economic complications and controversy, and for now are still in the earliest stages of what will likely be a long-term evolution.

One promising avenue from communication and social psychology research aims to preemptively debunk—or "prebunk" —misinformation, by preparing people to recognize and resist it before they encounter it (Roozenbeek et al., 2020). Fittingly enough, given rampant misinformation about health and vaccines circulates, the strategy is modeled on the idea of inoculation: exposing people to a controlled, weakened "dose" of misinformation can help build their defenses for when they are exposed to the real thing. Experiments in the contexts of the COVID-19 pandemic and climate change have produced promising results, with evidence that people are less susceptible to false claims if they are first provided with explanations of why and how misinformation distorts the facts (Cook et al., 2017; Pennycook et al., 2020).

CONCLUSION

Misinformation is far from a new phenomenon, but we are living in a time when it can spread far wider and faster than ever before. Our social media feeds, and with them our polarized public discourse, are inundated with it. Whether the consequences are trivial, or—as we have seen during the COVID-19 pandemic—tragic, the underlying cognitive biases and mechanisms remain the same. Misinformation thrives in the gaps of faulty memory, the appeal of congruent, familiar mental models, and the influence of repeated claims by trusted sources. The good news is that understanding why and how misinformation sticks also provide us with strategies to combat it. By staying alert to these points of susceptibility, we can cultivate a healthy skepticism of the information we encounter. Next time, you find yourself drawn in by a too-good-to-be-true life hack on Instagram, or a too-evil-to-be-true anecdote on Reddit, try asking yourself the following questions: Am I really remembering the details accurately? Do I *want* to believe this because it fits in neatly with my preexisting worldview? Is this source truly credible, or just likable? Am I conveniently ignoring other facts because they are less fluent, or familiar, or simply less engaging? Likewise, before you escalate into a shouting match with your conspiracytheorist relative over Thanksgiving dinner, remember that simply insisting that a claim is false will not do much to address the underlying factors at play. And remember that there's no shame in being taken in by a good story; people have been doing it for millennia. Although the spread of misinformation is far from solvable in the near future, raising awareness, understanding our own susceptibilities, and knowing where to concentrate resources are major steps in the right direction.

REFERENCES

Bebbington, K., MacLeod, C., Ellison, T. M., & Fay, N. (2017). The sky is falling: Evidence of a negativity bias in the social transmission of information. *Evolution and Human Behavior, 38*(1), 92–101. https://doi.org/10.1016/j.evolhumbehav.2016.07.004

Berinsky, A. J. (2017). Rumors and health care reform: Experiments in political misinformation. *British Journal of Political Science, 47*(2), 241–262. https://doi.org/10.1017/S0007123415000186

Cook, J., Lewandowsky, S., & Ecker, U. K. H. (2017). Neutralizing misinformation through inoculation: Exposing misleading argumentation techniques reduces their influence. *PLOS ONE, 12*(5), e0175799. https://doi.org/10.1371/journal.pone.0175799

Crew, B. (2013). *Animal or Vegetable? Legend of the Vegetable Lamb of Tartary.* Scientific American Blog Network. https://blogs.scientificamerican.com/running-ponies/animal-or-vegetable-legend-of-the-vegetable-lamb-of-tartary/

Desilver, D. (2022, March 10). The polarization in today's Congress has roots that go back decades. *Pew Research Center.* https://www.pewresearch.org/fact-tank/2022/03/10/the-polarization-in-todays-congress-has-roots-that-go-back-decades/

Festinger, L. (1957). *A theory of cognitive dissonance.* Stanford University Press.

Foster, J. L., Huthwaite, T., Yesberg, J. A., Garry, M., & Loftus, E. F. (2012). Repetition, not number of sources, increases both susceptibility to misinformation and confidence in the accuracy of eyewitnesses. *Acta Psychologica, 139*(2), 320–326. https://doi.org/10.1016/j.actpsy.2011.12.004

Funke, D., & Flamini, D. (2022). A guide to anti-misinformation actions around the world. *Poynter.* https://www.poynter.org/ifcn/anti-misinformation-actions/

Johnson, H. M., & Seifert, C. M. (1994). Sources of the continued influence effect: When misinformation in memory affects later inferences. *Journal of Experimental Psychology: Learning, Memory, and Cognition, 20*(6), 1420–1436. https://doi.org/10.1037/0278-7393.20.6.1420

Jones, N. A., Ross, H., Lynam, T., Perez, P., & Leitch, A. (2011). Mental models: an interdisciplinary synthesis of theory and methods. *Ecology and Society, 16*(1), 46. https://www.jstor.org/stable/26268859

Kennedy, B., Tyson, A., & Funk, C. (2022, February 15). Americans' Trust in scientists, other groups declines. *Pew Research Center Science & Society.* https://www.pewresearch.org/science/2022/02/15/americans-trust-in-scientists-other-groups-declines/

Kessler, G., Rizzo, S., & Kelly, M. (2021, January 24). Trump's false or misleading claims total 30,573 over 4 years. *Washington Post.* https://www.washingtonpost.com/politics/2021/01/24/trumps-false-or-misleading-claims-total-30573-over-four-years/

Lewandowsky, S., Ecker, U. K. H., Seifert, C. M., Schwarz, N., & Cook, J. (2012). Misinformation and its correction: Continued influence and successful debiasing. *Psychological Science in the Public Interest, 13*(3), 106–131. https://doi.org/10.1177/1529100612451018

Newman, E. J., Sanson, M., Miller, E. K., Quigley-McBride, A., Foster, J. L., Bernstein, D. M., & Garry, M. (2014). People with easier to pronounce names promote truthiness of claims. *PLoS ONE, 9*(2), e88671. https://doi.org/10.1371/journal.pone.0088671

Pennycook, G., McPhetres, J., Zhang, Y., Lu, J. G., & Rand, D. G. (2020). Fighting COVID-19 misinformation on social media: Experimental evidence for a scalable accuracy-nudge intervention. *Psychological Science, 31*(7), 770–780. https://doi.org/10.1177/0956797620939054

Petty, R. E., & Cacioppo, J. T. (1986). The elaboration likelihood model of persuasion. In L. Berkowitz (Ed.), *Advances in experimental social psychology* (Vol. 19, pp. 123–205). Academic Press.

Puddifoot, K. (2020). Re-evaluating the credibility of eyewitness testimony: The misinformation effect and the overcritical juror. *Episteme, 17*(2), 255–279. https://doi.org/10.1017/epi.2018.42

Roozenbeek, J., Linden, S. van der, & Nygren, T. (2020). Prebunking interventions based on "inoculation" theory can reduce susceptibility to misinformation across cultures. *Harvard Kennedy School Misinformation Review, 1*(2). https://doi.org/10.37016//mr-2020-008

Schwarz, N., Newman, E., & Leach, W. (2016). Making the truth stick & the myths fade: Lessons from cognitive psychology. *Behavioral Science & Policy, 2*(1), 85–95. https://doi.org/10.1353/bsp.2016.0009

Shapiro, N. L. (2018). Quackery and hype: Mesmerized by wizards. *Social Research, 85*(4), 889–911. https://doi.org/10.1353/sor.2018.0056

Shaw, J. (2020). Do false memories look real? Evidence that people struggle to identify rich false memories of committing crime and other emotional events. *Frontiers in Psychology, 11.* https://doi.org/10.3389/fpsyg.2020.00650

Shu, C., & Shieber, J. (2020, March 16). Facebook, Reddit, Google, LinkedIn, Microsoft, Twitter and YouTube issue joint statement on misinformation. *TechCrunch.* https://techcrunch.com/2020/03/16/facebook-reddit-google-linkedin-microsoft-twitter-and-youtube-issue-joint-statement-on-misinformation/

Skurnik, I., Yoon, C., & Schwarz, N. (2007). *"Myths & Facts" about the flu: Health education campaigns can reduce vaccination intentions.* Retrieved from http:// webuser.bus.umich. edu/ yoonc/research/Papers/Skurnik_Y oon_Schwarz_2005_Myths_Facts_Flu_Health_ Education_Campaigns_JAMA.pdf

Steele, C. M. (1988). The psychology of self-affirmation: Sustaining the integrity of the self. In *Advances in experimental social psychology* (Vol. 21, pp. 261–302). Academic Press.

Stencel, M. (2019, June 11). Number of fact-checking outlets surges to 188 in more than 60 countries. *Poynter.* https://www.poynter.org/fact-checking/2019/number-of-fact-checking-outlets-surges-to-188-in-more-than-60-countries/

Swancer, B. (2018, September 11). *The Mysterious World of the Homunculi.* Mysterious Universe. https://mysteriousuniverse.org/2018/09/the-mysterious-world-of-the-homunculi/

Swire, B., Berinsky, A. J., Lewandowsky, S., & Ecker, U. K. H. (2017). Processing political misinformation: Comprehending the Trump phenomenon. *Royal Society Open Science, 4*(3), 160802. https://doi.org/10.1098/rsos.160802

Talarico, J. M., & Rubin, D. C. (2007). Flashbulb memories are special after all; In phenomenology, not accuracy. *Applied Cognitive Psychology, 21*(5), 557–578. https://doi.org/10.1002/acp.1293

Taylor, S. E. (1991). Asymmetrical effects of positive and negative events: The mobilization-minimization hypothesis. *Psychological Bulletin, 110*(1), 67–85. https://doi.org/10.1037/0033-2909.110.1.67

van der Meer, T. G. L. A., & Jin, Y. (2020). Seeking formula for misinformation treatment in public health crises: The effects of corrective information type and source. *Health Communication, 35*(5), 560–575. https://doi.org/10.1080/10410236.2019.1573295

Vosoughi, S., Roy, D., & Aral, S. (2018). The spread of true and false news online. *Science, 359*(6380), 1146–1151. https://doi.org/10.1126/science.aap9559

Walter, N., & Tukachinsky, R. (2020). A meta-analytic examination of the continued influence of misinformation in the face of correction: How powerful is it, why does it happen, and how to stop it? *Communication Research, 47*(2), 155–177. https://doi.org/10.1177/0093650219854600

Walter, N., Cohen, J., Holbert, R. L., & Morag, Y. (2020). Fact-checking: A meta-analysis of what works and for whom. *Political Communication, 37*(3), 350–375. https://doi.org/10.1080/10584 609.2019.1668894

Weaver, K., Garcia, S. M., Schwarz, N., & Miller, D. T. (2007). Inferring the popularity of an opinion from its familiarity: A repetitive voice can sound like a chorus. *Journal of Personality and Social Psychology, 92*(5), 821–833. https://doi.org/10.1037/0022-3514.92.5.821

Yang, J., & Khan, S. (2022, April 26). How powerful conservatives pushed the "Big Lie" that the 2020 election was fraudulent. *PBS NewsHour.* https://www.pbs.org/newshour/show/how-powerful-conservatives-pushed-the-big-lie-that-the-2020-election-was-fraudulent

HOW I LEARNED TO STOP WORRYING ABOUT AND START ENJOYING VIDEO GAMES

Nicholas David Bowman
Syracuse University

September 13, 1993. I have been playing video games for as long as I can remember, but this date sticks out to me for reasons that will become clear in a bit.

As a child of the 1980s, I get to experience first-hand the rebirth of the home console industry—the Nintendo Entertainment System and Sega Master System were released right about the time I was learning the sensorimotor coordination necessary to hold a game controller, and I spent countless rainy days getting Mario to his next castle (*Super Mario Bros.*) or helping Link reassemble the Triforce (*Legend of Zelda*). Living in a small apartment, our video game system was in the living room, and as a result, I'd often play with my parents (a form of active parental mediation, as I'd come to learn later in my research career; Martins et al., 2015).

As I got older, the game system would move to the basement of our first house (it's a well-known Midwestern rule that "teenagers live in the basement") and of course, the video games got more mature. Games' focus on cartoonish graphics and scenarios was replaced with increased photorealistic content, and the early 1990s saw the rise of two video game genres that would challenge the "playfulness" of the medium: first-person shooters and fighting games. Both were marked by a focus on competition (beating your friends) and violence (beating them bloody, at least on-screen). Which takes us to September 13, 1993—known by gamers as Mortal Monday, as it marked the home release of one of the most controversial video games to date, *Mortal Kombat*. The game was based on a highly successful arcade game in which players would battle each other using fists and weapons, each punch or cut generating gallons of blood on contact. Once a player was sufficiently beaten, they would stand dazed while the victorious player was given the opportunity to, with a series of well-time button presses, commit a *Fatality* on the losing player (examples include an uppercut that punches the player's head clear off, or a punch that reaches in and allows the winner to pull out the still-beating heart of the loser; see YouTube for examples). Although the 1990s were not the first time that video games featured violence (see Korucek, 2012), *Mortal*

Kombat and a handful of other video games were among the first to receive widespread public scrutiny. Stores refused to sell the game, while many parents and policymakers railed against the blood and gore of what was generally seen as a children's toy. A firestorm of moral panic ensued (see Bowman, 2015) and pressure from the U.S. Congress compelled the gaming industry to create content labels for video games through an organization known as the Entertainment Software Ratings Board (Andrews, 1993).

I was 12 years old during the moral panic around Mortal Monday, and I was among the three million people to get a copy of the game on release (it would go on to earn more than $300 million in revenues). The game was a major point of discussion on the playground and in the school cafeteria, as the only way to learn the game's secrets—including how to execute fatalities—was by sorting through playground and lunchroom gossip (or finding the "lucky kid" who bought a rather expensive strategy guide from the local mall). After all, there was no Internet to look up these details. Unfortunately, these discussions also snuck their way into classrooms … and this is where I first learned that different people see video games very differently. After being caught discussing the game (and drawing some of the game's characters) in my art class, I was rather viciously yanked out of class and put in detention. A call to my parents placed my mother under the hot lights of an inquisition from my teachers, who questioned "What kind of parent would buy their child such a toy?" In that conversation, the teachers learned to their chagrin that our household had video games, comic books, and various other (in the views of the school) immoral and corrosive pieces of media. The face my teacher made when Mom explained that she'd learned to play *Mortal Kombat* with me was priceless—and even more flustered when Mom explained our plans to buy *Mortal Kombat 2*.

What does this story have to do with the study of video games? First and foremost, I should state clearly that *it would be irresponsible to presume that video games have no effect on their players*. Analyses of several studies on video game violence show that "violent video games do increase aggressive behavior but that these effects are almost always quite small" (Mathur & VandeWeele, 2019, p. 705). In other words, the fears people have that children who play violent video games will commit more violent crimes or get in more fights in school or with their friends are generally not supported by research—at best, there are very small correlations between video game play and having aggressive thoughts (a person might think about fighting after playing a fighting game, for example), but the evidence that these thoughts manifest as actual violence is not very strong. This is probably one reason why the current position of the American Psychological Association (the professional association for psychologists in the United States) is that:

> "Attributing violence to video gaming *is not scientifically sound and draws attention away from other factors*, such as a history of violence, which we know from the research is a major predictor of future violence" (APA, 2020, para 3; emphasis added).

So, if we move past research on video games to answer a singular (and somewhat myopic) question about video game violence, then we can ask ourselves, "Why do people play so many video games?" In the United States alone, more than 227 million people play video games (that's nearly 70% of the entire population). Despite presumptions that video games are "just for kids," the average age of a gamer in the U.S. is 31 years old, with more than 80% of gamers over the age of 18. Despite gender stereotype claims that gaming is "just for boys," more than 45% of gamers identify as female (ESA, 2021). In 2020, video games contributed over $90 billion to the U.S. economy alone and generated nearly $13 billion in tax revenues (Field Level Media, 2020), and global estimates suggest that video games generate more than $180 billion in revenues (Wijman, 2021). Video games in some form or fashion can be found in everything from entertainment to education, social media, corporate and industry training, health care, and more…and there's a good chance that if you open your laptop, tablet, or smartphone, you will be able to find a video game to play. Even better? This ready access to video games speaks to their functional role in our daily lives: gaming helps us manage our moods and achieve (at least temporary) psychological well-being, including the formation of meaningful relationships. I will talk about these three areas of research below.

VIDEO GAMES AND RELIVING BAD MOODS

Whenever I teach a course on video games, one of the very first questions that I ask my students is "when do you find yourself playing video games?" In nearly 20 years of asking this question to students of all ages, majors, and several cultures (having taught courses in five U.S. states and three other countries), many of the answers come down to some form of "whenever I'm bored…" or "whenever I'm stressed!" In other words, for many people (including myself) video games seem to be something that we turn to whenever we are having a bad time—media psychologists refer to this as the theory of affect-dependent model of stimulus arrangement (Zillmann & Bryant, 1985), but we will use the shortened name of *mood management theory* (see overview in Bowman & Tamborini, 2012; 2015).

What is particularly interesting about mood management processes is that they are not necessarily cognitive and deliberate processes. Instead, we learn through experience that certain activities are very good at addressing our psychological needs—in this case, getting rid of noxious mood states such as boredom or stress (which happen to the two most common "bad moods" that people experience). Of course, there are many different things that people could do to alleviate boredom and stress, but our research team wondered if video games might be superior to other options (such as watching television) for a key reason: video games are interactive, which means that they require much more of the person's attention. One of the features of media that make them especially effective at mood management (according to mood management theory) is their intervention potential—their ability to distract us from our moods. To test this, we did a series of experiments (Bowman & Tamborini, 2012; 2015. In both experiments, we asked people to indicate their current mood using a grid system (see Figure 1, below). Then, we randomly assigned them to do one of two tasks: sort a large bowl of metal washers and place them on a length of string (expected to be very boring) or take a set of very difficult logic puzzles as part of an intelligent test (expected to be very stressful). After completing the assigned task, we assessed their mood again. As you can see in Figure 1, the manipulations worked very well—as expected, people came into the lab (pre-manipulation) with neutral moods (i.e., directly in the center of the grid), but the two different tasks "moved" their moods toward the boredom (bottom-left) or stress (top-right) corners of the grid (see Russell et al., 1989 for more information about the affect grid measurement).

Figure 1. Self-reported mood in Bowman et al. (2015).

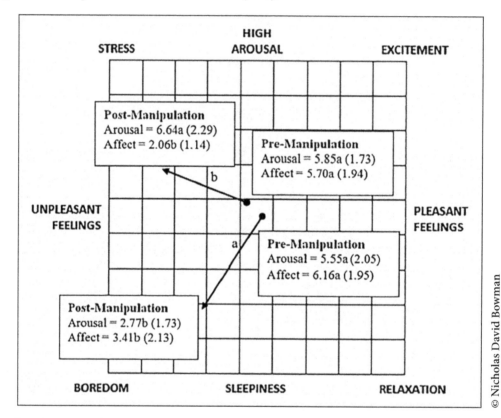

Data from Bowman and Tamborini (2015) showing pre- and post-mood manipulation moods. *A* represents the boredom manipulation (threading washers on string) and *B* represents the stress manipulation (answering a difficult set of logic puzzles).

Once we were able to make people bored or stressed, we were then ready to test our predictions about video games and mood management. For the first experiment (Bowman & Tamborini, 2012), we expected that interactivity in video games is what makes them useful for mood management, then giving the player more to do in-game should result in a better mood after gameplay. To test this, we asked these same people to then play a flight simulator video game in which they would land a fighter jet on a runway, but we manipulated how much control the players had over the jet itself: from a full autopilot mode (low intervention potential, similar to watching television), to having players use a flight stick and throttle to control the direction and speed of the airplane (moderate intervention potential), to giving them complete control over the airplane including the flight stick, throttle, and several other avionics such as airbrakes and landing gears (high intervention potential). After the game was over, we asked participants to again tell us their mood. What we found was a bit surprising: it turns out that increasing the intervention potential of a video game did result in better mood scores … but only to a point. Having some control over the jet fighter (the flight stick and throttle) required the players to focus more than just watching the game on autopilot, and players' scores were nearly 15% higher as a result. However, when players were given full control over the jet fighter, the findings became very interesting: for bored people, moderate and high intervention potential were equally useful for mood repair; for stressed people, high intervention potential *actually made their moods worse.* In other words, we found an important boundary condition for mood management theory that also helped us understand a bit more about video games—for bored people, video games are effective at mood management, but for stressed people, video games could be an additional source of stress if they are too difficult! In a follow-up study (Bowman & Tamborini, 2015), we replicated these findings with a key difference: in the second study, we allowed people to choose their own level of intervention potential from the three options above. When people chose for themselves, we found that moderate and high levels of intervention potential were useful for mood manipulation regardless of boredom or stress, although we saw overall levels of affect much higher for bored participants. Research into video games and mood management has since built on these initial studies, including emerging research into the use of video games (and other media) for psychological recovering and resilience against future stressors (Reinecke & Reiger, 2021). During COVID-19, researchers found that video games became an important source of mood management for people dealing with anxieties and stressors related to the pandemic (Barr & Copeland-Stewart, 2021).

PSYCHOLOGICAL WELL-BEING AND VIDEO GAME ENJOYMENT

As an extension of the research above, our research team was interested in understanding what other types of needs video games could satisfy in daily life. For example, video games seemed to us to be highly compatible with leading theories of psychological well-being that suggested a near-universal set of basic psychological needs for all people: competence (to feel skilled at a given action), autonomy (to have control over our actions), and relatedness (to form connections with others while doing a task; see Deci & Ryan, 2000). Early research had already suggested that features of video games could help satisfy these basic psychological needs (Ryan et al., 2006), and we wanted to replicate these findings by manipulating the experience of playing a single video game—demonstrating that specific changes in one game could reliably predict changes in need satisfaction. For the study, we chose a bowling video game for the Nintendo Wii system, because the Wii has a unique motion-control mechanism in which gameplay is controlled by motion sensors that allowed players to mimic "real-world" actions in the video game—in this case, rolling a bowling ball. Our expectation was that Wii's motion sensor controls would be both easier to use (increasing competence) and provide a greater sense of control (autonomy). However, we added a twist to the study in that *we designed our own version of a bowling ball controller* that would fit around the standard Wiimote (see Figure 2). We reasoned that using a controller similar to the "real world" would feel more natural in player's hands, which would even further increase competence and autonomy (as they would feel more "in control" of the video game).

Figure 2. Nintendo Wii controls used in Tamborini et al. (2010).

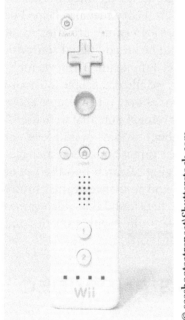
© seeshooteatrepeat\Shutterstock.com

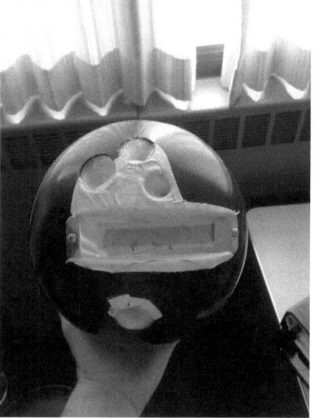
© Nicholas David Bowman

Standard Wiimote. To bowl, a player moves the wand-like controller back to their sides, and slides it forward, releasing the trigger button to toss the ball.

Customized controller. To bowl, a player holds the controller just as they would a bowling ball; Wiimote is affixed to the center, so the trigger can be released to toss the ball.

In this experiment, we randomly assigned players to use one of the two controllers, and then we also randomly assigned players to play with a human or a computer-based partner—we expected that a human partner would be easier to connect with and thus, feel a greater sense of relatedness. Then, we predicted that satisfying each need would increase enjoyment of the game.

Overall, we found that playing video games could satisfy basic psychological needs, but with some surprising results. Unsurprisingly, playing with humans did result in greater relatedness, but the bowling ball controller actually *lowered* feelings of competence and autonomy. People who had a human partner and who used the regular Wiimote felt the highest levels of competence, autonomy, and relatedness ... and also had the highest levels of enjoyment. These findings helped us answer two questions in that (a) video games can satisfy psychological needs useful to our daily lives, and (b) the context of that gameplay (such as playing socially or using different controller inputs) can also affect how well the game satisfies our needs. In later research, we followed up on the surprising finding that the bowling ball controller diminished need satisfaction (see Bowman et al., 2017; Rogers et al., 2015), and the answer became increasingly clear: unless players were experienced bowlers, the bowling ball controller was probably more difficult and frustrating to use—similar to the high intervention flight simulator controls from the studies mentioned earlier in this chapter.

Although it was not the focus of our research in the beginning, it became clear very quickly when talking with students that another key feature of video games was their ability to help people form relationships with each other. By the 2000s, massively multiplayer online video games were increasingly popular—one of the more famous being *World of Warcraft* (released in 2005). Gamers would often talk about logging on to meet family and friends, including people whom they would never otherwise meet in "real life" (see Steinkuehler & Williams, 2006), and this was not all too different to the social elements of video game arcades in the 1970s and 1980s (Egli & Meyers, 1984). In a recent review article, another one of our research teams (with scholars from the U.S., Germany, and Taiwan; Bowman, Rieger et al., 2022) reviewed several studies on the social mechanics of video games and found ample evidence that gamers can and do socialize in and around video games—players bond not only with each other, but with other in-game characters (Banks, 2015), and these relationships are meaningful. One of the more meaningful findings from this research involved interviews with college students talking about their personally nostalgic memories from playing video games when they were younger. In these memories, more than 25% of participants would specifically mention friends and family, with one answer sticking out more than any other: "My dad died when I was 10 so [playing Mario Kart with him] is one of my best memories of him" (Wulf et al., 2020, p. 91). In follow-up research, (Bowman, Yoshimura et al., 2022) we found that college students playing older video games (a game for the 1980s Nintendo Entertainment System), would often comment on feeling connected with their parents and older siblings as an "older generation" of gamers. Not only do video games help people socialize with others while playing, but they also provide common cultural touchstones for socializing across generations.

CONCLUSION

When I look back on Mortal Monday, I can understand why so many were concerned about the video games. Children were clamoring for the chance to pound each other's on-screen characters senseless, and the bloodier the better. However, when I think about these experiences through the lens of my research over the last 20 years, I see it very differently. Video games were a common outlet for lazy summer days, and it was easy enough to lose myself in a video game after getting into arguments with Mom, Dad, or my brother. Being good at a video game (even a fighting game) was less about being aggressive, and more about being competent at something—indeed, only the best players could pull off a fatality. Video games also gave "us" (as children) something that we had control over, in a schedule otherwise made for us by adults—we had autonomy over our gameplay. My friends and I bonded over sharing video game secrets and playing with and against each other—we formed relationships that last to this day. And of course, I have already mentioned memories of playing video games with my parents … and indeed, my students often ask me "what it was like blowing into cartridges" or "spending quarters at the mall arcade" (we can thank the popularity of Netflix's *Stranger Things* for a heavy dose of 80s nostalgia). I'm in my 40s now, and video games—played in moderation—are still a useful and ever-ready source of daily well-being.

Now if you'll excuse me, I'm *almost* done with this next level. =)

REFERENCES

American Psychological Association. (2020, March 3). APA reaffirms position on violent video games and violent behavior. *APA*. Retrieved from https://www.apa.org/news/press/releases/2020/03/violent-video-games-behavior

Andrews, E. L. (1993). Industry set to issue video game ratings as complaints rise. *The New York Times*. Retrieved from https://www.nytimes.com/1993/12/09/business/industry-set-to-issue-video-game-ratings-as-complaints-rise.html

Banks, J. (2015). Object, me, symbiote, other: A social typology of player-avatar relationships. *First Monday*. https://journals.uic.edu/ojs/index.php/fm/article/view/5433

Barr, M., & Copeland-Stewart, A. (2021). Playing video games during the COVID-19 pandemic and effects on players' well-being. *Games and Culture*. https://doi.org/10.1177%2F15554120211017036

Bowman, N. D. (2016). The rise (and refinement) of moral panic. In R. Kowert & T. Quandt (Eds.), *The video game debate: Unravelling the physical, social, and psychological effects of digital games* (pp. 22–38). Routledge/Taylor & Francis Group.

Bowman, N. D., Liebold, B., & Pietschmann, D. (2017). The Golden (Hands) Rule: Exploring user experiences with gamepad and natural-user interfaces in popular video games. *Journal of Gaming and Virtual Worlds, 19*(1), 69–83. https://doi.org/10.1386/jgvw.9.1.69_1

Bowman, N. D., Rieger, D., & Lin, J-H. T. (2022). Social video gaming and well-being. *Current Opinions in Psychology*. https://doi.org/10.1016/j.copsyc.2022.101316

Bowman, N. D., & Tamborini, R. (2012). Task demand and mood repair: The intervention potential of computer games. *New Media & Society, 14*(8), 1339–1357. https://doi.org/10.1177/1461444812450426

Bowman, N. D., & Tamborini, R (2015). "In the mood to game": Selective exposure and mood management processes in computer game play. *New Media & Society, 17*(3), 375–393. https://doi.org/10.1177/1461444813504274

Bowman, N. D., Yoshimura, K., & Bohaty, E. (2022, November). Makes me feel like I was born in the wrong era:" Gamer self-efficacy and appreciation are correlated with historical nostalgia when playing a retrogame. National Communication Association.

Deci, E. L., & Ryan, R. M. (2000). The "what" and "why" of goal pursuits: Human needs and the self-determination of behavior. *Psychological Inquiry, 11*(4), 227–268. https://doi.org/10.1207/S15327965PLI1104_01

Egli, E. A., & Meyers, L. S., (1984). The role of video game playing in adolescent life: Is there a reason to be concerned? *Bulletin of the Psychonomic Society, 22*, 309–312. https://link.springer.com/article/10.3758/BF03333828

Entertainment Software Association (2021). Essential facts about the video game industry. Retrieved from https://www.theesa.com/resource/2021-essential-facts-about-the-video-game-industry/

FieldLevelMedia.(2020,December3).Study:Gamingindustrycontributed$90BtotheU.S.economyin2019. *Reuters.* Retrieved from https://www.reuters.com/article/esports-business-gaming-economy/study-gaming-industry-contributed-90b-to-u-s-economy-in-2019-idUSFLM6F7yh2

Korucek, C. A. (2012). The agony and the Exidy: A history of video game violence and the legacy of Death Race. *Game Studies, 12*(1). http://gamestudies.org/1201/articles/carly_kocurek

Markey, P. M., Ivory, J. D., Slotter, E. B., Oliver, M. B., & Maglalang, O. (2020). He does not look like video games made him do it: Racial stereotypes and school shootings. *Psychology of Popular Media, 9*(4), 493–498. https://doi.org/10.1037/ppm0000255

Martins,N.,Matthews,N.L.,&Ratan,R.A.(2015).Playingbytherules:Parentalmediationofvideogame play. *Journal of Family Issues, 38*(9), 1215–1238. https://doi.org/10.1177%2F0192513X15613822

Mathur, M. B., & VanderWeele, T. J. (2019). Finding common ground in meta-analysis "wars" on violent video games. *Perspectives on Psychological Science, 14*(4), 705–708. https://doi.org/10.1177/1745691619850104

Reinecke, L., & Rieger, D. (2021). Media entertainment as a self-regulatory resource: The recovery and resilience in entertainment media use (R2EM) model. In P. Vorderer & C. Klimmt (Eds.), *Oxford handbook of entertainment theory.* Oxford University Press. https://doi.org/10.1093/oxfordhb/9780190072216.013.39

Rogers, R., Bowman, N.D., & Oliver, M. B. (2015). It's not the model that doesn't fit, it's the controller! The role of cognitive skills in understanding the links between natural mapping, performance, and enjoyment of console video games. *Computers in Human Behavior, 49*, 588–596. https://doi.org/10.1016/j.chb.03.027

Russell, J. A., Weiss, A., & Mendelsohn, G. A. (1989). A single-item scale of pleasure and arousal. *Journal of Personality and Social Psychology, 57*(3), 493–502. https://psycnet.apa.org/doi/10.1037/0022-3514.57.3.493

Ryan, R. M., Rigby, C. S., & Przybylski, A. (2006). The motivational pull of video games: A self-determination theory approach. *Motivation and Emotion, 30*, 344–360. https://doi.org/10.1007/s11031-006-9051-8

Steinkuehler, C. A. & Williams, D. (2006). Where everybody knows your (screen) name: Online games as "third places." *Journal of Computer-Mediated Communication, 11*(4), 885–909. https://doi.org/10.1111/j.1083-6101.2006.00300.x

Tamborini, R., Bowman, N. D., Eden, A., Grizzard, M., & Organ, A. (2010). Defining media enjoyment as the satisfaction of intrinsic needs. *Journal of Communication, 60*(4), 758–777. https://doi.org/10.1111/j.1460-2466.2010.01513.x

Wijman, T. (2021, December 22). The games market and beyond in 2021: The year in numbers. *NewZoo*. Retrieved from https://newzoo.com/insights/articles/the-games-market-in-2021-the-year-in-numbers-esports-cloud-gaming

Wulf, T., Bowman, N. D., Velez, J., & Breuer, J. (2020). Once upon a game: Exploring video game nostalgia and its impact on well-being. *Psychology of Popular Media Culture, 9*(1), 83–95. https://doi.org/10.1037/ppm0000208

Zillmann, D., & Bryant, J. (1985). Affect, mood, and emotion as determinants of selective exposure. In D. Zillmann & J. Bryant (Eds.), *Selective exposure to communication* (pp. 157–189). Lawrence Erlbaum Associates.

WHY DO WE BINGE-WATCH TELEVISION CONTENT, AND TO WHAT EFFECT?

Bridget Rubenking
University of Central Florida

Cheryl Campanella Bracken
Cleveland State University

Chances are that you have binge-watched something recently, especially if you are a college student. It may have been a new true crime limited series on Netflix, a critically acclaimed drama from HBO, a new anime series on a more niche streaming service, or may be a favorite comedy series after a long day, or week. You may have felt a rollercoaster of emotions—suspense, concern, anxiety, connected or identified with characters, happy, alarmed, and sad. Perhaps you curled up in bed and watched on your laptop, or may be you binge-watched on a large-screen television over dinner and snacks with a roommate or a family member

The experience should be familiar to most readers, as college students report more frequent binge watching than their older counterparts (Rubenking & Bracken, 2021). Industry players and researchers define and measure binge watching in different ways. This can lead to mixed findings when looking at the phenomenon and attempting to make conclusions. At a minimum, we all tend to agree that we are talking about watching multiple episodes of a serial program in one sitting. In our time spent researching binge watching, we have found a narrower definition allows us to focus on the behavior that we are most interested in. We define binge watching as *"Long periods of focused, deliberate viewing of sequential television content that is generally narrative, suspenseful, and dramatic in nature. Binge watching may be a planned, purposeful activity, or unintentional."* This focus on narrative content is purposeful—this allows us to distinguish from other sorts of entertainment content, such as sports or short social media videos, which we view as distinct, and worthy of their own study. While Netflix can report "binge watching data," they actually report on what a device accessing Netflix was doing. This allows everything from nonviewership to distracted viewing to get mischaracterized as binge watching, despite general agreement that binge watching is a focused, attentive way of viewing content.

It may seem like we have all always binge watched, but that is not the case. This chapter begins with briefly explaining the circumstances of how binge watching became a "new norm" in television viewing just over a decade ago. It then discusses academic research, some of which we conducted ourselves, that examines what *motivates* viewers to binge watch, as well as *to what effect* it has on us, as viewers. It concludes with notes on what to look out for in the future related to binge watching and our evolving television viewing styles.

WHAT ENABLES BINGE WATCHING?

Binge watching at home has been one way to view narrative series since VCRs enabled viewers to record television content and watch later, at their leisure, and cable television programmers scheduled "marathons" of various shows across time slots and dayparts. However, the modern era of streaming services afforded binge watching to become a "new norm," by changing distribution strategies, adding to the sheer quantity of content, taking advantage of faster Internet speeds in homes, and by reaching large segments of the population. The first streaming service to be considered nearly synonymous with binge watching is still the most common streaming service in the United States and beyond: Netflix (Attest, 2021, Rubenking et al., in press). In 2013, Netflix introduced their first slate of original programming (e.g., *House of Cards* and *Orange is the New Black*) and went on a press tour announcing that "binge watching is the new normal" (*"Netflix: Binge watching"* 2013; *"The Story of Netflix,"* n.d.).

Currently, Netflix remains the only streaming service with a default "all-at-once" distribution strategy. They are leaning into it, with a spokesperson saying, "We think our bingeable release model helps drive substantial engagement, especially for newer titles" (Webster, 2022). In 2019, just before the COVID-19 pandemic left most of the world at home, with little to do *except* binge-watch television, streaming service subscriptions first surpassed cable subscriptions in the United States (Deloitte, 2019). More recently, current subscribers have an average of four streaming service subscriptions (Spangler, 2021). Streaming services simply allow for on-demand binge watching wherever, and whenever, a viewer chooses. In the United States, 18–24-year-olds reported *more time* watching streaming services than every other adult age group, and the *least amount of time* watching traditional broadcast/cable television. Our own research has shown that over 90% of college students have regular access to Netflix alone (Rubenking et al., in press).

The onset of the COVID-19 pandemic spurred more time spent viewing streaming content and boosted subscriptions, followed by a dip since the height of stay-at-home orders. Current viewing and subscription levels are higher than just prior to the onset of the pandemic (Alexander, 2020; Rubenking et al., in press). In fact, we found that binge watching and episodic viewing (an in-between type of viewing, where viewers watch narrative seasons of content at their own pace, without the super-long binges) were both higher after COVID-19 stay-at-home orders had lifted than before they began. In contrast, traditional viewing of live television decreased. By all accounts, binge-watching television is a common leisure activity, easily enabled by widely accessible streaming services. Binge watching shows no signs of disappearing from our media entertainment repertoires as we look to the future.

WHY DO WE BINGE WATCH: A REVIEW OF MOTIVATIONS

When new media technologies or new ways of using media technologies begin to reach widespread adoption, media researchers often start their inquiry with a set of relatively basic questions: what is it? Who is using it, and how? And critically, *why are people adopting this new media technology behavior?* Binge watching was no exception. Early research on antecedents to the viewing style used both qualitative (Flayelle et al., 2017; Rubenking et al., 2018) and quantitative methodologies (Pittman & Sheehan, 2015; Rubenking & Bracken, 2018; Walton-Pattison et al., 2016). Together, this research largely paints motivations to binge watch in several related categories, including (1) *Engagement.* This engagement was often related to the type of content, such as anticipation and suspense in the content, the amount of content available, and quality of the narrative. This paints binge watching as an active, enjoyable type of viewing. (2) *Habit, automaticity, and part of daily routines.* Even within the first several years of academic investigation, binge watching has become a new norm in television viewing. Binge watching as an established, functional part of individuals' routines was a critical early finding (Rubenking & Bracken, 2018). (3) *Emotion responses, emotion regulation, and mood management.* Individuals express that binge watching has positive effects on their emotional states, and that they use binge watching to help regulate their emotions and moods. (4) *Social motives.* Whether binge watching so one could talk about a show with someone else, or watching together, there were social aspects reported by nearly all studies that explored it. Social movies include both supporting bonds with nonmediated others, as well as with mediated others via character identification and parasocial interaction.

What was *not* found to be an early motivation of binge watching behavior? Self-control (or lack thereof), addiction, and self-efficacy (or one's belief in their own ability to exert control over their behaviors, motivations, and environment) were all found not to predict binge watching. There have been more neutral and negative motives reported, such as procrastinating other tasks to binge watch, or being motivated to binge watch less due to regret or anticipated regret (although, of note, not guilt).

As the research on motivations to binge watch moved on from exploratory, preliminary research to more theoretically driven and empirically sound, our own research focused on parsing the differences between motivations to binge watch, and motivations to watch television, generally. In a study comparing and contrasting motivations to binge watch and motivations to view television via the old standard—tuning in to watch a show as it airs, live—we found binge watching frequency live, appointment-style viewing frequency to be unrelated (Rubenking & Bracken, 2018). Despite many media use variables sharing positive relationships, how often individuals appointment-viewed television content was unrelated to how frequently they binge- watched content. This may have been because different people were binge watching, with much greater binge watching frequency among our college student sample and much greater appointment viewing frequency observed in the adult sample. There was also evidence that women engaged in more binge watching than men, but this was a relatively small effect. The other major difference we saw in motivations to view in each of the two types explored was that viewing as a way to help regulate one's emotions was much greater for binge watching than appointment viewing. We think this is due to related results that suggest engagement is a critical component to the binge-watching experience: One can experience greater emotional responses when paying more attention to content that spurs anticipation and suspense. This experience was also reflected in our qualitative exploration of motives (Rubenking et al., 2018), where a full range of emotional responses while viewing was reported. Some reported enjoying nail-biter dramas, such as *Breaking Bad*, so they could feel "on edge," while others preferred viewing to relax and binge on content that let them relax and tune out.

Participants reported several dichotomies about their motives to binge watch as well. First, sometimes they planned to binge watch in a purposeful way, such as after completing homework, participants felt they earned a break. Other times they ended up watching just one more episode because they wanted to see what happened next, often staying up later than planned. Likewise, some participants differed about binging with others; some liked viewing together, setting time aside on the weekends to watch multiple episodes of a show with friends, partners, or roommates. Still others complained about trying to binge watch with others who talked too much and interrupted the viewing (Rubenking et al., 2018).

As noted in the beginning of this chapter, research on binge watching is often confused by each researcher using their own conceptual definitions (or dictionary-type definitions) of binge watching. Researchers also operationally define, (or measure and observe) binge watching in different ways, which can also lead to conflicting results. We explored this issue in Merrill and Rubenking (2019), where we looked at differences in antecedents of binge-watching *frequency*, or how often individuals report a binge-watching session, and binge-watching *duration*, or how long each of those sessions were, on average. Interestingly, we found that one set of predictors was related to frequency alone, and a completely non-overlapping set was related to duration. Watching as a reward, and as a means to procrastinate led to *more* frequent binge watching, whereas more regret experienced for viewing and self-regulation was related to *less* frequent binge watching. How long those binge-watching sessions were, however, was unrelated to those variables: women were more likely than men to binge watch longer, and greater enjoyment experienced while viewing also led to longer viewing sessions. How we define and measure binge watching is a critical part to developing a body of research that can make definitive statements about common and less common (or nonexistent) motivations to binge watch.

TO WHAT EFFECT FOR INDIVIDUALS

While the previous section detailed what we know about why we choose to binge watch, this section explores what we know to happen after we have elected to binge watch. The type of effect of media on an individual is influenced by who one studies, the content and form characteristics of the media, and how much media one is exposed to. Since academics first took an interest in binge-watching behaviors, research has often focused on the relationship between it and less than desirable outcomes, such as negative effects on well-being, loneliness, depression, and lack of high-quality/quantity of sleep (Exelmans & Van den Bulck, 2017; Wheeler, 2015). However, others have focused on other types of (more positive) effects such as sensations of entertainment (Rubenking & Bracken, 2018).

Many researchers, including ourselves and colleagues, have found that audiences engage in binge watching primarily because they enjoy it. Most people will not continue to watch a program they find uninteresting or boring for an extended period of time. Some people enjoy media content that is happy, fun, and light, while other people enjoy media content that is either sad or dark (think horror). Audiences who engage in binge watching view all types of programs.

Beyond entertainment and enjoyment effects, parasocial interactions/relationships have been a reported outcome of binge watching. When people watch television content, they may form parasocial relationships, or perceptions of closeness, friendships, or intimate bonds with mediated others. Tukachinsky and Eyal (2018) found that people who binge watched reported higher levels of parasocial relationships than people who watched the same program in a nonbinging way of viewing. Other media effects influenced by binge watching include successfully binge watching as a way of regulating our emotions: To either relax and destress or to improve our mood (Rubenking & Bracken, 2018).

However, not all media effects are positive. Researchers have found negative mental and physical health effects connected to binge watching. Within the binge watching literature there is debate about whether not binge watching is addictive. The term binge implies overindulgence, like binge drinking or binge eating. Although, it is important to note that some researchers prefer terminology with less negative connotations, such as Perks' (2015) use of "media marathoning." Flayelle and colleagues have compared nonproblematic and problematic binge watching and have found that excessive media use, including binge watching, is associated with greater levels of depression and a greater lack of self-control (Flayelle et al., 2019). Further, research has found that that when people binge watch because they are lonely, to escape, or looking for social interaction, that there is a stronger link to problematic viewing behaviors (Ort et al., 2021).

While other more interactive media, such as video games and Internet use, have been linked to addictive behaviors for an exceedingly small segment of users, our perspective is that for most media users, binge watching is merely one way to enjoy television entertainment. The term "binging" itself seems to have elicited the implementation of addiction and health-based theoretical models and measures, but empirical data generally finds support for the relationship between binge watching and enjoyment and engagement (Rubenking & Bracken, 2020). There is a lack of data or documentation of individuals in the throes of a terrible, life-threatening binge-watching addiction. In fact, the behavior is so typical that it is a regular media habit for many. Rubenking and Bracken (2018) examined how binge watching was becoming a part of people's lives. They found that people had developed frequent behaviors of watching the same show for an extended period of time, or binge watching. Media habits are defined as automatic media consumption behaviors (LaRose, 2010). For example, many people turn on their television or their computer as soon as they get home or listen to the same daily podcast or radio show during a commute. We found that binge watching had become a media habit, and for many people, it was a routine way of viewing that seems perfectly ordinary.

Recent research has explored several other effects of binge watching. Researchers have linked long binges to fear of being left out (FOMO), or relatedly, to catch up on a show to be able to talk with their friends (Starosta, & Izydorczyk, 2020). Specifically, Anghelcev et al. (2022) found that heavy binge-watchers actually spent more time daily interacting with their friends and family as compared to nonbinge-watchers. Research on the effects and experiences of binge watching continue to develop over time.

BINGE WATCHING AND THE FUTURE

TV viewing continues to evolve as new technologies are introduced, and sometimes it is not all smooth sailing. Some reports show overall time spent viewing television is down, post-pandemic (Attest, 2021). Further, viewers are increasingly *un*happy about their streaming service experiences (Deloitte, 2019) and others are frustrated with the ever-growing need for more subscriptions, at more of a cost (Rubenking et al., in press). Additionally, churn between streaming services is high, such that subscribers often drop one streaming service for another. This is often due to price hikes, the end of a complimentary subscription, or in favor of a streaming service with better quality content (Rubenking et al., in press; Spangler, 2021).

Fear not! There are still many data points that point to the longevity of binge watching and emerging viewing behaviors. First, the shift to streaming is clear. For the first time in 2021, more U.S.-based adults watch streaming content daily (83%) than live TV (81%). A full 44% of Gen Z and 43% of Millennials report watching streaming television for three or more hours daily, followed by 29% of Gen Xers and 20% of Baby Boomers (Attest, 2021). Interestingly, the average amount of leisure time for an American adult has held steady at between 5 and 5.5 hours per day for over a decade (U.S. Bureau of Labor, *n.d.*). And the most common way of spending that leisure time—by more than two-three times the next most common way. Watching television. While "traditional" binge watching has staying power, in our opinion, some other trends in emerging viewing behaviors should also be considered for both how they relate to binge watching, and how they will shape future behaviors. These include episodic, or serial, viewing, and media multitasking, including "social TV."

It is apparent that media audiences enjoy the ability to self-pace their viewing—including binge watching but also including episodic or serial viewing. In Rubenking and Bracken (2021), we studied episodic or serial viewing, defined as "Watching a series, a season, or several seasons of a TV show at your own pace over the course of several days, weeks, or months." We think this is more in line with what typical daily viewing looks like for most adults, although binge-watching sessions will likely still occur, and still occur more frequently for younger viewers. For working adults, busy students, and those with caretaking responsibilities, the endless nights of viewing cannot be a reality most nights. Episodic or serial viewing may be the best of both worlds between binge watching and appointment viewing.

Other threats to binge watching are different media habits. There are only so many hours in a day, and especially younger viewers report increasing amounts of time spent on both social media and gaming (Attest, 2021). Indeed, Westcott et al. (2021) report that among Gen Z, individuals report unintentionally spending more time than planned on social media more often than they do on streaming content. The attentional pull of these digital media alternatives should not be overlooked. One way around the zero-sum game of media choices is what many of us find ourselves doing when sitting in front of a television: media multitasking. Increasingly, people are engaging in second screen viewing, or using a second media device such as their smartphone, tablet, or laptop, while watching a program on another device, often a TV or computer. People have always engaged in multitasking while watching TV. However, what is changing now is the *prevalence* of multitasking during television viewing, the ease in which we have another connected device nearby, and the often *interrelated* nature of this type of multitasking. In 2018, Nielsen reported that 88% of U.S. adults were engaging with a secondary device while viewing television (Anderson, 2019). The majority of second screen activity was either related to the content they were viewing on the primary screen or spent messaging family and friends about the program they were viewing, according to Nielsen.

One new example of second screening is Social TV. Social TV is defined as the "simultaneous act of watching TV and engaging in communication about the TV program with other TV viewers connected online," (Kim et al., 2018). This discussion with others about television content can happen in public spaces, like Twitter, or in more personal spaces, with only known others via messaging apps etc. (Kim et al., 2019). Like binge watching, researchers have found different motivations and individual differences predicting Social TV viewing, enjoyment and engagement being chief among them (Kim et al., 2018; 2019).

As technologies change quickly, it is important to consider that individuals' viewing preferences are not always as quick to change. People are drawn to stories. New ways of accessing stories will continue to grab our attention, whether it is in one, condensed, sitting, or over several weeks. People also like having increased agency in their entertainment choices: The wealth of personalized content available on the wealth of streaming service options are good signs for the future of television viewing and binge watching.

REFERENCES

Alexander, J. (April 21, 2020). Netflix adds 15 million subscribers as people stream more than ever, but warns about tough road ahead. *The Verge.* Retrieved from https://www.theverge.com/2020/4/21/21229587/netflix-earnings-coronavirus-pandemic-streaming-entertainment.

Anderson, N. (2019, December). 88% of Americans use a second screen while watching TV. Why? *Arts Technica.* Retrieved from: https://arstechnica.com/gaming/2019/12/88-of-americans-use-a-second-screen-while-watching-tv-why/

Anghelcev, G., Sar, S., Martin, J., & Moultrie, J. L. (2022). Is heavy binge-watching a socially driven behaviour? Exploring differences between heavy, regular and non-binge-watchers. *Journal of Digital Media & Policy, 13*(2), 201–221. https://doi.org/10.1386/jdmp_00035_1

Attest. (No Author). US Media Consumption Report 2021. *Attest.* Retrieved from: https://www.askattest.com/reports-guides/us-media-consumption-report-2021-2

Deloitte (2019). Deloitte fan engagement survey. *Deloitte.com.* Retrieved from https://www2.deloitte.com/content/dam/Deloitte/us/Documents/technology-media-telecommunications/us-enhancing-digital-fan-engagement.pdf

Exelmans, L., & Van Den Bulck, J. (2017). Binge viewing, sleep, and the role of pre-sleep arousal. *Journal of Clinical Sleep Medicine, 13*(8), 1001–1008. https://doi.org/10.5664/jcsm.6704

Flayelle M., Canale N., Vögele C., Karila L., Maurage P., & Billieux J. (2019). Assessing binge-watching behaviours: Development and validation of the "Watching TV Series Motives" and "Binge-Watching Engagement and Symptoms" questionnaires. *Computers and Human Behavior, 90,* 26–36. https://doi.org/10.1016/j.chb.2018.08.022

Flayelle, M, Maurage, P, & Billieux, J. (2017). Toward a qualitative understanding of binge watching behaviors: a focus group approach. *Journal of Behavioral Addictions, 6*(4), 457–471. https://doi.org/10.1556/2006.6.2017.060

Kim, J., Song, H., & Lee, S. (2018). Extrovert and lonely individuals' social TV viewing experiences: A mediating and moderating role of social presence. *Mass Communication and Society, 21*(1), 50–70. https://doi.org/10.1080/15205436.2017.1350715

Kim, J., Merrill Jr, K., & Yang, H. (2019). Why we make the choices we do: Social tv viewing experiences and the mediating role of social presence. *Telematics and Informatics, 45,* 101281. https://doi.org/10.1016/j.tele.2019.101281

LaRose, R. (2010). The problem of media habits. *Communication Theory, 20*(2) 194–222. https://doi.org/10.1111/j.1468-2885.2010.01360.x

Merrill Jr., K. & Rubenking, B. (2019). Go long or go often: Influences on binge watching frequency and duration among college students. *Social Sciences, 8*(1), 1–12.https://doi.org/10.3390/socsci8010010

Netflix: Binge watching is the new normal for TV streamers. (2013, December). *Deadline*. Retrieved from: https://deadline.com/2013/12/netflix-binge-watching-tv-streaming-study-651962/

Ort, A., Wirz, D., & Fahr, A. (2021). Is binge-watching addictive? Effects of motives for TV series use on the relationship between excessive media consumption and problematic viewing habits. *Addictive Behaviors Reports, 13,* 100325. https://doi.org/10.1016/j.abrep.2020.100325

Perks, L. G. (2015). *Media marathoning: Immersions in morality*. Lexington Books.

Pittman, M., & Sheehan, K. (2015). Sprinting a media marathon: Uses and gratifications of binge watching television through Netflix. *First Monday, 20*(10). https://doi.org/10.5210/fm.v20i10.6138

Rubenking, B., & Bracken, C. C. (2018). Binge watching: A suspenseful, emotional habit. *Communication Research Reports, 35*(5), 381–391. https://doi.org/10.1080/08824096.2018.1525346.

Rubenking, B., & Bracken, C. C. (2020). *Binge watching: Implications and motivations of our changing viewing behaviors*. Peter Lang Publishing.

Rubenking, B. & Bracken, C. C. (2021). Binge watching and serial viewing: Comparing new media viewing habits in 2015 and 2020. *Addictive Behavior Reports, 14,* 100356. https://doi.org/10.1016/j.abrep.2021.100356

Rubenking, B., Bracken, C. C., Sandoval, J., & Rister, A. (2018). Defining new viewing behaviors: What makes and motivates TV binge watching. *International Journal of Digital Television, 9*(1), 69–85. https://doi.org/10.1386/jdtv.9.1.69_1

Rubenking, B., Lewis, N., & Bracken, C. C. (in press). COVID, cord-cutting and coping: A snapshot of university students' viewing behaviors. In R. Brookey, J. Phillips, and T. Pollard's (Eds.). *Triaging the streaming wars: Electronic media research series*. Routledge.

Spangler, T. (2021, April). Gen Z watching TV, movies as fifth among top 5 entertainment activities. *Variety*. Retrieved from: https://variety.com/2021/digital/news/gen-z-survey-deloitte-tv-movies-ranking-1234954207/

Starosta, J. A., & Izydorczyk, B. (2020). Understanding the phenomenon of binge-watching—A systematic review. *International Journal of Environmental Research and Public Health, 17*(12), 4469. https://doi.org/10.3390/ijerph17124469

"The Story of Netflix." (no date). Netflix. Retrieved from: https://about.netflix.com/en

Tukachinsky, R., & Eyal, K. (2018). The psychology of marathon television viewing: Antecedents and viewer involvement. *Mass Communication and Society, 21*(3), 275–295. https://doi.org/10.1080/15205436.2017.1422765

U. S. Bureaus of Labor Statistics. (*no date*). Average hours per day spent in selected leisure and sports activities by age. Retrieved from: https://www.bls.gov/charts/american-time-use/activity-leisure.htm

Walton-Pattison, E., Dombrowski, S. U., & Presseau, J. (2016). 'Just one more episode': Frequency and theoretical correlates of television binge watching. *Journal of Health Psychology, 23*(1), 14–24. https://doi.org/10.1177/1359105316643379

Webster, A. (2022, September). Netflix is all in on binging. *The Verge*. Retrieved from: https://www.theverge.com/2022/10/18/23411580/netflix-binge-watching-strategy-squid-game-dahmer

Westcott, K., & Arbanas, J. (2021). Commentary: Gen Z gamers could shake up the media and entertainment industries. *Fortune*. https://fortune.com/2021/04/19/gen-zgamers-video-games-media-entertainment-outlook-changes-future.

Wheeler, K. S. (2015). *The relationships between television viewing behaviors, attachment, loneliness, depression, and psychological well-being*. (Honors Thesis). Georgia Southern University, Georgia, United States.

NONVERBAL COMMUNICATION

The nonverbal communication context focuses on the messages we send without verbal communication or words/language. Nonverbal communication scholars typically examine different nonverbal codes including physical appearance, touch, eye behavior, space, time, facial behavior, gestures and movements, vocal cues, and environmental cues. Some major areas of research in nonverbal communication include physical attraction, impressions, identity displays, deception, nonverbal differences across cultures, and emotion displays. This section includes chapters focusing on three important areas of nonverbal communication research: (1) deception, (2) flirting, and (3) competent nonverbal skills. First, Timothy Levine (University of Alabama Birmingham) reviews deception research for answers about how we can tell if someone is lying to us. Second, Betty La France (Northern Illinois University) and Jeffrey Hall (University of Kansas) review flirting research to provide the nonverbal cues that are effective when flirting. Third, Brian Spitzberg (San Diego State University) reviews the nonverbal skills that are most important for displaying communicating competence. Many of us are unaware of the nonverbal messages we send and how important these messages can be. Whether it is interviewing for a job, meeting someone for a first date, or taking a video call with friends, our nonverbal cues provide important information to people who form impressions and perceptions about us. These chapters can help you sort out previous advice you may have been given about detecting lies, flirting with a potential partner, or communicating competence in general. Sometimes, the words we say are less important than the nonverbal cues we display, and these research programs explain the importance of our actions in commonly occurring situations.

HOW CAN WE TELL IF SOMEONE IS LYING TO US?

Timothy R. Levine
University of Alabama Birmingham

Hi. My name is Tim Levine and I am a Distinguished Professor and the Chair of Communication Studies at UAB (Alabama, Birmingham). Before UAB, I taught at Korea University, Michigan State University, and the University of Hawaii. I have been asked to write a little bit about myself and especially about my research. You might find what I do interesting. I study, among other things, deception. But really, I'm interested in everything social.

In the academic field of human communication, I am known for a variety of things. For one, I publish lots of research. Whenever analyses of scholarship come out, I'm usually near the top. I'm also known for my hard-core quantitative and experimental approach. I'm part of the open science and new statistics movements. My most cited article was about an error I discovered in a popular statistical software program. I also have a reputation as being more than a little bit feisty. I have been in several back-and-forth academic debates with other professors with whom I disagree.

These days, however, I am best known for my deception research, and especially a new theory I call Truth-Default Theory (TDT for short) and my book, *Duped*. TDT was the inspiration for Malcom Gladwell's book *Talking to Strangers*. Thanks to Malcom, my work has gained visibility outside academic circles. My work is now used by prosecutors, defense attorneys, the National Security Agency, and FBI profilers, among others.

Deception is good topic to research for many reasons. First up, it is just interesting. Almost all academics can give the "I'm interested in…" speech. With deception, its other people that are interested in my work. The topic has audience appeal.

There are also plenty of important applications for deception research. Currently, the topics of misinformation and disinformation are hot. There are applications in cyber security, criminal investigations, anti-terrorism, civil and criminal litigation, fraud prevention, online dating platforms, and so on.

A question I am often asked is how I came to study deception. I know a deception researcher who started researching deception in order to try and understand their own gullibility. They got burned by a big lie from someone they trusted. My path into deception research, however, was more mundane. I did not get involved in the topic because I was naturally interested in the topic in the first place, but instead, because one of my professors (Dr. Steve McCornack) was interested in deception. At first, I was just the research assistant and was along for the ride. I went to graduate school to study persuasion, not deception. But, one question led to another, and well, here I am. I got sucked in. Now I'm an internationally recognized expert in deception.

There are two big reasons I stuck with research on deception as my career evolved. One has to do with something called counterintuitive findings. One of the big criticisms of much social science research is that so much social science just documents the obvious. It is common sense. A counterintuitive finding is a result of research that goes against common sense. If all we needed were common sense, there is little need for research. But, when research brings you knowledge that you cannot come by otherwise, that makes research fun, interesting, and important. In deception, common sense does not always hold and this makes deception an interesting thing to research. To show you what I mean, try answering these three questions:

1. What is the best way to tell if someone is lying to you?

2. True or False: It is easier to detect a lie from someone you know well than from a stranger.

3. Truth or False: Most people lie less often than the average person.

The answers to these questions are interspersed throughout the rest of this chapter.

The second reason I got sucked into deception research was there was opportunity. I became convinced early on that most deception theory was wrong-headed. It was mythology, not science. It pointed attention in the wrong direction. Research findings, it seemed to me, disproved the theories. Because I believed that the existing theory was flawed, I saw opportunity. Deception and deception detection provided a puzzle to solve. If old theory was wrong, what was the truth about deception? It took me 30 years of research to come up with answers I am happy with, but the puzzle pieces finally fit together.

In short, the reason to do research is to learn something new. Deception provided me with a topic about which there was little existing valid knowledge, many misconceptions to correct, and so much to learn. Some people like researching topics upon which there is good prior research to build on and where knowledge needs only a little fine-tuning. Not me. I was looking for a challenge, and deception provided that for me. That other people found my research intriguing is a bonus.

Deception is defined as intentionally, knowingly, or purposely misleading another person (Levine, 2020). A **lie** is a subtype of deception that involves deceiving someone by saying something that is known to be false. For greater discussion of these definitions, see my book *Duped* where there is whole chapter devoted to defining deception. For ease, I use lying and deception interchangeably here.

First, consider question #1 above. How can you tell if someone is lying to you? Did you answer that a liar will not look you in the eye? Or may be you guessed that liars fidget or act nervous? This is what research says most people think. A psychologist by the name of Charley Bond (Bond & The Global Deception Research Team, 2006) surveyed people in 75 different countries asking just this question. By far, the #1 answer worldwide was a lack of eye contact. People everywhere think liars will not look you in the eye while lying. Other common answers had to do with acting nervous or anxious. Most people think that liars have nonverbal tells that give them away. Yet, in research looking at the behaviors of both truth-tellers and liars, there is no scientifically supported evidence that a lack of eye contact signals deceit (DePaulo et al., 2003). Eye contact has no validity as a deception tell. Zero. Fidgeting is not very informative either. In fact, most specific nonverbal behaviors are for practical purposes worthless as signals of lying. Some research supports some nonverbal deception cues, but other findings do not, and in the end, it tends to be a wash. Forty years of research on nonverbal deception cues has led to a dead end in lie detection. Not everyone agrees about this, but I find the evidence convincing. Research disproves common sense and conventional wisdom about nonverbal communication and deception.

It was findings such as these that clued me into the belief that most deception theory is probably misguided. You see, most older deception theory is all about nonverbal communication as the path to detecting lies. Since the 1970s, most thinking about deception and deception detection was guided by variations on Psychologist Paul Ekman's idea of **leakage**. If you have seen the TV show, *Lie to Me*, you will know something about this idea. Basically, the idea is that it is easy to control what you say, but the truth leaks out though facial expressions and body language. According to leakage and related theories, if you know how to read nonverbal behaviors, you can detect lies.

The idea that paying attention to nonverbal behaviors is actually misleading guided one of my most important series of experiments (Levine et al., 2011). This is the series of experiments that attracted Gladwell to my work. People who present themselves as confident, composed, and friendly tend to be believed. We say such people have an honest demeanor. Other people who come off as standoffish, anxious, or uncertain tend to be disbelieved and they have a dishonest demeanor. We found this to be true regardless of who was witnessing and judging the communication. We replicated our findings with college students, college professors, federal agents, and people from a different country who did not fully understand what was being said. Some people are just seen as more sincere than others. The thing is though, the things that make people believable are not the same things that are valid signals of actual honesty or deception. People believed sincere-acting people, not sincere people. It matters how smooth, confident, and friendly a communicator was, not how honest the person was. So, when people base judgments of other's honesty based on how those people are acting (i.e., their demeanor; do they look honest, have good eye contact, appear confident and composed, etc.), they are wrong much of the time. This makes accuracy at detecting deception near chance (Levine et al., 2011). And this is just what most deception detection experiments find. People are only slightly better at chance at distinguishing truths from lies in deception experiments (Bond & DePaulo, 2006).

If deception cues are not good ways to detect deception, then what are? My work points to two. If possible, fact-check. Use evidence. If hard evidence is not available, listen to what is said, that is, pay attention to message content. Second, people can be persuaded to be honest. You can talk people into admitting the truth.

My thinking about deception was initially influenced by a well-documented finding called **truth-bias**. Truth-bias is the tendency to believe others regardless of whether or not the person is actually honest (Levine et al., 1999). The term was originally coined by McCornack and Parks (1986). Every study I have ever done, and I have done many, has supported truth-bias. People tend to believe others more often than not.

The truth-bias finding led my wife (Dr. Hee Sun Park, also a communication professor, and also a deception researcher) to the idea of **the veracity effect** (Levine et al., 1999). Veracity has to do with if something is true or false, honest or dishonest. The idea is that a sender's honesty (or veracity) affects accuracy at detecting truths and lies. As I said previously, overall, research shows that people are near chance at distinguishing truths from lies (Bond & DePaulo, 2006). Research also finds that people are truth-biased. Because people tend to believe others more often than not, if the person they are talking to is honest, then they are correct in believing them. If the person is actually lying, however, they tend to be wrong and are fooled. Although people are a little better than chance at distinguishing truths and lies, they get honest statements right much more often than lies. Accuracy for truths is above 50%, but accuracy for lies is below 50%. The veracity of the message affects accuracy, hence the veracity effect.

By the way, people tend to believe the people they know even more often than strangers. That is, the closer your relationship with someone, the more you will tend to be truth-biased. Because truth-bias blinds us to other's lies, we tend to be slightly worse at detecting deception in people we know best. This is the answer to question two above. The answer is false. It is easier to detect lies in strangers (McCornack & Parks, 1986). It was cool findings like these that made me want to work with Professor McCornack and got me into deception research in the first place.

Truth-bias led to another of my recent interesting findings. As I mentioned, people are truth-biased in my studies. I began to wonder why. Generally, when students participate in research, they know things are not always what they seem. Especially if you know you are in a deception experiment, would not that make you suspicious? My thinking was, if people are truth-biased even when they know they are in a deception experiment, this truth-bias must really be powerful and deeply ingrained in people.

Back in the late 1980s and 1990s, I thought of truth-bias as flawed thinking. It is called a bias after all. It must be irrational. Or, is it? What if most people were honest most of time? Then believing others makes good sense. Truth bias might actually be functional. This led me to research how often people lie.

My colleagues and I (Serota et al., 2010) did a nationally representative survey asking 1,000 adults in the USA how often they had lied in the past 24 hours. How many lies have you told today? What do you think the results were?

The results were that the average was between one and two lies per day. But, most people said they did not lie at all. A few people, in contrast, lied a whole lot. Almost half of the reported lies were told by just 5% of the sample. I call this finding *a few prolific liars*. Most people are honest most of the time, but there are a few people who lie a whole lot. As a consequence, the average number of lies (1.6 lies per day) does not reflect the average person (who reports zero lies).

We have now replicated the few prolific liar findings several times. We have surveyed college students and high school students and got access to prior research as well as a new large survey data from China, England, Germany, Japan, Korea, and Mexico. The pattern holds up. Most people are usually honest, but there are few chronic liars out there. So, may be truth-bias is not so much of a bias after all. May be people believe others more often than not because people are in fact honest more often than not. Communication would not work well if you had to second guess everything you were told or read.

There is one interesting variable that we have found so far predicts how often people lie. Age. Older people lie less(Serota et al., 2010). High school students reporting lying twice as often as college students. College students lie more than older adults. Our findings suggest honesty increases with age for most people. Most (but not all) people grow out of lying so to speak, and only lie occasionally as needed.

So far, we have learned that people tend to be truth-biased and that truth-bias may not be a bias at all because people tend to be honest about most things most of the time. But, people are not always honest and people do not always believe others. This led me to research why people actually lie (Levine et al., 2010b) and when people think others lie (e.g., Levine et al., 2010a).

Generally, people lie for a reason. That is, they lie why they have a motive to do so. However, the motives that prompt deception are not any different than those that guide honest communication. People want to gain desirable outcomes and avoid undesirable outcomes. People want to create a positive impression and maintain autonomy. When the truth works in a person's favor, or at least does not interfere with their goals and desires, almost everyone is honest (Levine et al., 2010b). It is only when the truth is a problem that the question of deception arises. So, for example, if a significant other gives you a gift that you like, you would almost certainly be honest in expressing your opinion of the gift. It is only when the gift is disliked and you have to worry about hurting the gift-giver's feeling or appearing ungrateful that the temptation to lie occurs.

Perhaps because people lie for a reason and are typically honest absent a motive to lie, people consider motive when judging the honesty of others. I call this idea the **Projected Motive Model** (Levine et al., 2010b). Charlie Bond independently had the same idea (Bond et al., 2013). The idea of projecting motive is that we tend to believe others when they lack an obvious motivation to lie, but truth-bias is diminished greatly when we think someone might have a reason to lie. An obvious example is when someone is trying to sell us something. In my experiments, I showed people videos of people who denied cheating or confessed to cheating. The confessions were almost always believed. Why would someone say the cheated when they did not? They have no apparent motive. Denials, in contrast, were believed less often. Recently, we found additional support for the projected motive model in opinions about art forgeries in Korea (Lee et al., 2021).

How then can we know if someone is actually lying or not? I have already told you about Charlie Bond's study asking people that question. The number one answer was that they will not look you in the eye. Most other common answers, you will remember, centered on other aspects nonverbal communication like acting nervous. You will also remember, I hope, that such beliefs have little validity. Eye contact is not a valid deception cue.

Hee Sun Park had a clever idea. Together we did a study asking the question a slightly different way. Instead of asking people their beliefs about how to detect deception, we asked people to think of a recent but memorable situation where the actually discovered a lie. Try this yourself. Can you think of a time you discovered, uncovered, or recognized a lie? How did you do that? How did you know you were lied to?

In our study (Park et al., 2002) titled, **How People Really Detect Lies**, we asked 200 participants to describe, in detail, a lie that they had detected. The results were very different than Charley Bond's eye contact findings. The detected lies in our data were uncovered though the use of various sorts of evidence rather than through the observation of nonverbal behaviors. There was information from third parties. Other people provided information that contradicted the lie. People used physical evidence. For example, a roommate denied using a computer owned by another roommate, but her login name was in a login spot. People confessed. The person being lied to already knew the truth, so the lie failed. In all, 98% of the reported instances of discovered deception involved discovery methods other than eye contact and other nonverbal clues. Further, most lies were detected after the fact at some later point in time. Leakage and deception cues had little to do with it.

The Park et al. data led Pete Blair and I to the idea of **Content in Context** (Blair et al., 2010). By content, we mean paying attention to what someone says rather than how they say it. We distinguish between communication content (the words and what the words mean) and **demeanor** (how someone presents themselves; do they seem honest). While deception research has traditionally focused on demeanor and **deception cues**, we think content is more valuable so long as the communication context is understood. Context has to do with the situation surrounding the communication. We believe that listening to what is said and comparing that to what is known given the context can be useful in detecting lies. In our series of experiments, providing people with valid context information greatly improved their ability detect lies (Blair et al., 2010).

In conclusion, deception is an intriguing area of research. Over the past 30 or so years, I have become increasingly obsessed with investigating if people can detect lies, and if so, how. One finding has led to another and I think my persistence in research has finally paid off. When I started doing research on deception, most research was based on the idea that lies could be detected by careful and knowledgeable observation of nonverbal behaviors. My earlier understanding of the research findings was that people could not really detect lies at rates much better than chance, and that truth-bias was a nearly inescapable cloud obscuring people judgment. After years of research, I now think that truth-bias is healthy and adaptive. It makes good sense to believe most people most of the time because most people are for the most part honest. To catch lies, do not focus nonverbal behaviors. They are misleading. You are likely to mistake a friendly extrovert for an honest person. Instead consider if the person has a motive to lie, listen to what the person is saying, and assess if what is said makes sense given what you know about the context. If evidence is available to fact-check, use it. That is how you can detect a lie.

REFERENCES

Blair, J. P., Levine, T. R., & Shaw, A. J. (2010). Content in context improves deception detection accuracy. *Human Communication Research, 36*(3), 423–442. https://doi.org/10.1111/j.1468-2958.2010.01382.x

Bond, C. F., & DePaulo, B. M. (2006). Accuracy of deception judgments. *Personality and Social Psychology Review, 10*(3), 214–234. https://doi.org/10.1207/s15327957pspr1003_2

Bond, C. F., & The Global Deception Research Team (2006). A world of lies. *Journal of Cross-Cultural Psychology, 37*(1), 60–74. https://doi.org/10.1177/0022022105282295

Bond, C. F., Jr., Howard, A. R., Hutchison, J. L., & Masip, J. (2013). Overlooking the obvious: Incentives to lie. *Basic and Applied Social Psychology, 35*(2), 212–221. https://doi.org/10.1080/01973533.2013.764302

DePaulo, B. M., Lindsay, J. J., Malone, B. E., Muhlenbruck, L., Charlton, K., & Cooper, H. (2003). Cues to deception. *Psychological Bulletin, 129*(1), 74–118. https://doi.org/10.1037/0033-2909.129.1.74

Lee, S. A., Park, H. S., & Levine, T. R. (2021). Judgments of honest and deceptive communication in art forgery controversies: Two field studies testing truth-default theory's projected motive model in Korea. *Asian Journal of Communication, 31*(6), 536–549. https://doi.org/10.1080/01292986.2021.1977354

Levine, T. R. (2020). *Duped: Truth-default theory and the social science of lying and deception.* University of Alabama Press.

Levine, T. R., Kim, R. K., & Blair, J. P. (2010a). (In)accuracy at detecting true and false confessions and denials: An initial test of a projected motive model of veracity judgments. *Human Communication Research, 36*(1), 81–101. https://doi:org/10.1111/j.1468-2958.2009.01369.x

Levine, T. R., Kim, R. K., & Hamel, L. M. (2010b). People lie for a reason: An experimental test of the principle of veracity. *Communication Research Reports, 27*(4), 271–285. https://doi.org/10.1080/08824096.2010.496334

Levine, T. R., Park, H. S., & McCornack, S. A. (1999). Accuracy in detecting truths and lies: Documenting the "veracity effect." *Communication Monographs, 66*(2), 125–144. https://doi.org/10.1080/03637759909376468

Levine, T. R., Serota, K. B. Shulman, H., Clare, D. D., Park, H. S., Shaw, A. S., Shim, J. C., & Lee, J. H. (2011). Sender demeanor: Individual differences in sender believability have a powerful impact on deception detection judgments. *Human Communication Research, 37*(3), 377–403. https://doi.org/10.1111/j.1468-2958.2011.01407.x

McCornack, S. A., & Parks, M. R. (1986). Deception detection and relationship development: The other side of trust. In M. L. McLaughlin (Ed.), *Communication yearbook 9* (pp. 377–389). Sage.

Park, H. S., Levine, T. R., McCornack, S. A., Morrison, K., & Ferrara, M. (2002). How people really detect lies. *Communication Monographs, 69*(2), 144–157. https://doi.org/10.1080/714041710

Serota, K. B., Levine, T. R., & Boster, F. J. (2010). The prevalence of lying in America: Three studies of reported deception. *Human Communication Research, 36*(1), 1–24. https://doi.org/10.1111/j.1468-2958.2009.01366.x

EFFECTIVE NONVERBAL FLIRTING CUES

Betty H. La France
Northern Illinois University

Jeffrey A. Hall
University of Kansas

A look across a bar. A loud laugh at someone's joke. A coy smile. Brushing against someone's arm. Leaning forward. Making eye contact and attention during a one-on-one conversation. These nonverbal behaviors are examples of flirtatious cues in that they convey attraction and relational interest (Hall & Xing, 2015). Flirting is crucial for relationships—especially in the early stages (La France & Hall, 2021). This chapter will present a short summary of how flirting has been defined, results from research investigating people's use of nonverbal cues and verbal messages associated with flirting, and then we consider the flirtatious nonverbal behaviors that are perceived to be most effective. We end this chapter with further thoughts to consider about how and why we flirt.

FLIRTING DEFINED

Hall (2013) specified that "flirting occurs when one person expresses sexual or romantic interest in another person, is the target of such an expression," or is attempting to assess whether this interest is mutual (p. 7). In addition to verbal messages, these types of expressions can be categorized into the traditional nonverbal cue categories: kinesics (body movement), haptics (touch), proxemics (space), oculesics (eye movement), vocalics (vocal sounds), chronemics (time), physical appearance, and facial expressions (e.g., smiling and eyebrow flashes).

People generally think of flirting happens at the beginning stages of courtship (Hall & Xing, 2015). In one of the earliest models of courtship, Givens's (1978) explicitly acknowledged the function of nonverbal cues in the initiation of romantic relationships. His five-stage model of courtship explicitly highlights the use of nonverbal signals to demonstrate interest to gain someone's attention, communicate interest, interact using verbal messages and nonverbal cues to maintain a connection, use physical touch to increase the intimacy of a relationship, and finally, to engage in sexual interactions (Givens, 1978). As will be described below, however, courtship is just one relational context in which flirting occurs. To address this chapter's guiding question regarding the effectiveness of nonverbal cues, we present current research investigating flirting beginning with a discussion about how to think about what is meant by effective.

WHAT NONVERBAL CUES ARE EFFECTIVE?

Answering simple questions about the effectiveness of flirtatious nonverbal cues is not straightforward. There are two main reasons for this difficulty. First, effectiveness can only be determined after considering the goal or objective of a particular action. That is, there is often an assumption that people flirt only to accomplish the goal of communicating romantic sexual interest as part of the courtship process. Second, there have only been a few investigations that have specifically examined how a single nonverbal cue leads to some predicted outcome. In any given naturalistic setting, however, a single nonverbal behavior is unlikely to produce reliable judgments across all people, in all settings, and across all situations. We use verbal messages, nonverbal cues, and situational attributes together to interpret any given communicative act. The following paragraphs will address the different reasons why people flirt and discuss the assessments people make about the effectiveness of specific nonverbal cues.

WHY WE FLIRT

People flirt for a variety of reasons including to induce jealously, to explore relationship potential, or to increase relational intimacy (Wade et al., 2021). Henningsen (2004) adds the following to the list: to intensify an existing relationship, to explore whether someone may be interested in a romantic relationship, to feel better about themselves by increasing self-esteem, to engage in a fun conversation (independent of relational consequence), and to gain some sort of tangible reward (like a server who flirts to increase customers' tips). These different reasons point to a much broader definition of flirting, a definition that extends beyond sexual and romantic relationships and moves the function of flirting into cultivating platonic relationships (Henningsen, 2004).

To complicate matters further, people have different flirting styles. Hall et al. (2010) demonstrated that there are different ways to flirt, different types of flirters, and differential verbal messages and nonverbal cues that are used depending on the kind of flirting being engaged. The five flirting styles are differentiated by personality, interpersonal goals, identity presentation, and the kinds of communication cues associated with these elements of style. *Traditional* flirting is characterized by performing gendered courtship scripts where men are the initiators of romantic and sexual interactions, and women provide receptivity cues (i.e., nonverbal cues that signal interest) regarding those advances. Recently, Hall and La France (2022) have argued that this type of interaction might be more usefully explained using an interdependence perspective whereby the roles during courtship are reconceptualized into a pursuer (or initiator) and pursued dynamic. This change promotes inclusivity and allows for a more nuanced understanding regarding courtship interactions as foundationally interdependent. *Physical* flirting prioritizes interactions where sexual interest is more obvious, assertive, and demonstrative. People who flirt using the *sincere* style focuses on expressing romantic interest through the development of an emotional, meaningful bond that reflects an intimate connection. The *playful* flirting style highlights the lighthearted nature of interpersonal interactions—a type of adult play where interaction is seen less as initiating a romantic relationship and viewed more as a way of having fun and enjoying social ties. The *polite* flirting style reflects a reserved and respectful approach to communicating interest where people prioritize their concern for appearing too forward, aggressive, or sexual means that subtle cues are preferred, and overt cues are eschewed.

It is important to keep in mind, our goals for flirting lead to different relational outcomes, and two people may have incompatible goals. For example, imagine hanging out with someone you like at a bar. You are attracted to this person. You think things are going well, so you are anticipating that the likelihood of pursuing a sexual relationship is moderately high. Given this person's behaviors during the night, you think s/he is really into you, too. At the end of the night, however, the person turns to you and remarks that you are a nice person and good friend. These two different relational assessments were generated from the same interaction. Furthermore, if these interactants explicitly shared their perceptions with each other, they likely would experience confusion, hurt feelings, disappointment, frustration, or other negative feelings.

Clearly, the previous example highlights how flirting is an inherently ambiguous set of verbal messages and nonverbal cues. But, they are ambiguous for a good reason. The communicative behaviors that are considered flirtatious in one setting (e.g., eye contact between two patrons at a bar) are interpreted as friendly in another setting (e.g., eye contact between two coworkers in a hallway at work) (Abbey, 1987). The same verbal and nonverbal communicative behaviors that are typically associated with flirting appear in cross-sex romantic and platonic (i.e., nonsexual) relationships (Egland et al., 1996). They have even been seen in therapeutic settings (Scheflen, 1965). Most recently, Hall (2016) has empirically demonstrated that flirting is a combination of seductive and friendly relational frames.

Even if we *only* consider the courtship context, there remain challenges in understanding what specific nonverbal cues are effective. Effective from one perspective can even mean biased from another perspective. Knowing which nonverbal behaviors are effective lies in how evolution has driven our adaptations to evolutionary pressures that differ between men and women (Buss, 1998; Schmitt, 2005). Sexual Strategies Theory (SST; Buss & Schmitt, 1993) provides a lens for examining why people flirt the way they do. SST argues that men tend to overestimate women's sexual interest because that biased conclusion places them at an evolutionary advantage. This bias reduces the likelihood that a man misses a courtship opportunity with a woman. Women, on the other hand, are likely to underestimate men's interest in commitment because that biased assessment gives them an advantage: it reduces the chances that a woman will perceive a man is committed to her when he is, in fact, not committed. The largest evolutionary costs for men (i.e., missing a woman's nonverbal cue that signals her interest) and women (i.e., misperceiving a man's nonverbal behavior as an indicator of commitment) are avoided when men perceive a woman is flirting and women read men as noncommittal (Haselton, 2003; Haselton & Buss, 2000; La France et al., 2009).

Another significant challenge is people are very likely to signal rather than clearly express their attraction. During courtship, people signal social and romantic interest in one another while advertising oneself as a quality partner (Grammer, 1990). Moore (2002) calls these "courtship signals," which include "nonverbal behaviors [that] serve to attract and maintain the attention of a potential partner" (p. 97). In cross-sex interactions, heterosexual people have the potential to be sexually interested in each other, but whether they actually are interested in each other varies widely and is probably unknown. As such, the most effective nonverbal flirting may be the behaviors that allow a person to discover the other person's openness to courtship, while subtly signaling their own availability—all the while looking good when doing it. This version of effectiveness is in direct opposition to effectiveness as defined by clarifying people's sexual and romantic intent.

IDENTIFICATION OF FLIRTATIOUS CUES

One common theme in flirting research is the identification of specific verbal messages and nonverbal cues men and women use during interactions (see Tables 1 and 2). Recall Hall et al.'s (2010) discovery of the different flirting styles discussed above. Recently, Hall and Xing (2015) empirically demonstrated that those styles are predictably related to using particular nonverbal behaviors. They asked strangers in heterosexual dyads to engage in a brief 10-minute discussion about different topics, and this conversation was videotaped. Trained coders watched those videotaped interactions and systematically noted instances of established flirtatious behaviors (e.g., gazing, palming, self-touch, and head nods). They found that traditional female flirts acted demure by incorporating teasing, palming, and disclosing. Traditional male flirts assertively shook their heads, leaned forward, and were fluid conversationalists. Female physical flirts provided affirmations but refrained from asking questions, giving compliments, leaning forward, or touching their bodies. Male physical flirts avoided affirmations, compliments, teasing, and flirtatious glances, favoring leaning forward and palming. The sincere flirting style was associated with demonstratively less teasing. Sincere female flirts engaged in flirtatious glances, smiled, laughed, and exhibited verbal fluency early on during interactions. Sincere male flirts also smiled, laughed, flirtatiously gazed, leaned forward, and avoided crossing their arms. Playful flirts asked fewer questions overall. Playful female flirts moved away from their conversational partner, played with what they were holding, and engaged in flirtatious glancing, whereas male playful flirts crossed their arms infrequently but complemented and looked flirtatiously at their interactional partner.

Table 1 *Hall and Xing's (2015) Coded Verbal and Nonverbal Factors*

Factor	Example Cue
Self-Touch	Body touch Hair touch Touch face
Affirmation	Nodding Saying yes
Joyful	Smiling Laughing
Expressive	Facial expressiveness Expressive gesticulation
Lips	Lip biting Lip licking Putting objects/hand in mouth
Disclosure	Depth Amount of talk
Play objects	Adjusting clothes Adjusting artifacts
Gaze	Flirtatious gaze Coy gaze

Table 2 *Hall and Xing's (2015) Coded Verbal and Nonverbal Indicators*

Behavioral Indicators of Flirting
Affirmation (nod, yes)
Arms (open versus crossed)
Ask questions
Breast present
Compliments
Conversational fluency
Disclosure (depth, amount)
Expressive (hands, face)
Fall in chair
Flirtatious glance
Gazing (direct versus away)
Joyful (smile, laugh)
Leaning toward versus back
Leg cross
Lips (bite, lick, hands in mouth)
Move closer
Palming
Pitch (high versus low)
Play cards (constant versus not)
Play objects (artifacts, clothes)
Self-deprecating comment
Self-touch (hair, face, body)
Shake head
Shoulder shrug
Teasing Count
Vocal expression (animated versus monotone)

In perhaps the most recent extensive list of flirting tactics to date, White et al. (2018) identified 450(!) verbal messages and nonverbal cues that someone could use to flirt. In addition to behaviors they labeled *creative* (e.g., wear red-colored clothing, set up a scavenger hunt, write a poem, and blow in someone's ear) they included communication cues that reflected modern technology use in developing interpersonal relationships. Sending a message on social media, adding someone on Facebook, sending a flirty text, using emojis, adding someone on Instagram, emailing someone, asking to "Netflix and chill," and putting one's phone down when someone approaches were behaviors added to the list of flirting possibilities. These nonverbal behaviors were complemented by other more traditional nonverbal signals of interest including smiling, acting like a lady/gentleman, listening, exuding confidence, and sharing common interests.

Clark et al. (2021) recently challenged the predominant focus on heterosexual flirting behavior especially as it has been traditionally situated within the kind of evolutionary framework discussed in this chapter. Arguing for the purposive use of a sexual minority sample, they explored whether gender, masculinity/femininity, sexual orientation, and adherence to gender role ideologies may impact the likelihood of flirting. Their sample (22% men, 77% women; 80% straight, 4% gay/lesbian, and 16% bisexual) responded to a list of flirting techniques that included nonverbal cues like giggling, eye contact, flexed muscles, and head tilts. When considered together, gender (their label for being a man or woman) most strongly predicted someone's likelihood of flirting when compared to masculinity/femininity and beliefs in traditional gender roles. Curiously, their findings also classified flirting behaviors into those performed primarily by women (e.g., lip licking), primarily by men (e.g., rough-housing) or were considered gender neutral (e.g., smiling). Also contrary to their expectation, sexual orientation did not influence flirting behavior. Rather, people's identification with masculine or feminine behavioral norms contributed to their flirting behavior. Women's endorsement of traditional gender roles also led to them flirting more frequently than women who did not adhere to such roles. Clark et al. cautiously conclude, "the longstanding reliance on gender as a primary predictor of flirting techniques is viable; indeed … this reliance on gender may be more broadly generalizable to sexual minority individuals than previous work has suggested" (p. 1700).

The identification of specific nonverbal behaviors used to flirt leads us to answer the question posed at the beginning of this chapter. We now turn to addressing the nonverbal cues that are perceived as most effective.

EFFECTIVENESS

In their influential and foundational work in the identification of effective flirtatious cues, Greer and Buss (1994) explored 34 tactics and the 122 acts associated with those tactics. Practicing good hygiene was the top frequently performed behavior that both men and women reported engaging in to flirt with someone. Good grooming, humor use, and sharing proxemic space were also behaviors people frequently used to flirt. Men and women agreed that the most effective ways to flirt with someone were to increase contact (nonsexual), create a romantic atmosphere, increase attention, and use one's friendship network to support one's advances. It is important to point out that frequency and among of talk time and showing nonverbal indicators of attention (e.g., motor mimicry and gazing) are also among the best indicators of attraction (La France & Hall, 2021). What is effective may also be a good signal of interest.

Wade and Feldman's (2016) investigation into the perceived effectiveness of flirtatious tactics functioned, in part, to explore how nonverbal behaviors may have changed over the decades since Greer and Buss's (1994) work. Establishing eye contact, making body contact, asking someone out, talking, and smiling were flirtatious behaviors that men used. Women engaged in smiling, eye contact, talking, teasing, and laughing at jokes when they flirted. The acts men and women perceived as most effective, however, were acts where the man was presented as the initiator. Asking a woman out, spending time with someone, kissing, holding hands, acting interested, making a woman laugh, and complimenting a woman were all flirtatious cues that were perceived as the most effective. Similarly, Wade and Slemp (2015) found that men's verbal messages and nonverbal cues that were closely aligned with ideals of commitment (e.g., holding hands, spending time together, kissing, and asking for a date) were perceived by women as most effective. By comparison, women's flirtatious behaviors that signaled more sexual openness (e.g., kissing, rubbing, moving close, touching, and dancing) were rated by men as most effective. Overall, these results are consistent with the traditional sexual script in North America where men are the initiators of sexual activity, and women are the gatekeepers of sexual behavior (Byers, 1996; Gagnon, 1990; La France & Hall, 2021).

Wade et al. (2021) investigated the tactics heterosexual women employ to flirt competitively. They argue that men and women use different nonverbal cues to flirt and performing those specific flirtatious behaviors are driven by the distinct evolutionary pressures men and women face when finding a partner (as described above). Wade et al. argue that one such pressure is the existence of rival suitors. Their investigation explored how women use nonverbal behaviors to compete with other women by focusing their attention on tie-signs. A tie-sign is a nonverbal display that an interpersonal bond exists (e.g., a wedding band). In a competitive flirting situation, a woman presents a tie-sign that is a signal to the other women present that she has identified her target of interest. The top three most effective nonverbal cues that operated as tie-signs were touching a man (i.e., arm, shoulder, chest, or leg), initiating eye contact with a man, and hugging him. Other tie-signs were laughing at the man's jokes, physically invading the competitor's space, and smiling, dancing, bumping/brushing/squeezing past, and waving at the man. Showing distaste for her competitors and flirting with the other men present to invite jealousy were also seen as competitive ways that women flirt.

White et al. (2018) examined what they termed atypical or creative flirting tactics, which they defined as the subtler or nonobvious signs of sexual interest. They argue that versatile or unpredictable flirting tactics are used on people who have typically grown accustomed to predictable strategies. White et al. had respondents rate their 450 flirting behaviors based on assessments of their effectiveness and usualness. The top five creative flirting tactics—nonverbal behaviors that were rated as the most *unusual*—were running from the FBI, giving a dead animal as a gift, acting like a casting agent, licking someone's face, and doing cartwheels. As might be expected, they also found that these odd flirting behaviors—although creative—were perceived as the most ineffective. The most typical nonverbal behaviors were smiling, being nice, and having a drink. The nonverbal cues that were rated the highest for *both* effectiveness and usualness were: expressing confidence, listening/engaging in a conversation, smiling, asking questions, and being nice. White et al.'s results demonstrate that some creativity in flirting (e.g., wearing trendy clothing) does pay off, but flirting behaviors that are too unusual are perceived very negatively (i.e., not effective). They also noted that while people preferred to flirt creatively, targets of flirtatious overtures prefer typical cues.

Often people are interested in knowing what specific flirting cues are effective because they want to know when someone is *definitely* flirting with them. Given the available evidence, such cues are elusive (La France & Hall, 2021). Why? Gersick and Kurzban (2014) argue that overt or boorish flirting comes at considerable social risk. White et al. (2018) have referred to this mismatch as a double standard: Flirters prefer to use subtle cues, and targets of flirtatious overtures want those cues to be unambiguous. Covert cues come at significantly less social risk and allow for plausible deniability (Gersick & Kurzban, 2014), which is an opportunity to save face if rejected.

Another way of thinking about the social costs of flirting is to consider the social skills required to initiate relationships. Apostolou et al. (2019) argue that in our contemporary dating environment, free mate choice is the norm in the United States and differs from historical societies where free mate selection occurred less frequently. As a result, individual traits useful for courtship (e.g., flirting skills, ability to detect flirting cues accurately) are crucial for successful flirting. Indeed, Apostolou et al. found a strong positive relationship between people's self-assessments of their ability to flirt and their ability to determine whether someone was flirting with them. This idea of flirting competence suggests that flirting is one indication of how people can initiate relationships generally and that there is considerable variation in people's flirting skills.

SUMMARY

At the risk of sounding flippant, one conclusion to be drawn from the research presented in this chapter is that the nonverbal communication cues that are effective flirting behaviors are the tactics that benefit all relationships: good hygiene, smiling, laughing, being an engaged conversationalist by asking questions and active listening, complimenting someone, being nice, and spending time together. Examining flirtatious behavior as a courtship tactic, however, reveals that specific cues address the differential evolutionary pressures that men and women experience and to which they have adapted. In courtship, effective nonverbal cues for men are behaviors that signal commitment (e.g., holding hands), whereas nonverbal indicators of sexual openness, such as kissing and touching, are perceived as most effective for women.

One last thought to note. No matter who you are, being effective at flirting requires some risk of rejection. No set of nonverbal behaviors can make someone be attracted to you in the same way you are attracted to them. But, without taking a risk, there can be no relationship.

REFERENCES

Abbey, A. (1987). Misperceptions of friendly behavior as sexual interest: A survey of naturally occurring incidents. *Psychology of Women Quarterly, 11*(2), 173–194. https://doi.org/10.1111/j.1471-6402.1987.tb00782.x

Apostolou, M., Papadopoulou, I., Christofi, M., & Vrontis, D. (2019). Mating performance: Assessing flirting skills, mate signal-detection ability, and shyness effects. *Evolutionary Psychology, 17*(3), 1–8. https://doi.org/10.1177/1474704919872416

Buss, D. M. (1998). Sexual strategies theory: Historical origins and current status. *The Journal of Sex Research, 35*(1), 19–31. http://www.jstor.org/stable/3813162

Buss, D. M., & Schmitt, D. P. (1993). Sexual strategies theory: An evolutionary perspective on human mating. *Psychological Review, 100*(2), 204–232. https://doi.org/10.1037/0033-295X.100.2.204

Byers, E. S. (1996). How well does the traditional sexual script explain sexual coercion? Review of a program of research. In E. S. Byers & L. F. O'Sullivan (Eds.), *Sexual coercion in dating relationships* (pp. 7–25). Haworth.

Clark, J., Oswald, F., & Pedersen, C. (2021). Flirting with gender: The complexity of gender in flirting behavior. *Sexuality & Culture, 25*, 1690–1706. https://doi.org/10.1007/s12119-021-09843-8

Egland, K. L., Spitzberg, B. H., & Zormeier, M. M. (1996). Flirtation and conversational competence in cross-sex platonic and romantic relationships. *Communication Reports, 9*(2), 105–117. https://doi.org/10.1080/08934219609367643

Gagnon, J. H. (1990). The explicit and implicit use of the scripting perspective in sex research. *Annual Review of Sex Research, 1*(1), 1–43. https://doi.org/10.1080/10532528.1990.10559854

Gersick, A., & Kurzban, R. (2014). Covert sexual signaling: Human flirtation and implications for other social species. *Evolutionary Psychology, 12*(3), 549–569. https://doi.org/10.1177%2F147470491401200305

Givens, D. B. (1978). The nonverbal basis of attraction: Flirtation, courtship, and seduction. *Psychiatry, 41*(4), 346–359. https://doi.org/10.1080/00332747.1978.11023994

Greer, A. E., & Buss, D. M. (1994). Tactics for promoting sexual encounters. *The Journal of Sex Research, 31*(3), 185–201. https://doi.org/10.1080/00224499409551752

Grammer, K. (1990). Strangers meet: Laughter and nonverbal signs of interest in opposite-sex encounters. *Journal of Nonverbal Behavior, 14*(4), 209–236. https://doi.org/10.1007/BF00989317

Hall, J. A. (2013). *The five flirting styles: Use the science of flirting to attract the love you really want.* Harlequin Nonfiction.

Hall, J. A. (2016). Interpreting social-sexual communication: Relational framing theory and social-sexual communication, attraction, and intent. *Human Communication Research, 42*(1), 138–164. https://doi.org/10.1111/hcre.12071

Hall, J. A., Carter, S., Cody, M. J., & Albright, J. M. (2010). Individual differences in the communication of romantic interest: Development of the Flirting Styles Inventory. *Communication Quarterly, 58*(4), 365–393. https://doi.org/10.1080/01463373.2010.524874

Hall, J. A., & La France, B. H. (2022). The role of humor in initiating romantic relationships. In T. E. Ford, W. Chłopicki, & G. Kuipers (Eds.), *Handbook of Humor Studies*. De Gruyter.

Hall, J. A., & Xing, J. A. (2015). The verbal and nonverbal correlates of the five flirting styles. *Journal of Nonverbal Behavior, 39*, 41–68. https://doi.org/10.1007/s10919-014-0199-8

Haselton, M. G. (2003). The sexual overperception bias: Evidence of a systematic bias in men from a survey of naturally occurring events. *Journal of Research in Personality, 37*(1), 34–47. https://doi.org/10.1016/S0092-6566(02)00529-9

Haselton, M. G., & Buss, D. M. (2000). Error management theory: A new perspective on biases in cross-sex mind reading. *Journal of Personality and Social Psychology, 78*(1), 81–91. https://doi.org/10.1037/0022-3514.78.1.81

Henningsen, D. D. (2004). Flirting with meaning: An examination of miscommunication in flirting interactions. *Sex Roles, 50*(7–8), 481–489. https://doi.org/10.1023/B:SERS.0000023068.49352.4b

La France, B. H., & Hall, J. A. (2021). Communication, courtship, and the emerging adult. In T. Coffelt's (Ed.), *Interpersonal sexual communication across the Lifespan*. Peter Lang.

La France, B. H., Henningsen, D. D., Oates, A., & Shaw, C. M. (2009). Social-sexual interactions? Meta-analyses of sex differences in perceptions of flirtatiousness, seductiveness, and promiscuousness. *Communication Monographs, 76*(3), 263–285. https://doi.org/10.1080/03637750903074701

Moore, M. M. (2002). Courtship communication and perception. *Perceptual and Motor Skills, 94*(1), 97–105. https://doi.org/10.2466/pms.2002.94.1.97

Scheflen, A. E. (1965). Quasi-courtship behavior in psychotherapy. *Psychiatry, 28*(3), 245–257. https://doi.org/10.1080/00332747.1965.11023433

Schmitt, D. P. (2005). Fundamentals of human mating strategies. In D. M. Buss's (Ed.), *The handbook of evolutionary psychology* (pp. 258–291). John Wiley & Sons.

Wade, J. T., & Feldman, A. (2016). Sex and the perceived effectiveness of flirtation techniques. *Human Ethology Bulletin, 31*(2), 30–44. https://doi.org/10.22330/heb/312/030-044

Wade, T. J., Fisher, M. L, & Clark, E. (2021). I saw him first: Competitive nonverbal flirting among women, the tactics used and their perceived effectiveness. *Personality and Individual Differences, 179*, 110898. https://doi.org/10.1016/j.paid.2021.110898

Wade, J. T., & Slemp, J. (2015). How to flirt best: The perceived effectiveness of flirtation techniques. *Interpersona, 9*(1), 32–43. https://doi.org/10.5964/ijpr.v9i1.178

White, J., Lorenz, H., Perilloux, C., & Lee, A. (2018). Creative casanovas: Mating strategy predicts using—but not preferring—atypical flirting tactics. *Evolutionary Psychological Science, 4*, 443–455. https://doi.org/10.1007/s40806-018-0155-7

NONVERBAL SKILLS FOR COMMUNICATING COMPETENTLY

Brian H. Spitzberg
San Diego State University

A commonplace assumption is that nonverbal behavior matters more in the communication of meaning than verbal communication. This is not a very accurate claim, because meaning depends significantly on the context and what meanings are being interpreted (e.g., detecting deception versus communicating empathy; Nazione et al., 2020; ten Brinke & Weisbuch, 2020), and because nonverbal behavior is rarely separated from verbal behavior in everyday interactions (Hellmann et al., 2020). Communication and meaning, taken broadly, are neurologically overlapping in perception and production, multimodal (many channels), concurrent (simultaneous), jointly and sequentially coconstructed (Bezemer & Jewitt, 2018; Healey, 2021; Jacob et al., 2012). Furthermore, translating such an aphorism into practical advice is not easy. Consider the following train of thought:

- You never get a second chance to make a first impression.
- To make a good first impression, *make eye contact.*
- To make a good first impression, make an *appropriate* amount of eye contact.
- To make a good first impression, make an appropriate amount of eye contact for the particular type of *relationship* you have with the others in the situation.
- To make a good first impression, make an appropriate amount of eye contact for the particular type of relationship you have with the others *in the situation for that particular culture.*

We all know that making a good impression on others is vital to our success in life and that making a good impression depends on our nonverbal behavior. Skill in nonverbal communication can significantly affect who we develop intimate relationships with (Sharon-David et al., 2019; Vacharkulksemsuk et al., 2016) and sustain (Faure et al., 2018), our intellectual (Schlegel et al., 2020) and academic success (Brackett et al., 2011), our occupational success

(Spitzberg, 2020), and our mental and physical health (Hesse et al., 2020). In an era of digital communication, emojis, avatars, virtual reality, near-universal access to personal music and video streaming, and the collapse of distance (Spitzberg, 2019), nonverbal communication will play no less of a role in our relationships. But how can we translate such findings into learnable skills? It's easy to recommend things like "a firm handshake," "good eye contact," "dress for success," and "a friendly smile." What's far, far more difficult to know in advance is how *much of and in what manner in which contexts* such behaviors are needed in any given communication encounter (how firm a handshake, how much eye contact, how dressy, how big a smile, etc.). This chapter provides some guidance for these questions. In particular, it seeks to address *which nonverbal skills are important for communicating competence.*

KEY CONCEPTS

Nonverbal behavior consists of the entire domain of a person's observable actions, conscious and unconscious. This includes, for example, averting eye contact and the blush a person reveals at feeling embarrassed, as well as the firm handshake and the smile at greeting some-one. *Nonverbal communication* consists of all nonverbal behaviors that do not involve words that result in you or others attributing meaning to actions (Spitzberg & Andersen, 2020). Nonverbal communication has many potential relationships with verbal communication (Spitzberg & Andersen, 2020). Some nonverbal communication is highly symbolic, such as traffic sign shapes or *iconic* gestures in particular cultural contexts (e.g., the peace sign, the hitchhiking thumb, and the "crazy" sign of circling a finger at one's head).

In relationship to verbal communication, nonverbal communication can *complement* (e.g., pointing in a given direction while describing how to get to the bookstore), *contradict* (e.g., your eyes dilate while trying to keep a deadpan face when dealt a good hand in a game of poker), *substitute* (e.g., nodding "yes" or "no" instead of saying "yes" or "no"), or *regulate* (e.g., raising your hand to indicate you want a turn to talk in class) interaction. While we rely substantially on both verbal and nonverbal behaviors in judging another person's emotion, according to one study, nonverbal behavior is as much as eight times more important to such judgments than verbal communication (Jacob et al., 2013).

Although nonverbal communication generally lacks many features of language (e.g., it has less formal syntax and semantic rules), it is also very similar to language in many ways. American sign language, for example, is a set of nonverbal skills for representing language. Lip-reading and reading Braille are ways of understanding language through the nonverbal behaviors of sight and touch. Wearing a uniform or badge is a way of communicating a lot of information nonverbally that can also be communicated verbally. If a picture can say a thousand words, it illustrates the complex interrelation between these modes of communicating.

A nonverbal communication *skill* is a repeatable sequence of behaviors capable of achieving some specified goals (Greene, 2021; Spitzberg, 2015b). You might be able to toss a basketball into a hoop by accident, but this does not qualify you as a professional basketball player. To be considered skilled, you must be able to consciously identify a goal and be able to call forth a sequence of actions that provide a reasonable likelihood of achieving these goals at least to some preferred degree at least some of the time (e.g., Spitzberg, 2015b). As a skill, it is always capable of improvement, so that the level and quality of goal achievement can increase as you refine your skills through experience, practice, feedback, and analysis (Donner & Hardy, 2015). Experience alone, however, is rarely a predictor of expertise (Rassafiani, 2009). People often bake in bad habits they learn over time. Instead, aside from individual differences in social abilities, competence is achieved through systematic expert instruction, rehearsal, and feedback. So professional poker players and actors generally get better at their crafts the more they systematically study their craft, seek qualified feedback, and train toward improvement until their expertise is less about being able to articulate the rules of competent interaction and more about being able to perform to these rules without consciously thinking about the rules (McIlroy et al., 2012; Swan et al., 2020).

The reality is that people rarely care about a skill by itself—what they care about is whether or not a given skill produces desirable outcomes. We generally do not care whether or not someone can ask a question or make eye contact. We care whether they perform these skills in ways that competently lead to personally, relationally, or socially desirable outcomes (Spitzberg, 2013, 2015b). The judgment of a skill's competence is, in turn, generally based on two judgments—appropriateness and effectiveness (Spitzberg & Cupach, 1984).

Appropriateness is the judgment that a skill is legitimate or fitting in a given context. Smiling during a funeral tends to be evaluated differently than smiling at a party (unless the funeral is a wake or similar cultural episode). *Effectiveness* is the judgment that a skill has successfully accomplished a preferred outcome. This is not to say that the skill achieved a satisfying outcome, because there exist no-win situations in which the most effective thing to do is do what produces the least costly or harmful outcomes. Thus, competence hinges on forms of subjective human judgment, both from the communicator's and the cointeractant's perspective (i.e., judging the choices of action that will be judged as most appropriate and effective; MacIntyre & Ayers-Glassey, 2020). From this perspective, there are two key components to nonverbal skills: the things we are able to *do* nonverbally (i.e., skills), and the judgments we make about the competence of those skills (i.e., appropriateness and effectiveness).

GUIDING PRINCIPLES

Before identifying valuable nonverbal skills, a few important principles require consideration. First, having nonverbal skills is not the same thing as using them. You may be *able* to smile and make eye contact, but you may not be motivated to in a given situation, and you may not know how in a particular context (e.g., how much to smile when someone compliments you—too much and you might look egotistical, too little and you might look unappreciative). Thus, *competence is a function of motivation, knowledge, and skills* (Spitzberg & Cupach, 1984, 2011).

Second, *the competence of nonverbal skills depends on the context* (Spitzberg & Brunner, 1991). In general, we view people who match or synchronize with our own nonverbal behavior as more competent (Kim, 2015). Even this generalization, however, will depend in part on the context. There are at least five levels of understanding the nature of a context: cultural, chronological, situational, relational, and functional (Spitzberg, 2013).

At the *cultural* level, the context is the patterns of intergenerational and transmissible beliefs, values, attitudes, and behavioral rituals of a group of people (Spitzberg & Chagnon, 2009). Different cultures have somewhat different expectations for what constitutes competent nonverbal behavior in any of the other levels of a communication context. For example, although most college students perceive their professors as more competent when nonverbally expressive and relaxed in movement, there are also cultural differences in the relative importance of these factors (Georgakopoulos & Guerrero, 2010). At the *chronological* level, the context involves all those aspects of timing that affect communication, such as what constitutes "showing up on time," speaking pace or rate, the timing with which certain actions are considered appropriate or inappropriate (e.g., when should a "first kiss" occur in a dating relationship), and so forth. At the *situational* level, communication occurs in different physical environments. Temperature, expansiveness of physical space, background noise, the comfort or discomfort of seating or standing arrangements, the color of the environment, and so forth, all can significantly affect what nonverbal communication skills are most appropriate. At the *relational* level, different skills are likely to be considered competent in different types of relationships, and at different stages of relationships. You probably have a very different level of informality with a best friend or romantic partner than you do with your coworkers, or your teacher, or your boss, or your classmates who are mere acquaintances. Finally, at the *functional* level, which nonverbal skills are most competent depend significantly on the purpose or objectives of the communication encounter. You are likely to need somewhat different nonverbal skills to manage a conflict encounter than you do a courtship or flirtation encounter (unless the flirtation encounter becomes a conflict encounter).

Third, *too much (and often, too little) of any skill is likely to be judged incompetent.* Textbooks often say things like "make eye contact when meeting someone," "use a firm handshake" and "dress up for a job interview," when we intuitively understand that we can make too much or too little eye contact, grip too softly or firmly, and dress too elaborately or too informally for a job interview. People can stand too far and too close to you (Welsch et al., 2019). Most nonverbal skills are therefore curvilinear to competence—that is, a moderate amount of the skill is viewed as more competent than too little or too much (Spitzberg, 2013; Spitzberg & Cupach, 2011). For example, research shows that communicators who display too much confidence (Tenney et al., 2019) or are too emotionally or relationally expressive (Marinova et al., 2018) are viewed as less competent rather than more competent. Related to this principle is that having more skills does not mean they will be used in the most competent ways. For example, people may engage in skilled routine deception in relating with others (Horan & Booth-Butterfield, 2013).

Fourth, nonverbal skills in practice are always intertwined with verbal skills. Just as someone can look very physically attractive, until they open their mouth, so can any non-verbal skill be undone by the verbal skills that accompany it (or do not accompany it). For example, the ability to detect deception depends significantly on verbal interrogation skills; relying on nonverbal behaviors alone achieves accuracy rates no better than chance (Levine, 2018; Sporer & Schwandt, 2007).

Fifth, *nonverbal skills can (and should) be understood at both macro and micro levels* (Rasipuram & Jayagopi, 2018; Spitzberg, 2015a). Some nonverbal skills are best considered for the sake of learning at relatively specific levels of analysis. For example, it is relatively easy to think about smiling, eye contact, dress, and gestures as relatively specific and iso-lated types of skills that can be learned and enacted. Other skills, however, are far more macro or composite in nature. For example, research has investigated the holistic ability to accurately perceive, or "read" nonverbal behavior, including the skills of interpreting emotions (Elfenbein et al., 2010), romantic or sexual interest (Bello, 2010; Moore, 2010), and detecting deception (Hauch et al., 2016). Research has also examined the ability to accurately express emotions in ways that can be easily or accurately interpreted by others (Elfenbein et al., 2010), to communicate dominance or composure (Burgoon et al., 2021), to deceive (Verigin et al., 2019), and to communicate affection (Redlick & Vangelisti, 2018). Others have studied the ability to match (i.e., reciprocate similar skills and actions, such as smiling when another person smiles) or compensate (i.e., to reflect the opposite type of skill or action, such as leaning back when someone leans toward you) another's nonverbal actions (Andersen et al., 1998). Other examples of macro-level nonverbal skills include dis-playing charisma (Heide, 2013), immediacy or empathy (Kraft-Todd et al., 2017), which are holistic composites of behaviors such as moderately open body posture, eye contact, touch, relatively equal eye level, avoidance of physical barriers, and matching facial expression (Kraft-Todd et al., 2017).

NONVERBAL SKILLS

The study of nonverbal communication has historically divided nonverbal skills into domains of study that reflect a particular channel or mode of behavior: haptics (the study of touch), oculesics (the study of eye contact, gaze, dilation, etc.), kinesics (the study of body movement, including facial expressions, body lean, nodding, gestures, etc.), proxemics (the study of use of space, such as personal space), chronemics (the study of the use of time as communication), and paralinguistics (the study of the nonverbal aspects of speech, such as rate, pitch, prosody, volume, etc.). These domains work well enough for examining the more micro nonverbal skills but tend to blur when considering macro-level nonverbal skills, which tend to be comprised of multiple forms of behavior that cross over these domains of activity. There are two broad ways of considering macro-level nonverbal skills. One is a *dimensional* approach, which attempts to identify the underlying dimensions of nonverbal communication skills. You can think of an underlying dimension as an essential evaluative theme that ranges along two ends of a continuum, often from low-to-high, or across opposites. For example, Mehu and Scherer (2015) identified dimensions of facial emotion: *valence* (pleasant/unpleasant), *arousal* (low-to-high physical or physiological activation), *dominance* (low-to-high ability to control situation), and *unpredictability* (usual-familiar-expected to unusual-unpredictable-unexpected). They found that people process specific micro-facial behaviors (e.g., cheek raised jaw dropped, eyelids tight, and brow raised) and interpret them through the more macro-level dimensions in order to arrive at a judgment of what emotion is being experienced. These and similar dimensions have been identified across a variety of nonverbal interactions (e.g., Burgoon & Hale, 1987) and are often distinct to a particular topic. For example, judging a person's dishonesty appears to hinge on two dimensions (Hamlin et al., 2018): difficulty (i.e., cues of anxiety; e.g., gaze aversion, postural shifts, and nonfluencies) and involvement (i.e., cues of verbal and vocal involvement; e.g., expressive face, hand gestures, and response length).

Another approach to dimensions attempts to bridge the macro- and micro-levels of nonverbal communication skills. Research indicates that most nonverbal behaviors can be grouped into four skill clusters, or dimensions (Spitzberg et al., 1990). These skills include *attentiveness skills* (i.e., attention to, interest in, and concern for conversational partner), *composure skills* (i.e., confidence, assertiveness, and relaxation), *expressiveness skills* (i.e., animation and variation in verbal and nonverbal forms of expression, including face, voice, body, and opinion), and *coordination skills* (i.e., the nondisruptive negotiation of speaking turns, conversational initiation, and conversational closings). These skills appear to represent the vital functions of asserting oneself (i.e., composure and expressiveness) as well as orienting to the other person(s) in the encounter (i.e., attentiveness and coordination). In any communication encounter, competent nonverbal skills will function at their most macro-level to enable the appropriate and effective promotion of one's own interests, as well as the interests of the other persons involved in the encounter (Spitzberg, 2013; Spitzberg & Cupach, 2011).

A second approach to macro-level nonverbal skills is to identify specific skills that are important to particular contexts or interaction functions. Research has, for example, examined the nonverbal skills involved in competent flirtation (e.g., Egland et al., 1996), courtship (e.g., Moore, 2010; Vannier & O'Sullivan, 2011), negotiation (e.g., Semnani-Azad & Adair, 2011), teaching (Allen et al., 2006), health interactions (e.g., Henry et al., 2012), and successful sales (e.g., Pauser et al., 2018), just to name a few. The likelihood is that any given area of professional or career interest, hobby, sport, or interest, will have been investigated by scholars in the pursuit of identifying important nonverbal skills. If you have the motivation, then you can obtain the knowledge and the skills through further education, both through your own efforts, and the efforts of your instructors.

Given the principles discussed earlier, it is possible to consider research across these research traditions and speculate on the most general competent nonverbal skills. Research at the micro-level of nonverbal skills has tended to show, all other things being equal, that the communication skills listed in Table 1 tend to be strongly associated with competent communication (Spitzberg & Dillard, 2002).

Table 1 Generally Competent Micro-Level Nonverbal Skills

Appropriate lean toward partner (neither too forward nor too far back)
Appropriate posture (neither too closed/formal nor too open/informal)
Avoiding nonverbal adaptors (i.e., nervous "ticks" like twirling hair or tapping a foot or pen)
Avoiding response latencies (i.e., minimizing awkward silences between speaking turns)
Expressive or regulative head movements, such as head nods in response to partner statements
Facial expressiveness (neither blank nor exaggerated)
Moderate eye gaze (i.e., steady direction of eyes toward other interactants)
Moderated (adapted to context) speaking volume
Moderately disproportionate talk time (i.e., talking 60–70% of the proportionate time based on the interaction time allowed and the number of participants)
Occasional eye contact
Occasional moderated (adapted to context) smiles and/or laughter
Occasional, well-timed gestures to emphasize or regulate what is being said
Speaking fluency (pauses, silences, "uh," etc.)
Speaking rate (neither too slow nor too fast)
Vocal confidence (neither too tense/nervous nor overly confident sounding)
Vocal variety (neither overly monotone nor dramatic voice)

For any more macro-level contextual type of skill, research has indicated various skills that are associated with the function of interest. For example, both direct (e.g., kissing, hugging, and holding hands) and indirect (helping with a task and lending use of a car) nonverbal behaviors are used in communicating affection (Floyd, 2014). In contrast, communicating immediacy in an educational context involves making eye contact, relaxed body posture, gestures, casual touching (e.g., on the shoulder), smiles, less formal dress, open body position and posture, vocal expressiveness, and proximal movement through the classroom (Frymier et al., 2019). In contrast, if you want to communicate power rather than immediacy or affection, nonverbal skills portray inattention to others, initiation of handshake, invasive proximity behavior, touch initiation, gaze, eye contact while speaking, assertive or aggressive facial expression, gestures, fewer self-touching behaviors, upturned head orientation, and erect posture (Andersen et al., 1998; Burgoon et al., 2021).

CONCLUSION

Nonverbal communication research has generated a rich set of findings about how to communicate competently. In general, communication competence will be facilitated by nonverbal behaviors that reveal an interest in and attentiveness toward others, that display an ability to smoothly manage the ebb and flow of conversation, that reveal emotions and intended meanings through expressive behavior, and that demonstrate a calm and collected demeanor suggesting that one is in control of his or her own behavior. Beyond this, these actions should be adapted to the particular function of the situation, the place, the type of relationship, and the cultural expectations.

As the rapid evolution of media continues to converge across face-to-face and distance contexts, and as media become richer in allowing people to communicate their entire verbal and nonverbal presence in the encounter (Spitzberg, 2019), the more important nonverbal communication is likely to become, particularly given the extent to which our screen time with our devices may displace our face-to-face proximal interactions (Twenge & Spitzberg, 2020; Twenge et al., 2019). Even though nonverbal communication tends to be managed more unconsciously than verbal communication, it is still subject to learning, practice, and feedback. Assuming you are motivated to enhance your nonverbal skills in any given context, it is likely that scholars have already conducted important research in the area, pointing to specific activities or behaviors that you could identify and begin to incorporate into your everyday communication. As but one example that may apply to many of you reading this chapter, research has shown that a casual or incidental touch of a patron can significantly increase the tips that waiters earn and increase the sales a sales associate makes (Jacob & Guéguen, 2012; Jewell, 2008; Luangrath et al., 2020). It seems that research sometimes can pay off.

REFERENCES

Allen, M., Witt, P., & Wheeless, L. (2006). The role of teacher immediacy as a motivational factor in student learning: Using meta-analysis to test a causal model. *Communication Education, 55*(1), 21–31. https://doi.org/10.1080/03634520500343368

Andersen, P. A., Guerrero, L. K., Buller, D. B., & Jorgensen, P. (1998). An empirical comparison of three theories of nonverbal immediacy exchange. *Human Communication Research, 24,* 501–536. https://doi.org/10.1111/j.1468-2958.1998.tb00429.x

Bello, R. S. (2010). Verbal and nonverbal methods for expressing appreciation in friendships and romantic relationships: A cross-cultural comparison. *International Journal of Intercultural Relations, 34*(3), 294–302. https://doi.org/10.1016/j.ijintrel.2010.02.007

Bezemer, J., & Jewitt, C. (2018). Multimodality: A guide for linguists. In L. Litosseliti (Ed.), *Research methods in linguistics* (2nd ed., pp. 281–304). Bloomsbury Publishing. http://dx.doi.org/10.5040/9781350043466.ch-012

Brackett, M. A., Rivers, S. E., & Salovey, P. (2011). Emotional intelligence: Implications for personal, social, academic, and workplace success. *Social and Personality Psychology Compass, 5*(1), 88–103. https://doi.org/10.1111/j.1751-9004.2010.00334.x

Burgoon, J. K., & Hale, J. L. (1987). Validation and measurement of the fundamental themes of relational communication. *Communication Monographs, 54*, 18–41. https://doi.org/10.1080/03637758709390214

Burgoon, J. K., Wang, X., Chen, X., Pentland, S. J., & Dunbar, N. E. (2021). Nonverbal behaviors "speak" relational messages of dominance, trust, and composure. *Frontiers in Psychology, 12*, 624177. https://doi.org/10.3389/fpsyg.2021.624177

Donner, Y., & Hardy, J. (2015). Piecewise power laws in individual learning curves. *Psychonomic Bulletin & Review, 22*(5), 1308–1319. https://psycnet.apa.org/doi/10.3758/s13423-015-0811-x

Egland, K. L., Spitzberg, B. H., & Zormeier, M. M. (1996). Flirtation and conversational competence in cross-sex platonic and romantic relationships. *Communication Reports, 9*, 105–118. https://doi.org/10.1080/08934219609367643

Elfenbein, H. A., Foo, M. D., Mandal, M., Biswal, R., Eisenkraft, N., Lim, A., & Sharma, S. (2010). Individual differences in the accuracy of expressing and perceiving nonverbal cues: New data on an old question. *Journal of Research in Personality, 44*(2), 199–206. https://doi.org/10.1016/j.jrp.2010.01.001

Faure, R., Righetti, F., Seibel, M., & Hofmann, W. (2018). Speech is silver, nonverbal behavior is gold: How implicit partner evaluations affect dyadic interactions in close relationships. *Psychological Science, 29*(11), 1731–1741. https://doi.org/10.1177/0956797618785899

Floyd, K. (2014). Empathic listening as an expression of interpersonal affection. *International Journal of Listening, 28*(1), 1–12. https://doi.org/10.1080/10904018.2014.861293

Frymier, A. B., Goldman, Z. W., & Claus, C. J. (2019). Why nonverbal immediacy matters: A motivation explanation. *Communication Quarterly, 67*(5), 526–539. https://doi.org/10.1080/01463373.2019.1668442

Georgakopoulos, A., & Guerrero, L. K. (2010). Student perceptions of teachers' nonverbal and verbal communication: A comparison of best and worst professors across six cultures. *International Education Studies, 3*(2), 3–16. http://dx.doi.org/10.5539/ies.v3n2p3

Greene, J. O. (2021). *Essentials of communication skill and skill enhancement: A primer for students and professionals.* Routledge.

Hamlin, I., Wright, G. R. T., Van der Zee, S., & Wilson, S. (2018). The dimensions of deception detection: Self-reported deception cue use is underpinned by two broad factors. *Applied Cognitive Psychology, 32*(3), 307–314. http://dx.doi.org/10.1002/acp.3402

Hauch, V., Sporer, S. L., Michael, S. W., & Meissner, C. A. (2016). Does training improve the detection of deception? A meta-analysis. *Communication Research, 43*(3), 283–343. https://doi.org/10.1177/0093650214534974

Healey, P. G. T. (2021). Human-like communication. In S. Muggleton & N. Charter (Eds.), *Human like machine intelligence* (pp. 137–151). Oxford University Press.

Heide, F. J. (2013). "Easy to sense but hard to define": Charismatic nonverbal communication and the psychotherapist. *Journal of Psychotherapy Integration, 23*(3), 305–319. https://doi.org/10.1037/a0032481

Hellmann, A., Ang, L., & Sood, S. (2020). Towards a conceptual framework for analysing impression management during face-to-face communication. *Journal of Behavioral and Experimental Finance, 25*, 100265. https://doi.org/10.1016/j.jbef.2020.100265

Henry, S. G., Fuhrel-Forbis, A., Rogers, M. A. M., & Eggly, S. (2012). Association between nonverbal communication during clinical interactions and outcomes: A systematic review and meta-analysis. *Patient Education and Counseling, 86*(3), 297–315. https://doi.org/10.1016/j.pec.2011.07.006

Hesse, C., Floyd, K., Rains, S. A., Mikkelson, A. C., Pauley, P. M., Woo, N. T., Custer, B. E., & Duncan, K. L. (2020). Affectionate communication and health: A meta-analysis. *Communication Monographs, 88*(2), 194–218. https://doi.org/10.1080/03637751.2020.1805480

Horan, S., & Booth-Butterfield, M. (2013). Understanding the routine expression of deceptive affection in romantic relationships. *Communication Quarterly, 61*(2), 195–216. https://doi.org/10.1080/01463373.2012.751435

Jacob, C., & Guéguen, N. (2012). The effect of physical distance between patrons and servers on tipping. *Journal of Hospitality & Tourism Research, 36*(1), 25–31. https://doi.org/10.1177/1096348010388660

Jacob, H., Kreifelts, B., Brück, C., Erb, M., Hösl, F., & Wildgruber, D. (2012). Cerebral integration of verbal and nonverbal emotional cues: Impact of individual nonverbal dominance. *NeuroImage, 61*(3), 738–747. https://doi.org/10.1016/j.neuroimage.2012.03.085

Jacob, H., Kreifelts, B., Brück, C., Nizielski, S., Schütz, A., & Wildgruber, D. (2013). Nonverbal signals speak up: Association between perceptual nonverbal dominance and emotional intelligence. *Cognition & Emotion, 27*(5), 783–799. https://doi.org/10.1080/02699931.2012.739999

Jewell, C. N. (2008). Factors influencing tipping behavior in a restaurant. *Psi Chi Journal of Undergraduate Research, 13*(1), 38–48. https://doi.org/10.24839/1089-4136.jn13.1.38

Kim, Y. Y. (2015). Achieving synchrony: A foundational dimension of intercultural communication competence. *International Journal of Intercultural Relations, 48*, 27–37. https://doi.org/10.1016/j.ijintrel.2015.03.016

Kraft-Todd, G. T., Reinero, D. A., Kelley, J. M., Heberlein, A. S., Baer, L., & Riess, H. (2017). Empathic nonverbal behavior increases ratings of both warmth and competence in a medical context. *PLoS ONE, 12*(5), 1–16. https://doi.org/10.1371/journal.pone.0177758

Levine, T. R. (2018). Scientific evidence and cue theories in deception research: Reconciling findings from meta-analyses and primary experiments. *International Journal of Communication, 12*, 2461–2479. https://ijoc.org/index.php/ijoc/article/view/7838

Luangrath, A. W., Peck, J., & Gustafsson, A. (2020). Should I touch the customer? Rethinking interpersonal touch effects from the perspective of the touch initiator. *Journal of Consumer Research, 47*(4), 588–607. https://doi.org/10.1093/jcr/ucaa021

MacIntyre, P. D. & Ayers-Glassey, S. (2020). Competence appraisals: Dynamic judgements of communication competence in real time. In W. Lowie, M., Michel, M. Keijzer, & R. Steinkrauss (Eds.), *Usage-based dynamics in second language development* (pp. 155–175). Multilingual Matters. https://doi.org/10.21832/9781788925259-010

Marinova, D., Singh, S. K., & Singh, J. (2018). Frontline problem-solving effectiveness: A dynamic analysis of verbal and nonverbal cues. *Journal of Marketing Research, 55*(2), 178–192. https://doi.org/10.1509/jmr.15.0243

McIlroy, R., Stanton, N., & Remington, B. (2012). Developing expertise in military communications planning: Do verbal reports change with experience? *Behaviour & Information Technology, 31*(6), 617–629. https://doi.org/10.1080/0144929X.2010.492239

Mehu, M., & Scherer, K. R. (2015). Emotion categories and dimensions in the facial communication of affect: An integrated approach. *Emotion, 15*(6), 798–811. https://doi.org/10.1037/a0039416.supp

Moore, M. M. (2010). Human nonverbal courtship behavior—A brief historical review. *Journal of Sex Research, 47*(2), 171–180. https://doi.org/10.1080/00224490903402520

Nazione, S., Nazione, A., & Griner, T. (2020). How do perceptions of verbal statements and nonverbal actions as empathetic differ by medical appointment context? *Patient Education and Counseling, 103*(2), 410–413. https://doi.org/10.1016/j.pec.2019.08.016

Pauser, S., Wagner, U., & Ebster, C. (2018). An investigation of salespeople's nonverbal behaviors and their effect on charismatic appearance and favorable consumer responses. *Journal of Personal Selling & Sales Management, 38*(3), 344–369. https://doi.org/10.1080/08853134.2018.1480383

Rasipuram, S., & Jayagopi, D. B. (2018). Automatic assessment of communication skill in interview-based interactions. *Multimedia Tools and Applications, 77*(14), 18709–18739. https://doi.org/10.1007/s11042-018-5654-9

Rassafiani, M. (2009). Is length of experience an appropriate criterion to identify level of expertise? *Scandinavian Journal of Occupational Therapy, 16*(4), 247–256. https://doi.org/10.3109/11038120902795441

Redlick, M. H., & Vangelisti, A. L. (2018). Affection, deception, and evolution: Deceptive affectionate messages as mate retention behaviors. *Evolutionary Psychology, 16*(1). https://doi.org/10.1177/1474704917753857

Semnani-Azad, Z., & Adair, W. L. (2011). The display of "dominant" nonverbal cues in negotiation: The role of culture and gender. *International Negotiation, 16*(3), 451–479. https://doi.org/10.1163/157180611X592950

Sharon-David, H., Mizrahi, M., Rinott, M., Golland, Y., & Birnbaum, G. E. (2019). Being on the same wavelength: Behavioral synchrony between partners and its influence on the experience of intimacy. *Journal of Social and Personal Relationships, 36*(10), 2983–3008. https://doi.org/10.1177/0265407518809478

Spitzberg, B. H., & Cupach, W. R. (1984). *Interpersonal communication competence*. Sage.

Spitzberg, B. H. (2013). (Re)Introducing communication competence to the health professions (Special issue: Interdisciplinary Perspectives on Medical Error). *Journal of Public Health Research, 2*(3), 126–135. https://doi.org/10.4081/jphr.2013.e23

Spitzberg, B. H. (2015a). Assessing the state of assessment: Communication competence. In A. F. Hannawa & B. H. Spitzberg (Eds.), *Communication competence* (pp. 559–584). De Gruyter Mouton.

Spitzberg, B. H. (2015b). The composition of competence: Communication skills. In A. F. Hannawa & B. H. Spitzberg (Eds.), *Communication competence* (pp. 237–269). De Gruyter Mouton.

Spitzberg, B. H. (2019). Traces of pace, place and space in personal relationships: The chronogeometrics of studying relationships at scale [Distinguished Scholar lead essay]. *Personal Relationships, 26*(2), 184–208. https://doi.org/10.1111/pere.12280

Spitzberg, B. H. (2020). College, communication, and careers. In B. H. Spitzberg, H. E. Canary, & D. J. Canary (Eds.), *The communication capstone: The communication inquiry and theory experience* (pp. 338–351). Cognella.

Spitzberg, B. H. & Andersen, P. A. (2020). Orienting to communication: The nature of communication. In B. H. Spitzberg, H. E. Canary, & D. J. Canary (Eds.), *The communication capstone: The communication inquiry and theory experience* (pp. 14–30). Cognella.

Spitzberg, B. H., Brookshire, R. G., & Brunner, C. C. (1990). The factorial domain of interpersonal skills. *Social Behavior and Personality, 18*, 137–150. https://doi.org/10.2224/sbp.1990.18.1.137

Spitzberg, B. H., & Brunner, C. C. (1991). Toward a theoretical integration of context and competence inference research. *Western Journal of Speech Communication, 55*(1), 28–46. https://doi.org/10.1080/10570319109374369

Spitzberg, B. H., & Chagnon, G. (2009). Conceptualizing intercultural communication competence. In D. K. Deardorff (Ed.), *The SAGE handbook of intercultural competence* (pp. 2–52). Sage.

Spitzberg, B. H., & Cupach, W. R. (2011). Interpersonal skills. In M. L. Knapp & J. A. Daly (Eds.), *Handbook of interpersonal communication* (4th ed., pp. 481–524). Sage.

Spitzberg, B. H., & Dillard, J. P. (2002). Meta-analysis, social skills, and interpersonal competence. In M. Allen, R. Preiss, K. Dindia, B. Gayle, and N. Burrell (Eds.), *Interpersonal communication: Advances through meta-analysis* (pp. 89–107). Erlbaum.

Sporer, S. L., & Schwandt, B. (2007). Moderators of nonverbal indicators of deception: A meta-analytic synthesis. *Psychology, Public Policy, and Law, 13*(1), 1–34. https://doi.org/10.1037/1076-8971.13.1.1

Swan, R. H., Plummer, K. J., & West, R. E. (2020). Toward functional expertise through formal education: Identifying an opportunity for higher education. *Educational Technology Research and Development, 68*(5), 2551–2568. https://doi.org/10.1007/s11423-020-09778-1

ten Brinke, L., & Weisbuch, M. (2020). How verbal-nonverbal consistency shapes the truth. *Journal of Experimental Social Psychology, 89*, 103978. https://doi.org/10.1016/j.jesp.2020.103978

Tenney, E. R., Meikle, N. L., Hunsaker, D., Moore, D. A., & Anderson, C. (2019). Is overconfidence a social liability? The effect of verbal versus nonverbal expressions of confidence. *Journal of Personality and Social Psychology, 116*(3), 396–415. https://doi.org/10.1037/pspi0000150

Twenge, J. M., & Spitzberg, B. H. (2020). Declines in non-digital social interaction among Americans, 2003-2017. *Journal of Applied Social Psychology, 6*(1), 329–345. https://doi:10.1111/jasp.12665

Twenge, J. M., Spitzberg, B. H., & Campbell, W. K. (2019). Less in-person social interaction with peers among U.S. adolescents in the 21st century and links to loneliness. *Journal of Social and Personal Relationships, 36*(6), 1892–1913. https://doi.org/10.1177/0265407519836170

Vacharkulksemsuk, T., Reit, E., Khambatta, P., Eastwick, P. W., Finkel, E. J., & Carney, D. R. (2016). Dominant, open nonverbal displays are attractive at zero-acquaintance. *PNAS Proceedings of the National Academy of Sciences of the United States of America, 113*(15), 4009–4014. https://doi.org/10.1073/pnas.1508932113

Vannier, S., & O'Sullivan, L. (2011). Communicating interest in sex: Verbal and nonverbal initiation of sexual activity in young adults' romantic dating relationships. *Archives of Sexual Behavior, 40*(5), 961–969. https://doi.org/10.1007/s10508-010-9663-7

Verigin B. L. , Meijer, E. H., Bogaard, G., & Vrij, A. (2019). Lie prevalence, lie characteristics and strategies of self-reported good liars. *PLoS ONE, 14*(12): e0225566. https://doi.org/10.1371/journal.pone.0225566

Welsch, R., von Castell, C., & Hecht, H. (2019). The anisotropy of personal space. *PLoS ONE, 14*(6), 1–13. https://doi.org/10.1371/journal.pone.0217587

ORGANIZATIONAL COMMUNICATION

The organizational communication context focuses on how members of organizations communicate in and about work environments. Organizational communication scholars examine how workplace relationships are influenced at the macro (e.g., entire organization) and micro levels (e.g., individual coworker relationships). Some major areas of research in organizational communication include corporate social responsibility, organizational identification, organizational culture, workplace incivility, and communication technologies at work. This section includes chapters focusing on three important areas of organizational communication research: (1) work-family balance, (2) crisis communication, and (3) emotional labor, burnout, and compassion. First, Patrice Buzzanell (University of South Florida) examines research on sustaining commitments to our work, family, personal lives, and enacting work-life resilience. Second, W. Timothy Coombs (Centre for Crisis and Risk Communications) reviews research on how managers should respond to a crisis that might damage the organization. Third, Carsyn Endres and Sarah Tracy (Arizona State University) discuss the experiences of emotional labor and burnout at work, and how to engage in compassionate communication. As college students, you are not just enrolled to have fun (we hope!). We know that you have another goal too; to obtain a fulfilling career after graduation and to participate in meaningful work. The organizational communication research reviewed in these chapters will better prepare you for the inevitable difficulties we face in organizations while providing solutions for having a meaningful career throughout workplace challenges. Collectively, this research may help you prepare for communication that is relevant to any organization.

HOW CAN WE BALANCE WORK AND FAMILY?

Patrice M. Buzzanell
University of South Florida

To address the question of work-family balance, I first pull apart and examine what the language and assumptions in this question entail. Then I provide some strategies from work-life communication and interdisciplinary scholarship that can assist in negotiating the different aspects of our lives.

LANGUAGE AND ASSUMPTIONS OF WORK-FAMILY BALANCE

When people ask the question about how they can balance work and family, they make several assumptions. These assumptions attempt to bring the discourse, or everyday talk and interactions, and discourse, or cultural formations and institutional understandings that circulate in society, into harmony (for d/Discourses, see Alvesson & Kärreman, 2000). For instance, people's language indicates that these two aspects—"work" and "family"—and only these two are relevant and that they must be equally present at all times. In other words, the language does not adequately portray the constantly shifting, sometimes precarious, and fluid ways in which different conceptualizations and enactments of both work, from organizational employment to rising gig or sharing economy, AI-automation, and media influencer activities, and family, from marital partnerships to households with pets and friends, shift and reconfigure over lifespans and circumstances (Buzzanell & Medved, forthcoming; Katz & Krueger, 2019; West, 2018).

Drawing out these critiques further, work-family phrasing typically implies a traditional family structure (heterosexual couple with children) and with separate public (work) and private (family) gendered domains despite considerable evidence that multiple family forms, including childfree, and intersecting work-life domains are normative in the United States (e.g., Casper et al., 2016; Lucas & Buzzanell, 2006; Murphy et al., 2021; Rick & Meisenbach, 2017; Roeder et al., 2021). When conventional notions are held, these normative understandings affect everyday practices and carry a burden for those who might be perceived as different. For instance, when LGBTQ+ (lesbian, gay, bisexual, transgender, queer, and other identities), single, and immigrant employees are interacting with coworkers, they often use traditional family, career, and cultural discourses so as not to be scrutinized and perceived as nonnormative (Bishop & Medved, 2020; Dixon & Dougherty, 2014)

Moreover, work is prioritized over family—despite voiced "family first" discourses—such that work-to-family imbalances or conflicts are studied more and considered more significant than family-to-work conflicts (Kirby et al., 2003). These kinds of conflicts are often resolved by appealing to economic, gendered, moral, and classed Discourses such as when mothers make decisions to leave the labor force because the costs (e.g., expenses associated with childcare, commuting time and transportation, and personal stress) and the moral responsibilities to family life are perceived to outweigh the advantages of remaining in the workforce (Duncan & Irwin, 2004). These kinds of Discourses or prevailing logics for decisions are consistent with Kossek et al.'s (2021b) 50-year review of work–family research that noted a focus on women's careers and family–career incompatibilities that necessitate trade-off approaches. These costs became very visible during the COVID-19 pandemic when caregivers struggled to keep their jobs, to home-school their children, or to fulfill the needs of elderly and ill family members at times when the informal supports of afterschool programs, neighbors' assistance, and independent living or nursing homes became unavailable because of lockdowns and virus outbreaks (Bariola & Collins, 2021; Qian & Fuller, 2020). In often unconsciously relying upon economic, gendered, and classed Discourses, what often is not considered are the benefits of working for the mothers' well-being and the probable difficulties in workforce reentry for skilled and professional careers (e.g., Goldin, 2022).

Additionally, the label, work–family balance, neglects several other considerations. It prioritizes people with families, often those with young children. In doing so, it fails to recognize the very real dilemmas and struggles with which everyone contends in attempting to have satisfying and meaningful work and personal lives. To de-emphasize traditional family and balance and to reflect the ambivalences and tensions in work-life communication, descriptors such as work-life with transitions, negotiations, permeability, boundaries, integration, interface, enrichment, spillover, and diffusion have been used in theory and in practice (Berkelaar & Tronstad, 2017; Buzzanell, 2019b; Roeder et al., 2021). Making work-life choices is difficult when there are so many competing interests and needs that deserve attention. For example, you may be a college student who works part-time, takes a full load of classes, wants to date and/or go out with friends, needs to connect even virtually with grandparents and other loved ones, has to obtain food from the college food pantry at the end of every month, checks in on elderly neighbors or walks their dogs, attends religious services on occasion, and tries to volunteer time at the animal rescue center.

However, as an international student studying in the United States during the COVID-19 pandemic and racial protests, the ordinary strains experienced by more traditional college students were exacerbated. Adding to everyday disruptions, many students had lost part-time jobs, had limited technological access, and experienced loneliness, with international students contending with language and cultural mismatches and inabilities to travel home (Lederer et al., 2021). During the COVID-19 pandemic, college students' work-life imbalance predicted perceived stress and depression (Wright et al., 2022). Social support, living arrangements, and race/ethnicity and gender affected mental health (Wright et al., 2022).

Additionally, managers and coworkers behave as though employees who appear to not have dependents or significant others are able to work more hours and readily help if other employees need to pick up children from childcare or have sick family members (Blight et al., 2022; Casper et al., 2016). Managers and coworkers do not expect these supposedly single employees to need to engage in work-life balance. They do not consider the time and energy it takes to cultivate and maintain friendships and other voluntary relationships (Young, 1996).

The phrasing of "balance" also makes it seem as though anyone can accomplish this supposedly equal distribution of time, energy, and resources, without considering the very real material differences among people. These differences center around time, place, lifespan, career phase, and types of or precarity of work, as well as race/ethnicity, nationality, gender, education, sexual-social orientation, (dis)ability, and so on that complicate work-life negotiations. Ammons et al. (2017) found variations in work-to-family and family-to-work conflict levels based on gender, race/ethnicity, and their intersections. Conflict may also arise because fathers, particularly White professional middle-upper class heterosexual men, often benefit from fatherhood premiums or extra pay and perquisites as heads of household whereas mothers often suffer motherhood penalties in which they are paid less and are presumed to have lower commitment to and involvement in their paid labor (noting that there are national, classed, raced, occupational, and other identity and contextual variations in these fatherhood bonuses and motherhood penalties, see Budig et al., 2016; Casper et al., 2016; Correll et al., 2007; Dias et al., 2020).

These gendered conflicts are so profound that female graduate students in the STEM (science, technology, engineering, and math) disciplines fear any mention of motherhood might derail their career aspirations (Thébaud & Taylor, 2021). Yet the COVID-19 pandemic may have eased some of these gendered pressures, by enabling STEM women to reveal non-work challenges and prompting women to subvert ideal worker norms (Kossek et al. 2021a). However, it is not simply graduate students and female engineers and scientists who question whether to talk about personal life concerns and/or aspirations. Malhotra et al. (2021) found that members of elite law firms in the UK desired work-life balance but feared that discussing these interests would be inappropriate.

Work-life negotiation often is a more accurate way of depicting struggles yet the very idea of "negotiation" seems weighted toward those perceived to have power, desirable expertise, and material, especially financial, resources. Thus, a seemingly innocuous question such as "how do you manage work and family" results in highly complex and often paradoxical and ironic considerations. The accountability for work-life "balancing" is thrust in the hands of individuals and families in the United States because of societal neoliberal tendencies toward less governmental support and market prioritization (Amis et al., 2020). Yet work-life negotiations draw upon multi-level—individual and familial, organizational and institutional, and societal—and d/Discourses and material resources (see Bednarek & Lê, in Pradies et al., 2021).

WORK-LIFE STRATEGIES

If you asked someone about how they balanced work and life aspects, they probably would come up with a number of different tactics that have been successful (or not) for them. They might tell you to engage in work-life integration or to compartmentalize and allocate certain hours at different times of the day or week for each of your activities then reprioritize if something becomes urgent like project deadlines or illness (Kossek & Lautsch, 2008). These preferences for compartmentalization, integration, and/or sequencing are born out in individual and family preferences and modified based on practical issues. For instance, Knight (2022) found that college-enrolled emerging adults, roughly 18–29 year-old students, managed work and romantic partner balancing via pragmatic segmentation or compartmentalization (such that they might sacrifice relationships for longer-term school and career pursuits) and integration or enrichment strategies (such as when the right partner helps with other life aspects). They tried to find strategies that fit their life and career phases as well as their aspirations for their futures. Similarly, understanding your context, constraints, and opportunities helps you to develop work-life communication strategies that can be helpful in the present and adjusted for the future.

Ways to accomplish work-life goals means that you might consider engaging in the following strategies: (1) challenging the normal: work-life social construction and design; (2) creating the new normal: resilience; and (3) institutionalizing work-life resilience: a multi-layered approach.

CHALLENGING THE NORMAL: WORK-LIFE SOCIAL CONSTRUCTION AND DESIGN

As you may have guessed from the opening of this essay, I take a social constructionist and critical viewpoint, meaning that knowledge is coconstructed based on personal experiences, societal norms, and conditions and politics of our lives (see Buzzanell, 1995). This stance means that realities endure because of the historically, politically, culturally, and socially embedded nature of taken-for-granted views but also that these same realities can be revised or reinvented from scratch. To design sustainable work-life balancing, then, is not simply application of appropriate spatiotemporal distributions or technological use, but ongoing design. Design involves problem definition, application, construction, testing, and transformation of d/Discourses and materialities to create fulfilling lifestyles (see Buzzanell, 2022). These designs are influenced by powerful societal forces to maintain the status quo.

As you reflect on the conduct of your career and personal lives, you can ask whose interests are served by the ways you prioritize career, work, family, friends, volunteering, spirituality, and/or leisure. By prototyping or shifting work-life designs, you can change these priorities and results. For instance, when women entrepreneurs in China, the United States, and Denmark found that there were barriers to the ways they wanted to conduct their careers and personal lives, these women identified the problematic issues and iterated solutions to find ways to rescript their experiences (Long & Buzzanell, 2022). As another example, despite the strength of the male breadwinner and traditional father masculinity ideologies in the United States, Duckworth and Buzzanell (2009) interviewed fathers from different racial/ethnic backgrounds, forms of families, ages, occupations, and classes to find that fathers frame work-life considerations as a "multifaceted negotiation process" meaning that fatherhood ideologies have expanded (p. 569) and are associated with father–child relational quality (Fellers & Schrodt, 2021).

Taking critical and social constructionist lenses mean that you can envision change and work toward it; taking a design lens means that when a strategy or practice does not work, then this is not failure but an opportunity to use this new information to revise the prototype and try again. My own and others' communication research indicates that key processes involve disassembling and critiquing everyday discourses and cultural formations about work-life balance to determine how you can transform your talk and societal structures that prohibit sustainable and fulfilling lifestyles. The next step involves viewing disruptions as means of adapting to and constituting new normals.

CREATING THE NEW NORMAL: RESILIENCE

Individuals cannot create new normals for work and personal by themselves. You need others to discuss, interact, and support your identity, network, and resilience enactments. Ahn et al. (2021) advocated that you "fuck individual resilience" and build in the relationships, structures, and supports that you, and the academicians about whom they write, need to create viable lifestyles while you also commit to good work. Individuals and their families— rather than societal structures and work-family ideologies—are blamed when they cannot manage disruptions, including work-life conflicts (Buzzanell, 2021). However, the communication theory of resilience (CTR) offers insight and strategies for ways to not only adapt to losses, challenges, and transitions but also to change the systems that prevent fulfilling and authentic reintegration efforts on multiple levels (Buzzanell, 2010, 2018, 2022; Buzzanell & Houston, 2018).

According to CTR, trigger events are disruptions that require adaptation and change through five resilience processes that constitute reintegration and new normals (Buzzanell, 2010, 2017, 2018, 2019a). The five resilience processes help individuals, collectives, and societies "bounce" back and forth in this reintegration: crafting normalcy (talking and interacting so that things are getting back to normal); affirming identity anchors (enacting and gaining support for roles); using and creating networks (connecting with and maintaining strong and weak ties, while also creating new ties when former ties are dysfunctional); backgrounding negative feelings while foregrounding productive action (acknowledging the right to feel bad about the disruption, but focusing on goal-oriented actions); and creating alternative logics (constructing workarounds, reframing, finding silver linings and humor, improvising, and doing other nonconventional behaviors). Each of these processes can be converted into practices or strategies that fit the circumstances.

When examining higher education challenges experienced by undergraduate students in the United States, Rossetto and Martin (forthcoming) not only found that students enacted the five resilience processes but also found that several themes could be used to support students' resilience. These themes were: mattering and belonging, mentorship, reframing and reorientation, and reflection and finding strengths. Their essay examined what students did but also what faculty, administrators, student support personnel, and others could do to assist in multi-level resilience cultivation and enactment.

However, as noted earlier, work-life resilience enactment is not only discursive but also material, embodied, and symbolic. Wieland (2020) found that, when workers who experienced involuntary job loss engaged in dialectical resilience strategies and were treated with and enacted dignity, they were better able to manage the work and personal life issues that came with job loss. Hintz et al. (2021) used health care workers' Reddit stories to uncover how these workers dealt with personal protective equipment (PPE) shortages that made them angry with their employers, threatened their own and their family members' lives, and resulted in these workers sharing strategies online to make it through the COVID-19 pandemic when unable to locate or make their own PPE. They engaged in the five resilience processes but some also resisted their workplace mandates and others tried to transform their workplaces. They questioned health care organizational hierarchies and the messaging they experienced that they were expendable.

Furthermore, work-life resilience strategies may be difficult or near impossible to enact when people who are disenfranchised by class, economic hardships, race/ethnicity, and other identities try to enact productive action such as dealing with welfare stigma and job search agencies not attuned to their financial, attire, and transportation conditions—in other words, their agency and decision-making is bounded materially and their resilience enactment needs assistance from community and governmental sources (Gist-Mackey, 2018; Gist-Mackey & Guy, 2019; Kingsford et al., 2021; see also Lucas & Buzzanell, 2011, 2012). Finally, resilience can be enacted in extreme, ironic, and seemingly counterproductive ways when women are confronted with infertility and failed medical interventions to become pregnant (Jarvis, 2021). All of these examples indicate that resilience processes performed as discursive are necessary but not sufficient in many areas of our work and personal lives.

INSTITUTIONALIZING WORK-LIFE RESILIENCE: A MULTI-LAYERED APPROACH

In the United States, individuals and families often must come up with their own strategies for managing work-life issues. Some of these people do not have safety nets like extended family living nearby, funds to hire caregivers or outsource tasks, and resources such as time, good health, or energy to even consider creative solutions to unexpected disruptions in their careful balancing of work and family or personal life issues. What the COVID-19 pandemic exposed was the devasting effects that lack of safety nets had on ordinary people just trying to get by. The result was eye-opening for some who had not realized how much these health and educational disparities, racial/ethnic injustices, financial and scheduling precarities, digital divides, and lack of governmental resources and policies can affect work-life management and the socio-cultural, economic, and political infrastructures of nations and communities.

Kossek and Lee (2020) took U.S. policy to task by saying that the COVID-19 pandemic revealed the inadequacies of U.S. work-family policy, especially in contrast with other industrialized countries. They advanced their proposal for three federal governmental policy changes: paid sick and family leave, emergency back-up staffing, and rights–not choices—to request and use flexible and reasonable work scheduling.

They and other researchers and advocates have called for structural changes. These changes include and add to the policies and resources already mentioned. They include government- and corporate-supported quality child and elder care, paid family leaves, after-school/evening/weekend programs for dependents so that caregivers can work shifts, and adequate respite care for those handling the family members' and other loved ones' chronic or end-of-life needs. From a practical or utilitarian ethical standpoint, investments into families and children are less costly than lack of investment. If caregivers cannot earn a living wage through paid labor, then they need to acquire unemployment or supplemental funds. If children do not receive good quality care and education and elders (or dependents with chronic illnesses or disabilities) do not have adequate day facilities and home-based medical assistance, then businesses lose productivity as their employees' attention is diverted away from their work and taxpayers foot higher bills for remedial training, hospital care, and, in worst case scenarios, for rehabilitation centers and prisons (Collins & Bilge, 2020). Society loses their children's potential contributions. Many researchers have calculated these cost-benefit ratios, with the bottom line being that structural changes and investments in human resources pay for themselves. Even so, the human costs and social injustices supercede these utilitarian arguments.

With all these very different and compelling arguments, you would think that it would be fairly easy to set policies, laws, and practices in motion to create better quality of life. But it is not "simply" a matter of revising structures and policies. Nor is it simply a matter of showing people how to manage time or resources better. Kirby and Krone (2002) was a wake-up call for communication scholars with their article, "The policy exists but you can't really use it," showing how agency and structure co-orient to prevent use of work-family policies. Since then, similar findings about thwarted policy use have emerged from communication studies exploring a variety of different contexts. In terms of work-life considerations of emerging adults and students, recent communication scholarship has examined graduate student parents' work-life dilemmas upon the birth of their children (Long et al., 2022). Communication and interdisciplinary researchers have advocated for work and personal life investments and strategies that can make a difference to all societal members discursively, materially, and symbolically.

In short, when you are asked, or you yourself ask, how someone balances work-family or work and personal life issues, remember that there are many deep and profound considerations. These individual through societal factors affect your own and others' abilities to manage and change what is taken for granted. You might first consider how the language and its implications enable and constrain your creativity to devise innovative strategies. This opens up opportunities for (1) challenging the normal: work-life social construction and design; (2) creating the new normal: resilience; and (3) institutionalizing work-life resilience: a multi-layered approach.

REFERENCES

Ahn, S. J., Cripe, E. T., Foucault Welles, B., McGregor, S. C., Pearce, K. E., Usher, N., & Vitak, J. (2021). Academic caregivers on organizational and community resilience in academia (fuck individual resilience). *Communication, Culture & Critique, 14*(2), 301–305. https://doi.org/10.1093/ccc/tcab027

Alvesson, M., & Kärreman, D. (2000). Varieties of discourse: On the study of organizations through discourse analysis. *Human Relations, 53*(9), 1125–1149. https://doi.org/10.1177/0018726700539002

Amis, J., Mair, J., & Munir, K. (2020). The organizational reproduction of inequality. *Academy of Management Annals, 14*(1), 195–230. https://doi.org/10.5465/annals.2017.0033

Ammons, S., Dahlin, E., Edgell, P., & Santo, J. (2017). Work–family conflict among Black, White, and Hispanic men and women. *Community, Work & Family, 20*(4), 379–404. https://doi.org/10.1080/13668803.2016.1146231

Bariola, N., & Collins, C. (2021). The gendered politics of pandemic relief: Labor and family policies in Denmark, Germany, and the United States during COVID-19. *American Behavioral Scientist, 65*(12), 1671–1697. https://doi.org/10.1177/00027642211003140

Berkelaar, B., & Tronstad, L. (2017). Negotiating work–life. In *Oxford research encyclopedia of communication*. Oxford University Press.

Bishop, S. C., & Medved, C. E. (2020). Relational tensions, narrative, and materiality: intergenerational communication in families with undocumented immigrant parents. *Journal of Applied Communication Research, 48*(2), 227–247. https://doi.org/10.1080/00909882.2020.1735646

Blight, M., Lambertz-Berndt, M., Fetherston, M., & Fonner, L. (2022). "It's like you need a family to have a reason to leave on time": Family type and the perceived inclusiveness of work-life practices. *Western Journal of Communication, 86*(1), 39–59. https://doi.org/10.1080/10570314.2021.1994637

Budig, M. J., Misra, J., & Boeckmann, I. (2016). Work–family policy trade-offs for mothers? Unpacking the cross-national variation in motherhood earnings penalties. *Work and Occupations, 43*(2), 119–177. https://doi.org/10.1177/0730888415615385

Buzzanell, P. M. (1995). Reframing the glass ceiling as a socially constructed process: Implications for understanding and change. *Communication Monographs, 62*(4), 327–354. https://doi.org/10.1080/03637759509376366

Buzzanell, P. M. (2010). Resilience: Talking, resisting, and imagining new normalcies into being. *Journal of Communication, 60*(1), 1–14. https://doi.org/10.1111/j.1460-2466.2009.01469.x

Buzzanell, P. M. (2017). Communication theory of resilience: Enacting adaptive-transformative processes when families experience loss and disruption. In D. O. Braithwaite, E. A. Suter, & K. Floyd (Eds), *Engaging theories in family communication: Multiple perspectives* (2nd ed., pp. 98–109). Routledge.

Buzzanell, P. M. (2018). Organizing resilience as adaptive-transformational tensions. *Journal of Applied Communication Research, 46*(1), 14–18. https://doi.org/10.1080/00909882.2018.1426711

Buzzanell, P. M. (2019a). Communication theory of resilience in everyday talk, interactions, and network structures. In S. R. Wilson & S. W. Smith (Eds.), *Reflections on interpersonal communication research* (pp. 65–88). Cognella.

Buzzanell, P. M. (2019b). Work/family spillover. In J. Ponzetti & S. M. Horan (Eds.), *Encyclopedia of interpersonal and family relationships* (pp. 915–918). Macmillan.

Buzzanell, P. M. (2021). Designing feminist resilience. In S. Eckert & I. Bachmann (Eds.), *Reflections on feminist communication and media scholarship: Theory, method, impact* (pp. 43–58). Routledge.

Buzzanell, P. M. (2022). Constituting intercultural harmony by design thinking: Conflict management in, for, and about diversity, equity, and inclusion work. In X. Dai & G. Chen (Eds.), *Conflict management and intercultural communication* (pp. 38-55). Routledge.

Buzzanell, P. M., & Houston, J. B. (2018). Communication and resilience: Multi-level applications and insights – A *Journal of Applied Communication Research* Forum. *Journal of Applied Communication Research, 46*(1), 1–4. https://doi.org/10.1080/00909882.2017.1412086

Buzzanell, P. M., & Medved, C. (forthcoming). Work-family issues. In V. Miller & M. S. Poole (Eds.), *Handbook of organizational communication*. DeGruyter.

Casper, W. J., Marquardt, D. J., Roberto, K. J., & Buss, C. (2016). The hidden family lives of single adults without dependent children. In T. Allen & L Eby (Eds.), *The Oxford handbook of work and family* (pp. 182–195). Oxford University Press.

Collins, P. H., & Bilge, S. (2020). *Intersectionality*. John Wiley & Sons.

Correll, S. J., Benard, S., & Paik, I. (2007). Getting a job: Is there a motherhood penalty? *American Journal of Sociology, 112*(5), 1297–1338. https://doi.org/10.1086/511799

Dias, F. A., Chance, J., & Buchanan, A. (2020). The motherhood penalty and the fatherhood premium in employment during covid-19: Evidence from The United States. *Research in Social Stratification and Mobility, 69*, 100542. https://doi.org/10.1016/j.rssm.2020.100542

Dixon, J., & Dougherty, D. S. (2014). A language convergence/meaning divergence analysis exploring how LGBTQ and single employees manage traditional family expectations in the workplace. *Journal of Applied Communication Research, 42*(1), 1–19. https://doi.org/10.1080/00909882.2013.847275

Duckworth, J., & Buzzanell, P. M. (2009). Constructing work-life balance and fatherhood: Men's framing of the meanings of *both* work *and* family. *Communication Studies, 60*(5), 558–573. https://doi.org/10.1080/10510970903260392

Duncan, S., & Irwin, S. (2004). The social patterning of values and rationalities: mothers' choices in combining caring and employment. *Social Policy and Society, 3*(4), 391–399. https://doi.org/10.1017/S1474746404002076

Fellers, M., & Schrodt, P. (2021). Perceptions of fathers' confirmation and affection as mediators of masculinity and relational quality in father-child relationships. *Journal of Family Communication, 21*(1), 46–62. https://doi.org/10.1080/15267431.2020.1866574

Gist-Mackey, A. N. (2018). (Dis)embodied job search communication training: Comparative critical ethnographic analysis of materiality and discourse during the unequal search for work. *Organization Studies, 39*(9), 1251–1275. https://doi.org/10.1177/0170840617736936

Gist-Mackey, A. N., & Guy, A. (2019). "You get in a hole, it's like quicksand": A grounded theory analysis of social support amid materially bounded decision-making processes. *Journal of Applied Communication Research, 47*(3), 237–250. https://doi.org/10.1080/00909882.2019.1617430

Goldin, C. (2022). *Understanding the economic impact of COVID-19 on women* (No. w29974). National Bureau of Economic Research.

Hintz, E., Betts, T., & Buzzanell, P. M. (2021). Healthcare workers without PPE: Material conditions as multidimensional cascading triggers for resilience processes. *Health Communication.* Advance online publication. https://doi.org/10.1080/10410236.2021.1953727

Jarvis, C. M. (2021). Expanding feminist resilience theorizing: Conceptualizing embodied resilience as a material-discursive process during infertility. *Journal of Applied Communication Research.* Advance online publication. https://doi.org/10.1080/00909882.2021.2011373

Katz, L., & Krueger, A. (2019). The rise and nature of alternative work arrangements in the United States, 1995-2015. *ILR Review, 72*(2), 382–416. https://doi.org/10.1177/0019793918820008

Kingsford, A. N., Gist-Mackey, A. N., & Pastorek, A. E. (2021). Welfare recipients communicated pathways to resilience during stigma and material hardship in the heartland of America. *Journal of Applied Communication Research.* Advance online publication. https://doi.org/10.1080/00909882.2021.1987504

Kirby, E. L., Golden, A. G., Medved, C. E., Jorgenson, J., & Buzzanell, P. M. (2003). An organizational communication challenge to the discourse of work and family research: From problematics to empowerment. *Annals of the International Communication Association, 27*(1), 1–43. https://doi.org/10.1080/23808985.2003.11679020

Kirby, E., & Krone, K. J. (2002). "The policy exists but you can't really use it": Communication and the structuration of work-family policies. *Journal of Applied Communication Research, 30*(1), 50–77. https://doi.org/10.1080/00909880216577

Knight, K. (2022). Emerging adults' discursive construction of work/partnership boundary strategies. *Western Journal of Communication, 86*(3), 379–399. https://doi.org/10.1080/10570314.2022.2060521

Kossek, E., & Lautsch, B. A. (2008). *CEO of me: Creating a life that works in the flexible job age.* Pearson Education.

Kossek, E., & Lee, K. (2020). The coronavirus & work–life inequality: Three evidence-based initiatives to update US work–life employment policies. *Behavioral Science & Policy, 6*(2), 77–85. https://doi.org/ 10.1353/bsp.2020.0018

Kossek, E., Dumas, T. L., Piszczek, M. M., & Allen, T. D. (2021a). Pushing the boundaries: A qualitative study of how stem women adapted to disrupted work–nonwork boundaries during the COVID-19 pandemic. *Journal of Applied Psychology, 106*(11), 1615–1629. https://doi.org/10.1037/apl0000982

Kossek, E., Perrigino, M., & Rock, A. (2021b). From ideal workers to ideal work for all: A 50-year review integrating careers and work-family research with a future research agenda. *Journal of Vocational Behavior, 126*, 103504. https://doi.org/10.1016/j.jvb.2020.103504

Lederer, A., Hoban, M. T., Lipson, S. K., Zhou, S., & Eisenberg, D. (2021). More than inconvenienced: The unique needs of U.S. college students during the COVID-19 pandemic. *Health Education & Behavior, 48*(1), 14–19. https://doi.org/10.1177/1090198120969372

Long, Z., & Buzzanell, P. M. (2022). Constituting intersectional politics of reinscription: Women entrepreneurs' resistance practices in China, Denmark, and the United States. *Management Communication Quarterly, 36*(2), 207–234. https://doi.org/10.1177/08933189211030246

Long, Z., Buzzanell, P. M., & King, A. S. (2022). Pivoting multiple liminalities in working parenthood: Communicative negotiations of permanent, transitional, and limbo liminalities. *Management Communication Quarterly.* Advance online publication. https://doi.org/10.1177/08933189221095093

Lucas, K., & Buzzanell, P. M. (2006). Employees "without" families: Discourses of family as an external constraint to work-life balance. In L. H. Turner & R. West (Eds.), *The family communication sourcebook* (pp. 335–352). Sage.

Lucas, K., & Buzzanell, P. M. (2011). It's the cheese: Collective memory of hard times during deindustrialization. In J. M. Cramer, C. P. Greene, & L. M. Walters (Eds.), *Food as communication: Communication as food* (pp. 95–113). Peter Lang.

Lucas, K., & Buzzanell, P. M. (2012). Memorable messages of hard times: Constructing short-and long-term resiliencies through family communication. *Journal of Family Communication, 12*(3), 189–208. https://doi.org/10.1080/15267431.2012.687196

Malhotra, N., Zietsma, C., Morris, T., & Smets, M. (2021). Handling resistance to change when societal and workplace logics conflict. *Administrative Science Quarterly, 66*(2), 475–520. https://doi.org/10.1177/0001839220962760

Murphy, L. D., Thomas, C. L., Cobb, H. R., & Hartman, A. E. (2021). A review of the LGBTQ+ work–family interface: What do we know and where do we go from here? *Journal of Organizational Behavior, 42*(2), 139–161. https://doi.org/10.1002/job.2492

Pradies, C., Aust, I., Bednarek, R., Brandl, J., Carmine, S., Cheal, J., ... & Keller, J. (2021). The lived experience of paradox: How individuals navigate tensions during the pandemic crisis. *Journal of Management Inquiry, 30*(2), 154–167. https://doi.org/10.1177/1056492620986874

Qian, Y., & Fuller, S. (2020). COVID-19 and the gender employment gap among parents of young children. *Canadian Public Policy, 46*(S2), S89–S101. https://doi.org/10.3138/cpp.2020-077

Rick, J. M., & Meisenbach, R. J. (2017). Social stigma, childfree identities, and work–life balance. In E. Hatfield (Ed.), *Communication and the work-life balancing act: Intersections across identities, genders, and cultures* (pp. 205–221). Lexington.

Roeder, A. C., Bisel, R. S., & Morrissey, B. S. (2021). Weathering the financial storm: A professional forecaster team's domain diffusion of resilience. *Communication Studies, 72*(1), 1–16. https://doi.org/10.1080/10510974.2020.1807379

Rossetto, K. R., & Martin, E. (forthcoming). "It's always about challenging and supporting." Communicative processes of resilience in higher education. *Communication Education.*

Thébaud, S., & Taylor, C. J. (2021). The specter of motherhood: Culture and the production of gendered career aspirations in science and engineering. *Gender & Society, 35*(3), 395–421. https://doi.org/10.1177/08912432211006037

Young, M. (1996). Career issues for single adults without dependent children. In D. T. Hall & Associates (Eds.), *The career is dead—Long live the career: A relational approach to careers* (pp. 196–219). Jossey-Bass.

West, D. M. (2018). *The future of work: Robots, AI and automation.* Brookings Institute.

Wieland, S. M. (2020). Constituting resilience at work: Maintaining dialectics and cultivating dignity throughout a worksite closure. *Management Communication Quarterly, 34*(4), 463–494. https://doi.org/10.1177/0893318920949314

Wright, K. B., Riemann, W., & Fisher, C. L. (2022). Work–life-imbalance during the COVID-19 pandemic: exploring social support and health outcomes in the United States. *Journal of Applied Communication Research, 50*(1), 54–69. https://doi.org/10.1080/00909882.2021.1965186

HOW SHOULD ORGANIZATIONS RESPOND DURING A CRISIS?

W. Timothy Coombs
Centre for Crisis and Risk Communications

When I was teaching and researching in public relations, crisis communication seemed the most interesting topic to me because it was so challenging. A crisis can be defined as "the perceived violation of salient stakeholder expectations that can create negative outcomes for stakeholders and/or the organization" (Coombs, 2023, p. 4). Essentially, a crisis is a disruption for an organization and its stakeholders that damages the organization–stakeholder relationship. I along with other researchers wondered, "How can crisis managers use communication to lessen the damage and to rebuild the relationship?" My pursuit of that broad question resulted in the development of the situational crisis communication theory (SCCT). SCCT provides theory-based and research-tested advice on how to respond to a crisis. Research is an important component for evidence-based approaches to an intervention. In an evidence-based approach, professionals combine their experience with the latest evidence from research to enhance interventions (Briner et al., 2009). SCCT provides one source of evidence for an evidence-based approach to crisis communication.

CRISIS COMMUNICATION AND SCCT

Crisis communication emerged because managers wanted to know how to effectively respond to a crisis situation. Effectively involves addressing the concerns of the crisis victims (those adversely affected by the crisis) and the needs of the organization-in-crisis. Victims need to feel physically safe and to cope psychologically with the crisis (Sturges, 1994). The organization seeks to limit the negative effects of the crisis including damage to the organization's post-crisis reputation, drops in purchase intention, and an increase in negative word-of-mouth about the organization (Coombs, 2007). Both stakeholder and organizational concerns must be considered if the crisis communication is to enhance the disrupted relationship between the organization and its stakeholders (those who can affect the organization or are affected by the organization's actions). Common stakeholders affected by crises include customers, investors, communities living near a facility, and employees. I admire the work of crisis managers and their desire to help people in the type of distress. I wanted to help crisis managers by enhancing our understanding how to create effective crisis responses. Drawing upon accepted ideas in communication, I believed the effectiveness of the crisis response was tied to understanding the crisis situation. That meant I needed to find a way to define the crisis situation that connected it in a meaningful way to possible crisis responses. Attribution theory informed my effort to forge these connections.

Attribution theory holds that people naturally look for causes of events, especially negative events. Crises are negative events meaning people will seek to explain why the crisis occurred. People tend to attribute a crisis to the person involved in the situation or the circumstances (Weiner, 1995). Was it something the person did or did not do that caused the event or a matter of factors beyond their control? In a crisis, people tend to attribute the cause to either the organization-in-crisis or some external factors beyond the organization's control. In 2022, baby formula produced at Abbott Labs sickened infants. Abbott was responsible because it had not properly sanitized its production facility. Had it been product tampering by an external agent, the crisis situation would be viewed as caused by situational factors similar to the Tylenol poisonings in the 1980s.

Crisis managers have a range of crisis response options—what they might say and do in response to a crisis. Managers should begin any crisis response with the ethical base response. The ethical base response tells people how to protect themselves physically from the negative effects of a crisis and helps them to cope psychologically with the crisis (Sturges, 1994). From the earlier example, Abbott Lab warned parents not to use the tainted baby formula and to return the product (physical safety). Tops Friendly Markets offered condolences (psychological comfort) to the families of those killed at a 2022 shooting at one of the company's Buffalo, NY stores.

Other crisis response strategies can be used to rebuild the organizational reputation. These reputation building strategies vary in how accommodative they are to the needs of the crisis victims. Managers can use crisis responses to deny responsibility (no accommodation), seek to reduce responsibility (minimal accommodation), or accept responsibility (highly accommodative). Denial and scapegoating (blaming another actor for the crisis) are the least accommodative. Managers might choose to minimize the severity of the crisis or the organization's responsibility for a crisis in order to lessen the negative effects of the crisis on the organization. Minimization offers limited accommodation because it at least recognizes the crisis and the organization's connection to the crisis. Highly accommodative strategies include apologies (accepting responsibility for the crisis) and compensation (offering victims some material compensation for the crisis). Both apology and compensation focus on the crisis victims rather than the organization-in-crisis (Coombs, 1995).

For SCCT, understanding the crisis situation is predicated upon assessing the level of crisis responsibility a crisis situation will evoke. Crisis responsibility represents the amount of responsibility stakeholders are likely to assign to the organization-in-crisis (Coombs & Holladay, 2002). SCCT argues that the crisis type is the foundation for understanding perceptions of the crisis responsibility. The crisis type is the frame used to interpret the crisis event. The SCCT research finds that various crisis types can be organized by the attributions of crisis responsibility a crisis is likely to produce. SCCT groups similar crisis types into three clusters: victim, accidental, and preventable crises. Victim crises produce very low levels crisis responsibility and include workplace violence, natural disasters, and product tampering crises. Accidental crises produce low levels crisis responsibility and involve product harm and accidents caused by technical-errors such as the failure of a mechanical system or software glitch that was unexpected. Preventable crises produce high levels of crisis responsibility and include product harm and accidents caused by human-error as well as situations created when managers knowingly place stakeholders at risk (management misconduct) (Coombs & Holladay, 2002). A history of past crises and/or a negative reputation prior to a crisis intensify perceptions of crisis responsibility (Coombs & Holladay, 2006; Eaddy & Jin, 2018).

SCCT argues that as attributions of crisis responsibility increase, the crisis response must become more accommodative. A crisis manager should assess the potential attributions of crisis responsibility the crisis situation will produce then select a crisis response that fits with the that level. In April of 2022, Southwest Airlines had cancellations of thousands of flights due to a computer glitch. In the same year, Abbott Labs produced infant formula in a facility they knew had sanitation problems only to creating a foodborne illness outbreak with its product. Clearly the attributions of crisis responsibility will differ between these two crisis situations. Southwest would be perceived as less responsible for the crisis than Abbott Labs. Abbott labs would be perceived as having been able to prevent the crisis but Southwest was a victim of circumstances.

All theories have boundary conditions, points beyond which the theory no longer holds. A boundary condition is essentially the limits for the theory. Recent research has indicated that moral outrage is boundary condition for SCCT (Coombs & Tachkova, 2019). Moral outrage is a specific emotion that emerges when people perceive a situation was intentional, involves injustice, and motivated by greed (Antonetti & Maklan, 2016). Scansis is a unique crisis type that occurs when a crisis is also a scandal. Scandals have a strong moral component, hence, a scansis produces strong perceptions of moral outrage (Coombs et al., 2018). Furthermore, the moral outrage creates distance between stakeholders and the organization as stakeholders feel a lack of value congruence with the organization. The scansis found that the SCCT recommendations to use accommodative strategies produce no positive effect on post-crisis reputation, purchase intention, and negative word-of-mouth—created the same results as less accommodative crisis responses. This led to the conclusion that moral outrage was a boundary condition for SCCT (Coombs & Tachkova, 2019). Additional research found that management misconduct produced enough moral outrage to be past the boundary condition as well (Tachkova & Coombs, 2022). It seems that the recommendations from SCCT hold when moral outrage is low and that would include crises from the victim and accidental crisis clusters along with the human-error crises from the preventable crisis cluster.

TIMING AND CRISIS COMMUNICATION

Timing is another factor to consider for crisis communication. Crisis managers have long argued for a quick response to a crisis (Caruba, 1994). The stealing thunder research in crisis communication has repeatedly proven the value of being quick (e.g., Arpan & Pompper, 2003; Claeys & Cauberghe, 2014). Stealing thunder occurs when the organization is the first to report the existence of a crisis. People find out about the crisis from the organization rather than a new story or a social media post by some other entity. Research consistently finds a crisis does less damage to an organization and its relationship with stakeholders when the organization steals thunder (Claeys, 2017). As a manager, you cannot always steal thunder, but you should when given the option. In February of 2022, extraction giant Rio Tinto released an internal report that found a culture of bullying, racism, and harassment at the company. Rio Tinto was the source of the information about its own internal problems. This is in contrast to Wells Fargo whose management knew about its problem of charging customers for accounts the customers knew nothing about months before the problem was released by a newspaper expose. Wells Fargo had generated millions of dollars in revenue from these phantom accounts.

Oddly, managers are reluctant to steal thunder even though the evidence of its benefits are overwhelmingly positive. Managers do not want to disclose a crisis based on the hope that may be no one will learn about the crisis (Claeys & Opgenhaffen, 2016). That outcome could occur and probably has. However, with so many eyes watching organizational actions and the potential of employees to disclose the crisis through whistleblowing (reporting negative information to outside actors), it is more likely that a crisis will become known by others. Managers are simply victims of the human desire to avoid loss. Behavioral economics, a combination of psychology and traditional economics, tell us that people value avoiding loss far more than they value gains (Thaler, 2015). Stealing thunder will create loss by admitting there is a crisis. Not stealing thunder avoids loss for the moment and perhaps even in the future (Claeys & Coombs, 2020). The point is that even strong evidence can be ignored by crisis managers.

CONCLUSION

As we conclude, let us return to the question: "How can crisis managers use communication to lessen damage and to rebuild the relationship?" Most of you will not be crisis managers but SCCT and stealing thunder offers some useful guidance for those who will be. When you have the chance, steal thunder and be the first to disclose a crisis exists. This will lessen the negative effect of the crisis on the organization and warn stakeholders more quickly about a possible danger for themselves. Begin your crisis communication with the ethical base response and focus on crisis victims. Corrective action is an important component of the ethical base response. Corrective action are the steps being taken to prevent a repeat of the crisis. The fear of a future crisis creates psychological stress for stakeholders. Consider how parents would be concerned about using baby formula Abbott Lab produces after the product recall. Corrective action facilitates psychological coping with the crisis (Coombs, 2023). When crisis responsibility is likely to be high, you should add a very accommodative response such as an apology or compensation. Both apology and compensation reflect an organization being accountable for the crisis and keeps the focus the crisis victims. Never use denial if your organization has any responsibility for the crisis. A denial will only intensify the damage when the organization's connection to the crisis is revealed. When a crisis evokes moral outrage, accommodative strategies will no longer have a positive effect on post-crisis reputations, purchase intentions, or negative word-of-mouth. Your organization needs to be prepared to suffer for its actions. However, an accommodative response can help to re-establish value congruence between the organization and its stakeholders. Crises are disruptive and threat the organization–stakeholder relationship but an effective crisis response can limit the negative effects stakeholders and the organization might experience from the crisis. Crisis communication research has been integral to understanding what constitutes and effective response.

REFERENCES

Antonetti, P., & Maklan, S. (2016). An extended model of moral outrage at corporate social irresponsibility. *Journal of Business Ethics, 135*(3), 429–444. https://doi.org/10.1007/s10551-014-2487-y

Arpan, L. M., & Pompper, D. (2003). Stormy weather: Testing "stealing thunder" as a crisis communication strategy to improve communication flow between organizations and journalists. *Public Relations Review, 29*(3), 291–308. https://doi.org/10.1016/S0363-8111(03)00043-2

Briner, R. B., Denyer, D., & Rousseau, D. M. (2009). Evidence-based management: Concept cleanup time?. *Academy of Management Perspectives, 23*(4), 19–32. https://doi.org/10.5465/amp.23.4.19

Caruba, A. (1994). Crisis PR: Most are unprepared. *Occupational Hazards, 56*(9), 85.

Claeys, A. S. (2017). Better safe than sorry: Why organizations in crisis should never hesitate to steal thunder. *Business Horizons, 60*(3), 305–311. https://doi.org/10.1016/j.bushor.2017.01.003

Claeys, A. S., & Cauberghe, V. (2014). What makes crisis response strategies work? The impact of crisis involvement and message framing. *Journal of Business Research, 67*(2), 182–189. https://doi.org/10.1016/j.jbusres.2012.10.005

Claeys, A. S., & Coombs, W. T. (2020). Organizational crisis communication: Suboptimal crisis response selection decisions and behavioral economics. *Communication Theory, 30*(3), 290–309. https://doi.org/10.1093/ct/qtz002

Claeys, A.-S., & Opgenhaffen, M. (2016). Why practitioners do (not) apply crisis communication theory in practice. *Journal of Public Relations Research, 28*(5–6), 232–247. https://doi.org/10.1080/1062726X.2016.1261703

Coombs, W. T. (1995). Choosing the right words: The development of guidelines for the selection of the "Appropriate" crisis-response strategies. *Management Communication Quarterly, 8*(4), 447–476. https://doi.org/10.1177/0893318995008004003

Coombs, W. T. (2007). Protecting organization reputations during a crisis: The development and application of situational crisis communication theory. *Corporate Reputation Review, 10*(3), 163–176. https://doi.org/10.1057/palgrave.crr.1550049

Coombs, W. T. (2023). *Ongoing crisis communication: Planning, managing, and responding* (6th ed.). Sage.

Coombs, W. T., & Holladay, S. J. (2002). Helping crisis managers protect reputational assets initial tests of the situational crisis communication theory. *Management Communication Quarterly, 16*(2), 165–186. https://doi.org/10.1177/089331802237233

Coombs, W. T. & Holladay, S. J. (2006). Unpacking the halo effect: Reputation and crisis management. *Journal of Communication Management, 10*(2), 123–137. https://doi.org/10.1108/13632540610664698

Coombs, W. T., Holladay, S. J., & Tachkova, E. R. (2018). When a scandal and a crisis fuse: Exploring the communicative implication of scansis. In A. Haller, M. Hendrik, and M. Kraus (Eds.), *Scandalogy: An interdisciplinary field* (pp. 172–190). Herbert von Harlem Verlag.

Coombs, W. T. & Tachkova, E. R (2019). Scansis as a unique crisis type: Theoretical and practical implications. *Journal of Communication Management, 23*(1), 72–88. https://doi.org/10.1108/JCOM-08-2018-0078

Eaddy, L. L., & Jin, Y. (2018). Crisis history tellers matter: The effects of crisis history and crisis information source on publics' cognitive and affective responses to organizational crisis. *Corporate Communications: An International Journal, 23*(2), 226–241. https://doi.org/10.1108/CCIJ-04-2017-0039

Sturges. (1994). Communicating through Crisis. *Management Communication Quarterly, 7*(3), 297–316. https://doi.org/10.1177/0893318994007003004

Tachkova, E. R. & Coombs, W. T. (2022). *Communicating in extreme crises: Lessons from the edge.* Routledge.

Thaler, R. H. (2015). *The making of behavioral economics: Misbehaving.* W.W. Norton & Company.

Weiner, B. (1995). *Judgments of responsibility: A foundation for a theory of social conduct.* Guilford Press.

EMOTIONAL LABOR, BURNOUT, AND COMPASSION AT WORK

Carsyn J. Endres & Sarah J. Tracy
Arizona State University

Balancing schoolwork, social responsibilities, and relationships can be daunting. May be you are reading this chapter after a long day, and you can already feel your mind wandering to your other obligations. The juggling act of managing our personal and professional responsibilities involves managing our emotions, keeping our cool, and battling burnout—all topics that have been at the forefront of communication scholar Sarah Tracy's research program. Sarah J. Tracy, Ph.D., is an award-winning researcher, author, professor, administrator, mentor, and consultant whose research centers on fostering human flourishing. Tracy's research and writing explores communication that fosters resilience in the face of organizational disruption and stress.

In the narrative below, Sarah shared her experience of the complexity of emotional work during her early job as a public relations practitioner. (Tracy & Redden, 2019, p. 155):

> I gulped in several breaths of warm evening air from the penthouse suite balcony. It felt good to escape the air conditioning and drama inside. Gazing toward the glowing lights several miles away, I imagined the Friday night West Los Angeles scene—beautiful people enjoying the beginning of their weekend. My watch read 8:12 p.m. I needed to get my face back together before returning to my current reality: working late, again, in a toxic environment, under deadline. My boss had made it clear: if I wanted to succeed, not only did my public relations writing need to be impeccable but I also needed to get used to working long hours and towing the line. Further, I had to conveniently look away from coworkers frequently glossing over ethical missteps. One of my senior colleagues called it "dancing." I called it making things up. I was 22 years old and absolutely miserable.

Tracy's experience is unfortunately very common. Lots of people struggle with managing emotions and stress at work. This chapter overviews the role of emotions at work, burnout, and the importance of organizational compassion.

EMOTIONAL LABOR IN ORGANIZATIONS

Tracy's research journey began by evaluating the importance of emotional management. Early organizational scholars inappropriately labeled emotions at work as an interference to organizational goals and processes (Dougherty & Drumheller, 2006), with strong emotional expressions viewed as threats to the health of the workplace that needed regulation (Paul & Riforgiate, 2015). It's no surprise, then, that initial emotion research focused on rules around emotional expression. Emotional management is work that is conducted in "private contexts for actors' own purposes" (Tracy & Tracy, 1998, p. 392). Imagine, for example, that you receive some bad news right before a holiday gathering. If you think you must put a smile on your face to please your hosts, you may engage in emotional management to pretend that nothing is wrong. While emotional management is feeling work done in private contexts, *emotional labor* is "the management of feelings to create a publicly observable facial and bodily display" (Tracy & Tracy, 1998, p. 392). Therefore, while sadness of the pet's family members is a display of emotional management, a veterinarian's expression of sadness while preforming a euthanasia is emotional labor.

Tracy and Tracy (1998) explored multiple ways that 911 emergency call-takers engaged in emotional labor. One strategy, for example, was self-talk. This approach allowed call-takers to manage their emotions by speaking to themselves in order to make sense of their often-traumatic experiences. In the passage below Tracy and Tracy (1998) share an example of this phenomena for 911 call-takers (p. 403):

> *Call-Taker:* The part that I really hate is the fact that they take it out on me since they can't take it out on the person that did something to them.
> *Interviewer:* How do you deal with that?
> *Call-Taker:* I just sit there and try to understand. I don't get mad at them…they feel like nobody is going to be able to solve their crime. I can put myself in their position especially when they don't know who did it, especially burglaries.

This example highlights the use of sensemaking to manage emotions in a difficult occupation. This passage shows call-takers both simultaneously reminding themselves that it is not personal and that they can not take the feelings of the other person personally.

Emerging from Tracy and Tracy's exploration of 911 call-takers arose the concept of *double-faced emotion management*. The authors described how the call-takers not only channeled the feelings of hysteria or anger from the callers but also managed their own emotions of irritation, disgust, etc. (Tracy & Tracy, 1998). This means that call-takers had to simultaneously manage the emotions of themselves and the callers. This dual management of emotion is common in a range of jobs—especially those in customer service—where employees must not only calm and placate customers, but also manage their own feelings of anger, fear, or disgust.

You might consider the various ways you have managed your own emotions—whether that is stifling a giggle during a serious presentation, hiding your irritation when dealing with a pushy customer, or exaggerating a smile to hopefully command a better tip. This type of emotion work is common at work and during play. And the need for double faced emotional management is especially common in situations of high stress, say for example, an airline had to cancel a full flight and now the airline representatives must manage their own emotions and those of the frustrated passengers.

Emotional labor can be a major source of organizational suffering. Sociologist Arlie Hochschild (1983) described how individuals experience emotive dissonance in the form of discomfort stemming from a mismatch between one's own authentic feelings and "fake" outward expression. Inauthentic expressions could look like a retail worker being expected to smile and suppress their true irritation when dealing with a difficult customer, or someone trying to remain composed in a job interview after being broken up with moments before. This type of emotional labor can be alienating, and individuals can find difficulty in performing inauthentic versions of themselves.

But, the pain of emotional labor is not just because of dissonance. Emotional labor is also difficult when employees can never escape organizational norms and also when their emotional expression is deemed by larger societal discourses to be low status (Tracy, 2000). On a cruise ship, for example Tracy (2000) described the "macro" or larger cultural discourse that "the customer is the boss." This mindset complicates the emotions of the cruise ship worker as they may have to suppress their own feelings of frustration in order to please passengers and supervisors. And this maintenance of remaining composed and collected becomes even more difficult without a break. On a cruise ship in the middle of the ocean— and with absolutely no days off—there is nowhere to hide from the grueling responsibilities of "the customer is always right" discourse.

You might consider a time when you have had to create a certain identity for a job and have not been able to escape to a "backstage." Take working at a summer camp, for example. Similar to a cruise ship, a summer camp is another environment with few areas that are "off-duty." Even if the campers are sleeping, a counselor still faces the watchful eyes of other counselors. Imagine you are working as a camp counselor for the summer, and you get a call that a family member has passed away. Managing your emotions and dealing with your grief in this situation is especially challenging and you may feel the need to suppress your sadness and slap on a smile.

Indeed, the pain and difficulty of emotional labor are complicated in "total institutions" (Goffman, 1961) contexts like this because of their controlling nature. Sarah identified that on the cruise ship, for example how the "staff's uncritical strive to please passengers" led to some problematic events (Tracy, 2000, p. 109). Consider the example below from Cassie, a junior assistant cruise director:

> There was this man at the disco and he asked me to dance. He was grabbing and holding me close … and saying these weird things. I just played dumb and acted as though I didn't understand. In this type of situation … you don't want to piss someone off. I had only been on the ship few months, and I didn't know what I could get away with and what

I could not. I was so frustrated that I had no control. I took it as if he had paid for the cruise and that we, as the cruise staff, are part of his cruise. (Tracy, 2000, p. 110)

Cassie is describing the phenomena of panoptic control. Panoptic control is the idea that people follow and obey rules and norms when they feel like they are constantly surveilled and disciplined (Foucoult, 1975). Although no supervisor was present mandating that Cassie dance with this customer, the watchful eyes of other passengers coupled with the norm that the "customer is always right" led to Cassie's own self-monitoring. What's more, she was engaging in what Burawoy (1985) coined as self-subordination (1985), which is when people discipline themselves in accordance with management goals, even when they are *not* being watched. As one might imagine, emotional labor, especially in a controlling organization like a cruise ship, can also lead to stress and burnout.

BURNOUT

Most people have a pretty good idea of what burnout feels like. Metaphorically, we might imagine watching a beautiful campfire slowly die out. In this passage, Tracy (2009) draws a narrative picture of burnout at work.

My alarm blared, but I yearned to stay tucked under the covers. The idea of going to work seemed overwhelming. I was tired of dealing with everyone else's whines and needs. It was just too much—too much work, too many conflicting responsibilities, too high of expectations. All of it was dragging on me, pushing me into a puddle of cynicism. Whereas I used to greet my work with energy, aspiration and passion, the job had slowly but surely eaten away at my confidence, enthusiasm and sense of control. What used to feel meaningful now felt like a chore. I coped by going on automatic pilot, and turned my co-workers and clients into faceless, nameless others—trying to disable them from sapping the little energy I had left. I felt depleted, bored, disengaged and exhausted. I was burned out. (p. 77)

While this example illuminates what burnout can look like, cases of burnout vary based on individual experiences. Typically, burnout is a result of unmanaged stress, and takes the form of emotional exhaustion, depersonalization, and a decreased sense of personal accomplishment (Tracy, 2009). Emotional exhaustion is usually associated with work that involves caring or interacting with other people, and the exhaustion part comes in distancing oneself emotionally from work and peers. Depersonalization is a negative shift in responses to others. This can look like treating humans as objects and being overall more alienated from other people and one's own identity (Tracy, 2009). Finally, the third dimension is an overall decrease of a sense of personal accomplishment. It may be that people begin their work feeling very proud and good about themselves, and over time, they gradually feel less and less talented or skilled.

So, what causes burnout? Researchers have argued a number of factors that make one more or less susceptible to burnout—one of them emerging from overworking. Overwork is particularly difficult when the job does not align with a person's self-concept and values. Another cause of burnout is when employees are faced with double binds in their work—a type of contradiction that creates a dilemma that employees cannot escape. When you are faced with a double bind—like the edict of "be spontaneous"—you are dammed if you do and you are dammed if you do not. If you are spontaneous, you are following directions and therefore being predictable, but if you are *not* spontaneous, then you are defying the edict. As you might imagine, double binds lead to burnout when, for instance, you are feeling guilty when you are not working and trying to rest and then feeling bothered by work when you try to step away.

Some jobs are especially riddled with double binds. Tracy (2003) discussed the tensions faced by correctional officers and how it led to their experiences of burnout. For example, officers wanted to show empathy toward the inmates while at the same time had to remain emotionally detached to protect their own emotions. Similarly, officers struggled to maintain consistency with the inmates while also being flexible with them. Managing tensions in the total institution atmosphere of a correctional institution contributed to burnout. In sum, it is clear that burnout is a complex organizational problem that impacts people in numerous ways.

MOVING BEYOND BURNOUT AND EMOTIONAL LABOR TO ENGAGEMENT AND COMPASSION

Although much of Tracy's early career scholarship revolved around the difficulties and trials of emotional labor and burnout, her more recent scholarship has begun exploring the brighter side of organizing. She argues that instead of merely trying to prevent negative behaviors in organizations, we can actively work to construct positive ones. Following the framework set by (Maslach et al., 2001), Tracy centers engagement as the antipathy to burnout (Tracy, 2009). Even more recently, Tracy has focused on compassionate communication in organizations.

Past scholars who have explored emotions such as kindness and compassion have found that this type of work is consistently undervalued. In fact, research surrounding compassion in organizations is still fairly recent (Tracy & Huffman, 2017; Way & Tracy, 2012), yet scholars are increasingly addressing human flourishing. Work surrounding compassion is typically unpaid labor that is expected of women and is "not credentialed and is considered natural and instinctual rather than due to education or skill" (Tracy, 2008, p. 169). Most of the past research on compassion was focused on people who were thought to be the least likely to ask for and accept help (Miller, 2007).

Way and Tracy (2012) discuss that compassionate communication is a combination of three processes: (1) recognizing, (2) relating, and (3) (re)acting. The first component of compassionate communication is the journey from noticing to recognizing suffering. This "requires an openness and receptivity to what is going on in those around us, paying attention to others' emotions and reading subtle cues in our daily interactions with them" (Kanov et al., 2004, p. 812). Recognizing suffering also implies noting the means of communication behaviors as well as the meanings of what is *not* being communicated (Way & Tracy, 2012). Recognizing goes beyond noticing communicative cues to more deeply understand the value in the cues, timing, and context (Way & Tracy, 2012). Therefore, if you see that someone is struggling, recognizing involves taking the extra time and effort to understand the root cause of their experience.

The second component of compassion is relating. Relating "encompasses possibilities for both affective feeling and cognitive connecting, while not privileging one over the other or requiring both" (Way & Tracy, 2012, p. 303). Relating is identifying with or feeling and connecting with another person. Consider the last time someone stopped to ask how you were doing. Not just a passing "How are you?" but someone who actually took the time to be curious about your well-being. Relating takes mindful intentionality. Relating can involve vulnerability like opening up about a time when you were also struggling.

The final component of compassion is (re)acting, defined as "engaging in behaviors or communicating in ways that are seen, or could be seen, as compassionate by the provider, the recipient, and or another individual" (Tracy & Huffman, 2017, p. 2). The parentheses around "re" suggests that compassionate action might not just be a response to someone else's pain but can also be proactive (Way & Tracy, 2012). Intentional action is what makes compassion stand apart from empathy and can take many forms; it could be giving someone space to be with themselves, performing an act of service to try and lessen their load, or even just reaching out to let the other person that you are there if they need you.

CONCLUSION

Something that draws all of Sarah Tracy's work together is the hope that her scholarship may not only extend theory in the areas of emotion and organizing, but also provide actionable wisdom that people can put into practice in their own lives to improve flourishing. Tracy's research has served as a catalyst for other scholarship tackling complex problems within organizations.

So, as you reflect on this chapter, you might ask yourself how you can best use what you have learned. Everyone is managing emotional labor, burnout, and compassion in different ways. It's important to explore what tools you have in your toolbox to recognize, honor, and connect with your own and others' emotions.

Consider how your emotions are impacting you. We are all human beings, and human beings have emotions! Sarah Tracy's research would suggest that you give yourself permission to feel your emotions instead of bottling them up inside. Acknowledging your emotions and the toll they are taking is a crucial part of emotional management. If you find yourself experiencing burnout, brainstorm some ways that you can reduce your facetime or workload. Recognize the signs of burnout. In other words, what leads you to feel most energized and engaged? Consider how to be intentional with what you give your time and effort.

Finally, Tracy's work would encourage you to create more compassion for yourself and others. Remember that compassionate communication is a combination of (1) recognizing, (2) relating, and (3) (re)acting. Invite yourself and those around you to share in more authentic and open communication. The path to honoring our emotions is an ongoing commitment. While this work is difficult, acknowledging the importance of your emotional experiences at work is a great place to start.

REFERENCES

Dougherty, D. S., & Drumheller, K. (2006). Sensemaking and emotions in organizations: Accounting for emotions in a rational(ized) context. *Communication Studies, 57*(2), 215–238. https://doi.org/10.1080/10510970600667030

Burawoy, M. (1985). *The politics of production: Factory regimes under capitalism and socialism*. Verso.

Foucoult, M. (1975). Discipline and punish. *A. Sheridan, Tr., Paris, FR, Gallimard.*

Goffman, E. (1961). *Asylums*. Anchor.

Hochschild, A. R. (1983). *The managed heart: Commercialization of human feeling*. University of California Press.

Kanov, J. M., Maitlis, S., Worline, M. C., Dutton, J. E., Frost, P. J., & Lilius, J. M. (2004). Compassion in organizational life. *American Behavioral Scientist, 47*(6), 808–827. https://doi.org/10.1177/0002764203260211

Maslach, C., Schaufeli, W. B., & Leiter, M. P. (2001). Job burnout. *Annual Review of Psychology, 52*, 397–422. https://doi.org/10.1146/annurev.psych.52.1.397

Miller, K. I. (2007). Compassionate communication in the workplace: Exploring processes of noticing, connecting, and responding. *Journal of Applied Communication Research, 35*(3), 223–245. https://doi.org/10.1080/00909880701434208

Paul, G. D., & Riforgiate, S. E. (2015). "Putting on a happy face," "getting back to work," and "letting it go": Traditional and restorative justice understandings of emotions at work. *Electronic Journal of Communication, 25*(3 & 4). http://www.cios.org/getfile/025303_EJC

Tracy, S. J. (2000). Becoming a character for commerce: Emotion labor, self-subordination and discursive construction of identity in a total institution. *Management Communication Quarterly, 14*(1), 90–128. https://doi.org/10.1177/0893318900141004

Tracy, S. J. (2003). Corrections contradictions: A structural approach to addressing officer burnout. *Corrections Today, 65*, 90–95.

Tracy, S. J. (2008). Care as a common good. *Women's Studies in Communication, 31*(2), 166–174. https://doi.org/10.1080/07491409.2008.10162529

Tracy, S. J. (2009). Managing burnout and moving toward employee engagement: Reinvigorating the study of stress at work. In P. Lutgen-Sandvik & B. D. Sypher (Eds.), *Destructive organizational communication: Processes, consequences, and constructive ways of organizing* (pp. 77–98). Routledge.

Tracy, S. J., & Huffman, T. P. (2017). Compassion in the face of terror: A case study of recognizing suffering, co-creating hope, and developing trust in a would-be school shooting. *Communication Monographs, 84*(1), 30–53. https://doi.org/10.1080/03637751.2016.1218642

Tracy, S. J., & Redden, S. M. (2019). The structuration of emotion. In A. M. Nicotera (Ed.). *Origins and traditions of organizational communication: A comprehensive look into the field* (pp. 348–369). Routledge.

Tracy, S. J., & Tracy, K. (1998). Emotion labor at 911: A case study and theoretical critique. *Journal of Applied Communication Research, 26*(4), 390–411. http://doi.org/10.1080/00909889809365516

Way, D., & Tracy, S. J. (2012). Conceptualizing compassion as recognizing, relating and (re)acting: An ethnographic study of compassionate communication at hospice. *Communication Monographs, 79*(3), 292–315. https://doi.org/10.1080/03637751.2012.697630

PERSUASION AND RHETORIC

Persuasion is a pervasive phenomenon affecting our everyday lives on both an interpersonal and a social scale. Persuasion has been the subject of considerable and focused scholarship since antiquity, however, advances in technology have added a layer of complexity to its study. Altering the beliefs, attitudes, values, and behaviors of other people is a useful but challenging task. The three chapters in this section explore strategies for increasing our effectiveness in influencing others. First, Robin Nabi (University of California, Santa Barbara) examines how evoked emotions impact our attempts to be persuasive. She examines research to answer the question as to when and how inducing fear, guilt, or humor in an audience enhances the likelihood they are persuaded to agree with us. Second, Christina Foust (Metropolitan State University of Denver) provides strategies for ways we can engage more effectively in social movement activism in a digital age. By situating convergence of social movement and social media within larger conversations about what "effective" social movement rhetoric involves, Foust explores the impact of digital media on the ecology of social change. Foust utilized case studies to identify promising practices for engaging in consequential social movement activism in a digital age. Finally, Lijiang Shen (The Pennsylvania State University), introduces psychological reactance theory and explains why people do the opposite of what they are asked (or told) to do. Shen explains the process of psychological reactance and provides communication strategies to mitigate it.

THE PERSUASIVE INFLUENCE
OF EMOTION

Robin L. Nabi
University of California, Santa Barbara

In everyday life, we are bombarded with persuasive messages in the media. One cannot turn on the television, browse the Internet, or scroll through social media without exposure to attempts at persuasion. Yet, decades of persuasion research have documented just how challenging it can be to alter the beliefs, attitudes, and especially the behaviors of others. Indeed, one of the key challenges in persuasion is simply securing the attention of the audience in the first place. Given message exposure is a necessary condition for that message to have any chance at achieving its desired effect, this is a critical issue in all persuasion endeavors, particularly in the modern digital world. As such, numerous strategies have been employed to capture audience attention, and primary among these is the use of emotional appeals. The assumption is that by using scary, angering, or amusing messages, for example, the audience will not only be more likely to pay attention to the message but also, given their emotional state, be more motivated to yield to its claims. But is this truly the case? Are audiences more likely to yield to a persuasive message that evokes an emotional response?

As we look at the research literature on emotional appeals, it is clear that the answer to this question is not a simple one. Sometimes emotions facilitate attitude and behavior change; other times they actually interfere. Further, different emotions may affect the persuasive process differently, so generalizations across emotions are unlikely to hold. Understanding how each emotion influences how people think and choose to act, then, is critical not only to the choice of whether to use an emotional appeal or not but also how to design one that has the greatest chance of achieving its goals.

The overwhelming majority of the research on emotion and persuasion has centered around fear arousal and its effects on both message processing and the outcomes of attitudes, behavioral intentions, and behaviors, though increasing attention is being paid to the persuasive influence of other emotional states, like guilt and amusement. This chapter overviews what is currently known about the persuasive effect of different emotions and the implications of this knowledge for successful message design. In essence, the research question this chapter addresses is: "How do evoked emotions affect our attempts to be persuasive?"

FEAR APPEAL RESEARCH

The fear appeal literature has cycled through several theoretical perspectives over the past 50 years (see Myrick & Nabi, 2017, for a more detailed discussion). First, fear was thought to be akin to drive states, like hunger, motivating people to adopt message recommendations expected to alleviate their unpleasant feelings (Hovland et al., 1953). But when research showed fear appeals sometimes led to successful persuasion and other times backfired, scholars began thinking about fear not simply as a motivational state but as a cognitive one as well (Leventhal, 1970). That is, scholars asserted that sometimes fear may promote rational thought, allowing people to focus on how to best protect themselves from a threat, which increases the chances they will adopt the message's recommendations. However, fear as a motivational state would lead people to engage in counterproductive responses, like denial or reactance (message resistance stemming from perceiving an unjust restriction to one's freedom to choose; Brehm, 1966), and thus reject the message's recommendations. As conceptualization of fear's cognitive components progressed, scholars determined that four cognitions, or thoughts, are necessary for the success of a persuasive appeal. First, a person must see a threat as something that is severe, or potentially very dangerous. Second, a person must see themselves as susceptible to that threat. Combined, these two perceptions lead to the emotion of fear. Whether that fear leads to effective action is in part dependent on two other judgments: response efficacy, or whether there is an action that can help one to avoid that threat, and self-efficacy, or whether the person believes they can actually take that action (Witte, 1992).

So imagine we have the goal of changing the behavior of texting while driving. How might we try to persuade drivers to stop this dangerous behavior? Using the model of fear appeals outlined above, we must first point out how severe the consequences are for performing the behavior. We could use statistics (e.g., texting while driving is more than twice as dangerous as drinking and driving), or we might depict a fatal accident caused by a driver distracted while texting. We would also note that the audience is susceptible to those negative outcomes to the extent they text while driving, even if only on occasion. We then offer an effective response to help the audience see that they can avoid the scary possibility of a fatal car accident by, for example, suggesting the driver put the cell phone in the back seat, out of reach to avoid temptation. Finally, we would indicate that this is a behavior that is easily accomplished. According to theories like the protection motivation model (PMM; Rogers, 1975, 1983) and the extended parallel process model (EPPM; Witte, 1992), this message structure should increase the chances that this message will change the audience's behavior and thus reduce the incidence of texting while driving.

However, though this message design may increase the chances of persuasion over messages that do not evoke fear, it does not guarantee persuasive success. Some audience members will not perceive the danger, and thus will not experience fear. Some will not believe the outcome will happen to them, and thus have no motivation to change their behavior. And still other audience members will think the response will not work or that they can not actually do it. Indeed, some might even avoid listening to the message to avoid feeling fear at all. Thus, though our fear appeal may work for some, the audience's perception of the message information is highly variable, which makes persuasive success hard to secure.

Still, evidence does support a small to moderately sized positive relationship between fear arousal and attitude, behavioral intention, and behavior change, and meta-analyses, or statistical reviews, of the fear research suggest that the cognitions identified in the PMT, and later the EPPM, are important to fear appeal effectiveness (e.g., Tannenbaum et al., 2015; Witte & Allen, 2000). Still, there are significant holes in our knowledge. First, no model of fear appeals has been endorsed as fully capturing the process of fear's effects on decision-making and action. To the extent message features evoke perceptions of susceptibility and severity, as well as response and self-efficacy, fear may generate persuasion, but how these constructs relate to one another is still unclear. Additionally, questions about whether severity and susceptibility information should always be explicitly included in a message, or whether "implicit" fear appeals might be more effective, have also been raised (Nabi et al., 2008). That is, evidence suggests that when audiences are very knowledgeable about a subject, including information about the severity and susceptibility of a threat in a fear appeal may actually be more irritating than fear-inducing and thus less effective. Indeed, the research on fear appeals is rather complicated by the fact that fear appeals often evoke emotions other than just fear, like anger, sadness, or disgust (Dillard et al., 1996), which makes it difficult to assess the effects of fear versus these other emotions. Thus, in sum, though fear appeals generally give a persuasive advantage over nonfear-based messages, there is still much work to be done in linking the theory of fear appeals to appropriate message design.

THE PERSUASIVE EFFECT OF GUILT

Unlike fear appeals, there has been minimal theorizing regarding the effects of guilt on attitude change. Still, there is some discussion in the research literature about how one might evoke guilt and the conditions under which it may be effective in persuasive contexts (O'Keefe, 2002). Guilt is typically evoked when people feel they have violated an internalized norm (Lazarus, 1991), like "one shouldn't lie" or "one shouldn't cause harm to another." Thus, creating the perception that one has transgressed against, or harmed, another person is likely to evoke guilt in one's audience. Further, people are likely to feel more guilt over transgressions when there is some preexisting interpersonal relationship. That is, a person will likely feel more guilty after lying to a friend than to a stranger. Once guilt is aroused, a person is motivated to alleviate that uncomfortable state by making amends to the wronged party. For example, if you have lied to your parents, you might voluntarily do some extra chores around the house. This action may not undo the lie, but it does offer a benefit to the harmed party while also helping to reestablish your view of yourself as a good person, all of which help to alleviate guilt. Given guilt is such an uncomfortable state, people are motivated to reduce it quickly. Making amends is one way to reduce guilt, but people also eliminate guilt through various forms of rationalization, for example, by denying they did something wrong or convincing themselves the harmed party deserved what they got.

Of course, the question here is: does guilt help or harm persuasion? The answer is, unsurprisingly, it depends. Early studies of guilt in interpersonal contexts assumed that guilt would increase compliance with requests from strangers, and research seemed to support that hypothesis (e.g., Carlsmith & Gross, 1969; Freedman et al., 1967). Indeed, meta-analysis results support a positive linear relationship between guilt-inducing interpersonal transgression and compliance (O'Keefe, 2000). Further, guilt has also been shown to be effective in interpersonal contexts with stronger relational ties (Baumeister et al., 1994).

However, interestingly, evidence from media-based studies suggest a *negative* linear relationship in that the stronger the guilt appeal in a media message (e.g., a telethon to raise money for victims of a natural disaster), the less persuasive the message may be (O'Keefe, 2000). This effect tends to be attributed to the fact that high levels of guilt are associated with high levels of anger (Pinto & Priest, 1991), which short-circuits attitude change if the anger is directed at the source of the message (Nabi, 2002b). The striking contrast between guilt in interpersonal versus media contexts is likely a function of the lack of interpersonal connection between the media message source and the audience. This does not mean, however, that guilt cannot be a successful media strategy. Rather, care must be taken in message design to minimize the likelihood of resistance.

Based on the theoretical conceptualization of guilt as well as the small body of empirical literature, it is clear that media messages should be somewhat subtle in pointing out past transgressions (e.g., not eating healthy or exercising frequently enough) or anticipated transgressions (e.g., not donating to a worthy cause or sponsoring a child in a developing country) to keep guilt arousal moderate and minimize the chances of evoking reactance. Next, to the extent a familiar and likable source (e.g., a celebrity or influencer) can deliver the message, the perception of an interpersonal relationship may increase, thus increase the audience's tolerance for the guilt experience. Third, guilt messages should provide clear and easy-to-perform behaviors that can be performed quickly to alleviate the guilt. If there is too much time passage between message exposure and opportunity to act, the likelihood that the guilt will dissipate by some other means (e.g., denial) greatly increases, thus reducing the chances the audience will comply with the recommended action. Finally, media messages may wish to tap into anticipated guilt. That is, rather than leave the audience feeling guilty over past mistakes, messages can help audiences see how they can avoid feeling guilty by altering their behavior to avoid creating future harm (e.g., do not text and drive so that you will not feel guilty about causing an accident at some point in the future) (Carcioppolo et al., 2017; Lindsey,

2005). These are just a few suggestions for how to design more effective guilt appeals, though more theorizing and research are needed to substantiate these claims.

HUMOR AND PERSUASION

A third area of emotion and persuasion that has received notable attention is the role of humor in various forms of advertising. Although there is a general sense that funny advertisements are effective, in fact, reviews of the humor literature suggest little persuasive advantage compared to serious messaging. Meta-analyses of humorous advertising (Eisend, 2009; Walter et al., 2018) suggest that there is only a small relationship between humor in response to a persuasive message and changes in intentions to perform a behavior, like purchasing a new product or starting a new health behavior, and there is little evidence that humor translates into actual behavior. Further, to the extent that humor arousal generates some persuasive outcome, the relationship may be a curvilinear one. That is, the most persuasive benefit may come from messages that do not generate too much or too little amusement.

Importantly, however, such reviews have noted that humor may enhance message attention and source liking. Given, as noted earlier, that message attention is a necessary, though not sufficient, condition for persuasive success, the fact that funny messages garner greater attention means that they may, in fact, have an inherent persuasive advantage in a competitive media environment. However, though humor may offer an advantage in terms of capturing attention, if not implemented properly, it may undermine that advantage if the humor distracts from, rather than is integrated with, the main point of the message. For example, the classic Energizer bunny commercials are arguably effective because the bunny is so directly tied to the product name and slogan. However, the concepts of "bunny" and "batteries" are not naturally linked, so it is possible that though people may remember and like the commercials, they may have difficulty remember with what product or brand they are associated (e.g., Duracell rather than Energizer), thus undermining their effectiveness in terms of purchase behavior.

Finally, in light of the tremendous popularity of political satire programs, such as the *Daily Show* and the *Late Late Show*, there has been an upswing in interest in examining the process through which humor may have persuasive influence, especially given evidence that humorous messages seem to increase knowledge gain (Walter et al., 2018). Nabi et al. (2007) argue that humor may not have immediate persuasive effect because though audiences attend closely to the message, they discount it as a joke that is not intended to persuade, thus minimizing the message content's effects on their attitudes. However, they also posit that this type of processing may lead to a "sleeper effect" such that the persuasive effect of humor may emerge after some time has passed (see also Appel & Richter, 2007; Young, 2008). Although there is not consistent support for this hypothesis (see Walter et al., 2018), it raises the issue of the importance of considering how humor influences how deeply audiences engage with messages and the point at which persuasive outcomes should be assessed. Clearly, future research would benefit from closer examination of the contexts, processes, and timing of humor's effect in media-based persuasive efforts.

GENERAL THEORETICAL FRAMEWORKS FOR EMOTIONAL APPEALS

Despite the focus on a very limited number of emotions thus far, there is growing interest in understanding the effects of a range of emotions in the processing of persuasive messages (see Myrick, 2015, for a more extensive discussion), and emerging models attempt to examine those processes. For example, the cognitive functional model (CFM; Nabi, 1999) attempts to explain how message-relevant negative emotions (e.g., fear, anger, sadness, guilt, and disgust) affect the direction and stability of persuasive outcome based on three constructs—emotion-driven motivated attention to the issue at hand, motivated processing of the message, and expectation of that the message will provide reassurance from the negative situation presented. An initial test of the model (Nabi, 2002a) offered support for some, though not all, of the model's propositions, and other research suggests its usefulness in understanding the persuasive effects of emotions that have received less attention, like anger (Walter et al., 2019). As such, the CFM offers potentially useful insight into the processes through which a range of discrete emotions, not just fear, influence message outcomes.

In a similar vein, Nabi (2003, 2007) posits an emotions-as-frames model to explain the effects of more general media exposure on attitudinal and behavioral outcomes. In this model, emotions are conceptualized as frames, or perspectives, through which incoming stimuli are interpreted. The model first notes that certain message features are likely to evoke various discrete emotions. These emotional experiences, moderated by individual differences, like prior knowledge or coping style, are predicted to influence both accessibility of information in the mind as well as information seeking in the environment, which ultimately generate emotion-consistent decisions and action. Nabi argues that through this perspective, we may ultimately have a better understanding of the potentially central role emotions may play in understanding how message frames in a range of media messages, including those designed to persuade, might impact attitudes and behaviors. In fact, a recent meta-analysis demonstrated the central role that emotions aroused in response to differently framed messages play in understanding message effects (Nabi et al., 2019).

The most recent theoretical development in the emotion and persuasion literature is the introduction of the notion of emotional flow, which suggests that as different pieces of information are unveiled in a persuasive message, emotional responses shift, which can explain, in part, the success of emotion-based persuasive messages (Nabi, 2015). For example, in the case of fear appeals, when audiences are exposed to information about a severe threat to which they may be susceptible, they are likely to feel fear. But what do they feel in response to efficacy information? Nabi (2015) argues such information is likely associated with hope. Thus, it may be that fear appeals persuade people to enact the recommended behavior to the extent that they generate an emotional flow from fear to hope. Indeed, recent evidence suggests that hope associated with the recommended actions within a fear appeal increases persuasive success (Nabi et al., 2018). Importantly, emotional flow reflects not only shifts between emotions but also changes in the intensity of a single emotion. For example, research on the trajectory of fear in response to threat-based messages has shown that when fear peaks mid-message and then resolves, fear appeals are more persuasive (Dillard et al., 2017).

Despite these advances, there is much that is still unknown about the effects of emotions on persuasive outcomes. We know little about the conditions under which various negative emotions, like sadness or envy, contribute to persuasive outcome. Additionally, there has been very little attention to positive emotions, like hope, pride, and compassion, in motivating attitude and behavior change. Beyond the types of emotions investigated, we also need to know more about the conditions under which emotions draw attention to messages versus generate message avoidance. Of course, once attention is gained, it is critical that the rest of the message be structured appropriately for the audience. Understanding the delicate balance between gaining attention and harnessing it to intended effect has been an elusive challenge in the area of emotional appeals and persuasion, and future research would be well-served by tackling this difficult message design issue.

Further, there has been surprisingly little attention to the types of themes that are likely to evoke particular emotions in specific target audiences. For example, the assumption in fear appeal research is that people are scared by threats to their physical body, most especially thoughts of death. Yet fears of disability (e.g., paralysis and blindness) or disfigurement may prove equally, and sometimes more, frightening than death. Further, not all fears are rooted in physical well-being. Younger audiences are more likely to view themselves as invulnerable to serious physical calamity. However, given teenagers and young adults are still forming their identities, threats to social acceptance may be far more salient, and thus more frightening, to such audiences than threats to physical well-being. Thus, social harm-based fear appeals may be more effective for such audiences than physical harm-based fear appeals. Future research would be well-served by considering not simply a greater range of emotional responses, but also matching message content and features to the desired emotional arousal for particular target audiences.

CONCLUSION

At their most functional, emotional states can facilitate attention to persuasive messages and motivate productive action. However, they can also deter desire to attend to a message and lead to rationalization processes that interfere with persuasive success. To this point, fear is the only emotion that has been the focus of substantial theorizing in the domain of emotion and persuasion. Other emotions, like guilt and humor, are in their nascent stages of development, and still other emotions, like anger, sadness, and hope, have been subject to only very limited empirical attention. Indeed, there are still many open questions about the conditions under which fear appeals, as well as other emotional appeals, facilitate attitude and behavior change.

Ultimately, the successful use of emotion to persuade requires first, a solid understanding of the various emotional states so that one can choose the emotion that is most consistent with one's goals. For example, fear may be useful to alert people to behaviors they do not see as dangerous (e.g., texting while driving) whereas hope may be more useful to motivate people to continue to attempt to change hard-to-change behaviors (e.g., quitting smoking). Second, care must be taken not to arouse emotions that may be counterproductive, like anger, which may generate reactance against the message's goals, or shame, which may lead audience to avoid the message whenever possible. Finally, it is important that emotional appeals convey a sense of response and self-efficacy, so audiences know what they are to do and that they are able to do it. As we await greater theoretical development across the array of emotional appeals that may be used, these guidelines may help us achieve the benefits, while avoiding the pitfalls, of the use of emotion in persuasive contexts.

REFERENCES

Appel, M., & Richter, T. (2007). Persuasive effects of fictional narratives increase over time. *Media Psychology, 10*(1), 113–134. https://doi.org/10.1080/15213260701301194

Baumeister, R. F., Stillwell, A. M., & Heatherton, T. F. (1994). Guilt: An interpersonal approach. *Psychological Bulletin, 115*(2), 243–267. https://doi.org/10.1037/0033-2909.115.2.243

Brehm, J. (1966). *A theory of psychological reactance.* Academic Press.

Carcioppolo, N., Li, C., Chudnovskaya, E. V., Kharsa, R., Stephan, T., & Nickel, K. (2017). The comparative efficacy of a hybrid guilt-fear appeal and a traditional fear appeal to influence HPV vaccination intentions. *Communication Research, 44*(3), 437–458. https://doi.org/10.1177/0093650215616457

Carlsmith, J. M., & Gross, A. E. (1969). Some effects of guilt on compliance. *Journal of Personality and Social Psychology, 11*(3), 232–239. https://doi.org/10.1037/h0027039

Dillard, J. P., Li, R., & Huang, Y. (2017). Threat appeals: The fear-persuasion relationship is linear and curvilinear. *Health Communication, 32*(11), 1358–1367. https://doi.org/10.1080/10410236.2016.1220345

Dillard, J. P., Plotnick, C. A., Godbold, L. C., Freimuth, V. S., & Edgar, T. (1996). The multiple affective outcomes of AIDS PSAs: Fear appeals do more than scare people. *Communication Research, 23*(1), 44–72. https://doi.org/10.1177/009365096023001002

Eisend, M. (2009). A meta-analysis of humor in advertising. *Journal of the Academy of Marketing Science, 37*, 191–203. https://doi.org/10.1007/s11747-008-0096-y

Freedman, J. L., Wallington, S. A., & Bless, E. (1967). Compliance without pressure: The effect of guilt. *Journal of Personality and Social Psychology, 7*(2), 117–124. https://doi.org/10.1037/h0025009

Hovland, C. I., Janis, I. L., & Kelley, H. H. (1953). *Communication and persuasion.* Yale University Press.

Lazarus, R. S. (1991). *Emotion and adaptation.* Oxford University Press.

Leventhal, H. (1970). Findings and theory in the study of fear communications. In L. Berkowitz (Ed.), *Advances in experimental social psychology* (Vol. 5, pp. 119–186). Academic Press. https://doi.org/10.1016/S0065-2601(08)60091-X

Lindsey, L. L. M. (2005). Anticipated guilt as behavioral motivation: An examination of appeals to help unknown others through bone marrow donation. *Human Communication Research, 31*(4), 453–481. https://doi.org/10.1093/hcr/31.4.453

Myrick, J. G. (2015). *The role of emotions in preventative health communication.* Lexington Books.

Myrick, J. G., & Nabi, R. L. (2017). Fear arousal and health and risk messaging. In R. Parrott (Ed.), *Oxford research encyclopedia of health and risk message design and processing.* https://doi.org/10.1093/acrefore/9780190228613.013.266

Nabi, R. L. (1999). A cognitive-functional model for the effects of discrete negative emotions on information processing, attitude change, and recall. *Communication Theory, 9*(3), 292–320. https://doi.org/10.1111/j.1468-2885.1999.tb00172.x

Nabi, R. L. (2002a). Anger, fear, uncertainty, and attitudes: A test of the cognitive-functional model. *Communication Monographs, 69*(3), 204–216. https://doi.org/10.1080/03637750216541

Nabi, R. L. (2002b). Discrete emotions and persuasion. In J. Dillard & M. Pfau (Eds.), *Handbook of persuasion* (pp. 289–308). Sage. https://doi.org/10.4135/9781412976046.n15

Nabi, R. L. (2003). Exploring the framing effects of emotion: Do discrete emotions differentially influence information accessibility, information seeking, and policy preference? *Communication Research, 30*(2), 224–247. https://doi.org/10.1177/0093650202250881

Nabi, R. L. (2007). Emotion and persuasion: A social cognitive perspective. In D. R. Roskos-Ewoldsen & J. Monahan (Eds.), *Social cognition and communication: Theories and methods* (pp. 377–398). Erlbaum.

Nabi, R. L. (2015). Emotional flow in persuasive health messages. *Health Communication, 30*(2), 114–124. https://doi.org/10.1080/10410236.2014.974129

Nabi, R. L., & Gustafson, A., & Jensen, R. (2018). Framing climate change: Exploring the role of emotion in generating advocacy behavior. *Science Communication, 40*(4), 442–468. https://doi.org/10.1177/1075547018776019

Nabi, R. L., Moyer-Gusé, E. & Byrne, S. (2007). All joking aside: A serious investigation into the persuasive effect of funny social messages. *Communication Monographs, 74*(1), 29–54. https://doi.org/10.1080/03637750701196896

Nabi, R. L., Roskos-Ewoldsen, D., & Dillman-Carpentier, F. (2008). Subjective knowledge and fear appeal effectiveness: Implications for message design. *Health Communication, 23*(2), 191–201. https://doi.org/10.1080/10410230701808327

Nabi, R. L., Walter, N., Oshidary, N., Endacott, C., Love-Nicols, J., Lew, Z., & Aune, A. (2019). Can emotions capture the elusive gain-loss framing effect? A meta-analysis. *Communication Research, 47*(8), 1107–1130. https://doi.org/10.1177/0093650219861256

O'Keefe, D. J. (2000). Guilt and social influence. *Annals of the International Communication Association, 23*(1), 67–101. https://doi.org/10.1080/23808985.2000.11678970

O'Keefe, D. J. (2002). Guilt as a mechanism of persuasion. In J. P. Dillard & M. Pfau (Eds.), *The persuasion handbook: Developments in theory and practice* (pp. 329–344). Sage. https://doi.org/10.4135/9781412976046.n17

Pinto, M. B., & Priest, S. (1991). Guilt appeals in advertising: An exploratory study. *Psychological Reports, 69*(2), 375–385. https://doi.org/10.2466/pr0.1991.69.2.375

Rogers, R. W. (1975). A protection motivation theory of fear appeals and attitude change. *Journal of Psychology, 91*(1), 93–114. https://doi.org/10.1080/00223980.1975.9915803

Rogers, R. W. (1983). Cognitive and physiological processes in fear appeals and attitude change: A revised theory of protection motivation. In J. T. Cacioppo & R. E. Petty (Eds.), *Social psychophysiology* (pp. 153–176). Guilford Press.

Tannenbaum, M. B., Hepler, J., Zimmerman, R. S., Saul, L., Jacobs, S., Wilson, K., & Albarracín, D. (2015). Appealing to fear: A meta-analysis of fear appeal effectiveness and theories. *Psychological Bulletin, 141*(6), 1178–1204. https://doi.org/10.1037/a0039729

Walter, N., Cody, M. J., Xu, L. Z., & Murphy, S. T. (2018). A priest, a rabbi, and a minister walk into a bar: A meta-analysis of humor effects on persuasion. *Human Communication Research, 44*(4), 343–373. https://doi.org/10.1093/hcr/hqy005

Walter, N., Tukachinsky, R., Pelled, A., & Nabi, R. (2019). Meta-analysis of anger and persuasion: An empirical integration of four models. *Journal of Communication, 69*(1), 73–93. https://doi.org/10.1093/joc/jqy054

Witte, K. (1992). Putting the fear back into fear appeals: The extended parallel process model. *Communication Monographs, 59*(4), 329–349. https://doi.org/10.1080/03637759209376276

Witte, K., & Allen, M. (2000). A meta-analysis of fear appeals: Implications for effective public health campaigns. *Health Education & Behavior, 27*(5), 591–615. https://doi.org/10.1177/109019810002700506

Young, D. (2008). The privileged role of the late-night joke: Exploring humor's role in disrupting argument scrutiny. *Media Psychology, 11*(1), 119–142. https://doi.org/10.1080/15213260701837073

PROMISING PRACTICES FOR EFFECTIVE ACTIVISM IN A DIGITAL AGE

Christina Foust
Metropolitan State University of Denver

INTRODUCTION

I grew up in a small town in central Iowa, where I began developing a feminist consciousness from my mom. The 10th of 11 kids, and youngest girl, she had a unique place in this second generation (at least on my grandfather's side) Dutch farm family. Because her older siblings had moved on to their own nuclear (often farm) families or military service, and because her parents were in their late 50s and early 60s when she was a teen, she did all the physical labor that her brothers were expected to do. And, when she was not throwing hay bales or helping deliver calves (my mom is famous for having small but strong hands to support such a task), she was helping my grandmother clean, bake rolls, and care for others. My mom had (and still has) a sharp eye for contradiction. And in the U.S. Midwest, from the 1960s through the 1990s, double standards for boys and girls abounded.

My mom did not know it, but she was really passing me a baton. I took it and ran with what I had available to me in a small town in central Iowa as a teenager, strengthening not only my vision, but also my voice, when it came to calling out what was unfair and asking for change. When I was a senior in high school, for instance, I asked: Why wouldn't we stop calling teen girls names, while we celebrated teen boys' sexual promiscuity? Why wouldn't we supply birth control to teens to prevent pregnancy and STIs rather than stigmatizing sexuality, especially for girls? It did not make any sense. I was fortunate to have support from amazing teachers (like Mrs. P) to transform these questions into an original oratory. I went to undergraduate and found that the Speech Communication major would support my desire to figure this out and talk to others about it. I imagine for teens growing up today, state bans on gender affirming health care and even bathroom access, join a growing list of contradictions and injustices to which we should all be responsive.

Thirty years and three college degrees later, the puzzles have only grown with complexity and pathos. As the Internet and smart phones became more accessible in the early 2000s—and soon joined by platforms like YouTube, Facebook, Twitter, Instagram, and TikTok—I witnessed events such as the Arab Spring and Occupy Wall Street; protests led by #BlackLivesMatter and #SchoolStrike4Climate; and the explicit convergence of White supremacy with conservative activism. Some view digitally mediated movements as fundamentally new and different, for better and worse. Questions about the ethics of socially mediated protest, in particular, have followed the circulation of hate speech, racist and sexist tropes, and attacks on democracy. Others wonder if the "new" digital activism is as effective as "old school" protest, where showing up in public places quite literally puts one's body where one's heart and words are. The purpose of this chapter is to help us sort out claims about digitally mediated movements. Given the urgency of now—which includes threats to the carrying capacity of Earth, which have been building with centuries of colonial and racist systems—it is also wise to ask: How does one engage more effectively in social movement activism in a digital age?

I answer this question by first situating "social movement 2.0" (the convergence of social movement and social media), within larger conversations about what "effective" social movement rhetoric involves. I then consider whether or not social movements fundamentally change with digital media. Perhaps not surprisingly, I argue that there are a few key features of digital technology which shape communication in unique ways, but for the most part, the ecology of social change remains quite similar to social movements past. This leads me to identify promising practices for engaging in consequential social movement activism in a digital age, with the help of case studies.

"EFFECTIVE" SOCIAL MOVEMENT RHETORIC

When Griffin (1952) coined the rhetoric of historic movements as a sub-field within rhetoric and communication, his primary contribution was expanding what "counts" as the legitimate object of focus for rhetoric scholars. Not only the single orator's great works would occupy the student of social movement, wrote Griffin. Rhetoric scholars should especially study a multiplicity of voices, ideas, and individuals who nonetheless appeared as a collective—and who nonetheless changed the pattern of public conversation. Following successive waves of critique and reshaping,[i] rhetoric scholars advocate that not only should we study social movement to expand students' understanding of rhetoric, or to classify social movements. Instead, rhetoric scholars must focus the driving question of what *moves* the social?

---

i See, for instance, McGee (1980) who pushed the need to center questions of what moves the social against the tendency to instrumentalize social movement rhetoric; DeLuca (1999), who amplified McGee's arguments in a mediated context; Enck-Wanzer (2006), who advocated an intersectional rhetoric that was identity-conscious, and recognized the convergence of bodies, images, and words/stories; and Foust (2017), who challenged the proliferation of concepts against developing literature that is responsive to rhetorical situations.

Three primary schools of thought prioritize different grammatical facets of social movement to answer this question (Foust & Alvarado, 2019). First, borrowing from sociology, functional rhetoric scholars suggest that "a movement" (noun) uses rhetoric to achieve its goals. A movement operates like governments and other social movements past to realize changes in policy. Scholars value changes in law, since the law dictates individuals' behavior (while also reflecting a community's values). Effective social movements, Simons (1970) argued, followed effective leaders who faced problems and met requirements with effective rhetoric. Stewart (1980) identified persistent needs that social movements faced, suggesting that rhetoric met these nouns' needs to "alter audience perceptions of the past, the present, and the future, to convince [audiences] that an intolerable situation exists and demands urgent action" (p. 155). Digital media (like other channels of communication), nourishes a social movement by spreading messages of pride and hope, as in the use of Facebook to build a movement to oust Egyptian dictator Hosni Mubarak (Eltantawy & Wiest, 2011).

As Foust and Alvarado (2019) review, women's movements from the late 1960s on, troubled the noun focus on social movement, pushing an intersectional consciousness that recognized overlapping systems of oppression, marginalization, and power (Lorde, 1984). Liberal feminists practiced consciousness-raising and modes of organizing that did not fit neatly into noun theorizing (Campbell, 1973), while tactics flaunting bodies and identities (such as sit-ins, draft card burnings, and Black Panther actions) questioned the reasonability at the heart of a movement's effective use of rhetoric (Haiman, 1967). Two new schools of thought began emerging as alternatives to nouns, each with different answers to the question of effective movements—fiction and verb (Foust & Alvarado, 2019).

Scholars treating movements as fictions recognize the power of identification, where rhetoric inspires new ways of seeing oneself, of talking, relating, and acting in the world. A "social movement" does not exist empirically in the same way that an individual or a building does. But it *is* a meaningful collective identity to which individuals attach their own sense of self, and can be said to manifest "the social movement," in the real world. Rhetoric builds identifications of "friends" against "enemies," animating identities in political, cultural, and social struggle.

On October 15, 2017, actress Alyssa Milano tweeted a friend's post that suggested survivors of sexual harassment, assault, or/and abuse identify with the hashtag, #MeToo. Milano later credited activist Tarana Burke, who used the catchphrase to connect women of color survivors in networks of healing and support, since the early 2000s. The hashtag went viral, with tens of thousands of tweets and 4.7 million Facebook posts bearing #MeToo 24 hours after Milano's post (Khomami, 2017, October 20). Notorious Hollywood producer and serial harasser, Harvey Weinstein, was fired from his production company, and soon, other prominent men in government, media, and business were let go. Actress Salma Hayak, Olympic gymnast McKayla Moroney, Lisa Van Allen (who survived R. Kelly's abuse), and many others did not create an organized campaign or lobby Congress. Instead, their stories and perseverance rode tremendous waves of recognition, helping to articulate a collective consciousness that showed people would no longer stand for institutions ignoring or explaining away sexual harassment and violence. Though a resource mobilization approach, like other noun-based lenses, would suggest that social media made it quicker and easier to alter peoples' perceptions, the fiction view attunes more to how networks proliferate stories of friends-against-enemies. Foust and Drazner Hoyt (2018) note, "The ubiquity of digital media allows 'a movement' to seem even more like it exists, as it manifests repeatedly on smartphones, tablets, and laptops across the world" (p. 5). If we assume that peoples' actions follow their intentions, values, and identities, the achievement of collective identity is an indicator of social change. #MeToo powerfully demonstrates what can happen if people are persistent in narrating their stories together through rhetoric.

Finally, scholars join practitioners in recognizing that rhetoric *moves* the social, featuring the verb facet of movement. Rhetoric immediately intervenes (along with performances and physical actions) in stopping injustice. It enacts new ways of being and acting and relating in the world that do not replicate oppression. And if one attends to such changes as they happen, typically in smaller scale, everyday ways, one sees social change. For instance, as DeLuca (1999) shares, an environmental activist's body is buried in a forest road, only his head visible. This direct action immediately stops the ability of loggers to haul equipment to cut trees, while also interrupting typical meanings about the world. Here, we see the activist articulating (combining elements and speaking forth) new meanings, for instance, of the forest ecosystem's value superseding lumber or even his own life—since he willingly puts it at risk to save the forest. The activist's action is immediately moving the social by interrupting business as usual (in that moment). The potential for this *moving* to perpetuate further interruptions and new ways of being is, in some ways, up to those who witness the social moving, most likely on a screen in a different place and time. As in the moon's effects on the tide, rhetoric's force demands witnesses to translate or speak to its impacts, to share with others how rhetoric moves the social.

The noun, fiction, and verb approaches to social movement emphasize different ways that social movement rhetoric might be effective, including meeting needs patterned after policy-changing actions from the past; proliferating stories of friends against enemies; and materially halting injustices, with the potential to expand movement beyond the immediate moment. In order to more directly address this chapters driving question, we must first attend to a debate we have been engaging in since 2011: do social movements fundamentally change with digital media?

MEDIA ECOLOGY AND NAVIGATING SOCIAL MOVEMENT 2.0

In 2011 and 2012, several high-profile protests appeared in countries like Tunisia, Egypt, Spain, and the Unites States. They shared in common a deep engagement with new communication technologies (NCTs), particularly, the integration of smart phones and social media. Scholars began debating whether or not digitally mediated activism represented "a new species of social movement," as networks seemed "the fastest and most autonomous, interactive, reprogrammable and self-expanding means of communication in history" (Fuchs, 2012, p. 779; reviewing Castells, 2012). Other scholars questioned the "slacktivism" and "clicktivism" of digitally mediated movement, suggesting that the commitments, ties, and virtual expressions of online activism were shallower than face-to-face movement (Fuchs, 2012). Scholars are not immune from the technologically utopian and dystopian visions that often accompany NCTs (Lim, 2012). Utopian scholarship celebrates greater access and movement of ideas and information, and the potential for participatory democracy; dystopian scholarship emphasizes the potential for surveillance, as well as leverages face-to-face protest as more consequential than technologically mediated.

Rather than falling into a deterministic frame (whether utopian or dystopian), scholars like Treré and Mattoni (2016) advocate turning to media ecology as a better conceptual lens to understand digitally mediated activism. Media ecology frameworks assume that people use technology to suit their needs. The affordances (or features) of a NCT do not have to conform to what designers have chosen. Hashtags are a case in point. What was designed as a tool through which to quickly aggregate and archive posts (with a "#" symbol) served many different valuable uses in action, including self-expression, collective tone-setting, and even identification (Gómez García & Treré, 2014; Pappacharissi, 2015; Postill & Pink, 2012). Through media ecology, we are more prepared to see the complex uses of digital media as a neutral channel, refusing to treat digital media as inherently good or evil, intrinsically better or worse than other mediums. We are also more able to see digital media as one piece of complex communicative portfolios used by activists and advocates, rather than as some sort of golden key that unlocks activists' dreams of social change (or, as some have suggested of Twitter, inherently ruins democracy with its incivility).

Importantly, though, media ecology scholars recognize that new media differ from face-to-face, print, broadcast (radio and television), and other media due to their affordances, and their uses in action. Milan (2015) identifies six important differences in new media, which relate to its ability to present content in real-time … and its ability to subvert real-timeness through algorithms. Digital media's ability to immediately link users with something happening in the present moment has been crucial to the formation of movements like #BlackLivesMatter, where livestream and footage have prompted witnessing (e.g., bearing witness to racist brutality) outside of original contexts in which violence has occurred. When combined with *mobility* (as social media apps are engaged on smartphones, tablets, and other easily portable devices), digital media change space as well as time and frequency of content production.

Digital publicity, Millan argues, has a similar play of time that makes it differ from broadcast, print, and face-to-face publicity. In her words, "content, narratives and interactions are for the most part public, transparent and traceable—even if oftentimes within the users' 'walled gardens' of 'friends' or 'followers' " (p. 891). The aggregation and archiving of stories, reactions, and reviews allows us to see, in real-time *and* in retrospect, the negotia-tions of collective identities happening. In other words, as noted earlier, we can see the fic-tion of "a social movement" taking shape before our eyes through social media.

Milan continues that "social media quantify content, feelings, and interactions" (p. 891), with apps like Facebook or Twitter sharing numbers of reactions or shares as an easy exam-ple. Though other media quantify (e.g., television's Nielsen ratings), social media's "datafica-tion" is an affordance given to users—so networks can "interpret and strategically leverage" trends, "improving visibility, popularity and circulation of their content" (p. 891). This leads Milan to articulate the fifth main difference, that is, the intensity of "blur[ring] the bound-aries between the real and the virtual ... which social actors can exploit for strengthening the intensity of their voice, operating simultaneously on both levels" (p. 891). One's *platform* is a combined virtual and real presence, with the power to turn up the volume on what one says publicly. Finally, Milan concludes, the presence of "fake accounts and social bots," as well as algorithms—all of which have origin in human programming, but exceed human control, presence, and intention, to some degree—is peculiar to social media (p. 891). True to media ecology scholarship, Milan (2015) forces us to grapple with the complexity of NCTs and digital media. Like the fiction and verb facets of social movement theory introduced above, media ecology promotes humility. It focuses the inventiveness of people who will do whatever they can, using the tools available to them, to stop injustice and live life anew.

PROMISING PRACTICES IN DIGITALLY MEDIATED MOVEMENT

Knowing that digital media (like broadcast, print, and face-to-face channels prior to it) is no panacea to solving urgent problems, we finally identify some promising practices for effective activism in a digital age. The practices which I identify below derive from spe-cific case studies, so it is difficult to offer generalizations about what might work—save that, if action is attentive to context, if it amalgamates a portfolio of tactics and media, it is probably more likely to work. Diverse ecologies are more robust against disease and environmental stress than monocultures. Networks of interdependent relationships demonstrate more resilience than a social movement led by a figurehead—and if we are to look more closely at some of the great figureheads, we will likely see they are visible and important nodes in much more complex ecologies. So, the first promising practice I would suggest is getting to know the ecology of an issue you care about—a complex set of interdependent relationships, combining the technological (apps, platforms, devices), the social (people and how they organize), and the discursive (meanings and identities in communication) (Tacchi et al., 2003).

Other promising practices that consequential actions in "social movement 2.0" have included:

- **Sharing personal experiences of injustice**, especially if one has a platform. As Milan (2015) suggests, by platform, I refer not to celebrities or elected officials, but rather, a following or presence of networked relationships. Student government president, Payton Head, posted on Facebook his experiences dealing with racism at the University of Missouri campus. The action went viral with over 1000 repostings in 24 hours. But more importantly, Head's action would become a template for others to follow, as they shared publicly experiences of racism that would have been too easy to ignore, or blame the students of color for (Alfonzo & Foust, 2019).

- **Using social media to hold institutions accountable, particularly, asking them to live up to their values**. Again, drawing on the experience of #ConcernedStudent1950, students appealed to the University of Missouri's stated values (e.g., excellence, responsibility, and respect). They used @-handles of administrators and departments. They invoked Mizzou policies through which racist behavior should be held accountable (Alfonzo & Foust, 2019). Students rightfully questioned: Should someone who told his driver to proceed into students of color protesting at the homecoming parade be a university president in 2015? Did such a person represent well the university's values of responsibility and respect? And if not, should they continue on in the president role?

- **Taking advantage of social media affordances to build networks (and refusing to discipline networks on the basis of what worked well in the past)**. As noted above with the example of #MeToo, hashtags and sharing allows networks to spread, potentially quite quickly. Consequential actions play algorithms to signal boost, getting more views. Advocates repost others' social media with hashtags, they call on acquaintances with organizational accounts to use those accounts to amplify individual, small group, and other posts. In 2014–2015, teachers, students, and families led activism against a conservative school board in Jefferson County, Colorado. Their experience proved once again that social media affordances cannot be predicted in advance (Foust & Weathers, 2021). Oftentimes, it's the "one off" hashtags that go viral. In the case of Jefferson County, a hashtag meme that mocked the conservative board's plans to sanitize U.S. history (#JeffCoSchoolBoardHistory) intervened at a crucial moment to expand the power of activists. Riding the tide of such affordances—rather than fronting prescriptions for what worked for social movements past—helps promote consequential action.

- **Be a good node in the network. Share your story if you're called to, and "pass the mic" if you're in dominant identities.** Consequential actions are built through sharing, passing along posts, and being active in the building of collective identities. But, as survivors recognized in the #MeToo moment, those in marginalized positionalities should not feel forced to participate in story sharing. Likewise, for those in dominant identities, social media posts are like other forms of communication, and demand reflexivity to avoid replicating dominance in a network. Practically, this might mean seeking out activism that is already being led by people of color, women, members of the LGBTQIA+ community, rather than "leading" it by yourself. It might also mean "passing the mic" to someone in marginalized identity/ies, amplifying their story, rather than your own.

- **Create a symbiosis between online and offline rhetoric**. Consequential action emerges through the complex, organic portfolios of rhetoric. As Aboubakr (2013) noted in the context of Egypt, it is not Facebook that brings down dictators like Hosni Mubarak. Rather, immediate forms like street performance and graffiti were crucial at moments in the Arab Spring. Protests of the last 5 years underscore this as well, where protest signs take on a second (and possibly eternal?) life after a march, circulated on Instagram, TikTok, and Facebook. Consequential action does not draw ideological lines between different media, rather, it considers the potential of all of them together.

- **Refusing to "go low," and demonstrating respect for potential coconspirators in a collective identity**. Finally, given the state of some media ecologies as of this writing (which rely on conspiracy, White supremacy, misogyny, and on), I feel compelled to note that *just* consequential actions in digital media refuse to replicate oppression as a starting point. As noted in our exploration of #ConcernedStudent1950's digital archive, Black student activists ignored trolling, and "occasionally offered general statements that responded to cynicism, as in activist @justbeying's tweet: 'if you're a current student, condemning other students speaking out on things they find important, re-evaluate. We all deserve equality'" (Alfonzo & Foust, 2019, pp. 95–96). In another instance, @justbeying addressed a Twitter user's cynicism, suggesting that if concerned students held the university administration accountable to its values, they could see change. They could fight racism on campus.

It may be tempting to use "alternative facts," hate, or conspiracy, because we see a quick or easy payoff to their use happening all around us. It might also be tempting to turn to discourses of cynicism, and hopelessness, too, because change desperately needs to happen and institutions appear unresponsive. But we must remember, there are centuries of dominant ways of being and acting in the world supporting inaction and injustice. In the leaked Supreme Court majority opinion for what would overturn *Roe v. Wade*, for instance, Justice Samuel Alito leveraged 17th century writings from Sir Matthew Hale, a jurist who tried outspoken women as witches, thus justifying death sentences for them. Additionally, Hale popularized the idea that women could not be raped in marriage (Armstrong, 2022, May 6). It may seem like today's White hetero-patriarchal discourse is "new," but the manifestations of injustice are quite old. It may feel like it's less efficient or effective to use methods of activism that enact, in the current moment, a world you *want* to be a part of. But we cannot live with the anguish and violence of this injustice now, so we must act differently as we are trying to realize the world we want.

CONCLUSION

In conclusion, in this chapter, I have provided examples of promising practices of activism in digital media, grounding the discussion in media ecology and a complex view of social movement. Though digital media affordances change what is possible through social movement rhetoric, they do not make it easier, or better or worse. If anything, digital media allows us to witness the formation of movement as fiction, verb, and perhaps noun, invites us to consider the organic relationships that might be responding to injustice, and to join them.

REFERENCES

Aboubakr, R. (2013). New directions of internet activism in Egypt. *Communications: The European Journal of Communication Research, 38*(3), 251–265. https://doi.org/10.1515/commun-2013-0015

Alfonzo, P. & Foust, C. R. (2019). Campus activism in the digital age: An ecological chronology of #ConcernedStudent1950. *Journal of Contemporary Rhetoric, 9*(3/4), 87–111.

Armstrong, K. (2022, May 6). Draft overturning Roe v. Wade quotes infamous witch trial judge with long-discredited ideas on rape. *ProPublica.* Accessed June 12, 2022: https://www.propublica.org/article/abortion-roe-wade-alito-scotus-hale

Campbell, K. K. (1973). The rhetoric of women's liberation: An oxymoron. *Quarterly Journal of Speech, 59*(1), 74–86. https://doi.org/10.1080/00335637309383155

Castells, M. (2012). *Networks of outrage and hope: Social movements in the Internet age.* Polity.

DeLuca, K. M. (1999). *Image politics: The new rhetoric of environmental activism.* Guilford Press.

Eltantawy, N. & Wiest, J. (2011). Social media in the Egyptian revolution: Reconsidering resource mobilization theory. *International Journal of Communication, 5,* 1207–1224.

Foust, C. R. & Alvarado, R. F. (2019). "Rhetoric and social movements." In D. L. Cloud (Ed.), *Oxford encyclopedia of communication and critical studies.* Oxford University Press.

Foust, C. R., & Drazner Hoyt, K. (2018). Social movement 2.0: Integrating and assessing scholarship on social media and movement. *Review of Communication, 18*(1), 37–55. https://doi.org/10.1080/15358593.2017.1411970

Foust, C. R. & Weathers, C. (2021). #JeffCoSchoolBoardHistory and the tale of conservative "reformers" in Colorado: Evaluating the consequentiality of memes in social movement 2.0. In N. Crick (Ed.), *The rhetoric of social movements: Networks, power, and new Media* (pp. 135–155). Routledge.

Fuchs, C. (2012). Some reflections on Manuel Castells' book *Networks of Outrage and Hope,* social movements in the Internet age. *Triple C: Cognition, Communication, Co-Operation, 10*(2), 775–797. https://doi.org/10.31269/triplec.v10i2.459

Gómez García, R. & Treré, E. (2014). The #YoSoy132 Movement and the struggle for media democratization in Mexico. *Convergence: The Journal of Research into New Media Technologies, 20*(4), 496–510. https://doi.org/10.1177/1354856514541744

Griffin, L. (1952). The rhetoric of historical movements. *Quarterly Journal of Speech, 38*(2), 184–188. https://doi.org/10.1080/00335635209381762

Haiman, F. S. (1967). The rhetoric of the streets: Some legal and ethical implications. *Quarterly Journal of Speech, 53*(2), 99–114. https://doi.org/10.1080/00335636709382822

Khomami, N. (2017, October 20). #MeToo: How a hashtag became a rallying cry against sexual assault. *The Guardian.* Accessed April 15, 2022: https://www.theguardian.com/world/2017/oct/20/women-worldwide-use-hashtag-metoo-against-sexual-harassment

Lim, M. (2012). Clicks, cabs, and coffee houses: Social media and oppositional movements in Egypt, 2004–2011. *Journal of Communication, 62*(2), 231–248. https://doi.org/10.1111/j.1460-2466.2012.01628.x

Lorde, A. (1984). *Sister outsider: Essays and speeches.* Crossing Press.

Milan, S. (2015). From social movements to cloud protesting: The evolution of collective identity. *Information, Communication & Society, 18*(8), 887–900. https://doi.org/10.1080/1369118X.2015.1043135

Pappacharissi, Z. (2015). Affective publics and structures of storytelling: Sentiment, events and mediality. *Information, Communication & Society, 19*(3), 307–324. https://doi.org/10.1080/1369118X.2015.1109697

Postill, J. & Pink, S. (2012). Social media ethnography: The digital researcher in a messy web. *Media International Australia, 145*(1), 123–134. https://doi.org/10.1177/1329878X1214500114

Simons, H. W. (1970). Requirements, problems, and strategies: A theory of persuasion for social movements. *Quarterly Journal of Speech, 56*(1), 1–11. https://doi.org/10.1080/00335637009382977

Stewart, C. J. (1980). A functional approach to the rhetoric of social movements. *Central States Speech Journal, 31*(4), 298–305. https://doi.org/10.1080/10510978009368070

Tacchi, J. A., Slater, D., & Hearn, G. N. (2003). *Ethnographic action research: A user's handbook.* Unesco.

Treré, E. & Mattoni, A. (2016). Media ecologies and protest movements: Main perspectives and key lessons. *Information, Communication & Society, 19*(3), 290–306. https://doi.org/10.1080/1369118X.2015.1109699

PSYCHOLOGICAL REACTANCE AND PERSUASIVE COMMUNICATION

Lijiang Shen
The Pennsylvania State University

In the realm of physics, Newton's third law states: For every action, there is an equal and opposite reaction. Parallel to that law of motion, in the realm of psychology and communication studies, psychological reactance theory (PRT) (Brehm, 1966; Brehm & Brehm, 1981) posits that for every restriction on one's freedom, there is a reaction from the individual, although not necessarily equal in degree or magnitude, to regain or restore the lost or threatened freedom. The motivation underlying that opposite reaction is called psychological reactance. PRT contends that any attempt to influence individuals, be it a public campaign, a commercial, or a personal request, may be perceived as a restriction on their freedom; hence, arousing psychological reactance. The theory is often called upon to explain the outcomes of social influence attempts: some efforts succeed, others do not have any discernable effects, and others may even produce a boomerang effect, that is, telling someone to do something makes them less likely to act than if you had said nothing, and vice versa.

The explanation offered by PRT is based on the balance between the action (i.e., the influence attempt) and the reaction (i.e., psychological reactance): when the action is stronger than the reaction, intended outcomes follow; when the action is equal to the reaction, there is no change; and when the action is less than the reaction, the undesirable and unintended boomerang effects emerge. The purpose of this chapter is to introduce the theory of psychological reactance by (1) defining the antecedents to reactance: freedom and threat to freedom, (2) explicating the nature and measurement of reactance, (3) discussing the consequences of reactance arousal, freedom restoration, and (4) presenting communication strategies to mitigate reactance. Examples from daily lives will be provided to illustrate the concepts and highlight the implications for communication practices.

ANTECEDENTS TO PSYCHOLOGICAL REACTANCE

FREEDOM

The fundamental assumption of the PRT lies in the notion of freedom. Freedom here is "not abstract considerations, but concrete behavioral realities" (Brehm & Brehm, 1981, p. 12). In other words, freedom is interchangeable with free behavior, where behavior is broadly defined to include actions, attitudes, as well as thoughts and emotions. There are two prerequisites for freedom: knowledge (i.e., individuals are aware of the behavior) and ability (i.e., individuals believe they are capable of enacting the behavior). For example, posting videos on the social media platform TikTok is a freedom only when an individual knows about TikTok and knows how to produce and post videos on social media. Such perceived freedom can come from multiple sources: (1) one's past experience, (2) vicarious experience—observation of others performing the behavior, and (3) laws and social norms (in favor of the behavior). For example, most residents of mainland China know about but do not have access to Twitter because the App is blocked by the government. However, they may still perceive using Twitter as a freedom once they know ordinary people outside of China have free access.

Freedom also may vary in importance. The importance of a freedom is the degree to which the free behavior is attractive such that it satisfies certain needs that no other free behavior does (i.e., there is no alternative available). The importance of freedom can also be due to different levels of behavioral commitment and investment. For example, the freedom to smoke cigarettes is more important to smokers than to nonsmokers. Freedom to stay in a relationship one has invested a lot in is more important than a relationship in which one has little investment. The same freedom might vary in importance as a function of individual differences (see trait reactance below).

THREAT TO FREEDOM

Any force on the individual that makes it more difficult to exercise a freedom constitutes a threat to freedom. Restrictive laws and regulations (e.g., gun control regulations, banning of supersize soda cups, and booking banning efforts) might be the strongest form of threat to freedom. Persuasion and social influence attempts, by telling people what position to have and what to do (or not to do), obviously restrict their choices and options and are threats to freedom, especially when they come with high pressure (such as commands). Influence attempts with less pressure such as bribery and consensus information might also be perceived as freedom-restricting. The threat to freedom is magnified when such restrictions or influence attempts are perceived to be unjustified, illegitimate, or out of boundary. People playing hard-to-get makes it more difficult for their partners to accomplish their relational goals, hence, is also a form of threat to freedom. Likewise, it is a threat to freedom when one gives their relational partner the ultimatum. Even impersonal events such as the weather or the pandemic, when they make it more difficult to exercise a freedom, can become threats to freedom.

Threats to freedom can also be implied (Brehm, 1989). Once a particular freedom is threatened, the first type of implied threat is to the same freedom on future occasions. For example, if one's relational partner announces, "We will do whatever I want for the date tonight." The implied threat is that they would want the same for future dates. The second type of implied threat is to other freedoms of the same general nature, of equal or less importance, such as other things that the two of you do together.

The PRT posits that the magnitude of reactance arousal is a positive function of threats to freedom and individual differences in reactance. The more important the threatened freedom is, the stronger reactance. The higher the number or proportion of freedoms threatened, the more reactance.

Freedom-threatening language features. Research has identified a few language features that can magnify the inherent threat to freedom (see Rains, 2013). It is well documented that controlling, forceful, or dogmatic language with an explicit intent to persuade (e.g., "You *must* do X."), and with very concrete and specific demands (e.g., "You must do X, Y, and Z.") tends to highly threaten freedom. Language that highlights the negative consequences of noncompliance (i.e., the loss frame) tends to be more forceful and controlling, more explicit in the persuasion intent, and be perceived as more manipulative; therefore, also threatens freedom. Finally, language that restricts alternatives and forces choice is also freedom-threatening (e.g., masking and vaccine mandates and the ban on supersize soda cups introduced by former New York Mayor Michael Bloomberg).

THE NATURE OF PSYCHOLOGICAL REACTANCE

Originally, Brehm and Brehm (1981) conceptualized psychological reactance as "a motivational state that *is hypothesized to occur* [emphasis added] when a freedom is eliminated or threatened with elimination" (p. 37) (see also Brehm, 1966). That is, the arousal of psychological reactance (i.e., state reactance) is immeasurable and can only be inferred, which is contingent upon the boomerang effect. In other words, psychological reactance resides in a black box and is presumed to be absent unless the action of persuasion and social influence is larger than the reaction of resistance to persuasion. Since then, scholars have endeavored to measure psychological reactance as state arousal (i.e., in response to threats to freedom) and as a trait (i.e., dispositional differences in the tendency to experience psychological reactance).

STATE REACTANCE MEASURE

Scholars in social psychology and communication studies have analyzed and extended the PRT and identified four different ways in which state reactance can be measured (see Dillard & Shen, 2005): (1) Reactance can be considered as cognitive in the form of counter-arguments, (2) reactance might be conceived as the emotion of anger such as hostile and aggressive feelings, (3) the third approach proposes that individuals experience both counter-arguments and anger when reactance is aroused, but these two elements are separate and parallel to each other, and (4) the final approach suggests that the processes of counter-argument and anger can not be separated, but are intertwined. Dillard and Shen (2005) conducted two studies that provided evidence for the intertwined model of reactance. A comparison of different measures of reactance (Quick, 2012) and a meta-analysis of 20 primary studies (Rains, 2013) provided further evidence that psychological reactance is both cognitive and affective and is best be measured as the amalgam of counter-arguments and anger.

TRAIT REACTANCE MEASURE

Brehm and Brehm (1981) recognized that reactance could be a trait since people have different levels of desire for freedom in general. This is consistent with the theory's assumption that people have the need for autonomy and self-determination. There have been three measures for trait reactance: (1) The Questionnaire for Measuring Psychological Reactance in German (QMPR, Merz, 1983), (2) Hong and associated translated the QMPR into English and further refined it into the Hong Psychological Reactance Scale (HPRS, Hong & Faedda, 1996; Hong & Page, 1989), which captures trait reactance as four dimensions: emotional response to restricted choice, reactance to compliance, resisting influence from others, and reactance to advice and recommendations. Confirmatory factor analyses (Shen & Dillard, 2005; Yost & Finney, 2018) have demonstrated evidence that the four dimensions of the HPRS can be considered as components of a unidimensional scale, that is, trait reactance is best conceptualized and operationalized as a single construct. The third measure for trait reactance was the Therapeutic Reactance Scale (TRS) developed by Dowd et al. (1991). However, some of the TRS items do not correspond well to the construct of reactance and its application has been largely confined in the field of counseling and therapy, but not in communication studies.

RESTORATION OF FREEDOM

Once psychological reactance is aroused due to a perceived threat to freedom or loss of a freedom, the PRT posits that individuals are motivated to restore the freedom and regain control. The restoration of freedom can take multiple forms in addition to the expression of hostile and aggressive feelings (Brehm, 1966; Miron & Brehm, 2006): (1) direct restoration, (2) subjective change, and (3) vicarious restoration.

Direct restoration is to regain the lost freedom by performing the forbidden act, holding or expressing the position and attitude that the source of persuasion desires to rectify. For example, readers form banned book clubs in the face of book-banning efforts, and gun rights advocates rush to purchase guns when there are potential new gun control regulations under consideration (after incidents of mass shootings). Some New Yorkers who came out to protest against Michael Bloomberg's ban on supersize soda cups were drinking out of 32 oz soda cups in the rally.

However, threatened freedoms are not always restored directly; there are some restrictive factors that inhibit direct restoration. The first factor is the cost associated with the restoration. The cost of restoration might be sufficiently high to inhibit restorative efforts. The cost can be external. For example, restoring the freedom of owning one's wallet from a robber might be dangerous. The cost can also be internal. For example, if direct restoration of freedom might lead to one's responsibility for a negative consequence to another person, restorative attempts would be inhibited. Another restrictive factor is the option of other forms of restoration. When more than one alternative is available to restore one's threatened freedom, people tend to evaluate the costs of these different alternatives and choose less costly alternatives such as subjective change and vicarious restoration.

Subjective change can be negative reactions (i.e., derogation) to the source of persuasion or restriction. For example, protesters against Michael Bloomberg's ban on supersize soda cups called him "the nanny." It can also manifest as a more negative evaluation of the message, and a more positive evaluation of the forbidden act, a removed choice, or the target of restriction and regulation, but a more negative evaluation of a forced choice. For example, individuals tend to find movies, shows, and computer games with more restrictive ratings more desirable. When one plays hard to get, their relational partner might find them more attractive and more committed to the relationship (e.g., Dai et al., 2014). Giving the relational partner the ultimatum, on the other hand, might drive them away. Some consumers experience buyer's remorse and suddenly find the product they did not buy more attractive, especially when the purchase is important (e.g., a house) and the transaction cannot be reversed, because the completed purchase transaction means the alternative has been removed and no longer available as a choice. Psychological reactance might be the reason for why and how the scarcity heuristic (Cialdini, 2021) works in social influence and marketing.

Vicarious restoration is an indirect way of regaining freedom. It can be a vicarious or related boomerang. Vicarious boomerang occurs when one observes others performing the forbidden act to restore the freedom (Quick & Kim, 2009). Related boomerang refers to the individual engaging in some other rebellious behavior that is not the direct target of the restriction or regulation. Such vicarious restoration works in the opposite direction as well—when they are offered one thing, people would rather prefer something else that is not available or removed as a choice. *The Duck and the Lemonade Stand* song by Bryant Oden gives us the perfect example: The duck repeatedly passed on the lemonade offered to him by the man at the lemonade stand and asked for some grapes. When the man finally took the duck to the store, bought some grapes, and offered one to him, the duck thought lemonade sounded good and asked if the store had any.

Putting the antecedents, the measurement, and the consequences of psychological reactance together, we can see the experience of psychological reactance as a process: Controlling, forceful, and dogmatic language with explicit intent to persuade constitutes a high threat to freedom, especially when the freedom is important because of behavioral commitment. Threat to freedom activates psychological reactance, which motivates the individual to restore the lost/threatened freedom either directly or indirectly. A clip from the popular sitcom shows *Friends* (Episode 5, Season 9) where Monica and Chandler have a fight over his smoking.

> Chandler returns from Oklahoma where he has been smoking with co-workers at a meeting. Monica smells the smoke on him, and gives him a stern talking-to: "How can you smoke in this day and age?" Just as Chandler promises he is not going to smoke again, Monica says, "That's right, because I forbid you to smoke again." Chandler then defiantly lights up a cigarette in Monica's face just to further upset her. During the entire conversation, Chandler is visibly frustrated and angry. There is counter-arguing and subjective change: when Monica asks him "Don't you have any willpower?" Chandler reminds her that she eats ding-dongs without taking the tin foil during a movie, which he used to find sexy. Chandler also does not see her as a loving wife anymore. Later Monica apologizes and admits she should not have come down so hard on him about smoking (just to trick him into celebrating life). Chandler smiles, tells Monica she is incredible, and again promises not to smoke any more.

COMMUNICATION STRATEGIES TO MITIGATE PSYCHOLOGICAL REACTANCE

The majority of research studies have focused on the message features that are freedom-threatening and reactance-arousing, namely, language that is controlling, forceful, and dogmatic language, with negative valence and explicit intent to persuade. They are proscriptive in nature and only tell us what *not to do* in communication to avoid psychological reactance. Unfortunately, such message features also tend to have more persuasive prowess. That's why they have been utilized in persuasion in the first place. Along with this line of argument, although messages are less likely to threaten freedom and active reactance when they are mild and gentle, positive in valence, and without explicit intent to persuade, they do not necessarily enhance the overall persuasion output. To achieve better persuasion and social influence, we need strategies that mitigate psychological reactance without reducing the overall impact. Communication scholars have identified a few such strategies.

FREEDOM RESTORATION LINGUISTIC DEVICES

Linguistic devices can be added toward the end of a persuasive message to mitigate reactance. There is evidence that postscripts restore freedom, for example, by telling people they do not have to listen to the persuasive message because they know what is best for themselves (Miller et al., 2007), or by simply telling people they are free to refuse the request after a compliance-gaining message (Carpenter, 2013) could mitigate reactance and enhance persuasion. Providing multiple behavioral options in the message advocacy also reduces reactance, for example, to reduce one's risk of skin cancer, health messages can recommend multiple behaviors such as sunscreen use, protective clothing, visiting a dermatologist for a checkup, or performing self-exams, instead of one option only (Shen, 2015).

NARRATIVES

A narrative presents a representation of connected events and characters that has an identifiable structure and is bound in space and time (Kreuter et al., 2007). The intent to persuade is oftentimes embedded in the story of real people, hence, is implicit and indirect. The language in storytelling also does not tend to be controlling, forceful, or dogmatic. There is evidence that the use of narratives as a persuasion strategy (see also entertainment-education, Singhal & Rogers, 2002) can simultaneously enhance persuasion and reduce psychological reactance (Gardner & Leshner, 2016; Ratcliff & Sun, 2020).

EMPATHY APPEAL

Empathy is aroused when message recipients vicariously experience the characters' state, situation, and object; specifically, viewers share the characters' feelings and thoughts and feel a connection with them. Such nature of empathy is directly opposite to the nature of psychological reactance: sharing the characters' feelings means the message receivers do not experience anger (against the message or its source), having the same thoughts and perspectives as the characters mean they are not counter-arguing, and feeling a connection with the characters means they are not going to reject and attack the message or its source.

There are specific message features that arouse empathy including (1) the narrative is about some social relationship, (2) the characters share similarities with the audience, (3) music consonant with the characters' emotions, (4) vividness, (5) gaze from the characters, (6) portrayal of characters' pain and suffering, (7) characters being innocent, (8) the characters are expressive of their emotions, and (9) the message highlights the characters' point of view (Shen, 2019). There is evidence that empathy appeals can have a direct impact, and an indirect effect via the reduction of reactance on persuasion outcomes (Shen, 2010, 2011). An additional benefit of empathy appeal messages lies in that they can avoid inducing stigma against individuals who suffer from the health issues the persuasive messages strive to address (e.g., people who live with HIV/AIDS or who use drugs and substances) (Peng et al., 2020).

CONCLUSION

In this chapter, I reviewed the theory and research on PRT in communication studies by discussing the antecedents and the nature and measurement of psychological reactance, and its consequences—the different forms of freedom restoration. It is important to note that, (1) in persuasion and social influence attempts, we often strive to change behaviors that people are committed to, even their habits (e.g., smoking and drinking), that is, we are attacking some important freedoms and (2) the target audiences, therefore, are most likely to experience psychological reactance: smokers, drinkers, and rebellious adolescents. To achieve optimal persuasion outcomes, we have to be careful in our language style as well as more micro-linguistic devices so that reactance can be mitigated or avoided without limiting the direct message effects on persuasion. There is evidence for the effectiveness of the use of narratives and empathy appeals. On the other hand, given its motivational nature, reactance can be a persuasion tool itself. Playing hard to get might make one more attractive as a relational partner. The scarcity heuristic is a proven successful tool for marketing promotion (Cialdini, 2021). We also have to be aware that the intrinsic attractiveness of certain behaviors might override the freedom *not to* perform the act: If I were to tell my teenagers "I *forbid* you to do your homework and you *must* play computer games all day!," it would surely backfire on me instead of yielding the desired boomerang. I would be the best dad ever instead of a tyrant who takes away their freedom.

REFERENCES

Brehm, J. W. (1966). *A theory of psychological reactance.* Academic Press.

Brehm, J. W. (1989). Psychological reactance: Theory and applications. *Advances in Consumer Research, 16,* 72–75.

Brehm, S. S., & Brehm, J. W. (1981). *Psychological reactance: A theory of freedom and control.* Academic Press.

Carpenter, C. J. (2013). A meta-analysis of the effectiveness of the "But You Are Free" compliance-gaining technique. *Communication Studies, 64*(1), 6–17. https://doi.org/10.1080/10510874.2012.727941

Cialdini, R. (2021). *Influence, new and expanded: The psychology of persuasion.* HarperCollins Publishers.

Dai, X., Dong, P., & Jia, J. S. (2014). When does playing hard to get increase romantic attraction? *Journal of Experimental Psychology: General, 143*(2), 521–526. https://doi.org/10.1037/a0032989

Dillard, J. P., & Shen, L. (2005). On the nature of reactance and its role in persuasive health communication. *Communication Monographs, 72*(2), 144–168. https://doi.org/10.1080/03637750500111815

Dowd, E. T., Milne, C. R., & Wise, S. L. (1991). The therapeutic reactance scale: A measure of psychological reactance. *Journal of Counseling & Development, 69,* 541–545. http://dx.doi.org/10.1002/j.1556-6676.1991.tb02638.x

Hong, S. M., & Faedda, S. (1996). Refinement of the Hong psychological reactance scale. *Educational and Psychological Measurement, 56*(1), 173–182. https://doi.org/10.1177/0013164496056001014

Hong, S. M. & Page, S. (1989). A psychological reactance scale: Development, factor structure, and reliability. *Psychological Reports, 64*(3), 1323–1326. https://doi.org/10.2466%2Fpr0.1989.64.3c.1323

Kreuter, M. W., Green, M. C., Cappella, J. N., Slater, M. D., Wise, M. E., Storey, D., … Wooley, S. (2007). Narrative communication in cancer prevention and control: A framework to guide research and application. *Annals of Behavioral Medicine, 33*(3), 221–235. https://doi.org/10.1007/BF02879904

Gardner, L., & Leshner, G. (2016). The role of narrative and other-referencing in attenuating psychological reactance to diabetes self-care messages. *Health Communication, 31*(6), 738–751. https://doi.org/10.1080/10410236.2014.993498

Merz, J. (1983). A questionnaire for the measurement of psychological reactance. [German]. *Diagnostica, 29,* 75–82.

Miller, C. H., Lane, L. T., Deatrick, L. M., Young, A. M., & Potts, K. A. (2007). Psychological reactance and promotional health messages: The effects of controlling language, lexical concreteness, and the restoration of freedom. *Human Communication Research, 33*(2), 219–240. https://doi.org/10.1111/j.1468-2958.2007.00297.x

Miron, A. M., & Brehm, J. W. (2006). Reactance theory – 40 years later. *Zeitschrift für Sozialpsychologie, 37*(1), 9–18. https://doi.org/10.1024/0044-3514.37.1.9

Peng, L., Shen, L., Vanderbilt, R., & Forley, K. (2020). The impact of fear versus state empathy on persuasion and social stigma. *Media Psychology, 23*(1), 1–24. https://doi.org/10.1080/15213269.2018.1535321.

Quick, B. L. (2012). What is the best measure of psychological reactance? An empirical test of two measures. *Health Communication, 27*(1), 1–9. https://doi.org/10.1080/10410236.2011.567446

Quick, B. L., & Kim, D. K. (2009). Examining reactance and reactance restoration with South Korean adolescents: A test of psychological reactance within a collectivist culture. *Communication Research, 36*(6), 765–782. https://doi.org/10.1177/0093650290346797

Rains, S. A. (2013). The nature of psychological reactance revisited: A meta-analytic review. *Human Communication Research, 39*(1), 47–73. https://doi.org/10.1111/j.1468-2958.2012.01443.x

Ratcliff, C. L., & Sun, Y. (2020). Overcoming resistance through narratives: Findings from a meta-analytic review. *Human Communication Research, 46*(4), 412–443. https://doi.org/10.1093/hcr/hqz017

Shen, L. (2010). Mitigating psychological reactance: The role of message-induced empathy in persuasion. *Human Communication Research, 36*(3), 397–422. http://dx.doi.org/10.1111/j.1468-2958.2010.01381.x

Shen, L. (2011). The effectiveness of empathy-versus fear-arousing antismoking PSAs. *Health Communication, 26*(5), 404–415. http://dx.doi.org/10.1080/10410236.2011.552480

Shen, L. (2015). Antecedents to psychological reactance: The impact of threat, message frame, and choice. *Health Communication, 30*(10), 975–985. https://doi.org/10.1080/10410236.2014.910882

Shen, L. (2019). Features of empathy-arousing strategic messages. *Health Communication, 34*(11), 1329–1339. https://doi.org/10.1080/10410236.2018.1485078

Shen, L., & Dillard, J. P. (2005). The psychometric properties of the Hong Psychological Reactance Scale. *Journal of Personality Assessment, 85*(1), 72–79. https://doi.org/10.1207/s15327752jpa8501_07

Singhal, A., & Rogers, E. M. (2002). A theoretical agenda for *entertain-education*. *Communication Theory, 12*(2), 117–135. https://doi.org/10.1111/j.1468-2885.2002.tb00262.x

Yost, A. B., & Finney, S. J. (2018). Assessing the unidimensionality of trait reactance using a multifaceted model assessment approach. *Journal of Personality Assessment, 100*(2), 186–196. https://doi.org/10.1080/00223891.2017.1280044

POLITICAL COMMUNICATION
AND PUBLIC DELIBERATION

It is not uncommon to hear an undergraduate student proclaim they are uninterested in "political stuff." So one might reasonably ask the question of who exactly is or should be interested in political communication. The context of political communication addresses how people come together in attempting to influence their world. Political communication can occur at the local, regional, national, or even international (or global) level. The three chapters in this section explore our engagement in contemporary political life. First, Joshua Scacco (University of South Florida), focuses attention on how the changing media ecology has brought dynamic alterations to how political leaders govern as well as how news is produced and delivered. From traditional or "legacy" media (television, radio, and newspapers) to digital and social media (Facebook, YouTube, and Twitter), Scacco explores the present challenges and opportunities for representative democracy and technologies to influence American political life. Second, Brooke Molokach, Erin Oittinen, Robert Stise, and Dannagal Young (University of Delaware) discuss research of political satire as a preferred political information genre of the left and "opinion talk" (also called outrage programming) as a preferred political information genre on the right. They explore what is it about conservatives and liberals that may draw them to produce and consume two different genres of political content and the ways that people with different political beliefs may also differ psychologically, resulting in a predisposition to particular types of political communication. Third, Katherine Knobloch (Colorado State University), examines the decline (both in the United States and globally) of freedom and democracy by exploring the scholarship and practice of public deliberation to expand the ways you can take steps to make your community more informed, more inclusive, and more respectful.

COMMUNICATION TECHNOLOGIES AND AMERICAN POLITICAL LIFE

Joshua M. Scacco
University of South Florida

When I interned for a United States senator many years ago, one of my responsibilities was constituent service. In addition to reading and responding to public messages, I also answered the phone and talked with constituents calling the senator's Washington, D.C. office. In constituent letters, I observed how messages I saw in news stories or online message boards were echoed almost verbatim. On phone calls, I timed particular messages during the day based on when talk radio or cable television programming ended. It helped me, as a person interested in political communication, respond better to the senator's constituents. Later as a political communication researcher, these experiences and observations continued to inform my thinking.

How people and political agents navigate democratic life, including a variety of governmental and news media sources, inspires my work. My research has focused on how emerging communication technologies continue to present challenges and opportunities for representative democracy. From traditional or "legacy" media (television, radio, and newspapers) to digital and social media (Facebook, YouTube, and Twitter), I approach media as potential catalysts for democratic and antidemocratic processes.

In the sections that follow, *I detail how emerging technologies influence American political life, including the presidency and news organizations.* To illustrate for you how researchers approach their craft, I highlight how my own observations, questions, and concerns lead me to explore particular topics in my research. And I offer thoughts on how the research I conduct provides insights in the practice of politics and governance.

THE PRESIDENCY

Observing the presidency, especially from a research perspective, is a bit different from the work that you may read in this book on interpersonal communication, online relationships, or organizations. In many instances, researchers observe first-hand how couples navigate relational turbulence or how organizations communicate as an expression of explicit and implicit structures. Few researchers observe the presidency first-hand, though political scientist Martha Joynt Kumar's work observing the president's communications operation inside the White House is an important exception (Kumar, 2007). My curiosities began through mediated observations—watching the president on television and YouTube, listening to the president on radio, or reading presidential speeches.

My observations crystallized that *something* may be changing with the presidency as an institution (or enduring organization with constitutional roles and political norms) when then-President Barack Obama decided to transition the weekly radio address to YouTube at the beginning of his administration (Scacco, 2011). The conversational and informal speech given regularly since President Ronald Reagan (and dates to Franklin Roosevelt) suddenly became visual, digital, and interactive. Such a change also corresponded with a dramatic expansion of the settings where Obama appeared, including social media platforms, late night comedy programming, and sporting events, as well as an increased frequency of his presidential communication. Writing in *New York Magazine*, Jennifer Senior labeled this "ubiquity" as "a deliberate strategy" (Senior, 2009, para. 7). The president seemed to be chasing media platforms and their respective audiences.

When Kevin Coe and I explained the rise of the ubiquitous presidency (Scacco & Coe, 2016, 2017), our purpose was to explain how the institutional presidency had evolved alongside audiences and media technologies. We confronted a dominant paradigm in presidential communication—the rhetorical presidency—and had to explain how and where it did or did not apply (Ceaser et al., 1981). Firmly rooted communication practices where presidents give formal, infrequent, and policy-based speeches remain. Inaugural addresses and State of the Union speeches continue to be constants. However, such practices of the rhetorical presidency are shaded with modern practices of the president being everywhere and engaging in frequent, recurring, and more informal messaging (Scacco & Coe, 2016). The ubiquitous presidency, as an institutional adaptation, is characterized by accessible, personal, and pluralistic communication to respond to changing audience demands and shifting media platforms. As we note in the work that became our book *The Ubiquitous Presidency*, this institutional response to the contemporary context ensures that enduring communication goals of visibility, adaptation, and control are met (Scacco & Coe, 2021b).

In envisioning a ubiquitous presidency, we hoped to spark new research on the presidency adapted to the contemporary circumstances of American democracy, media, and audiences. For practitioners, the goal was to explain modern presidential leadership—including how some communication acts that may be deemed "unpresidential" (such as Barack Obama with a selfie stick appearing in a *Buzzfeed* video) are nonetheless adapted to the needs and wants of the communicative ecology. As communication researcher Kathleen Hall Jamieson noted several decades ago, communication eloquence involves the adaptability of a speaker to the means of the moment (Jamieson, 1988). Such examinations of presidential leadership and eloquence extend to how effective public communication can be in general. Indeed, leaders in industries beyond politics increasingly use accessible digital media technologies to project a more personalized image to a variety of audiences.

A second area that focuses the attention of presidential communication researchers is how White House messaging can influence agents in the political system. Presidents attempt to influence the public, other political actors domestically and internationally, business and cultural leaders, and journalists. The president is a prominent political "influencer" in a cluttered environment of influencers across politics, sports, and culture. We know, for instance, that the president's words can move company standing on the stock market, as then-President-elect Trump did when he tweeted negative sentiments about Boeing (Kilgore, 2016). When former President Obama appeared on the Netflix show "My Next Guest Needs No Introduction with David Letterman," he exclaimed to the former late night host "part of your ability to lead a country doesn't have to do with legislation, doesn't have to do with regulation, it has to do with shaping attitudes, shaping culture, increasing awareness" (Bonfiglio, 2018). President Joe Biden also understands this power, noting repeatedly during his successful 2020 campaign "The words of a president matter. They can move markets. They can send our brave men and women to war. They can bring peace" (Pager & Viser, 2022). This shaping and moving function of presidential communication interests both the general public and academic researchers.

Traditionally, researchers have studied how presidential communication can move public opinion regarding a chief executive's job performance and the issues the public deems as important. Such approaches use surveys and experiments to track such speech effects. Job performance indicators, including approval ratings, are an often-reported metric in news media reports (Groeling, 2008). For instance, news outlets sometimes report presidential approval rating changes following a major speech, such as the annual State of the Union address. Some experimental research has found robust changes in approval with presidential messages (Druckman & Holmes, 2004). Conversely, survey-based studies point to minimal effects of such public communication (Edwards, 2003). A mixed set of results also have been reported by researchers studying how presidential communication sets the policy agenda for the public. Political scientist Brandon Rottinghaus, for example, notes that presidential messaging success is "provisional" when discussing policy issues, but can be achieved in some circumstances, such as consistent repetition of a particular issue (Rottinghaus, 2010).

As a political communication researcher working in this area at the beginning of my career, I was struck by studies pointing to changing media technologies as a contributor to such a range of strong and weak effects of presidential communication. Cable television and media fragmentation scattered the audiences presidents could rely upon for their messages (Baum & Kernell, 2009). I explain to my students that a diverse media environment means that viewers can choose between the president, shows like the HGTV series *Property Brothers*, or the latest viral video on YouTube. Research suggests many audiences opt for the latter options (Prior, 2005). In this vein, research found presidential policy agenda leadership was strongest when there were fewer media programs to occupy the public's attention (Young & Perkins, 2005). As audiences scattered, the president is increasingly "preaching to their party choir and losing the capacity to influence public opinion more broadly" (Kernell & Rice, 2011, p. 693). However, such audiences may be more susceptible to opinion polarization (i.e., extremism) from presidential communication.

If opinion indicators of presidential influence, such as approval ratings, no longer can capture the potential ways presidents sway audiences in a modern media ecology, the range of indicators researchers assess needs to expand. The trajectory of studies on presidential communication, in addition to my own observations of presidential behavior during the Bush and Obama administrations, would inspire some of my work. For example, Eric Wiemer and I used a network-based approach to track how President Trump's tweet messages were echoed online from news outlets and the public (Wiemer & Scacco, 2018). We examined the extent to which presidential tweets about tax reform and North Korea were "echoed," finding instances where Trump and the public's messaging on Twitter aligned around these issues. Using a similar methodological approach in *The Ubiquitous Presidency*, Kevin Coe and I document how Barack Obama's health care messaging aligned with news outlets on Twitter (agenda-building) and Donald Trump's health care communication aligned with the public on Twitter (agenda-setting). These influences warrant additional study, as well as extension to how President Biden communicates. Nonetheless, the findings illustrate the possibilities for an expanded set of indicators of presidential communication influence (Scacco & Coe, 2021b).

The contemporary media environment pushes researchers to expand the scope of effects possibilities. Individuals can find likeminded others in digital spaces, while also attending to mediated information that affirms preexisting political beliefs (Stroud, 2011). These audience dynamics provide political leaders opportunities to target supporters with messages designed to strengthen (polarize) a variety of attitudes. Recent work illustrates that then-President Trump's tweeted criticisms of companies such as Nike and Macy's led to short-term changes in brand perceptions (Endres et al., 2021). As Kyle Endres and colleagues note, "the polarizing effects of presidential tweets are driven, in large part, by their ability to rally copartisans to take a hostile view of the brand under fire" (p. 839). Similarly, Trump's tweets challenging the integrity of U.S. elections led to reductions in public trust in elections among the former president's supporters (Clayton et al., 2021). The January 6, 2021 attack on the U.S. Capitol also raised critical questions (and an impeachment investigation) of how presidential communication contributes to polarization, incitement, and violent acts. It is a basket of effects worthy of research inquiry to ensure presidential accountability for their public messaging (Scacco & Coe, 2021a). For all of us reading this chapter, it also is important to understand how our political leaders attempt to influence us.

NEWS ORGANIZATIONS

How news organizations and audiences adapt to evolving media technologies also has interested me since my days interning in the United States Senate and as a graduate student. News, or events that deviate from what is expected (Tuchman, 1973), is a critical orienting force in society. Yet, a fragmented media environment where trained journalists' stories appear alongside the musings of an amateur influencer presents challenges for information acquisition. Moreover, a plethora of media options makes opting out of news for entertainment much more likely (Prior, 2005), accidentally stumbling upon public affairs information more difficult (Stroud et al., forthcoming), and encountering attitude-supporting news content possible (Stroud, 2011). The same technology contexts that alter presidential communication also influence news outlets.

My interests in news grew from observations of presidential communication practices. Specifically, I was fascinated by the collision of seemingly disparate institutions—the presidency and the press. An examination of the presidential press conference led to the conclusion that journalists increasingly struggle to hold modern presidents accountable in the setting (Hart & Scacco, 2014). Over time, journalists questioning the president exhibit a less interrogative (questioning) tone—the type of tone to be expected when reporters hold political leaders accountable for their decisions. In turn, presidents are more promotional in the press conference setting over time. This work, as well as my encounter with a Federal Communication Commission report on the economic and informational challenges confronting local news outlets nationwide (Waldman et al., 2011), were some of my first indicators that news may struggle in the current political and technological ecology.

When I joined the Engaging News Project as a graduate student researcher, and later the Center for Media Engagement (CME) as a faculty research associate, my interests in news were tied to a mission to empower "the public to understand, appreciate, and participate in the democratic exchange of ideas" (CME About Us, 2022). The goal remains to create a news environment that is both commercially viable and democratically beneficial. This mission and goal inspire my work examining how journalist and news audience practices change due to communication technologies.

An obvious place to look for changes in news practices is headlines. Traditionally, news is conveyed in a certain, clear, and informative manner (Rubin, 2010). These presentational practices harken to a moment where audiences had a more limited set of choices to consume print, television, or radio news. Famously, CBS News reporter and television anchor Walter Cronkite would end his evening news broadcasts with "And that's the way it is." However, the contemporary media environment with fragmented information outlets centers practices designed to garner and keep audience attention (Stroud, 2017). A competitive information environment means that news outlets must adapt their practices to stay visible.

"You'll never believe what happened next." "Click here to learn more." Clickbait-based writing practices coax audiences to select particular digital content by presenting it in ways that pique curiosity or uncertainty (Scacco & Muddiman, 2020). Such approaches are designed to boost the metrics newsrooms use to attract advertisers (advertising remains a critical way many newsrooms fund their operations; Hindman, 2015). For instance, in work examining local news coverage of the 2016 election in eight newspapers across six states, one-in-ten headlines on newspaper websites featured curiosity or question-based clickbait (Scacco et al., 2016a, 2017). Moreover, the initial findings from this research suggested that these clickbait headlines actually *reduced* the page views on news stories compared to traditionally written news headlines. In other words, clickbait backfired.

My curiosity, piqued by these findings, led me to explore why clickbait might backfire. With my colleague Ashley Muddiman, we hypothesized that clickbait may backfire because the style violates normative expectations of how news should be presented (i.e., it should be clear, informative, and certain; Scacco & Muddiman, 2020). Information seeking mechanisms suggest such outcomes because expectations of information quality and certainty are built into decision-making about whether to select information sources (Afifi & Weiner, 2004; Mokros & Aakhus, 2002; Ramirez et al., 2002). We experimentally tested different types of headlines to determine whether clickbait presentations influence perceptions of information adequacy in the headline itself and expectations of information adequacy in the news article. Our findings pointed to question-based headlines as a main driver of backfire effects. Question headlines, such as "Will it rain tomorrow?," reduce perceptions of the adequacy of information in a headline as well as expectations of information adequacy in the news article. The ultimate result is a reduced likelihood of engaging with the news story.

Information quality and attainment in digital spaces animates quite a bit of my news research. Amid digital spaces rife with mis- and disinformation, news outlets must find ways to break through the noise with quality information. One way for news outlets to elevate quality information while engaging audiences is through news quizzes (Scacco et al., 2016b). Similar to the underpinnings of the clickbait work, our research team started with the assumption that audiences seek out quality information. We experimentally tested news quizzes that included either multiple choice or slider options for individuals to answer public affairs information. Then, individuals were provided with the correct answer (as a means of affirming correct cognitions or attempting to remediate incorrect ones). Individuals not only learned from the quizzes, but also spent more time with information presented as part of a quiz as opposed to a paragraph snippet with the same information. We then partnered with a local news outlet to test the quizzes on a live news website. The field test results showed that time on page increased by approximately 20 seconds with a mixture of multiple choice and slider quizzes on a news page compared to the same type of quiz displayed more than once.

An important aim of CME projects is to use them in the service of journalism practice. At each stage of the research process, I try to incorporate the perspectives of newsrooms and journalism entities. This first-hand work with journalists provides an important perspective to how I approach, discuss, and analyze current news practices. Study results can then guide journalists through possible best practices for navigating digital contexts. In the case of headlines, traditional news headlines (compared to clickbait) meet both the information needs of audiences and assist in the commercial aims of newsrooms. Quizzes, similarly, provide opportunities for quality information acquisition while assisting a metric (time on page) that newsrooms use for advertising revenue generation. Greater than 150 newsrooms have adopted the quiz tool developed by CME, an important achievement in our work toward a news system adapted to the present circumstances (Scacco & Muddiman, 2019). It also inspired later CME research examining how quizzes spark interest in political news (Masullo Chen et al., 2020).

News outlets continue to navigate multiple economic and technological challenges, as well as heightened degradation of the profession by elected and political officials (Scacco & Coe, 2021). The challenges are not altogether separate. Digital technologies accelerate attacks, bullying, and threats against journalists. For instance, in *The Ubiquitous Presidency*, we document how then-President Trump's attacks on journalists correlated with an increasingly hostile environment toward news that included harassment and threats. The Committee for the Protection of Journalists warned that Trump's "treatment of the press [was] emulated by leaders in their own countries to crack down on the media and justify repression" (CPJ, 2019). Such concerns animate the work of my colleagues at CME as well. Specifically, the Center has focused on guiding news organizations through the digital media ecology on topics related to harassment of women journalists (Masullo Chen et al., 2018). A vital democracy is based on a solid foundation of verifiable information. And journalists are a critical component of democracy.

CONCLUSION

This chapter is animated by the question of *how emerging technologies influence American political life, including the presidency and news organizations.* The media ecology has brought dynamic alterations to how political leaders govern as well as how news is produced and delivered. I have illustrated how my observations, questions, and concerns lead me to explore particular topics in my research. And I offered potential ties between the research I conduct and the practices of leadership, governance, and politics.

Returning to that congressional intern working the phones for his boss, I am reminded of how what I learned then helps me understand what I research now. I differentiated quality information and misinformation, sparking my continued concern about the adequacy of information in a democracy. The repetition of constituent messages at particular times during the day or the echoed phrasing of a news article in a constituent letter all raised questions about influence for me. Such questions, when coupled with theoretical considerations and rigorous research methods, led to some of the insights mentioned in this chapter. Our observations about the world, whether of close relationships or nonprofit organizations or democratic institutions, are an important component to the practice of communication.

REFERENCES

About Us. (2022). Center for Media Engagement. Retrieved from https://mediaengagement.org/about-us/

Afifi, W. A., & Weiner, J. L. (2004). Toward a theory of motivated information management. *Communication Theory, 14*(2), 167–190. https://doi.org/10.1111/j.1468-2885.2004.tb00310.x

Baum, M. A., & Kernell, S. (2009). How cable ended the golden age of presidential television: From 1969–2006. In S. Kernell & S. S. Smith (Eds.), *Principles and practice of American politics: Classic and contemporary readings* (4th ed., pp. 311–326). CQ Press.

Bonfiglio, M. (Director). (2018, January 12). Barack Obama [Television series episode]. In Barclay, M. (Producer), My Next Guest Needs No Introduction with David Letterman. United States: Netflix.

Ceaser, J. W., Thurow, G. E., Tulis, J., & Bessette, J. M. (1981). The rise of the rhetorical presidency. *Presidential Studies Quarterly, 11*(2), 158–171. https://www.jstor.org/stable/27547683

Clayton, K., Davis, N. T., Nyhan, B., Porter, E., Ryan, T. J., & Wood, T. J. (2021). Elite rhetoric can undermine democratic norms. *Proceedings of the National Academy of Sciences, 118*(23), e2024125118. https://doi.org/10.1073/pnas.2024125118

CPJ raises press freedom concerns in meeting with U.S. Vice President Pence. (2019, November 18). Committee to Protect Journalists. Retrieved from https://cpj.org/2019/11/cpj-raises-press-freedom-concerns-in-meeting-with-.php

Druckman, J. N., & Holmes, J. W. (2004). Does presidential rhetoric matter? Priming and presidential approval. *Presidential Studies Quarterly, 34*(4), 755–778. https://doi.org/10.1111/j.1741-5705.2004.00222.x

Edwards, G. C. III (2003). *On deaf ears: The limits of the bully pulpit.* Yale University Press.

Endres, K., Panagopoulos, C., & Green, D. P. (2021). Elite messaging and partisan consumerism: An evaluation of President Trump's tweets and polarization of corporate brand images. *Political Research Quarterly, 74*(4), 834–851. https://doi.org/10.1177%2F1065912920939188

Groeling, T. (2008). Who's the fairest of them all? An empirical test for partisan bias on ABC, CBS, NBC, and Fox News. *Presidential Studies Quarterly, 38*(4), 631–657. https://doi.org/10.1111/j.1741-5705.2008.02668.x

Hart, R. P., & Scacco, J. M. (2014). Rhetorical negotiation and the presidential press conference. In R. P. Hart (Ed.), *Communication and language analysis in the public sphere* (pp. 59–80). IGI Global.

Hindman, M. (2015, April). Stickier news: What newspapers don't know about web traffic has hurt them badly – but there is a better way. Discussion Paper Series #D-93. Retrieved from http://shorensteincenter.org/stickier-news-matthew-hindman/

Jamieson, K. H. (1988). *Eloquence in an electronic age: The transformation of political speechmaking.* Oxford University Press.

Kernell, S., & Rice, L. L. (2011). Cable and the partisan polarization of the president's audience. *Presidential Studies Quarterly, 41*(4), 693–711. https://doi.org/10.1111/j.1741-5705.2011.03910.x

Kilgore, T. (2016, December 6). Boeing's stock drops after Trump tweet about canceling Air Force One order. Market Watch. Retrieved from http://www.marketwatch.com/story/boeings-stock-drops-after-trump-tweet-to-cancel-air-force-one-order-2016-12-06

Kumar, M. J. (2007). *Managing the president's message: The White House communications operation.* Johns Hopkins University Press.

Masullo Chen, G., Ng, Y. M. M., Riedl, M. J., & Chen, V. Y. (2020). Exploring how online political quizzes boost interest in politics, political news, and political engagement. *Journal of Information Technology & Politics, 17*(1), 33–47. https://doi.org/10.1080/19331681.2019.1680475

Masullo Chen, G., Pain, P., Chen, V. Y., Mekelburg, M., Springer, N., and Troger, F. (April, 2018). Women journalists and online harassment. Center for Media Engagement. https://mediaengagement.org/research/women-journalists

Mokros, H. B., & Aakhus, M. (2002). From information-seeking behavior to meaning engagement practice. *Human Communication Research, 28*(2), 298–312. https://doi.org/10.1111/j.1468-2958.2002.tb00810.x

Pager, T., & Viser, M. (2022, March 26). How Biden sparked a global uproar with nine ad-libbed words about Putin. *The Washington Post.* Retrieved from https://www.washingtonpost.com/politics/2022/03/26/biden-putin-regime-change/

Prior, M. (2005). News vs. entertainment: How increasing media choice widens gaps in political knowledge and turnout. *American Journal of Political Science, 49*(3), 577–592. https://doi.org/10.1111/j.1540-5907.2005.00143.x

Ramirez, A., Walther, J. B., Burgoon, J. K., & Sunnafrank, M. (2002). Information-seeking strategies, uncertainty, and computer-mediated communication. *Human Communication Research, 28*(2), 213–228. https://doi.org/10.1111/j.1468-2958.2002.tb00804.x

Rottinghaus, B. (2010). *The provisional pulpit: Modern presidential leadership of public opinion.* Texas A&M University Press.

Rubin, V. L. (2010). Epistemic modality: From uncertainty to certainty in the context of information seeking as interactions with texts. *Information Processing and Management, 46*(5), 533–540. https://doi.org/10.1016/j.ipm.2010.02.006

Scacco, J. M. (2011). A weekend routine: The functions of the weekly presidential address from Clinton to Obama. *Electronic Media & Politics, 1*(4), 66–88.

Scacco, J. M., & Coe, K. (2016). The ubiquitous presidency: Toward a new paradigm for studying presidential communication. *International Journal of Communication, 10*, 2014–2037. https://doi.org/1932–8036/20160005

Scacco, J. M., & Coe, K. (2017). Talk this way: The ubiquitous presidency and expectations of presidential communication. *American Behavioral Scientist, 61*(3), 298–314. https://doi.org/10.1177/0002764217704321

Scacco, J. M., & Coe, K. (2021). Securing the guardrails of democracy? Accountability and presidential communication in the 2020 election. *Quarterly Journal of Speech, 107*(4), 423–429. https://doi.org/10.1080/00335630.2021.1983191

Scacco, J. M., & Coe, K. (2021a). Securing the guardrails of democracy? Accountability and presidential communication in the 2020 election. *Quarterly Journal of Speech, 107*(4), 423–429. https://doi.org/10.1080/00335630.2021.1983191

Scacco, J. M., & Coe, K. (2021b). *The ubiquitous presidency: Presidential communication and digital democracy in tumultuous times.* Oxford University Press.

Scacco, J. M., Hearit, L., Potts, L., Sonderman, J., & Stroud, N. J. (2016a). *Primary election coverage: What types of news engage audiences.* Engaging News Project. Retrieved from https://mediaengagement.org/wp-content/uploads/2016/10/ENP-What-Types-of-Primary-Election-Coverage-Engage-Audiences.pdf

Scacco, J. M., & Muddiman, A. (2019). Using controlled and field experiments to create and test digital news quizzes. *SAGE Research Methods Cases,* Part 2, 1–16. https://doi.org/10.4135/9781526479617

Scacco, J. M., & Muddiman, A. (2020). The curiosity effect: Information seeking in the contemporary news environment. *New Media & Society, 22*(3), 429–448. https://doi.org/10.1177/1461444819863408

Scacco, J. M., Muddiman, A., & Stroud, N. J. (2016b). The influence of online quizzes on the acquisition of public affairs knowledge. *Journal of Information Technology & Politics, 13*(4), 311–325. doi:10.1080/19331681.2016.1230920

Scacco, J. M., Potts, L., Hearit, L., Sonderman, J., & Stroud, N. J. (2017). General election news coverage: What engages audiences down the ballot. Center for Media Engagement. https://mediaengagement.org/research/general-election-news-coverage-what-engages-audiences-down-the-ballot/ (In partnership with the American Press Institute).

Senior, J. (2009, July 31). The message is the message. *New York Magazine.* Retrieved from http://nymag.com/news/politics/58199/

Stroud, N. J. (2011). *Niche news: The politics of news choice.* New York, NY: Oxford University Press.

Stroud, N. J. (2017). Attention as a valuable resource. *Political Communication, 34*(3), 479–489. https://doi.org/10.1080/10584609.2017.1330077

Stroud, N. J., Scacco, J. M., & Kim, Y. (forthcoming). Passive learning and incidental exposure to news. *Journal of Communication.*

Tuchman, G. (1973). Making news by doing work: Routinizing the unexpected. *American Journal of Sociology, 79*(1), 110–131. https://doi.org/10.1086/225510

Waldman, S. and the Working Group on Information Needs of Communities. (2011). The information needs of communities: The changing media landscape in a broadband age. Report prepared for the Federal Communication Commission. Retrieved from www.fcc.gov/infoneedsreport.

Wiemer, E. C., & Scacco, J. M. (2018). Disruptor-in-chief? The networked influence of President Trump in building and setting the agenda. *The Agenda Setting Journal: Theory, Practice, Critique, 2*(2), 191–213. https://doi.org/10.1075/asj.18020.wie

Young, G., & Perkins, W. B. (2005). Presidential rhetoric, the public agenda, and the end of presidential television's "golden age". *The Journal of Politics, 67*(4), 1190–1205. https://doi.org/10.1111/j.1468-2508.2005.00356.x

THE AESTHETIC PREFERENCES OF LIBERALS AND CONSERVATIVES

Brooke Molokach, Erin Oittinen, Robert Stise, and Dannagal G. Young
University of Delaware

After almost 20 years studying the effects of exposure to late-night political jokes on attitudes and behaviors, Danna Young (one of the authors on this chapter) received the same question over and over after delivering public lectures. After discussing the impact of political satire on public opinion, inevitably someone would raise their hand and ask: "Why is satire so liberal?" or "Why aren't there many examples of political humor from the right?" After two decades providing largely unsatisfying answers to this predictable question, Young decided to study it empirically. Was it true that satire was the domain of liberals? If so, was there a parallel political information genre that was popular among conservatives? And so began her study of political satire as a preferred political information genre of the left and "opinion talk" (also called outrage programming; see Berry & Sobieraj, 2014) as a preferred political information genre on the right.

Research on media history revealed that this pattern (liberal satire and conservative opinion talk) was not new. Contemporary American political satire had its roots in stand-up comedy and improvisational theater, while conservative talk shows were an outgrowth of the talk radio movement of the 1950s and 1960s. Counterculture comic and satirist Lenny Bruce got his start in the strip joint precursors to the modern comedy club, and his influence on contemporary satire is unmistakable—with many satirists, including former Daily Show host Jon Stewart, citing him as an influence. Meanwhile, Dan Smoot and Clarence Manion, also culturally significant voices of the late 1950s–1960s hosted popular conservative radio talk shows where they railed against immorality and communism. The two worlds could not have been more different, and yet they seem to have grown into forms of entertainment that scratched a similar itch for their respective audiences: satire on the left, and outrage on the right.

This distinction between liberal satire and conservative political talk speaks to a larger question: Are some aesthetic forms—from art to music, literature to media genres—naturally appealing to liberals or conservatives? Satire is not *inherently* liberal; it's not as though satire stops working if it's not engaging with a liberal topic. Yet, liberals seem to produce and consume satire (think *The Colbert Report, The Daily Show,* or *Last Week Tonight*), while conservatives seem drawn to make and watch political talk shows (like *Hannity, Tucker Carlson Tonight*, and *The Ingraham Angle*).

So what is it about conservatives and liberals that may draw them to produce and consume two different genres of political content? *Why* do conservatives gravitate to outrage talk, and liberals to ironic satire? As social scientists—specifically political psychologists—have discovered, the answer may be—at least partly—in our heads.

POLITICAL PSYCHOLOGY: WHAT IS GOING ON IN OUR HEADS?

At its most basic level, political psychology is concerned with the psychological roots of political values and beliefs. For example, do people who hold certain political preferences have distinct psychological traits, and conversely, do people with certain psychological traits tend toward certain political preferences? At the heart of this literature is research on how different kinds of people monitor for and manage interpersonal threat. The motivated social cognition framework suggests that people who are organically (perhaps biologically or even genetically) (see Smith et al., 2011) predisposed to monitor for threats are also less tolerant of situations that are uncertain or ambiguous. They act quickly and prioritize efficiency in decision-making. And those who are less prone to monitor for threat are more tolerant of ambiguity and uncertainty. These people tend to enjoy thinking for the sake of thinking (a trait called need for cognition) (Cacioppo & Petty, 1982).

Through numerous studies, surveys, and experiments, social scientists have found that liberals are more likely to enjoy thinking for the sake of thinking and coming up with solutions to complex problems more than conservatives (Jost et al., 2003; Leone & Chirumbolo, 2008, Stern et al., 2013). Additional studies have found that tolerance for ambiguity is higher among liberals than conservatives, too (Amodio et al., 2007; Anderson & Singer, 2008; Kemmelmeier, 1997), with liberals more comfortable with unpredictability and conservatives less favorable toward statements that could mean many different things. Interestingly, the lower tolerance for ambiguity found among conservatives is most pronounced when examining social and cultural conservatism, rather than fiscal conservatism, meaning it is linked more to people's political attitudes related to crime, race, and sexuality.

It is important to note that these relationships are not fixed. They are not deterministic. It cannot be said that all liberals will always have a certain set of traits or that conservatives will always engage with unpredictability in a certain way. What can be said is that people tend to organize their cognitive selves in patterns and those patterns are somewhat predictable.

An obvious next question would be: "How and why are these traits related to specific political beliefs?." Let's take two issues on which public opinion is clearly tied to psychological traits: issues of transgender rights and criminal justice reforms. In 2022, conservative

Republicans remain largely opposed to a broader social acceptance of transgender people and largely opposed to transgender rights (Brown, 2022). Meanwhile liberal Democrats try to push reforms to the judicial system, including softening sentencing guidelines and moderating punishment for felons (Gramlich, 2021). The psychological traits discussed here are linked to beliefs about both of these issues, with studies showing that people higher in tolerance for ambiguity are more supportive of transgender people and their rights (Jones et al., 2017); and that need for cognition is negatively associated with support for punitive criminal measures (Sargent, 2004). And so we see the way that people engage with the world—in terms of how much they tolerate uncertainty and like coming up with solutions to complex problems, are closely related to how they think about social and cultural issues.

ARTISTIC PREFERENCES: THE PSYCHOLOGY OF TASTE

Interestingly, these differing psychological traits do not *just* relate to political preferences. It turns out that they *also* help to explain the kinds of art, music, and forms of communication that we enjoy. Since people with a high need for cognition enjoy thinking, they respond in a certain way to ads, literature, and art. They prefer books that require more complex thought and they are more likely to carefully evaluate the arguments contained in advertisements. And people who do not mind uncertainty or vagueness have different aesthetic preferences from those who have a high "need for cognitive closure." Aesthetically, these ambiguity-tolerant folks enjoy abstract art (Ostrofsky & Shobe, 2015; Wilson et al, 1973) open-ended plots (Weirsema et al., 2012), and have a greater appreciation for art in general (Chamorro-Premuzic et al., 2009). In contrast, people who are low in tolerance for ambiguity appreciate realistic art and stories with a clear resolution (Weirsema et al., 2012). Related work shows that cultural conservatives tend to dislike the blurring of boundaries in a wide variety of contexts, ranging from visually blurred edges or patterns to divisions of labor in organizations. Boundaries, whether as literal frames around paintings or as literal walls separating national borders, seem to appeal to a culturally conservative psychological profile (Hiel & Mervielde, 2004).

FUNNY DEPENDS ON THE AUDIENCE: THE POLITICAL PSYCHOLOGY OF HUMOR

In *Irony and Outrage: The Polarized Landscape of Rage, Fear, and Laughter in the* United States, Young explains how traits like need for cognition and tolerance for ambiguity also help explain why individuals with different political preferences have a different appreciation for ironic humor and political opinion outrage programming. Because many jokes (especially irony) are created by juxtaposing two seemingly incompatible frames of reference, joke appreciation, especially of the ironic kind, requires a lot of cognitive work to "reconcile the incongruity" and for the listener to find the punchline. For example, take the following joke delivered by Trevor Noah at the 2022 White House National Correspondents' Association Dinner: "[addressing President Joseph Biden directly] … these people have been so hard on you, which I don't get. I really don't. I think ever since you've come into office, things are really looking up, you know? Gas is up, rent is up, food is up, everything!" First, the audience needs to activate knowledge of the common colloquial phrase "things are looking up" and its association with a positive outlook. Then, the audience must *also* activate previous knowledge about the negative or highly uncertain economic climate characterizing Biden's presidency. To resolve the incongruity introduced by "things looking up" and the economy, the audience must answer the question: when might something being "up" be a bad thing? In order to get the joke, the audience must activate their understanding that a major challenge characterizing the economy during the Biden administration has been inflation, wherein prices for items such as gas and food have increased. While it feels automatic, the cognitive work required to unpack even this simple joke is a pretty heavy lift. An even heavier cognitive lift is required to comprehend Irony. Irony is a special kind of incongruity—one where what is literally stated is the opposite of what is actually meant. This kind of communication is steeped in ambiguity and requires a lot of mental gymnastics to get the joke. For those low in tolerance for ambiguity and low need for cognition, irony is not a great fit. In fact conservatives tend to appreciate irony less than liberals do—and that they are less likely to understand its ironic meaning—instead interpreting it literally (LaMarre et al., 2009; Young, 2020a).

While playful ironic humor appeals to an audience high in tolerance for ambiguity and need for cognition, for those who are *more* likely to be monitoring for threat, a more direct, efficient approach would be more appealing. Outrage programming is a more efficient approach. Outrage is emotional, threat-oriented programming delivered by a dominant voice using ridicule, character attacks, exaggeration, extreme language, sensationalism, and accusations of hypocrisy (Berry & Sobieraj, 2014). Given the research on conservatives' higher likelihood to monitor for and attend to threats compared to liberals (Jost & Amodio, 2012; Oxley et al., 2008), their engagement with outrage programming begins to make sense. For people with a low tolerance for ambiguity, the experience of outrage may provide a righteous clarity and sense of confidence in-group membership. Plus, outrage programming's use of symbolic references can provide mental shortcuts to help identify threats—or make it easier to understand who "the bad guys" are (Berry & Sobieraj, 2014). For all of these reasons, outrage has asymmetric appeal for conservatives compared to liberals, as evidenced by the greater ratings success enjoyed by conservative outrage compared to liberal outrage. In fact, while liberal-leaning outrage shows do exist, their content tends to be less "outrageous" than that of conservative outrage shows (Berry & Sobieraj, 2014), and their audiences are less extreme in their political views (Young, 2020a). Similarly, conservative shows that employ satirical formats exist, but still often rely on the outrage tactic of targeting "the other" (Sienkeiwicz & Marx, 2021). We can also see this dichotomy play out on social media, where the most liked and shared Facebook posts among liberals employ humor, and the most engaging content among conservatives is more threat oriented, targeting "the other" (Nave et al., 2018).

Put simply, irony and outrage each emerges as communicative expressions of the political left and right, driven by their respective needs. Liberals are drawn to the world of satire, which suits their aesthetic preferences for messy, abstract, playful invitations to engage their need for cognition, comfort with ambiguity, and enjoyment of open-minded experimentation. Conservatives (particularly social and cultural conservatives) are drawn to clarity and boundaries, and react strongly to threats and negativity, all of which are present in outrage programming.

It's important to remember that these observed psychological differences between liberals and conservatives explain broad *trends*, rather than hard-and-fast rules. Since the 2020 publication of *Irony and Outrage*, other researchers have specifically explored media that "plays against type"—conservative irony and liberal outrage. Some found that the line between liberal irony and conservative outrage is far blurrier when it comes from user-generated political content (Nissenbaum & Shifman, 2022) or written satire (Brugman et al., 2020) than Young's prior theorizing would suggest. Plenty of liberals express outrage while conservatives crack ironic jokes. And the aesthetic divide between liberal and conservative media may be specific to the United States, as it does not always hold up in international contexts (Koivukoski & Ödmark, 2020).

Finally, we can never fully divorce media from its commercial context: if liberal satire is what "sells best," then there's no reason for networks to try investing in conservative satire (Sienkeiwicz & Marx, 2021). This framework would suggest that the partisan gap in political programming aesthetics is more about the market's sense of what "ought to work" than it is about what liberals and conservatives actually prefer. Some researchers have also found that conservative shows mimic the *format* of liberal political satire—like Gutfeld! On the *Fox News Network*—are finding success in the conservative media sphere (Sienkeiwicz & Marx, 2021). Yet, the successful conservative shows in the political comedy genre are making use of humor that is decidedly *unironic,* but rather embraces hyperbole and exaggeration—two common features of *outrage* programming (Young, 2020a).

DIVIDED: IMPROVED UNDERSTANDING OF HOW TO REACH THE OTHER SIDE

So liberals and conservatives are different—not just in ideology, but also in the psychological traits that drive them and their aesthetic preferences. Where does that leave us more broadly in terms of our understanding of political communication? Is it time to throw in the towel and wash our hands of attempts to reach across the aisle? Obviously not—but this research suggests that communicating across ideology will require understanding and effort. By understanding the differences between liberal and conservative aesthetic preferences, we can start to better identify ways to reach both groups—and understand what kinds of messages might be alienating—or just misunderstood.

Take, for example, the anti-Trump Super-PAC the Lincoln Project, created by conservative Republicans who saw Donald Trump as a threat to American democracy. Through the use of threatening, hyperbolic imagery and video footage, coupled with ominous narration, the group produced viral videos that may have been more compatible with the psychological profile of conservatives than liberals (Young, 2020b). In an international context, research points to distinct messaging aesthetics on the side of anti-government revolutionaries versus pro-government messaging (Makhortykh & González Aguilar, 2020). Researchers studying the memes used during anti-government protests in Venezuela and Ukraine found that the anti-government memes were more nuanced and creative while the pro-government memes were simpler and more emotion-based. Given that the protests in Venezuela were aimed at an authoritarian leader and the protesters in Ukraine were opposing the creation of closer ties with authoritarian Russia, these relationships between aesthetics and political movements make sense (Makhortykh & González Aguilar, 2020).

The notion that messaging aesthetics are more appreciated and understood by those with certain political preferences has important implications for the correction of misinformation as well. There are many ways to tackle mis- and disinformation online and discussing all of them would be far beyond the scope of a textbook chapter. But research has shown that the use of humor can be an effective way to increase attention to misinformation correction efforts because it increases attention to the message—simply by virtue of humor always requiring additional cognitive effort (Vraga et al., 2020). This raises important questions about the differences we see in misinformation adoption between the left and the right. It might also point us in the direction of more effective misinformation correction for both liberals and conservatives: if we know that the psychological traits associated with political leaning are also associated with certain aesthetic preferences, we can tailor our messages to ensure they reach the people we are targeting (Young, 2020a; Young & Bleakley, 2020).

Similarly, social media disproportionately amplifies partisan and emotional information (Hasell, 2021), which makes it a perfect breeding ground for people looking to spread political lies or sew divisiveness. Social media users disproportionately gravitate toward and employ outrage in their posts, especially in circles that already prioritize outrage (Brady et al., 2021). This means that conservatives may be uniquely vulnerable to misinformation spread via social media, but it also means that researchers and social media platforms, having identified a particular vulnerability, can work to correct it.

Finally, partisan differences in aesthetic preferences might help us better understand where people receive their news. While political satire shows are considered a valid news source by many liberal and liberal-leaning Americans (Becker, 2020; Edgerly & Vraga, 2020), the lack of clear boundaries and hybrid, playful format of these shows means that conservatives may be less likely to consume them—and even *less* likely to consider them newsworthy, if they do consume them. This intolerance of the ambiguity inherent in political satire, along with a preference for clear boundaries and definitions, may drive conservatives to networks and platforms with programming that follows rigid, predictable guidelines—like *Fox News*. This in turn can help explain some of the outsize influence that Fox has on its audience, as compared to other news networks (Hoewe et al., 2021). Conversely, the knowledge that liberals may be consuming political satire not just as a form of entertainment but also to help them understand their political world might pose problems, as analysis of the content of political satire has found that satirical news shows frequently play with blending fact seamlessly with fiction, leaving it to the audience to suss out which is which (Brugman et al., 2021).

Discussing the ways that people with different political beliefs may also differ psychologically often makes people uncomfortable. If we have free will and can engage with the world however we want and can believe whatever we want, then the notion that some of our beliefs and preferences are the result of underlying—innate—predispositions ... feels like a violation of some kind. But the framework advanced here does not say that a social conservative cannot like ironic humor or that a social liberal cannot prefer content that is didactic and threat oriented. It merely says it is more likely, given the traits that tend to accompany these political inclinations, that they will not. Given how today's media environment—especially our social media environment—is driven by data analytics, user behaviors, and preferences, the entities that have the most to gain from the understanding of these relationships (advertisers, media executives, political operatives, and foreign governments) probably already know about them. If you are in the business of efficiently appealing to certain types of people to mobilize them to vote or buy something, then understanding their preferred messaging aesthetic is key. But if political information producers are always catering to their target audiences' psychographic profile and accompanying aesthetic tastes, citizens will become increasingly siloed simply due to the distilling impact of market forces. If we have any hope of disrupting exploitative forces that take advantage of these dynamics—especially on the political right where emotion-based, threat-oriented messaging is helping to mobilize emotionally-responsive, threat-monitoring citizens—we as communication scholars need to understand them, too.

REFERENCES

Amodio, D. M., Jost, J. T., Master, S. L., & Yee, C. M. (2007). Neurocognitive correlates of liberalism and conservatism. *Nature Neuroscience, 10*(10), 1246–1247. https://doi.org/10.1038/nn1979

Anderson, C. J., & Singer, M. M. (2008). The sensitive left and the impervious right: Multilevel models and the politics of inequality, ideology, and legitimacy in Europe. *Comparative Political Studies, 41*(4–5), 564–599. https://doi.org/10.1177/0010414007313113

Becker, A. B. (2020). Applying mass communication frameworks to study humor's impact: advancing the study of political satire. *Annals of the International Communication Association, 44*(3), 273–288. https://doi.org/10.1080/23808985.2020.1794925

Berry, J. M., & Sobieraj, S. (2014). *The outrage industry: Political opinion media and the new incivility.* Oxford University Press.

Brady, W. J., McLoughlin, K., Doan, T. N., & Crockett, M. J. (2021). How social learning amplifies moral outrage expression in online social networks. *Science Advances, 33*(7). https://doi.org/10.1126/sciadv.abe5641

Brown, A. (2022). *Deep partisan divide on whether greater acceptance of transgender people is good for society*, Pew Research Center. Retrieved from https://policycommons.net/artifacts/2256849/deep-partisan-divide-on-whether-greater-acceptance-of-transgender-people-is-good-for-society/3015513/

Brugman, B. C., Burgers, C., Beukeboom, C. J., & Konijn, E. A. (2020). Satirical news from left to right: Discursive integration in written online satire. *Journalism*. Advance online publication. https://doi.org/10.1177/1464884920979090

Brugman, B. C., Burgers, C., Beukeboom C. J., & Konijn, E. A. (2021). From The Daily Show to Last Week Tonight: A quantitative analysis of discursive integration in satirical television news, *Journalism Studies, 22*(9), 1181–1199. https://doi.org/10.1080/1461670X.2021.1929416

Cacioppo, J. T., & Petty, R. E. (1982). The need for cognition. *Journal of Personality and Social Psychology, 42*(1), 116. https://doi.org/10.1037/0022-3514.42.1.116

Chamorro-Premuzic, T., Reimers, S., Hsu, A., & Ahmetoglu, G. (2009). Who art thou? Personality predictors of artistic preferences in a large UK sample: The importance of openness. *British Journal of Psychology, 100*(3), 501–516. https://doi.org/10.1348/000712608X366867

Edgerly, S., & Vraga, E. K. (2020). Deciding what's news: News-ness as an audience concept for the hybrid media environment. *Journalism & Mass Communication Quarterly, 97*(2), 416–434. https://doi.org/10.1177/1077699020916808

Gramlich, J. (2021). *US public divided over whether people convicted of crimes spend too much or too little time in prison.* Retrieved from https://policycommons.net/artifacts/2005055/us/2757295/

Hasell, A. (2021) Shared emotion: The social amplification of partisan news on Twitter. *Digital Journalism, 9*(8), 1085–1102. https://doi.org/10.1080/21670811.2020.1831937

Hiel, A. V., & Mervielde, I. (2004). Openness to experience and boundaries in the mind: Relationships with cultural and economic conservative beliefs. *Journal of Personality, 72*(4), 659–686. https://doi.org/10.1111/j.0022-3506.2004.00276.x

Hoewe, J., Brownell, K. C., & Wiemer, E. C. (2021). The role and impact of Fox News. *The Forum, 18*(3), 367–388. https://doi.org/10.1515/for-2020-2014

Jones, P. E., Brewer, P. R., Young, D. G., Lambe, J. L., & Hoffman, L. H. (2017). Explaining public opinion toward transgender people, rights, and candidates. *Public Opinion Quarterly, 82*(2), 252–278. https://doi.org/10.1093/poq/nfy009

Jost, J. T., & Amodio, D. M. (2012). Political ideology as motivated social cognition: Behavioral and neuroscientific evidence. *Motivation and Emotion, 36*, 55–64. https://doi.org/10.1007/s11031-011-9260-7

Jost, J. T., Glaser, J., Kruglanski, A. W., & Sulloway, F. J. (2003). Political conservatism as motivated social cognition. *Psychological Bulletin, 129*(3), 339–375. https://doi.org/10.1037/0033-2909.129.3.339

Kemmelmeier, M. (1997). Need for closure and political orientation among German university students. *The Journal of Social Psychology, 137*(6), 787–789. https://doi.org/10.1080/00224549709595501

Koivukoski, J., & Ödmark, S. (2020). Producing journalistic news satire: How Nordic satirists negotiate a hybrid genre, *Journalism Studies, 21*(6), 731–747. https://doi.org/10.1080/1461670X.2020.1720522

LaMarre, H. L., Landreville, K. D., & Beam, M. A. (2009). The irony of satire: Political ideology and the motivation to see what you want to see in The Colbert Report. *The International Journal of Press/Politics, 14*(2), 212–231. https://doi.org/10.1177/1940161208330904

Leone, L., & Chirumbolo, A. (2008). Conservatism as motivated avoidance of affect: Need for affect scales predict conservatism measures. *Journal of Research in Personality, 42*(3), 755–762. https://doi.org/10.1016/j.jrp.2007.08.001

Makhortykh, M., & González Aguilar, J. M. (2020). Memory, politics and emotions: Internet memes and protests in Venezuela and Ukraine. *Continuum, 34*(3), 342–362. https://doi.org/10.1080/10304312.2020.1764782

Nave, N. N., Shifman, L., & Tenenboim-Weinblatt, K. (2018). Talking it personally: Features of successful political posts on Facebook. *Social Media+ Society, 4*(3), 1–12. https://doi.org/10.1177/2056305118784771

Nissenbaum, A., & Shifman, L. (2022). Laughing alone, together: local user-generated satirical responses to a global event. *Information, Communication & Society, 25*(7), 924–941. https://doi.org/10.1080/1369118X.2020.1804979

Ostrofsky, J., & Shobe, E. (2015). The relationship between need for cognitive closure and the appreciation, understanding, and viewing times of realistic and nonrealistic figurative paintings. *Empirical Studies of the Arts, 33*(1), 106–113. https://doi.org/10.1177/0276237415570016

Oxley, D. R., Smith, K. B., Alford, J. R., Hibbing, M. V., Miller, J. L., Scalora, M., … & Hibbing, J. R. (2008). Political attitudes vary with physiological traits. *Science, 321*(5896), 1667–1670. https://doi.org/10.1126/science.1157627

Sargent, M. J. (2004). Less thought, more punishment: Need for cognition predicts support for punitive responses to crime. *Personality and Social Psychology Bulletin, 30*(11), 1485–1493. https://doi.org/10.1177/0146167204264481

Sienkeiwicz, M. & Marx, N. (2021). Appropriating irony: Conservative comedy, Trump-Era satire, and the politics of television humor. *Journal of Cinema and Media Studies, 60*(4), 85–108. https://doi.org/10.1353/cj.2021.0046

Smith, K. B., Oxley, D. R., Hibbing, M. V., Alford, J. R., & Hibbing, J. R. (2011). Linking genetics and political attitudes: Reconceptualizing political ideology. *Political Psychology, 32*(3), 369–397. https://doi.org/10.1111/j.1467-9221.2010.00821.x

Stern, C., West, T. V., Jost, J. T., & Rule, N. O. (2013). The politics of gaydar: Ideological differences in the use of gendered cues in categorizing sexual orientation. *Journal of Personality and Social Psychology, 104*(3), 520–541. https://doi.org/10.1037/a0031187

Vraga, E. K., Kim, S. C., Cook, J., & Bode, L. (2020). Testing the effectiveness of correction placement and type on Instagram. *The International Journal of Press/Politics, 25*(4), 632–652. https://doi.org/10.1177/1940161220919082

Wiersema, D. V., Van Der Schalk, J., & van Kleef, G. A. (2012). Who's afraid of red, yellow, and blue? Need for cognitive closure predicts aesthetic preferences. *Psychology of Aesthetics, Creativity, and the Arts, 6*(2), 168–174. https://doi.org/10.1037/a0025878

Wilson, G. D., Ausman, J., & Mathews, T. R. (1973). Conservatism and art preferences. *Journal of Personality and Social Psychology, 25*(2), 286–288. https://doi.org/10.1037/h0033972

Young, D. G. (2020a). *Irony and outrage: The polarized landscape of rage, fear, and laughter in the United States.* Oxford University Press.

Young, D. G. (2020b). The Lincoln Project and the conservative aesthetic. *Society, 57,* 562–568. https://doi.org/10.1007/s12115-020-00537-9

Young, D. G., & Bleakley, A. (2020). Ideological health spirals: An integrated political and health communication approach to COVID interventions. *International Journal of Communication, 14*(17), 3508–3524.

HOW TO TALK POLITICS AND SAVE DEMOCRACY

Katherine R. Knobloch
Colorado State University

Let's start with the bad news. Freedom and democracy are on the decline, both in the United States and globally (Gorokhovskaia et al., 2023; Papada et al., 2023). Rises in polarization and disinformation undermine the ability for publics to collectively govern, and citizens are facing increasing restrictions on their freedom of expression and personal rights. These findings likely align with your own experiences. Members of the public are polarized and alienated from our government and from one another, and perpetual propaganda machines further divide us and blur the lines between fact and fiction (Citrin & Stoker, 2018; Freelon & Wells, 2020; Iyengar et al., 2019). So even if you do not study democracy or political communication, you likely see it in your communities and in your own behaviors. But hope is not lost. For several decades now, scholars of democracy working alongside civic practitioners have been advancing a solution: public deliberation.

Deliberation asks community members to come together across difference, to learn from one another, and, ultimately, to make decisions and take actions that are responsive to public needs and goals. Decades of research in the field have both allowed practitioners to experiment with new process designs and understand the potential impacts of deliberative interventions, and the field of deliberative democracy is ripe with examples of communities that are working together to reclaim their democratic power (Gastil & Levine, 2005; Nabatchi et al., 2012; Smith, 2009). In the sections below, I will introduce you to the study of public deliberation, using some of my own stories to show how scholarship and practice have merged to expand the possibilities for empowered and informed collective governance.

PUBLIC DELIBERATION

During deliberative discussion, community members have conversations in which they share their own experiences, learn about the experiences of others, and develop a mutual understanding of the big issues that they collectively face (Gastil, 2008; Mansbridge et al., 2006; Young, 2000). Unlike most forms of political communication, which tend to be goal-oriented, deliberation asks community members to focus on learning rather than winning (Habermas, 1984) and seeks to be inclusive of diverse perspectives (Young, 2000).

Deliberative democracy, then, attempts to realize those ideal speech conditions in the wider public sphere. To achieve these objectives, practitioners, and scholars create opportunities for structured conversations across traditional divides in which members of the public learn about an issue, consider multiple policy options, and seriously weigh the tradeoffs of any decision they might make (Burkhalter et al., 2002; Carcasson, 2013). These conversations are usually guided by an impartial facilitator, both to ensure that all members of the group have an equal opportunity to speak and to encourage group members to respect one another and consider diverse perspectives (Carcasson & Sprain, 2010; Dillard, 2013; Mansbridge et al., 2006; Ryfe, 2006). Ultimately, deliberation is a decision-making process designed to empower an inclusive public to make more informed decisions that better respond to community needs and goals.

Deliberation often takes place through community forums or meetings—formal and highly structured processes that encourage deep listening and learning—but deliberation can take place anytime people are engaged in a conversation about public life. In this sense, deliberation is both a practice and an ideal. It is a theory about how members of the public *could* work together if given the appropriate circumstances and a way of organizing the public to reach those ideals. Deliberative scholarship then, attempts to test these innovations, exploring whether public deliberation can live up to its ideals and understanding how design choices can influence individual and community-level impacts.

Because deliberation is both a theory and a practice, many scholars of deliberation live somewhere between scholar and practitioner. We get to both design and study new ways of gathering folks together, and we often bring our students along for the ride, training them in facilitation and community organizing and then asking for their help to implement community projects (Shaffer et al., 2017). The remainder of this chapter will introduce you to this work.

DELIBERATIVE DESIGN AND RESEARCH

Perhaps the most studied form of deliberation takes place in the context of minipublics, highly structured deliberative processes that ask a representative sample of the public to engage in formal deliberation (Curato et al., 2021). During these events, participants, generally numbered between 20 and a few hundred, hear from experts and engage in small-group conversation about a public issue. Through conversation, they analyze evidence about the problem and the potential impacts of any solution. They discuss the values underlying the issue and the reasons why different people might support different solutions. After their conversations, participants usually come to some sort of decision or recommendation that is then passed along to decision-makers. Sometimes these recommendations serve more as a suggestion for what decision-makers should do and other times the recommendations have a more direct influence. Minipublics have been practiced all over the world, ranging from worldwide deliberations on environmental sustainability to local conversations on budgetary allocations, and researchers across the globe are studying their quality and impacts to learn how to build more empowering and effective methods for democratic decision-making.

One process that my colleagues and I have spent years studying, the Citizens' Initiative Review, offers a good example. For about four full days, 20–25 members of the public come together to learn about a ballot measure.[1] The members are randomly selected to be reflective of the wider population in terms of characteristics like race, gender, age, education level, and political ideology. During their time together, these ordinary community members hear from advocates campaigning for and against the measure and some neutral experts, such as university and government researchers. After the presentations, participants spend time in small groups weighing arguments and evidence against one another and discussing the ways that the law might impact their community. At the end of their time, they produce a Citizens' Statement containing information and arguments that they think the public should know. Members of the public can then use that information to make their own decisions when casting their ballots for or against the measure.

For several years, my colleagues and I sat in on these meetings, taking copious notes and trying not to make faces when an advocate made a particularly illogical statement (Gastil & Knobloch, 2020). We also interviewed and surveyed participants to understand how the experience impacted them and ran state-wide surveys and experiments to learn how the Citizens' Statement affected voters. In short, we conducted a long-term case study to explore the implications of inserting a new deliberative institution into the governing system. Our work used qualitative and quantitative methods to deeply explore the impact of this deliberative innovation and the ways it affected the larger democratic systems in which it operates.

Our findings demonstrate the potential for deliberative interventions to create a more informed and empowered democratic system. Though advocates did not always behave, and participants sometimes got confused, the processes were both analytically rigorous and respectful (Knobloch et al., 2013). Participants came away with a much deeper understanding of the issue they studied and created Citizens' Statements that were factually accurate and helpful for readers (Gastil et al., 2018; Knobloch et al., 2013). Our state-wide experiments found that voters learned new information through the Statements, and for some, reading the statement shifted their position on the issue (Gastil et al., 2018; Már & Gastil, 2020).

Aside from these benefits, the process also changed the ways that participants and members of the public understood their civic role. Participants generally came away from their

---

1 Ballot measures are laws that the public vote on directly.

experience with an increased sense of political power, and after the CIR, they were more likely to talk about politics and engage in their community (Knobloch & Gastil, 2015). For some, the experience was transformative. Participants recalled using the CIR's discussion guidelines years later to encourage better listening at a city council meeting. One reported that they went back to school because the process reminded them of their love of learning. Another founded a community group to address underfunded local schools after participating in a review that focused on a tax measure designed to increase school funding (Gastil & Knobloch, in press).

Voters, too, saw some of these benefits. Our state-wide surveys showed that participants who knew about the CIR increased their belief that the government is responsive to the public, and people who read the Statement became more confident in their own ability to make governing decisions (Knobloch et al., 2019). Though the CIR represents a single deliberative intervention, it produces a wealth of civic benefits that move communities closer to democracy.

Other minipublics and deliberative interventions have produced similar results, and scholars have conducted research on processes representing a variety of designs, contexts, and issues. Participants who engage in deliberative discussion generally learn new information about the issue in question (Gastil & Dillard, 1999; Luskin et al., 2002), and well-designed processes can heighten a sense of empowerment for participants and the public and increase their sense of connection to one another (Boulianne, 2019; Fishkin, 2009; Hartz Karp et al., 2010; Nabatchi, 2010).

And these processes are taking place all over the world (Curato et al., 2021; Gastil & Levine, 2005; Nabatchi et al., 2012; Smith, 2009). Participatory Budgeting allows community members to make proposals for how public funds should be spent and conducts engagement processes that give community members the power to allocate funds (Cabannes, 2004; Russon Gilman, 2016). Citizens' Assemblies and Constitutional Conventions have allowed community members to weigh in on proposals such as changes to British Columbia's electoral process (Warren & Pearse, 2008) and the legalization of abortion and same-sex marriage in Ireland (Farrell et al., 2019). Scholars and practitioners continue to innovate and implement new designs all the time and use the research produced by others to build processes that are more likely to reach deliberative ideals.

DELIBERATIVE SYSTEMS

Not all deliberative experiences, however, are so formal. The work my colleagues and I do at the Center for Public Deliberation (CPD) at Colorado State University (CSU) illustrates the variety of ways that deliberation might be implemented in the community and poses a whole new set of research opportunities for scholars. At the CPD, we tend to take a systemic approach to democracy, focusing on how deliberative ideals might be implemented across the wider civic system. Though deliberative discussions can try to create the ideal conditions for democratic governance within the confines of their processes, collective governance requires us to engage in public life in a myriad of ways. In short, politics takes place outside of the highly regulated deliberative processes like minipublics, and scholars are interested in understanding how deliberative ideals can be implemented across a range of civic institutions (Bohman, 2012; Dryzek, 2012; Hendriks, 2016; Parkinson & Mansbridge, 2012). To truly reach the ideals of deliberative democracy, we must identify ways to implement those ideals, like inclusion, quality information, and respect, into the diverse ways that communities learn, talk, and act politically.

To give you a sense of what that looks like, I will start with a description of our work at CSU. The CPD recruits about 15 students every semester and through coursework we train them in deliberative facilitation, community engagement, and participatory research. As students develop these skills, they begin to help us design, facilitate, and research community projects and get a chance to use their deliberative skills to enhance community empowerment and deliberative decision-making. For those projects, we work with community partners, like our city government, the school district, and nonprofits to design and implement community programs intended to connect residents across difference and solicit their input on public decisions. Some of our processes look a lot like minipublics; we gather a diverse group of folks together to learn about issues and then ask for their input on policy decisions. Others take different approaches, finding ways to create the wider civic structures that enable a deliberative democracy.

For example, our Community Guide program trains local community members, such as representatives from nonprofit or advocacy groups, in facilitation and then asks them to have conversations with other members of their community about upcoming local policy decisions. In these conversations, we do not focus on decision-making across difference; rather, we attempt to create opportunities for community members who share similar experiences to understand and express their shared interests. We then collect data from these conversations to frame the larger public discussion, using that information to understand how distinct communities are impacted by local issues. This process serves an agenda-setting function for our community because it helps us understand what issues our community thinks are most important to address. Policymakers in our local government then use that data to build proposals that best respond to public needs and goals (Knobloch, 2022). In this model, and in similar programs we conduct at the CPD, we focus on helping existent organizations become more deliberative and better connect to decision-making processes.

Another CPD program focuses on fostering local journalism that is better rooted in community interests and more tethered to quality information. Yet another connects high school students with our college students to understand and address issues of inclusion in equity in their classrooms and communities, and in one, we work with local organizations in rural communities to help residents build connections with one another and develop projects aimed at bolstering community capacity. Like other deliberative practitioners, we sometimes implement dialogic processes rather than deliberative ones. In these conversations, individuals are focused on simply listening to and learning from one another so that they can better understand each other across difference without the additional burden of trying to make collective decisions.

In all these efforts, we are attempting to build a more deliberative system that creates the building blocks for democracy. Though on their own, each of these efforts does not fulfill the entirety of the deliberative ideal, together they help improve the quality of information available to the public, reduce polarization, and increase opportunities for expression, correcting the antidemocratic trends emerging from traditional political institutions.

WHAT CAN YOU DO?

"Cool," you might be saying, "but what about me?" Well, the title of this chapter promised instructions for how to talk politics and save democracy, so here goes. One of the easiest things that you can do is start reflecting on your own political habits. Do you only pay attention to information that supports your preexisting ideas? Do you talk more than you listen? Are you open to new perspectives? In its simplest form, deliberative democracy asks us to broaden our own perspectives and allow for deliberation within (Goodin, 2000).

In this sense, deliberation starts with a mindset, an openness to learning that allows you to consider multiple perspectives before reaching a decision (Barabas, 2004; Burkhalter et al., 2002; Sprain & Ivancic, 2017). If you want to foster such a mindset, it likely makes sense to reevaluate where you are already getting your political information. If people pay attention to politics at all, they tend to give their attention to those media outlets that reaffirm their political ideologies, and people tend to socialize in similar manners, gravitating toward individuals who support the things that we support (Stroud, 2010; Sunstein, 2009, 2018). While this type of engagement is not inherently bad,[2] when the public only listens to people who already agree with them, they reduce the potential for learning from and understanding people who hold different beliefs (Iyengar et al., 2019; Mutz, 2002). Moreover, this tends to further polarize the public as individuals believe all the good things about their own side and all the bad things about the other side. That rising polarization makes it increasingly difficult for the public to make sustainable and informed decisions across political and identity-based divides.

So, a first step toward being more deliberative in your everyday life might be to assess the information you pay attention to. Try to make sure that you are listening to diverse perspectives from credible sources committed to providing quality information. It may feel good to only listen to the things that support our viewpoints, but it's definitely not good for democracy.

---

2 For groups that have been historically excluded from political decision making, this type of enclave communication, or communication among individuals who hold similar experiences and perspectives, can be deeply empowering because it creates the opportunity for community members to understand their collective needs and develop strategies for advocating for their distinct interests (Karpowitz et al., 2009; Mansbridge, 1994).

You can also practice deliberating in your everyday life. How often do you actually listen and ask follow-up questions rather than waiting for your turn to speak? Now think about your political conversations with people you disagree with. If you are honest, you might avoid them entirely. Or if you do talk politics, you likely focus on convincing the other person why *they* are *wrong* and *you* are *right*. When we do this, we close off the possibilities for learning and connection. Next time, try listening more than you talk.

At the CPD, we always start our facilitation training with active listening exercises. We ask our students and folks at our community trainings to tell each other stories, and instead of responding, the listener focuses on making sure that the person telling the story feels heard. We then ask them to practice asking questions so they can get a deeper understanding of the values and information that motivates the speaker. Another thing you might do is share your own stories and encourage others to share theirs. Storytelling plays a key role in deliberative discussion, allowing us to express our values and share evidence and creating opportunities for empathy and perspective taking that fosters understanding across difference (Black, 2008; Ryfe, 2006). When we share our own stories, we can connect with others across difference and create the space for learning and understanding.

So the next time, you are in a political conversation, practice listening and storytelling. Ask other people questions about their experiences and then share your own experiences.[3] You will likely find that when you are open to learning, you have better conversations and make better connections with others. Of course there is a lot more to learn about how to deliberate. We teach our students how to identify and discuss the values that are often at the heart of disagreements and offer trainings in bias intervention and responding to misinformation. The really radical act, however, is a shift toward listening, learning, and sharing, rather than winning.

So now that you have learned to talk politics, how might you save democracy? As we discussed earlier, democracy requires the public to engage in all sorts of ways, and deliberation is just one of them. See if there are folks who are already doing important work and figure out how you can help. Attend community meetings and vote in your local elections[4]; make your voice heard in public conversations and through advocacy efforts. Go outside and talk to your neighbor. All of these things matter, but they matter most when we do them together (Dryzek, 2012; Parkinson & Mansbridge, 2012). The point is not for you to save democracy on your own; that's impossible. But what you can do is take steps to make your community more informed, more inclusive, and more respectful. If more of us do that work, we can create the conditions that make a better democracy possible.

---

3 Research shows that's likely to be more convincing in any case. Studies exploring how to change people's minds on deeply polarizing issues find that approaches focused on perspective-taking, those instances when we ask people to share their stories in an effort to understand their perspective and share ours in return, are highly effective (Broockman & Kalla, 2016; Kubin et al., 2021).

4 Seriously, y'all, voting is important. If you have the privilege of citizenship, make sure you're registered to vote and that you exercise your voice every time you get the chance. We can't create a better democracy if we don't vote.

REFERENCES

Barabas, J. (2004). How deliberation affects policy opinions. *American Political Science Review, 98*(4), 687–701. https://doi.org/10.1017/S0003055404041425

Black, L. W. (2008). Deliberation, storytelling, and dialogic moments. *Communication Theory, 18*(1), 93–116. https://doi.org/10.1111/j.1468-2885.2007.00315.x

Bohman, J. (2012). Representation in the deliberative system. In J. Parkinson & J. Mansbridge (Eds.), *Deliberative systems: Deliberative democracy at the large scale* (pp. 72–94). Cambridge.

Boulianne, S. (2019). Building faith in democracy: Deliberative events, political trust and efficacy. *Political Studies, 67*(1), 4–30. https://doi.org/10.1177/0032321718761466

Broockman, D., & Kalla, J. (2016). Durably reducing transphobia: A field experiment on door-to-door canvassing. *Science, 352*(6282), 220–224. https://doi.org/10.1126/science.aad9713

Burkhalter, S., Gastil, J., & Kelshaw, T. (2002). A conceptual definition and theoretical model of public deliberation in small face—to—face groups. *Communication Theory, 12*(4), 398–422. https://doi.org/10.1111/j.1468-2885.2002.tb00276.x

Cabannes, Y. (2004). Participatory budgeting: a significant contribution to participatory democracy. *Environment and Urbanization, 16*(1), 27–46. https://doi.org/10.1177/095624780401600104

Carcasson, M. (2013). Tackling wicked problems through deliberative engagement. *National Civic Review, 105*(1), 44–47. https://doi.org/10.1002/ncr.21258

Carcasson, M., & Sprain, L. (2010). Key aspects of the deliberative democracy movement. *Public Sector Digest*, 1–5.

Citrin, J., & Stoker, L. (2018). Political trust in a cynical age. *Annual Review of Political Science, 21*, 49–70. https://doi.org/10.1146/annurev-polisci-050316-092550

Curato, N., Farrell, D. M., Geissel, B., Grönlund, K., Mockler, P., Pilet, J. B., Renwick, A., Rose, J., Setälä, M., & Suiter, J. (Eds.). (2021). *Deliberative mini publics: Core design features.* Bristol University Press.

Dillard, K. N. (2013). Envisioning the role of facilitation in public deliberation. *Journal of Applied Communication Research, 41*(3), 217–235. https://doi.org/10.1080/00909882.2013.826813

Dryzek, J. S. (2012). *Foundations and frontiers of deliberative governance.* Oxford University Press.

Gorokhovskaia, Y., Shahbaz, A., & Slipowitz, A. (2022). *Freedom in the world 2023: Marking fifty years in the struggle for democracy.* Freedom House.

Farrell, D. M., Suiter, J., & Harris, C. (2019). 'Systematizing' constitutional deliberation: the 2016–18 citizens' assembly in Ireland. *Irish Political Studies, 34*(1), 113–123. https://doi.org/10.1080/07907184.2018.1534832

Fishkin, J. S. (2009). *When the people speak: Deliberative democracy and public consultation.* Oxford University Press.

Freelon, D., & Wells, C. (2020). Disinformation as political communication. *Political Communication, 37*(2), 145–156. https://doi.org/10.1080/10584609.2020.1723755

Gastil, J. (2008). *Political communication and deliberation.* Sage.

Gastil, J., & Dillard, J. P. (1999). Increasing political sophistication through public deliberation. *Political Communication, 16*(1), 3–23. https://doi.org/10.1080/105846099198749

Gastil, J. & Knobloch, K. R. (2020). *Hope for democracy: How citizens can bring reason back into politics.* Oxford University Press.

Gastil, J. & Knobloch, K. R. (in press). Assessing long-term attitudinal and behavioral impacts of the Oregon Citizens' Initiative Review minipublic. In V. Jacquet, R. Van Der Does, & M. Ryan (Eds.), *The power of democratic innovations. The impact of participatory and deliberative institutions.* ECPR Press.

Gastil, J., Knobloch, K. R., Henkels, M., Reedy, J., & Cramer, K. (2018). Assessing the electoral impact of the 2010 Oregon Citizens' Initiative Review. *American Politics Research, 46*(3), 534–563. https://doi.org/10.1177/1532673X1771562

Gastil, J., & Levine, P. (2005). *The deliberative democracy handbook: Strategies for effective civic engagement in the twenty-first century.* Jossey-Bass.

Goodin, R. E. (2000). Democratic deliberation within. *Philosophy & Public Affairs, 29*(1), 81–109. https://www.jstor.org/stable/2672865

Habermas, J. (1984). *The theory of communicative action, vol. 1: Reason and the rationalization of society*, trans. Thomas McCarthy. Beacon.

Hartz-Karp, J., Anderson, P., Gasti, J., & Felicetti, A. (2010). The Australian Citizens' Parliament: Forging shared identity through public deliberation. *Journal of Public Affairs, 10*(4), 353–371. https://doi.org/10.1002/pa.370

Hendriks, C. M. (2016). Coupling citizens and elites in deliberative systems: The role of institutional design. *European Journal of Political Research, 55*(1), 43–60. https://doi.org/10.1111/1475-6765.12123

Iyengar, S., Lelkes, Y., Levendusky, M., Malhotra, N., & Westwood, S. J. (2019). The origins and consequences of affective polarization in the United States. *Annual Review of Political Science, 22*, 129–146. https://doi.org/10.1146/annurev-polisci-051117-073034

Karpowitz, C. F., Raphael, C., & Hammond IV, A. S. (2009). Deliberative democracy and inequality: Two cheers for enclave deliberation among the disempowered. *Politics & Society, 37*(4), 576–615. https://doi.org/10.1177/0032329209349226

Knobloch, K. R. (2022). Listening to the public: An inductive analysis of the good citizen in the deliberative system. *Journal of Deliberative Democracy, 18*(1), 1–13. https://doi.org/10.16997/10.16997/jdd.955

Knobloch, K. R., Barthel, M. L., & Gastil, J. (2019). Emanating effects: the impact of the Oregon Citizens' Initiative Review on voters' political efficacy. *Political Studies, 68*(2), 426–445. https://doi.org/10.1177/0032321719852254

Knobloch, K. R., & Gastil, J. (2015). Civic (re)socialisation: The educative effects of deliberative participation. *Politics, 35*(2), 183–200. https://doi.org/10.1111/1467-9256.12069

Knobloch, K. R., Gastil, J., Reedy, J., & Walsh, K. C. (2013). Did they deliberate? Applying an evaluative model of democratic deliberation to the Oregon Citizens' Initiative Review. *Journal of Applied Communication Research, 44*(2), 105–125. https://doi.org/10.1080/0090 9882.2012.760746

Kubin, E., Puryear, C., Schein, C., & Gray, K. (2021). Personal experiences bridge moral and political divides better than facts. *Proceedings of the National Academy of Sciences, 118*(6), e2008389118. https://doi.org/10.1073/pnas.2008389118

Luskin, R. C., Fishkin, J. S., & Jowell, R. (2002). Considered opinions: Deliberative polling in Britain. *British Journal of Political Science, 32*(3), 455–487. https://doi.org/10.1017/ S0007123402000194

Mansbridge, J. (1994). Using power/fighting power. *Constellations, 1*(1), 53–73. https://doi. org/10.1111/j.1467-8675.1994.tb00004.x

Mansbridge, J., Hartz-Karp, J., Amengual, M., & Gastil, J. (2006). Norms of deliberation: An inductive study. *Journal of Deliberative Democracy, 2*(1), Article 1. https://doi.org/10.16997/jdd.35

Már, K., & Gastil, J. (2020). Tracing the boundaries of motivated reasoning: How deliberative minipublics can improve voter knowledge. *Political Psychology, 41*(1), 107–127. https://doi. org/10.1111/pops.12591

Mutz, D. C. (2002). Cross-cutting social networks: Testing democratic theory in practice. *American Political Science Review, 96*(1), 111–126. https://doi.org/10.1017/S0003055402004264

Nabatchi, T. (2010). Addressing the citizenship and democratic deficits: The potential of deliberative democracy for public administration. *The American Review of Public Administration, 40*(4), 376–399. https://doi.org/10.1177/0275074009356467

Nabatchi, T., Gastil, J., Weiksner, G. M., & Leighninger, M. (Eds.). (2012). *Democracy in motion: Evaluating the practice and impact of deliberative civic engagement.* Oxford University Press.

Papada, E., Altman, D., Angiolillo, F., Gastaldi, L., Köhler, T., Lundstedt, M., Natsika, N., Nord, M., Sato, Y., Wiebrecht, F., & Lindberg, S. I. (2023). Defiance in the face of autocratization: Democracy report 2023. University of Gothenburg: Varieties of Democracy Institute.

Parkinson, J., & Mansbridge, J. (Eds.). (2012). *Deliberative systems: Deliberative democracy at the large scale.* Cambridge University Press.

Russon Gilman, H. (2016). *Democracy reinvented: Participatory budgeting and civic innovation in America.* Brookings Institution Press.

Ryfe, D. M. (2006). Narrative and deliberation in small group forums. *Journal of Applied Communication Research, 34*(1), 72–93. https://doi.org/10.1080/00909880500420226

Shaffer, T. J., Longo, N. V., Manosevitch, I., & Thomas, M. S. (2017). *Deliberative pedagogy: Teaching and learning for democratic engagement.* MSU Press.

Smith, G. (2009). *Democratic innovations: Designing institutions for citizen participation.* Cambridge University Press.

Sprain, L., & Ivancic, S. (2017). Communicating openness in deliberation. *Communication Monographs, 84*(2), 241–257. https://doi.org/10.1080/03637751.2016.1257141

Stroud, N. J. (2010). Polarization and partisan selective exposure. *Journal of Communication, 60*(3), 556–576. https://doi.org/10.1111/j.1460-2466.2010.01497.x

Sunstein, C. R. (2009). *Going to extremes: How like minds unite and divide.* Oxford University Press.

Sunstein, C. R. (2018). # Republic. In *# Republic.* Princeton University Press.

Warren, M. E. & Pearse, H. (2008). *Designing deliberative democracy: The British Columbia Citizens' Assembly.* Cambridge University Press.

Young, I. M. (2000). *Inclusion and democracy.* Oxford University Press.

SCIENCE COMMUNICATION

The science communication context focuses on how scientific information and evidence is presented and received by the public. Thus, science communication scholarship examines how experts communicate about scientific advancements to inform society by raising awareness, generating interest, and facilitating understanding of science. Some major areas of research in science communication include communication about climate change, the environment, human–machine communication, vaccinations, and food labeling. This section includes chapters focusing on three important areas of science communication research: (1) the rhetoric of science, health, and medicine, (2) artificial intelligence and social agents, and (3) aggressive communication in science conversations. First, Lisa Keränen (University of Colorado Denver) and Jennifer Malkowski (California State University, Chico) explore the rhetoric of health and discuss how language choices shape scientific, health, and medical understanding and (in)action. Second, Jaime Banks (Syracuse University) and Kevin Koban (University of Vienna, Austria) explore human–machine communication and theorize about how we view and think about social machines as artificially intelligent agents. Third, Shupei Yuan (Northern Illinois University) reviews how aggressive communication styles are interpreted in science messaging (e.g., about vaccination and climate change). Scientific advancements occur rapidly and change society as we know it. The ways in which people choose to communicate about these science advancements will shape the future and influence how people will adopt and understand medicine and machines alike.

HOW CAN RHETORIC HELP US UNDERSTAND SCIENCE, HEALTH, AND MEDICINE?

Lisa Keränen
University of Colorado Denver

Jennifer Malkowski
California State University, Chico

COVID-19 illustrated the importance of timely, accurate public health communication. The pandemic also demonstrated that the global communication environment is flooded with health information, disinformation, and misinformation, what the World Health Organization (WHO, 2022) has called an "infodemic." The relentless public discourse about science, health, and medicine can make it difficult to distinguish credible information from misleading or harmful claims, highlighting the importance of trust, truthfulness, transparency, and accountability when crafting and consuming scientific and health-related messages. According to WHO (2022), infodemics—the proliferation of health information during disease outbreaks—can cause confusion, erode trust, undermine health, and lengthen the course of disease. Even when people's intentions are good, communication about health needs and risks is fraught with the potential for unreliable information and misunderstanding. Because health care occupies such a significant part of everyday life, and because it bridges both biomedical *science* and the *art* of caregiving, communication about health and medicine spans public and private, corporate and nonprofit, and national and international contexts.

Unlike health communication researchers, who tend to prioritize social science methods to understand and improve health messages (see, for example, the chapter by Gary Kreps), a growing number of researchers examine health and medical discourses and practices using the lens of persuasion, or rhetoric, along with the tools of rhetorical analysis. This chapter explores how a distinctly rhetorical perspective can help us understand the roles of science and medicine in shaping our views of health, disease, wellness, ability, the body, and illness. To address the question, "how can rhetoric help us understand science, health, and medicine?," we begin by reviewing the history, characteristics, and current trends of a growing research area known as the rhetoric of health and medicine (RHM). We then outline some research that illustrates how a rhetorical approach can improve understanding and potentially influence professional, public, and clinical discourses about medicine and health. Ultimately, we show that a rhetorical perspective allows the identification, tracking, and assessment of how and why particular language choices shape scientific, health, and medical understanding and action (and sometimes inaction as well), and how the productive aspects of rhetoric enable us to create, challenge, or reinvent new patterns of thought and action.

RHETORICAL STUDIES OF HEALTH AND MEDICINE

The term *rhetoric* refers most broadly to the ancient practice and analysis of persuasion and originally meant persuasive speaking or oratory. In the mid-twentieth century, rhetoric's scope broadened from the realm of speeches to include any use of symbols and now encompasses all types of persuasive texts and artifacts, including art and digital images, film, writing, speeches, nonverbal symbols, pharmaceutical advertisements, digital communication, and even doctor-patient conversations. The scholarly methods used by rhetorical scholars often involve some sort of textual analysis, wherein the researcher identifies symbolic properties and patterns and assesses their dynamics and consequences. While rhetoric was long considered an essential part of the humanities, rhetoric scholars increasingly use multiple means of analysis, including social scientific methods and critical perspectives, especially when conducting rhetorical studies of health and medical discourses and practices. These include interviewing, content analysis, participant observation and field methods, statistical and network analyses of big data, and more (Melonçon & Scott, 2017). The term *rhetorical criticism* refers to the use of rhetorical concepts or theory to reveal how patterns of language structure understanding and action in a text, discourse, or object. For instance, Molloy (2019) uses the classical concept of *ethos*, or appeals to character, to explore how patients seeking mental health care attempt to establish their credibility in the face of stigma and misdiagnosis related to race, class, and gender.

The study and practice of the rhetoric of health and medicine grew out of a scholarly field known as the rhetoric of science (Harris, 2020; Roundtree, 2013), which examines how persuasion functions in scientific and technical discourses. Scholars trained in rhetorical theory and methods who began to study persuasion in and around health and medicine eventually formed a field now known as the rhetoric of health and medicine (Melonçon et al., 2020; see also Heifferon & Brown, 2008; Jensen, 2015; Leach & Dysart-Gale, 2011; Malkowski et al., 2016; Melonçon & Frost, 2015; Segal, 2005, 2009). Galvanizing resources and coordinating conversations across disciplines, publications, professional events, and organizations since the early 2000s, the subfield of RHM forged a distinct interdisciplinary identity. Although clear affinities exist with other disciplines and sub-fields, including health communication (Zoller & Dutta, 2008), the health humanities (Campbell, 2018; Jones et al., 2014) and critical health communication (Dutta, 2010; Lynch & Zoller, 2015; Sastry et al., 2021), RHM cemented its standing as a distinct research area in 2018 with the launch of its award-winning, namesake journal, *Rhetoric of Health and Medicine.* With collaborative publications focused on what it means to adopt a rhetorical approach to the study of health and medicine (Melonçon & Scott, 2017; Melonçon et al., 2020), the field attracts scholars from a variety of backgrounds and disciplines. Recent work in the rhetoric of health and medicine has focused on vaccine rhetorics (Hausman, 2019; Lawrence, 2020), gendered pathologies (Emmons, 2010; Frost & Eble, 2020; Jensen, 2016; Koerber, 2018; Segal, 2015; Stormer, 2015); mental health rhetorics (Hanganu-Bresch & Berkenkotter, 2019; Molloy & Melonçon, 2022; Molloy et al, 2020), public health rhetoric (Malkowski & Melonçon, 2019; Winderman et al., 2019), Caribbean and Latinx health rhetoric and practices (Bloom-Pojar, 2018; Pigozzi, 2020), and pandemic and disease rhetorics (Bennett, 2019; Ding, 2014; Levina, 2022). What broadly unites these researchers is a common focus on how health messages function as persuasive exchange and how such communication is ethically and politically laden.

A primary concern for rhetoricians of health and medicine is the use of language to define health, wellness, disease, dis/ability, and illness. For example, rhetoric plays a pivotal role in *medicalization*, the process used to redefine broad human concerns as medical issues that require diagnosis, treatment, therapy, and medicine (Conrad, 2007; Jensen et al., 2019; Lane, 2007). Shyness and obesity, for example, are two conditions that used to be defined socially but that have, through rhetoric, become subject to medical authority, counseling, and an ever-expanding array of pharmaceuticals. As a result, patients, medical providers, and everyday citizens use rhetoric to define and redefine both well-known and emerging conditions in ways that create health and illness identities and inform health behaviors and responses. As Derkatch and Segal (2005, p. 139) explain:

> The phrase "social anxiety disorder" persuades the very shy person that he or she may be a candidate for drug therapy; the word "breakthrough" persuades the public to imagine medical research as a particularly dramatic sort of enterprise; the phrase "fighting disease" persuades persons that they have failed at something when they cannot stop being ill; the term "survivor" leaves the dead person looking somehow culpable.

These examples illustrate how the rhetoric we use to talk about health and disease is far from neutral; it subtly asks us to adopt particular health identities ("the cancer survivor," "the heart patient," "the person with ADHD") and to think of health conditions in certain ways ("as invaders to be *fought*," "as problems to be *managed*") in order to pursue certain courses of action (to take medication, to forgo surgery, to get a vaccine). As the domains of science and technology become further entwined with health care, scholars suggest that rhetoric is now also heavily implicated in *biomedicalization*, the transformation of health and bodies through technoscientific enhancement (see e.g., Clarke et al., 2010; Happe et al., 2018). Beyond defining health and disease and shaping their social, professional, and identity meanings, rhetoric also influences expectations for what health and health care *should* look and feel like for patients and publics alike.

To deepen understanding of how rhetoric helps us understand science, health, and medicine, for the remainder of this chapter we will consider the work of the first author across professional, public, and clinical contexts. Specifically, we will discuss how Lisa Keränen's work illuminates the rhetoric used in both caregiving and care-receiving and in public discourses about biological threats and security. In exploring these two areas of scholarship, we demonstrate how rhetorical tools develop knowledge and contribute to practical recommendations in the rhetoric of health and medicine across contexts.

PERSUASION IN GIVING AND RECEIVING HEALTH CARE

One strand of Keränen's work investigates persuasion in the context of giving and receiving health care. This work has spanned her first published rhetorical analysis of the significance of the Hippocratic Oath (Keränen, 2001) through analyses of end-of-life rhetoric (Keränen, 2013) and breast cancer research and treatment (Keränen, 2010). One of her case studies that is taught in medical humanities classes examines how language functions when giving or seeking care for Morgellons Disease. Morgellons is what sociologists call a "contested illness," meaning that health care providers and patients disagree about the nature of the condition and its treatment (Keränen, 2014). The name *Morgellons* was adopted in 2001 by the mother of the first patient named as having the condition, then 2-year-old Drew Leitao, who complained of "bugs" while touching his lips. Mary Leitao found baffling fibers erupting from lesions on her son's lip, a condition eventually shared by family members. She scoured the medical literature for something that might explain these symptoms, and eventually, she borrowed the name *Morgellons* from a reference to a centuries-old French medical case report that mentioned fibers erupting from skin. Leitao sought help from numerous, often skeptical, physicians; one even suggested she had Munchausen's by proxy, meaning the doctor thought she was attention seeking by faking symptoms in her child. When the medical community was unable to provide the answers she was seeking, Leitao created an online support group, the Morgellons Research Foundation (MRF), which at its peak included more than 10,000 members from the United States and other nations, all of whom claimed to be affected by Morgellons.

The MRF promoted media and congressional attention in the early 2000s, which in turn prompted public awareness of the symptoms, and the number of care seekers mushroomed. The singer/songwriter Joni Mitchell and former Oakland A's baseball pitcher Billy Koch both spoke publicly about having the condition, triggering further public interest. Meanwhile, patients who self-diagnosed with Morgellons continued to arrive at their dermatologists' offices complaining of unusual fibers erupting from their skin and a host of neurological symptoms. Their physicians would typically diagnose them with a classic condition known as *delusional parasitosis*, or DP, which, as its name suggests, suggested that patients sincerely believed they were infected with parasites when they were not. The recommended treatment regimen for DP involves psychiatric medicine. Understandably, self-diagnosed Morgellons patients did not appreciate being called "delusional," nor did they agree that their problem was psychiatric, and so caregivers and care receivers found themselves at a rhetorical impasse: how could patients who self-identified as having Morgellons persuade their health care providers to take their concerns seriously, and how could physicians persuade Morgellons suffers to consider that psychiatric medicines seemed to alleviate many of the symptoms? To make matters worse, the act of bringing in samples of bugs, fibers, or bodily debris, which is called the matchbox or baggy sign in medical literature (because patients suffering from delusions would bring in samples in a matchbox or small plastic bag), was listed as a classic diagnostic sign of DP.

Keränen's rhetorical analysis of Morgellons tracked the different language choices of both Morgellons sufferers and the mainstream medical community in medical publications produced by both groups and in their public accounts of how each adapted their language to appeal to the other. Identifying patterns in their word choice and frames, she found that Morgellons sympathizers appealed mainly to visual evidence and framed Morgellons as a medical mystery, while dermatologists and psychiatrists offered mostly cultural and psychological explanations that identified Morgellons as Internet-fueled hysteria. Some of these rhetors used stigmatizing language to frame Morgellons patients as lonely and hysterical, attention-seeking women, although people of all genders identified as having the condition. Beyond these incompatible frames, Keränen's analysis further demonstrated how both groups accommodated their language to one another in an effort to be persuasive. Some physicians gradually adopted the name "Morgellons" and urged a staged approach to medication. Meanwhile, sufferers used the genre of the medical case report to lend credibility to their symptoms and launched their own studies of the condition. Keränen maintained that the incommensurate beliefs of each group evidenced by their rhetoric meant that they were unlikely to resolve the controversy about the nature Morgellons, even in the face of rigorous scientific study. The lack of shared understanding about the nature of and treatment for the condition was simply too great. Although its prominence has waned since the MRF shut down in 2012, the controversy over Morgellons continues and was featured in a 2019 Netflix documentary *Skin Deep: The Battle Over Morgellons.* By highlighting the power of the Internet to mobilize patients and illuminating the gulf of understanding between the world of mainstream medicine and patient advocates, the case of Morgellons shows how important publicly circulating rhetoric can be to understandings of health and illness, to patients receiving the care they need, and to health care providers' efforts to establish trusting therapeutic relationships.

How Can Rhetoric Help Us Understand Science, Health, and Medicine?

THE CONSTRUCTION OF BIOLOGICAL THREATS AND BIOSECURITY

While one strand of Keränen's research examines rhetoric in caregiving and receiving, a second major strand of her research explores the public construction and understanding of biological threats. She has published numerous analyses of how the rhetoric of bioterrorism threat construction obscured concern for more mundane but pervasive killers like HIV/ AIDS, tuberculosis, and malaria (see e.g., Keränen, 2011, 2019). This work has culminated in a recent book that is forthcoming from Johns Hopkins University Press, *Envisioning Viral Apocalypse: Rhetorics of Biosecurity, Risk, and Resilience from Anthrax to COVID*. This book explores how biological threats and responses have been framed in U.S. public discourse from 1989 to the present by offering a rhetorical history of the concept of biosecurity. A rhetorical history investigates "how specific discourses, their meanings, and their effects have changed over time by examining historical records or traces of those discourses" (Malkowski et al., 2016, p. 12). Here, Keränen sets her sights on the relationships between a widely circulating vision of viral apocalypse and U.S. policy rhetorics.

The dominant contemporary vision of viral apocalypse, which depicts global civil and economic collapse following contagion, appears across films (e.g., *Outbreak, I am Legend, 28 Days Later, Contagion*), television shows (e.g., *The Walking Dead* and *Station Eleven*), preparedness simulations (e.g., *Atlantic Storm* and *Dark Winter*), and policy documents (e.g., *Biodefense for the 21ˢᵗ Century* and *U.S. National Pandemic Preparedness Plan*). Keränen's book chronicles how concerns about biological insecurity promoted a recurring but evolving vision of viral apocalypse that helped fuel the rise of a global health security paradigm, which, despite billions of dollars of funding over decades of preparation, ultimately left the U.S. radically unprepared for the novel threat of pandemic COVID.

The book begins at the end of the Cold War when concerns about Soviet biological weapons programs emerged as a security issue. Here, Keränen demonstrates how a group of predominantly White, male security analysts persuaded government officials that state made biological weapons were easily accessible by terrorists and that bioterrorism constituted an inevitable, existential threat to the United States. Across government reports, simulation exercises, and think tank documents, she catalogs the construction of bioterrorism as a "catastrophic" or "apocalyptic" risk to the United States more than a decade before the anthrax mailings of 2001 (also see Keränen, 2011).

When the 9/11 attacks became symbolically, albeit misleadingly, associated with the anthrax mailings, government leaders used them as rhetorical justification for a new era of "biodefense," centered around the concept of "biopreparedness." In this vision of viral apocalypse, governments and citizens needed to prepare for either bioterrorism or a novel emerging infectious disease, requiring a focus on the *preemption* or *prevention* of biological attacks. Although critics claimed the focus on bioterrorism was an inflated and sensationalistic risk rhetoric, the construction of bioterrorism as an existential threat persuaded

Congress and other nations to fund a growing array of actions intended to prevent a biological attack. Keränen shows how this vision merged with concerns about a pandemic, directing global attention to avian influenza in the mid-2000s. This rhetoric portrayed infectious disease as a national security issue that required improved disease surveillance, detection, and communication networks to prepare the nation for what was framed as inevitable.

During the Obama administration, official visions of "biodefense" from the post-9/11 era evolved into a broader concern for global health security. Through close readings of pivotal government texts, including the *2009 National Strategy for Biological Threats* and the *2014 Global Health Security Agenda*, Keränen charts a growing concern with a wider array of biological threats. Instead of a rogue bioterrorist quietly releasing a bioweapon into an unsuspecting city or a novel avian influenza killing millions, multiplying germ threats were configured as threatening not only humanity but also the natural world. This emerging global health security agenda with its accompanying notion of "resilience" confronted a viral emergency during the Ebola outbreak in 2014 in Western Africa. Keränen here explores how U.S. public discourses pushed racialized and gendered imaginings that inflated the perceived risk of Ebola, and later Zika, among wealthy Western audiences and furthered the securitization of public health, exemplified by the U.S. military's role in the Ebola response abroad.

The book then brings readers into the era of COVID-19, when fears of a pandemic were realized. By analyzing the purported links between the novel coronavirus and either United States or Chinese bioweapons in official and social media discourses from both nations, Keränen shows how the old links between biological attack and pandemic resurfaced. She then analyzes how United States and Chinese state-supported narratives blamed each other for spreading the infection, revealing how nationalism and contagion often intertwine in harmful ways. Even as the rhetoric of world leaders often undermined global and national responses to the pandemic, conspiracy rhetoric and disinformation campaigns performed the harmful work of division, sowing hatred, promoting ignorance, and breeding confusion in ways that cost lives and extended the life of the pandemic. Keränen concludes by asking readers to consider how contagion is linked to visions of belonging and Otherness, inviting readers to shed old narratives about biological threats and instead focus on the shared humanity seen in pandemic times, to embrace what Eugene T. Richardson (2020) calls *pandemicity*, "the linking of humanity through contagion" (p. 1). In erecting systems of health security, she asks *who* and *what* are being secured? Whose bodies are vulnerable and left out? And at what cost? Keränen argues that in a time of radical interdependence between people and their environment, humanity must learn to thrive together in various states of sickness/health and dis/ability while creating alternate viral rhetorics that embrace an ethic of care instead of scapegoating and blame.

Theoretical analyses of health and medical texts like the ones discussed in this essay can help readers become more informed patients, critical consumers of scientific and health information, and trained observers of health and illness discourses through the close examination of real-world examples. A rhetorical perspective offers understanding of the persuasive mechanisms at work in public, private, and clinical discourses, a vocabulary for assessing potentially problematic and promising trends in health and medicine, and a platform to begin discussion about the consequences of representing people and institutions in public spaces. Rhetorical studies of health and medicine allow people to weigh in more thoughtfully in public discussions of science, health, and medicine, and they allow us to reconsider our experiences of illness and our roles as patients.

CONCLUSION

Our contemporary digital communication environment ensures we are each more embedded in and accountable to a world that extends far beyond our individual daily lives. That our own health experiences are connected so closely to those of others, that the management of our own health depends on networks of professional experts across industries and continents, and that our own physical and mental health statuses rely on how we communicate about them, means that the rhetoric of health and medicine constitutes an important site of inquiry. In the wake of COVID-19, many people have come to realize that persuasion matters to the experience and management of health and disease. The rhetoric of health and medicine provides theories, concepts, and tools to recognize and respond to that which ails us in more thoughtful, effective, and ethical ways.

In this chapter, we have taken a closer look at how research in the rhetoric of medicine helps us understand the consequential role language plays across professional, public, and clinical health settings. Based on what you have read, take a moment to assess the medical and health rhetoric that you encounter. What forms of medical and health communication do you participate in daily, weekly, and annually? Which health messages are most persuasive to you, where do they come from, and why? Are your sources of health information credible and trustworthy? How are distinct genres of medical rhetoric (hospital forms, direct-to-consumer advertisements, medical websites) and new technologies (electronic medical records, email to providers, health-related smart-phone "apps") changing your communication with health care professionals? Of what are they attempting to persuade you? How much of your information about health and wellness is gleaned from online sources? How do public discourses about health, medicine, and science affect your understanding of yourself and your health? How is and should health be linked to national and international security? And overall, how does your health care communication stack up to the communication discussed in this chapter?

The next time you visit a health care professional, take stock of how the language of medicine and the institutional imperatives shape your communication. Who does the talking? How much time is scheduled? Who is trying to persuade whom of what using which means? How do patients and health care providers identify or misidentify with one another? How do forms, charts, and computer screens enable and constrain your communication? In adopting a rhetorical perspective on health and medicine, you will be examining how your health care communication is shaped by social and symbolic processes with unique but consequential histories, contexts, and functions. In short, you will be examining how rhetoric about medicine and health structures identities, coordinates care, and shapes personal and societal understandings of illness and health.

REFERENCES

Bennett, J. A. (2019). *Managing diabetes: The cultural politics of disease.* New York University Press.

Bloom-Pojar, R. (2018). *Translanguaging outside the academy: Negotiating rhetoric and healthcare in the Spanish Caribbean.* National Council of Teachers of English.

Campbell, L. (2018). The rhetoric of health and medicine as a "teaching subject": Lessons from the medical humanities and simulation pedagogy. *Technical Communication Quarterly, 27*(1), 7–20. https://doi.org/10.1080/10572252.2018.1401348

Clarke, A. E., Mamo, J., Fosket, R., Fishman, J. R., & Shim, J. K. (Eds.) (2010). *Biomedicalization: Technoscience, health, and illness in the U.S.* Duke University Press.

Conrad, J. (2007). *The medicalization of society: On the transformation of human conditions into treatable disorders.* Johns Hopkins University Press.

Derkatch, C., & Segal, J. Z. (2005). Realms of rhetoric in health and medicine. *University of Toronto Medical Journal, 83*, 138–142. Retrieved from http://www.colleenderkatch.com/wp-content/uploads/2018/09/Derkatch-and-Segal-2005-Realms-of-Rhetoric-in-Health-and-Medicine.pdf

Ding, H. (2014). *Rhetoric of a global epidemic: Transcultural communication about SARS.* Southern Illinois University Press.

Dutta, M. J. (2010). The critical cultural turn in health communication: Reflexivity, solidarity, and praxis. *Health Communication, 25*(6–7), 534–539. https://doi.org/10.1080/10410236.2010.497995

Emmons, K. (2010). *Black dogs and blue words: Depression and gender in the age of self-care.* Rutgers University Press.

Frost, E. A., & Eble, M. F. (Eds.). (2020). *Interrogating gendered pathologies.* Utah State University Press.

Hanganu-Bresch, C., & Berkenkotter, C. (2019). *Diagnosing madness: The discursive construction of the psychiatric patient, 1850-1920.* The University of South Carolina Press.

Happe, K., Johnson, J., & Levina, M. (Eds.) (2018). *Bio-citizenship: The politics of bodies, governance, and power.* New York University Press.

Harris, R. A. (Ed). (2020). *Landmark essays on rhetoric of science: Issues and methods.* Routledge.

Hausman, B. L. (2019). *Anti/Vax: Reframing the vaccination controversy.* Cornell University Press.

Heifferon, B., & Brown, S. (Eds.). (2008). *The rhetoric of healthcare: Essays toward a new disciplinary inquiry.* Hampton Press.

Jensen, R. E. (2015). An ecological turn in rhetoric of health scholarship: Attending to the historical flow and percolation of ideas, assumptions, and arguments. *Communication Quarterly, 63*(5), 522–526. https://doi.org/10.1080/01463373.2015.1103600

Jensen, R. E. (2016). *Infertility: Tracing the history of a transformative term.* Pennsylvania University Press.

Jensen, R. E., Maison, K., Mann, B. W., Krall, M. A., & Parks, M. M. (2019). Medicalization's communicative infrastructure: Seventy years of 'brain chemistry' in the *New York Times. Health Communication, 36*(3), 272–279. https://doi.org/10.1080/10410236.2019.1673951

Jones, T., Friedman, L., & Wear, D. (Eds.). (2014). *Health humanities reader.* Rutgers University Press.

Keränen, L. (2001). The Hippocratic Oath as epideictic rhetoric: Reanimating medicine's past for its future. *Journal of Medical Humanities, 22*, 55–68.

Keränen, L. (2010). *Scientific characters: Rhetoric, politics, and trust in breast cancer research.* University of Alabama Press.

Keränen, L. (2011). Concocting viral apocalypse: Catastrophic risk and the construction of bio(in)security. *Western Journal of Communication, 75*(5), 451–472. https://doi.org/10.1080/1057031 4.2011.614507

Keränen, L. (2013). Technologies of self at the end of life: Pastoral power and the rhetoric of advance care Planning. In M. Hyde & J. Herrick (Eds.), *The language of our biotechnological future* (pp. 193–218). Baylor University Press.

Keränen, L. (2014). "This weird, incurable disease": Competing diagnoses in the rhetoric of Morgellons. In T. Jones, L. Friedman, and D. Wear (Eds.), *Health humanities reader* (pp. 36–49). Rutgers University Press.

Keränen, L. (2019). Biosecurity and communication. In B. C. Taylor & H. Bean (Eds.), *Handbook of security and communication* (pp. 223–246). Routledge.

Keränen, L. (forthcoming). *Envisioning viral apocalypse: Rhetorics of risk, resilience, and biosecurity from Anthrax to Covid.* Johns Hopkins University Press.

Koerber, A. (2018). *From hysteria to hormones: A rhetorical history.* Pennsylvania University Press.

Lane, C. (2007). *Shyness: How a normal behavior became a sickness.* Yale University Press.

Lawrence, H. Y. (2020). *Vaccine rhetorics.* The Ohio State University Press.

Leach, J., & Dysart-Gale, D. (Eds.). (2011). *Rhetorical questions of health and medicine.* Lexington Books.

Levina, M. (2022). Forum: Cultural chronicles of COVID-19, part 1: Language. *Communication and Critical/Cultural Studies, 19*(1), 5–7. https://doi.org/10.1080/14791420.2021.2020859

Lynch, J. A., & Zoller, H. (2015). Recognizing differences and commonalities: The rhetoric of health and medicine and critical-interpretive health communication. *Communication Quarterly, 63*(5), 498–503. https://doi.org/10.1080/01463373.2015.1103592

Malkowski, J., & Melonçon, L. (2019). The rhetoric of public health for RHM scholarship and beyond. *Rhetoric of Health & Medicine, 2*(2), iii–xiii. https://doi.org/10.5744/rhm.2019.1007

Malkowski, J., Scott, J. B., & Keränen, L. (2016). Rhetorical approaches to health and medicine. In *Oxford research encyclopedia of communication.* Oxford University Press.

Melonçon, L., & Frost, E. A. (2015). Charting an emerging field: The rhetorics of health and medicine and its importance in communication design. *Communication Design Quarterly, 3*(4), 7–14. https://doi.org/10.1145/2826972.2826973

Melonçon, L., Graham, S. S., Johnson, J., Lynch, J. A., & Ryan, C. (Eds.) (2020). *Rhetoric of medicine as/is: Theories and approaches for the field.* The Ohio State University Press.

Melonçon, L., & Scott, B. (2017). *Methodologies for the rhetoric of health and medicine.* Routledge.

Molloy, C. (2019). *Rhetorical ethos in health and medicine: Patient credibility, stigma, and misdiagnosis.* Routledge.

Molloy, C., Holladay, D., & Melonçon, L. (2020). The place of mental health rhetoric research (MHRR) in rhetoric of health and medicine and beyond. *Rhetoric of Health and Medicine, 3*(2), iii–x. https://doi.org/10.5744/rhm.2020.1011

Molloy, C., & Melonçon, L. (Eds.) (2022). *Strategic interventions in mental health rhetoric.* Routledge.

Pigozzi, L. M. (2020). *Caring for and understanding Latinx patients in health care settings.* University of British Columbia Press.

Richardson, E. T. (2020). Pandemicity, COVID-19 and the limits of public health 'science.' *BMJ Global Health, 5,* e00257. http://dx.doi.org/10.1136/bmjgh-2020-002571

Roundtree, A. K. (2013). *Computer simulation, rhetoric, and the scientific imagination: How Virtual evidence shapes science in the making and in the news.* Roman & Littlefield.

Sastry, S., Zoller, H. M., & Basu, A. (2021). Doing critical health communication: A forum on methods. *Frontiers in Communication, 5.* https://doi.org/10.3389/fcomm.2020.637579

Segal, J. Z. (2005). *Health and the rhetoric of medicine.* Southern Illinois University Press.

Segal, J. Z. (2009). Rhetoric of health and medicine. In A. A. Lundsford, K. H. Wilson, & R. A. Eberly (Eds.), *The Sage handbook of rhetorical studies* (pp. 227–246). Sage.

Segal, J. Z. (2015). The rhetoric of female sexual dysfunction: Faux feminism and the FDA. *Canadian Medical Association Journal, 187*(12), 915–916. https://doi.org/10.1503/cmaj.150363

Stormer. N. (2015). *Sign of pathology: U.S. medical rhetoric on abortion, 1800s–1960s.* Pennsylvania State University Press.

Winderman, E., Mejia, R., & Rogers, B. (2019). "All smell is disease": Miasma, sensory rhetoric, and the sanitary-bacteriologic of visceral public health. *Rhetoric of Health and Medicine, 2*(2), 115–146. https://doi.org/10.5744/rhm.2019.1006

World Health Organization (WHO). (2022). Infodemic. Retrieved from https://www.who.int/health-topics/infodemic

Zoller, H. M., & Dutta, M. J. (Eds.). (2008). *Emerging perspectives in health communication: Meaning, culture, and power.* Routledge.

HOW DOES MEDIA SHAPE HOW WE SEE SOCIAL MACHINES?

Jaime Banks
Syracuse University

Kevin Koban
University of Vienna, Austria

Artificially intelligent (AI) agents were once only the stuff of science fiction. Today, they are starting to play a role in communities and spaces traditionally reserved for humans (and sometimes animals). From the living room to the operating room, AI agents are technologies that in some way mimic natural intelligence. Sometimes these technologies are broadly called "smart" devices, but there is an important distinction: AI agents must have the ability to act on their own to some degree. In other words. they must have *agency*.

THINKING ABOUT THE SOCIALNESS OF MACHINES

One kind of AI agent is a "social machine," a technology designed to mimic our social behaviors. For instance, Amazon's Alexa is a voice assistant that performs tasks by processing and generating audible human language. Although Alexa functions across different devices, social machines are also sometimes contained in just one body. NASA's Valkyrie robot, as an example, has a human-like body equipped with sensors so it can navigate complicated human environments. Then again, other social machines (like social media bots) do not have bodies at all. Instead, they rely on programming to interpret and generate texts as they engage in conversations with humans.

These kinds of AI agents are technologies considered in the social-scientific field of *human-machine communication* (HMC). HMC is broadly characterized as the study of how humans and machines make meaning together (Guzman, 2019). We can think about meaning-making in terms of the Shannon-Weaver model of communication (Figure 1; Shannon & Weaver, 1949). That model illustrates a process in which a sender *encodes* information into a message, which is then sent over a *channel* (ideally persisting through some noise) until it is *decoded* by a receiver. Communication can be considered effective when the sent/encoded and received/decoded information have similar or identical meanings. In traditional communication science, machines have only been considered tools for encoding, channels, or decoding. For instance, CMC research considers the ways that computers serve as channels through which humans communicate with one another. However, HMC scholars have argued that social machines can create, send, and receive meaningful messages, so in addition to considering how people communicate *through* technology it is also important to think about how people communicate *with* technology (Banks & de Graaf, 2020).

Figure 1.

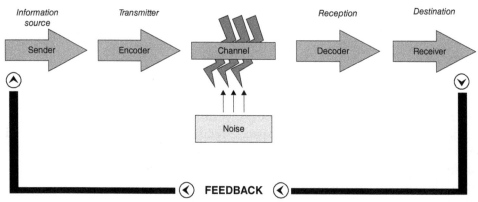

SHANNON-WEAVER'S MODEL OF COMMUNICATION

If AI agents are popping up in human social spaces and behaving like social agents, this idea of machines as meaning-making partners should be pretty intuitive, right? In some ways, it is! The Computers are Social Actors (CASA; Nass & Moon, 2000) paradigm argues that people intuitively apply social expectations to machines as soon as they show the slightest hint of behaving socially. The most famous illustration of this tendency concerns politeness, as it was shown that we are often polite to machines when they ask us directly for feedback. Interestingly, though, many people would not openly admit to seeing a machine as really social. What explains this disconnect between how people behave toward machines and how they think about social machines? Our research on androids—a kind of social machine with a humanoid body—suggests that people have a common but narrow understanding of what they are, even if they actually have never met one (Banks, 2020c). People's understanding could be shaped by media representations about what robots are and how we should communicate with them. Because of their strong presence in popular culture, social robots are a useful way to think about how media may shape how we think and feel about technologies.

MEDIA SHAPES HOW WE SEE MACHINES

In the 2021 film *The Matrix Resurrections*, we see various representations of agentic technologies; the film's online forums are packed with discussions of those representations, from the potential for humans and sentient machines to coexist to the notion that AI agents could have mundane lives. Although these ideas may seem far-fetched, it is important to remember that many current technologies were first imagined in popular media: mobile phones popped up in 1940s sci-fi and later in the *Star Trek* television series, the Roomba robot vacuum looks conspicuously like one in *The Jetsons* cartoons, and the idea of an immersive, persistent virtual environment like the emerging Metaverse appeared in the 1990s cyberpunk fiction *Snow Crash*. Popular media are remarkably important in shaping people's ideas about social machines, especially since people seldom have direct experiences with them (Banks, 2020b).

To understand how this shaping happens, we can look to Cultivation Theory. Originally devised by communication scholar George Gerbner (see Gerbner & Gross, 1976), Cultivation Theory argues (in part) that media messages *cultivate* audiences' perceptions of reality. Over time, as people consume media, they combine information from media representations with direct experiences and other information sources to form ideas about what is normal, appropriate, or expected in the world. Sometimes this consumption is purposeful (like if you really enjoy sci-fi and purposefully seek out robot films) and sometimes incidental (like if you were to scroll through Twitter and see a post about a new kind of robot). The more you see some kinds of representations (like robots as silver humanoids trying to take over the world), the more it becomes part of your perceived reality (like thinking that robots are strange and terrifying).

We think it is useful to understand cultivated perceptions of reality in terms of *mental models* (MMs). A MM is your mind's internal picture of something that exists in the world around you, and you can think of it as a collection of information chunks that are linked together. Depending on the media you consume and other experiences you have had (let's say you have spent a lot of time battling synths in a *Fallout* franchise game), you might have a robot MM that includes the concepts of "silver," "wheels," "talking," "dangerous," "computer," and "laser" and the concept is 'dangerous' might be the most powerful. In other people's minds, different concepts might be more present, for instance, "shiny," "cute," "friendly," "helper," and "lively," where "cute" is most central. If we have not had direct experiences with robots, media representations can play a stronger role in adding, removing, shifting, or reinforcing the concepts in our MMs. For instance, if the person whose MM emphasizes robots as dangerous were to watch *Wall-E, Chappie*, or *ALITA: Battle Angel*, were to play *Portal 2* or *Ratchet & Clank*, and perhaps were to read comics about DC character Cyborg and the *Transformers* character Bumblebee, this person's MM could shift from harm-focused concepts to a more positive understanding.

HEURISTICS FOR SOCIAL MACHINES

These cultivated mental models are important because they help us make sense of new experiences by guiding us to consider some information and avoid other information (see Tversky & Kahneman, 1974). MMs can include heuristics, which are mental shortcuts where we replace a very complex idea or decision with a much simpler one. To make quick judgments, we rely on the concepts contained in the mental models. As you might guess, many heuristics become relevant to our MMs through their repeated representations in popular media. Related to the examples above, the more robot characters you see that are cute and friendly, the more likely you are to assume that other cute robots are also friendly.

Research shows that we have various heuristics that we use to judge social machines, including:

- Social heuristics—these are shortcuts we use to make decisions in social contexts, especially related to what counts as "social," how we should be social, or what could result from socializing. These heuristics are triggered by a cue from someone we are interacting with. Examples include the tit-for-tat heuristic (if someone smiles you should smile back) or the majority-rule heuristic (whatever most people do is best).

- Ontological heuristics—this class of shortcuts relies on assumptions about the *kind* of thing a robot is. Examples include the machine heuristic (if machine, then efficient and unemotional) and nature heuristic (if unnatural, then bad; see Banks, Edwards, & Westerman, 2021) or robotypicality heuristics (if robot, then like other robots; Banks & Koban, 2021).

- Moral heuristics—these are shortcuts for what counts as morally good and bad, guiding how we behave and how we judge others' behaviors. Examples include the affect heuristic (what we have positive feelings about is good) or the familiarity heuristic (what is good in past situations is good in a new situation).

Although heuristics are helpful in making fast decisions—especially when we are faced with uncertainty and must act quickly—they can lead to biased behavior that is not optimal or rationale. This is not to say that heuristics are *bad*. In fact, heuristics are inevitable for human functioning and are hard to suppress once we have learned them. However, we should try to be aware of our heuristic thinking as we make decisions in daily life. So how do media-cultivated heuristics play a role in how we think about robots?

MIND AND MORALITY IN MACHINES?

Whether you realize it or not, as we go about our daily lives, we are constantly making evaluations of other people—especially about what they might be thinking and what they might do next. These judgments are essential for human communication because we use them to make sense of what others are doing and how we will behave in response. For example, imagine if you walk into a department store looking for a particular brand of shoes you saw on TikTok and you see a clerk who might be able to assist. You may decide whether or not to ask for help based on clues about the clerk's demeanor (do they seem to be in a helpful mood?), knowledge (do they seem like they'd be savvy to the trend?), and availability (are they too busy to be approached?). It seems likely that similar kinds of inferences will be important to how we communicate with social machines—and our ability to make those judgments depends on how we see them as having *mental* and *moral* capacities.

Thinking first about mental capacities, popular media often presents robots as being conscious of their actions and meaning to do what they do. For instance, think about the small pit droids in *The Mandalorian* and *Boba Fett* series. Even though they have a very practical purpose (fixing ships on command), their behaviors are suggested to be intentional and self-interested: they fear for their safety (e.g., retracting like a turtle when there is a threat), cheat at games (e.g., passing each other cards while a human is looking away), and tease each other (e.g., poking in the eye and Three Stooges style). In other words, they are presented as having motivations and goals that indicate they have a mind. Think also about the nonfictional Mars Rover "Curiosity" whose Twitter account frequently tweets in first person *as* the rover. It sometimes says things like "thanks for joining me," calls engineers and scientists "my team," and refers to things it does along "my mission." These seemingly small uses of pronouns may move people to see the rover as having agency so that it *means to* pick up rocks or take selfies.

Our research shows that people intuitively behave in ways that indicate they are inferring mental states in a robot as long as that robot is delivering human-like social cues like facial expressions or vocal inflections (Banks, 2020c). For instance, people thought that robots with expressive, animated eyes had emotional capacities while that was less so for robots with static, hardware eyes. However, when asked if the robot has a mind, many people will say no—even if just moments before they behaved as though the robot was thinking or feeling (Banks, 2021). We think these tendencies are a matter of mentalizing or automatically inferring what someone else is thinking. Although mentalizing is automatic and a very natural response to social cues, those assumptions can be revised later after some more thought. Existing research suggests that humanizing nonhumans may be a kind of mental shortcut in itself (Dacey, 2017)—just as we see the man in the moon or assign emotions to our pets. If all of this is not complicated enough, we can actually make *multiple kinds* of inferences that, altogether, form a "theory of mind" (see Banks, 2020c) This is no formal scientific theory but a capacity that people have to guess what is going on in others' minds—and that capacity is the foundation of most of our social interactions.

If we turn to thinking about moral capacities, media narratives often present robots as being morally good or bad. These representations highlight the potential to have *moral agency*, which is the capacity to think and purposefully do good or bad things. For example, in the Marvel comics universe, the robot Ultron was created to be an engineering marvel but it rebelled and became evil; in contrast, Ultron created the Vision for evil but it turned against Ultron and joined the heroic Avengers. In both instances, the characters rebelled against their programmed natures and *chose* to be good or bad. In another example, even the logical and morally neutral Data of Star Trek fame can be interpreted as good because it adopts human norms.

Media narratives also frequently show robots being treated well or poorly by humans, illustrating *moral patiency*, which is the capacity to benefit or suffer from others' actions. We have looked at many different kinds of moral patiency based on how humans might treat robots: the values of *caring* or being *fair* to them, respecting their *authority* and skill, being *loyal* to them, keeping them *pure* and unbroken, and supporting their *liberty*. These moral treatments are all based on Moral Foundations Theory (MFT; Graham et al., 2013) which argues that the ways we judge "good" and "bad" are essentially gut reactions to these six notions of goodness. Think for a moment about the social-media sensation hitchBOT, a robot designed to hitchhike long distances based on the kindness of humans. The original version crossed Canada three times, as people helped it to board buses, spend the night in their homes, and otherwise be welcomed into human spaces. A second version was made, successfully traveling Germany and the Netherlands before attempting to cross the United States where it was soon beheaded and stripped of all wiring. In this way, hitchBOT was shown benefiting and suffering from humans' arguably (im)moral actions.

Our research shows that people see robots as moral agents in the same way they see humans—good behavior means a good person or robot, and bad behavior means a bad one. However, compared to humans, people see robots as having more responsibility to be good and greater blame when they are bad, *even when their behavior is identical* (Banks, 2020a). In other words, humans get more credit and less blame—the robots can not get a break! When it comes to moral patiency, we see that lots of people can imagine many different ways that robots can benefit and suffer as a result of human treatment (Banks, 2021a). Sometimes benefits and suffering are similar to human experiences (e.g., being taken care of, getting hurt, or being humiliated), but sometimes they are very different like humans assisting them in an uprising against other humans or having their warranties voided. Both perceptions that a robot is a moral agent and a moral patient are associated with trusting that robot (Banks et al., 2022) and they could be important in promoting other relational outcomes—from whether people adopt the technology in the first place to developing empathetic feelings for it.

WHAT THIS MEANS FOR HOW WE COMMUNICATE WITH SOCIAL MACHINES IN EVERYDAY LIFE

Understanding how media representations of social machines contribute to many of our mental defaults can matter for how we communicate with them in everyday life. One thing that occurred in our studies was that many students (even tech-savvy ones) did not realize that their expectations about artificial agents and social machines did not match how current state-of-the-art machines actually work.

The impact of (mostly fictional) media representations explains a lot of what people typically expect of machines—and often people expect too much (Horstmann & Krämer, 2019). When robot characters are repeatedly framed as dangerous or helpful—because they have mental and moral capacities—that helps to cultivate expectations about their characters. Cultivation theory also helps us understand why many people are quick to accept (and even panic over) new robots that are marketed and sold as having features that are not realistically possible any time soon. For instance, a robot called "Buddy" is sold as an "emotional robot" even though the state-of-the-art has not yet achieved authentic AI that would allow a robot to have something equivalent to emotions (Darmanin, 2019). While high social and functional expectations could be seen as beneficial because they help us to rationalize a machine's actions and feel more comfortable (Duffy, 2003), some scholars have argued that they open the door for deceptive exploitation of natural tendencies (see Bryson, 2019)—perhaps for financial profit (as with phishing bots) or to reinforce an ideological agenda (like expecting subservience from female-cued machines). These questions are still very much open to scientific debate and given that many technologies are already presented as human-like, it may ultimately be up to each person to decide whether or not they think it is reasonable to connect with a robot that *seems* mindful and moral, even if it really is not.

It can also be helpful to think about how the other communication processes detailed in this textbook could possibly unfold between humans and robots. For instance, social interactions may make us more uncomfortable with robots and task-focused interactions can make us more comfortable because the latter aligns with our *expectations* for what a robot should do (Banks et al., 2021). Or consider how relatively simple persuasive appeals from a robot can motivate people to ignore security tools (i.e., CAPTCHAs) and help a robot access some information (Koban et al., 2022). Even further, a news story written by an AI journalist can reduce the perception that the story is biased against either side of an issue (Cloudy et al., 2021). Knowing about what happens when humans communicate with social machines and why will help you to think critically about your media-influenced ideas about today's technological developments—both for the possible problems and the meaningful possibilities.

Ultimately, being aware of how quickly humans tend to perceive mind and morality in social machines may also change the ways you see yourself, others, and society at large. Philosophers like David J. Gunkel, John Danaher, and Mark Coeckelbergh think that how we humans treat artificial agents might say a lot about who we are and how we understand ourselves as human beings. For instance, instead of judging other "beings" (be it unfamiliar humans, animals, or robots) in relation to ourselves, we might be better off by first appreciating them as they are before considering how they are different from us. You can also think of it as an extension of how we now see many animals; society has slowly acknowledged certain unalienable rights at least to some animals (for instance, the United Kingdom in 2021 granted welfare protections to octopi, crabs, and lobsters because scientific evidence emerged showing they can experience pain). In other words, those movements are focusing on what makes some animals like us in some ways without washing over their otherness—and it is possible that we could see similar movements unfolding for what counts as morally and legally correct behavior for social machines. In short, these theorists suggest that considering how machines are somewhat like us could make you more considerate when communicating with both machines and other humans.

CONCLUSION

Certainly, these are some BIG questions, and communication researchers are only just beginning to unpack them—and social machines' abilities could evolve before we fully understand the implications of communicating with them. In the meantime, it can be useful to be conscious of how we tend to think in *automatic ways* about social machines, especially based on the media we have consumed—and that we may want to be more purposeful in our thinking, depending on whether we think it is good and useful to see a robot as social when it really is not … yet.

REFERENCES

Banks, J. (2020a). Good robots, bad robots: Morally valenced behavior effects. *International Journal of Social Robotics* [online before print]. https://doi.org/10.1007/s12369-020-00692-3

Banks, J. (2020b). Optimus primed: Media cultivation of robot mental models and social judgments. *Frontiers in Robotics and AI, 7*, no. 62.

Banks, J. (2020c). Theory of mind in social robots: Replication of five established human tests. *International Journal of Social Robotics, 12*, 403–414. https://doi.org/10.1007/s12369-019-00588-x

Banks, J. (2021a). From warranty voids to uprising advocacy: Human action and the perceived moral patiency of social robots. *Frontiers in Robotics & AI, 8*, article 670503. https://doi.org/10.3389/frobt.2021.670503

Banks, J. (2021b). Of like mind: The (mostly) similar mentalizing of robots and humans. *Technology, Mind, and Behavior, 1*(2). https://doi.org/10.1037/tmb0000025

Banks, J., & Koban, K. (2021). Framing effects on judgments of social robots' (im)moral behaviors. *Frontiers in Robotics and AI, 8*, 627233. https://doi.org/10.3389/frobt.2021.627233

Banks, J., & de Graaf, M. M. (2020). Toward an agent-agnostic transmission model: Integrating anthropocentric and technocentric paradigms in communication. *Human-Machine Communication, 1*, 19–36. https://doi.org/10.30658/hmc.1.2

Banks, J., & Edwards, A. P. (2019). A common social distance scale for robots and humans. *28th IEEE International Conference on Robot and Human Interactive Communication* [online before print]. Piscataway, NJ: IEEE.

Banks, J., Edwards, A. P., & Westerman, D. (2021). The space between: Nature and machine heuristics in evaluations of organisms, cyborgs, and robots. *Cyberpsychology, Behavior, and Social Networking [online before print]*. https://doi.org/10.1089/cyber.2020.0165

Banks, J., Koban, K., & Chauveau, P. de V. (2021). Forms and frames: Mind, morality, and trust in robots across prototypical interactions. *Human-Machine Communication, 2*, 81–103. https://doi.org/10.30658/hmc.2.4

Banks, J., Koban, K., & Haggadone, B. (2022). Breaking the typecast? Moral status and trust in robotic moral patients. In R. Hakli, P. Mäkelä, & J. Seibt (Eds.), *Social robots in social institutions* (pp. 315–324). IOS Press

Bryson, J.J. (2019). Robot, all too human. *XRDS: Crossroads, The ACM Magazine for Students. XRDS: Crossroads, The ACM Magazine for Students, 25*(3), 56–59. https://doi.org/10.1145/3313131

Cloudy, J., Banks, J., & Bowman, N.D. (2021). The str(AI)ght scoop: Artificial intelligence cues reduce perceptions of hostile media bias. *Digital Journalism* [online ahead of print]. https://doi.org/10.1080/21670811.2021.1969974

Dacey, M. (2017). Anthropomorphism as cognitive bias. *Philosophy of Science, 84*(5), 1152–1164. https://doi.org/10.1086/694039

Darmanin, G. (2019). On the possibility of emotional robots. *Revista De Filosofia Aurora, 31*(54). https://doi.org/10.7213/1980-5934.31.054.DS08

Duffy, B. R. (2003). Anthropomorphism and the social robot. *Robotics and Autonomous Systems, 42*(3), 177–190. https://doi.org/10.1016/S0921-8890(02)00374-3

Graham, J., Haidt, J., Koleva, S., Motyl, M., Iyer, R., Wojcik, S. P., & Ditto, P. H. (2013). Moral foundations theory: The pragmatic validity of moral pluralism. In P. Devine & A. Plant (Eds.), *Advances in experimental social psychology* (Vol. 47, pp. 55–130). Academic Press

Gerbner, G., & Gross, L. (1976). The scary world of TV's heavy viewer. *Psychology Today, 9*(11), 41–45.

Guzman, A. L. (2019). *Human-machine communication: Rethinking communication, technology, and ourselves.* Peter Lang.

Horstmann, A. C., & Krämer, N. C. (2019). Great expectations? Relation of previous experiences with social robots in real life or in the media and expectancies based on qualitative and quantitative assessment. *Frontiers in Psychology, 10*(939). https://doi.org/10.3389/fpsyg.2019.00939

Koban, K., Banks, J., & Haggadone, B. (2022, May). *Avoiding the abject and seeking the script: Perceived mind, morality, and trust in a persuasive social robot.* Paper presented at the aannual convention of the International Communication Association, Paris, France.

Shannon, C. E., & Weaver, W. (1949). *The mathematical theory of communication.* University of Illinois Press.

Nass, C., & Moon, Y. (2000). Machines and mindlessness: Social responses to computers. *Journal of Social Issues, 56*(1), 81–103. https://doi.org/10.1111/0022-4537.00153

Tversky, A., & Kahneman, D. (1974). Judgment under uncertainty: Heuristics and biases: Biases in judgments reveal some heuristics of thinking under uncertainty. *Science, 185*(4157), 1124–1131. https://doi.org/10.1126/science.185.4157.1124

THE INFLUENCE OF AGGRESSIVE COMMUNICATION STYLES IN SCIENCE CONVERSATIONS

Shupei Yuan
Northern Illinois University

INTRODUCTION

From Chelsea Handler's (2017) "Hey dumbass, global warming doesn't only mean extreme heat; it means extreme weather. Hot and cold. Maybe buy a thermometer and shove it up your ass" to Bernie Sanders's (2019) "Donald Trump believes climate change is a hoax. Donald Trump is an idiot," we started to observe emotional and uncivil attacks happening in scientific debates, especially in controversial topics like climate change. Whether it is name-calling, cursing, teasing, or personal attacks, we can find these non-neutral, aggressive styles in both online messages and comments. The commonality between an individual's uncivil comments online versus a science communicator's message that uses an aggressive style, is that they both show the emotional expression of the person. The difference is that online comments are more of a *response* to a message while a communicator's message has original intent. Also, initial messages, especially those by famous communicators, receive more exposure. Here we focus on the style of an initial message, such as a blog, YouTube video, or original tweet. When we see these messages in debates regarding climate change, vaccine, or other controversial science debates, we could not stop wondering, what will message styles do to readers? Outside of possibly giving an impression that the communicator is angry or mean, will the style affect the message quality itself positively or negatively?

Aggression is not a new concept in communication, especially in political communication, which often involves attack ads or hostile tones used in political debates. However, we need to recognize that findings in political communications may not be carried out in science communication directly for a couple of reasons. First, in political communication such as electoral debates, there is a specific target—the competitor or his/her party (McNair, 2017). However, in science communication, the target could vary. It could be "climate change deniers," "conservative politicians" or a specific person. Second, electoral debates have a clear deadline (the election day), where all the attacks could end in one day and the conversations will move forward afterward. But in science communication, there is no such deadline; the conversation about climate change will go on as long as climate change still exists. The communication of vaccine acceptance is needed as long as there is concern regarding vaccine uptake. The essential research questions are: how do communication styles influence the message's effect? How do individuals perceive communication styles, especially those extreme ones?

DEVELOPMENT OF COMMUNICATION STYLES

To answer these research questions, the first step is to understand what is *communication style*. Defining and categorizing communication styles have been a research area for communication scholars for many years. Communication style is described as: "the characteristic way a person sends verbal, paraverbal, and nonverbal signals in social interactions denoting (1) who he or she is or wants to (appear to) be, (2) how he or she tends to relate to people with whom he or she interacts, and (3) in what way his or her messages should usually be interpreted" (De Vries et al., 2009, p. 2). The term "communication style" and "communication tone" are used interchangeably sometimes (Edwards & Noller, 1998). Communication styles are primarily presented through verbal language, such as the choices of words. However, communication styles can also be delivered through paraverbal signals, such as pitch or pace, or nonverbal communication such as body language. Researchers have attempted to categorize communication styles. Many used binary classifications, such as dominance versus supportiveness (Sorenson & Savage, 1989), or dominance versus affiliation (Dillard et al., 1999). Some further expanded into several categories, such as dominating, respectful, warm, patronizing, supportive, and nurturing (Edwards & Noller, 1998). In this chapter, we mainly focus on the aggressive communication style because of its unique characteristics and unexpected effects in science communication.

Similar to how research into communication styles began, research on aggressive styles initiated from interpersonal communication, and then later explored in mass science communication contexts such as climate change or vaccination. Upon reviewing related literature, we found that the aggressive style generally has two characteristics: (1) intense language, such as words like "extremely" or "absolutely," and (2) words that are insulting or attacking a person such as "ignorant" and "stupid," or name-calling, such as "anti-vaxxers" "Covidiot" (Chu et al., 2021). Before discussing the specific effects of aggressive styles in science debates, I would like to highlight why understanding communication style matters to effective science communication. Researchers have found that to help the public make decisions based on scientific evidence, just informing and educating the public with scientific knowledge is not sufficient (Seethaler et al., 2019). Individuals' decision-making is not always based on the evidence but instead on subjective intuitive judgments oftentimes (Lamond & Thompson, 2000). A good example is that the negative health effect of smoking is well known, but messages focusing on this scientific fact is far from enough (Roth & Taylor, 2001), and thus anti-smoking campaigns also use emotional approaches or fear appeals to motivate people to quit (Jeong et al., 2021). Thus, communication styles could be one important factor that influences an individual's subjective intuitive judgment, and understanding the specific effect of aggressive style could maximize the desired message effect.

MAIN EFFECTS OF AGGRESSIVE STYLE

In science communication, messages are not only intended to inform the public about scientific information, but also to persuade the public to make decisions based on scientific evidence. For instance, science communicators would want the public to realize that climate change is real and human-caused, and therefore be more willing to perform pro-environment activities to mitigate climate change. Health communicators or doctors would want the public to receive accurate information about vaccines and become more likely to accept vaccination. When heated debates around these topics happen, we want to know to what extent using an aggressive style would influence the persuasiveness of the message, such as whether audiences find the message compelling and perform desired behaviors. Research in other contexts showed mixed results; in some situations, it would hurt the persuasiveness of the message (Thorson et al., 2010) but in other situations, it could be more memorable and engaging (Brooks & Geer, 2007; Lau et al., 2007). After reviewing studies conducted in science communication, we have a short answer: aggressive styles in science communication have a negative effect on communication outcomes.

Some negative consequences are expected. Using an aggressive style will make the communicator less likable, and readers also find the message lower in quality, and less likely to share the message and other desired behavioral outcomes (Hardy et al., 2019; Yuan & Besley, 2018; Yuan & Lu, 2020; Yuan et al., 2019). In other words, when a science communicator uses aggressive styles, it not only harms the persuasive effects of the message, but also jeopardizes the relationship between the communicator and the audience, and reduces an individual's willingness to act. In science communication these negative effects could be more specific; conflict in the climate change discussion has the potential to polarize an individual's perceptions of climate change (Anderson & Huntington, 2017) and endanger the goal of mobilizing the public toward climate change mitigation (Yuan & Lu, 2020).

The next question becomes, why does the aggressive style cause these consequences? Researchers have looked into the mechanism behind it, and one theory provided a logical explanation here—expectancy violations theory (EVT: Burgoon & Hale, 1988). The theory states that each individual has developed an expectation on how each individual should speak and interact with others, and when the conversation is different from what they expected, they will adjust their responding behavior accordingly as well. While we may expect one person to say certain things in certain ways, we may also have expectations toward how certain groups of people talk or how we should talk about certain conversations. For example, should scientists always be serious? Or should doctors talk nicely? Should we joke about scientific topics like climate change? EVT gives a good explanation of how expectation works and what forms expectations. We applied EVT to multiple studies which examined the effects of aggressive messages on different science communication contexts, such as child vaccination, genetically modified organisms (GMO), or climate change. The findings of studies of EVT in these contexts have been pretty consistent. They suggest that the reason why individuals respond to aggressive message differently is that the message violates their expectation, and the level of expectation negatively influence people's willingness to perform the science behavior advocated by the communicator (Chu et al., 2021; Yuan & Lu, 2022).

However, when the mechanism of expectancy violation is introduced, we raised one more question: What if the expectation is not violated? In other words, what will happen when readers are not surprised by the aggressive style? We found that, when expectancy violation is controlled, individuals would find the message as higher quality. For example, when a communicator has always seen as mean or aggressive, when he or she uses such language to talk about science issues, not only are people not surprised, but they also find the message of *higher quality* (Yuan et al., 2018) compared nonaggressive messages. As studies have suggested that aggressive or uncivil messages could be more intense and more powerful (Bon & Walter, 2021; Fridkin & Kenney, 2011), the key is to understand and manage audiences' expectations. In science communication, the expectation could be formed through our stereotype of scientists (Scholes & Stahl, 2022), how science information is normally shared via mass media, and many other reasons.

OTHER INFLUENCING FACTORS

Although it seems to be a straightforward answer, the expectation is not easily captured and it shifts constantly (Pinquart et al., 2021). In this case, are the effects of aggressive styles consistent? Are there other factors that influence such effects? Expectancy Violations Theory offered us some way to explore other influencing factors. Specifically, Burgoon and Hale (1988) proposed three determinants that may form an individual's expectation of a person's action: first, communicator characteristics which describe the characters of the person, such as gender, age, or the affiliation of a communicator; second is relationship characteristics, which indicate status inequality and degree of acquaintance between the communicator and the audiences (e.g., teachers with students, scientists with the public; or interaction between peers); and the third determinant is the context, which indicates situational definition and formality, such as discussing serious environmental risks, or sharing basic science knowledge such as the necessity of handwashing. We may also want to pay attention to the relationship between these three factors and the scenario. When the scenario changes, the three factors could yield different effects. For instance, a scientist may be expected to have a more formal or serious communication style with the public on a science issue but may be expected to have a casual or warm style if the conversation is about his/her/their family. Thus, we want to highlight that the investigation of other influencing factors may be limited to specific scenarios, but they could provide some indications for us to understand the effects of communication styles more thoroughly.

Some studies focused on the communicator's characteristics by investigating whether the communicator's gender, level of expertise, and psychological distance from the audience (such as physical, temporal, or social status distance between the communicator and the audience) would affect the level of expectancy violation. Specifically, researchers found that audiences are less surprised by female communicators who use aggressive styles and therefore the negative effect of aggression is less perceived compared with those from male communicators (Yuan & Besley, 2018). People are more surprised when an expert (such as a scientist or doctor, compared with a lay person) speaks aggressively about a science topic, and therefore the negative effect of aggressive messages from an expert will be larger as well (Yuan et al., 2019). These studies were conducted in contexts including GMO and childhood vaccination. During the pandemic, doctors, scientists, and many others also made significant efforts to advocate COVID-19 vaccines. Meanwhile, the perspectives which were anti-vaccination joined the conversation again and the debates around COVID-19 vaccination heated up. Researchers (Chu et al., 2021) investigated the effects of aggressive style from experts with different psychological distances. A good example of experts in different psychological distances is a doctor from the reader's nearby health institute versus a doctor from a faraway state. The findings showed that individuals have more tolerance of community doctors who use aggressive styles compared with a doctor who is far away.

Meanwhile, some studies investigated how audiences' characteristics could affect how they perceive an aggressive science message. As we can imagine, people with different backgrounds may see science information differently, especially when some science topics are tied to a political agenda, such as climate change (Bayes et al., 2020) or COVID-19 vaccination (Jiang et al., 2021). These recent projects found that political ideology would significantly affect how they view a message, not just the content of the message, but also the styles. What has been found was interesting: liberals (who are more likely to support climate change or pro-vaccination policies) are finding aggressive messages more surprising and therefore find the message quality lower. Similar to ideology, an individual's preexisting attitude toward the topic would also affect how they view the style of the message as well. A person who holds a similar view on the topic to the author (e.g., pro-environment and pro-vaccine) is more likely to be offended by an aggressive message (Yuan et al., 2019). In other words, starting "fights" and attacking the "deniers" may not receive resonance from people who already support this issue. It could backfire because of the violation of what people expected. It is also worth mentioning that because of the complexity of human reactions and behaviors, there is more to explore in this category for certain. We also want to recognize other communication styles, such as humor or politeness. Studying emotional tones such as anger, fear, or hope and their potential effect on the message quality as well. Although we may not have a comprehensive investigation at this time, knowing some of the influencing factors would help science communicators choose their communication styles more strategically.

CONCLUSION

The rationale for studying communication tones or styles is that science communication can no longer be simply addressed by providing public science information. It is also called the "information deficit model," which suggests that the public's misunderstanding or hostility to science is due to a lack of understanding or a lack of information). To persuade the public to accept science information and trust science, communication strategies such as proper communication styles are needed. While many science debates can turn into heated arguments, and some of these arguments may seem powerful, research still suggests that aggressive communication could have a negative effect on the message effect itself. The takeaway is that an individual's response to an extreme message style varies by how their expectation is formed How expectations are formed is related to the mass and interpersonal communication we have every day. When we read, view, or share science information, we want to recognize the style of communicators being used, and finally understand the powerful influence of message styles.

REFERENCES

Anderson, A. A., & Huntington, H. E. (2017). Social media, science, and attack discourse: How Twitter discussions of climate change use sarcasm and incivility. *Science Communication, 39*(5), 598–620. https://doi.org/10.1177/1075547017735113

Bayes, R., Bolsen, T., & Druckman, J. N. (2020). A research agenda for climate change communication and public opinion: The role of scientific consensus messaging and beyond. *Environmental Communication.* Advanced online publication. https://doi.org/10.1080/17524032.2020.1805343

Bon, E. V., & Walter, A. S. (2021). The 2016 EU referendum campaign on social media: Uncivil MPs and campaign groups? In E. V. Bon & A. S. Walter (Eds.), *Political incivility in the parliamentary, electoral and media arena* (pp. 161–180). Routledge.

Burgoon, J. K., & Hale, J. L. (1988). Nonverbal expectancy violations: Model elaboration and application to immediacy behaviors. *Communications Monographs, 55*(1), 58–79. https://doi.org/10.1080/03637758809376158

Chu, H., Yuan, S., & Liu, S. (2021). Call them COVIDiots: Exploring the effects of aggressive communication style and psychological distance in the communication of COVID-19. *Public Understanding of Science, 30*(3), 240–257. https://doi.org/10.1177/0963662521989191

De Vries, R. E., Bakker-Pieper, A., Alting Siberg, R., van Gameren, K., & Vlug, M. (2009). The content and dimensionality of communication styles. *Communication Research, 36*(2), 178–206. https://doi.org/10.1177/0093650208330250

Dillard, J. P., Solomon, D. H., & Palmer, M. T. (1999). Structuring the concept of relational communication. *Communications Monographs, 66*(1), 49–65. https://doi.org/10.1080/03637759909376462

Edwards, H., & Noller, P. (1998). Factors influencing caregiver-care receiver communication and its impact on the well-being older care receivers. *Health Communication, 10*(4), 317–341. https://doi.org/10.1207/s15327027hc1004_2

Fridkin, K. L., & Kenney, P. (2011). Variability in citizens' reactions to different types of negative campaigns. *American Journal of Political Science, 55*(2), 307–325. https://doi.org/10.1111/j.1540-5907.2010.00494.x

Handler C. (2017, December 28) Hey dumbass, global warming doesn't only mean extreme heat; it means extreme weather. Hot and cold. Maybe buy a thermometer and shove it up your ass. [Tweet]. Twitter. Retrieved from https://twitter.com/chelseahandler/status/946567438761521152?lang=en

Hardy, B. W., Tallapragada, M., Besley, J. C., & Yuan, S. (2019). The effects of the "war on science" frame on scientists' credibility. *Science Communication, 41*(1), 90–112. https://doi.org/10.1177/1075547018822081

Jeong, J. S., Choi, J., & Noh, G. Y. (2021). Fear appeal effectiveness in antismoking campaigns: Do anger and smoking matter? *Psychology, Health & Medicine.* Advance online publication. https://doi.org/10.1080/13548506.2021.2006251

Jiang, X., Su, M. H., Hwang, J., Lian, R., Brauer, M., Kim, S., & Shah, D. (2021). Polarization over Vaccination: Ideological differences in twitter expression about COVID-19 vaccine favorability and specific hesitancy concerns. *Social Media + Society, 7*(3). https://doi.org/10.1177/20563051211048413

Lamond, D., & Thompson, C. (2000). Intuition and analysis in decision making and choice. *Journal of Nursing Scholarship, 32*(4), 411–414. https://doi.org/10.1111/j.1547-5069.2000.00411.x

McNair, B. (2017). *An introduction to political communication.* Routledge.

Pinquart, M., Endres, D., Teige-Mocigemba, S., Panitz, C., & Schütz, A. C. (2021). Why expectations do or do not change after expectation violation: a comparison of seven models. *Consciousness and Cognition, 89*, 103086. https://doi.org/10.1016/j.concog.2021.103086

Roth, L. K., & Taylor, H. S. (2001). Risks of smoking to reproductive health: assessment of women's knowledge. *American Journal of Obstetrics and Gynecology, 184*(5), 934–939. https://doi.org/10.1067/mob.2001.112103

Sanders B. (2019, August 10) Donald Trump believes climate change is a hoax. Donald Trump is an idiot. [Tweet]. Twitter. https://twitter.com/berniesanders/status/1160305065325977600?lang=en

Scholes, L., & Stahl, G. (2022). 'I'm good at science but I don't want to be a scientist': Australian primary school student stereotypes of science and scientists. *International Journal of Inclusive Education, 26*(9), 927–942. https://doi.org/10.1080/13603116.2020.1751316

Seethaler, S., Evans, J. H., Gere, C., & Rajagopalan, R. M. (2019). Science, values, and science communication: Competencies for pushing beyond the deficit model. *Science Communication, 41*(3), 378–388. https://doi.org/10.1177/1075547019847484

Sorenson, R. L., & Savage, G. T. (1989). Signaling participation through relational communication: A test of the leader interpersonal influence model. *Group & Organization Studies, 14*(3), 325–354. https://doi.org/10.1177/105960118901400307

Thorson, K., Vraga, E., & Ekdale, B. (2010). Credibility in context: How uncivil online commentary affects news credibility. *Mass Communication and Society, 13*(3), 289–313. https://doi.org/10.1080/15205430903225571

Yuan, S., & Besley, J. C. (2018). Talking aggressively about GMOs? Examining the effect of aggressive risk communication with communicator's facial expression and gender. *Journal of Risk Research, 21*(12), 1592–1607. https://doi.org/10.1080/13669877.2017.1351480

Yuan, S., Besley, J. C., & Lou, C. (2018). Does being a jerk work? Examining the effect of aggressive risk communication in the context of science blogs. *Journal of Risk Research, 21*(4), 502–520. https://doi.org/10.1080/13669877.2016.1223159

Yuan, S., & Lu, H. (2020). "It's global warming, stupid": Aggressive communication styles and political ideology in science blog debates about climate change. *Journalism & Mass Communication Quarterly, 97*(4), 1003–1025. https://doi.org/10.1177/1077699020904791

Yuan, S., & Lu, H. (2022). Examining a conceptual framework of aggressive and humorous styles in science YouTube videos about climate change and vaccination. *Public understanding of science.* Advance online publication. https://doi.org/10.1177/09636625221091490

Yuan, S., Ma, W., & Besley, J. C. (2019). Should scientists talk about GMOs nicely? Exploring the effects of communication styles, source expertise, and preexisting attitude. *Science Communication, 41*(3), 267–290. https://doi.org/10.1177/1075547019837623

SPORT COMMUNICATION

The sport communication context focuses on communication within and about sports. This is a newer area of study in the communication discipline that includes major areas such as media coverage of sports, athletic coaching, communication among teammates, watching sports, and sport fan culture. This section includes chapters focusing on three important areas of sport communication: (1) sports media and societal senses of identity, (2) sport socialization, and (3) sport fandom. First, Andrew Billings (University of Alabama) reviews research on sport media coverage pertaining to gender, sexual orientation, and nationality. Second, Gregory Cranmer (Clemson University) reviews research on how athletes are prepared and integrated safely into sports. Third, Michael Devlin (Texas State University) reviews research on highly-identified fans of sports teams. For many college students, watching and playing sports is an enjoyable hobby, and for some students, it is central to their identity. That said, these chapters will help you understand how sport communication impacts our culture and identities, and perhaps impacts you personally as former or current player, or avid fan of sports.

HOW TO USE SPORTS MEDIA FOR IDENTITY INSIGHTS

Andrew C. Billings
The University of Alabama

For decades, we had very little sports communication research. The rationale was simple: sports are fun and games, so why should they be taken seriously? Of course, as anyone who's ever witnessed the parent screaming at their 8-year-old to be more aggressive or the friend who can not get out of bed the next morning because "the Steelers lost," there is no shortage of people taking elements of sport as heavy business.

Over the course of about 25 years, an entire cohort of scholars have challenged the premise that sports are not worthy of investigation. In my own work, I often say that I study gaps in sports. Perhaps that's between how men and women athletes are treated; perhaps it's the difference between sports fan perceptions and realities. Often, I find that the gap I study the most is the difference between what should be and what is. Sports, somewhat paradoxically, are frequently depicted as both the "first" and "last" hurdles in social movements. As legendary UCLA basketball coach John Wooden was known to argue, sports do not *build* character as much as they *reveal* it. My own work reveals the character of various stakeholders, including sports fans, athletes, and media rights holders. I often focus on issues of identity to compare how one group is treated as opposed to another. Here, I will explain three examples of how sports communication can be used to reveal differences pertaining to (1) gender, (2) sexual orientation, and (3) nationality.

SPORTS APPLICATION #1: GENDERED VALUES

It likely does not surprise you that sports have a very masculine history. Many of the presumptions made about women in sports have been wrong. For instance, any presumption of women athletes being weaker is typically mitigated by historical oppression; women tennis players still only play best two-of-three sets in Grand Slams (instead of three-of-five as the men do), but this decision can be traced to the sport's origins, where women were required to wear corsets while playing, which would lower anyone's stamina. Or, for instance, there used to be the assumption that women were not interested in playing or watching sport. The 1972 adoption of Title IX resulted in millions of American girls and women eager to debunk the first part of that myth and the fact that 47% of all NFL fans are women (Graham, 2020) now debunks the second part.

Where women's sports still struggle is in media representation. Even the inclusion of espnW is advanced for women who love sports, not for those who wish to watch women's sports. Outlets like ESPN's *SportsCenter* highlight women's sports just 5% of the time (Cooky et al., 2021) with competitors like Fox Sports 1 often faring worse (Billings & Young, 2015). When women's stories are shown, they tend to be of a "one and done" nature (Cooky et al., 2021, p. 347), inserted as single stories that provide a change of pace to the heavily-covered men's team sports.

One major stream of my research has been showing that this meager coverage is not always the case. Women's World Cup coverage can garner roughly the same viewership as a college football national championship game and higher than a World Series or NBA Finals. Moreover, NBC's primetime Olympic telecasts have proven to be leaders in highlighting women's sports. In the 1990s and 2000s, women athletes were consistently highlighted at least 40–45% of the time (Billings, 2008; Billings et al., 2018) and the 2010s brought even more equity (Billings & Angelini, 2019). In fact, the past three Summer Olympics (London, Rio, Tokyo) each featured women athletes even more than men athletes (fiveringtv.com, 2022). Some now even argue that women can be overrepresented in such broadcasts (DeLorme, 2014), yet I argue that the reason women are now shown even more than the men is the higher rates of Olympic successes (Billings & Gentile, 2022), as the American women now frequently out-medal American men by almost an identical margin to how NBC highlights them.

Still, beyond the amount of coverage given to women in sports, there are also troubling signs still present regarding the language used (and not used) to depict women athletes. Decades ago, these stereotypes were more overt, with female attractiveness accentuated considerably more than for men (Billings et al., 2010); I still recall an early analysis of NBC's Olympics where a gymnast was called "easy on the eyes." This problematic focus on the sexualization of women is not uniquely American (see Licen & Billings, 2013), yet it does lend credence to how one might prescribe to the notion that "sex sells" and yet, somehow what it is selling is not women's sporting competitions (Kane et al., 2013).

Indeed, it appears that the sports that are most popular are different than the women who are often depicted in media coverage and features. Denham (2022) studied men's magazine covers, finding that when women athletes were featured, they were almost always White and frequently from questionable parts of sports culture (more than a third were women athletes from professional wrestling or sports entertainment). This appears to be part of the problem: a desire to shoehorn in "women in sports" without a desire to cover women's sports. One woman managed to grace not one but two *Sports Illustrated* covers in 2013, yet that woman was supermodel Kate Upton, not a female athlete.

Thus, part of what sport communication can reveal about society relates to power. In terms of gender, it seems resistance comes in a presumed zero-sum game where more coverage for women's sports means less for men's sports. When "media" was still largely defined as newspapers, magazines, and linear television, perhaps there was at least some veracity in that claim as pages and minutes were limited. Now, with unlimited Internet bandwidth and social media posting possibilities, that seems much less credible as a form of resistance. Often, the desire to diminish women's sports comes in what is not said (perhaps a lack of a comment about their expertise) or what is tangentially said in different contexts. For that latter point, I still recall an analysis (Billings et al., 2006) we did of Annika Sorenstam's competing in the 2003 Men's Colonial tournament, where we compared characterizations of her performance with other PGA golfers. During the first round, she led the field in driving accuracy and was in the top 20 in greens in regulation, yet the most deflating comment about her came hours after her round was complete, when another male golfer hit a shot that bounced off a tree and fortuitously ricocheted onto the green. The commentator called it an "Annika bounce." Such comments show the gaps I referenced earlier: the difference between what should be and what is.

SPORTS APPLICATION #2: VALUES ABOUT SEXUAL ORIENTATION

Arguably the most noticeable identity shift in sports media coverage since I started working in the field has involved portrayals of sexual orientation. Sport has traditionally been a space for heterosexual and masculine conformity (Anderson, 2005) with problematic derogatory phrases like "you throw/run like a girl" and homophobic games like "smear the queer." While those elements still can be found in modern sports, they are much less frequent and far less accepted (Magrath, 2019). As public sentiment has shifted dramatically about issues such as gay marriage, even questioning the notion of binary male/female classifications is much more likely to occur.

Some of the work I have done with a colleague (Billings & Moscowitz, 2018) has attempted to understand how depictions of out athletes have shifted in media over time. For instance,

National Basketball Association (NBA) player Jason Collins came out as gay in 2013, using a *Sports Illustrated* cover story to offer his first-person narrative. Because Collins was the first active NBA player to ever do this, we worked to understand what themes and trends happened within responses to Collins' story (Billings et al., 2015c). For example, we found that newspapers used social media posts as a form of surrogate/substitute support. A journalist could be called an activist if saying Collins' announcement is great, but is just reporting the story if showing that other athletes like Kobe Bryant or leaders like then-President Obama applauded Collins' announcement. We also discovered that Collins was gradually quoted less and less in media stories; of his first-person quotes were in the majority of the articles in the first two days, but less than a third of the stories by the end of the first week. As such, he moved from being the athlete speaking to the athlete being spoken *about*. Themes got deeper in print news coverage, later focusing on Collins' race (Black) or religious upbringing. In contrast, Twitter posts about Collins quickly became more random; by the end of the first week of media coverage, the majority of posts about Collins were not about him at all, instead using his hashtag and personae to promote products and other media stories unrelated to his coming out story.

We then went on to contrast Collins' story to one that followed just months later, as National Football League (NFL) hopeful Michael Sam announced that he was gay just 3 months before the 2014 NFL draft. We contrasted the Collins and Sam storylines (Billings et al., 2021), showing that in virtually every imaginable way, Michael Sam's response was rockier than Jason Collins's—largely for reasons outside of his control. For instance, Collins was a 12-year NBA veteran who had played for six different NBA teams; Sam was an aspiring rookie who was ultimately taken in the last round of the NFL Draft. Thus, Collins had a large cohort of colleagues in the league that were supporting him and vouching for his inclusion while Sam had people questioning whether he belonged on the team. As another example, Michael Sam had a boyfriend during the media story and they kissed during ESPN's coverage of the NFL Draft. Some fence-sitters of potential support for Sam took to social media and other forms of communication to say that they felt the televised kiss was inappropriate. Meanwhile, Jason Collins announced that he was gay but that he had never even been on a date with another man, making him perceived as less threatening to people who might have felt resistance to wholesale acceptance of his announcement.

As we go on to explain (Moscowitz et al., 2019) "the paradox of both celebratory and cautious assertions was subtle and tenuous, often relying on coded homophobic language of distraction and complication" (p. 260).   Traditional media was generally applauding these athletes' announcements even while homophobia was percolating in less formal social media circles.   We continue to explore these types of representations (Moscowitz et al., 2022), including more recently looking to the Instagram announcement from NFL player Carl Nassib, who came out as gay before the 2021 season. Media coverage was less pronounced than for Collins or Sam, but in odd and paradoxical ways. Media content seemed to be arguing two converse things, namely that Nassib's announcement was big and also a nonstory. The notion that American society is somehow beyond needing to report on these coming out stories seems to be at odds with the fact that there are so few of them relative to the general population, particularly in American male team sports.

SPORTS APPLICATION #3: NATIONALIZED VALUES

The final way I will explain insights from my type of sports communication about broader societal senses of identity pertains to nationality. Even as there are more than 200 nations that compete on various international stages, sports inevitably get unpacked in a sense of dichotomies: home/away, me/you, us/them. Such nationalism is not ideal, as the protagonist tends to become the home nation and its athletes (no matter how flawed they may be) with the antagonist being every other nation and its athletes (no matter how ideal they may be). As Bachman (2017) explains, "it's just as easy to be exclusive as it is to be inclusive, just as easy to create an Us as a Them" (p. 226). Nevertheless, great insight can be attained by exploring divisions by nationality.

Ties that one feels to their home nation is argued to be one of the "most emotive issues in the modern world" (Bairner, 2001, p. xi). There are debates about whether such divisions are better than the alternative. 1984 author George Orwell once described international sporting contests as "war minus the shooting," equating sport as a feasible substitute to other forms of battle. However, Anderson's (1983, p. 6) conception of an "imagined political community" can also be invoked, as affiliations with a nation's citizens still involves kinship with people who are almost all strangers. The average Facebook account has 338 friends; the population of the United States is approximately 330 million. Thus, the chances that rooting for someone in an international sporting event is actually a friend is, quite literally, approaching one in a million.

Still, social identity theory (Tajfel & Turner, 1985) explains this type of fanship via the formulation of ingroups (who should be affirmed) and outgroups (who should be rejected). Sports make the lines between groups quite easy. Soccer's World Cup pits team by nation; no nicknames or mascots needed. When that happens, media content tends to evolve—or perhaps devolve—into "fragment of us, fragments of them" (Billings et al., 2015b, p. 726). Depictions also tend to differ between the home team and those of other nations, with the home athletes being much more three-dimensional and dynamic and the foreign athletes being static and often emotionless in their depiction (Billings et al., 2018). For instance, American athletes have been characterized as possessing qualities that are difficult to assess, ranging from being more determined, hard-working, or courageous. Meanwhile, foreign athletes are more frequently shown as athletic powerhouses, with strength and strong athletic prowess being accentuated. Essentially, this becomes the modern equivalent of the 1980s film *Rocky IV*, where the gritty, pugnacious Rocky Balboa somehow managing to secure a victory over the robotic and athletically superior Ivan Drago.

There's a reason why we pit nations against each other: people love to have a vested interest and there are some who will consider it their patriotic duty to support their home nation in any competition, even if that would involve which nation could flick rubber bands across the room more effectively. Media consumption spikes when international fervor is invoked (Devlin & Billings, 2016) as there are different types of identification enacted simultaneously. Perhaps you watch a World Cup soccer match because you love the sport; perhaps you watch because you love a player on the team; perhaps you watch because you love the red, white, and blue and everything represented in the American team. In any of these cases, people now have a reason to watch. These "rings of fandom" (Brown et al., 2020) form the crux of the international sporting context. All you need is an affiliation with one of these motivations for watching and the result may be hours of intense viewing.

These "us vs. them" allegiances have been found to be stoked in sports media content. For instance, the Olympics features a "medals table" which becomes a form of pseudo world domination for some viewers, even if they are flawed at their core. For instance, if a nation is good at basketball, the maximum number of medals it can win is two (women's, men's), but if a nation is good at swimming, dozens can be secured. The United States won 30 swimming medals in the 2020 (2021) Tokyo Summer Olympics, yet some in the media were disappointed from the performances. Meanwhile, the construction of the table is in constant debate: China, for example, typically orders the table by number of *gold* medals won, whereas the United States orders the table by number of *overall* medals won. Still, the table gets shown because of its popularity, seen as an essential element to the overall product and bolstering ratings in the process (Billings et al., 2015a).

It's important to note that there's little unusual about the American international sporting experience. Yes, there is an added level of adrenaline that seems to be evoked into the Summer Olympics for Americans; one study I was a part of (Billings et al., 2013) showed the United States was the highest in smugness but lowest in internationalism amongst a six-nation composite studied immediately after the 2012 London Games. Still, this seemed to be at least mitigated somewhat by the fact that the United States "won" the medals table. One would surmise that if Germany won the World Cup, smugness scores would similarly spike in the days after if one chose to measure it.

Still, other works have found that the way a nation shows international sports shapes a story tremendously (Xu et al., 2018). When Chinese female swimmer Ye Shiwen not only won gold but swam a faster final 50 meters than most of the top men (including decorated American Ryan Lochte), I worked with a colleague (Bie & Billings, 2015) to compare media coverage in China as opposed to the United States. Somewhat unsurprisingly, Chinese media was more likely to either defend Ye Shiwen or deflect/diminish the concerns whereas American media leaned into the story, finding her performance not only noteworthy, but suspiciously so.

CONCLUSION

There are many more identity-oriented insights that you can attain through studying sports communication processes and effects. Certainly issues of race, ethnicity, class, age, and many other elements have been studied before and could be included here if time and space permitted. The key aspect to understand is that in many ways it's the perceived lack of seriousness of sports (at least compared to other forms of hard news, health, war, and beyond) that makes them compelling to study. Why? Because when we do not take things as seriously, we do not think as critically about what is going on. In the case of sports, a *lot* is going on. When it does, sports are shaping our worldviews—whether we are a fan or not.

REFERENCES

Anderson, B. (1983). *Imagined communities* (2nd ed.). Verso.

Anderson, E. (2005). *In the game: Gay athletes and the cult of masculinity*. SUNY Press.

Bachman, F. (2017). *Beartown*. Atria Books.

Bairner, A. (2001). *Sport, nationalization, and globalization: European and North American perspectives*. SUNY Press.

Bie, B., & Billings, A. C. (2015). 'Too good to be true?': U.S. and Chinese media coverage of Chinese swimmer Ye Shiwen in the 2012 Olympic Games. *International Review for the Sociology of Sport, 50*(7), 785–803. https://doi.org/10.1177/1012690213495746

Billings, A. C. (2008). Clocking gender differences: Televised Olympic clock-time in the 1996–2006 Summer and Winter Olympics. *Television & New Media, 9*(5), 429–441. https://doi.org/10.1177/1527476408315502

Billings, A. C., & Angelini, J. R. (2019). Equity achieved?: A longitudinal examination of biological sex representation in the NBC Olympic telecast (2000–2018). *Communication & Sport, 7*(5), 551–564. https://doi.org/10.1177/2167479519863652

Billings, A. C., Angelini, J. R., & Duke, A. H. (2010). Gendered profiles of Olympic history: Sportscaster dialogue in the 2008 Beijing Olympics. *Journal of Broadcasting & Electronic Media, 54*(1), 9–23. https://doi.org/10.1080/08838150903550352

Billings, A. C, Angelini, J. R., & MacArthur, P. J. (2018). *Olympic television: Broadcasting the biggest show on Earth*. Routledge.

Billings, A. C., Brown, N., & Brown, K. (2015a). Everyone loves a winner?: Relationships between medal counts, media exposure, and nationalism within a six-nation composite. *Journal of Sports Media, 10*(1), 101–118. https://doi.org/10.1353/jsm.2015.0004.

Billings, A. C., Brown, N. A., Brown, K. A., Guo, Q., Leeman, M., Licen, S., Novak, D., & Rowe, D. (2013). From pride to smugness and the nationalism between: Olympic media consumption effects on nationalism across the globe. *Mass Communication & Society, 16*(6), 910–932. https://doi.org/10.1080/15205436.2013.822519

Billings, A. C., Burch, L. M, & Zimmerman, M. H. (2015b). Fragments of us, fragments of them: Social media, nationality, and U.S. perceptions of the 2014 FIFA World Cup. *Soccer & Society, 16*(5–6), 726–744. https://doi.org/10.1080/14660970.2014.963307

Billings, A. C., Craig, C. C., Croce, R., Cross, K. M., Moore, K. M., Vigodsky, W., & Watson, V. G. (2006). Just one of 'the guys': An analysis of Annika Sorenstam at the 2003 PGA Colonial golf tournament. *Journal of Sport & Social Issues, 30*(1), 137–143. https://doi.org/10.1177/0193723505284278

Billings, A. C., & Gentile, P. C. (2022). Flag before gender biases?: The case for national identity bolstering women athlete visibility in sports mega-events. In K. Dashper (Ed.), *Gender, sport, and mega-events* (pp. 221–238). Routledge.

Billings, A. C., & Moscowitz, L. M. (2018). *Media and the coming out of gay male athletes in American team sports.* Peter Lang.

Billings, A. C., Moscowitz, L. M., & Lewis, M. (2021). Jason Collins, Michael Sam, and the spectacle of coming out in men's team sport. In L. D. Alexander & J. N. Rosen (Eds.), *The circus is in town: Sport, celebrity, and spectacle* (pp. 165–179). University of Mississippi Press.

Billings, A. C., Moscowitz, L. M., Rae, C., & Brown-Devlin, N. (2015c). The art of coming out: Traditional and social media frames surrounding the NBA's Jason Collins. *Journalism & Mass Communication Quarterly, 92*(1), 142–160. https://doi.org/10.1177/1077699014560516

Billings, A. C., & Young, B. D. (2015). Comparing flagship news programs: Women's sport coverage in ESPN's *SportsCenter* and FOX Sports 1's *FOX Sports Live. Electronic News, 9*(1), 3–16. https://doi.org/10.1177/1931243115572824

Brown, K. A., Billings, A. C., Devlin, M. B., & Brown-Devlin, N. A. (2020). Rings of fandom: Overlapping motivations of sport, Olympic, team, and home nation fans in the 2018 Winter Olympic Games. *Journal of Broadcasting & Electronic Media, 64*(1), 20–40. https://doi.org/10.1080/08838151.2019.1689741

Cooky, C., Council, L. D., Mears, M. A., & Messner, M. A. (2021). One and done: The long eclipse of women's televised sports, 1989-2019. *Communication & Sport, 9*(3), 347–371. https://doi.org/10.1177/21674795211003524

DeLorme, N. (2014). Were women really underrepresented in media coverage of Summer Olympic Games (1984-2008)?: An invitation to open a methodological discussion regarding sex equity in sports media. *Mass Communication & Society, 17*(1), 121–147. https://doi.org/10.1080/15205436.2013.816740

Denham, B. E. (2022). Media representations as a form of stacking: Male and female athletes featured on men's magazine covers, 1980-2019. *Communication & Sport, 10*(1), 30–51. https://doi.org/10.1177/2167479520927993

Devlin, M. B., & Billings, A. C. (2016). Examining the world's game in the United States: Impact of nationalized qualities on fan identification and consumption of the 2014 FIFA World Cup. *Journal of Broadcasting & Electronic Media, 60*(1), 40–60. https://doi.org/10.1080/08838151.2015.1127243

Fiveringtv.com (2022). Olympic television: News. https://fiveringtv.com/news/

Graham, M. (2020, February 2). Women are watching the NFL in record numbers, and Super Bowl ads are finally starting to reflect that. *CNBC*. Retrieved from https://www.cnbc.com/2020/02/01/women-nfl-fans-are-at-a-record-and-super-bowl-ads-finally-reflect-that.html

Licen, S., & Billings, A. C. (2013). Cheering for 'our' champs while watching 'sexy' female throwers: Representation of nationality and gender in Slovenian 2008 Summer Olympic television coverage. *European Journal of Communication, 28*(4), 379–396. https://doi.org/10.1177/0267323113484438

Kane, M. J., LaVoi, N. M., & Fink, J. S. (2013). Exploring elite female athletes' interpretations of sport media images: A window into the construction of social identity and 'selling sex' in women's sports. *Communication & Sport, 1*(3), 231–236. https://doi.org/10.1177/2167479512473585

Magrath, R. (2019). *LGBT athletes in the sports media*. Palgrave-Macmillan/Springer.

Moscowitz, L. M., Billings, A. C., Ejaz, K., & O'Boyle, J. (2019). Outside the sports closet: News discourses of professional gay male athletes in the mainstream. *Journal of Communication Inquiry, 43*(3), 249–271. https://doi.org/10.1177/0196859918808333

Moscowitz, L., Billings, A. C., Gentile, P. C., & Jackson, J. R. (2022, May). The paradoxical big non-story: Traditional and social media frames surrounding Carl Nassib, the NFL's first openly gay player. International Communication Association, Paris, France.

Tajfel, H., & Turner, J. C. (1985). The social identity theory of intergroup behavior. In S. Worchel & W. G. Austin (Eds.), *Psychology of intergroup relations* (2nd ed., pp. 7–24). Nelson-Hall.

Xu, Q., Billings, A. C., & Fan, M. (2018). When women fail to 'hold up more than half the sky': Gendered frames of CCTV's coverage of gymnastics at the 2016 Summer Olympics. *Communication & Sport, 6*(2), 154–174. https://doi.org/10.1177/2167479517695542

SPORT SOCIALIZATION: HOW DO WE IMPROVE SPORTING EXPERIENCES?

Gregory A. Cranmer
Clemson University

Just like millions of Americans (and may be you), sport participation has always been a central aspect of my life and that of my family for as long as I can remember. I began wrestling at three years old and played a variety of sports—football, soccer, baseball, track, basketball, wrestling, and cross country—during my youth, and until I graduated high school. Most of my friendships and memories from my youth and adolescence revolve around sport, as it was a cause for family gathering, traveling to new places, passing time on weekends, and releasing pent-up energy. Because of the efforts of countless coaches and my parents, these experiences ultimately equipped me with the attitudes and skills from which I attribute much of my success in life as a scholar, father, and husband. Needless to say, the academic study of such experiences spoke to me—as the saying goes, "research is me-search."

I was first introduced to sport socialization scholarship, which originated in sport sociology and was taken up within psychology and sport management, as part of my Ph.D. coursework at West Virginia University. *Sport socialization* is an umbrella term for a host of research efforts that consider distinct but interconnected processes that span how athletes are prepared for and integrated into sport, as well as how these experiences inform their broader adjustment to society (Coakley, 1993; McPherson, 1981). Naturally, I was drawn to this scholarship. But as a communication scholar, my perspective and approach to sport socialization differ from my interdisciplinary peers in notable ways. I position sports participation and its meaning as a product of interaction between stakeholders, as its potential benefits and detriments are only realized through communication—not predetermined as structural functionalists and critical theorists assert. Such a perspective underscores the possibility of providing coaches, parents, and athletes with messages and behaviors that aid in socialization experiences.

My scholarship has provided me with numerous opportunities that illustrate the utility of communication research for sports practitioners; spanning assisting with Clemson

University's student-athlete orientation program, helping design the professional and personal development program for its football team (known as PAW Journey), and consulting for the Atlantic Coast Athletic conference regarding the socialization of basketball officials. There are a host of sporting occupations that can benefit from socialization knowledge: athletic directors, coaches, academic advisors, and various support staff positions within the field of sport management. Keeping these stakeholders in mind, I have focused on three interrelated questions: (1) *How are student-athletes prepared for collegiate athletics?* (2) *How can sport practitioners integrate student-athletes into their roles and teams more efficiently?* and (3) *How can sporting stakeholders (primarily parents, teammates, and coaches) structure sporting experiences so that they are safe and beneficial for athletes?*

HOW ARE STUDENT-ATHLETES PREPARE FOR COLLEGIATE ATHLETICS?

At the heart of sport socialization scholarship is the consideration for how we get individuals involved in sport and keep them interested in playing—a process known as *socialization into sport*. Such efforts are paramount in the modern sporting landscape where 70% of youth athletes quit sport by age 13—mostly because of a lack of enjoyment (Miner, 2016). Unfortunately, these trends will probably continue because the youth and adolescent sporting culture of the United States is increasingly professionalized, specialized, and commercialized. The result being year-round sports participation (often) in a single sport for many children, which commonly leads to burnout and overuse injuries (e.g., Tommy John surgery in Little Leaguers which replaces the ulnar collateral ligament in the elbow with tendons from the body) (Hyman, 2009). The rising costs of equipment, travel, private coaching, and membership with elite/travel clubs and teams have only encouraged parental overinvolvement and pressure. Many parents adopt a "return on investment" mindset whereby an expectation for children is to "pay back" their parents in the form of a collegiate scholarship (Hyman, 2012). But on average, only 7% of high school athletes will play in college, and a sizeable portion of those athletes will play at the Division III level where athletic scholarships are not offered (National Collegiate Athletic Association, 2020).

Like many sports parents, I also find myself intrigued by how athletes are prepared for collegiate athletics (i.e., scholars call the period of preparation for joining a group or organization *anticipatory socialization*)—although for very different reasons. Rather than viewing it as a viable option for my children's future or an affirmation of my parental choices, my interest stems from my perspective that participation in sport is a great tool to aid human development if structured properly. That is exactly how collegiate athletics sells itself (whether accurate or not) to prospective athletes and their families, as an exchange of talent and effort for an education and developmental experiences. Interestingly, many of the messages that are meant to prepare student-athletes for collegiate athletics mirror those shared with high school and youth athletes—that sport and being an athlete is about developing good character (e.g., responsibility, autonomy, or honesty), forming social connections with others, having fun, and learning to work hard (cf., Cranmer & Myers, 2017; Kassing & Pappas, 2007; Starcher, 2015). The ubiquity of these types of messages is of note for two reasons. First, it demonstrates that collegiate student-athletes receive the same messages as their peers who failed to reach these elite levels of athletics; meaning these messages alone cannot explain their success. Second, it reveals that meta-narratives are baked into sporting culture, whereby sport is seen as a universal developmental benefit that teaches desirable attitudes and characteristics. This narrative is then shared with athletes in the form of common scripts that we have all likely heard many times (e.g., "practice makes perfect," "you miss 100% of the shots you don't take," and "pain is temporary"). Despite the commonality of these messages, athletes draw appreciation and respect toward themselves, their teams, and sport from them (Cranmer, 2017).

Collegiate student-athletes, however, have a unique experience as so few athletes ever get to this competitive level of athletics. Unsurprisingly, prior to enrollment, athletes receive messages specific to the challenges (e.g., time demands) and opportunities (e.g., pride, public figure, or education) associated with participation in collegiate athletics (Cranmer & Myers, 2017). These messages are subsequently utilized to determine if and where athletes will play in college (Cranmer, 2017). Most of these communicative exchanges occur during athletes' recruitment, which is ideally a period in which athletes and collegiate teams engage in assessments to determine mutual fit in abilities, interest, and culture. The recruitment of collegiate student-athletes, however, seldom accomplishes these aims as elite athletic talent is rare and coaches' tenure rests on their abilities to acquire it. Such issues are exacerbated in the revenue-generating sports of football and basketball, where coaches' have millions of dollars at stake and universities gamble excessive amounts of resources in hopes of winning seasons. As such, collegiate recruitment is plagued with concerning realities: (1) impossible to keep promises, (2) inflated senses of rewards, (3) ill-informed understandings of day-to-day tasks and roles, (4) unhealthy orientations toward the educational aspects of college, and (5) a host of illicit behaviors (Cranmer et al., 2019; Posteher, 2019). In summary, most collegiate student-athletes step onto campus with vague and/or inaccurate understandings of their roles and responsibilities and inflated expectations for their future experiences.

The best means of preparing student-athletes for collegiate athletics is with realistic previews of their future experiences and accurate information that allows them to make informed decisions to join teams that provide mutual fit. To give such an experience requires a collective effort and deviation from common sporting practices. Coaches and sport practitioners should seek to establish authentic relationships with athletes and set expectations that are consistent with team cultures and future collegiate realities; doing so is beneficial for reinforcing established norms, athlete retention, and development. Athletes and parents also need to be proactive and seek out authentic experiences. For example, visit campus beyond game days, sit in on classes, use sources of information that are not provided by athletic departments, and consciously guard against the human nature of inflating expectations for future experiences.

HOW ARE STUDENT-ATHLETES INTEGRATED INTO THEIR TEAMS?

Once student-athletes arrive on campus, they must be onboarded to their university, athletic department, and team culture as quickly as possible—a process of *socialization into teams*. Joining new teams is often a stressful, uncertain, and anxiety-inducing process—think back to how you felt during the first few weeks of being a college student and add the role and social demands of being an elite athlete. If prolonged, these experiences can be destructive to team cultures, cause athlete turnover, and inspire resistance to coaching efforts (Cranmer, 2021b). At the start of this period, student-athletes may rely on their preparation and the expectations created during their anticipatory socialization. If accurate or shared by their teammates, these experiences allow student-athletes to socially integrate with their peers and acquire support, information, and feedback throughout their careers (Cranmer, 2017). In most cases, athletes are not well prepared with accurate information and are unsure of how to manage the demands placed upon them in the classroom and on the playing field (Cranmer et al., 2019). To remedy these disparities, a concerted effort to instill new understandings and knowledge are required. The infamous football coach, Urban Meyer, deemed the process of bringing athletes back to reality after inflating their expectations as *de-recruitment* while at the University of Florida.

During socialization into teams, the efforts of athletic departments, teammates, and coaches are required to aid student-athletes' adjustment to their new realities. These efforts should include the provision of needed information, support, feedback, and relationships that strive to enhance development (all of which are known as *socialization resources*). Such resources may be transmitted as part of orientations, team bonding events, mentoring programs, meetings, or informal interactions. The various sources and means of obtaining resources underscore a need for synergy and shared culture/vision during socialization, as athletes often piecemeal types of information and resources from different sources. For instance, while head coaches may shape overall team goals and objectives, teammates reveal internal power dynamics, and assistant coaches provide understanding of team histories that precede membership (Cranmer, 2018). Likewise, personal development staff (e.g., counselors and advisors) can be relied upon to help address challenges and stressors stemming from personal and academic concerns, as well as for issues student-athletes are afraid to take to coaches (Cranmer et al., 2019). Together, these stakeholders can reduce the stress and uncertainty of the initial transition into college athletics—at which point student-athletes can be considered socialized (i.e., know their roles, can competently perform sport and academic tasks, and have quality relationships).

Socialization, however, continues beyond the initial joining of a team because of the dynamic nature of team and sporting environments. Sporting structures and culture—its limitations on eligibility, demands for victory, and cultural importance—ensure that athletic careers present continual change and uncertainty. Throughout their careers, student-athletes may experience coaching changes, conference realignment, rule or governance changes (e.g., Name Image Likeness legislation), cohorts of new athletes, the departures of teammates, injuries, position changes, or professional opportunities (Cranmer et al., 2020; Fontana et al., 2021). As these events arise, they affect sporting experiences by altering team membership, social dynamics, task and role assignments or demands, and organizational cultures. Such events can be leveraged toward bringing teams together as shared experiences but are best navigated when directly and openly discussed, with student-athlete involvement in decision-making (Fontana et al., 2021).

Collectively, socializing student-athletes into teams speaks to two general stages of adjustment. An immediate and difficult stage defined by being a newcomer and the resolution of inflated expectations and uncertainty; and a subsequent stage is defined by periodic events that alter the status quo. The best way to navigate such experiences is with accurate and useful information and feedback. Relationships are central to these efforts. Coaches must carefully hire staff who share the same values and understandings to promote synergy (Cranmer, 2018). Additionally, the cultivation of trusting and respectful relationships will allow for better exchanges of accurate information—as such characteristics ease the face threats of unflattering feedback (Jowett, 2017).

HOW DO WE ENSURE SAFE AND ENJOYABLE SPORTING EXPERIENCES?

For socialization both into sport and teams, as well as into society, to be successful, sporting environments need to be made safe and enjoyable. Reflect on what you know about the hierarchy of human needs; it becomes difficult to teach meaningful life lessons and to promote positive development when more immediate needs go unsatiated. Boredom, burnout, excessive pressure, stress, antisocial team environments, and injuries are common causes of withdrawal from sport and detract from socialization efforts (West & Strand, 2016; Witt & Dangi, 2018). Both parents and coaches have vital roles in ensuring beneficial environments by promoting safety and enjoyment, which enhance sports participation and its potential benefits. Yet, there is little research from communication scholars regarding these issues (Cranmer, 2021a).

Starting with safety there are various health crises confronting modern athletes, including concussion, overuse injuries, eating disorders (especially for female athletes), and mental health (Cranmer et al., 2022). These issues are particularly pressing within sporting environments because of the nature and culture of sports. For example, injuries and concussions are expected outcomes of sport participation, especially in contact sports (e.g., football), and physical characteristics (e.g., weight) are often prominent features of eligibility and do influence performance. However, sporting cultures are exacerbating these experiences, as playing through injuries and pain are not only framed as a means of revealing character but developing it (i.e., the *pain principle*) (Sabo, 2004) and sports media have traditionally lionized injured athletes who have succeeded on the field of play (e.g., Michael Jordan's "Flu Game"). These cultural forces stigmatize the prioritization of health and the disclosure of illnesses. Fortunately, research demonstrates that when teammates, coaches, and parents encourage and support such disclosures, the effects of perceived stigma are reduced and health-conscious decisions are more readily made by athletes (e.g., Burke et al., 2022; Cranmer & LaBelle, 2018). Simply, the societal-level, cultural norms can be offset by supportive and concerned teammates, coaches, and parents that encourage healthy behaviors. The challenge, however, is inspiring those individuals to become proactive in promoting healthy environments and decisions.

So how do we inspire others to discuss and encourage healthy behaviors? An early answer appears to be through the strategic use of narratives, whereby health-conscious stories that feature relatable figures (e.g., other coaches, parents, or athletes) and promote strong emotional reactions can inspire health intentions, acceptance of messaging, and information-seeking behaviors (Tallapragada & Cranmer, 2022). Other promising efforts use the team structures found within sport to shift health initiatives toward shared social responsibility frameworks (e.g., bystander intervention models) whereby the role of teammates is leveraged to looking out for the health of others (Burke et al., 2022). In this manner, initiatives—like the Concussion Legacy Foundation's *Team Up against Concussions* and *Legacy Stories* initiatives, or the Center of Disease Control's *Heads Up* campaign—have sought to encourage sporting stakeholders to address health issues more actively. Parents have especially been a relevant referent target for shaping their children's sporting behaviors (e.g., Arthur-Banning et al., 2009), but challenges with these efforts remain. In particular, parents are susceptible to the influence of other parents and coaches (e.g., Boneau et al., 2020; Fontana et al., 2022), and those that prioritize sport participation as central to their identity or are highly involved as volunteers or coaches are less open to health concerns (Boneau et al., 2020; Cranmer et al., 2021).

In addition to health concerns, trends indicate that athlete enjoyment of sport is vulnerable to parental pressures, hyper-competitive environments, and adult intervention that professionalizes youth sport. These dynamics become especially unhealthy when parents have difficulty assuming their roles as supporters or rely on extrinsic rewards to encourage sport participation (Turman, 2007). One must only look to local sporting events to find examples of parents demonstrating vicarious living, poor sportsmanship, verbal aggression, and sometimes violence (Meân & Kassing, 2008). Athletes more readily rely on parents (as opposed to coaches) when role-modeling sporting behaviors during sporting contests (Arthur-Banning et al., 2009)—exacerbating the detrimental impacts of such antisocial behaviors. Most concerning (at least as a parent), parents' emphasis on successful sporting performance over enjoyment is associated with lower relational quality later in their children's life (Starcher, 2015). Most likely some of your least favorite moments from your sporting careers were the drives home with a mom or dad who wanted to critique your performances.

The unfortunate reality is the solutions needed to address sport safety and athlete enjoyment are largely cultural. As such, there are no quick or easy remedies, and it will take time, effort, and buy-in from numerous entities. Thankfully, numerous organizations and nonprofits have begun investing in such changes, including the Concussion Legacy Foundation, Positive Coaching Alliance, and Aspen Institute's "Project Play."

CONCLUSION

Sport socialization is a broad program of research with various foci and efforts. My research only addresses a fraction of the potential of this scholarship, but it addresses a core question for sporting practitioners; most centrally *how do provide sporting experiences that are beneficial for athletes*? A central theme within my research is the need to leverage relationships in a way that is athlete-centric. By focusing first on athletes' needs and their development the common causes of destructive practices (e.g., parental pressures, manipulative recruiting practices, and disregard for athlete well-being) become marginalized. Communication students like yourself are well positioned to help change sporting culture as you assume parental, coaching, and (may be) professional sporting roles.

REFERENCES

Arthur-Banning, S., Wells, M. S., Baker, B. L., & Hegreness, R. (2009). Parents behaving badly? The relationship between the sportsmanship behaviors. *Journal of Sport Behavior, 32*(1), 3–18.

Boneau, R. D., Richardson, B. K., & McGlynn, J. (2020). "We are a football family": Making sense of parents' decisions to allow their children to play tackle football. *Communication & Sport, 8*(1), 26–49. https://doi.org/1177/2167479518816104

Burke, M., Tallapragada, M., Bell, T., & Cranmer, G. A. (2022). Bystander intervention for concussion reporting: Putting Team Up Speak Up into practice. *Strategies: A Journal for Physical and Sport Educators, 35*(4), 45–48. https://doi.org/10.1080/08924562.2022.2070388

Coakley, J. (1993). Sport and socialization. *Exercise and Sport Sciences Reviews, 21*(1), 169–200. https://doi.org/10.1249/00003677-199301000-00006

Cranmer, G. A. (2017). A communicative approach to sport socialization: The functions of memorable messages in Division-I student-athletes' socialization. *International Journal of Sport Communication, 10*(2), 233–257. https://doi.org/10.1123/IJSC.2017-0031

Cranmer, G. A. (2018). An application of socialization resources theory: Collegiate student-athletes' team socialization as a function of their social exchanges with coaches and teammates. *Communication & Sport, 6*(2), 349–367. https://doi.org/10.1177/2167479517714458

Cranmer, G. A. (2021a). Setting the agenda: A playbook for tackling family communication in sport. *Journal of Family Communication, 21*(1), 70–75. https://doi.org/10.1080/15267431.2020.1856852

Cranmer, G. A. (2021b). The organizational processes of athletic coaching. In M. Butterworth (Ed.), *Handbook of communication and sport* (pp. 83–102). De Gruyter Mouton.

Cranmer, G. A., & LaBelle, S. (2018). Using the disclosure decision-making model to understand high school football players' disclosures of concussion symptoms. *International Journal of Sport Communication, 11*(2), 241–260. https://doi.org/10.1123/ijsc.2017-0120

Cranmer, G. A., & Myers, S. A. (2017). Exploring Division-I student-athletes' memorable messages from their anticipatory socialization. *Communication Quarterly, 65*, 125–143. https://doi.org/10.1080/01463373.2016.1197292

Cranmer, G. A., Rey, R., & Mikkilineni, S. (2022). Coach-athlete communication and implications for health. In J. Sanderson & M. Weathers (Eds.), *Health communication and sport: Connections, applications, and opportunities* (pp. 79–94). Rowman & Littlefield.

Cranmer, G. A., Rey, R., & Tallapragada, M. (2021). Exploring the role of parents' sport orientations in the efficacy of concussion intervention materials. *Communication Research Reports, 38*(4), 250–261. https://doi.org/10.1080/08824096.2021.1936480

Cranmer, G. A., Troutman, B., & Legacy, S. (2020). Female golfers' uncertainty management during their transition into professional golf. *Qualitative Research Reports in Communication.* Advance online publication. https://doi.org/10.1080/17459435.2020.1853207

Cranmer, G. A., Yeargin, R., & Spinda, J. (2019). Life after signing: The recruiting process as a resource of college football players' socialization. In T. L. Rentner & D. P. Burns (Eds.), *Case studies in sport communication: You make the call* (pp. 77–84). Routledge.

Fontana, J., Cranmer, G. A., Ash, E., Mazer, J., & Denham, B. (2022). Parent-child communication regarding sport-related concussion: An application of the theory of planned behavior. *Health Communication, 37*(8), 923–934. https://doi.org/10.1080/10410236.2021.1876326

Fontana, J., Cranmer, G. A., & Sollitto, M. (2021). "Next person up": Understanding collegiate student-athletes' socialization experiences with teammate exit. *Communication & Sport, 9*(2), 308–329. https://doi.org/10.1177/2167479519859864

Hyman, M. (2009). *Until it hurts: America's obsession with youth sports and how it harms our kids.* Beacon Press.

Hyman, M. (2012). *The most expensive game in town: The rising cost of youth sports and the toll on today's families.* Beacon Press.

Jowett, S. (2017). Coaching effectiveness: The coach–athlete relationship at its heart. *Current Opinion in Psychology, 16*(5), 154–158. https://doi.org/10.1016/j.copsyc.2017.05.006

Kassing, J. W., & Pappas, M. E. (2007). "Champions are built in the off season": An exploration of high school coaches' memorable messages. *Human Communication, 10*, 537–546.

McPherson, B. D. (1981). Socialization into and through sport involvement. In G. R. F. Luschen & G. H. Sage (Eds.), *Handbook of social science of sport* (pp. 246–273). Stipes.

Meân, L. J., & Kassing, J. W. (2008). Identities at youth sporting events: A critical discourse analysis. *International Journal of Sport Communication, 1*(1), 42–66. https://doi.org/10.1123/ijsc.1.1.42

Miner, J. W. (2016, June 1). Why 70 percent of kids quit sports by age 13. *Washingtonpost.com*. Retrieved from https://www.washingtonpost.com/news/parenting/wp/2016/06/01/why-70-percent-of-kids-quit-sports-by-age-13/

National Collegiate Athletic Association (April 8, 2020). Estimated probability of competing in college athletics. *NCAA.org*. Retrieved from https://www.ncaa.org/sports/2015/3/2/estimated-probability-of-competing-in-college-athletics.aspx

Posteher, K. (2019). *Winning the recruiting game: The student-athlete perspective* [Unpublished doctoral dissertation]. Arizona State University.

Sabo, D. (2004). The politics of sport injury: Hierarchy, power, and the pain principle. In K. Young (Ed.), *Sporting bodies, damaged selves: Sociological studies of sports-related injuries* (pp. 59–80). Emerald.

Starcher, S. C. (2015). Memorable messages from fathers to children through sports: Perspectives from sons and daughters. *Communication Quarterly, 63*(2), 204–220. https://doi.org/10.1080/01463373.2015.1012221

Tallapragada, M., & Cranmer, G. A. (2022). Media narratives about concussions: Effects on parents' intention and willingness to discuss concussions with their children. *Communication & Sport, 10*(3), 517–540. https://doi.org/10.1177/2167479520944549

Turman, P. D. (2007). Parental sport involvement: Parental influence to encourage young athlete continued sport participation. *Journal of Family Communication, 7*(3), 151–175. https://doi.org/10.1080/15267430701221602

West, G. S., & Strand, B. (2016). Preventing youth sports dropouts. *Louisiana Association of Health, Physical Education, Recreation, and Dance Journal, 79*(2), 13–15.

Witt, P. A., & Dangi, T. B. (2018). Why children/youth drop out of sports. *Journal of Park and Recreation Administration, 36*(3), 191–199. https://doi.org/10.18666/JPRA-2018-V36-I3-8618

THE HIGHLY IDENTIFIED SPORTS FAN: A BRIEF INTRODUCTION INTO THE PERSONALITY AND CONSEQUENCES OF A SPORT FAN

Michael B. Devlin
Texas State University

Humans routinely self-identify and self-categorize in order to cognitively place themselves into various groups. Researchers have utilized social identification (Tajfel & Turner, 1986) and self-categorization (Turner et al., 1987) to better understand how and why humans desire to be part of a larger group. Results commonly suggest that belonging to groups not only helps increase your self-esteem, but it also helps define who you are, your beliefs, and how you want others to see you. We may belong to many different groups at one time, and we place emphasis on groups that are important during specific times (Spears et al., 1999). As a result, "each of us has a range of different, cross-cutting, social identities, including those derived from highly meaningful and clearly delineated groups" (Ellemers et al., 2002, p. 164).

For example, I identify as a college professor, as a parent, and as a highly-identified fan of my favorite team during the season. More specifically, I self-identify as a University of Alabama football fan. Before you roll your eyes, let me explain how I became a fan. If you are a college football fan, you probably hate Alabama. I know because I hated them too before attending the University of Alabama. I cheered against them in the 2009 Sugar Bowl against Utah—and not because I particularly liked Utah; I just did not like Alabama. So, what changed?

In 2010, I was invited to enroll into the University of Alabama's doctoral program by then director, Dr. Jennings Bryant—editor of the *Handbook of Sports and Media*, which I encourage you to check it out if you find this chapter interesting. I went to the first home game because that's what many of my peers were doing that weekend. I immediately sensed the passion and excitement in the city of Tuscaloosa, Alabama. Football was an escape for many of us in the doctoral program. My peer social groups would chat about the upcoming game throughout the week, plan cookouts on gamedays, or even schedule trips for away games. Being a fan gave us new layer to our academic identity, and one that allowed us to assimilate into the University and town. I gradually went from simply watching games on Saturday to learning the customs and traditions, participating in pregame rituals, and of course buying team-related merchandise. I eventually became a raging fan who consumes college-football media throughout the week and schedules weekend activities completely around kick-off. I bask-in-reflected-glory (BIRG) when my team wins and find pleasure when our rivals lose.

While studying at Alabama, I learned sport fandom is ripe with research opportunities, ranging from theoretical sociological and psychological perspectives (Donavan et al., 2005; Funk & James, 2001, 2006; Wann et al., 1996), marketing and public relations (Devlin, 2016; Devlin & Billings, 2018; Devlin & Sheehan, 2017), and consumer behavior (Madrigal, 2001; Wakefield, 2016). Since then, I have researched and written about fandom for over a decade focusing on the development of fandom from a psychological approach to better understand how individuals navigate cross-cutting identities, and the consequences of being a highly-identified fan as it relates consumer behavior.

DEFINING THE HIGHLY-IDENTIFIED FAN

As noted by Funk and James (2001), "any effort to review the literature becomes an exercise in untangling semantic differences" (p. 120) when differentiating between fan attachment, loyalty, and allegiance. However, fandom uniformly agreed upon to explain a level of obsessive passion with an object. There is some nuance between fandom and being a highly-identified fan. The concept of team identification is based on the theories of self-categorization (Turner, 1985) and social identification (Tajfel & Turner, 1986), suggesting team identity is more than an obsessive passion with an object, but rather a connection to one's team whereby their team's performance becomes self-relevant (Wann, 2006). As one becomes a highly identified fan, their favorite team's victories feel like personal victories, and consequently, their team's losses feel like a personal loss. This psychological connection prevents fans from simply walking away from their team, which explains why so many fans are willing to endure years of disappointment when their team fails to win.

The path to becoming a highly-identified fans happens in stages and occurs for a variety of reasons. Researchers have categorized reasons as *environmental, team-related,* and *psychological*. Environmental causes refer to external variables, such as geography and influence from family and friends (Greenwood et al., 2006; Kolbe & James, 2000; Wann et al., 1996). Because socialization is important to individuals, it is easy to understand how pure proximity to a sport team based on where they live, and their friends' and family's preference can influence one's identity. I, for example, never would have become a fan of Alabama had I not attended the university and lived in Tuscaloosa.

Team-related causes refer to the on-the-field product, such as players and coaches (Gladden & Funk, 2001; Mahony et al., 2000). This can also refer to the team's prestige (Gwinner & Swanson, 2003) and its distinctiveness (Jetten et al., 1999). It is worth noting that winning is not a requirement for identity. For example, scholars conducing a 10-year study of Chicago Cubs fans found they basked in their failure, and the identity as the "lovable losers" is what made their group distinct (Jensen et al., 2018). Consequently, off-putting characteristics from owners, coaches, and players can however de-escalate one's fandom (Hyatt & Foster, 2015).

Daniel Wann describes fan identification as the extent to which a fan feels a *psychological* connection to the team and the team's performances are viewed as self-relevant (Wann, 2006). While the definition hinges on a *psychological* connection, much of the work in this area has approached the study of fandom from a sociological perspective. Some scholars have focused on the need for affiliation to address the psychological causes of team identification (Donavan et al., 2005), but if being a sport fan relied only on the desire to be part of a group, then you would expect very little difference between someone wanting to join a quiet book-club and a highly-identified sport fan ardently cheering for their team on game day.

PERSONALITY TRAITS OF HIGHLY IDENTIFIED FAN

I became increasingly curious as to what extent personality coincided with being a highly identified fan. Burgeoning research in this area seeks to answer not only *why* people became fans, but *who* was likely to become a fan, suggesting underlying personality traits are likely to influence one's draw to sport and then predict subsequent fan behaviors. Scant evidence supports the notion that the development of being a highly-identified fan can be approached from the personality perspective. Wann and colleagues (2004) initially found that those who were extraverts and open to experiences were more likely to be sports fans. Additional researchers noted that one's need for arousal and desire for material goods increased a need for affiliation, which correlated with increased team identification (Donavan et al., 2005).

Using more robust personality measurement scales provided an opportunity to recognize several core personality traits that predict the likelihood of becoming a highly identified fan. The HEXACO Personality Inventory (Ashton & Lee, 2007, 2009) proposed the existence of 6 broad domains (Honesty–Humility, Emotionality, eXtraversion, Agreeableness, Conscientiousness, and Openness to Experience) along with 24 narrower traits that contribute to the larger 6 personality domains. Using this scale allowed researchers to garner a more accurate persona of who was likely to become a highly identified fan.

Throughout several studies, researchers noted several emerging personality traits that exist among highly-identified sport fans. Highly-identified fans typically have lower modesty, fearfulness, prudence, and anxiety coupled with increased sincerity, sociability, and diligence

(Brown-Devlin & Devlin, 2019; Brown-Devlin et al., 2018; Devlin, 2016; Devlin & Brown-Devlin, 2017). Lowered modesty explains why fans may be drawn to prestigious teams (Gwinner & Swanson, 2003) and why they are more likely to bask in reflected glory after a win. The association between highly-identified fans and lowered prudence scores, which is used to describe impulsive behavior (Ashton & Lee, 2009), helps explain some of the seemingly irrational behavior among ardent fans. One of the tenants of being a highly-identified fans is group affiliation, which requires members to act in accordance of the group to maintain membership (Ashforth & Mael, 1989), therefore increased sincerity and sociability scores are expected. While work in this area is still being conducted, the amount of research already provides an argument that certain personality traits draw people to sport under specific circumstances and predict behaviors ranging from media consumption (Devlin & Brown-Devlin, 2017); basking-in and cutting-off behaviors (Brown-Devlin et al., 2018), and may provide nuance to specific motivations for becoming a fan (Brown-Devlin & Devlin, 2019).

THE EFFECTS OF FAN IDENTITY

A need for belonging is one of the primary reasons people assimilate into groups, and research shows that being a highly-identified fan of a team is associated with psychological well-being and self-esteem (Wann et al., 2004). Scholars have found that being a highly-identified fan is also related to several other outcomes. Highly-identified fans are more likely to consume more media related to their team, purchase team-related merchandise, and exhibit higher self-esteem (Fisher, 1998; Gantz & Wenner, 1995; Madrigal, 2000, 2004; Wann, 2006). One of the more interesting topics related to fan behavior is their willingness to bask in reflected glory after their team's win.

As Cialdini and colleagues (1976) found, people tend to "share in the glory of a successful other with whom they are in some way associated …. [even] when the one who basks in the glory of another has done nothing to bring about the other's success (p. 366). This behavior has been coined as basking-in-reflected glory or BIRGing. The more one identifies with their team, the more they are likely to BIRG, and exhibit behaviors such as showcasing their team's colors and logo and using the term "we" or "us" to describe victories. Listen carefully the next time a friend's team wins a big game—you will likely hear them describe the results in terms of "we won" even though they likely did nothing more that watch.

Some researchers have argued that after a loss, some fans will cut-off-reflected failure (CORF) (Snyder et al., 1986) in order to protect their self-esteem, and will try to distance themselves from a losing team and use the term "they" when describing a loss (Cialdini et al., 1976). However, more research suggests that the more highly identified one is with their team, the less likely they are to CORF. This helps explain bandwagon and fair-weather fans who cheer when the team is doing well, but retreat during bad times (Wann & Branscombe, 1990).

Other scholars have taken a different approach to addressing this phenomenon. Rather than broadly advocating *all* fans are likely to BIRG, Brown-Devlin and colleagues (2018) examined to what extent certain personality traits among highly identified fans influenced BIRGing and CORFing behaviors. Increased liveliness and sentimentality emerged as two key traits predicting likelihood to BIRG, suggesting people who seek out meaningful relationships and have strong emotional attachments are more likely to BIRG. Additionally, those who are less prudent, meaning they are less likely to consider consequences of their actions and are impulsive (Lee & Ashton, 2004), are also more likely to BIRG. This explains why *some* fans are impulsive and potentially destructive when they celebrate a team's victory.

SPORT SPONSORSHIPS AND FANS

Sport is more than a game; it is a multi-billion-dollar business that generates revenue for not only teams, but sponsoring partners. Globally, sport sponsorship spending was approximately $65 billion in 2020. Sport sponsorships can reach a wide array of demographics and provide high levels of brand exposure to audiences attending the event and those watching on television, making a sponsorship extremely flexible. Sports fans are great audiences for marketers because an emotional link between the brand and the team or event that the fan values is readily available. It is the hope that the loyalty and attachment fans express toward their team will transfer onto the brand (Pracejus, 2004).

Previous research has shown the extent to which team identification influences the effectiveness of sports sponsorships, finding a positive relationship between team identification and sponsor purchase intentions (Bee & Dalakas, 2015; Brown et al., 2013; Koo et al., 2006; Madrigal, 2000) and positive attitudes toward sponsors (Grohs et al., 2015). Other work in this area has noted the importance of team identity as it relates to sponsor success, noting that brands that are congruent to the sport are more likely to be recalled and liked by highly identified fans than brands that are tangential to the sport (Devlin & Billings, 2018). Researchers have also noted that highly identified fans are likely to purchase sponsoring brands' products even if they do not particularly like the product (Madrigal, 2000) in order to maintain group affiliation. Madrigal (2004) wrote that "fans view supporting their team's sponsors favorably because by doing so they are acting in a way that is consistent with the goals and values of the team" (p. 249).

NATIONAL IDENTITY AND FANS

There is a long-established link between sport and the bolstering of patriotism (love of one's country), nationalism (belief that your country is better than other countries), and internationalism (belief that global connectedness and inclusion is beneficial) during international competitions. Megaevents, like the World Cup and the Olympic games, instill nationalistic angles into their television production (Devlin & Billings, 2016). The Olympics medal table and focus on each country's medal count during the Olympics provides an overarching narrative of global supremacy (Van Hilvoorde et al., 2010), and "a forum for fervent nationalism" (Butterworth, 2007, p. 187). As a result of these televised narratives, multiple identities, namely team identities and national identities, emerge and influence how networks craft messages that appeal to audiences with different levels of interest and points of attachment.

Research has examined to what extent one's national identity and fan identity influence their consumption of these international sport megaevents in hopes of understanding how different identities influence media consumption. Take the World Cup for example—highly identified soccer fans may already be primed to watch a month-long coverage regardless of how their preferred team/country performs. However, nonsoccer fans with strong national identities may feel a sense of patriotic duty to watch the World Cup and cheer on their country's team as long as they are competing. Devlin et al. (2017) found that national identity did not directly influence one's media consumption of international sport events, suggesting team identity is still a stronger predictor for media consumption and the heavily nationalized media messages are likely unnecessary to garner ratings. However, both smugness (the belief your country is the best), and internationalism influenced sport fandom for the U.S. Men's National Soccer Team (USMNT) during the 2014 World Cup. The results indicated that multiple, simultaneously interwoven identities influence sport media consumption. It was also posited that fans who know their team is unlikely to advance or succeed are likely to limit their sport media consumption to only when their country/team is playing. This again underscores the nuance between a sport fan who may watch regardless who is playing and a highly identified fan, who is likely to watch only their team.

Since "each of us has a range of different, cross-cutting, social identities," (Ellemers et al., 2002, p. 164), emphasis is placed on which category or categories are most salient to that person at a given time. We can examine how identities predict likelihood of watching sport, but we can also examine how our identities are affected by watching international sport. Succulently stated, what is more important, being a sport fan or a stateman during an international event? To answer this, U.S. citizens were surveyed at six points over the course of the 2014 FIFA Men's World Cup and asked about their levels of team identification with Team USA, the fan identification toward the World Cup, and the degree of patriotism, nationalism, smugness, and internationalism (Devlin & Billings, 2016).

Devlin and Billings found that media consumption of the World Cup did not shape or influenced U.S. citizens' national identity, suggesting that our national identity is somewhat fixed and unlikely to be changed by a sporting event. However, when controlling people's level of fandom with the U.S. Men's team, a significant decrease in nationalism scores over time was reported, suggesting that fans of the U.S. Men's Team actualized their national standing in the world was less favorable than hoped. What was more telling was sports fans smugness scores, or belief that one's country is superior to every other country by nearly every respect, increased to an all-time high once the U.S. Men's team was eliminated from the World Cup. This equated to the proverbial "we're picking up our ball and going home, and we still think we are better than the rest of the world." Fans were unable to BIRG, so instead retreated and shifted their identity back to national identities.

CONCLUSION

Sports fans are as integral as athletes for sport to remain a profitable business. The business of sport does not show any signs of slowing down, evident by the ever-growing audience size and economic impact. Sport generates a predictable audience, which is why networks are willing to administer lucrative contracts with sport leagues in the hopes of garnering large audiences. Being a sport fan is more than just cheering for one's team though. It is understanding rituals and traditions and adopting the team as part of one's identity. The reason one becomes a fan varies from their environment to the underpinnings of their personality. The impact of being a highly identified fan, however, transcends just consuming media. It can influence our self-esteem, can affect ancillary partnerships and sponsorships, and influence how we see the rest of the world during mega sporting events.

REFERENCES

Ashforth, B., & Mael, F. (1989). Social identity theory and the organization. *Academy of Management Review, 14*(1), 20–39. https://doi.org/10.5465/amr.1989.4278999

Ashton, M. C., & Lee, K. (2007). Empirical, theoretical, and practical advantages of the HEXACO model of personality structure. *Personality and Social Psychology Review, 11* (2), 150–166. https://doi.org/10.1177/1088868306294907

Ashton, M. C., & Lee, K. (2009). The HEXACO-60: A short measure of the major dimensions of personality. *Journal of Personality Assessment, 91*(4), 340–345. https://doi.org/10.1080/00223890902935878

Bee, C., & Dalakas, V. (2015). Rivalries and sponsor affiliation: Examining the effects of social identity and argument strength on responses to sponsorship-related advertising messages. *Journal of Marketing Communications, 21*(6), 408–424. https://doi.org/10.1080/13527266.2013.828768

Brown, N., Devlin, M. B., & Billings, A. C. (2013). When fan identity levels go extreme: An exploratory study of the highly identified fans of the Ultimate Fighting Championship. *International Journal of Sports Communication, 6*(1), 19–32.

Brown-Devlin, N. & Devlin, M. (2019). Winning with personality: Underscoring antecedents for college students' motives for team identification. *Communication & Sport, 8*(3), 364–388. https://doi.org/10.1177/2167479519832017

Brown-Devlin, N., Devlin, M., & Vaughan, P. (2018). Why fans act that way: Using personality to predict BIRGing and CORFing behaviors. *Communication & Sport, 6*(4), 395–417. https://doi.org/10.1177/2167479517725011

Butterworth, M. L. (2007). The politics of the pitch: Claiming and contesting democracy through the Iraqi national soccer team. *Communication and Critical/Cultural Studies, 4*(2), 184–203. https://doi.org/10.1080/14791420701296554

Cialdini, R. B., Borden, R. J., Thorne, A., Walker, M. R., Freeman, S., & Sloan, L. R. (1976). Basking in reflected glory: Three (football) field studies. *Journal of Personality and Social Psychology, 34*(3), 366–375. https://doi.org/10.1037/0022-3514.34.3.366

Devlin, M. (2016). Sport and advertising. In A.C. Billings (Ed.), *Defining sport communication* (pp. 312–325). Routledge.

Devlin, M., & Billings, A. C. (2016). Examining the world's game in the United States: Impact of nationalized qualities on fan identification and consumption of the 2014 FIFA World Cup. *Journal of Broadcasting & Electronic Media, 60*(1), 40–60. https://doi.org/10.1080/08838151.2015.1127243

Devlin, M. & Billings, A. C. (2018). Examining confirmation biases: implications of sponsorCongruency. *International Journal of Sports Marketing and Sponsorship, 19*(1), 58–73, https://doi.org/10.1108/IJSMS-10-2016-0078

Devlin, M., Billings, A. C., & Brown, K. A. (2017). Interwoven statesmanship and sports fandom: World Cup consumption antecedents through joint lenses of nationalism and fanship. *Communication & Sport, 5*(2), 186–204. https://doi.org/10.1177/2167479515593417

Devlin, M. & Brown-Devlin, N. (2017). Using personality and team identity to predict sports media consumption. *International Journal of Sport Communication, 10*, 371–392.

Devlin, M. & Sheehan, K. (2017). A 'Crucial Catch': Examining responses to NFL teams' corporate social responsibility messaging on facebook. *Communication & Sport, 6*(4), 477–498. https://doi.org/10.1177/2167479517719683

Donavan, D., Carlson, B. D., & Zimmerman, M. (2005). The influence of personality traits on sports fan identification. *Sport Marketing Quarterly, 14*(1), 31–42.

Ellemers, N., Spears, R., & Doosje, B. (2002). Self and social identity. *Annual Review Psychology, 53*, 161–186. https://doi.org/10.1146/annurev.psych.53.100901.135228

Fisher, R. J. (1998). Group-derived consumption: The role of similarity and attractiveness in identification with a favorite sports team. *Advances in Consumer Research, 25*, 283–288.

Funk, D. C., & James, J. D. (2001). The psychological continuum model: A conceptual framework for understanding an individual's psychological connection to sport. *Sport Management Review, 4*(2), 119–150. https://doi.org/10.1016/S1441-3523(01)70072-1

Funk, D. C., & James, J. D. (2006). Consumer loyalty: The meaning of attachment in the Development of sport team allegiance. *Journal of Sport Management, 20*(2), 189–217. https://doi.org/10.1123/jsm.20.2.189

Gantz, W., & Wenner, L. A. (1995). Fanship and the television sports viewing experience. *Sociology of Sport Journal, 12*(1), 56–74. https://doi.org/10.1123/ssj.12.1.56

Gladden, J. M. & Funk, D. C. (2001). Understanding brand loyalty in professional sport: Examining the link between brand association and brand loyalty. *International Journal of Sports Marketing & Sponsorship, 3*(1), 54–81. https://doi.org/10.1108/IJSMS-03-01-2001-B006

Greenwood, P. B., Kanters, M. A., & Casper, J. M. (2006). Sport fan team identification formation in mid-level professional sport. *European Sport Management Quarterly, 6*(3), 253–265. https://doi.org/10.1080/16184740601095016

Grohs, R., Reisginer, H. & Woisetschlager, D. M. (2015). Attenuation of negative sponsorship effects in the context of rival sports teams' fans. *European Journal of Marketing, 49*(11/12), 1880–1901. https://doi.org/10.1108/EJM-01-2013-0010

Gwinner, K., & Swanson, S. R. (2003). A model of fan identification antecedents and sponsor-ship outcomes. *Journal of Services Marketing, 17*(3), 275–294. https://doi.org/10.1108/08876040310474828

Hyatt, C. G. & Foster, W. M. (2015). Using identity work theory to understand the de-escalation of fandom: A study of former fans of national hockey league teams. *Journal of Sport Management, 29*(4), 443–460. https://doi.org/10.1123/jsm.2013-0327

Jensen, J. A., Greenwell, T. C., Coleman, C., Stitsinger, M., & Andrew, D. (2018). From BIRFing to BIRGing: A 10-year study of the psychology of Cubs fans. *Sport Marketing Quarterly, 27*(4), 237–250.

Jetten, J., Spears, R., & Manstead, A. S. (1999). Distinctiveness and intergroup discrimination. In N. Ellemers, R. Spears, & B. Doosje (Eds.), *Social identity: Context, commitment, content* (pp. 107–126). Basil Blackwell.

Kolbe, R. H., & James, J. D. (2000). An identification and examination of influences that shape the creation of a professional team fan. *International Journal of Sports Marketing and Sponsorship, 2*(1), 23–37.

Koo, G. Y., Quarterman, J., & Flynn, L. (2006). Effect of perceived sport event and sponsor image fit on consumers' cognition, affect, and behavioral intentions. *Sport Marketing Quarterly, 15*(2), 80–90.

Lee, K., & Ashton, M. C. (2004). Psychometric properties of the HEXACO personality inventory. *Multivariate Behavioral Research, 39*(2), 329–358. https://doi.org/10.1207/s15327906mbr3902_8

Madrigal, R. (2000). The influence of social alliances with sports teams on intentions to purchase corporate sponsors' products. *Journal of Advertising, 29*(4), 13–27. https://doi.org/10.1080/00913367.2000.10673621

Madrigal, R. (2001). Social identity effects in a belief-attitude-intentions hierarchy: Implications for corporate sponsorship. *Psychology & Marketing, 18*(2), 145–165. https://doi.org/10.1002/1520-6793(200102)18:2<145::AID-MAR1003>3.0.CO;2-T

Madrigal, R. (2004). A review of team identification and its influence on consumers' responses toward corporate sponsors. In L. R. Kahle & C. Riley (Eds.), *Sports marketing and the psychology of marketing communication* (pp. 241–255). Erlbaum.

Mahony, D. F., Madrigal, R., & Howard, D. (2000). Using the psychological commitment to team (PCT) scale to segment sport consumers based on loyalty. *Sport Marketing Quarterly, 9*(1), 15–25.

Pracejus, J. W. (2004). Seven psychological mechanisms through which sponsorship can influence consumers. In L. R. Kahle & C. Riley (Eds.), *Sports marketing and the psychology of marketing communication* (pp. 175–189). Erlbaum.

Snyder, C. R., Lassegard, M. A., & Ford, C. E. (1986). Distancing after group success and failure: Basking in reflected glory and cutting off reflected failure. *Journal of Personality and Social Psychology, 51*, 382–388. https://doi.org/10.1037/0022-3514.51.2.382

Spears, R., Doosje, B., & Ellemers, N. (1999). Commitment and the context of social perception. In N. Ellemers, R. Spears, & B. Doosje (Eds.), *Social identity: Context, commitment, content* (pp. 59–83). Blackwell Science.

Tajfel, H., & Turner, J. C. (1986). The social identity theory of intergroup behavior. In S. Worchel & L. W. Austin (Eds.), *Psychology of intergroup relations* (pp. 7–24). Nelson-Hall.

Turner, J. C. (1985). Social categorization and the self-concept: A social cognitive theory of group behaviour. In E. J. Lawler (Ed.), *Advances in group processes* (pp. 77–122). JAI Press.

Turner, J. C, Hogg, M. A., Oakes, P. J., Reicher, S. D., & Wetherell, M. S. (1987). *Rediscovering the social group: A self-categorization theory.* Basil Blackwell.

van Hilvoorde, I., Elling, A., & Stovkis, R. (2010). How to influence national pride? The Olympic medal index as a unifying narrative. *International Review for the Sociology of Sport, 45*(1), 87–102. https://doi.org/10.1177/1012690209356989

Wakefield, K. (2016). Using fan passion to predict attendance, media consumption, and social media behaviors. *Journal of Sport Management, 30*, 229–247. http://dx.doi.org/10.1123/jsm.2015-0039

Wann, D. L. (2006). The causes and consequences of sport team identification. In A. Raney & J. Bryant (Eds.), *Handbook of sport and media* (pp. 331–352). Erlbaum.

Wann, D. L., & Branscombe, N. R. (1990). Die-hard and fair-weather fans: Effects of identification on BIRGing and CORFing tendencies. *Journal of Sport and Social Issues, 14*(2), 103–117. https://doi.org/10.1177/019372359001400203

Wann, D. L., Dunham, M. D., Byrd, M. L., & Keenan, B. L. (2004). The five-factor model of personality and the psychological health of highly identified sport fans. *International Sports Journal, 8*(2), 28–36.

Wann, D. L., Tucker, K. B., & Schrader, M. P. (1996). An exploratory examination of the factors influencing the origination, continuation, and cessation of identification with sports teams. *Perceptual and Motor Skills, 82*(3), 995–1001. https://doi.org/10.2466/pms.1996.82.3.995

Printed in the USA
CPSIA information can be obtained
at www.ICGtesting.com
JSHW060432300824
68839JS00005B/1

9 781792 494